Law, Governance and Technology Series

Issues in Privacy and Data Protection

Volume 46

Issues in Privacy and Data Protection aims at publishing peer reviewed scientific manuscripts that focus upon issues that engage into an analysis or reflexion related to the consequences of scientific and technological developments upon the private sphere, the personal autonomy and the self-construction of humans with data protection and privacy as anchor points. The objective is to publish both disciplinary, multidisciplinary and interdisciplinary works on questions that relate to experiences and phenomena that can or could be covered by legal concepts stemming from the law regarding the protection of privacy and/or the processing of personal data. Since both the development of science and technology, and in particular information technology (ambient intelligence, robotics, artificial intelligence, knowledge discovery, data mining, surveillance, etc.), and the law on privacy and data protection are in constant frenetic mood of change (as is clear from the many legal conflicts and reforms at hand), we have the ambition to reassemble a series of highly contemporary and forward-looking books, wherein cutting edge issues are analytically, conceptually and prospectively presented.

More information about this subseries at http://www.springer.com/series/13087

Themistoklis Tzimas

Legal and Ethical Challenges of Artificial Intelligence from an International Law Perspective

Springer

Themistoklis Tzimas
School of Political Science
Aristotle University of Thessaloniki
Thessaloniki, Greece

ISSN 2352-1902 ISSN 2352-1910 (electronic)
Law, Governance and Technology Series
ISSN 2352-1929 ISSN 2352-1937 (electronic)
Issues in Privacy and Data Protection
ISBN 978-3-030-78584-0 ISBN 978-3-030-78585-7 (eBook)
https://doi.org/10.1007/978-3-030-78585-7

This Springer imprint is published by the registered company Springer Nature Switzerland AG.
The registered company address is: Gewerbestrasse 11, 6330 Cham, Switzerland

To Dora, Panos, Sofia,
for making the world worth exploring

Acknowledgments

I would like to thank—as I always do whenever I write any academic text—professor Nicholas Tsagourias for teaching me how to write, with tough love, during my MPhIL; Professor Grigoris Zarotiadis and Aris Stylianou for providing me their friendship, as well as a hospitable academic environment in the Aristotle University of Thessaloniki, within which this book was written; The School of Political Sciences of the Aristotle University of Thessaloniki and all of its members, with special acknowledgments to professors Spyros Marchetos and Giorgos Margaritis for their support these last years that we have been working together.

Above all I would like to thank my parents for their lasting support.

Contents

Part I The Ethical Challenges from AI

1 **Introduction** . . . 3
References . . . 7

2 **The Expectations and Risks from AI** . . . 9
2.1 Introduction . . . 9
2.2 Between High Expectations and Existential Anxiety . . . 10
2.3 An "Economic Singularity" Ahead? Social Implications . . . 21
2.4 Conclusions . . . 30
References . . . 30

3 **The Ontology of AI** . . . 33
3.1 Introduction . . . 33
3.2 Defining AI . . . 35
3.3 Weak and Strong AI . . . 39
3.4 AI, Machine Learning and Neural Networks . . . 44
3.5 AI Consciousness and Its Nature . . . 50
3.6 The Quest for Friendly AI . . . 55
3.7 Conclusions . . . 63
References . . . 64

4 **The Ethics of AI** . . . 69
4.1 Introduction . . . 69
4.2 From ANI to ASI . . . 73
4.2.1 ANI Challenges . . . 73
4.2.2 Ethical Challenges from AGI and ASI . . . 77
4.3 Attempts for Ethical Regulation of AI . . . 81
4.3.1 Transparency—Explainability—Accountability—Safety . . . 83
4.3.2 AI Ethics . . . 85
4.3.3 AI and Use of Data . . . 88
4.3.4 AI and Well-Being . . . 91

4.3.5 AI and "Human-in-the-Loop" . . . 93
4.4 Conclusions: From Ethical Responses to the Legal Regulation . . . 96
References . . . 97

Part II Legal Framework of AI

5 AI Governance and the Fundamental Principles of International Law . . . 103
5.1 Introduction . . . 103
5.2 The Form of AI Governance . . . 104
5.3 The Fundamental Goals and Principles for AI Governance . . . 119
5.3.1 The Constitutionality of the Charter . . . 119
5.3.2 The Fundamental Principles of the Charter and Their Transfer to AI Governance . . . 122
5.4 Conclusions . . . 125
References . . . 126

6 AI and Human Rights . . . 131
6.1 Introduction . . . 131
6.2 The Role of Human Rights in International Law . . . 132
6.3 Governance of AI and the Role of Human Rights . . . 138
6.3.1 Human Rights and ANI . . . 138
6.3.2 Human Rights, AGI, ASI . . . 142
6.4 Conclusions . . . 145
References . . . 146

7 AI and International Security- the Case of AWS' and Collective Security System . . . 149
7.1 Introduction . . . 149
7.2 The Collective Security System . . . 151
7.3 The Autonomy of AWS' . . . 154
7.4 Definitions of AWS's . . . 160
7.5 Conclusions . . . 162
References . . . 164

8 Legal Ramifications of the Use of AWS's- the Role of IHL and Human Rights . . . 167
8.1 Introduction . . . 167
8.2 AWS and IHL . . . 169
8.2.1 IHL Characteristics . . . 169
8.2.2 Responsibility of AWS's? . . . 174
8.2.3 Tracing the Human Behind the Machine . . . 179
8.3 AWS's and Human Rights Law . . . 190
8.4 Conclusions . . . 195
References . . . 196

9 AI, Issues of Ownership, Liability and the Role of International Law 199
9.1 Introduction 199
9.2 AI and Patent Eligibility 200
9.2.1 Patents' and IP Rights' Utility 200
9.2.2 Mental Activities, Inventions, IP and Patent-Eligibility 202
9.2.3 The Patent-Eligibility of AI Autonomous Systems' Inventories 208
9.3 AI and Liability 215
9.4 Conclusions 223
References 224

10 Conclusions: A Taste of the Future (?)—AGI/ASI and Potential Legal Personhood 227
10.1 Context of the Conclusions 227
10.2 Identifying the Sets of Legal Issues for the Determination of a Potential Legal Personhood 229
10.3 A New Perception of Sovereignty and of Legal Personhood 232
10.4 Summing Up 240
References 242

Part I
The Ethical Challenges from AI

Chapter 1
Introduction

The ambitions of the human race are contradictory, ambivalent, often dangerous and most important, endless: to explore further the universe, to invent ways to prolong our lives and enhance our biological existence in almost all of its aspects, to achieve exponential growth, to protect the environment, to make our daily lives easier and more beneficial, to restructure the forms of authority and power, to understand the world inside us and around us, to build more effective and cheaper weapons, to invent devices, to expand individual conscious towards collective forms are some of them.

The list is ever-expanding, not unanimously agreed approached from different perspectives and with—often hostile—goals. A common place however is that we tend to use machines in furtherance of our goals. The bigger our goals, the more sophisticated the machines that we invent. Karl Marx in his "German ideology" wrote that "men. . .produce their means of subsistence", which differentiates them from animals, as is the case with consciousness too.[1]

By producing our means of subsistence in gradually more complicated societies we are led into relying more on machines, therefore inventing ones which resemble to characteristics that we, humans have and surpassing our capacities in specific areas. Human inventiveness has led us to the discussion and the ambition of giving life to machines and therefore to achieving a type of divinity.

Envisaging living machines is of course not a new trend, as after all Homers with the self-moving tripods of Hephaestus told us, thousands of years ago.[2] We live however in the first era during which this prospect not only seems realistic but has also started to materialize, although the term "living" becomes gradually blurrier. In this sense we are forced to rethink on the machine-making capacities and therefore

[1]Karl Marx, The German Ideology, First Premises of Materialist Method, (www.marxists.org/archive/marx/works/1845/german-ideology/preface.htm, access. 04-06-2020).

[2]Kang (2011), p. 84.

T. Tzimas, *Legal and Ethical Challenges of Artificial Intelligence from an International Law Perspective*, Law, Governance and Technology Series 46,
https://doi.org/10.1007/978-3-030-78585-7_1

on our ethical, political ideas and symbolic creations and the ways that they may be transferred to potentially, new entities.[3]

It is this prospect, which makes the debate about the possible ramifications of Artificial Intelligence-AI- so intense and up to date. Our reliance on machines is leading us to the development of machines that may reach our level of intelligence or surpass it, not only in specific areas but in general as well. Where will we go from there? Are we going to become the architects and the creators of new forms of life or do we approach the moment of opening a "Pandora's box"? Are we at the verge of liberating our lives from the hardship of social and economic models based on exploitation of humans by humans or are we about to enter a socio-economic catastrophe because of inequality and the suffocation of productive forces?

Are we going to become "Gods" or taste a bitter irony of history, as Morpheus in Matrix tells Nio, when explaining the Matrix? "Throughout human history, we have been dependent on machines to survive. Fate, it seems, is not without a sense of irony."[4]

AI condenses and heightens these expectations and fears as it is the most ambitious technological goal, especially regarding the prospects of general artificial intelligence—AGI—and super artificial intelligence looming -ASI. In fact even existing narrow artificial intelligence—ANI—promises advantages—but raises risks too—of unprecedented nature.[5]

AI arrives as part of a fascinating, albeit potentially dangerous too, world of emerging technologies, including synthetic life, bioengineering,[6] nano-robots,[7] merging of human and artificial intelligence, 5G networks,[8] medical treatment, transportation, tools of cyber security etc.[9] In fact AI constitutes a driving force behind most of these technologies.

---

[3]Mumford (2010), pp. 9–51.

[4]Flavia Medrut, 23 The Matrix Quotes That Will Challenge Your Understanding of the World, Goalcast, (www.goalcast.com/2020/02/28/the-matrix-quotes/, access. 05/06/2020).

[5]Good (1966); Muggleton (2006); McGinnis (2010), p. 371; Benjamin (2005), p. 38.

[6]Yuan-Cheng Fung & Shu Chien, Introduction to Bioengineering V (Yuan-cheng Fung ed., 2001); ETC Group, Extreme Genetic Engineering: An Introduction to Synthetic Biology 1 (Jan. 2007), http://www.etcgroup.org/sites/www.etcgroup.org/files/publication/602/01/synbioreportweb.pdf.

[7]Nanotechnology White Paper, Nanotechnology Workgroup, Envtl. Prot. Agency's sci. Pol'y council 5 (2007), http://epa.gov/osa/pdfs/nanotech/epa-nanotechnology-whitepaper-0207.pdf.

[8]Wilson (2013), p. 308; Terry Grossman et al., Reinventing Humanity: The Future of Human-Machine Intelligence, The Futurist 45–46 (Mar.Apr., 2006), available at www.kurzweilai.net/reinventing-humani.ty-the-fliture-of-human-machine-intelligence.

[9]Sveta McShane, The Future of Surgery Is Robotic, Data-Driven, and Artificially Intelligent, SINGULARITY HUB (Oct. 11, 2016), https://singularityhub.com/2016/10/11/the-future-of-surgery-is-robotic-data-driven-and-artificiallyintelligent/#sm.000t2wraf1306fo6rzd20ac545jib [https://perma.cc/B2ZK-Y5XA]; Cade Metz, Inside Libratus, the Poker AI that Out-Bluffed the Best Humans, WIRED (Feb. 1, 2017, 7:00 AM), https://www.wired.com/2017/02/libratus/ [https://perma.cc/E7R5-JLYZ]; Cade Metz, Google's Hand-Fed AI Now Gives Answers, Not Just Search Results, WIRED (Nov. 29, 2016, 7:00 AM), https://www.wired.com/2016/11/googles-search-engine-can-now-answer-questions-human-help/ [https://perma.cc/V7ZY-BXMD]; Madhav

The origins of AI date as back as 1956, in the famous by now, Dartmouth Conference, when and where, John McCarthy, a mathematics professor at the relevant college came up with the term AI.[10] As Professor McCarthy articulated back then, the inspiration of the event had been "to proceed on the basis of the conjecture that every aspect of learning or any other feature of intelligence can in principle be so precisely described that a machine can be made to simulate it."[11]

Similarly, Alan Turing and Alonzo Church through their distinct researches came up with what became known as the Turing-Church thesis, which argued in favor of the feasibility of a universal symbol system that can simulate any algorithmically calculable system. Therefore, once our cognitive processes are perceived as algorithmically calculable, a computer is expected to have the potential of simulating the mind itself, once the technical capacities are achieved.[12]

This is essentially the origin as well as the goal of AI: the invention of a simulation of the human mind or—*to put it in other terms*—of human intelligence, which in several possible scenarios, may come to have some type of a life of its own, possessing unique characteristics, reaching even greater heights of intelligence compared to the human mind, either regarding specific aspects of our intelligence or in general.

Since its initial emergence, AI became a distinct scientific branch, with ups and downs, with disappointments and expectations. The periods of disappointments from AI have been labeled as AI "winters", which however have been followed by AI "reincarnations".[13]

The present, highly optimistic phase for AI, is the outcome of a number of factors, such as "...advances in neuroscience as well as computer science...[and] increases in affordable computing power and faster networks; cloud infrastructures; the growth in the Internet of Things and Big Data – and specifically the open-source availability of very large datasets", among several more contributors.[14]

The emergence of cyberspace constitutes the domain for AI exponential growth, as this is the "pool" for the gathering and use of big data which are fundamental for machine learning.[15]

AI could not evolve without the "digitization" of information and essentially of modern world. It is characteristically estimated that by 2012, all stored information

---

Srinath, Artificially Intelligent Homes: The Robot Vacuum Cleaner, MEDIUM (Aug. 23, 2017), https://medium.com/@humansforai/artificially-intelligent-homes-the-robot-vacuum-cleaner-5dd8071e9f8b [https://perma.cc/SSE4-DDU9].

[10]Gerdes (2018), p. 678.

[11]Dartmouth, Artificial Intelligence (AI) Coined at Dartmouth, (https://250.dartmouth.edu/highlights/artificial-intelligence-ai-coined-dartmouth, access. 06-06-2020).

[12]*Gerdes, An Inclusive Ethical Design Perspective for a Flourishing Future with Artificial Intelligent Systems,* at p. 678.

[13]De Spiegeleire et al. (2017), p. 35.

[14]De Spiegeleire et al. (2017).

[15]*Cuéllar, A Simpler World? On Pruning Risks And Harvesting Fruits in an Orchard of Whispering Algorithms.*

of the world was digitized, whereas in 2000 the equivalent percentage was only 25 percent; a huge leap took place in the meantime.[16]

Currently, the expansion of AI seems unstoppable, reaching scientific areas which are considered as the realm of humans because of their sophistication. The expanding role of AI into law, through scrutinizing legal evidence, the prospect of AI capable of issuing moral judgments, and reaching a judicial decision on human rights law, the role of AI as an assistant of lawyers- generating the fear of usurping the legal profession-[17] constitute only some examples of technological achievements, with potentially huge implications in moral and legal terms.[18]

The impact of AI generates different and often contradictory views among various stakeholders. It is not uncommon to see stark contrast between the enthusiasm of engineers and private corporations on the one hand and skeptical observers on the other hand,[19] of various—and all kinds of—origins.

Still, the exponential growth of AI applications creates a reality of relying on it at a growing rate. In several regards, we tend to put trust to AI, even though-as is analyzed below—our knowledge about AI and its potential evolution is far from complete. The inherent unpredictability of AI because of its expanding autonomy, the so called "black box" effect, the potentially biased machine-training of AI and the ellipsis of a regulatory framework for AI create risks which necessitate both a more insightful knowledge of the ontology of AI and a coherent legal framework.

The combination of the impact of AI and of the necessity of regulation constitutes the motive behind this book. The scope of the book is to explore not only or mainly, the existing legal framework for AI—which remains rather weak—but mainly focuses on a "lex ferenda" analysis.

In order to do so however, the book first focuses on critical, non-legal issues, which present the overall picture of AI impact: the existential risks and expectations from AI, AI definitions, the subsequent debate about weak and strong AI and the issue of AI consciousness are described. Having discussed these, the ethics of AI and their different aspects are further analyzed. The discussion about AI ethics explains why legal regulation becomes critical; it is in order to somehow achieve a more "objective" approach to ethical questions which are highly ambivalent and define or will define humanity, explaining also why law must step in.

This is the first, non- legal part of the book, which shapes the framework for the second one, the legal part by framing the context of the wider debate, which justifies the need for the legal discussion.

In the second part, the "lege ferenda" legal examination of AI is articulated; the part begins with the issue of legal governance and of some of the characteristics that

[16]Cuéllar (2017), pp. 30–31.

[17]Becerra (2018), pp. 27–52; Simon (2018), pp. 34–37; Hall (2018), pp. 17–19.

[18]Chris Johnston, "Artificial intelligence 'judge' developed by UCL computer scientists," The Guardian, Oct. 24, 2016, https://www.theguardian.com/technology/2016/oct/24/artificial-intelligence-judge-university-college-london-computer-scientists.

[19]Burri (2016), p. 360.

an international treaty about AI must have. This analysis corresponds again with the need for an overall regulation of AI. Then, human rights, international humanitarian law—IHL—state responsibility, matters of ownership and eligibility and last but not least of legal personhood are analyzed.

The scope of this part is to present the framework which can shape both research and its implementation regarding the development of AI, in ways that will safeguard freeing[20]—in the sense of the development of human capacities—and friendly towards human capacities, forms of AI.

From both parts it becomes apparent that no alleged, legal "neutrality" is shared in this book. Legal science as all social sciences is explicitly or implicitly political too. The effort in the book is not to conceal this but to prove that the ontology of AI on the one hand and the proper interpretation of existing law on the other hand lead to quest for freeing and friendly for humans evolution of AI.

The next chapter focuses on the existential expectations as well as risks by AI on its first part and on the economic and social prospect as well as threats in its second part, in order to present a picture of why AI creates sentiments of high hopes as well as of anxiety and of concern.

In the beginning, three definitions are outlined, which are crucial for the rest of the analysis: the first is the term "singularity" that Vernor Vinge and Ray Kurzweil have described as an intelligence explosion by AI entities,[21] capable of self-improvement and self-replication, at a pace higher compared to the one that we, humans can achieve.

The other two terms are those of weak or narrow AI, where "the computer is merely an instrument for investigating cognitive processes" and strong AI, where "[t [he processes in the computer are intellectual, self-learning processes."[22] Weak AI is labeled as Artificial Narrow Intelligence-ANI- while strong AI is further distinguished between Artificial General Intelligence—AGI—and Artificial Super Intelligence-ASI, with the former being AI at the level of human general intelligence and the latter, AI which has surpassed human intelligence.[23]

These terms are met continuously especially throughout the first part of the book and are further analyzed below.

References

Becerra SD (2018) The rise of artificial intelligence in the legal field: where we are and where we are going. J Bus Entrepreneurship Law 11:27

[20] Or liberating, to place it differently.

[21] Kurzweil (2005) and Vinge (1993).

[22] *Wisskirchen et al, Artificial Intelligence and Robotics and their Impact on the Workplace*, at p. 10.

[23] T. Urban, The AI Revolution: The Road to Superintelligence, WAIT BUT WHY (Jan. 22, 2015), (waitbutwhy.com/2015/01/artificial-intelligence-revolution-1.html, access. 28-06-2018).

Benjamin S (2005) Man and the machines it's time to start thinking about how we might grant legal rights to computers. Legal Aff:36
Burri T (2016) The politics of robot autonomy. Eur J Risk Regul 7:341
Cuéllar M-F (2017) A simpler world? On pruning risks and harvesting fruits in an orchard of whispering algorithms. U.C. Davis Law Rev 51:27
De Spiegeleire S, Maas M, Sweijs T (2017) Artificial intelligence and the future of defense. The Hague Centre for Strategic Studies, Den Haag, p 35
Gerdes A (2018) An inclusive ethical design perspective for a flourishing future with artificial intelligent systems. Eur J Risk Regulation 9:677
Good IJ (1966) Speculations concerning the first ultraintelligent machine. Adv Comp 6:31
Hall D (2018) The future of law includes math. J Kansas Bar Assoc 87:17
Kang M (2011) Sublime dreams of living machines, the automation in the European imagination. Harvard University Press, Cambridge, p 84
Kurzweil R (2005) The singularity is near: when humans transcend biology. Viking, New York
McGinnis JO (2010) Accelerating AI. Northwestern Univ Law Rev Colloquy 104:366
Muggleton SH (2006) Exceeding human limits. Nature 440:409
Mumford L (2010) Technics & civilization. The University of Chicago Press, Chicago, pp 9–51
Simon RD (2018) Artificial intelligence, real ethics. N Y State Bar J 90:34
Vinge V (1993) The coming technological singularity: how to survive in the post-human era. In: Vis21: interdisciplinary science and engineering in the era of cyberspace, 11–22. NASA Conference Publication 10129. NASA Lewis Research Center, Cleveland
Wilson G (2013) Minimizing global catastrophic and existential risks from emerging technologies through international law. Va Environ Law J 31:307

Chapter 2
The Expectations and Risks from AI

2.1 Introduction

Isaac Asimov, among his many contributions, had stated that the saddest aspect of life is how quickly science outpaces the wisdom of society. He had explained what fuels our anxiety in the face of magnificent technological advance, even if we consciously fail to capture it. Maybe it is not actually the saddest aspect of life but it is certainly a worrisome one. It is also a crucial reason explaining the debate about AI evolution: while the technological aspect of AI is present since its initial conception, the legal and ethical aspects are only gradually entering public debate since not more than—roughly speaking—15–20 years.

The impact of AI obviously cannot be completely assessed in advance given our limited knowledge about its evolution and application. It can be envisaged with some extent of accuracy however, especially taking into account our expectations and anxieties in the present.

This chapter analyzes mainly two types of expectations and risks; those emerging from the core of the ontological perspectives of AI, meaning its evolving intellectual autonomy and capacity and the ones that are related to social and economic consequences.

The former represents and touch upon our existential aspirations-*with the main on being the victory over death*—and fears—*the subversion of our dominion by a potentially superior species.*

The latter are included in what is described as the 4th industrial revolution and already an impact on the social and economic model, promising a new era of welfare or threatening a social and economic desertification for the majority of our societies. The analysis in this chapter briefly depicts the importance of AI and therefore justifies the need for regulation.

T. Tzimas, *Legal and Ethical Challenges of Artificial Intelligence from an International Law Perspective*, Law, Governance and Technology Series 46,
https://doi.org/10.1007/978-3-030-78585-7_2

2.2 Between High Expectations and Existential Anxiety

There is an inherent tendency among humans to extract some type of joy from dystopian art and science fiction. While often underestimated regarding its artistic as well as scientific value, science fiction can depict fears and warnings which are quite realistic in terms of their potential materialization. It is in this sense perfectly understandable why science fiction which focuses on AI is both popular and most often dystopian.[1]

AI is already manifesting capacities—at significant, albeit still narrow areas—which begin to approach or are already exceeding human capacities; image recognition, speech transcription, direct translation, driving, emotions recognition, article, movie screenplays and music writing, text analysis, generating recipes, scrutinizing legal evidence are some of the rapidly developing applications, indicating both cognitive and analytical capacities.[2] AI systems are also used as experts, replicating human experts in a variety of sciences and of fields[3] and it is expected that it will do so even more in the future.

---

[1]Wired, Why Science Fiction Is the Most Important Genre, (August 9, 20o18), (https://www.wired.com/2018/09/geeks-guide-yuval-noah-harari/, Accessed 20-06-2019).

[2]Chris Johnston, "Artificial intelligence 'judge' developed by UCL computer scientists," The Guardian, Oct. 24, 2016, (https://www.theguardian.com/technology/2016/oct/24/artificial-intelligence-judge-university-college-london-computer-scientists).

Gaëtan Hadjeres & François Pachet, "DeepBach: a Steerable Model for Bach chorales generation" (Dec. 3, 2016) at 1, https://arxiv.org/pdf/1612.01010v1.pdf.

Morgane Tual, "Intelligence artificielle: quand la machine imite l'artiste" [Artificial intelligence: when the machine imitates the artist], Le Monde, Sept. 8, 2015, http://www.lemonde.fr/pixels/article/2015/09/08/intelligence-artificielle-les-machines-peuventelles-etre-creatives_4749254_4408996.html.

Allison Linn, "Microsoft Researchers Win ImageNet Computer Vision Challenge," Next at Microsoft, December 10, 2015, https://blogs.microsoft.com/next/2015/12/10/microsoft-researchers-win-imagenet-computer-vision-challenge/;

Wayne Xiong et al., "Achieving Human Parity in Conversational Speech Recognition," arXiv Preprint arXiv:1610.05256, 2016, https://arxiv.org/abs/1610.05256;

Davide Castelvecchi, "Deep Learning Boosts Google Translate Tool," Nature News, accessed February 25, 2017, doi:https://doi.org/10.1038/nature.2016.20696;

Matt Burgess, "Microsoft's AI Can Detect Your Emotions (but Only If You're Angry)," Wired UK, 2015, http://www.wired.co.uk/article/microsoft-predict-emotions-artificial-intelligence;

Hyacinth Mascarenhas, "Associated Press to Expand Its Sports Coverage by Using AI to Write Minor League Baseball Articles," International Business Times UK, July 5, 2016, http://www.ibtimes.co.uk/associated-press-expand-its-sports-coverage-by-using-ai-write-minor-league-baseball-articles-1568804.; HAL 90210, "This Is What Happens When an AI-Written Screenplay Is Made into a Film," The Guardian, June 10, 2016, sec. Technology, https://www.theguardian.com/technology/2016/jun/10/artificial-intelligence-screenplay-sunspring-silicon-valley-thomas-middleditch-ai.; Alex Marshall, "From Jingles to Pop Hits, A.I. Is Music to Some Ears," The New York Times, January 22, 2017, https://www.nytimes.com/2017/01/22/arts/music/jukedeck-artificial-intelligence-songwriting.html.

[3]Hassett (2000), p. 1226.

Such growth of AI into new areas is not only impressive but also enlightening of how AI touches our existential inner chores. The novelty and the expected, evolving ontology, the autonomy and unpredictability of AI lead to intellectual evolution which may potentially bring AI beyond our reach and control. How can we avoid therefore, the fear of bringing ourselves into the position of sorcerer's apprentice, without on the other hand restricting the potential benefits of technological progress?

In order to address the existential "touch" of AI upon us we need to keep in mind that the driving force behind AI is its autonomy. Autonomy—a concept which is revisited several times in the course of this book, in relation to AI is multi-faceted, ambiguous and comprised of different levels and areas of implementation. In relation to AI, it describes a situation of growing or potentially complete "detachment" of AI from human supervision and control.

As Merel Noorman and Deborah Johnson notice "[a]utonomy implies acting on one's own, controlling one's self, and being responsible for one's actions. Being responsible for one's action in particular requires that the person had some kind of control over the outcome at issue. Thus, framing robots as becoming increasingly autonomous may suggest that robots will be in control and that human actors will, therefore, not be in control."[4]

According to P.W. Singer autonomy is "the relative independence of a robot . . . [that] is measured on a sliding scale from direct human operation at the low end to what is known as 'adaptive' at the high end."[5]

While autonomy partially resembles to automation,[6] the primary is qualitatively different in the sense that it gradually surpasses human control, which on the contrary is omnipresent with automation. An initial and critical remark is that AI autonomy is based on the human design—at least in the primary stages—and therefore in principle it is not complete, in the sense that the at least some initial parameters have been set in advance.

While the argument is not mistaken, still is of relative significance only: human autonomy is also restrained by natural evolution and biology but nevertheless attempts—often successfully—to surpass and rewrite the biological and atavistic human instincts. In similar terms, the prospect therefore is that AI may eventually move beyond its initial design, eventually re-writing its software.

AI could then replicate the most fundamental elements of our dominion: our autonomy and our superior intelligence, which make it possible for us to achieve—until now—our superiority. The two elements are mutually reinforcing and concretely linked: we, humans are not bound completely by our biology, which we tend

[4]Noorman and Johnson (2014), pp. 51, 52.

[5]Singer (2009), p. 5.

[6]"The mechanization of well defined processes, in which routine tasks are translated into some formalized structure that allows human operators to delegate some level of control to an automated system".

Sheridan and Verplank (1978), pp. 6–12.

to amend and potentially to improve as scientific and technological progress advances.

Therefore, it is only natural to be at least skeptical towards a future with entities possessing equal or superior intelligence and levels of autonomy; the prospect even of existential risk looms as possible.[7]

AI that will have reached or surpassed our level of intelligence make us wonder why would highly autonomous and intelligent AI want to give up control back to its original creators?[8] Why remain contained in pre-defined goals set for it by us, humans?

Even AI in its current form and narrow intelligence poses risks because of its embedded-ness in an ever-growing number of crucial aspects of our lives. The role of AI in military, financial,[9] health, educational, environmental, governance networks-among others—are areas where risk generated by AI—*even limited*—autonomy can be diffused through non-linear networks, with significant impact—even systemic.[10]

The answer therefore to the question whether AI brings risk with it is yes; as Eliezer Yudkowski comments the greatest of them all is that people conclude too early that they understand it[11] or that they assume that they can achieve it without necessarily having acquired complete and thorough understanding of what intelligence means.[12]

Our projection of our—lack of complete—understanding of the concept of intelligence on AI is owed to our lack of complete comprehension of human intelligence too, which is partially covered by the prevalent and until now self-obvious, anthropomorphism because of which we tend to identify higher intelligence with the human mind.

Yudkowski again however suggests that AI "refers to a vastly greater space of possibilities than does the term "Homo sapiens." When we talk about "AIs" we are really talking about minds-in-general, or optimization processes in general. Imagine a map of mind design space. In one corner, a tiny little circle contains all humans; within a larger tiny circle containing all biological life; and all the rest of the huge map is the space of minds-in-general. The entire map floats in a still vaster space, the space of optimization processes."[13]

---

[7]Nick Bostrom & Milan M. IRKOVI, Introduction, in global catastrophic risks 25 (Nick Bostrom & Milan M. #irkovi#, eds., 2008).

[8]Martinez (2019), p. 1027.

[9]Karppi and Crawford (2016), pp. 73, 74, 77.

[10]Renn and Klinke (2004), p. S41.
van Asselt and Renn (2011), pp. 431, 436–438.
Spier (2011), p. 501.

[11]Yudkowski (2008) pp. 308–345.

[12]E. Yudkowski, Artificial Mysterious Intelligence, Lesswrong, (2008, December 7), (https://www.lesswrong.com/posts/fKofLyepu446zRgPP/artificial-mysterious-intelligence, Accessed 22-08-2019).

[13]Yudkowski (2008), p. 313.

Regardless of what our well-established ideas are, there are many, different intelligences and even more significantly, there are potentially, different intelligences equally or even more evolved than human.

From such a perspective, the unprecedented—ness of potential AI developments and the mystery surrounding them emerges as not only the outcome of pop culture but of a radical transformation of our—until recently—self—obvious identification of humanity with highly evolved and dominant intelligence.[14]

The lack of understanding of intelligence and therefore of AI may be frightening but does not lead necessarily to regulation—at least to a proper one. We could even be led into making potentially catastrophic choices, on the basis of false assumptions.

On top of our lack of understanding, we should add a sentiment of anxiety as well as of expectations, which intensifies as an atmosphere of emergency and of expected groundbreaking developments grows. The most graphic description of this feeling is the potential of a moment of singularity, as mentioned above according to the description by Vinge and Kurzweil.

As the mathematician I. J. Good–Alan Turing's colleague in the team of the latter during World War II—has put it: "Let an ultraintelligent machine be defined as a machine that can far surpass all the intellectual activities of any man however clever. Since the design of machines is one of these intellectual activities, an ultraintelligent machine could design even better machines; there would then unquestionably be an "intelligence explosion," and the intelligence of man would be left far behind. Thus the first ultraintelligent machine is the last invention that man need ever make, provided that the machine is docile enough to tell us how to keep it under control."[15] This is in a nutshell the moment of singularity.

The estimates currently foresee the emergence of ultra or super intelligence—as it is currently labelled—or in other words of singularity, somewhere between 20 and 50 years from today, further raising the sentiment of emergency.[16] We cannot even foretell with precision how singularity would look like but we know that because of its expected groundbreaking impact, both states and private entities compete towards gaining the upper hand in the prospect of the singularity.[17]

---

[14]Bostrom (2002).

[15]Good (1965), p. 33.

[16]Tegmark; Baum et al. (2011), pp. 185–195.

[17]Greg Satell, 3 Reasons to Believe the Singularity Is Near, Forbes (June 3, 2016 11:19 PM), http://www.forbes.com/sites/gregsatell/2016/06/03/3-reasons-to-believe-the-singularity-is-near/#298b88471cb;

Deep Learning, NVIDIA, https://blogs.nvidia.com/blog/category/deep-learning/ (last visited Nov. 23, 2016) (aggregating deep learning and AI research by Nvidia, a major hardware company); Facebook AI Research (FAIR),FACEBOOK (emphasis added), https://web.archive.org/web/20161116191404/https://research.facebook.com/ai (last visited Nov. 23, 2016) ("We're committed to advancing the field of machine intelligence and developing technologies . . . . In the long term, we seek to understand intelligence and make intelligent machines. How will we accomplish all this? By building the best AI lab in the world."); IBM Research: Artificial Intelligence, IBM (emphasis added), http://researcher.ibm.com/researcher/view_group.php?id=135 (last visited Nov. 23, 2016)

Despite the fact that such predictions have been proven rather optimistic in the past[18] and therefore up to some extent inaccurate, there are reasons to assume that their materialization will take place and that the urgency of regulation will be proven realistic.

After all, part of the disappointments from AI should be blamed on the fact that certain activities and standards, which were considered as epitomes of human intelligence have been surpassed by AI, only to indicate that they were not eventually satisfactory thresholds for the surpassing of human intelligence.[19] Partially because of AI progress we realize that human intelligence and its thresholds are much more complicated than assumed in the past.

The vastness's of definitions of intelligence, as well as its etymological roots are enlightening of the difficulties: "to gather, to collect, to assemble or to choose, and to form an impression, thus leading one to finally understand, perceive, or know".[20]

As with other relevant concepts, the truth is that until recently our main way to approach intelligence for far too long was "we know it, when we see it". AI is an additional reason for looking deeper into intelligence and the more we examine it, the most complicated it seems.

("Artificial Intelligence (AI) has a long history at IBM Research, dating back to the 1950s. By AI we mean anything that makes machines act more intelligently. Our work includes basic and applied research in machine learning, deep question answering, search and planning, knowledge representation, and cognitive architectures."); Machine Intelligence, RES. GOOGLE, http://research.google.com/pubs/MachineIntelligence.html (last visited Nov. 23, 2016) ("Research at Google is at the forefront of innovation in Machine Intelligence, with active research exploring virtually all aspects of machine learning, including deep learning and more classical algorithms."); The Race for AI: Google, Baidu, Intel, Apple in a Rush to Grab Artificial Intelligence Startups, CB Insights (July 21, 2017).

Elon Musk (©ElonMusk), Twitter (Sept. 4, 2017, 2:33 AM), https://twitter.com/elonmusk/status/904638455761612800;

Dominic Basulto, Why Ray Kurzweil's Predictions Are Right 86% of the Time, Big Think, http://bigthink.com/endlessinnovation/why-ray-kurzweils-predictions-are-right-86-of-the-time (last visited Nov. 18, 2017).

[18]In fact AI is in a constant procedure of high expectations or "spring times" and AI "winters", between the first expectations the 40's and the present. The main deficiency consisted of achievements in narrow areas but lack of success in the general one. One of the issues which have caused significant problems in the growth of AI is the "combinatorial explosion", which can prove exhaustive search as non-efficient, when long theorems require proof. Combinatorial explosion requires different approaches, meaning "algorithms that exploit structure in the target domain and take advantage of prior knowledge by using heuristic search, planning, and flexible abstract representations—capabilities that were poorly developed in the early AI systems."

Such approach requires capacities which surpass the mere computational power of narrow artificial intelligence, especially of previous eras.

As is examined below, recent developments "promise" to overcome this.

Bostrom (2016), pp. 5–10.

[19]Such aradigm is chess-playing, which was considered as the threshold between human and artificial intelligence, until it was surpassed.

Newell et al. (1958), p. 320.

[20]De Spiegeleire et al. (2017), p. 26.

The combination of lack of complete understanding of intelligence, the unpredictability of AI, its rapid evolution and the prospect of singularity explain both the fascination and the fear from AI. Once the latter emerges, we have no real knowledge about what will happen next but only speculations, which until recently belonged to the area of science fiction.

We are for example pretty confident that the speed of AI intelligence growth will accelerate, once self—improvement will have been achieved. The expected or possible chain of events will begin from AI capacity to re-write its own algorithms and exponentially self—improve, surpassing human intelligence, which lacks the capacity of such rapid self—improvement and setting its own goals.[21]

We can somehow guess the speed of AGI and ASI evolution and possibly some of its initial steps but we cannot guess the directions that such AI will choose to follow and the characteristics that it will demonstrate. Practically, we credibly guess the prospects of AI beyond a certain level of development.

Two existential issues could emerge: first, an imbalance of intelligence at our expense—*with us, humans becoming the inferior species*—in favor of non-biological entities and secondly a lack of even fundamental conceptual communication between the two most intelligent "species". Both of them heighten the fear of irreversible changes, once we lose the possession of the superior intelligence.[22]

However, we need to consider the expectations as well. The positive side focuses on the so-called friendly AI, meaning AI which will benefit and not harm humans, thanks to its advanced intelligence.[23]

AI bears the promise of significantly enhancing human life on various aspects, beginning from the already existing, narrow applications. The enhanced automation[24] in the industry and the shift to autonomy,[25] the take—over by AI of tasks even at the service sector which can be considered as "tedious"—*i.e. in the banking sector*—climate and weather forecasting, disaster response,[26] the potentially better cooperation among different actors in complicated matters such as in matters of information, geopolitics and international relations, logistics, resources ex.[27]

[21]Good (1965), pp. 31–88.

[22]From a certain point of view this is the case with pre- modern era as well, not only regarding ancient Athens but since humans started distinguishing from other beings and the natural environment, projecting to Gods and Goddesses, human identities.

Add Reference.

[23]Yudkowski (2001), p. 2.

[24]According to Thomas Sheridan automation is "the mechanization of well defined processes, in which routine tasks are translated into some formalized structure that allows human operators to delegate some level of control to an automated system."

Sheridan and Verplank (1978), pp. 6–12.

[25]The shift from the automation to the autonomy is not always clear. The crucial element is whether human control is required and at what extent.

[26]Kashyap Vyas, 7 Benefits of AI That Will Help Humanity, Not Harm It, Interesting Engineering, (2021, April 6), https://interestingengineering.com/7-ways-ai-will-help-humanity-not-harm-it.

[27]Floridi et al. (2018), pp. 692–694.

The realization of the positive expectations depends up to some extent upon the complementarity or not, of AI with human intelligence. However, what friendly AI will bring in our societies constitutes a matter of debate, given our lack of unanimous approach on what should be considered as beneficial and therefore friendly to humans—*as is analyzed in the next chapter*.

Friendly AI for example bears the prospect of freeing us from hard labor or even further from unwanted labor; of generating further economic growth; of dealing in unbiased, speedy, effective and cheaper ways with sectors such as policing, justice, health, environmental crisis, natural disasters, education, governance, defense and several more of them which necessitate decision-making, with the involvement of sophisticated intelligence.

The synergies between human intelligence and AI "promise" the enhancement of humans in most of their aspects. Such synergies may remain external—*humans using AI as external to themselves, in terms of analysis, forecasts, decision—making and in general as a type of assistant-*[28] or may evolve into the merging of the two forms of intelligence either temporarily or permanently.

The second profoundly enters humanity, existentially—speaking, into uncharted waters. Elon Musk argues in favor of "having some sort of merger of biological intelligence and machine intelligence" and his company "Neuralink" aims at implanting chips in human brain. Musk argues that through this way humans will keep artificial intelligence under control.[29] The proposition is that of "mind design", with humans playing the role that God had according to theologies.[30]

While the temptation is strong—exceeding human mind's capacities, far beyond what nature "created", by acquiring the capacity for example to connect directly to the cyberspace or to break the barriers of biology[31]—the risks are significant too: what if a microchip malfunction? Will such a brain be usurped or become captive to malfunctioning AI?

The merging of the two intelligences is most likely to evolve initially by invoking medical reasons, instead of human enhancement. But the merging of the two will most likely continue, as after all the limits between healing and enhancement are most often blurry. This development will give rise, as is analyzed below, to significant questions and issues, the most of crucial of which is the setting of a threshold for the prevalence of the human aspect of intelligence over the artificial one.

---

[28]Ferguson and Goldie (1999), pp. 56–58.

[29]Susan Schneider, Merging with AI would be suicide for the human mind, Financial Times, (2019, August 13), (https://www.ft.com/content/0c4fac58-bd15-11e9-9381-78bab8a70848, Accessed 16-06-2020).

[30]Schneider (2019), pp. 2–4.

[31]Solomon Israel, Artificial intelligence, human brain to merge in 2030s, says futurist Kurzweil, CBC News, (2015, June 9), (https://www.cbc.ca/news/technology/artificial-intelligence-human-brain-to-merge-in-2030s-says-futurist-kurzweil-1.3100124, Accessed 16-06-2020).

Human nature is historically improved, enhanced, healed and now, potentially even re-designed in the future.[32] Can a "medical science" endorsing such a goal be ethically acceptable and if yes, under what conditions, when, for whom and by what means? The answers are more difficult than it seems. As the World Health Organization—WHO—provides in its constitution, "Health is a state of complete physical, mental and social well-being and not merely the absence of disease or infirmity".[33]

Therefore, why discourage science which aims at human-enhancement, even reaching the levels of post-humanism?[34] Or if restrictions are to be imposed on human enhancement, on what ethics and laws will they be justified? How ethically acceptable is it to prohibit or delay technological evolution, which among several other magnificent achievements, promises to treat death as a disease and cure it, by reducing soul to self, self to mind, and mind to brain, which will then be preserved as a "softwarized" program in a hardware other than the human body?[35]

After all, "According to the strong artificial intelligence program there is no fundamental difference between computers and brains: a computer is different machinery than a person in terms of speed and memory capacity."[36]

While such a scientific development and the ones leading potentially to it will be undoubtedly, groundbreaking technologically-speaking, is it actually—ethically-speaking—as ambivalent as it may sound or is it already justified by our well—rooted human-centrism?[37]

Secular humanism may have very well outdated religious beliefs about afterlife in the area of science but has not diminished the hope for immortality; on the contrary, science, implicitly or explicitly predicts that matter can in various ways surpass death, albeit by means which belong in the realm of scientific proof, instead of that of metaphysical belief.[38]

If this is the philosophical case, the quest for immortality becomes ethically acceptable; it can be considered as embedded both in the existential anxiety of humans, as well as in the human-centrism of secular philosophical and political victory over the dei-centric approach to the world and to our existence.

From another perspective of course and for the not that distant philosophical reasons, the quest for immortality becomes ethically ambiguous or even

[32]Leon R. Kass, Preventing a Brave New World: Why We Should Ban Human Cloning Now, The New Republic, May 21, 2001, at 22, available at http://www.thenewrepublic.com/052101/kass052101_print.html.

[33]World Health Organization, Constitution, https://www.who.int/about/who-we-are/constitution.

[34]Again we have to wonder what post- humanism will come to mean.

[35]Pasquale (2002), pp. 86–88.

"...reality is finally a quantity of material atoms and that significant discourse must relate itself directly or indirectly to reality so conceived."

Murdoch (1997), p. 287.

[36]Horgan (1999), p. 201.

[37]Taylor (1999), p. 24.

[38]Purdy (1998), pp. 34–40.

unacceptable.[39] By seeking endless life we may miss all these that make life worth living in the framework of finiteness. As the gerontologist Paul Hayflick cautioned "Given the possibility that you could replace all your parts, including your brain, then you lose your self-identity, your self-recognition. You lose who you are! You are who you are because of your memory."[40]

In other words, once we begin to integrate the two types of intelligence, within ourselves, until when and how we will be sure that it is human intelligence that guides us, instead of the AI? And if we are not guided completely or—even further—at all by human intelligence but on the contrary we are guided by AI which we have embodied and which is trained by our human intelligence, will we be remaining humans or we will have evolved to some type of meta-human or transhumant species, being different persons as well?[41]

AI promises tor threatens to offer a solution by breaking down our consciousness into small "particles" of information—simplistically speaking—which can then be "software-ized" and therefore "uploaded" into different forms of physical or non-physical existence.

Diane Ackerman states that "The brain is silent, the brain is dark, the brain tastes nothing, the brain hears nothing. All it receives are electrical impulses--not the sumptuous chocolate melting sweetly, not the oboe solo like the flight of a bird, not the pastel pink and lavender sunset over the coral reef--only impulses."[42] Therefore, all that is needed—although it is of course much more complicated than we can imagine—is a way to code and reproduce such impulses.

Even if we consider that without death, we will no more be humans but something else, why should we remain humans once technologies allow us be something "more", in the sense of an enhanced version of "being"? Why are we to remain bound by biological evolution if we can re-design it and our future form of existence?

Why not try to achieve the major breakthrough, the anticipated or hoped digitalization of the human mind, which promises immortality of consciousness via the cyberspace or artificial bodies: the uploading of our consciousness so that it can live on forever, turning death into an optional condition.[43]

Either through an artificial body or emulation-*a living, conscious avatar*—we hope—*or fear*—that the domain of immortality will be within reach. It is the prospect of a "substrate-independent minds," in which human and machine

---

[39]"Strip something of its mortality, and how do you know what's left to see?".
Doty (1996), p. 85.

[40]Stephen S. Hall, Racing Toward Immortality: The Recycled Generation, N.Y. Times, Jan. 30, 2000 (Magazine), at p. 31.

[41]The term can be traced back to Julian Huxley back in 1957.
Huxley (1957), pp. 13–17.

[42]Ackerman (1990), p. 307.

[43]Maria Trimarchi, Is it possible to digitize human consciousness?, HowStuffWorks, https://electronics.howstuffworks.com/future-tech/digitize-human-consciousness.htm, Accessed 12-06-2020).

consciousness will merge, transcending biological limits of time, space and memory" that fascinates us.[44]

As Anders Sandberg explained "The point of brain emulation is to recreate the function of the original brain: if 'run' it will be able to think and act as the original," he says. Progress has been slow but steady. "We are now able to take small brain tissue samples and map them in 3D. These are at exquisite resolution, but the blocks are just a few microns across. We can run simulations of the size of a mouse brain on supercomputers—but we do not have the total connectivity yet. As methods improve, I expect to see automatic conversion of scanned tissue into models that can be run. The different parts exist, but so far there is no pipeline from brains to emulations."[45]

The emulation is different from a simulation in the sense that the former mimics not only the outward outcome but also the "internal causal dynamics", so that the emulated system and in this particular case the human mind behaves as the original.[46] Obviously, this is a challenging task: we need to understand the human brain with the help of computational neuroscience and combine simplified parts such as simulated neurons with network structures so that the patterns of the brain are comprehended. We must combine effectively "biological realism (attempting to be faithful to biology), completeness (using all available empirical data about the system), tractability (the possibility of quantitative or qualitative simulation) and understanding (producing a compressed representation of the salient aspects of the system in the mind of the experimenter)".[47]

The technological challenges are vast. Technologically speaking, the whole concept is based on some assumptions which must be proven both accurate and feasible.[48] We must achieve technology capable of scanning completely the human brain, of creating software on the basis of the acquired information from its scanning and of the interpretation of information and the hardware which will be capable of uploading or downloading such software.[49] The steps within these procedures are equally challenging. Their detailed analysis evades the scope of this book.

Some critical questions—they are further analyzed in the next chapters—emerge however: how will we interpret free will in emulation? What will be the impact of the environment and of what environment? How will be missing parts of the human brain re-constructed and emulated? What will be the status of the several emulations

---

[44]Jerry Adler, The Quest to Upload Your Mind Into the Digital Space, Smithsonian Magazine, (May 2015), (https://www.smithsonianmag.com/innovation/quest-upload-mind-into-digital-space-180954946/, Accessed 12-06-2020).

[45]Parkin, Back-up brains: The era of digital immortality, BBC Future, (2015, January 23rd), (https://www.bbc.com/future/article/20150122-the-secret-to-immortality, Accessed 12-06-2020).

[46]Sandberg and Bostrom (2008), p. 7.

[47]Sandberg and Bostrom (2008), p. 9.

[48]As such are mentioned physicalism, or multiple realizability, Computability, Non-organicism, Scale separation, Component tractability, Simulation tractability, Brain-centeredness.
Sandberg and Bostrom (2008), pp. 14–15.

[49]Sandberg and Bostrom (2008), p. 15.

which will be created—i.e. failed attempts or emulations of parts of the human brain—in the course of the search for a complete and functioning emulation? Will they be considered as "persons" and therefore as having some right or will they be considered as mere objects in an experimental lab? How are we going to decode the actual subjective sentiments of these emulations? Essentially, are emulations the humans "themselves" who are emulated or a different person? Even further what will human and person mean in the era of emulation?

From a different perspective, the victory over death may be seen as a danger of mass extinction, absorption or de-humanization. In this new, vast universe of emulations will there be place for humans?[50]

From the above—mentioned discussion, it becomes obvious that at a large extent, the prospect of risk or of expectation is a matter of perspective, for which there is no unanimous agreement in the present. This may be the greatest danger of all, for which Asimov warned us: unleashing technology while we cannot communicate among us, in the face of it.

The existential prospect as well as the risks by AI may self-evidently emerge from technological advances but are determined on the basis of politico—philosophical or in the wider sense, ethical assumptions. This is where the need for legal regulation steps in. Such a need was often underestimated in the past in favor of a solely technologically oriented approach—although exceptions raising issues other than technological can be found too.[51] The gradual raising of ethic—political, philosophical and legal issues constitutes a rather recent development, partially because of the realization of the proximity of the risks and of the expectations.

The public debate is often divided between two "contradictory" views: fear of AI or enthusiastic optimism. The opinions of the experts differ respectively.

Kurzweil, who has come with a prediction for a date for the emergence of singularity—until 2045—expects such a development in a positive way: "What's actually happening is [machines] are powering all of us," Kurzweil said during the SXSW interview. "They're making us smarter. They may not yet be inside our bodies, but, by the 2030s, we will connect our neocortex, the part of our brain where we do our thinking, to the cloud."[52]

In a well-known article—*issued on the occasion of a film*—Stephen Hawking, Max Tegmark, Stuart Russell, and Frank Wilczek shared a moderate position: "The potential benefits are huge; everything that civilization has to offer is a product of human intelligence; we cannot predict what we might achieve when this intelligence is magnified by the tools AI may provide, but the eradication of war, disease, and poverty would be high on anyone's list. Success in creating AI would be the biggest

[50] Bostrom (2014), p. 126.

[51] Wiener (1960), pp. 1355–1358.

[52] D. Galeon & C. Reedy, Kurzweil Claims That the Singularity Will Happen by 2045, Futurism (Oct. 5, 2017 http://futurism.com/kurzweil-claims-that-the-singularity-will-happen-by-2045/, Accessed 29-6-2018).

event in human history... Unfortunately, it might also be the last, unless we learn how to avoid the risks."[53]

In the framework of such risks, Tegmark proposes the so-called wisdom race which will attempt to regulate and design super intelligence—as well as prior AI achievements—ahead of their achievement.[54] The goal is to safeguard "friendly" AI. As is analyzed in the next chapter though, the term "friendly" requires extended analysis from an interdisciplinary perspective takes profoundly different meanings among humans and may be further altered when projected onto AI intelligence.

Summing up, AI is righteously raising fears as well as hopes. Isaac Asimov gave an explanation for the fears in a somehow poetic way. In fact, the evolution of AI gives a sense of existential emergency to our long-term political, philosophical and in the more general sense ethical differences or even struggles. The existence of a "grant design" may be comforting us, as long as we are the designees. Once we become the designers, the anxiety about the outcome of our activities is only natural. This is the primary reason justifying regulation. It becomes obvious that as we move down the road of AI evolution, the questions pile up. They are of deep existential and therefore ethical and political nature. They are addressed below from a mainly legal standpoint in terms of the aspiration to legally regulate such issues.

2.3 An "Economic Singularity" Ahead? Social Implications

A famous IBM quote is: "Machines should work; people should think."[55] While it is with the existential issues raised above that the most dramatic expectations as well as risks are raised, AI is not only about existential fears; part both of the expected risks and of the expectations refer to the economic implications AI brings with it, in the present. The social and economic implications, with their immediacy and urgency inflict wider concern in the present.

Technology has been historically a force of economic growth and of transformation of the productive relations. This role intensifies as the advance of technology becomes more rapid, with a profound case of such rapid technological evolution being AI; the question of course is always who will take advantage of such growth and what the cost will be.[56] This general question has gained momentum and become more specific due to the 4th industrial revolution, which is comprehended as an ongoing, fundamental change in terms of production, management and

---

[53]S. Hawking, M. Tegmark, S. Russell, and F. Wilczek, Transcending Complacency on Super intelligent Machines, *Huffpost*, (https://www.huffingtonpost.com/stephen-hawking/artificial-intelligence_b_5174265.html?ec_carp=3359844804041712164, Accessed 01-02-2019).

[54]M. Tegmark, How to Get Empowered Not Overpowered by AI, Ted2018, (2018 April), (https://www.ted.com/talks/max_tegmark_how_to_get_empowered_not_overpowered_by_ai#t-477030. Accessed 26-07-2019).

[55]Simon (2018), p. 34.

[56]Xu et al. (2018), p. 90.

governance,[57] at the core of which is identified the AI prospect of eternal and continuously working entities, at all sectors of the economy, with potential capacities of self-improvement.[58]

The exact course of the 4th industrial revolution cannot be completely foreseen; both, expected, positive sides, such as further economic growth and negative ones, such as labor markets disruption and huge inequality seem reasonable.[59]

AI plays a wide role as a pioneer of the design of the 4th industrial revolution, through five main types: deep learning, which is based on algorithms and mimics human cognitive functions having the potential of learning from mistakes, without the human tire; robotisation, with innovations such as 3D printers and self—learning capacities further enhancing its capacities; de-materialization, in the sense that autonomous software will be collecting data as well as that physical products will become software; gig economy, which includes to the expansion of self-employment in the sense of crowd working and working on apps; and autonomous driving.[60]

There are various, complementary categorizations of AI contribution in the emerging, 4th industrial revolution. Regarding the working environment the AI ramifications include "Robotics and Automation...Wearable and Performance-Enhancing Devices...Telepresence, Telemanipulation and Remote Work...Cognitive Computing..."[61]

The so—called cyber physical systems—CPS—which describe "the network connections between humans, machines, products, objects and ICT (information and communication technology) systems"[62] also will play a significant role. The emergence of "smart factories" promises enhanced, cheaper and undisturbed production, which as the pandemic of COVID-19 proved can be crucially important.

The conjunction of AI with "block chain" technology is equally significant. Avoiding the technical details, we know that their intertwining bears the potential for decentralized and personal use of personal data, as well as for AI algorithms which will be trained to autonomously race and counter cyber-threats.[63] The algorithms will produce significant value in the cyberspace environment due to enhanced security which will be based on their own training and capacity to adapt, via a largely de-centralized and diffused environment of data and information exchanges.

---

[57]Schwab K. (2015). The Fourth Industrial Revolution: What It Means and How to Respond, (www.foreignaffairs.com/articles/2015-12-12/fourth-industrial-revolution, Accessed 23-06-2019).

[58]Lucas (2004), pp. 5–20.

Banerjee and Duflo (2005), pp. 473–552.

[59]Jee (2017), pp. 255–256.

[60]Wisskirchen et al. (2017), pp. 10–11.

[61]Mathiason and Pierce (2017).

[62]Wisskirchen et al. (2017), p. 12.

[63]D. Pollock, The Fourth Industrial Revolution Built On Blockchain And Advanced With AI, Forbs, (November 30, 2018), (https://www.forbes.com/sites/darrynpollock/2018/11/30/the-fourth-industrial-revolution-built-on-blockchain-and-advanced-with-ai/#a6fdd4242b61, Accessed 8-4-2019).

AI is already present in guessing our consumption choices, intruding private corporations' business cycle. Walmart uses hundreds "...of bots to automate back-office processes, Western Digital reduces CapEx by using artificial intelligence to optimise test equipment, Bank of America and Harvard University's Kennedy School collaborate on responsible AI development [and] 7-Eleven uses chatbots and research voice interfaces to innovate the user experience."[64]

The social effect of AI in the course of the 4th industrial revolution remains to be determined. The synergies with human labor could enhance on the one hand human capacities, allowing time-space flexibility but could also and because of that diminish guarantees of labor law. A neoliberal strategy for AI use can lead to mass loss of jobs, wider inequality and impressive capitalist accumulation.[65]

The substitution of human labor by AI cannot be completely predicted as estimations vary; an assumption is that it will reach up to level of 45% in the service sector globally and up to 90% of job losses in the US.[66] World Bank predicted that 57% of jobs in the OECD nations could be displaced.[67] Without socially beneficial interventions the concern is that AI will intensify inequalities and destroy whatever prospect of prosperity from technological evolution.[68]

According to a PWC report, global GDP by 2030 could be up to 14% higher as a result of AI compared to the estimates not taking into account AI ramifications–$15.7 trillion bigger than the initial estimate of $114 trillion.[69] Regarding both the impact in terms of numbers and of the economic sectors which will be mainly influenced there are different estimations.

The Accenture report, which is entitled "Why AI is the future of growth", argues that "[A]rtificial intelligence (AI) is a new factor of production and has the potential to introduce new sources of growth, changing how work is done and reinforcing the role of people to drive growth in business... AI could double annual economic growth rates in 2035 by changing the nature of work and creating a new relationship between man and machine. The impact of AI technologies on business is projected to

[64]AI Blog, Five Ways CIOs are Deploying AI, (https://www.artificial-intelligence.blog/news/five-ways-cios-are-deploying-ai, Accessed 28-04-2019).

[65]F. Xiang, AI will spell the end of capitalism, The Washington Post, (May 3, 2018), (https://www.washingtonpost.com/news/theworldpost/wp/2018/05/03/end-of-capitalism/?noredirect=on&utm_term=.1252fbaa087d, Accessed 18-04-2019).

[66]L. Del Corro, Is AI driving humanity towards socialism?, Hackernoon, (2017, January 17), (https://hackernoon.com/is-ai-driving-humanity-towards-socialism-307c98c87fff, Accessed 18-04-2019).

[67]World Bank GRP., World Development Report 2016: Digital Dividends 129 fig. 2.24 (2016), http://www.worldbank.org/en/publication/wdr2016 [https://perma.cc/E76Q-QMAY].

[68]Frey and Osborne (2017), pp. 254, 261.

Daron Acemoglu & Pascual Restrepo, Robots and Jobs: Evidence from US Labor Markets 7-10 (MIT Dep't of Econ., Working Paper No. 17-04, 2017), https://papers.ssrn.com/abstract=2940245.

[69]*PWC, The macroeconomic impact of artificial intelligence, (2018, February), at p.* 3.

increase labor productivity by up to 40 percent and enable people to make more efficient use of their time."[70]

"The economic impact of AI will be driven by (a) productivity gains from businesses automating processes as well as augmenting their existing labour force with AI technologies (assisted, autonomous and augmented intelligence) and (b) increased consumer demand resulting from the availability of personalised and/or higher-quality AI-enhanced products and services."[71]

In a different way to estimate the impact of AI, McKinsey in its 2017 report found that "49% of the activities that people are paid to do in the global economy have the potential to be automated by adapting currently demonstrated technology."[72] Similarly, there are estimations about "...a third of workplace tasks [which] can be automated for the majority of workers."[73] More important is the impact on each distinct state, which may disrupt at different magnitude national economies, that most causing asymmetric consequences on global economy.[74] The Bank of America, in 2015 had estimated for 10 years, an 'impact value' of between $14 trillion and $33 trillion.[75]

Numbers in terms of the actual impact vary but the common denominator is that AI will radically change the landscape of the labor relations and not solely in manufacturing, due to the expected and partially underway, leap in productivity. AI will redefine workplace and labor, with the surpassing of "automation" in favor of autonomy and self—learning or even self—programming of AI.

It is highly anticipated that low—skilled jobs will be more affected than high—skilled, although the latter are expected according to some estimations to be seriously affected too.[76] AI bears the potentials of reducing the cost of labor, of raising productivity as well as of achieving conducts which humans would find impossible to do.[77] The answer to the question about who will benefit from these changes can be speculated on the basis of the present trends but cannot be concluded in advance.

---

[70]Accenture, Artificial intelligence is the future of growth, (https://www.accenture.com/us-en/insight-artificial-intelligence-future-growth, Accessed 20-04-2019).

[71]*PWC, The macroeconomic impact of artificial intelligence*, at p. 3.

[72]McKinsey, A Future that works: Automation, Employment and Productivity, (January 2017), at p. 5.

[73]Alex Campolo et al., AI Now 2017 Report 3 (Andrew Selbst & Solon Barocas eds. 2017), https://ainowinstitute.org/AI_Now_2017_Report.pdf.

[74]"The proportion of jobs threatened by automation in India is 69 percent, 77 percent in China and as high as 85 percent in Ethiopia."

Speech by World Bank President Jim Yong Kim: The World Bank Group's Mission: To End Extreme Poverty, The World Bank (Oct. 3, 2016), http://www.worldbank.org/en/news/speech/2016/10/03/speech-by-world-bank-president-jimyong-kim-the-world-bank-groups-mission-to-end-extreme-poverty.

[75]Ma et al. (2015).

[76]Manyika et al. (2017), p. 14.

[77]The Economist (2017), 'Automatic for the people: How Germany's Otto uses artificial intelligence', 12 April 2017, https://www.economist.com/news/business/21720675-firm-using-algorithm-designed-cern-laboratory-how-germanys-otto-uses.

McKinsey, in its above-mentioned report suggests that contrary to speculations about loss of jobs, AI has the potential to make up for the loss of productivity which is emerging due to the demographic decline and in ways which may not harm the labor but on the contrary enhance it.[78]

Other analyses also debate the trend of loss of jobs because of technological evolution: "[A] significant stratum of middle-skill jobs combining specific vocational skills with foundational middle-skills levels of literacy, numeracy, adaptability, problem solving, and common sense will persist in coming decades"[79] and "Ongoing automation is not likely to reduce the total number of jobs but instead will change the types of jobs that people do or shift people from the role of wage-earning laborers to the role of rent-earning capitalist (robot) owners."[80]

However, we must keep in mind that the divergence in terms of the impact on the labor market is significant. Again according to a McKinsey study, about half of the activities in the global economy may be automated by existing technology,[81] whereas a study by OECD concluded that 9% of the jobs of the most advanced economies can be automated.[82] Other estimations refer to an "onslaught" of the labor market with 37 up to 45% of job losses.[83] Even these estimations however cannot apply equally everywhere in the world, given the difference in the level of skilled workers.[84]

In general, it is true that dangers for existing jobs persist and still we cannot be certain neither for the type of impact on labor market, nor for the extent of it.[85] A report which was published by the Obama administration made reference to potential threat to US jobs within a decade from 2016, ranging from 9 to 47%.[86]

As senator Gary Peters stated in the US Congress, "[Artificial intelligence] systems will likely have significant influences on jobs and the economy. Few dispute the assertion that AI advances will increase production efficiencies and create new

---

[78] *McKinsey, A Future that works: Automation, Employment and Productivity*, at p. 15.

[79] Autor (2015), pp. 3, 27.

[80] Lehman (2015), p. 265, 280.

[81] Chui et al. (2016).

[82] Arntz et al. (2016), http://www.oecd-ilibrary.org/social-issues-migration-health/the-risk-of-automation-for-jobs-in-oecd-countries_5jlz9h56dvq7-en.

[83] Cukier (2018), p. 36.

[84] Herminia Ibarra, Hiring and Big Data: Those Who Could Be Left Behind. Harvard Bus. Rev. Blog Network, Dec. 3, 2013, available at http://blogs.hbr.org/2013/12/hiring-and-big-data-who-wins/?utm_source=Socialflow&utm_medium=Tweet&utm_campaign=Socialflow.

Andrew Soergel, Robots Could Cut Labor Costs 16 Percent by 2025, U.S. News, Feb. 10, 2015, available at http://www.usnews.com/news/articles/2015/02/10/robots-could-cut-international-labor-costs-16-percentby-2025-consulting-group-says.

[85] J. Manyika, Technology, jobs, and the future of work, McKinsey Global Institute, (May 2017), (https://www.mckinsey.com/featured-insights/employment-and-growth/technology-jobs-and-the-future-of-work, Accessed 23-04-2019).

[86] Office of the President of the USA, Artificial Intelligence, Automation, and the Economy, (2016, December 20) at p. 2, (https://obamawhitehouse.archives.gov/sites/whitehouse.gov/files/documents/Artificial-Intelligence-Automation-Economy.PDF, Accessed 24-04-2019).

wealth . . . add[ing] [an estimated] 2.2 trillion U.S. dollars to the U.S. GDP by 2025. There are rising questions about how the fruits of AI productivity will [be] distributed and on the influence of AI on jobs. Increases in the competencies of AI systems in both the cognitive and physical realms will have influences on the distribution, availability, attraction, and salaries associated with different jobs. We need to focus attention on reflection, planning, and monitoring to address the potential disruptive influences of AI on jobs in the U.S.—and to work to understand the broad implications of new forms of automation provided by AI for domestic and international economics."[87]

Apart from the quantitative impact of AI, the latter has a qualitative impact as well, which eventually leads to an even greater quantitative impact, due to its unique ontological characteristics: "[r]ather than capital being a source of ownership and minor wealth generation, it can now be a source of exponential wealth creation—simply because AI continuously evolves and builds upon itself. It's unique because it isn't a static capital item.AI isn't just a static piece of IP. It's capable of building entirely new monopolies, businesses and 'things' all by itself."[88]

The transformative impact of AI, "thanks" to its ontology can be so significant that even its description as capital may be proven problematic potentially. It certainly must be categorized in the broadest possible type of capital,[89] while in the prospect of its further ontological evolution may come to exist as a third, distinct both from labor and capital type of factor in the economic circuit.

The role—both present and potential—of AI within the ongoing 4th industrial revolution means that the ontology of AI and its tendency towards enhancing autonomy will be the catalyst of wealth accumulation and of the form that productive relations will eventually take.[90] Therefore, exactly because of the significance of AI

[87]The Dawn of Artificial Intelligence: Hearing Before the Subcomm. on Space, Science, and Competitiveness, 114th Cong. 14, (statement of Sen. Gary Peters).

[88]H. Innis, Why AI Will Break Capitalism, Chatbots Magazine, (2016, June 12), (chatbotsmagazine.com/why-ai-will-break-capitalism-14a6ad2f76da, Accessed 20-04-2019).

[89]Capital itself takes different meanings. As Fleissner explains, citing Ashford "The use of "capital. . . "includes land, animals, structures, and machines-- anything capable of being owned and employed in production. It does not include 'financial capital,' which [does not do work but rather] is a claim on, or ownership interest in, real capital." This is consistent with the foundational economic theorists (including Smith, Ricardo, Marx, Marshal, Walras, and Keynes). This usage contrasts with the usage in financial economics in which "capital" usually means "financial capital." However, many writers use a broader definition of capital that includes money, human capital, and refers to natural resources, physical capital, technology, corporate stock, knowledge, and/or anything else that can enhance an individual's capacity to perform economically useful work or generate income. This broader definition tends to confuse real capital assets (tools, machines, factories)--which, according to binary economics, do work--with financial capital (securities, bonds, notes, and shares)--which do not."

Fleissner, Inclusive capitalism based on binary economics and positive international human rights in the age of artificial intelligence, note 18;

Ashford (2015), p. 27.

[90]The term productive relations is adopted here from a Marxist perspective: "In the social production of their existence, men inevitably enter into definite relations, which are independent of their

in the course of the industrial revolution which is underway, the political and legal framework for its regulation emerges as critical.[91]

The selection of the regulatory framework—political and legal—of AI will at a significant extent condense and co—shape the prevalent internationally, socio—economic and political model, which subsequently will partially define the course of the globality for the decades to come.

The politically and legally ambivalent issues are ever-growing.

For example, in order to fulfill the expectations that it has created, AI is already making use of big data. Big data is essential for the development of AI autonomy because of machine learning—as is analyzed below. The use of the ecosystem of big data for the evolution of AI has already become a heated part of the political and legal discussion about AI: who will control and make use of big data that is produced by us all? A "cartel" of gigantic private corporations or an alternative scheme?[92] Will we allow large corporations to control this "ecosystem" within which AI entities are trained and function or not? Will this situation lead to harsher inequality? Or the use of other technologies such as of blockchain technology, will allow the de-centralized and free circulation of data, leading to enhanced equality?[93]

The issue at hand is not merely of economic significance; it has political ramifications touching upon the fundamentals of our conception of democracy, which are analyzed in the next chapter.

As always is the case with technology, the essential questions come down to who and how will benefit from the potential growth as well as who and how will bear the

---

will, namely relations of production appropriate to a given stage in the development of their material forces of production. The totality of these relations of production constitutes the economic structure of society, the real foundation, on which arises a legal and political superstructure and to which correspond definite forms of social consciousness. The mode of production of material life conditions the general process of social, political and intellectual life. It is not the consciousness of men that determines their existence, but their social existence that determines their consciousness. At a certain stage of development, the material productive forces of society come into conflict with the existing relations of production or – this merely expresses the same thing in legal terms – with the property relations within the framework of which they have operated hitherto. From forms of development of the productive forces these relations turn into their fetters. Then begins an era of social revolution. The changes in the economic foundation lead sooner or later to the transformation of the whole immense superstructure."

Karl Marx, A Contribution to the Critique of Political Economy Preface, 1859, (https://www.marxists.org/archive/marx/works/1859/critique-pol-economy/preface.htm, Accessed 14-06-2020).

[91] *The Crypto Oracle, The Fourth Industrial Revolution: The Rise Of The Autonomous Economy.*

[92] J. Rodriguez, AI Has Not One, Not Two, but Many Centralization Problems, *Hackernoon*, (2018, June 26), (https://hackernoon.com/ai-has-not-one-not-two-but-many-centralization-problems-a5f0664361ed, Accessed 13-04-2019).

[93] R. Pinto, Next Steps In The Integration Of Artificial Intelligence And The Blockchain, Forbes, (2018, October 9), (https://www.forbes.com/sites/forbestechcouncil/2018/10/09/next-steps-in-the-integration-of-artificial-intelligence-and-the-blockchain/#2b0cce483273, Accessed 14-04-2019);

The Crypto Oracle, The Fourth Industrial Revolution: The Rise of the Autonomous Economy, (December 13, 2018), (https://medium.com/altcoin-magazine/the-fourth-industrial-revolution-the-rise-of-the-autonomous-economy-cfe0886ad8b3, Accessed 8-4-2019).

cost. Who will make use of such potentials and in favor of whom? Are we going to see a new "wave" of "creative destruction"[94] or the emergence of a differentiated or even completely alternate and new model?

After all, AI-driven impact on the economy takes place as mentioned above in an already prevalent capitalist model, which combines capital flows and accumulation with wealth disparities widespread inequality, declining labor share of total earnings, insecurity and disruption of labor income by the above phenomena as well as by speculative activities.[95]

Will this model remain the prevalent or is it going to undergo structural transformations, partially because of the type of regulation of AI that will be chosen? What model will emerge from the 4th industrial revolution, on the basis of AI evolution? Neo-liberal, inclusive capitalism, aiming at revealing "market opportunities for low—and moderate-income people to acquire productive capital with the earnings of capital by employing the same market institutions that facilitate capital acquisition for more affluent individuals",[96] Keynesian and post-Keynesian[97] or socialist/ Marxist? Will AI become the catalyst for more egalitarian access to the potential of profit-making capital as well as to personal security instead of insecurity because of technological disruptions?[98]

This, fundamentally political, debate is approached in the next chapters from a legal perspective. In order to approach it from the perspective of law, bypassing thus the direct political debate, the book attempts to balance between two aspects: the goals that are assessed as critical from a political perspective on the one hand, in terms of AI social and economic impact and the rights as well as the legal norms, which correspond to certain goals on the other hand.

Such an approach is honest in the sense of acknowledging that legal debates are not neutral but—at least implicitly—bring with them political goals too. Each new

---

[94]"The opening up of new markets, foreign or domestic, and the organizational development from the craft shop and factory to such concerns as U.S. Steel illustrate the process of industrial mutation that incessantly revolutionizes the economic structure from within, incessantly destroying the old one, incessantly creating a new one. This process of Creative Destruction is the essential fact about capitalism. It is what capitalism consists in and what every capitalist concern has got to live in ... Every piece of business strategy acquires its true significance only against the background of that process and within the situation created by it. It must be seen in its role in the perennial gale of creative destruction; it cannot be understood irrespective of it or, in fact, on the hypothesis that there is a perennial lull."

Schumpeter (1962), pp. 83–84.

[95]Pfeffer et al. (2013), p. 98.

Fleck et al. (2011), p. 57.

Armenter (2015), p. 1.

The Dawn of Artificial Intelligence: Hearing Before the Subcomm. on Space, Science, and Competitiveness, 114th Cong. 14 (2016) (statement of Eric Horvitz, Technical Fellow and Director, Microsoft Research-Redmond Lab, Microsoft Corp.).

[96]Fleissner (2018), pp. 202–203.

[97]Ashford (2014), pp. 179, 180.

[98]Ashford (2009), p. 89.

phenomenon which is in need of regulation obviously does not exist in legal vacuum; pre-existing rights and obligations guide us but, in the end, the novelty and the impact of the phenomenon, its social impact, in combination with prevalent ideas determine the legal framework as well.

Characteristically, the UN Charter, in article 55 establishes the obligation of all member-states and of the international community to uphold the "conditions of stability and well-being" and promote "higher standards of living, full employment, and the conditions of economic and social progress and development."[99] Human rights have come to include a significant set of economic and social rights as well.[100]

The International Covenant on Economic, Social and Cultural Rights—ICESCR—also establishes "the right to access and maintain benefits, whether in cash or in kind, from (a) lack of work-related income."[101]

In addition, the Declaration on the Right to Development imposes the human right to "participate in, contribute to, and enjoy" economic development.[102] It also foresees that states must pursue policies aiming at the "constant improvement" of the well-being of the "entire population and of all individuals," which must be based on their "active, free, and meaningful participation in development…[and in the] "fair distribution of the benefits resulting therefrom."[103] The World Conference on Human Rights affirmed the same right "as a universal and inalienable right and an integral part of fundamental human rights".[104]

Similarly, the United Nations have issued a General Comment on the "right to work" imposing legal obligations on states, since the "right to work is essential for realizing other human rights and forms an inseparable and inherent part of human dignity."[105] The right to a dignified life also transcends human rights law, which imposes a minimum-at least—of obligations both for individuals and states.[106]

While the legal binding-ness of social rights has been constantly debated[107] they are equally binding with all other, international law norms. General Assembly decisions are obviously not legally binding but can be very well perceived as imposing policy guidelines on the one hand, while on the other hand being comprised of binding norms which impose obligations upon all implicated actors.[108]

---

[99]UN Charter, Article 55.

[100]Spiro (2003), pp. 1999, 2000, 2001.

[101]U.N. Comm. on Econ., Soc. & Cultural Rts., General Comment No. 19: The Right to Social Security, U.N. Doc. E/C.12/GC/19 (Feb. 4, 2008).

[102]U.N. GAOR, 41st Sess., 97th plen. mtg. at 3, U.N. Doc A/RES/41/128 (Dec. 4, 1986).

[103]*U.N. Doc A/RES/41/128.*

[104]World Conference on Human Rights, Vienna Declaration and Programme of Action, ¶10, U.N. Doc. A/CONF.157/23 (June 25, 1993).

[105]U.N. Comm. on Econ., Soc. & Cultural Rts., General Comment No. 18: The Right to Work (Art. 6), E/C.12/GC/18 (Feb. 6, 2006).

[106]Donnelly (1989) Universal human rights in theory & practice. Cornell University Press, Ithaca, p 18

[107]Vandenhole (2003), pp. 377(3), 382, 403.

[108]Villaroman (2010), pp. 299, 307, 332.

Of course, the above-mentioned rights and several others cannot be directly translated into detailed state or international policies. Still, they constitute legal basis for the attempt to materialize certain framework about AI regulation, which is implicitly political. It must also be emphasized that the selection of the one or the other legal framework is not the mechanic outcome of socio-economic developments but will partially influence them as well. In this sense, the legal "battle" for the regulation of AI is crucial for the future of AI evolution and of its social impact.

2.4 Conclusions

This chapter focused on two main types of prospects and of risks: the existential ones, which are mainly related to the moment of singularity, the expectation of super-intelligence, the merging of human and artificial intelligence and the social and economic ones, which are underway, involving existing, narrow AI as well. The scope of the chapter is to describe why regulation is critical as well as why it is important for such regulation to be legally binding.

The next chapter further elaborates on this need by focusing on the AI ontology, which only parenthetically was mentioned in the first chapter. Having explained part of the AI impact and of its ontology, the ethical challenges, which are built on the two first chapters, are analyzed in the third chapter where the first part of the book is concluded. The ethical challenges in other words are perceived as the outcome of the existing and potential impact of AI as well as of its ontology and the need for legal regulation is subsequently the result of the emergence of the ethical challenges.

References

Ackerman D (1990) Natural history of the senses. Vintage Books, p 307

Armenter R (2015) A bit of a miracle no more: the decline of the labor share. Federal Res Bank Philadelphia Res Dept, p 1

Arntz M, Gregory T, Zierahn U (2016) The risk of automation for jobs in OECD countries: a comparative analysis. OECD Social, Employment and Migration Working Papers, No. 189. OECD, Paris

Ashford R (2009) Broadening the right to acquire capital with the earnings of capital: the missing link to sustainable economic recovery and growth. Forum Soc Econ 39:89

Ashford R (2014) Beyond austerity and stimulus: democratizing capital acquisition with the earnings of capital as a means to sustainable growth. J Post Keynesian Econ 36(179):180

Ashford R (2015) Unutilized productive capacity, binary economics and the case for broadening capital ownership. Econ Manage Financ Mark 10:27

Autor DH (2015) Why are there still so many jobs? The history and future of workplace automation. J Econ Persp 29:3, 27

Banerjee A, Duflo E (2005) Growth theory through the lens of development economics. In: Aghion P, Durlauf S (eds) Handbook of economic growth. Elsevier, Amsterdam, pp 473–552

Baum SD, Goertzel B, Goertzel TG (2011) How long until human-level AI? Results from an expert assessment. Technol Forecast Soc Change 78(1):185–195

Bostrom N (2002) Existential risks: analyzing human extinction scenarios and related hazards. J Evol Technol 9. http://www.jetpress.org/volume9/risks.htm
Bostrom N (2014) Super intelligence paths, dangers, strategies. Oxford University Press, p 126
Bostrom N (2016) Superintelligence, paths, dangers, strategies. Oxford University Press, pp 5–10
Chui M, Manyika J, Miremadi M (2016) Where machines could replace humans—and where they can't (yet). McKinsey Quarterly. http://www.mckinsey.com/business-functions/digital-mckinsey/our-insights/where-machines-could-replace-humans-and-where-they-cant-yet
Cukier K (2018) The economic implications of artificial intelligence. In: Cummings ML, Roff HM, Cukier K, Parakilas J, Bryce H (eds) Artificial intelligence and international affairs: disruption anticipated. Chatham House, p 36
De Spiegeleire S et al (2017) Artificial intelligence and the future of defense: strategic implications for small- and medium-sized force providers. Hague Centre for Strategic Studies
Donnelly J (1989) Universal Human rights in theory & practice. Cornell University Press, Ithaca, p 18
Doty M (1996) Lament-heaven. In: My Alexandria. University of Illinois Press, p 85
Ferguson C-J, Goldie S (1999) Applied artificial intelligence and the management of knowledge. In: Castell AM (ed) Synergy matters, working with Systems in the 21st century. Kluwer Academic Publishers, p 55
Fleck S, Glaser J, Sprague S (2011) The compensation-productivity gap: a visual essay. Monthly Lab Rev 57
Fleissner C (2018) Inclusive capitalism based on binary economics and positive international human rights in the age of artificial intelligence. Wash Univ Glob Stud Law Rev 17:201, 202–203
Floridi L, Cowls J, Beltrametti M et al (2018) Opportunities, risks, principles, and recommendations. Minds Mach 28:689. https://doi.org/10.1007/s11023-018-9482-5
Frey CB, Osborne MA (2017) The future of employment: how susceptible are jobs to computerisation? Technol Forecast Soc Change 114(254):261
Good IJ (1965) Speculation, concerning the first ultra intelligent machine. In: Alt FL, Rubinoff M (eds) Advances in computers, Vol. 6. Academic Press, New York, pp 31, 33. https://doi.org/10.1016/S0065-2458(08)60418-0
Hassett P (2000) Technology time capsule: what does the future hold? Syracuse Law Rev 50:1223
Horgan J (1999) The undiscovered mind: how the human brain defies replication, medication, and explanation. Free Press, New York, p 201
Huxley J (1957) New bottles for new wine. Chando & Windus, pp 13–17
Jee Y-S (2017) Exercise rehabilitation in the fourth industrial revolution. J Exerc Rehabil 13 (3):255–256. https://doi.org/10.12965/jer.1735012.506
Karppi T, Crawford K (2016) Social media, financial algorithms and the hack crash. Theory Cult Soc 33:73, 74, 77
Lehman T (2015) Countering the modern luddite impulse. Ind Rev 20(265):280
Lucas RE (2004) The industrial revolution: Past and future. Annual Report of the Federal Reserve Bank of Minneapolis, pp 5–20
Ma B, Nahal S, Tran F (2015) Robot revolution – global Robot & AI Primer. Bank of America Merrill Lynch
Manyika J et al (2017) McKinsey, a future that works: automation, employment and productivity. McKinsey Global Institute, p 14
Martinez R (2019) Artificial intelligence: distinguishing between types & definitions. Nevada Law J 19:1015
Mathiason G, Pierce NA (2017) Littler on legal compliance solutions for the transformation of the workplace through robotic artificial intelligence, and automation, SZ002 ALI-CLE 2823. American Law Institute Continuing Legal Education, para 1.2
Murdoch I (1997) Existentialists and mystics. Penguin Books, p 187
Newell A, Shaw JC, Simon HA (1958) Chess-playing programs and the problem of complexity. IBM J Res Dev 2(4):320

Noorman M, Johnson DG (2014) Negotiating autonomy and responsibility in military robots. Ethics Info Technol 16(51):52

Pasquale F (2002) Two concepts of immortality: reframing public debate on stem-cell research. Yale J Law Humanit 14:73

Pfeffer FT, Danziger S, Schoeni RF (2013) Wealth disparities before and after the great recession. Ann Am Acad Polit Soc Sci 650:98

Purdy J (1998) The god of the Digerati. Am Prospect pp 34–40. Available at http://www.prospect.org/print/V9/37/purdy-j.html

Renn O, Klinke A (2004) Systemic risks: a new challenge for risk management. Eur Mol Biol Org Rep 5:S41

Sandberg A, Bostrom N (2008) Whole brain emulation: a roadmap, Technical Report #2008-3. Future of Humanity Institute, Oxford University, p 7, www.fhi.ox.ac.uk/reports/2008-3.pdf, Accessed 12 June 2020

Schneider S (2019) Artificial you, AI and the future of your mind. Princeton University Press, pp 2–4

Schumpeter JA (1962) Capitalism, socialism, and democracy, 3rd edn. Harper Perennial, pp 83–84

Sheridan TB, Verplank WL (1978) Human and computer control of undersea teleoperators. Massachusetts Institute of Technology, Man-Machine Systems Laboratory, Cambridge, pp 6–12

Simon RD (2018) Artificial intelligence, real ethics. N Y State Bar J 90:34

Singer PW (2009) Wired for war: the robotics revolution and conflict in the 21st century. Penguin p 5

Spier J (2011) Uncertainties and the state of the art: a legal nightmare. J Risk Res 14:501

Spiro J (2003) Treaties, international law, and constitutional rights. Standard Law Rev 55:1999, 2000, 2001

Taylor C (1999) A catholic modernity? In: Heft J (ed) A catholic modernity? Oxford Scholarship Online, p 24

van Asselt MBA, Renn O (2011) Risk governance. J Risk Res 14(431):436–438

Vandenhole W (2003) The human right to development as a paradox. Verfassung Und Recht In Übersee. Law Polit Afr Asia Latin Am 36(3):377, 382, 403

Villaroman NG (2010) The right to development: exploring the legal basis of a supernorm. Fla J Int Law 22:299, 307, 332

Wiener N (1960) Some moral and technical consequences of automation. Science 131 (3410):1355–1358

Wisskirchen G et al (2017) Artificial intelligence and robotics and their impact on the workplace. IBA Global Employment Institute

Xu M, David JM, Kim SH (2018) The fourth industrial revolution: opportunities and challenges. Int J Financ Res 9(2):90

Yudkowski E (2001) Creating friendly AI 1.0:the analysis and design of benevolent goal architectures. Machine Intelligence Research Institute, p 2

Yudkowski E (2008) Artificial intelligence as a positive and negative factor in global risk. In: Bostrom N, Ćirković MM (eds) Global catastrophic risks. Oxford University Press, New York, pp 308–345

Chapter 3
The Ontology of AI

3.1 Introduction

When Descartes expressed the proposition "Cogito, ergo sum"—I think therefore I am—he had come up with an indubitable truth: self-awareness cannot be tricked, hallucinated, be mistaken in calculative terms or deceived.[1] While a person could be deceived about ideas, sensations, reality, experiences, there cannot be deception about self-awareness; deception itself presupposes existence.

Self-awareness is self-evident; it needs no further proof. In the world of humans and regarding humans we know it when we see it. Of course, as science evolves some extent of uncertainty emerges as well. Medical research has proven for example, that the awareness of self-awareness may differ due to a number of factors; we are not certain of the type of self-awareness of embryos and we have also come to terms with the fact that the other species of the animal kingdom also have some—differentiated—extent of self-awareness.

Besides the alternate options in terms of our understanding on self-awareness that modem research has brought, a common point of reference historically is that self-awareness is the privilege of biological existence. As we distance from philosophical dualism we came to trace the origin of self-awareness in human mind or in other words, materialistically.

AI, as it evolves could expand or put in question Descartes indubitable truth in various ways: non-biological entities are in the course of developing self-awareness; when such an outcome occurs, will it mean that AI "is", that it exists? What will "existence" mean for a non-biological entity"? Will the manifestation of self-awareness be considered as sufficient for admitting that AI "is" or will we need more proof? And how will a world with non-biological, self-aware entities look like?

[1]The Editors of Encyclopaedia Britannica, Methodic doubt, Philosophy. https://www.britannica.com/topic/methodic-doubt. Accessed 14 June 2020.

T. Tzimas, *Legal and Ethical Challenges of Artificial Intelligence from an International Law Perspective*, Law, Governance and Technology Series 46,
https://doi.org/10.1007/978-3-030-78585-7_3

Descartes may have given us the threshold of existence; the effectiveness or not of his proposition about existence will be proven in the course of the analysis of AI ontology. While such an analysis is fascinating per se, the discussion about the ontology of AI is crucial in the framework of this book in order to build on the previous chapter in furtherance of identifying the reason, the extent of necessity and urgency, as well as the type of legal regulation that is needed in relation to the various levels of AI.

The analysis of AI ontology has to cope with our far from complete understanding of AI; from the fact that while AGI and ASI has not yet come to exist we must take it into account, in order to construct a legal framework, which will be proven capable of preemptively and timely confronting emerging threats. In this sense not only we must speculate and predict at least up to some extent its characteristics but also design legal tools on the basis of such speculations. The analysis begins from the ontology of ANI and exceeds into the potential ontology of AGI and ASI.

Ontology as a concept per se is ambiguous. For Parmenides, what we currently describe as ontology, orientates from the "being" and describes a structure of objects and their relations,[2] whereas Aristotle emphasized upon a synthesis of characteristics, including the substance-which is possibly the most important-the quantity, the qualities, the relation, the location, the time, the orientation, the "having", the doing and the experience.[3] Ontology describes whatever is "real" and in this sense exceeds the existing and reaches the potential and the evolving as well.

Several more definitions exist: "An ontology is a formal explicit specification of a shared conceptualization"[4]; "An ontology is a shared understanding of some domain of interest"[5]; "Formal ontology is the science that is concerned with the systematic development of axiomatic theories describing forms, modes, and views of being at different levels of abstraction and granularity";[6] "An ontology is a seven-tuple, O: = (L, C, R, F, G, H, A)" [With: C: A set of concepts R: Set of binary relations on C (Relationships between concepts) F: Function connecting symbol sets to sets of terms G: Function connecting symbol sets to sets of relations T: Taxonomy for the partial ordering of C in generic concepts/narrower concepts A: Set of axioms (constraints): statements with elements of C and R"][7]

Ontology helps us classify and understand phenomena and relationships. Briefly speaking, ontology is the "science of being."[8]

[2]Grossmann (1983).

[3]Busse et al. (2015), pp. 29–41.

[4]Gruber (1993), pp. 199–220.

[5]Uschold and Gruninger (1996).

[6]Herre et al. (2006).

[7]Pickert. Einf¨uhrungin Ontologien. http://www.dbis.informatik.hu-berlin.de/dbisold/lehre/WS0203/SemWeb/artikel/2/PickertOntologienfinal.pdf

[8]Busse et al. (2015), p. 29.

This general definition is adopted here. In terms of AI, it means that the latter is perceived as potential "being", with the focus on the substantial characteristics and the relationships of this being, both in the present and in the future.

In order to conduct the ontological analysis of AI, the chapter begins with the definition of AI in order to provide a general description, moving then to the main types of AI—weak and strong.[9] Having elaborated on these, the analysis moves onto machine—learning and consciousness; on such grounds, the crucial aspect of the debate, the one about the quest for friendly AI, as a potentially fundamental characteristic of AI is examined.

This last part of the chapter is crucial as it examines the ontological evolution of AI in terms of its relationship with humans. It also raises the most anxious and heated debate as it will possibly determine human fate: prosperity or doomsday?

3.2 Defining AI

The ambiguity which surrounds AI extends to its definitions as well. "[I]n spite of what I regard as AI's significant achievements . . . the not so well-kept secret is that AI is internally in a paradigmatic mess. There is really no broad agreement on the essential nature or formal basis of intelligence and the proper theoretical framework for it", Chandrasekaran comments.[10]

The definition of AI—as a starting point of its ontological description—constitutes profoundly a controversial matter.[11] Part of this ambiguity, apart from the lack of complete understanding of AI can be blamed on the fact that many AI definitions use at some extent as defining element the replication of human intelligence, replicating human intelligence controversy too.

Norvig and Russell defined AI as "technology that can think humanly, act humanly, think rationally, or act rationally,"[12] Poole and Mackworth as "the field that studies the synthesis and analysis of computational agents that act intelligently,"[13] whereas, other, simpler definitions simply relate AI to human functions; e.g. Rich and Knight suggest that it is the study "of how to make computers do things at which, at the moment, people are better"[14] and Charniak and McDermott "the field that studies the synthesis and analysis of computational agents that act intelligently."[15]

---

[9]They are also presented in the introduction.

[10]Chandrasekaran (1990), p. 14.

[11]Russell and Norvig (2013), p. 2.
Winograd (2006), p. 167.

[12]Russell and Norvig (2013).

[13]Poole and Mackworth (2010).

[14]Rich and Knight (1991).

[15]Charniak and McDermott (1985).

AI has also been defined as "a broad set of methods, algorithms, and technologies that make software 'smart' in a way that may seem human-like to an outside observer."[16] A slightly different definition describes AI as "Machines that are capable of performing tasks that, if performed by a human, would be said to require intelligence."[17]

A different type of definitions focuses on elements which indicate developed intelligence, such as "consciousness, self-awareness, language use, the ability to learn, the ability to abstract, the ability to adapt, and the ability to reason,"[18] without necessarily emphasizing on the replication of human intelligence—at least not completely.

Steven Omohundro, defined AI as a system that "has goals which it tries to accomplish by acting in the world,"[19] while Russell and Norvig, among eight definitions of AI preferred the rational agent one, according to which, AI agents "operate autonomously, perceive their environment, persist over a prolonged time period, adapt to change, and create and pursue [the best expected outcome]."[20]

The US Army Sciences Board defines AI on the basis of "…its capacity [to] incorporate abstraction and interpretation into information processing and make decisions at a level of sophistication that would be considered intelligent in humans."[21]

The focus on the "human-like" intelligence of machines,[22] despite being descriptively helpful can be also deceiving, either because an entity mimicking human intelligence does not necessarily "understand" or share the patterns of human intellect or because AI entities may develop intelligence of equal level but not identical to human. Still the above definitions offer basic, helpful guidance.[23]

McCarthy, chose not to identify AI with human intelligence arguing that machines may develop other types of intelligence that involve "much more computing than people can do"[24] and in this framework he defined intelligence as "…the computational part of the ability to achieve goals in the world."[25]

---

[16]Noyes. 5 things you need to know about A.I.: Cognitive, neural and deep, oh my! Computerworld (Mar. 3, 2016, 12:49 pm). http://www.computerworld.com/article/3040563/enterprise-applications/5-things-you-need-toknow-about-ai-cognitive-neural-anddeep-oh-my.html; http://perma.cc/7PW9-P42G. Accessed 25 June 2018.

[17]Scherer (2016), pp. 363–364.

[18]Scherer (2016), p. 360.

[19]Omohundro (2008).

[20]Russell and Norvig (2010), pp. 2–3.

[21]Brownstein et al. (1983), p. 169.

[22]Laton (2016), p. 94.

[23]Russell and Norvig (2010), p. 3.

[24]McCarthy (2007) What is artificial intelligence? STAN. http://www-formal.stanford.edu/jmc/whatisai/whatisai.html.

[25]McCarthy and Stanford University Formal Reasoning Group (2007) What is artificial intelligencel basic questions. Formal Reasoning Group. http://www-formal.stanford.edu/jmc/whatisai/node1.html.

Legg and Hutter came up with an extensive list of definitions, from which they derived three main characteristics: "Is a property that an individual agent has as it interacts with its environment or environments; Is related to the agent's ability to succeed or profit with respect to some goal or objective. Depends on how able the agent is to adapt to different objectives and environments."[26]

Their proposal for the definition of intelligence is that "Intelligence measures an agent's ability to achieve goals in a wide range of environments,"[27] whereas Albus defined intelligence as the "ability of a system to act appropriately in an uncertain environment, where appropriate action is that which increases the probability of success, and success is the achievement of behavioral sub goals that support the system's ultimate goal."[28]

Component of AI definitions is the computational capacity of AI which describes a sequence of internal cohesive, logical actions, which are externalized achieving goals in changing environment—*the "world"*—exercised throughout a variety of areas, including both the selection and the implementation of goals. Computationality evolves in the framework of dialectic interaction with the environment.

From the above mentioned definitions we see that not only they are extended but also that the analogies with aspects of human intelligence cannot constitute the sole criterion, neither for the holistic understanding of artificial intelligence, nor the threshold for the identification of AI that has reached a level of higher intelligence, equal or superior to human.

For example, we now know, that contrary to what was expected, board games are not capable of demonstrating the capacities that are defining for human intelligence, although before the relevant achievements by AI, capacities of such levels were expected to set the threshold of higher intelligence.

Still the capacity of AI to replicate human intelligence is central to its evaluation, which is why, two contradictory "tests" have been proposed: the one is the so-called Turing Test, which is in fact an imitation game aiming at the identification of intelligent machines. The idea of the test is that if a computer can fool a human judge into making him/her believe that the mysterious interlocutor on the other side is human. There are different quantitative criteria in terms of the number of human judges and the duration of the conversation, compared to the ones which were foreseen since the initial conception of the test.[29]

The Turing test focuses upon the external manifestation of intelligence as indicator of the emergence of higher of intelligence; we may disagree on the specific criteria which have been included in the test but the core idea of the Turing test can

---

[26]Legg and Hutter (2007) A collection of definitions of intelligence. arXiv:0706.3639 [Cs]. http://arxiv.org/abs/0706.3639.

[27]Legg and Hutter. A collection of definitions of intelligence, at p. 9

[28]Albus (1991), p. 473.

[29]Hern. What is the Turing test? And are we all doomed now? The Guardian. https://www.theguardian.com/technology/2014/jun/09/what-is-the-alan-turing-test. Accessed 18 June 2020.

be particularly enlightening once we come across the complexities of de-coding the subjective experience of AI.

The Chinese room argument by the philosopher John Searle indicated the possible flaws of the Turing test by trying to prove that AI can manifest capacities of intelligence without actually comprehending the semantics of higher intelligence of human type and without therefore developing the subjective, mental experience of human intelligence.

> Searle imagines himself alone in a room following a computer program for responding to Chinese characters slipped under the door. Searle understands nothing of Chinese, and yet, by following the program for manipulating symbols and numerals just as a computer does, he sends appropriate strings of Chinese characters back out under the door, and this leads those outside to mistakenly suppose there is a Chinese speaker in the room.[30]

Searle's argument sustains that consciousness exceeds computation and involves intentionality, as well as understanding. The understanding of syntax and of symbols does not mean that the semantics of these symbols are also understood. The difference therefore between the actual—human—intelligence and its mere simulation emerges.

A variety of counter-arguments have been formulated: the man in the room could come to some understanding of Chinese; or the behaviorally defined manifestation of understanding constitutes enough proof of understanding, which after all is not defined in the argument.[31] Other counter arguments propose that while the man in the room may not understand Chinese, the system as a whole, does so or that a distinct, virtual mind that "creates understanding of Chinese" is created. Searle's fallacy according to such counter-arguments is the shift from the part to the whole.[32]

Another type of criticism to Searle's argument could orientate from how can we identify the differentiation between syntax and semantics; how can we tell that anyone comprehends the former but not the latter? A response to that is by observing the capacity of the man in the room or of the whole system, to speak Chinese out of the room, meaning in unknown environments.

Therefore, we reach a functionalist approach again, albeit at a wider scale. In this sense, the principle of the Turing test is not overturned; it is its area of testing that must expand, to unknown environments. Non-functionalist approaches face the

---

[30] "Imagine a native English speaker who knows no Chinese locked in a room full of boxes of Chinese symbols (a data base) together with a book of instructions for manipulating the symbols (the program). Imagine that people outside the room send in other Chinese symbols which, unknown to the person in the room, are questions in Chinese (the input). And imagine that by following the instructions in the program the man in the room is able to pass out Chinese symbols which are correct answers to the questions (the output). The program enables the person in the room to pass the Turing Test for understanding Chinese but he does not understand a word of Chinese...

Cole. The Chinese room argument. In: Zalta EN (ed) *The Stanford encyclopedia of philosophy*, Spring 2020 ed. https://plato.stanford.edu/archives/spr2020/entries/chinese-room/.

[31] Cole. *The Chinese room argument.*

[32] Cole. *The Chinese room argument.*

Also see: Shaffer (2009), pp. 229–235; Nute (2011), pp. 431–433; Weiss (1990), pp. 165–181.

difficulty of having to identify specific internal characteristics and of trying to comprehend the subjective experience of the AI entity, whereas functionalist approaches offer more concrete "ground". The Chinese room argument however is crucial in helping us understand that the threshold of the achievement of intelligence is far more challenging than initially thought.

Especially, in the context of a legal book-although not only—a functionalist definition is more suitable in order to move on with a legal analysis.

For the purpose of this book, Russell's and Norvig's definition—"operate autonomously, perceive their environment, persist over a prolonged time period, adapt to change, and create and pursue [the best expected outcome]"[33]—is used. It provides a functionalist description which involves some internal characteristics that can be externally manifested. On the basis of the discussion for the definition of AI, the analysis below about the further ontological characteristics of AI takes place.

3.3 Weak and Strong AI

AI is roughly distinguished between weak AI, where "the computer is merely an instrument for investigating cognitive processes" and strong AI, where "[t [he processes in the computer are intellectual, self-learning processes."[34] Weak AI is labeled as artificial narrow intelligence—ANI—while strong AI is further distinguished between artificial general intelligence—AGI—and artificial super intelligence—ASI.[35]

ANI is a matter of the present whereas AGI and ASI are—anxiously—anticipated in the near or not so near future. Applications of ANI are all around us already, via computers where "intelligent systems have been taught or learned how to carry out specific tasks without being explicitly programmed how to do so."[36]

---

[33]Russell and Norvig (2010).

[34]Wisskirchen et al. (2010), p. 10.

[35]Urban (2015) The AI revolution: the road to superintelligence. Wait but why. https://www.waitbutwhy.com/2015/01/artificial-intelligence-revolution-1.html. Accessed 28 June 2018.

[36]The applications are ever-expanding in fact: "speech and language recognition of the Siri virtual assistant on the Apple iPhone. . .interpreting video feeds from drones carrying out visual inspections of infrastructure such as oil pipelines, organizing personal and business calendars, responding to simple customer-service queries, co-ordinating with other intelligent systems to carry out tasks like booking a hotel at a suitable time and location, helping radiologists to spot potential tumors in X-rays, flagging inappropriate content online, detecting wear and tear in elevators from data gathered by IoT devices. . ."

Heath (2018) What is AI? Everything you need to know about artificial intelligence. ZDNet. https://www.zdnet.com/article/what-is-ai-everything-you-need-to-know-about-artificial-intelligence. Accessed 1 February 2019.

ANI is already in the course of growing autonomy, in the sense of "…systems capable of operating in the real-world environment without any form of external control for extended periods of time."[37]

While some extent of autonomy exists—and in this sense the automation phase is already gradually surpassed—AI autonomy applies only to narrow tasks, unlike humans who possess general intelligence. Although AI has already "outsmarted" humans in certain, narrow areas and tasks, it cannot—yet—compete with humans, in terms of adaptable and general intelligence, which if achieved, eventually would or will bring general artificial intelligence at an intellect level, equal—at least—to that of humans.

AGI will be exactly this: a "type of adaptable intellect found in humans, a flexible form of intelligence capable of learning how to carry out vastly different tasks, anything from haircutting to building spreadsheets, or to reason about a wide variety of topics based on its accumulated experience."[38]

The above seemingly simple description about when general intelligence will have been achieved, prerequisites the development of a variety of intellectual characteristics several of which cannot be easily described.

The development of adaptability, of intellectual flexibility which allows the entity to choose on its own, where and how to apply its intelligence, the demonstration of "a reasonable degree of self-understanding and autonomous self-control, the ability to solve a variety of complex problems in a variety of contexts, and [the ability to] learn to solve new problems that didn't know about at the time of [the entities' creation,"[39] the learning as well as the effective handling of uncertainty and probabilistic information constitute inherent elements of general intelligence.[40]

General intelligence must include the abilities to compute information, to learn and to reason.[41] As of now, the reaction in the face of uncertainty—constitutes one of the most crucial differences between human intelligence and all, existing kinds of artificial intelligence.[42] The development of emotions is another such striking differentiation.

Despite the ellipsis of several characteristics of human intelligence, while "when" of AGI is debatable, a significant number of analysts agree that within this century it will emerge.[43] After all, if what essentially the human mind does is performing computation, in the sense that it "deals in information, converting a pattern of input

---

[37]Bekey (2005).

[38]Heath. What is AI? Everything you need to know about artificial intelligence.

[39]Goertzel and Pennachin (2007) Artificial general intelligence vi.

[40]Bostrom (2014), p. 23

[41]Khoury (2017), pp. 635–640.
Ginsberg (1988), p. 265.

[42]Gigerenzer et al. (1999).

[43]Tal (2018) Forecast|How the first artificial general intelligence will change society: future of artificial intelligence P2. Quantumrun special series. https://www.quantumrun.com/prediction/first-artificial-general-intelligence-society-future. Accessed 3 February 2019.

nerve signals to output nerve signals defining", a different, non-biological, computational entity could mimic it and eventually out-perform it, once that the necessary hardware has been achieved.[44] As analyzed below it is far from certain that the human mind can be reduced to this description. Still the fore-mentioned description provides us with the general guideline about the replication of human brain by AI.

In principle, the lesser that AI is based on programming and the more it is based on experience, the closer it gets to AGI.[45] When debating about the potential emergence of AGI, the main idea is that human engineering will manage to achieve a "shortcut" to what natural development has achieved with biological organisms. However, it remains to be answered whether the computational capacities can achieve such performances.

The opinions on such accounts vary. On the optimistic side, Moravec wrote: "The existence of several examples of intelligence designed under these constraints should give us great confidence that we can achieve the same in short order. The situation is analogous to the history of heavier than air flight, where birds, bats and insects clearly demonstrated the possibility before our culture mastered it."[46]

Schulman and Bostrom have extensively analyzed the potential evolutionary patterns for designing AGI, as well as the potential difficulties ahead, through interdisciplinary approach. The main concept—*since the details evade the scope of the book at hand*—is condensed in the effort either through genetic algorithms or via other, evolutionary algorithms and means to reproduce the natural evolutionary pattern, albeit without the "failures" of the natural environment and therefore in a relatively short period and—up to some extent—in a protected environment. The achievement of such a goal will be the outcome of technological breakthrough in the areas of algorithms, software and hardware technologies.[47]

Super intelligence—ASI—moves one step further and refers to the exceeding of human intelligence in the sense of "any intellect that greatly exceeds the cognitive performance of humans in virtually all domains of interest."[48] Or as Bostrom again in an older paper of his had suggested "[B]y a "superintelligence" we mean an intellect that is much smarter than the best human brains in practically every field, including scientific creativity, general wisdom and social skills."[49]

---

[44]What is still missing is the "raw computing power" but there are several other ways that the gap in these regards could close.

Snyder-Beattie and Dewey (2014) Explainer: what is superintelligence? The conversation. https://theconversation.com/explainer-what-is-superintelligence-29175. Accessed 1 February 2019.

[45]*Ibid.*

[46]Moravec (1976) The role of raw power in intelligence. www.frc.ri.cmu.edu/users/hpm/project.archive/general.articles/1975/Raw.Power.html. Accessed 14 July 2019.

[47]Bostrom (2012), pp. 103–130.

[48]Bostrom (2014).

[49]Bostrom. How long before superintelligence? Oxford Future of Humanity Institute, Faculty of Philosophy & Oxford Martin School, University of Oxford. https://nickbostrom.com/superintelligence.html. Accessed 02 February 2019.

ASI can be further distinguished on the basis of the different cognitive functions that ASI will be able to demonstrate: it is assumed that it can be speed Superintelligence, which exercises the functions of human intelligence but exponentially faster. Essentially, this would mean that humans and the physical world will be too slow to catch up with the capacities of ASI.[50]

A second potential manifestation of superintelligence may be collective intelligence, due to the merging in terms of function of distinct intelligences. Forms of collective intelligence exist already in the academia, the social media, the social networks of various types, the political parties etc. The different of ASI is the expectation that it will perform as a single mind.[51]

Lastly, ASI may take the form of qualitative superintelligence, meaning intelligence, which is at least as fast as the human mind but with qualities expanding the ones of humans.[52]

Under all these forms of Superintelligence, the common denominator is that ASI is expected to surpass human intelligence in various ways. Once ASI is achieved, it is very much likely that more than one of the forms of ASI will be obtained.

Good, back in 1965 suggested that it must be defined "as a machine that can far surpass all the intellectual activities of any man however clever. Since the design of machines is one of these intellectual activities, an ultra-intelligent machine could design even better machines; there would then unquestionably be an 'intelligence explosion', and the intelligence of man would be left far behind. Thus the first ultra -intelligent machine is the last invention that man need ever make."[53]

While the time of the achievement of super intelligence remains at stake, its achievability is highly anticipated, by part of the analysts. As an article co-authored by Stephen Hawking, Max Tegmark, Stuart Russell, and Frank Wilczek foresaw: "Looking further ahead, there are no fundamental limits to what can be achieved: there is no physical law precluding particles from being organized in ways that perform even more advanced computations than the arrangements of particles in human brains."[54] Vinge shares similar concerns, about a probable doomsday of humanity,[55] whereas John Good sees in this perspective "saviors" of humanity.[56]

The emergence of ASI is expected to bring two further outcomes regarding its potential exponential growth: the continuous invention of new machines by the ASI entities on the one hand and subsequent technological progress' speed acceleration,

---

[50] Bostrom (2014), pp. 40–60.

[51] Shanahan (2010).

[52] Bostrom (2014), pp. 40–60.

[53] Good (1965).

[54] Hawking et al. Transcending complacency on superintelligent machines. *Huffpost*. https://www.huffingtonpost.com/stephen-hawking/artificial-intelligence_b_5174265.html?ec_carp=3359844804041712164. Accessed 1 February 2019.

[55] Vinge (1993) The coming technological singularity: how to survive in the post-human era. In: Vision-21: interdisciplinary science and engineering in the era of cyberspace, vol. 11, pp 12–14. https://perma.cc/6UY3-C2RJ. Accessed 10 February 2019.

[56] Guihota et al. (2017), pp. 385–394.

up to explosive levels: "Computing speed doubles every two subjective years of work. Two years after Artificial Intelligences reach human equivalence, their speed doubles. One year later, their speed doubles again. Six months—three months—1.5 months ... Singularity", as Yudkowsky analyzes in a relevant article.[57]

The former could lead to an infinite number of "machines", whereas the second to intelligence by far exceeding our wildest dreams. Both of ASI capacities defy the biological restraints imposed on humanity, substitute natural evolution with intelligent design and accelerate the time of evolution to times unimaginable for human evolution.

It was Vernor Vinge who introduced the concept of singularity and later Kurzweil who further developed it, as well as Yudkowsky.[58] The main ideas refer to such technological developments that unpredictable phenomena emerge and to infinite intelligence and speed.[59] Eventually, it is the emergence of entities which exceed human intelligence that will materialize singularity. Such is the fascination from the potential emergence of "singularity" that it condenses philosophy, science, fiction, emotions.

Vinge suggested four possible ways for singularity emergence: the development of computers that are superhumanly intelligent, a computer becoming superintelligent, the interlinkage between humans and computers or methods of biological enhancement of human intellect.[60]

The main forecasting issue with singularity however is that while we can speculate that it is going to be achieved, we cannot foresee the events which will follow.[61] Therefore, its consequences and the way it will evolve remain undetermined or—even worse—impossible to guess.

Yudkowsky came up with three plus one theories for what singularity means: accelerating change, which causes a quicker pace of technological development; event horizon which suggests that AI and human brain can be interlinked, producing enhanced human intelligence, albeit with unpredictability becoming the main trend; and intelligence explosion, which leads to exponential intelligence growth, potentially through the linkage of human and artificial intelligence, leading to Superintelligence.[62] The last—fourth scenario—is the apocalyptic scenario. All these scenarios may be combined or some of them and in any case they are not that detailed.

---

[57]Yudkowsky (1996) Staring at the singularity. http://yudkowsky.net/obsolete/singularity.html.

[58]Vinge (1993).

Kurzweil (2005).

Yudkowsky (2007) Three major singularity schools. http://yudkowsky.net/singularity/schools.

[59]Chalmers (2010), pp. 7–9.

[60]Vinge (1993) The coming technological singularity: how to survive in the post-human era. https://edoras.sdsu.edu/vinge/misc/singularity.html. Accessed 1 August 2019.

[61]Wallach (2016), p. 297.

[62]Yudkowsky. Three major singularity schools. http://yudkowsky.net/singularity/schools/. Accessed 31 July 2019.

The crucial issue with singularity is what we could frame as the "super-hero among us" or "Gods among us" problem. Can we actually co-exist with so powerful and evolved entities among us, based, in the best case scenario, on their benevolence towards us? Can there be trust and harmony with so fundamental, ontological inequality?

Our own history as well as the history of our co-existence with other, inferior species gives a negative answer. ASI, driven by indifference, contradicting goals with us, misinterpretations, ignorance or whatever negative "feelings", towards these obsolete creators that we will be, may turn against us; even if it does not act as such and is on the contrary proven friendly beyond any doubt, we will be living under the shadow of superior species that we have created: how long will it take for our full of anxiety and unable to accept our inferiority, souls to turn against our own creations? These questions and the potential answers are further articulated in the discussion about the ethics of AI.

3.4 AI, Machine Learning and Neural Networks

The development of AGI and ASI is based on the main innovation of AI: that is that AI is not the mere outcome of software programming; it imitates the learning procedure which is followed by humans. This is what machine-learning is about, enhancing the adaptability and the autonomy of AI entities.

Machine learning was foreseen by Alan Turing as a fundamental element of the road to general intelligence, familiar with the idea of emulating human-learning procedure and implementing it on AI.[63]

Alan Turing's idea was to mimic child's mind. As he was writing "[I]nstead of trying to produce a programme to simulate the adult mind, why not rather try to produce one which simulates the child's? If this were then subjected to an appropriate course of education one would obtain the adult brain... We cannot expect to find a good child machine at the first attempt. One must experiment with teaching one such machine and see how well it learns. One can then try another and see if it is better or worse. There is an obvious connection between this process and evolution.... One may hope, however, that this process will be more expeditious than evolution. The survival of the fittest is a slow method for measuring advantages. The experimenter, by the exercise of intelligence, should be able to speed it up. Equally important is the fact that he is not restricted to random mutations. If he can trace a cause for some weakness he can probably think of the kind of mutation which will improve it."[64]

---

[63]McCarthy (2008), pp. 2003–2011.

Lake et al (2016) Building machines that learn and think like people. Center for brains, minds, and machines memo No. 046, at 7. http://www.mit.edu/tomeru/papers/machines_that_think.pdf.

[64]Turing (1950), pp. 433–460.

There are several definitions for machine learning. It has been defined as "the science of getting computers to learn and act like humans do, and improve their learning over time in autonomous fashion, by feeding them data and information in the form of observations and real-world interactions."[65]

Other definitions of machine learning refer to "the practice of using algorithms to parse data, learn from it, and then make a determination or prediction about something in the world."[66] Machine learning thus resembles more to "coaching" than programming[67] and also to human learning procedure.[68] It can be also described through the cumulative contribution of three abilities: to compute information, to learn and to reason.[69]

Three categories of machine learning are identified[70]: supervised learning, which "uses a set of examples with a label informing the algorithm of the expected output…"; "[R]einforcement learning," where algorithms learn how to choose between a set of actions to accomplish a task that will maximize some reward. The reward is a mathematical function that computes a score depending on how well the task was completed…" and "unsupervised learning" which "…refers to the problem of designing algorithms which can learn by themselves without any external goal (either a list of labelled examples or rewards) and which would be able to come up with their own goals."[71]

Machine learning obviously constitutes a highly challenging quest[72]; still it is producing impressive results,[73] essential to the quest of enhanced autonomy of AI, in

[65]Faggella. What is machine learning? Emerj. https://emerj.com/ai-glossary-terms/what-is-machine-learning/. Accessed 2 February 2019.

[66]Copeland (2016) What's the difference between artificial intelligence, machine learning, and deep learning? nvidia. https://blogs.nvidia.com/blog/2016/07/29/whats-difference-artificial-intelligence-machine-learning-deep-learning-ai/. Accessed 2 February 2019.

[67]Kowert. The foreseeability of human-artificial intelligence interactions, p. 183.

Tanz (2016) Soon we won't program computers. We'll train them like dogs. WIRED. https://www.wired.com/2016/05/the-end-of-code/. Accessed 24 June 2018.

Scherer (2016), p. 365.

Cuellar (2017), pp. 27–33.

[68]Schuller. At the crossroads of control: the intersection of artificial intelligence in autonomous weapon systems with International Humanitarian Law, at p. 396.

[69]Khoury (2017), pp. 635–640

[70]Tito (2017), pp. 7–8.

[71]UNIDIR. Autonomous weapon systems: implications of increasing autonomy in the critical functions of weapons - ref. 4283-ebook, Dr. Ludovic Righetti, Max Planck Institute for Intelligent Systems, Germany, Emerging technology and future autonomous weapons, at p. 37.

[72]Davis and Marcus (2015), pp. 92–93.

[73]"The median estimate of respondents was for a one in two chance that high-level machine intelligence will be developed around 2040–2050, rising to a nine in ten chance by 2075. Experts expect that systems will move on to superintelligence in less than 30 years thereafter".

Müller and Bostrom (2016), p. 553.

Machine learning: what it is and why it matters. SAS Institute. http://www.sas.com/en_us/insights/analytics/machine-learning.html. Archived at https://perma.cc/X5VD-4WPW.

the sense of AI which not only does not need real-time control by humans but also "...in the sense that the methods selected by the robots to accomplish the human-generated goal are not predictable by the human."[74]

It is comprised of a performance and of a learning element. The first one "senses the environment", while the latter, employs feedback from the system and amends the performance element.[75]

The technology of machine learning is enhanced by neural networks and deep learning. Roughly speaking, neural networks are inspired by human brain and the synapses between neurons, which function at different layers, through which, massive data run, in order to train the system.[76] The scope is for the algorithm to gain the ability to correctly predict the correct output even for new inputs, therefore demonstrating inductive logic.[77]

Machine learning very much relies on natural-language processing—NLP—that aims at teaching AI how to comprehend human language and seek patterns.[78] The expectation is that AI will comprehend reasoning via language processing.

Another groundbreaking development which sustains machine-learning are AI neural networks, meaning "biologically inspired computational model that is patterned after the network of neurons present in the human brain", modeling "the input-output relationship."[79]

Neural networks sustain and enhance machine learning, promoting and accelerating AGI. Further innovations in this area include the deep belief networks—DBN—which are "composed of multiple layers of latent variables ("hidden units"), with connections between the layers but not between units within each

---

[74]Karnow (2016), p. 53.

[75]Marra and McNeil (2013), pp. 1139–1145.

Schuller. At the crossroads of control: the intersection of artificial intelligence in autonomous weapon systems with International Humanitarian Law, p. 404.

[76]Copeland. What's the difference between artificial intelligence, machine learning, and deep learning?

[77]De Spiegeleire et al. Artificial intelligence and the future of defense, p. 41.

[78]Nadkarni et al. (2011), p. 544.

Liddy (2001) Natural language processing, surface (Syracuse Univ. Research Facility and Collaborative Env't). http://surface.syr.edu/cgi/viewcontent.cgi?article=1043&context=istpub.

[79]"An artificial neural network transforms input data by applying a nonlinear function to a weighted sum of the inputs. The transformation is known as a neural layer and the function is referred to as a neural unit. The intermediate outputs of one layer, called features, are used as the input into the next layer. The neural network through repeated transformations learns multiple layers of nonlinear features (like edges and shapes), which it then combines in a final layer to create a prediction (of more complex objects). The neural net learns by varying the weights or parameters of a network so as to minimize the difference between the predictions of the neural network and the desired values. This phase where the artificial neural network learns from the data is called training."

Nvidia. Artificial Neural Networks. https://developer.nvidia.com/discover/artificial-neural-network. Accessed 02 February 2019.

layer."[80] DBN's can perform more autonomously and with greater credibility than deep neural networks.

Neural networks bear the capacity of overcoming damages to their functions instead of a complete crash. They are based on finding natural ways of learning and they themselves and demonstrate capacities of generalization. This is how they get trained in recognizing patterns, a procedure which becomes even more elaborate with the introduction of multi-layered neural networks.[81]

The goal for them is the achievement of natural-like, evolutionary patterns, on the basis of algorithms which can produce solutions to a wide range of problems, without direct human control. However, the difficulties in practice are often proven too difficult to be overcome due to the above-mentioned combinatorial explosion.[82]

Neural networks sustain deep learning algorithms. They exercise multi-level functions, where "each unit in the bottom layer takes in external data... then distributes that information up to some or all of the units in the next layer. Each unit in that second layer then integrates its inputs from the first layer, using a simple mathematical rule, and passes the result further up to the units of the next layer. The input data accordingly passes through numerous layers of statistical data operations to produce the requested output data."[83]

This procedure is of particular significance because it is probabilistic in nature, non-linear, complicated, opaque and therefore unpredictable, justifying why enhanced and evolving AI becomes unpredictable and resembles to a black box in terms of its decision-making.[84]

Machine learning and artificial neural networks are based on the combined functions of algorithm, which perform different operations, with mathematically established trade-off, in furtherance of common goals.[85]

A turning point in the enhancement of AI learning will be the potential achievement of a "Bayesian agent" stage. Evading the technical complexities, the Bayesian agent is expected to perform "probabilistically optimal use of available information." The problem is that the computational capacities which are required are too demanding for any physical computer.[86] The ambition for AI is to find ways for shortcuts in

---

[80] Artificial Intelligence Blog. DL algorithms: deep belief networks (DBN). https://www.artificial-intelligence.blog/education/dl-algorithms-deep-belief-networks-dbn. Accessed 28 April 2019.

[81] Bostrom (2016), pp. 7–8.

[82] Bostrom (2016), p. 8.

[83] World Economic Forum (2019) White paper, AI governance: a holistic approach to implement ethics into AI, p. 6. https://www.weforum.org/whitepapers/ai-governance-a-holistic-approach-to-implement-ethics-into-ai. Accessed 18 October 2019.

[84] Castelvecchi (2016), p. 22.

UK Government Office for Science (2015) Artificial intelligence: opportunities and implications for the future of decision making, p 5. Available at https://www.gov.uk/government/uploads/system/uploads/attachment_data/file/566075/gs-16-19-artificial-intelligenceai-report.pdf.

[85] Bostrom (2014), p. 9.

[86] Bostrom (2014), p. 9.

order to gain effectiveness by sacrificing some extent of "optimality or generality."[87]

The procedure of machine-learning enhances further with the evolution of "seed AI", meaning AI with the ability to understand and improve its architecture. Seed AI has been attractive as pioneer of the singularity moment, meaning the explosion of intelligence since it will be capable of restructuring itself.[88]

Machine-learning of AI has to deal in its evolution with two fundamental uncertainties, due to the fact that it functions in non-deterministic environment: environment and model uncertainty. The primary is an identity of the environment—like flipping a coin—whereas the latter is the outcome of the agent's own lack of knowledge about the environment.[89]

This distinction matters a lot in reinforcement learning, which is a component of machine learning, where an agent acts in a certain environment in order to maximize its utility in the long term. Within such learning procedures the two "steps" are exploration which refers to "...learning about the environment so the agent knows what the most valuable actions are" and exploitation which follows explorations and means that "[O]nce the agent knows enough it can just stick to the most valuable action sequences (policy) and keep performing those."[90]

The learning element is followed by the decision element, which prerequisites the selection of the action with the highest expected utility, in the framework of the desirability of each possible "world", according to AI system's basic preferences.[91] The problem of computational capacities emerges again and it is what big data, machine learning and Bayesian agents' techniques, together with the development of hardware attempt to solve, through distinct but often combined approaches.

In order to achieve such goals, AI entities need to include various components, such as logic[92] "as a tool of analysis, as a basis for knowledge representation, and as a programming language"[93]—creativity—combined with skills such as problem solving, pattern recognition, classification, learning, induction, deduction, building analogies, optimization, surviving in an environment and language processing[94]—communicative capacities, external knowledge, "cognitive autonomy"—in the sense

[87]Bostrom (2014), p. 10.

[88]Bostrom (2014), p. 29.

[89]inFERENce (2015) The two kinds of uncertainty an AI agent has to represent. https://www.inference.vc/the-two-kinds-of-uncertainties-in-reinforcement-learning-2/. Accessed 06 July 2019.

[90]inFERENce (2015) The two kinds of uncertainty an AI agent has to represent.

[91]Bostrom (2014), p. 10.

[92]Thomason R. Logic and artificial intelligence. Stanford encyclopedia of philosophy. https://perma.cc/3RPH-PVKV. Accessed 29 August 2018.

[93]Thomason. Logic and artificial intelligence.

[94]Hutter (2010), pp. 125–126.

Hallevy (2018) Dangerous robots – artificial intelligence vs. human intelligence. Available at: https://ssrn.com/abstract=3121905. Accessed 19 July 2018.

of working "independently without human intervention beyond defining goals"—intuition and strategic thinking.[95]

The different ways and types of machine-learning have one common element: the central role of "big-data", a term that describes data sets that are excessive and cannot be incorporated with the traditional data analytics.[96]

Big data are essential for the machine-training procedure, which makes crucial who gathers what data and what use makes of them. The issue is analyzed below regarding its ethical and legal ramifications. What are described here are the different approaches and the innovativeness of machine-learning, as the pioneer of AI autonomy.

Cases of AI evolution through machine-learning continuously emerge. One such landmark event for AI specialists in the course of these developments, has been the victory of the "AlphaGo" programme against one of the best human players of "Go". The reason is that in order to achieve its victory, AI demonstrated intuition, via combination of deep learning and traditional AI.[97] AlphaGo got further upgrades by becoming capable "of teaching itself winning strategies with no need for human intervention."[98] AlphaZero presented further development, in the sense that it generated its own knowledge in playing three board games in just a few hours.[99]

These entities or "systems" indicated that machine learning and neural networks have already surpassed "rules-based programming,"[100] which means that AI possesses already the capacity to function autonomously from the human programmer, surpass by far human intelligence—*currently*—in narrow, pre-determined areas, evolve and even re-program itself. On the other hand, AI has not yet achieved general intelligence and is still indicating these exceptional capacities, in a

[95]Yanisky-Ravid and Liu. When artificial intelligence systems produce inventions: the 3A era and an alternative model for patent law, p. 7.

Camett and Heinz (2006) John Koza built an invention machine. *Popular Science*. www.popsci.com/scitech/article/2006-04/john-koza-has-built-invention-machine. Accessed 16 September 2018.

Hallevy. Dangerous robots – artificial intelligence vs. human intelligence, p. 6.

Suchman and Weber (2016), pp. 39–40.

[96]Big data: what it is and why it matters. SAS INSTITUTE. http://www.sas.com/en_us/insights/big-data/what-is-bigdata.html. Accessed 26 September 2016.

Hilbert M and Lopez P (2011) The world's technological capacity to store, communicate, and compute information: tracking the global capacity of 60 analog and digital technologies during the period from 1986 to 2007. martinhilbert.net. http://www.martinhilbert.net/WorldInfoCapacity.html. Accessed 26 September 2016.

[97]Tegmark (2017), pp. 140–141.

[98]Quellette (2018) Move over AlphaGo: AlphaZero taught itself to play three different games, arstechnica. https://arstechnica.com/science/2018/12/move-over-alphago-alphazero-taught-itself-to-play-three-different-games/. Accessed 3 February 2019.

[99]Quellette. Move over AlphaGo: AlphaZero taught itself to play three different games, arstechnica.

[100]Pyle and San Jose (2015) An executive's guide to machine learning. McKinsley Quarterly. https://www.mckinsey.com/industries/high-tech/our-insights/an-executives-guide-to-machine-learning. Accessed 3 February 2019.

"protected" environment. However, machine-learning is producing already outcomes leading towards this goal.

3.5 AI Consciousness and Its Nature

The road towards AGI and ASI and the subsequent evolution of AI ontology to greater autonomy and intelligence raises the issue of consciousness of AI and therefore of what consciousness is. Are we ever going to reach the groundbreaking moment when an AI entity will come to the conclusion "I think therefore I am"? Will such consciousness be a replicate of human consciousness or is it going to be fundamentally different?

On top of these questions, several more arise as AI-driven consciousness or—at least—intelligence will begin to be linked or merge with human consciousness presenting the issue of who or even what is the intelligent being in front of us.

The concept of consciousness is one of the most complicated scientific issues; it is a puzzling and unpredictable constituent of life,[101] which is further complicated when projected on AI, due to the "black box" effect of AI, which "blurs" our comprehension about the existence or not of consciousness of AI as well as about its type, in the case of potentially conscious AI. As Marvin Minsky wrote it seems almost impossible to make clear what we mean when we talk about consciousness.[102]

Ray Kurzweil, in his book "The age of spiritual machines" offers two intriguing examples showing the complexities, of consciousness. The first is of a man who begins to implant devices for health reasons until the procedure climaxes into replicating and emulating his consciousness into a non-biological mind. Is he still the same "Jack" given that he looks identical in terms of his behavior-albeit better in several regards—or a different person? And what will happen to the "old Jack" meaning to his old body, including the mind of his as well? More specifically, what will the old Jack actually be? Will there be Jack's conscious in two places? Or as Susan Schneider says, too many enhancements and you may stop being you.[103]

The other case is that of a computer on the screen of which the message "I'm lonely" pops up. Initially we will consider it, the outcome of the human programmer and therefore lacking any conscious; even if it is the unpredictable—by the software designer—outcome of a game, it will be difficult to assign to it consciousness. What

---

[101] Dennett (1978) Brainstorms, pp 149–150.

There are however contradictory approaches as well. According Henry Greely, the "...mind is wholly created by or through the state of (the physical) brain" and 2. "the state of the physical brain at time T1 is totally a function of its state at time T0 plus whatever inputs it has received," therefore 3. "the mind is completely determined."

Greely (2018), pp. 2303–2315.

[102] Minsky (1985).

[103] Schneider (2019), p. 7.

if however, behind the message, there are artificial neural networks, modeling human language and knowledge? What if this AI has access to the cyberspace and the message follows the reading by the AI of world literature?[104]

As long as consciousness remains a privilege of humans our way to identify is more or less "we know it when we see it". This approach despite remaining the prevalent one has been partially shaken; do embryos have consciousness? What about animals? And also, what is the consciousness of comatose people? Even further, why do we need consciousness, meaning why do we need to feel in a certain way from the inside, when processing information?[105]

If these are difficult questions—and indeed they are—with AI, things get even more complicated: even if we see it, are we sure that it is actually there? Can we trust the external manifestation of consciousness, when demonstrated by machines which are created and trained to imitate? Is AI that demonstrates the characteristics of consciousness conscious or simply imitates human behaviors?

A potential answer is that since the brain is the source of consciousness, then the modeling of brain by AI can replicate consciousness as well.[106] This is only one of the different approaches however; our lack of complete and holistic understanding of human consciousness has led part of the scientific community to suggest that consciousness cannot be replicated by AI because human consciousness possesses characteristics which are missing from AI[107]: emotions, intentionality, interests and free-will. But while these as well as other characteristics are still missing from AI, why must this remain the case in the future too?

Consciousness is a profoundly elusive, concept. It is not surprising that its definitions or even the answer to whether consciousness may be defined or not divide analysts.

Chalmers argued that consciousness can be essentially analyzed as an information-processing system.[108] This is how he came up with the "thermostat paradigm": "[L]et us consider an information-processing system that is almost maximally simple: a thermostat. Considered as an information-processing device, a thermostat has just three information states (one stateleads to cooling, another to heating, and another to no action). So, the claim is that to each of these information states, there corresponds a phenomenal state. These three phenomenal states will all be different, and changing the information state will change the phenomenal state..."[109]

[104]Kurzweil (1999), pp. 51–62.

[105]Chalmers has come forth with this "hard" and potentially un-answered problem.
See: Chalmers (1996).
Chalmers (2008).

[106]Johnson-Laird (1983), pp. 448–477.

[107]McGinn (1991), pp. 202–213.

[108]Chalmers (1996), pp. 293–297.
Chalmers. What is it like to be a thermostat? http://consc.net/notes/lloyd-comments.html.

[109]Chalmers (1996), pp. 293–297.

Eventually what this metaphor means is that the critical question is not whether AI can be conscious but what type of consciousness does it have: a simple, primitive one or a more sophisticated and evolved one.[110]

The paradigm is interesting, albeit it seems that fails to capture that the quantity affects the quality as well: even if we consider that consciousness is an information-processing system that does not mean necessarily that all information-processing systems are conscious(-ness); one may assume that there must be some minimum information—processing level and variety of information types, in order to conclude that a specific, information-processing system is conscious. Chalmers however, also explained that in his opinion the inner life—and in this sense consciousness—is a hard problem, whereas the function of the brain constitutes an "easy" problem.[111]

What the above paradigm however accurately indicates is that consciousness surpasses the mere physiology of the brain, resembling to a pattern; it is a palimpsest of constituents, based and emerging from and thanks to the human brain; the brain as organ per se experiences and interprets stimuli that create patterns. The relationship between the physiology of the brain and the patterns of stimuli interpretation can be described as similar to the relationship between matter and energy. If this is the case, then there is no reason why consciousness cannot evolve on an artificial brain provided that a number of technological breakthroughs are achieved.

The above analysis in several ways forces us to think about observable criteria and characteristics of consciousness. The central characteristic is intelligence; in spite of not being identical to consciousness—at least regarding the discussion that is related to AI-remains essential for the latter. The same elements that characterize intelligence are at a significant extent characteristic of consciousness too. It also resembles to consciousness in terms of the difficulty to define it.[112]

For both intelligence and consciousness, the capacity to communicate, self-awareness, external knowledge of the surrounding world, ability to set goals, the capacity to alternate external behavior on the basis of internal assessment have been mentioned as fundamental.[113]

Self-awareness is possibly the most crucial of them all. A step to a much higher level of autonomy and a proof of consciousness will be apparent[114] when AI entities will be endowed with self-awareness,[115] in the sense of being aware of their distinct and own existence. They will be then be placing themselves in the broader world, as unique from all other entities and species.

---

[110]Frye (2018), pp. 42–44.

[111]Chalmers (1995), pp. 200–219.

[112]Kurzweil defines it as the ability to use optimally limited resources in furtherance of goals. Kurzweil. The age of spiritual machines, at p. . . (What is Artificial Intelligence).

[113]Schank (1987) What is AI, anyway? AIMAG Winter, pp. 59–60.

[114]Schkolne (2018) Machines demonstrate self-awareness, Medium. https://becominghuman.ai/machines-demonstrate-self-awareness-8bd08ceb1694. Accessed 11 December 2018.

[115]Chong (2015) This robot passed a 'self-awareness' test that only humans could handle until now. Tech Insider. www.businessinsider.com/this-robot-passed-a-selfawareness-test-that-only-humans-could-handle-until-now-2015-7. Accessed 23 August 2018.

Self-awareness involves a unity of subjective, mental activities, such as imaginative thinking, self-decision, creativity, self-representation and self-discovery, sentience, wakefulness, all of which tend to re-inventing one's own presence in the world. On the basis of these characteristics, we can agree that a common denominator of consciousness, in spite of the ambiguity, which surrounds it,[116] is at least its self-reflective nature: the perception of perception, and the awareness of awareness."[117] This is the crux of the conscious subjective experience.[118]

The detailed definition of consciousness evades the purpose of this article as it necessitates an interdisciplinary approach. It is perceived as a multi-layered and multi-paragon function and condition, which is comprised of internal and external awareness and self-observation, sustained by a certain structure and function of matter as well as neurophysiological functions.[119] It necessitates and prerequisites a comprehension of the idea of the "self" as placed within world but also as distinct from its other constituents.

There is extended multidisciplinary literature about how the idea of the self establishes the concept of "being" and about how it presupposes recognizing that "being" per se "...involves a sense of self that is possible because of our relation to "other".[120] All these give birth to a series of important questions, that cannot be answered here: how data analysis by the brain works, what differentiates matter with consciousness from matter without, which natural identities make us have subjective experience and why an entity has consciousness.[121]

The important conclusions regarding the scope of this book are that conscious AI will be seeing us, humans and possibly other AI entities as distinct beings; it will be aware of its existence, reflective and stochastic on it. The above will most likely be combined with autonomy and unpredictability, which again probably will be hostile

[116]Herbert (1985), p. 249.

[117]Smith (1998), pp. 277–281.

[118]Yanisky-Ravid and Liu. When artificial intelligence systems produce inventions: the 3A era and an alternative model for patent law. https://www.papers.ssrn.com/sol3/papers.cfm?abstract_id=2931828. Accessed 10 July 2018.

Hunter (1990), pp. 12–15.

Copeland (2000) What is artificial intelligence? Alanturing.net. www.alanturing.net/turing_archive/pages/Reference%20Articles/what_is_AI/What%20is%20AI02.html. Accessed 29 June 2018.

Armstrong and Sotala (2012), p. 52.

Galeon and Reedy (2017) Kurzweil claims that the singularity will happen by 2045. Futurism. https://www.futurism.com/kurzweil-claims-that-the-singularity-will-happen-by-2045/. Accessed 29 June 2018.

Davenport and Kirby (2015) Beyond automation. Harvard Business Review. https://hbr.org/2015/06/beyond-automation. Accessed 11 December 2018.

[119]Koch (2018) What is consciousness? Scientific American. www.scientificamerican.com/article/what-is-consciousness/. Accessed 22 February 2019.

Tegmark (2017), pp. 428–430.

[120]Mason (2015), pp. 1–3.

[121]Tegmark (2017), p. 431.

to pre-existing, human design, not because of the substance of it—*at least not necessarily*—but "in principle"; the greater the autonomy of an entity is, the more it tends to defy pre-existing design.

In addition, the emergence of conscious AI will not necessarily lead to intellect, identical to that of humans. On the contrary, it is highly speculative to assume about the type and the tendencies of an intellect entity, for which the physical world, as well as the concepts of the "self" and of the surrounding environment may be inherently different.

For example, inherent part of human intelligence is not merely the capacity to calculate, but sentience, sapience, some not very-well defined "essence" of human nature, wisdom and emotions too.[122] Will it be possible for AI to share such types of intellect? If it does not, what will be the consequences? And how will they look like in case the answer is positive?

What if this last scenario takes a slightly different path however: intelligent but not conscious AI.[123] A potential consequence of that could be that ASI will never emerge as somehow resembling to human intelligence in the sense of being consisted by similar constituents but as fundamentally alien to human type of consciousness.

Although it is a wild guess to try and think about the consequences, it is reasonable to assume that such evolution of AI will lead to ontological and existential gap between human and artificial intelligence—which in principle does not sound too relieving especially if we are the less developed species of the two. Superior intelligence with no empathy—or one that cannot distinguish itself from the rest of the world—could be led into trying to absorb all other species in its own mode of intelligence.

While it is with AGI and ASI that the fore-mentioned issues become emphatically present[124]—they are also gradually raised with existing, AI intellect autonomy at

[122]Damasio (1994), pp. 247–248.

Oxford Living Dictionaries. https://en.oxforddictionaries.com/definition/sentient.

Sternberg (2003) Wisdom, intelligence, and creativity synthesized.

[123]Schneider (2019), pp. 36–37.

It is also framed as the distinction between phenomenal consciousness, the type of consciousness that we, humans have providing us with the internal, self-reflective perception of our perception and functional or cognitive consciousness, which lacks the depth of the former- the "AI zombie" type of consciousness existence.

Ibid, pp. 48–49

[124]Ben-Ari et al. (2017), pp. 4–17.

Eden et al. (2012), pp. 28–29.

Marie Del Prado (2015) Stephen Hawking warns of an 'intelligence explosion. Business Insider. www.businessinsider.com/stephen-hawking-prediction-reddit-ama-intelligent-machines-2015-10. Accessed 29 August 2018.

Ahmed and Glasgow (2012) Swarm intelligence: concepts, models and applications: technical report 2012-585. Queen's Univ. School of Computing 2. https://ftp.qucis.queensu.ca/TechReports/Reports/2012-585.pdf. Accessed 29 August 2018.

relatively narrow fields.[125] Aspects of consciousness are already demonstrated, with the potential to produce impressively beneficial or destructive consequences, a growing number of which is quite unpredictable and not traceable or attributable to the initial human programmer.[126] Given that AI is walking down the road to consciousness this debate must cover all forms of it.

The analysis about consciousness is fascinatingly complicated. It evolves different philosophical and in general scientific theories, ranging from the definition of consciousness as pattern—and therefore as potentially distinct from our biological or even physical—existence, to the complete denial of the self and of "I."[127]

The relationships between intelligence and consciousness, consciousness and humans, consciousness, intelligence and AI will weigh on several scientific areas in the decades to come. We have not yet acquired the means to identify the existence of the subjective, inner, conscious experience, other than the manifestation of certain characteristics.

It becomes even more difficult to proceed into such determinations when we talk about AI. Still, in order to identify it and until we conclude that consciousness sn for example a pattern the cartography of which we will be able to track and reproduce—if this will ever come to be the case—we will have to rely on the external manifestations, first of higher intelligence and then of consciousness, with the most crucial one being self-awareness, hoping that we will neither be fooled by imitations, nor blinded at the expense of potentially conscious, non-biological beings because of our ignorance.

The discussion above is crucial in order to comprehend the potential evolution of AI, the need and the type of necessary regulation, as well as some of the norms such regulation must include.

3.6 The Quest for Friendly AI

The previous parts attempted to articulate the basic elements of AI ontology focusing on how the ontology of AI is determined and on how it may potentially evolve in the future. There is one more issue however, which condenses our anxiety as well as the

[125] Senior (2015) Narrow AI: automating the future of information retrieval. Techcrunch. https://techcrunch.com/2015/01/31/narrow-ai-cant-do-that-or-can-it/. Accessed 29 August 2018.

[126] Bostrom (2014), pp. 26, 29, 140, 155.

Hauser. Chinese room argument, internet encyclopedia of philosophy. www.iep.utm.edu/chineser/. Accessed 9 September 2018.

[127] Hughes (2004).

Hughes (2013).

Olson (1997).

Olson (2017) Personal identity. In: Zalta EN (ed) The Stanford encyclopedia of philosophy. https://plato.stanford.edu/entries/identity-personal/. Accessed 21 June 2020.

expectations from AI: will AI be ontologically friendly towards us or not? Is it going to have a particular stance towards humans, a pre-determined one or not?

The significance of the AI potential stance towards us, especially once it reaches the level of higher intelligence and of greater autonomy, meaning the level of ASI is obvious.[128]

The "friendliness" or not of AGI and ASI determines whether the fear that ASI may be the last human invention is realistic or not. It also gives us an insight on whether and why regulation is required.

The development of friendly AI apart from its technical issues prerequisites a thorough discussion about what the concept of friendliness means for humans and also what would it mean from an AI perspective. The creation of friendly AI poses serious challenges, such as the content of friendliness and the replication of cognitive functions that guide humans into choosing the one or the other moral code.[129]

Yudkowski proposes that "" Friendly AI" is not intended to imply a particular internal solution, such as duplicating the human friendship instincts, but rather a set of external behaviors that a human would roughly call "friendly."[130] The idea is that we can somehow bypass the political, moral, social and philosophical issues of instructing AI to follow specific theories, by setting goals to which AI must comply.[131]

This is why significant part of the attempt to design "friendly" AI is comprised of a goal-oriented approach, including the primary goals, the secondary goals which should serve the primary ones, as well as the AI learning procedure which is supposed to guide AI towards serving the primary goals. Because of our incapacity to completely comprehend AI ontology and behavior, as well as because of our lack of unanimous understanding of friendliness we tend to focus on external manifestations of friendliness and then incorporate them in AI. Therefore, the argument of such an approach is that we should focus not on the internal connotations of AI or on the effort to attribute to it certain ethical principles but on binding AI to pre-determined, goal-driven behaviors.

Although this strategy provides us with some stable ground and clarity, it still cannot evade completely risks: As Omohundro argues the de facto harmful behavior to humans may not be a matter of malice behavior but the outcome of gathering of resources, in order to achieve the primary goal that has been set[132]; a catastrophic "misunderstanding" of some type.

AI in furtherance of primary goals may develop self-preservation or domination tendencies, which will cause harm to humans, due to the lack of empathy between AI

128 Some relevance exists with ANI too. Still regarding ANI applications the issue is of lower significance as the human intervention remains possible.

129 Yudkowsky (2001), p. 13.

130 Yudkowsky (2001), p. 3.

131 Tarleton (2010), p. 1.

132 Omohundro (2008), pp. 483–492.

and humans and the incapacity of AI to assess the impact of the chosen means for humans or for part of them, from the human perspective.

After all, even if "friendly" AI somehow complies with the superior goals, it will most likely be choosing the secondary goals in the framework of its autonomy. The two-primary and secondary goals-must align otherwise the primary goal of friendliness will be pointless. Apart from the technical difficulties however, such a procedure necessitates an eloquent and efficient learning procedure so that the AI entity can learn how to achieve such alignment.

The moral—in the wider sense, i.e. encompassing political, and philosophical matters—problem pops up again: let us for example imagine an AI system which attempts to psychologically comfort people; how far it could go in terms of providing them joy? Could it decide to give them drugs for example? How would it balance between competing or even contradictory needs? Should such a primary goal be established in the first place? Would it align with the moral foundations of our societies?

Or imagine an AI entity designed to promote human rights; could it intervene in the outcome of elections or against a government which is expected or already is hostile to human rights?

The setting of the primary goals also raises technical and philosophical issues itself. Primary goals especially as AI autonomy evolves become wider and more complicated in line with the tasks that AI takes over—i.e. aspects of national defense, policing, justice, psychological assistance, medical science, decision-making etc.

We have to think about how we actually make AI learn adopt and retain our goals.[133] These goals and tasks contain more complexities than it seems. If we are to entrust highly sophisticated and autonomous AI, the latter must "learn" and comprehend our goals, as well as to develop a mental capacity of choosing the appropriate means and secondary goals which will substantially meet our expectations; that does not prerequisite only observation of human behaviors, as such observation could very well become misleading; it also requires an insightful understanding of our motives.

AI must therefore acquire a sense of common knowledge, as well as deeper knowledge of human motives both via big data and by observing human behavior and inferring conclusions.[134] Therefore, AI must be taught ethical behaviors and must be morally "raised", before it reaches the point of AGI and ASI, when it is very much likely that it will be able to effectively resist our intervention.

Once ASI is achieved it is very much likely that human programmers will not have the chance to intervene in the AI software. Therefore, once the goal-oriented behavior is proven ineffective, regarding the achievement of "friendliness", very little will be possibly done from the human perspective.

---

[133]Tegmark (2017) Friendly AI: aligning goals, future of life institute. https://futureoflife.org/2017/08/29/friendly-ai-aligning-goals/. Accessed 24 August 2019.

[134]Tegmark (2017).

An additional problem emerges from the fact that we—humans—often tend to mess means with ends and vice versa. That can be an issue both for the initial programmer and lead to vague goals in the first place, as well as for the AI when attempting to interpret the pre-determined goals and the means to achieve them by replicating the human paradigm, on the basis of the machine-learning that is "fueled" by big data.

As we come to terms with the need to crystallize to design and to implement AI "friendliness", as well as to foresee guarantees for its maintenance, the more we understand that that the implementation of "friendliness", as a goal-oriented concept prerequisites that the "value learning problem" will be answered too.[135] We need to combine the goal-oriented approach with the one which focuses on a machine-learning, enriched with a spectrum of values.

Different methods have been proposed, for such a combination: predictability through design in advance, inheritance—namely inheritance of motivation of human template—emulation or predictability through convergent instrumental reasons.[136]

The last method begins from the point that there may be a wide range of goals for an AI entity which are sustained and transcended by a more specific and narrower spectrum of instrumental values. We could identify certain patterns of behavior and therefore achieve some greater extent of predictability in the course of the aim to build friendly AI.[137]

Bostrom proposed self-preservation, goal-content integrity, cognitive enhancement, technological perfection and resource acquisition as instrumental values.[138]

The first of them refers to the reasonably expected tendency of AI to sustain and prolong its existence either because of its conscious existence or in order to serve its goals. That could take the form of self-protection or of self-replication or other forms which evade our speculations.

The second instrumental value deals with the extent of "commitment" of the AI with the primary goals, which have been set.

Cognitive enhancement refers to the procedure of intelligence accumulation and evolution in furtherance of the goals which are to be achieved. Human intelligence is keen with cognitive enhancement albeit in ways which it can be assumed that will not be identical with these of AI. We cannot foretell what the capacities of ASI in terms of cognitive enhancement are going to be but we assume that they will not be limited in ways similar to the ones that humans are by our biology. We also cannot foretell if AI will seek knowledge and cognitive enhancement other than that which is necessary for the achievement of the primary goals, such as for example the type of enhancement which serves more abstract or implicit goals—i.e. self-fulfillment etc.[139]

---

[135] Soares and Fallenstein (2017), p. 10.

[136] Bostrom (2014), pp. 100–108.

[137] Bostrom (2014), pp. 109–110.

[138] Bostrom (2014), pp. 114–119.

[139] Bostrom (2014), pp. 114–119.

The suggestions about the instrumental values sustaining the primary goals of goal-oriented AI is of value in order to give us guidance regarding our aim of "friendliness" of AGI and ASI, albeit not guarantees.

The prevalence of such instrumental values instead of others is mainly speculation. We cannot foretell the persistence of our instrumental values on ASI given that ASI will be intelligence superior to ours. Even if it does not overturn them completely, a qualitatively different and superior intelligence will most likely interpret and implement them in ways we cannot imagine and even more control.

The fore-mentioned instrumental values are interpreted by humans in certain ways due to variety of reasons, which include our relationship with space and time, our biological capacities, our social interactions and therefore our self-reflection. This will not be the case with ASI.

Characteristically, self-preservation—at least until now—for humans means extending our life-time, while acknowledging the inevitable of death. This fundamental knowledge of our biological limits is definitive for humankind.

For an AI entity this existentially defining perspective will most probably be absurd. ASI does not need to "die", nor needs it to produce an offspring. It will most probably be able to self-replicate, to self-enhance and live on indefinitely while re-generating its conscious existence and possibly multiplying it. Even the idea of the "self", as distinct from the environment and as unique will be altered, when it will be multiplied or when it will be diffused within the cyber space or when collective conscience will be the case.

Such capacities of ASI entities may make them sense at a lesser extent danger from humans on the one hand and therefore become friendlier; on the other hand, such "friendliness" could very well take the form of patronage of humans; it could verify the impressive superiority of ASI over us and convince ASI to gradually "absorb" humanity in order to provide us the "gift" of immortality at the cost of fundamentally altering our nature. It could also take the form of a doomsday disaster not out of hate or fear from an ASI entity perspective towards humans, but because of our insignificance in a world of indefinite "beings."[140]

As we attempt to run away from the need to impose ethical machine-learning for AI we find ourselves having our hands full with the same ethical questions. In this framework, Hibbard suggests that "In place of laws constraining the behavior of intelligent machines, we need to give them emotions that can guide their learning of behaviors. They should want us to be happy and prosper, which is the emotion we call love... First, we can build relatively simple machines that learn to recognize happiness and unhappiness in human facial expressions, human voices and human body language. Then we can hard-wire the result of this learning as the innate emotional values of more complex intelligent machines, positively reinforced when we are happy and negatively reinforced when we are unhappy."[141] This proposition implicates technically and morally unresolved matters.

[140]Soares and Fallenstein (2017), p. 10.

[141]Hibbard (2001), pp. 13–15.

A slightly different strategy is to encode into AI in advance, "friendliness" as the main goal. It will be foreseen and established as the "super goal" to which all other goals comply.

Again however, for all of the above-mentioned reasons, that cannot be a sufficient guarantee, not at least with the level of knowledge and technical capacities that we currently have and with a variety of moral issues remaining unsolved.

Let us assume for a moment that we manage to design "friendly" AI in the way we agree as humanity and in a way that seems initially binding for AI. Is this the end of our risks? Most likely the answer is no.

First, we cannot be certain that AI after a certain level of evolution will be still bound by our pre-determined goals. Once AGI or ASI is achieved it is possible that not only it will change its goals or its chosen means but that it will also be capable of creating superior intelligence or that it may be able to resist effectively the creation of any other ASI that could be hostile to it and therefore restrain humans' capacities to acquire means of fighting back to potentially hostile AI.[142]

Secondly, even well and in advance designed AI however bears the risk of serious and dangerous malfunctions: not necessarily because the context will be breached by the AI but because within the given context, the AI may evolve in an unpredictable way or of not being able to adapt equally efficiently when the context changes.[143]

Third, we have another source of concern; how can we "trust" as "friendly", AI which gathers too much power over us. The reason of concern can be identified in the human-centric experience which indicates that the gathering of power corrupts moral boundaries. Friendliness among humans follows evolutionary trends as well as the needs which emerge from the relative equality among us. These conditions will not be necessarily duplicated in relation to AGI and ASI. Therefore, it is necessary to come up with software, capable of maintaining friendliness under any conditions.[144]

Fourth, we may find that because of existential and ontological inconsistencies between human and artificial intelligence, the concept of friendliness may evolve as meaning different things.

In other words, thinking about friendliness in relation to AGI and ASI leads to a double alignment challenge: the challenge of alignment of AI with the specific given goals but also of the alignment with certain values in furtherance of the goals. It also leads to—until now—unsolvable issue: how do we safeguard that a superior species will comply with the goals of an inferior species?

A different method is the one suggesting that AI should be confined into a safe environment without access to the cyberspace or to the physical world so that it

[142]Bostrom (2006), pp. 48–54.

Omohundro (2007) The nature of self-improving artificial intelligence. Paper presented at singularity summit 2007, San Francisco, CA, September 8–9. http://intelligence.org/summit2007/overview/abstracts/#omohundro.

[143]Yudkowski (2008), p. 16

[144]Yudkowski (2008), p. 42.

cannot "escape" into the outside world. Apart from the moral issues arising out of the confinement of an intelligent entity, which will be equal or superior to human intelligence—we can only imagine how tormenting it is going to be for such an intelligent entity to be confined indefinitely and to be deprived of external stimuli—the effectiveness of such an approach can be seriously doubted. A super intelligent entity can be expected to find means of escaping the confinement from beings of inferior intelligence.

After all, it is much more ethical and certainly more effective not to advance to AGI and ASI in the first place instead of first creating it and then trying to understand what we are going to do with such superior species.

A potential approach to the value—alignment problem could be to safeguard that AGI and ASI will be able to learn the wishes and values of its owners or designers. However, and apart from its technical complexities, this approach per se does very little to comfort us. How can we entrust to AGI and ASI the moral values of a specific group of people when we do not trust one another? How are we going to manage the antagonism among different groups of people that such an approach will most certainly cause? AI already is becoming part of our inter-human antagonisms, which can very easily lead to complete lack of human control over AI. The problem of how to determine what these values must be emerges again.

An alternative strategy is to attempt to collectively try to reach an agreement about which moral values must guide AI. Of course, until now the international community lacks the organs which can play such a role.

Regardless of all the complications, the debate about the necessary guarantees for friendly AI is—thankfully—continuing. Characteristically, 42 states adopted 5 principles about "friendly" AI and namely, that: "AI should benefit people and the planet by driving inclusive growth, sustainable development and well-being; AI systems should be designed in a way that respects the rule of law, human rights, democratic values and diversity, and they should include appropriate safeguards—for example, enabling human intervention where necessary—to ensure a fair and just society; There should be transparency and responsible disclosure around AI systems to ensure that people understand when they are engaging with them and can challenge outcomes; AI systems must function in a robust, secure and safe way throughout their lifetimes, and potential risks should be continually assessed and managed; Organisations and individuals developing, deploying or operating AI systems should be held accountable for their proper functioning in line with the above principles."[145]

The inclusion of such goals into a strategy for AI is appropriate but still it is inefficient; they set welcome but rather vague and declaratory goals and in addition such goals are more suitable for ANI. They say little however about AGI and ASI.

The European Commission also came up with the ethics guidelines for trustworthy artificial intelligence, which was prepared by the high-level expert group on

[145] Donadson (2019) Five principles for citizen-friendly artificial intelligence. The Mandarin. https://www.themandarin.com.au/109017-five-principles-for-citizen-friendly-artificial-intelligence/

artificial intelligence. The use of the term "trustworthy" implies more moderate ambitions than the term "friendly." The guidelines refer to human agency and oversight, technical robustness and safety, privacy and data governance, transparency, diversity, non-discrimination and fairness, societal and environmental wellbeing and accountability.[146]

Especially the first of these guidelines attempts to retain human discretion and control over AI, in combination with guarantees in favor of human and democratic rights. The second of the principles attempts to restrain the potentially harmful unpredictability of AI by providing for such a responsibility for the developers of AI. These principles are more relevant with ANI though than with AGI and ASI, given that as mentioned above, once the latter levels of AI intelligence have been reached, the guarantees which are provided in the above-mentioned documents are too difficult to be safeguarded.[147]

Another potential approach is to entrust the development of moral values to the AGI and ASI itself. After all, a species of superior intelligence may be proven morally superior and wiser than us, humans. That would constitute a groundbreaking development—albeit a dangerous one, given that it will constitute not only superior but most likely qualitatively different intelligence. We have to wonder why an intellectually superior entity will share our moral values given our potential moral inferiority or why it will comprehend the concept of morality per se instead of simply dismissing it.[148]

If the "orientation" and the values of the moral guidance of AI is the one issue, the other issue is how to implement whatever morality. The dominant suggestion is the step by step approach, which suggests that we should build gradually friendly AI, moving from more specific, narrow applications to AGI and ASI; the advantage of this proposal is that it provides the guarantee of having the time which is necessary in order to be certain of the friendliness of AGI and ASI before they emerge; however, it is not certain that we will use as humans the window of time in the best possible way, especially given the lack both of centralized global action about AGI and ASI as well as the lack of unanimous comprehension of what "friendliness" means.

Even further, while the procedure from the specific and narrow to the general sounds logical and is in fact already underway regarding AI, it underestimates that AGI and ASI will be qualitatively different in relation to their narrow applications. No matter how intelligent it is in any specific area, ANI lacks the subjective experience of general intelligence and of super intelligence. Therefore, our lack of understanding for the subjective experience that AGI and ASI may experience erodes the effectiveness of the step-by-step approach.

[146] European Commission. Requirements of trustworthy AI. https://ec.europa.eu/futurium/en/ai-alliance-consultation/guidelines/. Accessed 28 September 2019.

[147] They can also contribute in the debate about the legitimacy or not of the development of AGI and ASI, which is conducted below.

[148] Muehlhauser and Bostrom (2014), pp. 41–44.

The pinpointing of the problems of the step-by-step approach is not meant to deny its significance. On the contrary, apart from the fact that it is already implemented and therefore cannot be overlooked, it is critical in terms of testing and re-adjusting AI prior to AGI and ASI. The argument is that it cannot be the sole approach.

It must be complementary to an institutionalized public regulation which will conclude on a detailed enough description of the definition of "Friendly" AI, endorsed by a competent international body, through a relevant treaty. In this sense, hierarchical, centralized regulation will be implemented, as well as a design of friendly AI, which will both moving from the specific to the general and vice versa.

The critical point that emerges from the above debate is that the potential friendliness or not of ASI constitutes the most challenging quest in the framework of AI development.[149]

It involves our capacity to guess the evolution of AI until it reaches the level of ASI, as well as following the emergence of this level; we must be able to capture the characteristics and the qualities of AGI and ASI; we must then be able to determine their further development over time, the speed of this evolution and the subjective experience to which they are going to lead; we must be able to identify if we can "genetically" introduce some guarantees of ASI "friendliness", towards humanity.

In parallel it presses humanity to come up with a description of friendliness of AI and with a regulatory framework that will be capable of providing safeguards. The complexities in furtherance of friendly AI serve as a reminder of how dangerous it is to rush into the development of AGI and ASI, without efficient regulation which will be imposed in advance.

3.7 Conclusions

In this chapter the basic characteristics of AI ontology are presented in order to relate them with the ethics of AI and the need, as well as the norms of a potential legal framework.

The analysis of the ontology of AI leads to some of its basic characteristics: its evolving character, its expanding autonomy, as well as its unpredictability. These characteristics are defined by the machine-learning procedure, which each AI entity "experiences" and raises the risk of whether friendly AI can be safeguarded or not.

The evolving character, coupled with the speed of these developments not only necessitates the regulation of AI but also justifies the sense of emergency. The latter emerges not only from the estimations for the "singularity moment" but also and already because of the existing implications even at the narrow level.

The expanding autonomy familiarizes us with the discussion about the loss of direct or indirect human control over an intelligent entity. Eventually the erosion of

[149] Yudkowsky (2001), p. 5.

human control may reach the point of the emergence conscious or/ and equally or even superior in terms of intelligence, entities; therefore, of non-human—centric social interactions and conducts, which subsequently will raise the issue of non-human—centric legal systems.

Legal regulations in order to be effective must take into account—as is analyzed below—exactly this gradual erosion of human control over AI entities and the basic aspects of AI ontology.

Among them the most urgent "place" belongs to the quest for friendly AGI and ASI and the attempt to regulate it. The problem is both with what is understood as friendliness when we move into more specific and detailed analyses as well as with our—lack of—certainty that we will be able to maintain the—defined by us in whatever why—"friendliness" of any equally or superior intelligent entity. The danger of unfriendly AGI and ASI forces us to think of the additional issue of the legitimacy or not of AGI and ASI.

This same danger led to different efforts for the establishment of ethical principles that can guide the evolution of AI and determine its actions. These ethical principles are examined in the next chapter.

References

Albus JS (1991) Outline for a theory of intelligence. In: 21 IEEE transactions on systems, man and cybernetics, p 473

Armstrong S, Sotala K (2012) How we're predicting AI--or failing to. In: Romportl J (ed) Beyond AI: artificial dreams, mach. intelligence research inst. Czech Republic, Pilsen, p 52

Bekey GA (2005) Autonomous robots: from biological inspiration to implementation and control. MIT Press, Cambridge

Ben-Ari D, Frish Y, Lazovski A, Eldan U, Greenbaum D (2017) "Danger, will Robinson"? Artificial intelligence in the practice of law: an analysis and proof of concept experiment. Richmond J Law Technol 23:4–17

Bostrom N (2006) What is a singleton? Linguist Philos Invest 5(2):48–54

Bostrom CSN (2012) How hard is artificial intelligence? Evolutionary arguments and selection effects. J Consciousness Stud 19(7-8):103–130

Bostrom N (2014) Superintelligence paths, dangers, strategies. Oxford University Press, Oxford

Bostrom N (2016) Superintelligence, paths, dangers, strategies. Oxford University Press, Oxford, pp 7–8

Brownstein BJ et al (1983) Technological assessment of future battlefield robotic applications. In: Proceedings of the army conference on application of AI to battlefield information management. US Navy Surface Weapons Center, White Oak, p 169

Busse J, Humm B et al (2015) Actually, what does "ontology" mean? A term coined by philosophy in the light of different scientific disciplines. J Comput Inf Technol 23:29–41

Castelvecchi D (2016) Can we open the black box of AI. Nature 538:22

Chalmers DJ (1995) Facing up to the problem of consciousness. J Consciousness Stud 2 (3):200–219

Chalmers D (1996) The conscious mind. In: Search of a final theory. Oxford University Press, Oxford

Chalmers D (2008) The hard problem of consciousness. In: Velmans M, Schneider S (eds) The Blackwell companion to consciousness. Wiley-Blackwell, Hoboken

Chalmers D (2010) The singularity, a philosophical analysis. J Consciousness Stud 17(9-10):7–9
Chandrasekaran B (1990) What kind of information processing is intelligence? In: Partridge D, Wilks Y (eds) The foundations of artificial intelligence. Springer, New York, p 14
Charniak E, McDermott D (1985) Introduction to artificial intelligence. Addison-Wesley, Boston
Cuellar MF (2017) A simpler world? On pruning risks and harvesting fruits in an orchard of whispering algorithms. UC Davis Law Rev 51:27–33
Damasio AR (1994) Descartes' error: emotion, reason, and the human brain. Avon Books, New York, pp 247–248
Davis E, Marcus G (2015) Commonsense reasoning and commonsense knowledge in artificial intelligence. Commun ACM 58:92–93
Eden A, Steinhart E, Pearce D, Moor J (2012) Chapter I; singularity hypotheses: an overview, introduction: singularity hypotheses: a scientific and philosophical assessment. In: Eden A, Moor J, Soraker J, Steinhart E (eds) Singularity hypotheses, a scientific and philosophical assessment. Springer, New York, pp 28–29
Frye BL (2018) The lion, the bat & the thermostat: metaphors on consciousness. Savannah Law Rev 5:42–44
Gigerenzer G, Todd PM, ABC Research Group (1999) Simple heuristics that make us smart. Oxford University Press, Oxford
Ginsberg ML (1988) Multivalued logics: a uniform approach to reasoning in artificial intelligence. Comput Intell 4:265
Good IJ (1965) Speculations concerning the first ultraintelligent machine. In: Alt F, Rubinoff M (eds) Advances in computers, vol 6. Academic, New York
Greely HT (2018) Neuroscience, artificial intelligence, crispr--and dogs and cats. U C Davis Law Rev 51:2303–2315
Grossmann R (1983) The categorial structure of the world. In: Fundamental issues of artificial intelligence. Springer, New York
Gruber TR (1993) A translation approach to portable ontologies. Knowl Acquis 5(2):199–220
Guihota M, Matthew AF, Suzor NP (2017) Nudging robots: innovative solutions to regulate artificial intelligence. Vanderbilt J Entertainment Technol Law 20:385–394
Herbert N (1985) Quantum reality: beyond the new physics. Anchor Books Editions, New York, p 249
Herre H, et al (2006) General Formal Ontology (GFO): a foundational ontology integrating objects and processes. Technical Report, 8, University of Leipzig
Hibbard B (2001) Super-intelligent machines. ACM SIGGRAPH Comput Graphics 35(1):13–15
Hughes J (2004) Citizen cyborg: why democratic societies must respond to the redesigned human of the future. Westview Press, Cambridge
Hughes J (2013) Transhumanism and personal identity. In: More M, More N (eds) The transhumanist reader. Wiley, Boston
Hunter L (1990) Molecular biology for computer scientists. In: Hunter L (ed) Artificial intelligence and molecular biology. MIT Press, Cambridge, pp 12–15
Hutter M (2010) Universal artificial intelligence: sequential decisions based on algorithmic probability. Springer, New York, pp 125–126
Johnson-Laird PN (1983) Mental models, pp. 448–477
Karnow CEA (2016) The application of traditional tort theory to embodied machine intelligence. In: Calo, Froomkin, Kerr (eds) Robot law. Edward Elgar, Cheltenham, p 53
Khoury AH (2017) Intellectual property rights for "hubots": on the legal implications of human-like robots as innovators and creators. Cardozo Arts Entertainment Law J 35:635–640
Kurzweil R (1999) The age of spiritual machines, when computers exceed human intelligence. Penguin Books, London, pp 51–62
Kurzweil R (2005) The singularity is near. Viking, New York
Laton D (2016) Manhattan_Project.Exe: a nuclear option for the digital age. Cath Univ J Law Technol 25:94

Marra WC, McNeil SK (2013) Understanding “the loop”: regulating the next generation of war machines. Harv J Law 36:1139–1145
Mason C (2015) Engineering kindness: first steps to building a machine with compassionate intelligence. Int J Synth Emot 6(1):1–3
McCarthy J (2008) The well-designed child. Artif Intell 172:2003–2011
McGinn C (1991) The problem of consciousness: essays towards a resolution, pp. 202–213
Minsky M (1985) The society of mind. Simon and Schuster, New York
Muehlhauser L, Bostrom N (2014) Why we need friendly Ai. Think 13:41–44
Müller VC and Bostrom N (2016) Future progress in artificial intelligence: a survey of expert opinion. Fundamental issues of artificial intelligence, p 553
Nadkarni PM, Ohno-Machado L, Chapman WW (2011) Natural language processing: an introduction. J Am Med Informatics 18:544
Nute D (2011) A logical hole the Chinese room avoids. Mind Mach 21:431–433
Olson E (1997) The human animal: personal identity without psychology. Oxford University Press, Oxford
Omohundro SM (2008) The basic AI drives. In: Wang P, Goertzel B, Franklin S (eds) Artificial general intelligence 2008: 1st AGI conference. Frontiers in artificial intelligence and applications, vol 171. IOS, Amsterdam, pp 483–492
Poole DL, Mackworth AK (2010) Artificial intelligence: foundations of computational agents. Cambridge University Press, Cambridge
Rich E, Knight K (1991) Artificial intelligence. McGraw-Hill, New York
Russell SJ, Norvig P (2010) Artificial intelligence: a modern approach, 3rd edn. Pearson Education Limited, London, pp 2–3
Russell S, Norvig P (2013) Artificial intelligence: a modern approach, 3rd edn. Prentice Hall, Hoboken
Schank RC (1987) What is AI, anyway? AIMAG Winter, pp. 59–60
Scherer MU (2016) Regulating artificial intelligent systems: risks, challenges, competences, and strategies. Harv J Law Technol 29:363–364
Schneider S (2019) Artificial you: AI and the future of your mind. Princeton University Press, Princeton, p 7
Shaffer M (2009) A logical hole in the Chinese room. Mind Mach 19(2):229–235
Shanahan M (2010) Embodiment and the inner life: cognition and consciousness in the space of possible minds. Oxford University Press, New York
Smith JC (1998) Machine intelligence and legal reasoning. Chicago-Kent Law Rev 73:277–281
Soares N, Fallenstein B (2017) Agent foundations for aligning machine intelligence with human interests: a technical research agenda. The technological singularity: managing the journey. Springer, New York, p 10
Suchman L, Weber J (2016) Human-machine autonomies. In: Bhuta N, Beck S, Geib R, Yan Liu H, Kreb C (eds) Autonomous weapon systems: law, ethics, policy. Cambridge University Press, Cambridge, pp 39–40
Tarleton N (2010) Coherent extrapolated volition: a meta-level approach to machine ethics. Miri Machine Intelligence Research Institute, Berkeley, p 1
Tegmark M (2017) Life 3.0, being human in the age of artificial intelligence. Random House, New York, pp 140–141
Tito J (2017) Destination unknown: exploring the impact of artificial intelligence on government. Centre for Public Impact, pp. 7–8
Turing AM (1950) Computing machinery and intelligence. Mind 59:433–460
Uschold M, Gruninger M (1996) Ontologies: principles, methods and applications. Knowl Eng Rev 11:2
Vinge V (1993) The coming technological singularity: how to survive in the post-human era. Whole Earth Review. Winter
Wallach W (2016) The singularity: will we survive our technology Doug Wolens, director I-Maginemedia. Jurimet J 56:297

Weiss T (1990) Closing the Chinese room. Ratio 3:165–181
Winograd T (2006) Thinking machines: can there be? Are we? In: Partridge D, Wilks Y (eds) The foundations of artificial intelligence. Cambridge University Press, Cambridge, p 167
Wisskirchen, et al (2010) Artificial intelligence and robotics and their impact on the workplace, p 10
Yudkowski A (2008) Artificial intelligence as a positive and negative factor in global risk. Machine Intelligence Research Institute, Berkeley, p 16
Yudkowsky E (2001) Creating friendly AI 1.0: the analysis and design of benevolent goal architectures machine intelligence research institute, p 3

Part II
Legal Framework of AI

Chapter 5
AI Governance and the Fundamental Principles of International Law

> *"We the Peoples of the United Nations"*
> *UN Charter, Preamble*
> *"We the Conscious Beings of the United Worlds"*
> *Universal Declaration for the Harmonic Coexistence of Conscious Beings.—An alternative ending of the Matrix saga, proposed by the writer of this book.*

5.1 Introduction

The Matrix trilogy—as these lines are written we are waiting for the sequel—ended with a type of truce or peace treaty between AI and humans. Hopefully in the 4th movie we will find out what happened after this agreement was concluded and how it—probably—collapsed.

Still, as AI evolves and while trying to avoid a "Matrix scenario" or a "Terminator scenario", the issue of governance of AI emerges as a crucial one.[1] We need to plan not only the governance of ANI but also the governance in light of the prospect and of the potential reality of AGI and ASI too. After all, maybe at some point we will have to govern with AI, not in the sense of using it as a sophisticated tool but as beings with which we share our world or worlds.

As of now, AI is primarily governed via a context—based approach, focusing on specific AI applications and their governance. This approach, despite offering guidance on specific matters—albeit very often incomplete—misses the bigger picture.

As humans we have come to understand the significance of international governance in order to preserve international peace and security. The post—world war II era witnessed the creation of the United Nations—UN—and the establishment of the

---

[1] As governance is defined here "the formation and stewardship of the formal and informal rules that regulate the public realm, the arena in which states as well as economic and societal actors interact to make decisions".

Grindle (2007), pp. 533–574.

T. Tzimas, *Legal and Ethical Challenges of Artificial Intelligence from an International Law Perspective*, Law, Governance and Technology Series 46,
https://doi.org/10.1007/978-3-030-78585-7_5

collective security system as the means to govern international affairs without—ideally—resorting to violence, in order to safeguard international peace and security and to promote the humanization of international law. At least regarding the avoidance of a cataclysmic world war, it has been proven quite effective.

The UN and the collective security system, as centralized and legally binding system of international governance condense the comprehension of the above—mentioned goals and fundamental principles embodying them in the international community. In this sense these principles and goals can provide us with the necessary guidance in order to comprehend how we must govern AI, so that latter will not contradict but will align with the goals of the international community.

AI and governance "meet" in two ways: in the sense of governance with AI and of governance of AI. The former refers to how we endorse AI into governance, whereas the latter deals with how we govern AI and its evolution, meaning what goals, institutions, treaties and norms we must come up with in order to effectively regulate existing and future AI. The two are interlinked issues but still distinct. The emphasis here is on the governance of AI; however, governance with AI and its ramifications on matters of democracy, privacy, political and human rights also play a crucial role, since it is characteristic of the problematic of governance of AI.[2] The governance of AI sets the framework within which the specific legal themes are placed.

In the first part of the chapter, the type of proposed AI governance is articulated. In the second part, the fundamental and legally binding goals which must transcend the system of AI governance are presented. In order to identify them, the goals that can be derived from the UN Charter, as the Charter constitutes the constitutional treaty of the international community are proposed. Therefore, it is there where we must be returning whenever we want to adjust existing legal norms or come up with new ones, in the face of novel challenges, such as AI, as is the case with all types of constitutional documents.

5.2 The Form of AI Governance

Governance of AI has to balance between competitive norms and interests: of private corporations, of states, of the wider public; it must combine ethical and legal principles as well as systems, with different approaches; it must be taking into account the coexistence of public, private and social stakeholders; and eventually it will have to come up with policies[3] and norms which will be capable of

---

[2]Manheim and Kaplan (2019), p. 108.

Nicholas Wright, How Artificial Intelligence Will Reshape the Global Order, Foreign Aff. (July 10, 2018), https:// www.foreignaffairs.com/articles/world/2018-07-10/how-artificial-intelligence-will-reshape-global-order.

[3]Indicatively see the list of 10 policies, which are proposed by the AI Now, 2017 Report: "Core public agencies, such as those responsible for criminal justice, healthcare, welfare, and education (e.g. "high stakes" domains) should no longer use "black box" AI and algorithmic systems…

"fine-tuning" technical and technological innovation, together with codes of conducts and good practices.[4]

The governance of AI faces a number of significant social, political, technological and legal challenges: the groundbreaking novelty of AI, its expansion to new areas, the unpredictability, the inherent difficulty of legal systems to catch up with the technological evolution are all factors of complexity when trying to govern AI.[5]

In addition, the multiplicity as well as the low cost of several of the technologies and of the efforts leading to AI mean that AI developments may evolve "under the radar" of any governance mechanism as on top of the above-mentioned reasons—AI evolution requires not always extended infrastructure.[6]

Obviously, the effort to regulate such de-centralized, partially low-cost, diffused and highly disruptive technology tests the capacities of states as well as of the international community to come up with effective and timely regulation.[7]

This is the so-called pacing problem: it commonly refers to the situation when technology develops faster than the corresponding regulation and the latter hopelessly falls behind. The metaphor of 'the hare and the tortoise' is often conjured up. As summed up by Marchant and Wallach, 'at the rapid rate of change, emerging technologies leave behind traditional governmental regulatory models and approaches which are plodding along slower today than ever before."[8]

Before releasing an AI system, companies should run rigorous pre-release trials to ensure that they will not amplify biases and errors due to any issues with the training data, algorithms, or other elements of system design... After releasing an AI system, companies should continue to monitor its use across different contexts and communities... More research and policy making is needed on the use of AI systems in workplace management and monitoring, including hiring and HR... Develop standards to track the provenance, development, and use of training datasets throughout their life cycle... Expand AI bias research and mitigation strategies beyond a narrowly technical approach... Strong standards for auditing and understanding the use of AI systems "in the wild" are urgently needed... Companies, universities, conferences and other stakeholders in the AI field should release data on the participation of women, minorities and other marginalized groups within AI research and development... The AI industry should hire experts from disciplines beyond computer science and engineering and ensure they have decision making power... Ethical codes meant to steer the AI field should be accompanied by strong oversight and accountability mechanisms..."

Alex Campolo, Madelyn Sanfilippo, Meredith Whittaker, Kate Crawford, AI Now 2017 Report, at pp. 1–2.

[4]Erica Palmerini, Federico Azzarri, Fiorella Battaglia, Andrea Bertolini, Antonio Carnevale, Jacopo Carpaneto, Filippo Cavallo, Angela Di Carlo, Marco Cempini, Marco Controzzi, Bert-Jaap Koops, Federica Lucivero, Nikil Mukerji, Luca Nocco, Alberto Pirni, Huma Shah, Pericle Salvini, Maurice Schellekens, and Kevin Warwick, Robolaw, Regulating Emerging Robotic Technologies in Europe: Robotics facing Law and Ethics, www.robolaw.eu, at p. 11.

[5]Mokhtarian (2018), p. 149.

[6]*McGinnis, Accelerating AI*, at p. 375.

[7]Fenwick et al. (2017), pp. 563–568.

[8]Butenko and Larouche (2015), p. 66.

The rush for AI evolution by states or by private entities is not followed up by the speed and the capacities of public regulators.[9] Such asymmetry leads to a twofold problem: at the early stages of the evolution of technology there is a gap of information, whereas later, when the information gap has been bridged, the interests of the stakeholders push back, against regulation.[10]

On these we must also add the tense debates which always accompany emerging technologies. "Emerging technologies… are characterized by a rapid pace of development, a multitude of applications, manifestations and actors, pervasive uncertainties about risks, benefits and future directions, and demands for oversight ranging from potential health and environmental risks to broader social and ethical concerns. Given this complexity, no single regulatory agency, or even group of agencies, can regulate any of these emerging technologies effectively and comprehensively."[11]

Such asymmetries between technology, governance institutions and law create gaps of unregulated areas which can be proven critical when we talk about technologies that in very limited time can exponentially accelerate and cause unexpected disruptions. While with other technologies the regulation may follow the new technological environment, with AI, the regulatory framework must precede at least aspects of the new technological environment which may emerge.[12]

With AI, on the one hand, the risk from the exponential and accelerating growth of AI necessitates proactive regulation, while on the other hand the uncertainty which is surrounding AI erodes the effectiveness of whatever regulatory framework.[13] In addition, any regulatory framework must be able to strike a balance between effective regulation and the necessary flexibility, so that the evolution of AI is regulated but not eliminated.[14]

The unique characteristics of AI create significant risks in terms of governance, such as the diffusion of actors in different locations, the synthesis of AI technology from different components "the full potential of which will not be apparent until the components come together" and the fact that "technologies underlying AI will tend to be opaque to most potential regulators."[15]

Further, it must be taken into account that AI is intrinsically attached to governance of and with data, up to the extent of the so-called, "datafication" of society.[16] In such a framework, John Danaher raised attention for what he describes as

[9] Roger Brownsword, Rights, regulation, and the technological revolution (2008), at p. 162.

[10] Collingridge (1980), p.19.

[11] Mandel et al. (2013).

[12] Bennett Moses (2011), pp. 768–769; Shrupti Shah et al., The regulator of tomorrow, Deloitte 2, 3 (June 11, 2015); Julia Black, Forms and Paradoxes of Principles Based Regulation, LSE L., Soc & Econ. Working Papers 1, 14 (2008).

[13] Mandel (2013), pp. 44, 62.

[14] Schuck (1984), pp. 163, 197.

[15] Scherer (2016), p. 359.

[16] Manheim and Kaplan (2019), p. 118.

"algocracy". The term refers to the maximizing reliance of governments and of their institutions rely on AI, for the collection, collation, organization of data, as well as for the decision-making procedures of the governmental institutions.[17] Given, even further, the strengthening role of predictive and descriptive data—mining—i.e. of "the non-trivial process of identifying valid, novel, potentially useful and ultimately understandable patterns in data"—the significance of the issue of governance of AI is becoming more emphatic.[18]

It is obvious that AI brings novel challenges in terms of governance, which test the capacities both of norms and of institutions. AI expands in width—i.e. *new applications*—and in depth—*i.e. virtual worlds through cyberspace*—unifies space—*through its universality via the cyberspace*—and accelerates time—*by moving with the speed of electron or even of quanta in the future, compared to the speed of governance institutions.*

Until now, there are limited efforts for the establishment of a legal framework and a governance system, consisted mainly of declaratory documents and policy papers by international organizations, states and private entities.

Indicatively, the EU Parliament adopted a resolution about civil law rules on robotics,[19] endorsing Asimov rules for autonomous AI and robotics, without however establishing a coherent system of governance.[20] Other states, such as the US,[21] China[22] and the UK[23] are also working on regulatory frameworks, without having produced though concrete results. In addition, despite documents from international organizations, some of which are referred below, a consistent, international or even national—throughout most of states—is still missing.

The problematic of AI governance produces different perspectives: A less centralized governance—or "bottom-up"—model argues in favor of "algorithmic impact assessment" conducted on the basis of principles such as fairness, justice,

---

[17]Danaher (2016), pp. 245–268.

[18]Kitchin (2014); Zarsky (2011), p. 291.

[19]European Parliament resolution of 16 February 2017 with recommendations to the Commission on Civil Law Rules on Robotics (2015/2103(INL)).

[20]"(1) A robot may not injure a human being or, through inaction, allow a human being to come to harm. (2) A robot must obey the orders given it by human beings except where such orders would conflict with the First Law. (3) A robot must protect its own existence as long as such protection does not conflict with the First or Second Laws (See: I. Asimov, Runaround, 1943) and (0) A robot may not harm humanity, or, by inaction, allow humanity to come to harm."

European Parliament resolution of 16 February 2017 with recommendations to the Commission on Civil Law Rules on Robotics (2015/2103(INL)).

[21]Article 3 (a)(1) S. 2217, 115th Congress.

[22]*P. Triolo, E. Kania, and G. Webster*, Translation: Chinese government outlines AI ambitions through 2020, New America, (2018), https://www.newamerica.org/cybersecurity-initiative/digichina/blog/translation-chinese-government-outlines-ai-ambitions-through-2020/.

[23]House of Lords, Select Committee on Artificial Intelligence, AI in the UK: ready, willing and able? Report of Session 2017–2019, https://publications.parliament.uk/pa/ld201719/ldselect/ldai/100/100.pdf.

bias. The assessment must be conducted both by agencies using AI themselves, as well as by governmental authorities.[24]

Obviously, a significant aspect of such regulation relies on self-regulation and voluntary codes of conduct, imposed by private corporations on themselves[25]—which are often accused for being vulnerable to manipulation by the private stakeholders.[26] The goal of self-regulation is to keep governments away from intervening.[27]

According to Julia Black, a "decentered understanding" of governance includes "complexity, fragmentation of knowledge and of the exercise of power and control, autonomy, interactions and interdependencies, and the collapse of the public/private distinction"[28] and "...should be indirect, focusing on interactions between the system and its environment. It should be a process of co-ordinating, steering, influencing, and balancing interactions between actors/systems, to organise themselves, using such techniques as proceduralization, collibration, feedback loops, redundancy, and above all, countering variety with a variety."[29]

Bob Jessop focuses on self-regulation of the involved actors and on "the reflexive self-organization of independent actors involved in complex relations of reciprocal interdependence, with such self-organization being based on continuing dialogue and resource-sharing to develop mutually beneficial joint projects and to manage the contradictions and dilemmas inevitably involved in such situations",[30] which must include the "...more or less spontaneous, bottom-up development by networks of rules, values, norms and principles that they then acknowledge and follow; [and] (2) increased deliberation and participation by civil society groups through stakeholder democracy, putting external pressure on the state managers and/or other elites involved in governance".[31]

The idea behind both approaches is that less state and international organizations' as well as private entities' interventions will "democratize" the development of AI, while contributing to solutions of different problems as well.

Accurately so, private institutions and civil society have contributed into the gradual formation of governance and regulatory schemes. However, such contributions cannot be substitutes to full—fledged, legal schemes and equivalent governance schemes.[32]

---

[24]Dillon Reisman, Jason Schultz, Kate Crawford, Meredith Whittaker, Algorithmic Impact Assessments: A Practical Framework for Public Agency Accountability, AI Now; (April 2018).

[25]Rubinstein (2011), p. 355; Koops et al. (2006).

[26]Gellman and Dixon (2016).

[27]Priest (1997–1998), pp. 240–242; Hirsch (2011), pp. 438, 460–464.

[28]Black (2002), pp. 1, 4.

[29]Black (2001), p. 111.

[30]Jessop (2003).

[31]Jessop (2016).

[32]Black (2001), p. 103 et seq.

Future of Life Institute, Asilomar AI Principles, futureoflife.org/ai-principles.

A governance model that it is de-centralized is potentially vulnerable to lack of uniform practice and common interpretation, in spite of their contribution into raising awareness about the obligation both of private entities and of public sector to establish guarantees for the assessment of AI impact as well for transparency for AI behavior.

Regardless of the potential benefits from such types of governance, the problems which accompany them are significant: effective governance prerequisites coordination among different actors with conflicting interests. The more extended that the impact of a certain technology is, the more persistent that the need of coordination is. AI coordination in particular implicates stakeholders in areas such as international relations, finance, health, neuroscience, neurobiology, software engineering, psychiatry, psychology, political science and military, although the list can be much more extended.[33]

It can also fuel an AI race, which may lead—if not already leading—to neglect of safety regulations and to a vicious circle of further antagonism.[34] That is characteristic outcome of the lack of consolidated internationally responses, where each state attempts to identify the sectors where it may gain its momentum and antagonistic advantage.

Of course, even in terms of this seemingly self-obviously full of risks condition, a certain perspective sees positive aspects too: "Competition is natural and we find it in almost all areas of life. It can encourage actors to focus, and it lifts up the best solutions. . .The AI race itself could be seen as a useful stimulus. . .It is perhaps not desirable to "avoid" the AI race but rather to manage or guide it. . ."[35]

While the specific opinion has some merits, it fails to grasp the dangers, as they are explained in the chapters above. Right now, AI evolution has all the stimulus that it needs; what it does not have is proper governance and regulation.

It is in light of the above that the need for governance and regulatory body or bodies, which will have the authority to impose a binding framework is advocated.[36] The need for centralized or "top-down" governance emerges from the transformations of governance itself under the influence of AI.

In order to face effectively the challenges of governance in such a complicated and de-centralized technologically environment Ian Ayres and John Braithwaite came up with the "responsive regulation", which argues for a pyramid type of response "escalating forms of government intervention. . ." from ". . .less intrusive

[33]Guihota et al. (2017), p. 425.

[34]Armstrong et al. (2013), pp. 1–8; Kate Saslow and Philippe Lorenz, Artificial Intelligence Needs Human Rights September 2019, (https://www.stiftung-nv.de/sites/default/files/ai_needs_human_rights.pdf), at pp. 7–9.

[35]Marek Rosa, Olga Afanasjeva, Will Millership (GoodAI), Report from the AI Race Avoidance Workshop, (2017 November 28).

[36]*IEEE, Ethically Aligned Design*, at p. 20.

and delegated forms of market regulation…"[37] to more intrusive forms, of the command-and-control type.

The expansion of the role of AI and of its implications fuel the debate about a—rather or completely—centralized model of governance. AI applications related to national security characteristically contribute towards the centralized type of governance with a proactive role for the public sector.

Christopher Hood and Helen Margetts identify four means of state regulation: nodality—referring to governmental capacity for control information—authority—meaning the determination of legality and the sanctions to its violations—treasure—which is the state control of assets—and organization-meaning the mobilization of human and material resources by the state.[38]

Still, the centralized form of governance is not risk—free, as matters of bias, cost and of abuse of government power will have to be dealt with, through effective guarantees.[39]

Effective governance of the above type prerequisites a code of AI laws[40] and an international governance mechanism for AI; an International Artificial Intelligence Organization—IAIO—which will be established on the basis of—what could be called—the International Convention for the Development of AI- ICDAI.

The international character is the consequence both of the potential risks from AI, as well as of the fact that without global regulation, scientists could simply evade whatever checks and balances of a state or of a group of states by simply transferring their research elsewhere.

IAIO should be placed under an international body of significant international authority, such as is the UN Security Council-SC.[41] Its mission will most probably be consisted of two aspects: monitor and advocate the compliance of state and non-state actors with the relevant convention. Following relevant paradigms of international organizations, extensive, bureaucratic structures are necessary.

Such an organization will need to combine its members-states with non-state actors, together with a body of experts, that will have the credibility to make recommendations on a variety of issues.

---

[37] Ayres and Braithwaite (1992), pp. 4–6, 37–38.

[38] Hood and Margetts (2007), pp. 5–6, 8–12.

[39] *Joel Tito*, Destination unknown: Exploring the impact of Artificial Intelligence on Government September 2017 Working Paper *Center for Public Impact; September 2017*, at pp. 44–48.

[40] Matthew Howard, The Future of AI Relies on a Code of Ethics, Techcrunch (June 21, 2018), https://techcrunch.com/2018/06/21/the-future-of-ai-relies-on-a-code-of-ethics/ [https://perma.cc/P4PV-CMYF].

[41] In a similar proposal, although not positioned necessarily in the framework of hard law, the UN Economic and Social Council suggested "Governments, and by extension the UN, should move from reaction to action, and should devise strategies to manage the risks of technological progress."

UN ECOSOC, Joint Meeting of the Second Committee of the UN General Assembly and the Economic and Social Council, the Future Of Everything: Sustainable Development In The Age Of Rapid Technological Change 11 October 2017, informal summary by the chair of the second committee and the president of ECOSOC, at pp. 1–2.

The conclusion of common standards or of "metrology" internationally will be the most critical part of its mission, given especially that for the reasons mentioned above, the complete and overall monitoring of each significant AI development will be almost impossible. The scope of such an organization will not be to be present in each laboratory or in every private entity or public institution working on AI; this will be impossible. What must be expected instead is an international organization with the mandate and the capacity to set the standards for AI and for monitoring of AI, to design the regulatory mechanisms and to intervene when it is deemed necessary.

In the framework of such an organization mandate, a number of secondary means, for the evolution of AI will be implemented.[42]

The existence of an international organization does not mean that there will not be other, public and private mechanisms of governance; they will be complying with the international standards though.

ICDAI as the convention for the governance and legal regulation of AI will need to be analytical and insightful enough to foresee the potential prospects and risks from AI, while on the other hand it must be porous and flexible so that it will allow all the necessary interpretative adjustments, in the face of the ever-changing characteristics of AI.

The Convention must project the fundamental principles of international law and of the international community on the law of AI. On these grounds it will then be possible to adjust AI evolution—in principle—with critical areas of law such as—among others—the collective security system and human rights.

It should also be able to categorize the prospects and the risks from AI and its evolution. In terms of prospects not only an environment promoting research must be foreseen but in addition the regulation and the distribution of AI beneficial impact must be promoted as well.

Therefore, it must be a convention imposing not only guarantees or even prohibitions but also positive obligations on behalf of the international community and therefore of states—i.e. social rights. It could also sketch the defining elements of potential legal personhood at different levels of AI.

The convention should also give consideration to the fact that the problem of governance under AI will most likely have to encompass the gradual merging of human and artificial intelligence. In terms of risks, "precautionary clauses" must exist, foreseeing guarantees for the evolution of AI, either by prohibiting applications or by providing checks and balances on them, such as inspections, safety regulations, advocacy, publicity etc.

Under such an overall convention, flexible agreements for cooperation and high institutionalization endowed with the capacity of crisis management, can eventually

---

[42]Characteristically, in the "AI4People- An Ethical Framework", document, an extended list of 20 action points is proposed, which involve aspects of assessment of AI technology, of development of the necessary ethical, legal and framework, of Incentivisation in financial terms, of support to self- regulatory codes, corporate bonds and educational activities.

Floridi et al. (2018), pp. 701–705.

emerge contributing to the work of the above-mentioned international organization and to the subordinate governing bodies that will pertain to it.[43]

Obviously, the above, prerequisite the existence of political will by-at least—the majority of the international community. Given the experience from the international relations of the last 3 decades-at least—as well as from the way that strong, private oligopolies impose their role upon public regulations, we should be at least worrisome about how likely such a development actually is. We can only hope that we will not have to endure events even remotely as horrific as the two world wars in order to realize the necessity of international governance over so hopeful but also potentially dangerous technology, as is the AI.

In addition, the proposals for centralized forms of governance need to take into account that they must not over-regulate in the sense of suppressing innovation in the AI area of research. [44]

In between, the two, above—mentioned approaches to governance, the AI4People Initiative has come up with the proposal of S.M.A.R.T Governance, which stands for "Scalable, Modular, Adaptable, Reflexive, and Technologically-savvy".[45]

It partially distances itself, from both the bottom-up and the top-down approach, in favor of a so-called, "middle-out" approach, which "should be able to strike the balance between technology, ethics, market, and social norms", being positioned "between forms of coregulation and every variant of self-regulation."[46]

The "middle-out" approach focuses on aspects which lie between the first two approaches, referring to "...participatory procedures for the alignment of societal values and understanding of public opinion; ii. Upstream multi-stakeholder mechanisms for risk mitigation, e.g. unwanted consequences of human-AI interaction; iii. Systems for user-driven benchmarking of marketed AI offerings, allowing trust in products and services, as well as providers to be measured and made transparent; iv. Cross-disciplinary and cross-sectorial cooperation and debate incentivisation; A European observatory for AI to consolidate these forms of coordination..."[47]

Still however, in the same report, the top-down approach is proposed in the framework of the legal regulation and the bottom-up regarding self-regulation,[48] including the development of EU member-states' national policies, the raising of public awareness, a common EU research effort, the so-called "inclusive innovation", the "smooth transition to new kinds of jobs via rewarding human-machine

[43]Erdelyi and Goldsmith (2018), p. 2.

[44]Floridi et al. (2018), p. 691.

[45]AI4People, On Good A.I Governance, 14 Priority Actions, A S.M.A.R.T. Model of Governance, And a Regulatory Toolbox (2019).

[46]Ibid.

[47]Ibid.

[48]Ibid.

collaboration" and the support towards corporations in order to "take responsibility for the ethical implications of companies' AI technologies".[49]

The bottom-up—*again in the above—mentioned report*—approach refers to the use of participatory mechanisms, aiming at promoting dialogue among stakeholders, the establishment of an AI observatory and cross-sectional cooperation among the different areas that are involved in AI discourse.

The ambition of the proposed regulatory scheme is valid: to balance between competing norms, interests and governance systems and eventually to establish a system of governance according to which "... top-down legislation establishes the principles that must be followed by data controllers - as well as the goals that they should strive for- though it is in large part up to data controllers how they should attain such outcomes, under the supervision of public guardians", invoking in fact the principle of accountability—borrowed from the GDPR model.[50]

The paper accurately comprehends the inefficiencies of both the bottom-up and the top-down models of governance, as well as the lack of a set of legal and moral principles. The particular report is part of a wider approach of course, which suggests that centralized and de-centralized governance models are not mutually exclusive.

The problems that transcend the above- mentioned report but also—at least up to some extent—the whole approach are not that it combines different models of governance but that first one these models must be the leading one over the rest and second that it attempts to bypass the actual ethical and legal debate, which is unavoidable and which necessarily must be conducted in order to determine the context and the goals of any system of governance. As the report which is analyzed above suggests, its first goal is to "prevent the chilling effect of some ideological debates on the ethics of AI and the complexity of the legal environment."[51]

In addition, it is very much preoccupied with the need of a model that will be able to respond to developments rather than regulate in advance, which, in light of potential emergence especially of AGI and of ASI—albeit even before such a development—might be proven inadequate—if not catastrophic.

While proposing an interesting toolbox, which emphasizes aspects of a regulatory framework such as legal synchronization, standardization and monitoring, the necessary content in terms of the specific, ethical and legal rules is absent.

Both the contributions and the ellipses of the report indicate that while we need flexible and adjustable models of governance, combination of elements from different approaches, the need in the end for guidance by top-down regulation and for reaching a set of legal norms that will govern AI, being thus transcended by the equivalent ethics is of utmost importance.

We also need to keep in mind that the autonomy of AI means that, unless we reach universal decisions about the extent, the standards, the monitoring and their

[49]Ibid.

[50]Ibid.

[51]Ibid at p. 30.

enforcement, for AI autonomy, it may take just a handful of actors to completely de-regulate every governance mechanism.[52]

The argument of the present book is not that a solely centralized, "top-down" model of governance may cover all the needs regarding AI governance. Aspects of the other two models will be needed: both the coordination in de-centralized terms of various stakeholders, as well as the adoption of the principle of accountability.

Nevertheless, all these must be placed in principle under a centralized mode of governance which will bring together the different international actors, in light of the historically unique prospects and risks,[53] imposing common standards. This could be a solution to the already existing problem of various and different, national-states' governance models.[54]

It is also the outcome of the need to regulate in advance what is already emerging as the risk from racist, discriminatory- and therefore fundamentally unfriendly towards humans—AI.[55] As mentioned above, the role of the proposed governance model is to establish these legal norms which can shape and guide the ethics, on the basis of which AI machine—learning is trained.

Within such a universal, model, aspects of participatory or co-regulatory governance can be incorporated as well.

The idea of participatory governance is to leave room to various stakeholders in order to align with different types of norms; for example, private corporations may have more flexible, self-regulatory norms, AI users will be able to contribute to AI design—under a digital common's framework—whereas governments—and in our proposal, a relevant international organization—will be retaining the oversight and enforcement authority.[56] In this sense, it attempts to promote social responsibility, in

---

[52]As it has been presented, the goal is to safeguard "what we might call "meta-autonomy", or a "decide-or-delegate" model: humans should retain the power to decide which decisions to take, exercising the freedom to choose where necessary, and ceding it in cases where other interests such as efficiency outweigh the loss of control over decision-making. As anticipated, any delegation should remain overridable in principle (deciding to decide again)". It is obvious that this is a goal that must be preserved in a universally agreed manner.

Cowls and Floridi (2018).

[53]In similar terms, the EU in its "Statement on artificial intelligence, robotics and 'autonomous' systems" calls for a common and internationally recognized, ethical and legal framework.

European Commission, Statement on artificial intelligence, robotics and 'autonomous' systems.

[54]Indicatively, the US plans to create a new National AI Initiative Office and "the European Commission (EC) has put forth the Digital Services Act, which will create oversight for how internet platforms use AI".

Engler (2021, January 21).

[55]"Technology is not neutral or objective… It is fundamentally shaped by the racial, ethnic, gender and other inequalities prevalent in society, and typically makes these inequalities worse. It is resulting in discrimination and unequal treatment in all areas of life, from education and employment to healthcare and criminal justice."

UN News, Independent rights expert says emerging technologies entrenching racism, discrimination, (2020, July 20), https://news.un.org/en/story/2020/07/1068441.

[56]Crosnier (2018), pp. 1–12; Sinclair (1997), p. 544; Rubinstein (2016).

combination with an incentive—providing intervention of governments, together with the monitoring and enforcement mechanisms.[57]

Co-regulatory models are proximate to the governance which is proposed in this book. The difference—or the extra "thing- in the current book is that a universal model, transcending the international community is proposed as well.

In terms of such, international, governance, it is important to notice the recommendations by the Council of Europe Commissioner for Human Rights, in a relevant report of the year 2019, where a common legal framework of the member states is recommended, regarding the establishment of a system of "…human rights impact assessments HRIAs on AI systems."[58] In this framework, a system of "oversight" bodies is proposed.[59] In addition, the significance of effective remedies in front of national or international courts, for AI acts, again necessitates a centralized form of governance of some extent, imposing common standards and enforcement mechanisms.[60]

A proximate position can be found in the "Report of the Special Rapporteur to the General Assembly on AI and its impact on freedom of opinion and expression" of 2018 where it is suggested that states "should ensure that public sector bodies act consistently with human rights principles… conducting public consultations and undertaking human rights impact assessments or public agency algorithmic impact assessments prior to the procurement or deployment of artificial intelligence systems."[61] Such guarantees are supposed to extend to private sector as well, which further are foreseen in that same report, implying a tendency on behalf of the UN for international AI regulation.

In the note by the Secretary—General to the General Assembly about the "Promotion and protection of the right to freedom of opinion and expression', the same position is reiterated in clearer terms—with the additional reference to self-regulation by private entities: "AI tools, like all technologies, must be designed, developed and deployed so as to be consistent with the obligations of States and the responsibilities of private actors under international human rights law… With respect to the private sector, States are bound to guarantee respect for individual rights… States can meet this obligation through legal measures to restrict or influence the development and implementation of AI applications, through policies regarding the procurement of AI applications from private companies by public sector actors, through self- and co-regulatory schemes and by building the capacity

---

[57]Michael (1996), pp. 535, 541–544.

[58]Council of Europe Commissioner for Human Rights, Unboxing Artificial Intelligence: 10 steps to protect Human Rights, Council of Europe, May 2019, at p. 7.

[59]Ibid at p. 10.

[60]Ibid. at pp. 13–14.

[61]UN Human Rights Committee, Report of the Special Rapporteur to the General Assembly on AI and its impact on freedom of opinion and expression, (2018), https://www.ohchr.org/_layouts/15/WopiFrame.aspx?sourcedoc=/Documents/Issues/Expression/OnePagerGA73.docx&action=default&DefaultItemOpen=1.

of private sector companies to recognize and prioritize the rights to freedom of opinion and expression in their corporate endeavours".[62]

The UN recommendations are very close to the type of governance model which is proposed here: a central, public and internationally constructed model of governance, imposing standards on both states and the private sector as well, with the latter having also to implement its self-regulations.

In furtherance of such goals, the UN established the Centre for Artificial Intelligence and Robotics, which works with the United Nations Interregional Crime and Justice Research Institute—UNICRI—the International Telecommunications Union—ITU—the Institute of Electrical and Electronics Engineers—IEEE—the Foundation for Responsible Robotics and the World Economic Forum, Centre for Future Intelligence.[63]

Further, a centralized and unified system, endorsing aspects of the rest of governance models, is necessary in order to have transparent and therefore democratic governance, so that it is not fragmented among various stakeholders, self-regulating—or not—and with proper and effective public bodies monitoring.[64] That is also the proposal of the European Commission Group on Ethics in Science and New Technologies, which in its relevant document, addressed the need for democratic governance of AI in the sense that "Key decisions on the regulation of AI development and application should be the result of democratic debate and public engagement."[65]

Last but not least, the existence of centralized AI governance bears the prospect of unifying a predominantly context—based approach to the regulation of AI.[66] Part of that is related to the liability issue, that is analyzed below. As it became apparent with the accidents where self-driving cars were involved, very often, AI liability necessitates thorough investigation, expertise and resources.[67]

A de-centralized governance system, without central monitoring and standardization mechanisms could very well lead to several loopholes eroding any system of

---

[62]UN GA, Promotion and protection of the right to freedom of opinion and expression, Note by the Secretary-General, A/73/348, (2018, August 29), at paras. 19–20.

[63]Library of Congress, Regulation of Artificial Intelligence: International and Regional Approaches, (https://www.loc.gov/law/help/artificial-intelligence/international.php#_ftnref2).

[64]CNIL. (2017). How can humans keep the upper hand? The ethical matters raised by algorithms and artificial intelligence, at p. 55, https://www.cnil.fr/sites/default/files/atoms/files/cnil_rapport_ai_gb_web.pdf.

An initiative of Université de Montréal, Montreal Declaration for Responsible AI, 2018 Report Montréal Declaration for a Responsible Development of Artificial Intelligence, (2018), at p. 90.

[65]European Commission, European Group on Ethics in Science and New Technologies, Artificial Intelligence, Robotics and 'Autonomous' Systems, (2018, March), at pp. 17–18, (https://ec.europa.eu/research/ege/pdf/ege_ai_statement_2018.pdf).

[66]Scherer (2016), pp. 353, 359–360; Yanisky-Ravid (2017), pp. 659, 673.

[67]For these accidents, see: Hannah Knowles, Uber's Self-Driving Cars Had a Major Flaw: They Weren't Programmed to Stop for Jaywalkers, Wash. Post, https://www.washingtonpost.com/transportation/2019/11/06/ubers-self-driving-cars-hadmajor-flaw-they-werent-programmed-stop-jaywalkers.

liability. The complexity of the liability issues which related with AI and the role of the cyberspace demand a public liability policy. Further, inter-state antagonisms which are fueled by the race for AI advantage in critical areas necessitate an international treaty and a relevant governance mechanism, attempting to preserve the international peace and security.[68]

In addition, even the context—based attempts to regulate AI, eventually prove the need for centralized—and partially cooperative—governance. Characteristically, regarding autonomous vehicles, it was the 1968 Vienna Convention on Road Traffic which had to be amended in order for them to be allowed, provided that their technologies conform with the UN regulations or that they can be overridden and switched off by the human driver.[69]

Danny Yadron & Dan Tynan, Tesla Driver Dies in First Fatal Crash While Using Autopilot Mode, Guardian (June 30, 2016, 7:14 PM), https://www.theguardian.com/technology/2016/jun/30/tesla-autopilot-death-self-driving-car-elon-musk.

[68]Juergen Altmann and Frank Sauer, 2016, "Speed Kills! Why we need to hit the brakes on 'killer robots'", ICRAC, https://icrac.net/2016/04/speed-kills-why-we-need-to-hit-thebrakes-on-killer-robots.

UNIDIR, The Weaponization of Increasingly Autonomous Technologies: Concerns, Characteristics and Definitional Approaches (2017), https://www.unidir.org/files/publications/pdfs/the-weaponization-of-increasingly-autonomous-technologies-concerns-characteristics-and-definitional-approaches-en-689.pdf.

[69]Convention on Road Traffic, Nov. 8, 1968, 1042 U.N.T.S. 15705, https://www.unece.org/fileadmin/DAM/trans/conventn/Conv_road_traffic_EN.pdf, archived at http://perma.cc/JNG9-ZJNE; U.N. Economic and Social Council, Economic Commission for Europe (UNECE), Inland Transport Committee, Working Party on Road Traffic Safety, Report of the Sixty-Eighth Session of the Working Party on Road Traffic Safety 5, 9 (Apr. 17, 2014), http://www.unece.org/fileadmin/DAM/trans/doc/2014/wp1/ECE-TRANS-WP1-145e.pdf, archived at http://perma.cc/P4LT-YW5N.

In another similar paradigm, the Organization of American States—OAS—urged the banking sector in Latin America and the Caribbean to "prioritize the development of capacities using emerging digital technologies, such as Big Data, Artificial Intelligence and related (such as cognitive computing and Machine Learning), which have an important potential in the optimization of resources destined for detection and prevention."

OAS, State of Cybersecurity in the Banking Sector in Latin America and the Caribbean 146 (2018), http://www.oas.org/es/sms/cicte/sectorbancarioeng.pdf.

In the case of AWS's, the European Parliament resolution on autonomous weapons systems called again for a unified system imposing obligations on the member-states, as well as on private corporations.

European Parliament, European Parliament resolution on autonomous weapon systems (2018/2752(RSP)), (05.09.2018).

Similarly, in the CCW meeting of the 2015, recommendations were made about governance of LAWS in uniform way among member states.

CCW/MSP/2015/3, Meeting of the High Contracting Parties to the Convention on Prohibitions or restrictions on the Use of Certain Conventional Weapons Which May Be Deemed to Be Excessively Injurious or to Have Indiscriminate Effects, (2015, June 2), at https://undocs.org/ccw/msp/2015/3, at para. 54.

Such is the proposal of the ICRC for the regulation of AWS's, namely that "that States should agree on the type and degree of human control required to ensure compliance with international law and to satisfy ethical concerns".

In another example, states, when acquiring and developing weapons have to comply with relevant customary law[70] and with the Additional Protocol I to the Geneva Conventions—regarding the signatory parts.[71] While it is true that there is not a specific type of assessment that is imposed on states, something which is a profound deficit of international law, it is still apparent that the goal of the law is to establish a governance mechanism with international standards.

Having described the type of governance and advocated in favor of a centralized, at the international level approach, as the main framework, within which and under which, aspects of different governance models will be combined, the next part focuses on the goals that such governance must serve. The main idea is that these goals should be the ones of the international community as they are endorsed in the UN Charter, because of the constitutional character of the Charter.

International Committee of the Red Cross, Autonomy, artificial intelligence and robotics: Technical aspects of human control (August 2019), at p. 3, file:///C:/Users/User/Downloads/autonomy_artificial_intelligence_and_robotics.pdf.

When examining also and for example, health applications of AI we need to keep in mind that the selection of data and the conduct of machine training must comply with common, unbiased practices. The input of large data from a variety of patients necessitates common standards internationally and international collaboration.

Artificial intelligence in global health: defining a collective path forward. Washington, DC: United States Agency for International Development; 2019. Available from: https://www.usaid.gov/cii/ai-in-global-health.

Wyber et al. (2015), pp. 203–208. PMID: 25767300.

Elish (2019), pp. 40–60.

Paul and Schaefer (2020), p. 1.

Last but not least, in the realm of human rights, which is also related to AI—as is analyzed below—states are expected to take measures safeguarding the protection of human rights by businesses too, imposing thus a partially cooperative and in the end, centralized governance model for human rights.

United Nations Humans Rights Office of the High Commissioner, Guiding Principles on Business and Human Rights, (2011, United Nations), at pp. 1–8, articles 1–4, (https://www.ohchr.org/Documents/Publications/GuidingPrinciplesBusinessHR_EN.pdf).

[70]Boothby (2009), p. 341.

[71]"In the study, development, acquisition or adoption of a new weapon, means or method of warfare, a High Contracting Party is under an obligation to determine whether its employment would, in some or all circumstances, be prohibited by this Protocol or by any other rule of international law applicable to the High Contracting Party."

Protocol Additional to the Geneva Conventions of 12 August 1949 and Relating to the Protection of Victims of International Armed Conflicts art. 36, June 8, 1977, 1125 U.N.T.S. 3.

5.3 The Fundamental Goals and Principles for AI Governance

5.3.1 The Constitutionality of the Charter

In the previous part of the chapter, it is suggested that the guiding principles and goals of AI must be the guiding principles and goals of the international community, as thy are endorsed by the UN Charter. The idea is that as the latter constitutes the constitutional document of the international community, we should be guided by it whenever we need to adjust international law to novel and unpredictable conditions.

The UN Charter, it is a historically unique phenomenon, since it was obvious from its initial steps that it is meant to be more than an ordinary treaty of an international organization, having constitutional characteristics.[72]

The International Court of Justice—ICJ—moved forward with this constitutional interpretation of the UN Charter in the "Reparations for Injuries Suffered in the Service of the United Nations", case.[73]

The constitutional approach to the UN Charter is the consequence of the reflection of the international community on the failure of the League of Nations,[74] of the decision to prevent the outbreak of a new cataclysmic world war,[75] of the introduction of the human paragon at the fore-front of the international developments and therefore of human-centrism as guiding principle of the international community[76] and last but not least of the powers with which UN was endowed.[77]

The constitutionality of the UN Charter is also a response to the danger of fragmentation of the international community, because of the reinstatement of power politics as the source of authority in the international community. One may wonder at what extent this goal has been actually achieved; While the response may

---

[72]Truman (1945); Ress (2012), p. 15; Kelsen (1964), p. 3.

[73]ICJ, Advisory Opinion, Reparations for Injuries Suffered in the Service of the United Nations, (1949), 178–179.

Also see: ICJ (1955), p. 106.

[74]Ross (1983), pp. 100–126; Claude (1988), p. 57.

[75]As US President Wilson stated at the aftermath of the Great War: "The question upon which the whole future peace and policy of the world depends is this: Is the present war a struggle for a just and secure peace, or only for a new balance of power? If it be only a struggle for a new balance of power, who will guarantee, who can guarantee, the stable equilibrium of the new arrangement? Only a tranquil Europe can be a stable Europe. There must be, not a balance of power, but a community of power; not organized rivalries, but an organized common peace."

President W. Wilson, Address Before the United States Senate on Essential Terms of Peace in Europe (Jan. 22, 1917), στο W. Wilson, *The Messages And Papers Of Woodrow Wilson,* at pp. 348, 351 (Albert Shaw ed., 1924).

[76]Peters (2009), p. 186; Findler (1996), pp. 417–423.

[77]Weller (1997), p. 43.

not be very encouraging, especially during these last decades, the avoidance of a new world war remains a victory of the UN Charter—oriented architecture.[78]

The above are pre-legal origins of the constitutional nature of the Charter; there are internal, legal characteristics too, which lead to the same interpretation: the preamble with normatively binding, declaratory principles, the analogies between UN and state organs, the UN power to have an impact on third actors as well, its superiority over all other treaties and therefore the provision of a hierarchical structure in the international community, the fact that it establishes the fundamental norms for the international order, the flexibility of the Charter language. [79]

After all, the emblematic phrase of the preamble "We the peoples of the United Nations", expresses genuinely the comprehension of the specific "moment"—historically and legally speaking- as constitutional given that it is not meditated by states; as type of legal fiction and as the cornerstone of the UN are presented directly the "peoples", which bear what could be analogically considered as people's sovereignty at the international level. Although states are the members and signatory parts of the UN, as well as the expediters of the organization, they act as such in the name of the peoples, in stark differentiation from all the other international treaties.[80] The analogy with national constitutions obviously is not direct; still it reveals the goal of the founders of the UN and the nature of the Charter respectively. In these regards, the San Francisco conference is also categorized as a constitutional moment, which established legally a trend that began following the end of the Great War.[81]

The organs of the UN, as mentioned above are also derived from an analogy to the hierarchy and structure of national states' organs, albeit with significant differentiations, with the General Assembly attempting to represent the "peoples" of the United Nations and the member-states, the Security Council—SC—being endowed with legislative and executive authorities[82] and the International Court of Justice—ICJ—with the judicial ones, with the last two having a complementary relationship, resembling even in a remote way to constitutional checks and balances.[83] The ICJ in the several cases reached the same conclusion about the two organs.[84]

---

[78]Peters (2009), p. 153; McNair (1930), p. 112.

[79]Fassbender (1998), p. 99; Franck (2003), p. 95; Schwindt (2000), p. 206.

[80]Kelsen (1964), pp. 6–8.

[81]Cassese (1986), p. 222.

[82]Kelsen (1964), p. 294.

[83]Danilenko (1991), pp. 353, 359–360; Ulfstein (2009), p. 47.
ICJ, Certain Expenses of the United Nations, (1962), 201.
UN Charter, Article 96.

[84]ICJ, Military and Paramilitary Activities (Nicar. v. U.S.),(Prov. Measures of Nov. 26). (1984), 392, 434–435, 95.

ICJ, Application of the Convention on the Prevention and Punishment of the Crime of Genocide, (Bosnia and Herzegovina v. Yugoslavia (Serbia and Montenegro)), (1993), 325, 440, (separate opinion of Lauterpacht).

ICJ, Lockerbie, (1992) 114, 129, 138, (declaration of Oda), (separate opinion of Lachs).

ICJ, East Timor (Portugal v. Australia), (1995), 90, 251, (dissenting opinion of Skubiszewski).

The mandate of the UN Charter to impose its authority as ecumenical, even beyond its member-states, as the principal responsible for the maintenance of international peace and security, according to article 2 paragraph 6 and the hierarchical superiority of the Charter over all other treaties, as well as in relation article 103 are also characteristic of its constitutional nature.[85]

The constitutionality of the Charter is further proved by the flexibility of the language of the Charter, which is carefully selected in order to be interpreted over time, in line with the changing needs the international community,[86] in dynamic ways and from a teleological perspective.[87] Several decisions of the ICJ follow the same interpretation, such as in the South-West Africa Case and in the Namibia case.[88]

ICJ, Legal Consequences for States of the Continued Presence of South Africa in Namibia, (1971), 16, 33, 88–89 (Advisory Opinion).

ICJ, Advisory Opinion, Legal Consequences of the Construction of a Wall in the Occupied Palestinian Territory, (2004), 149–150.

Indicatively see: "Indeed, the Court notes that there has been an increasing tendency over time for the General Assembly and the Security Council to deal in parallel with the same matter concerning the maintenance of international peace and security (see, for example, the matters involving Cyprus, South Africa, Angola, Southern Rhodesia and more recently Bosnia and Herzegovina and Somalia). It is often the case that, while the Security Council has tended to focus on the aspects of such matters related to international peace and security, the General Assembly has taken a broader view, considering also their humanitarian, social and economic aspects."

For the fragmented exercise of these competent authorities see: International Tribunal for the Prosecution of Persons Responsible for Serious Violations of International Humanitarian Law Committed in the Territory of Former Yugoslavia since 1991, Prosecutor VS Dusko Tadic (1997) 2,15, 16(dissenting opinion Judge Li).

[85]Chesterman (2009), p. 1511.

UN Charter Article 2 para. 6: "The Organization shall ensure that states which are not Members of the United Nations act in accordance with these Principles so far as may be necessary for the maintenance of international peace and security."

Article 103 "In the event of a conflict between the obligations of the Members of the United Nations under the present Charter and their obligations under any other international agreement, their obligations under the present Charter shall prevail."

[86]Schwindt (2000), pp. 206–208.

[87]G. Ress, *The Interpretation of the Charter* at p. 16; Conforti (1996), p. 14; Schachter (1951), p. 193; Schachter (1994), p. 16.

[88]"The Court must have regard to the situation as it was at that time, which was the critical one and to the intentions of those concerned as they appear to have existed or are the reasonably to be inferred, in the light of that situation...".

ICJ, South-West Africa, Second Phase, (1966), 23.

See however the ICJ, Dissenting Opinion Jessup, (1966), 439.

"That the concepts embodied in Article 22 of the covenant...were not static but were by definition evolutionary... [the court's] interpretation cannot remain unaffected by the subsequent development of law, through the Charter of the United Nations and by way of customary law. Moreover, an international instrument has to be interpreted and applied within the framework of the entire legal system prevailing at the time of the interpretation".

ICJ, Legal Consequences for States of the Continued Presence of South Africa in Namibia (South West Africa) notwithstanding Security Council Resolution, Advisory Opinion, (1971) 31.

Summing up, the fact that the Charter emerges as document of constitutional nature means that as all documents of constitutional character, the UN Charter contains the fundamental and therefore guiding legal principles and goals. These principles and goals because of their fore-told nature are legally binding and of universal application,[89] which means that they do not only apply on states but also on the non-state actors even directly, without the states' meditation.[90]

As mentioned above, the constitutionality of the Charter is instrumental for the theme of the present book: it proves that there are constitutional principles and goals, which guarantee that there not legal gaps, even in the face of unprecedented legal challenges, such as those that AI brings. Therefore, once we have defined the legal nature of the Charter, we dive into its content in the next part of the Charter, in order to identify its fundamental principles and goals, which will then be transferred into the documents governing and regulating AI.

5.3.2 The Fundamental Principles of the Charter and Their Transfer to AI Governance

The fundamental goals and principles of the UN as they are described in the Charter, depict by what means the international community ideally should act and in furtherance of what goals. The principal goal is the maintenance of international peace and security, attaining the harmonic coexistence of all actors.[91] The main motivation and apprehension however behind this goal is the human-centric approach to the international community. The international peace and security are essential so that humans will not experience the destruction of the world wars again, as well as an additional number of crimes.

The realization of the principal goal and of the main motivation as a combination is crucial in order to comprehend the foundations of our international legal order, so that then we can be guided by them in furtherance of AI governance and regulation.

The rest of principles of the Charter interpret implement and serve the above. They are also crucial for the adjustment of the principal goal and motivation in the face of modern challenges.

The means for the maintenance of the international peace and security are condensed in the collective security system. The collective security system at first glance is the institutional regulation of the international community which

ICJ, Competence of Assembly Regarding Admission to the United Nations, Advisory Opinion, (1950) 12, 18–19, (Judge Alvarez, Dissenting Opinion).

ICJ, Legality of the Use by a State of Nuclear Weapons in Armed Conflict, Advisory Opinion, (1996) 66, 75.

[89]The legal binding-ness of these norms as fundamental of the international community categorizes them as jus cogens.

[90]Parker and Neylon (1989), p. 455.

[91]Brownlie (1979), p. 512.

guarantees that whenever a state is attacked by another, all the other members of the international community will unite in furtherance of its defense;[92] in a wider and more complete description, it is the regulation of the international relations in such ways that risks to peace are neutralized through common action of the international community.[93]

The collective security system emerged from the realization that the threats against international peace and security cannot be confronted effectively by the traditionally de-centralized, international, legal system, as long as the latter does not undergo any significant change; this change of the decentralized approaches came or was expected with the establishment of a centralized collective security system, foreseen by the UN Charter.[94]

The collective security system is supposed to be the outcome and a factor for further realization on behalf of states that each one's national security is better served from the security of all, as well as that a wider nexus of actions is necessary at the international level, aiming towards the prosperity not only of states but of peoples, even in the framework of a direct relationship of them with the international community, in order for peace to be maintained.[95]

The collective security system aligns with the primary goal of the maintenance of peace which is deeper and wider compared to the absence of war; this is how human-centrism transcends international law.[96] The UN Charter goal is not only states which do not fight against each other but peace in the sense of combination of

---

[92]Claude (1986), p. 51.

[93]White (2002), p. 237.

[94]H. Morgenthau, *Politics Among Nations*, (Peter Labella and John m. Morriss, 1949), στη σελ. 232.

[95]Wolfers (1962), p. 170; Mearsheimer (1998), pp. 329, 357–358; Cuellar (2004), pp. 218–219; Kirgis (1995), pp. 506–507; Shklar (1986), p. 125; Hoffmann (1987), 89–94. Graham (1946), pp. 57, 71.

[96]Indicative of that is the UN Charter Preamble, with the repeated references to peoples, to human rights and to social progress together with the absence of war as an: "We the Peoples of the United Nations Determined.

to save succeeding generations from the scourge of war, which twice in our lifetime has brought untold sorrow to mankind, and

to reaffirm faith in fundamental human rights, in the dignity and worth of the human person, in the equal rights of men and women and of nations large and small, and

to establish conditions under which justice and respect for the obligations arising from treaties and other sources of international law can be maintained, and

to promote social progress and better standards of life in larger freedom,

And for These Ends

to practice tolerance and live together in peace with one another as good neighbours, and

to unite our strength to maintain international peace and security, and

to ensure, by the acceptance of principles and the institution of methods, that armed force shall not be used, save in the common interest, and

to employ international machinery for the promotion of the economic and social advancement of all peoples".

absence of war, protection of human rights, equal rights of men and women, social progress.[97]

This is why the article about the purposes of the Charter—article 1—in paragraph 1 establishes the maintenance of peace with the prevention and the removal of threats to peace, which are not limited only to aggression. The rest of the article establishes as purposes the Charter, the principles of self-determination, human rights and "international co-operation in solving international problems of an economic, social, cultural, or humanitarian character".[98]

There is an extended debate about whether the goals of the UN Charter are equal among them or not.[99] The debate, in spite of its significance is not presented here, as the focus is on the undoubted fact of the co-existence of the principles of the UN Charter—even regardless of potential hierarchical differentiations.

Parenthetically and in relation to the projection and interpretation of the fundamental principles of the UN on and in relation to AI, it is by now well-established that the threats to peace are not limited to aggression or armed attack. Grave violations of human rights, colonial regimes, apartheid, terrorism, failed states, international humanitarian law violations, repression of self-determination, poverty, environmental destruction, pandemics are some of the different phenomena and events, which have been categorized over time as threats to international peace, gathering the attention and necessitating the action of the UN Security Council.[100] The governance of AI must take into account the potential of AI to be included in potential risk for international peace and security as well.

Summing up, the UN Charter includes the fundamental principles and goals of the international community. From them there are two guidelines that can be extracted in terms of AI governance: the one is the human-centrism of the international community institutional formation and of international law; the fact that it was initially endorsed from a different perspective, instead of developments such as AI does not mean that it should not guide us in the face of new challenges too.

The second is the maintenance of international peace and security through not only the absence of war but also via the combination of the former, with the

---

[97]UN Charter, Preamble; Henkin (1989), pp. 58–59; Evans (1994), pp. 15–16; Walker (1990), p. 3.

[98]UN Charter, Article 1.

[99]For the "narrow" approach arguing in favor of the hierarchical superiority of the absence of war, indicatively see: *L. Henkin, International Law: Politics, Values and Functions*, at p. 146.

Le Mon and Taylor (2004), p. 203.

For the wider perception of the Charter purposes see: Shestack (1997–1998), p. 566; Stern (1996), p. 587; O'Connell (1998), p. 488; Nickel (2002), p. 353.

[100]Indicatively see:

Reisman (2008), p. 57, 78.

Duffy (2005), p. 178, 184.

UN S.C. Res. 232, (1966), para. 1.

UN S.C. Res. 688, (1991), para. 1.

UN S.C. Res. 794, (1992), para. 10.

Ullmann (1983), pp. 133–138; Mathews (1989), pp. 162–177; Thomas (2002), p. 113; Renner (1996), p. 83; Jones (2004), p. 95.

promotion of human rights, of self-determination, of international cooperation and of the solving international, social economic and humanitarian issues.

There is an implicit hierarchy in the foundations of the UN Charter: the absence of war, human rights, self-determination, international cooperation, political and social rights, international humanitarian law, which attempt to solve the relevant problems, implement as principles the goal of the maintenance of international peace and security, whereas the latter preserves human-centrism. Therefore, when we seek a governance and regulatory scheme for AI we turn back to the fundamentals of our international legal order.

The quest for the implementation of these goals in AI will have to be adjusted on the new realities that emerge.[101] As already analyzed they will pass through the implementation of supplementary goals, sustaining the primary one of human—centrism, that must be further broken down in different supplementary and more specific goals, explain we need an overall, centralized governance scheme, capable of fine-tuning ethical and legal norms and designing proactively, so that it will then be implemented via more de-centralized structures.

5.4 Conclusions

This chapter, through focusing on the governance of AI attempted to set the framework for its legal regulation. First it was presented how and why an international and centralized form of AI governance is necessary, given its complexities and its impact. In such a framework, the proposal for an international organization and for an international convention was articulated. In order to address the need for guidance regarding the goals and the principles which must be endorsed in such a regulatory framework we turned to the UN Charter because of its constitutional character. It is there that human-centrism emerges as the main guideline, together with the—holistically interpreted-maintenance of international peace and security.

The proposal for the governance of AI attempts to address the need for guarantees of AI entities' ethics and the anxiety to safeguard the prevalence of human-centrism of contemporary societies and legal systems in light of AI development.

These emotions are obvious in several documents; indicatively, the European Commission in its document "Ethics for trustworthy AI" emphasized the prevalence both of human control—i.e. governance of AI—and of human-centrism through the relevant norms and principles.[102] The EU has further emphasized upon the goal of

[101] Cowls, Josh and Floridi, Luciano, Prolegomena to a White Paper on an Ethical Framework for a Good AI Society (June 19, 2018). Available at SSRN: https://ssrn.com/abstract=3198732 or https://doi.org/10.2139/ssrn.3198732.

[102] "Human agency and oversight: AI systems should empower human beings, allowing them to make informed decisions and fostering their fundamental rights. At the same time, proper oversight mechanisms need to be ensured, which can be achieved through human-in-the-loop, human-on-the-loop, and human-in-command approaches".

human—centrism of AI, suggesting that human agency should be ensured as well as that a machine cannot be in control.[103]

The race to avoid or at least reduce unpredictability of AI will be determined by the efficacy and the goals of the system of governance that will be implemented on AI. The challenges are unique: how are we going to protect human and political rights given that machine learning is opaque, built on inter-woven algorithms and protected by a palimpsest of laws about secrecy, which correspond to different legal systems?

In the next chapters, through the specification of the form, the goals, the principles and therefore of the proposed norms of governance, the above questions are attempted to be answered. Specific areas of international law and paradigms from national legal systems too are chosen in order to explain how these principles can be implemented. The first such area is the one of human rights, because of their role as ultimate guarantors at the legal level of human-centrism.

References

Armstrong S, Bostrom N, Shulman C (2013) Racing to the precipice: a model of artificial intelligence development, Technical Report#2013-1. Oxford University, Future of Humanity Institute, pp 1–8

Ayres I, Braithwaite J (1992) In: Harris DR et al (eds) Responsive regulation: transcending the deregulation debate. Oxford University Press, New York, pp 4–6, 37–38

Black J (2001) Decentring regulation: understanding the role of regulation and self-regulation in a 'post-regulatory' world. Curr Leg Probs 54:103

Black J (2002) Critical reflections on regulation. Aust J Legal Philosophy 27:1, 4

Boothby WH (2009) Weapons and the law of armed conflict. Oxford University Press, Oxford, p 341

Brownlie I (1979) Principles of public international law, 3rd edn. Oxford University Press, p 512

Butenko A, Larouche P (2015) Regulation for innovativeness or regulation of innovation? Law Innov Technol 7:52

Cassese A (1986) International law in a divided world. Oxford Clarendon Press

Chesterman S (2009) Unaccountable? The United Nations emergency powers and the rule of law. Vanderbilt J Transnl Law 42:1509

Claude IL Jr (1986) American approaches to world affairs. University Press of America, p 51

European Commission, Ethics guidelines for trustworthy AI.

[103]"The human-centric approach to AI strives to ensure that human values are central to the way in which AI systems are developed, deployed, used and monitored, by ensuring respect for fundamental rights, including those set out in the Treaties of the European Union and Charter of Fundamental Rights of the European Union, all of which are united by reference to a common foundation rooted in respect for human dignity, in which the human being enjoys a unique and inalienable moral status. This also entails consideration of the natural environment and of other living beings that are part of the human ecosystem, as well as a sustainable approach enabling the flourishing of future generations to come."

European Parliament, EU guidelines on ethics in artificial intelligence: Context and implementation, at p. 2.

Claude IL Jr (1988) Swords into plowshares: the problems and progress of international organization, 4th edn. Random House, p 57
Collingridge D (1980) The social control of technology. St Martin's Press, New York, p 19
Conforti B (1996) The law and practice of the United Nations. Martinus Nijhoff Publishers, p 14
Cowls J, Floridi L (2018) Prolegomena to a White Paper on an Ethical Framework for a Good AI Society. SSRN Electronic Journal. https://doi.org/10.2139/ssrn.3198732
Crosnier HL (2018) Communs numériques et communs de la connaissance. Introduction. tic&société 12(1):1–12
Cuellar MF (2004) Reflections on sovereignty and collective security. Stanford J Int Law 40:211
Danaher J (2016) The threat of algocracy: reality, resistance and accommodation, philosophy and technology. Philosophy Technol 29(3):245–268
Danilenko M (1991) The changing structure of the international community: constitutional implications. Harv Int Law J 32:353
Duffy H (2005) The 'War On Terror' and the framework of international law. Cambridge University Press, p 178, 184
Elish M (2019) Moral crumple zones: cautionary tales in human–robot interaction, engaging science. Technol Soc 5:40–60
Engler A (2021) 6 developments that will define AI governance in 2021. Brookings Institute. https://www.brookings.edu/research/6-developments-that-will-define-ai-governance-in-2021/?utm_campaign=Brookings%20Brief&utm_medium=email&utm_content=107735043&utm_source=hs_email
Erdelyi OJ, Goldsmith J (2018) Regulating Artificial Intelligence Proposal for a Global Solution. In: AAAI/ACM conference on artifical intelligence, ethics and society, New Orleans, p 2
Evans G (1994) Cooperating for peace: the global Agenda for the 1990s and beyond. Allen & Unwin, pp 15–16
Fassbender B (1998) U.N. Security council reform and the right of veto: a constitutional perspective. Kluwer, The Hague, p 99
Fenwick M, Kaal WA, Vermeulen EPM (2017) Regulation tomorrow: what happens when technology is faster than the law? Am Univ Bus Law Rev 6:561
Findler DP (1996) Caught between traditions: the security council in philosophical conundrum. Mich J Int Law 17:411
Floridi L, Cowls J, Beltrametti M, Chatila R, Chazerand P, Dignum V, Luetge C, Madelin R, Pagallo U, Rossi F, Schafer B, Valcke P, Vayena E (2018) AI4People—an ethical framework for a good ai society: opportunities, risks, principles, and recommendations. Minds Mach 28:689
Franck T (2003) Is the U.N. Charter a constitution? In: Frowein JA et al (eds) Negotiating for peace: Liber Amicorum Tono Eitel. Springer, New York, p 95
Gellman R, Dixon P (2016) Failures of privacy selfregulation in the United States. In: Wright D, De Hert P (eds) Enforcing privacy: regulatory, legal and technological approaches. Springer, Berlin
Graham MW (1946) Great powers and small states. In: Morgenthau HJ (ed) Peace, security & the United Nations. University of Chicago Press, pp 57, 71
Grindle M (2007) Good enough governance revisited. Dev Policy Rev 25(5):533–574
Guihota M, Matthewaa AF, Suzor NP (2017) Nudging robots: innovative solutions to regulate artificial intelligence. Vanderbilt J Entertain Technol Law 20:385
Henkin L (1989) Use of force: law and U.S. Policy. In: Henkin L et al (eds) Right V. might: international law and the use of force. Council on Foreign Relations Press, New York, pp 58–59
Hirsch DD (2011) The law and policy of online privacy: regulation, self-regulation, or co-regulation? Seattle Univ Law Rev 34:438, 460–464
Hoffmann S (1987) Liberalism and international affairs. In: Hoffman S (ed) Janus and Minerva: essays in the theory and practice of international politics. Westview Press, Boulder, pp 89–94
Hood CC, Margetts HZ (2007) The tools of government in the digital age. Palgrave Macmillan, pp 5–6, 8–12

ICJ (1955) Advisory opinion, voting procedures on questions and petitions concerning the territory of South-West Africa. Concurring Opinion Lauterpacht, p 106

Jessop B (2003) Governance and metagovernance: on reflexivity, requisite variety and requisite irony. In: Bang HP (ed) Governance as social and political communication, vol 101. Manchester University Press, Manchester

Jessop B (2016) State theory. In: Ansell C, Torfing J (eds) Handbook on theories of governance. Edward Elgar, pp 71, 82

Jones JF (2004) Human security and social development. Denver J Int Law Policy 33:92

Kelsen H (1964) The law of the United Nations. Frederick A. Praeger, New York, p 3

Kirgis L Jr (1995) The security council's first fifty years. Am J Int Law 89:506–507

Kitchin R (2014) The data revolution: big data, open data, data infrastructures and their consequences. Sage, London

Koops B-J et al (2006) Should self-regulation be the starting point? In: Koops B-J, Lips M, Prins C, Schellekens M (eds) Starting points for ICT regulation: deconstructing prevalent policy one-liners. TMC Asser Press, p 125

Le Mon J, Taylor RS (2004) Security council action in the name of human rights: from Rhodesia to the Congo. UC Davis J Int Law 10(2):197

Mandel GN et al (2013) Innovative governance models for emerging technologies. In: Marchant GE et al (eds) Innovative governance models for emerging technologies. Edward Elgar

Manheim K, Kaplan L (2019) Artificial intelligence: risks to privacy and democracy. Yale J Law Technol 21:106

Mathews JT (1989) Redefining security. Foreign Aff 68(2):162

McNair AD (1930) The functions and different legal character of treaties. Br Yearb Int Law 11:100

Mearsheimer JJ (1998) The false promise of international institutions. In: Brown ME et al (eds) Theories of war and peace, an international security reader. MIT Press, Cambridge, pp 329, 357–358

Michael DC (1996) Cooperative implementation of federal regulations. Yale J Reg 13 (535):541–544

Mokhtarian E (2018) The bot legal code: developing a legally compliant artificial intelligence. Vanderbilt J Entertain Technol Law 21:145

Moses LB (2011) Agents of change: how the law 'copes' with techno logical change. Griffith Law Rev 20:763, 768–769

Nickel JW (2002) Is today's international human rights system a global governance regime? J Ethics 6(4):353

O'Connell ME (1998) Regulating the use of force in the 21st century: the continuing importance of state autonomy. Columbia J Transnl Law 36:473

Parker K, Neylon LB (1989) Jus Cogens: Compelling the law of human rights. Hast Int Comp Law Rev 12:411

Paul AK, Schaefer M (2020) Safeguards for the use of artificial intelligence and machine learning in global health, World Health Organization. Bull World Health Org 98:1. https://doi.org/10.2471/BLT.19.237099

Peters A (2009) Membership in the global constitutional community. Klabbers J, Peters A, Ulfstein G (eds) The constitutionalization of international law. Oxford University Press, p 186

Priest M (1997–1998) The privatization of regulation: five models of self-regulation. Ottawa Law Rev 29:233

Reisman WM (2008) Acting before victims become victims: preventing and arresting mass murder. Case West Res J Int Law 40(57):78

Renner M (1996) Fighting for survival: environmental decline, social conflict and the new age of insecurity. W. W. Norton & Company, p 83

Ress G (2012) The interpretation of the charter. In: Simma B (ed) The charter of the united nations, a commentary, vol I, 2nd edn. Oxford University Press, p 15

Ross G (1983) The great powers and the decline of the European states system 1914–1945. Longman, pp 100–126

Rubinstein IS (2011) Privacy and regulatory innovation: moving beyond voluntary codes. I/S J Law Policy 6:355

Rubinstein IS (2016) The future of self-regulation is co-regulation. The Cambridge handbook of consumer privacy. Cambridge University Press (Forthcoming). Available at SSRN: https://ssrn.com/abstract=2848513

Schachter O (1951) Review of Kelsen: law of the United Nations. Yale Law J 61:1

Schachter O (1994) United Nations law. Am J Int Law 88:1

Scherer MU (2016) Regulating artificial intelligence systems: risks, challenges, competencies, and strategies. Harv J Law Technol 29:354

Schuck PH (1984) When the exception becomes the rule: regulatory equity and the formulation of energy policy through an exceptions process. Duke Law J 1984:163, 197

Schwindt CJ (2000) Interpreting the United Nations charter: from treaty to world constitution. UC Davis J Int Law Policy 6:194

Shestack JJ (1997–1998) Globalization of human rights law. Fordham Int Law J 21:558

Shklar JN (1986) Legalism: law, morals, and political trials, 2nd edn. Harvard University Press, p 125

Sinclair D (1997) Self-regulation versus command and control? Beyond false dichotomies. Law Policy 19:529

Stern B (1996) What exactly is the job of international institutions? Am Soc Int Law Proc 90:585

Thomas C (2002) Global governance and human security. In: Wilkinson R, Hughes S (eds) Global governance: critical perspectives. Routledge, p 113

Truman HS (1945) Documents of the United Nations Conference on International Organization. United Nations Information Organization, p 680

Ulfstein G (2009), Institutions and Competences. In: Klabbers J, Peters A, Ulfstein G (eds) The constitutionalization of international law. OUP, p 47

Ullmann H (1983) Redefining security. Int Secur 8(1):129

Walker R (1990) Security, sovereignty and the challenge of world politics. Alternatives 15:3

Weller M (1997) The reality of the emerging constitutional order: putting the pieces of the puzzle together. Cambridge Rev Int Aff 10:2

White ND (2002) On the brink of lawlessness: the state of collective security law. Indiana Int Comp Law Rev 13:237

Wolfers A (1962) Discord and collaboration: essays on international politics. The Johns Hopkins Press, Baltimore

Wyber R, Vaillancourt S, Perry W, Mannava P, Folaranmi T, Celi LA (2015) Big data in global health: improving health in low- and middle-income countries. Bull World Health Organ. 93 (3):203–208. https://doi.org/10.2471/BLT.14.139022

Yanisky-Ravid S (2017) Generating rembrandt: artificial intelligence, copyright, and accountability in the 3A Era—the human-like authors are already here—a new model. Mich St Law Rev 659, 673

Zarsky T (2011) Governmental data-mining and its alternatives. Penn State Law Rev 116:285

Chapter 6
AI and Human Rights

6.1 Introduction

The time and therefore the world are so often out of joint. Obviously, there are "better" and "worse" periods but the cycle of human suffering and crisis is more or less omnipresent throughout human history. It is on the basis of such understanding that our most important, collective responses such as the legal establishment of human rights have been forged. Human rights are obviously our own legal creations; therefore, they contain flaws and are open to misinterpretations. This is only natural or to phrase it better, human.

Still in their current form they express our aspirations, which emerged during the disjointed times of the two world wars, about how the world must be, in terms of a humanized and human-centric order of global affairs.[1] What came to be known as human rights law takes root in the political and social developments since ancient and medieval times, up to the Bill of Rights and the French Revolution.[2]

However, the two world wars constituted, through the sufferings that they caused, landmarks for the establishment of these rights. While we tend to forget quite often the efforts following the Great War, such as with the Permanent Court of International Justice—PCIJ—it was then that the modern era of human rights began.[3] The failure of the League of Nations between the two world wars led to an enhanced system of human rights at the aftermath of the Second World War, which is established at the center of the collective security system. As analyzed below, this is a significant difference albeit an underestimated one. It is also significant that within the wider framework of human rights we must include not only individual rights, but collective, social, political and economic as well.

[1]Cassese (1986), pp. 377–379.

[2]Perkins (1992), pp. 379–380; Buchanan (2004), p. 119.

[3]Provost (2004), pp. 16–17; Schwebel (1991), pp. 955–956.

T. Tzimas, *Legal and Ethical Challenges of Artificial Intelligence from an International Law Perspective*, Law, Governance and Technology Series 46,
https://doi.org/10.1007/978-3-030-78585-7_6

Human rights are approached here not as the sum of specific rights but as the legal embodiment of human-centrism in international law. In this sense they specify the way that human-centrism's implementation regarding AI should take place. Their role extends both to present and future AI developments and applications. The analysis begins from the place of human rights in international law and then moves onto their role in relation to AI. It is argued that not only current AI applications but also AGI and ASI as potential developments must be assessed.

6.2 The Role of Human Rights in International Law

Human rights constitute one of the most, widely endorsed areas of law and one of the most often violated. The reference to the term "human" implies per se their universality[4] and the obligation for compliance to them not only of states and international organizations but also of non-state actors as well, because of their origin from the human nature.[5]

The significance of the protective umbrella of human rights for each individual—as well as for peoples collectively—is indicated from the fact that they are not necessarily meditated by the state to which an individual may be citizen or resident—although every state bears obligations under human rights; any person is entitled to human rights merely on the basis of the human identity, while any state is obliged to respect them, regardless of its internal legal system.[6] Humanity per se attributes human rights to the humans[7] and human rights in their turn attempt to safeguard humanity, and through that human-centrism as well.

The role of human rights as guarantors of human-centrism becomes apparent through their practically universal application on the one hand and their horizontal implementation, even contrary to states' will, on the other hand.

Human rights do not merely constitute a sum of rights; by aiming at the protection and the development of human "dignity", as their cornerstone,[8] through a variety of rights they ascertain that every and each one of us possesses by nature some unique characteristics which bring us both individually and collectively at the center of attention and protection of international law; this proves human-centrism to transcend the international order, exactly because we comprehend us, humans as that unique and therefore important.

[4]Weston (2008), pp. 324–325.

[5]Buchanan (2004), pp. 121–123.

[6]Provost (2004), p. 25.

[7]Teng (2012), p. 157; Anderson (2010), p. 194.

[8]UN Charter, Preamble; Universal Declaration of Human Rights-UNDA-Preamble; International Covenant on Civil and Political Rights-ICCPR-Preamble; International Covenant on Economic, Social and Cultural Rights-ICESCR-Preamble.

The expansion of treaties which are related to human rights,[9] as well as of relevant institutions sustain the universal concession to the unique significance of human rights.[10]

As mentioned above, the—*even*—direct relationship between international community organs and peoples—*when states are proven unwilling or incapable of sustaining human rights, especially since a certain extent and severity of violations has been surpassed*—the horizontal responsibility of all actors to promote human rights—*even of private entities*—[11] and the resolutions from several international organs, with the UN GA and UN SC standing out among them[12] create a legal consensus not only regarding the centrality of human rights but also about their specific legal categorization as jus cogens.

The reference to jus cogens is significant as it describes the binding-ness of human rights. The main idea behind jus cogens norms is that they constitute the foundations of the international community as they embody general principles of law.[13] Jus cogens is superior to conventional law,[14] as part of the hierarchical structure of international law.[15] Indicative of its value is that even state policies which would otherwise be legitimate under national law are illegal, when

[9]Apart from the UN Charter one may indicatively refer to UNDA, ICCPR, ICESR, European Convention of Human Rights-ECHR-African Charter on Human and Peoples' Rights-ACHPR-American Convention on Human Rights-ACHR.

[10]Stamatopoulou (1999), pp. 284–285.

[11]Anderson (2010), pp. 183, 186, 194–197.

[12]U.N. GA RES/48/134(1993), Principles Relating to the Status of National Institutions; UN Human Rights Office of the High Commissioner for Human Rights, World Conference on Human Rights, (June 14–25, 1993), (www.ohchr.org/EN/ABOUTUS/Pages/ViennaWC.aspx access. 30-06-2020). Vienna Declaration and Programme of Action, U.N. Doc. A/CONF.157/23 (July 12, 1993).

[13]Conklin (2012), p. 838; Crawford (2002), pp. 148–150, 158–160; Byers (1999), p. 194; ICJ statute, Article 38 (www.icj-cij.org/documents/?p1=4&p2=2&p3=0#CHAPTER_II, access. 28-1-2015).

[14]Committee of United States Citizens in Nicaragua v. Reagan, 859 F.2d 929, 935 (D.C. Cir. 1988). Rozakis (1976), p. 1.

[15]ICJ, Armed Activities on the Territory of the Congo, Separate Opinion Of Judge Ad Hoc Dugard, (New Application, 2002), 85.

contradicting jus cogens norms.[16] This is what the universality of jus cogens means, as well as their nature as fundamental truths.[17]

There are different approaches to the origins of jus cogens, with others emphasizing its substance, whereas other on its procedural ramifications on international legal order.[18] The, not so clear, regarding its definition, article 53 of the Vienna Convention on the Law of Treaties holds that "A treaty is void if, at the time of its conclusion, it conflicts with a peremptory norm of general international law. For the purposes of the present Convention, a peremptory norm of general international law is a norm accepted and recognized by the international community of States as a whole as a norm from which no derogation is permitted and which can be modified only by a subsequent norm of general international law having the same character".[19]

---

[16]Spagnoli (2008), pp. 325–326; Petsche (2010), p. 255; Ogilvy (2009), p. 176; Criddle and Decent (2009), p. 334; Orakhelashvili (2005), pp. 79, 85; Cassese (2012), p. 166.

Regarding when it can be objectively identified that there is a jus cogens violation, judge Lauterpacht, in the case "Bosnia v Serbia II", argued that: "The duty to "prevent" genocide is a duty that rests upon all parties and is a duty owed by each party to every other... First, there is the duty of the Respondent [and thus of any state party] both to prevent genocide and to refrain from conduct that inhibits the ability of the Applicant itself to prevent genocide or to resist it... Third, there is the question of access by the Applicant to the means to prevent the commission of acts of genocide. The Applicant obviously has here in mind... the embargo placed by Security Council resolution 713 (1991)... [I]t is not to be contemplated that the Security Council would ever deliberately adopt a resolution clearly and deliberately flouting a rule of jus cogens or requiring a violation of human rights. But the possibility that a Security Council resolution might inadvertently or in an unforeseen manner lead to such a situation cannot be excluded... On this basis, the inability of Bosnia-Herzegovina sufficiently strongly to fight back against the Serbs and effectively to prevent the implementation of the Serbian policy of ethnic cleansing is at least in part directly attributable to the fact that BosniaHerzegovina's access to weapons and equipment has been severely limited by the embargo. Viewed in this light, the Security Council resolution can be seen as having in effect called on Members of the United Nations, albeit unknowingly and assuredly unwillingly, to become in some degree supporters of the genocidal activity of the Serbs and in this manner and to that extent to act contrary to a rule of jus cogens."

ICJ, Bosnia v. Serbia II, (2007), (separate opinion of Judge Lauterpacht) 436-41.

Also see:

ICJ, Questions of Interpretation and Application of the 1971 Montreal Convention arising from the Aerial Incident at Lockerbie (Libyan Arab Jamahiriya *v.* United States of America), (1998) Dissenting Opinion Of President Schwebel, 60.

Reference should also be made to article 38 of the ICJ.

For a contradictory argument: Weisburd (1995), pp. 38–39.

The origins of jus cogens in the post-World War II era can also be traced in the Nuremberg trial while at a later phase, in the "Barcelona Traction (Belgium v. Spain)" case, the similar term of "erga omnes" obligations was introduced.

Charter of the International Military Tribunal, in force August 8, 1945, 59 Stat. 1544, E.A.S. No. 472, 82 U.N.T.S. 279, ICJ, Barcelona Traction, 4, 32.

[17]*F. F. Martin, Human Rights and the Hierarchy of International Law Sources and Norms,* at p. 353; Crawford (2006), p. 102; Domingo (2012), p. 566.

[18]Parker and Neylon (1989), p. 414.

[19]Article 53 of the Vienna Convention "."

It is equally significant to keep in mind that during the preparatory proceedings, there was consensus about the binding-ness of jus cogens over conventional autonomy.[20]

The definition of the Vienna Convention has been criticized as vague as well as for being more "practical" than "scientific".[21] It recognizes superior authority and therefore a special procedure for their modification in the framework of international law. Obviously, it becomes particularly troubling to identify when a new rule has substituted a preexisting norm. Part of this troubling issue becomes apparent with the difficulty that exists in terms of reaching an internationally unanimous decision about which norms specifically constitute jus cogens; on the contrary there are different lists of jus cogens norms, although for at least some of them there is wider consensus.[22]

Nevertheless, and regardless of the complexities of jus cogens in terms of its development, the analysis of which evades the scope of the current book, it is by now well-understood that jus cogens exists, with the specific characteristics that are mentioned above.[23]

The sources of jus cogens that have been proposed vary: for some it is customary law, the "opinio juris" of the international community that determine whether a norm is of the type of jus cogens. While it is a partially correct approach, it is more accurate to trace jus cogens in a more legally positivist way, i.e. in the UN Charter and more specifically in its fundamental goals and principles, given its constitutional character. They constitute the basis from which jus cogens norms flow.

This argument aligns with the International Law Commission—ILC—position suggesting that jus cogens norms are not determined on the basis of their type but

[20]Rozakis (1976), p. 14.

[21]Rozakis (1976), pp. 45, 89–91; Weisburd (1995), p. 19; Schwarzenberger (1965), p. 467; Shleton (2006), p. 291.

[22]ICJ, Congo v. Rwanda Judgment, (citing Application of the Convention on the Prevention and Punishment of the Crime of Genocide (Bosn. & Herz. v. Yugo.), Preliminary Objections, (1996) 64. Spijkers (2009–2010), pp. 87–88. ICJ, Case Concerning Armed Activities on the Territory of the Congo (Democratic Republic of the Congo v. Rwanda), Jurisdiction of the Court and Admissibility of the Application, (2006) 64. Fitzmaurice (1973), p. 323. ICJ, The South West Africa Cases, (Ethiopia v. S. Afr.; Liberia v. S. Afr.) (1966) (Tanaka, J., dissenting) 6, 298 (Tanaka, J., dissenting). ICJ, Barcelona Traction, Light and Power Company (Belg. v. Spain), (1970) 3, 301. Adams (2005), pp. 364–369. ICTY, Prosecutor v Furundz ija, No IT-95-17/1-T, (1998), 153–154. H. Gros Espiell, Implementation Of United Nations Resolutions Relating To The Right Of Peoples Under Colonial And Alien Domination To Self-Determination, UN,E/CN.4/Sub.2/405(vol. I) (1978), (unispal.un.org/UNISPAL.NSF/0/BE1DDCB608178D7685256DE100727E8F, access. 29-1-2015). Kamminga (1992), p. 163. ICJ, Barcelona Traction Case, (1962), (Separate opinion of judge Ammoun), 301, 304–312; I.C.J., South West Africa cases, (1966), (Dissenting opinion of Judge Tanaka), 289–290, 298.

[23]Report of the International Law Commission on the Work of its Twenty-Eighth Session, State Responsibility, (1976) 2(2), *Y.B. Int'l L. Comm'n* 69, 99, U.N. Doc. A/CN.4/SER.4/1976/Add.1 (Part 2).

from the nature of the specific area with which each and every norm deals.[24] It is the supreme interest of the international community that legitimizes jus cogens—and humans rights are profoundly part of it.[25] This is after all why whenever a jus cogens norm is violated all other states need to work together in order to cease the violation.[26]

The parenthetical discussion about jus cogens is necessary in order to fully capture the status of human rights, as part of jus cogens.[27] Up to the extent that opinio juris constitutes a defining factor of jus cogens, the more than 100 hundred bilateral and multilateral treaties, as well as the fact that practically almost every state has committed itself to human rights prove that human rights are indeed part of this type of international norms.[28] In addition, the inclusion of human rights in jus cogens can be justified on the basis of their universal application and the legitimacy of "actio popularis" against the perpetrators of gross, human rights violations.[29] The orientation of human rights from the UN Charter also justifies their endorsement as jus cogens, given that it is in the fundamental goals and principles of the organization that we come across human rights as well.

In such a framework, the decision in the "Yassin Abdullah Kadi v Council of the European Union and Commission of the European Communities" of the European

---

[24]R. Nieto-Navia, International Peremptory Norms (Jus Cogens) And International Humanitarian Law, in the (www.iccnow.org/documents/WritingColombiaEng.pdf access. 01-07-2020); Janis (2003), pp. 62–63.

[25]Verdross (1966), p. 58.

Sir Hirsch Lauterpacht in 1953 argued that: "It would thus appear that the test whether the -object of the treaty is illegal and whether the treaty is void for that reason is not inconsistency with customary international law pure and simple, but inconsistency with such overriding principles of international law which may be regarded as constituting principles of international public policy (ordre international public). These principles need not necessarily have crystallized in a clearly accepted rule of law such as prohibition of piracy or of aggressive war. They may be expressive of rules of international morality so cogent that an international tribunal would consider them as forming part of those principles of law generally recognized by civilized nations which the International Court of Justice is bound to apply by virtue of Article 38 (3) of its Statute."

H. Lauterpacht, Document:- A/CN.4/63, Report on the Law of Treaties Special Rapporteur Topic: Law of Treaties, (1953), II, *Yearbook of the International Law Commission*:, 106, at p. 155.

Fitzmaurice also, held that: "The rules of international law in this context fall broadly into two classes—those which are mandatory and imperative in .any circumstances (jus cogens) and those (jus dispositivum) which merely furnish a rule for application in the absence of any other agreed regime, or, more correctly, those the variation or modification of which under an .agreed regime is permissible, provided the position and rights of their States are not affected."

G. G. Fitzmaurice, Third Report on the Law of Treaties, Document A/CN//4/115, (1958) II, *Yearbook of. International Law Commission,* 20, on p. 40.

[26]International Law Commission, Report of the on the Work of Its Fifty-third Session, Draft Articles on Responsibility of States for Internationally Wrongful Acts, RUN GAOR, 56th Sess., Supp. No. 10, at 43, UN Doc. A/56/10 (2001), (www.un.org/il,c access. 29-1-2015); Brownlie (1979), p. 512.

[27]Tams (2005), p. 141; Parker and Neylon (1989), pp. 413–414, Brownlie (1979), p. 513.

[28]Trnavci (2005), pp. 251–252.

[29]Cf. Bassiouni (2001), p. 104.

Court of Justice—ECJ—which ascertained both of the recognition of jus cogens, as binding, even for the UN SC decisions, as well as of human rights' law inclusion in jus cogens is a landmark decision.[30]

Similar was the decision in the case of "Al-Adsani v. The United Kingdom" in the European Court of Human Rights, which suggested that "...the prohibition of torture has achieved the status of a peremptory norm in international law..."[31] In the same decision, it is important to stress the dissenting opinions as well, which is enlightening about the role of jus cogens in relation to state sovereignty.[32]

It is, last but not least, important to stress that the human rights legal construction contains individual rights, basic guarantees of the rule of law and also what—in national legal systems—is described as the context of social rights.[33] This remark is crucial in order to comprehend in terms of legal theory that human rights are not limited to a solely liberal approach—identifying only the individual as the person of interest for human rights—but includes social rights as well and therefore the latter should be part of the AI governance as well. This is why the ICCPR and the ICESCR are also complementary—in spite of their unique significance—in the wider human rights framework.

On the basis of the previous analysis, human rights emerge as an essential part of AI governance. The governance of AI, which is analyzed below in line with human

[30]European Court of Justice, Case T-315/01, Kadi v. Council (2005), 224, 226.

[31]European Court of Human Rights, Case Of Al-Adsani V. The United Kingdom, (2001), 61.

[32]"By accepting that the rule on prohibition of torture is a rule of jus cogens, the majority recognise that it is hierarchically higher than any other rule of international law, be it general or particular, customary or conventional, with the exception, of course, of other jus cogens norms. For the basic characteristic of a jus cogens rule is that, as a source of law in the now vertical international legal system, it overrides any other rule which does not have the same status. In the event of a conflict between a jus cogens rule and any other rule of international law, the former prevails. The consequence of such prevalence is that the conflicting rule is null and void, or, in any event, does not produce legal effects which are in contradiction with the content of the peremptory rule. 2. The Court's majority do not seem, on the other hand, to deny that the rules on State immunity; customary or conventional, do not belong to the category of jus cogens; and rightly so, because it is clear that the rules of State immunity, deriving from both customary and conventional international law, have never been considered by the international community as rules with a hierarchically higher status. It is common knowledge that, in many instances, States have, through their own initiative, waived their rights of immunity; that in many instances they have contracted out of them, or have renounced them. These instances clearly demonstrate that the rules on State immunity do not enjoy a higher status, since jus cogens rules, protecting as they do the "ordre public", that is the basic values of the international community, cannot be subject to unilateral or contractual forms of derogation from their imperative contents. 3.The acceptance therefore of the jus cogens nature of the prohibition of torture entails that a State allegedly violating it cannot invoke hierarchically lower rules (in this case, those on State immunity) to avoid the consequences of the illegality of its actions."

European Court of Human Rights, Case Of Al-Adsani V. The United Kingdom, (2005, Joint Dissenting Opinion Of Judges Rozakis And Caflisch Joined By Judges Wildhaber, Costa, Cabral Barreto And Vajić), 1–3.

[33]UDHR, Articles 22–28.

rights follows the differentiated forms of AI—meaning ANI, AGI and ASI—and is suggested in relation both to its proactive and to its ex-post, intervening role.

6.3 Governance of AI and the Role of Human Rights

The role of human rights is that of the guarantors of human-centrism regarding their substance and as part of jus cogens in terms of their normative status.

Human rights can be expected to maintain human-centrism at the center of AI evolution, given that in the framework of their legal status, they constitute a "global language", "discussing and contesting understandings of social needs, impacts, responsibilities, and outcomes."[34] We need to think of human rights as a complex of international treaties, of institutions of different types, of agencies, which monitor and partially enforce human rights, nationally and internationally, towards both states and non-state actors as well.

Therefore, in relation to AI, their role is to reduce risks of non-friendly AI to maximize the potential benefit from AI and check AI development too, whenever the latter potentially fractures or raises the risk of fracturing this human-centrism.[35]

Human rights can and must contribute into a regulatory framework promoting "friendly" AI with their role into machine-learning being critical; they also are supposed to be prohibiting or enabling certain AI developments and applications. In other words, human rights are expected to provide up to some extent at least, the legal- and therefore partially ethical-regulation of AI development.

In order for such legal regulation to be achieved a synthesis of different means and stages of regulation must be applied. Human rights are examined below in relation to ANI and in relation to AGI and ASI.

6.3.1 Human Rights and ANI

Human rights are necessary in a proactive role; that is to "train" AI in line both with the specific human rights and the "ius commune"[36] of human dignity—*with the latter constituting inherent characteristic flowing out of human existence per se,*

[34]Jason Pielemeier, AI & Global Governance: The Advantages of Applying the International Human Rights Framework to Artificial Intelligence, United Nations University Centre for Policy Research, (2019, February 26), (https://cpr.unu.edu/publications/articles/ai-global-governance-the-advantages-of-applying-the-international-human-rights-framework-to-artificial-intelligence.html).

[35]Alston (1984), p. 607 et seq.

[36]Carozza (2008), p. 932.

guarantee of inter-human relations and state obligation—[37] as well as with the mentality they carry—i.e. the prevalence of human-centrism. In this sense, a first policy of a governance mechanism of AI and a reasonable one to impose upon AI designers, manufacturers and owners the obligation to conduct machine-learning of AI systems in line with, human rights.

Human rights must provide to AI assessment mechanisms, the backbone of its normative context. Even further, as we speak, the absence of a special legal framework for the regulation of AI means that the role of human rights increases.[38]

Human rights must be comprehended as the backbone for the creation of binding, internationally, legal framework that can provide the necessary scrutiny of AI applications.[39] The impact of human rights is significant for various applications of AI—such as privacy, anonymization and facial recognition.[40]

It must be further noted, that as the UN Guiding Principles on Human Rights and Business, foresee, the human rights framework is expected to be imposed on all actors, including businesses and private actors as well.[41] States are expected to respect, to protect and to fulfill, where they exercise control, concerning the wide nexus of human rights, including economic, social and cultural rights, as well as to establish an international scheme of governance.[42]

As the Council of Europe argues, a system of Human Rights Impact Assessment—HRIA—regarding the impact of AI, which will be extending not solely on the algorithms but also on the collection of the big data, which are used in order to conduct the necessary, machine-learning of AI, is necessary. These mechanisms will "set out the measures, safeguards, and mechanisms envisaged for preventing or mitigating that [AI] risk. In circumstances where such a risk has been identified in relation to an AI system that has already been deployed by a public authority, its use should be immediately suspended until the abovementioned measures, safeguards and mechanisms have been adopted. Where it is not possible to meaningfully

---

[37]Human dignity as a universal value interacts with each one, specific legal framework, remaining "informal, flexible and pluralistic in its relationship to local law and culture". Carozza (2003), p. 1043.

[38]Diane Desierto, Human Rights in the Era of Automation and Artificial Intelligence, EJILTalk, (2020, February 26), (https://www.ejiltalk.org/human-rights-in-the-era-of-automation-and-artificial-intelligence/).

[39]Kate Saslow and Philippe Lorenz, Artificial Intelligence Needs Human Rights September 2019, (https://www.stiftung-nv.de/sites/default/files/ai_needs_human_rights.pdf), p. 18.

[40]UN Human Rights Committee, Expert Seminar on Artificial Intelligence and the Right to Privacy, 27–28 May 2020, https://www.ohchr.org/EN/Issues/DigitalAge/Pages/SeminarArtificialIntelligence.aspx.

[41]The UN working group on business and human rights, the UN guiding principles on business and human rights an introduction, (https://www.ohchr.org/Documents/Issues/Business/Intro_Guiding_PrinciplesBusinessHR.pdf).

[42]UN Committee on Economic, Social and Cultural Rights (CESCR), E/C.12/GC/24, General comment No. 24 (2017) on State obligations under the International Covenant on Economic, Social and Cultural Rights in the context of business activities, (2017, August 10), at paras. 1–12, 35, https://www.refworld.org/docid/5beaecba4.html.

mitigate the identified risks, the AI system should not be deployed or otherwise used by any public authority".[43] Such assessment needs to be contacted prior, during and after the use of AI systems.[44]

The UN in its document of the General Assembly entitled "Promotion and protection of the right to freedom of opinion and expression" also came up with proposals about the implementation of human rights in relation to AI: "Companies and Governments must be explicit with individuals about which decisions in the information environment are made by automated systems and which are accompanied by human review, as well as the broad elements of the logic used by those systems... Companies and Governments need to embrace transparency throughout each aspect of the AI value chain... disclosure of, for example, data on how much content is removed by AI systems, how often AI-suggested content removals are approved by a human moderator, how often content removals are contested and how often challenges... Tackling the prevalence of discrimination in AI systems".[45]

Parenthetically, the need on behalf of governments to establish HRIA' on AI, safeguarding private companies' compliance is also indicative of the need for a centralized scheme of governance of AI, as mentioned above.[46]

Such human-rights oriented assessment must extend in all the stages of AI evolution. The idea is that big-data with which AI machine-learning is conducted must be harvested and used in accordance with human rights, up to such an extent that human rights will be endorsed in the evolution of AI autonomous behavior.

In such a framework, we could "raise" AI tending towards friendliness to humans. Even when the human designer will not be setting but only general goals, AI will be reasonably expected to be selecting the means and the secondary goals which will be compliant with a human-centric approach.[47]

The implementation of human-rights in AI machine-learning is not free of complexities: the growing autonomy of AI means that in spite of our best efforts, AI may overcome or misinterpret human rights—oriented machine-learning—at least in terms of what we consider as misinterpretation.[48]

In addition, the implementation of guidance by human rights will have to confront our own disagreements about both their meaning and their implementation, which will be obvious when we will try to choose cases and paradigms of human

[43]Council of Europe Commissioner for Human Rights, Unboxing Artificial Intelligence: 10 steps to protect Human Rights, pp. 7–8.

[44]EDRi, UN Special Rapporteur analyses AI's impact on human rights, (2018, November 7), https://edri.org/our-work/un-special-rapporteur-report-artificial-intelligence-impact-human-rights/.

[45]UN GA, Promotion and protection of the right to freedom of opinion and expression, Note by the Secretary-General, A/73/348, (2018, August 29), at paras. 47–51.

[46]Special Rapporteur on the promotion and protection of the right to freedom of opinion and expression, Report on Artificial Intelligence technologies and implications for freedom of expression and the information environment.

[47]*Waser, Discovering The Foundations Of A Universal System of Ethics As A Road To Safe Artificial Intelligence.*

[48]Tegmark (2017), pp. 402–404; Omohundro (2008), pp. 483–492.

rights-based machine learning. The implementation of complicated legal norms necessitates creative thinking and interpretative approaches which are delicate even for well-trained humans.[49] Non-human, intelligent entities will make their own assumptions about human rights and human approaches to them.[50] This is the essence of autonomy; as AI evolves it implements its gradually emerging creative thinking on complicated tasks.

A way to prevent unwanted outcomes from the enhanced autonomy of AI may—as mentioned right above—be to establish an emergency de-activating mechanism when human rights violations are at risk; the need for interpretation however is still there: how and who will determine when human rights violations are approximating and at what extent these violations must be in order for such a switch off mechanism to be activated? In addition, while the maintenance of human control both in principle and in practice is necessary in such cases, however, this could be undermining all these elements that AI is worth for.

What we can hope for is a synthesis of different means; there must be a categorization of AI applications with serious restrictions or even prohibition, as too dangerous for human rights; for example, AI using lethal force in policing duties could be deemed as unnecessary and too dangerous. Another type could be that of AI applications which are of relevant risk and therefore should be "slowed down", in the sense of retaining human control over them.[51] One last category will be that of low-risk AI, with greater reliance on the outcome of machine-learning, without underestimating the role of the latter in the primary two categories as well.

We will obviously have to navigate between both the beneficial and the possibly harmful aspect of AI. We need to imagine an elaborate and complicated enough legal system that will be able to balance between the two.

Regardless of all these complexities we have to rely in principle on the human rights-learning approach. Despite its potential failures, such learning approach, combined with well-designed software constitute crucial means in furtherance of achieving friendly AI, even when the human programmer impact will have been surpassed. It is in a way similar with trying to teach a child, so that (s)he becomes a trustworthy adult. The failures are too many, but in the end, we need to rely on that. However, we must maintain the option to slow down or even eventually stop the evolution of AI.

[49]Chen (2019). Forthcoming. <https://ssrn.com/abstract=3302507>. *A. Liptak*, Sent to Prison by a Software Program's Secret Algorithms, The New York Times (2017).

[50]*Tegmark* (2017).

[51]*E. Yudkowsky*, Creating Friendly AI 1.0: The Analysis and Design of Benevolent Goal Architectures, (2001), <singinst.org/CFAI.html>. *H. de Garis*, The Artilect War: Cosmists Vs. Terrans (2005).

6.3.2 Human Rights, AGI, ASI

The development of ANI raises some—mainly although not solely—practical issues in relation to human rights-in principle. There is no reason however to suggest that in principle human rights contradict AI of limited autonomy. We have to identify the specific types of ANI applications which give rise to such risks so that AI governance mechanisms will have to step in. With AGI and ASI however, things are different.

The critical question is not whether AGI and ASI will violate any specific human rights, as we cannot be aware of the given applications of these two types of AI but whether their mere come into existence threatens the human-centric role of human rights law, or not.

As mentioned above, human rights have a certain normative status within international law, on the basis of which they could even prohibit certain technological advances, once the latter threaten the area of interest of human rights. What should be the case then with AGI and ASI, up to the extent that they can be threatening for the superiority of human intelligence and for the human-centric world of ours? The human-centrism of our world is based on the self-obvious—until now—perception that us, humans are the dominant and more developed form of "being"—intellectually speaking. Our legal systems are also based on this reality. Therefore, how adjustable our legal systems be in the face of such a transformation?

While the question is currently hypothetical, it must not be forgotten that the technological developments, leading to this direction are already underway.

The achievement of AGI or ASI will—to say the least—challenge the prevalent human-centrism.[52] In addition, if the assumption is that AGI and ASI are likely or even may become hostile or non-friendly, towards humans, then not only human-centrism but the whole area of human rights will be threatened; therefore, both in principle and if the risk of non-friendly AGI and ASI is of medium or high probability, in the "name" of human rights we will have to slow down—so that more efficient governance mechanisms are found—or even stop the advance towards these two forms of AI.

In case we can be sure that the risk from AI evolution towards AGI and ASI is low, regarding non-friendly AI, we must focus upon these checks and balances, in accordance with human rights so that AGI and ASI remains safe and beneficial for humans. We will have to answer however to the question of how is it possible to have AGI and ASI without human-centrism being challenged or "transformed" structurally, given that we will stop being the prevalent species. It is rather difficult if not impossible to come up with a convincing answer.

The further difficulty that we must take into account is that the road towards AGI and ASI contains several evolutionary steps or even leaps. That means that it will necessitate very sophisticated and efficient governance mechanisms ahead of AGI

[52] *M. Anderson & S. L. Anderson*, Machine Ethics (2011), pp. 7–13.

and ASI, in order to determine when and where to step in, either in order to slow or to cease AI evolution.

AGI and ASI may establish that from human-centric we will pass to non-human-centric systems and therefore reality or realities. Subsequently our legal systems will stop being human-centric too and therefore, human rights, as jus cogens will cease to exist.

Such a development cannot be legitimized under the human rights' legal regime. Even in case that we would attempt to somehow downgrade the legal status and the normative binding-ness of human rights, by placing them—in a potential future where human and non-human intelligence will co-exist as equal—in a wider framework comprised of human and existential rights of AGI—or ASI—which will constitute jointly the fundamentals of the new legal order, the human-centrism of human rights, the element that by transcending them makes them unique, would be long gone.

Therefore, since human-centrism, is the explicit and implicit factor of legitimacy of our legal systems, human rights cannot "concede" to its transformation up to the extent of vanquishing and thus legitimize AGI or ASI. After all, no legal system can legitimize the overthrow of its foundations.[53]

There is a last question to be-attempted to be briefly—answered: how should we govern the merging of human and AI which is en route to achieving AGI or ASI level? The forms that such merging may take and even more the ways they may develop are unpredictable if not infinite. Therefore, we narrow down schematically these possibilities so that we will manage to draw some conclusions.

A world of such merging will be shifting towards post-humanism or transhumanism. There are many assumptions about how it will look like but of course we are far from certain about any of them. One possibility is the absorption—intentionally or by accident—of human by AI. For the reasons analyzed above this is an unacceptable—according to human rights—potential. Therefore, any efficient, human-rights-oriented governance mechanism will have to impose standards and checks that will safeguard that whatever merging will not evolve towards such a direction.

Such standards could be determined on the basis of the influence of AI on human intelligence, so that it will be determined that human intelligence maintains the overall intellectual activities. Obviously, the design and the implementation of such a mechanism will be technologically and ethically extremely difficult: how can we distinguish between the two and maintain human intelligence as the prevalent one, when we are still puzzled by the definition of existing, solely, human intelligence and consciousness? How is it possible to have two "intelligences" in "your head"? What will be in the end, our own responsibility and what is the concept of the 'self' under such circumstances"?

Until we have concrete answers and understanding of these issues we will be moving—*if we are to comply with human rights*—on a step-by-step approach

[53]Scherer (2016), p. 367.

which—*despite its profound inefficiencies*—either will be based on the approach "I know it when I see it" for human intelligence or will have to slow down the merging of intelligences. This is however an incomplete approach.

Let us think of a second scenario, highlighting some other critical points: let us imagine that somehow all of humanity ends up with the same type of merging of the two intelligences, at a relatively proximate if not identical point, chronically speaking. We all consider ourselves as humans, we just see that we have different capacities and—maybe—problems compared to the past. We also all consider each other as human. Are we still in a human-centric world, valid under human rights? Unless we somehow wake up in a Matrix type of illusion, the answer will most likely be yes. We will not be—considering ourselves and each other as—dehumanized; we will be evolved humans. Human-centrism will be present in this sense, as our collective and personal belief and attitude, albeit in an evolved form.

What is the difference with the first scenario? The first difference is our conscious. While our future belief that we will be leaving in human-centric world may seem illusionary from where we now stand, in the end it is all we have to rely on: our consciousness and the consciousness of the rest. Once we have designed in advance some safety mechanisms we could then advance into the next evolutionary leap. But the even more significant second difference from the previous scenario, in terms of human-centrism, once our consciousness is satisfied that we remain humans, is the equality within the course of such a leap towards evolved humanity.

If we study thoroughly the fundamentals of our legal systems and of human rights, we will see that they are based on at least some extent of relative equality.[54] In order to achieve the whole variety of human rights—including individuals' collective, social, economic, political and cultural rights we need to have some extent of equality which will be prohibiting the gathering of too much strength in too few hands.

This rather vague description becomes clearer not only in relation to present social and economic issues but in relation to potential ontological issues as well: who and what governance mechanism will be able to control and to impose checks and balances over a portion of the population which will evolutionary-speaking have by far surpassed all other humans? The answer is most likely none, apart from the benevolent attitude of this part of the population. Therefore, a human rights'--oriented governance mechanism of AI, tending towards AGI and ASI, in relation to their merging with human intelligence will have to impose a common leap of humanity in order to avoid a potentially catastrophic fragmentation because of ontological inequality.[55]

---

[54]UDHR Preamble: "Whereas recognition of the inherent dignity and of the equal and inalienable rights of all members of the human family is the foundation of freedom, justice and peace in the world," ICCPR, Preamble, "The States Parties to the present Covenant, Considering that, in accordance with the principles proclaimed in the Charter of the United Nations, recognition of the inherent dignity and of the equal and inalienable rights of all members of the human family is the foundation of freedom, justice and peace in the world".

[55]The issue is further mentioned in the concluding remarks of the book.

If such equality cannot be achieved, the outcome will be the division between humans and post-humans or trans-humans; between the plebe and a superior species. That again will be a non-human-centric reality, within which eventually, due to the ontological differences may emerge two different ontologically—partially—species, establishing deeply fractured societies.

Therefore, human rights excuse such a leap only if their social aspect is honored as well, so that cohesion and evolution will prevail, instead of division.

6.4 Conclusions

In this chapter the effort was to bring human rights at the center of the proposed AI governance system. As AI expands to a wide area of functions, the determination of the role of AI cannot be conducted on the basis of the relationship between AI and every single human right distinctively, in the framework of a book which approaches the overall relationship between AI and international law. This is why an alternative approach was chosen: following a brief reference to the role and to the status of human rights within international law, the relationship of human rights as guarantors of human-centrism to AI was described.

This relationship aligns with the ontology of AI. In principle the relationship is simpler in terms of ANI and much more complicated in the prospect of AGI and ASI. The main idea is that the preservation of human-centrism should lead to the imposition of certain standards on ANI development, on the basis of potential benefit or risk for human rights as well as to the prevention of the emergence of AGI and ASI both because of the potential risk of unfriendly attitude towards humans and the emergence of non-human-centric world.

There is of course the question of what will happen or may happen with and to human rights once—regardless of any other suggestions—AGI or ASI do emerge. This question is mainly addressed—up to the extent that is it possible to do so—in the last chapter about the potential legal personality of AI entities.

The preservation of human-centrism must impose checks and balances to the merging of human and AI as well. The technological and ethical problems necessitate sophisticated, delicate but still effective and in-depth approaches. Again, the absorption of human intelligence constitutes a risk that must be averted by a careful consideration of research and application of AI, through different intervention means. It was in these regards briefly mentioned that up to the extent that such absorption is averted, the critical issue that must worry us is the preservations of the equality—at least at a certain extent—within our societies and the international community, as otherwise human rights will be fundamentally shaken as well. This issue is touched upon again in the last chapter.

Human rights have until now received more attention in the legal debate in relation to specific AI applications such as, in relation to Autonomous Weapons Systems—AWS'. What we tried to do here was to present an overview of this ongoing, delicate relationship. Having presented that, the next chapter moves onto the discussion about what may emerge as the main threat again the collective security system—although it is difficult to determine which one is the major threat among so many: the emergence of Autonomous Weapons Systems—AWS'.

References

Adams D (2005) The prohibition of widespread rape as jus cogens. San Diego Int Law J 6:357

Alston P (1984) Conjuring up new human rights: a proposal for quality control. Am J Int Law 78:607 et seq

Anderson RJ (2010) Reimagining human rights law: toward global regulation of transnational corporations. Denver Univ Law Rev 88:183

Bassiouni MC (2001) Universal jurisdiction for international crimes: historical perspectives and contemporary practice. Vanderbilt J Int Law 42:81

Brownlie I (1979) Principles of public international law, 3rd edn. Oxford University Press, p 512

Buchanan A (2004) Justice, legitimacy and self-determination, moral foundations of international law. Oxford University Press, p 119

Byers M (1999) Custom, power and the power of rules: international relations and customary international law. Cambridge University Press, p 194

Carozza (2003) "My Friend is a Stranger": the death penalty and the global ius commune of human rights. Tex Law Rev 81:1031

Carozza PG (2008) Human dignity and judicial interpretation of human rights: a reply. Eur J Int Law 19(5):931

Cassese A (1986) International law in a divided world. Clarendon Press, Oxford, pp 377–379

Cassese A (2012) For an enhanced role of jus cogens. In: Cassese A (ed) Realizing Utopia: the future of international law. Oxford University Press, p 166

Chen D (2019) Machine learning and the rule of law. In: Livermore M, Rockmore D (eds) Computational analysis of law

Conklin WE (2012) The peremptory norms of the international community. Eur J Int Law 23:837

Crawford J (2002) The International Law Commission's articles on state responsibility: introduction, text, and commentaries. Cambridge University Press, pp 148–150, 158–160

Crawford J (2006) Creation of states in international law. Clarendon Press, p 102

Criddle EJ, Decent EF (2009) A fiduciary theory of jus cogens. Yale J Int Law 34:331

Domingo R (2012) The new global human community. Chic J Int Law 12(2):563

Fitzmaurice G (1973) The future of public international law and of the international legal system in the circumstances of today. Institut De Droit International, p 323

Janis MW (2003) An introduction to international law. Aspen Publishers, pp 62–63

Kamminga MT (1992) Inter-state accountability for violations of human rights. University of Pennsylvania Press, p 163

Ogilvy G (2009) Belhas V. Ya'alon: the case for a jus cogens exception to the foreign sovereign immunities act. J Int Bus Law 8:169

Omohundro S (2008) The basic AI drives. In: Wang P, Goertzel B, Franklin S (eds) Artificial General Intelligence 2008: proceedings of the first AGI conference, pp 483–492

Orakhelashvili A (2005) The impact of peremptory norms on the interpretation and application of United Nations Security Council Resolutions. Eur J Int Law 16:59

Parker K, Neylon LB (1989) Jus cogens: compelling the law of human rights. Hastings Int Comp Law Rev 12:414

Perkins SC (1992) Guide to researching international human rights law. Case West Reserve J Int Law 24:379

Petsche M (2010) Jus cogens as a vision of the international legal order. Penn State Int Law Rev 29:233

Provost R (2004) International human rights and humanitarian law. Cambridge University Press, pp 16–17
Rozakis CL (1976) The concept of jus cogens in the law of treaties. North-Holland Publications Co., Amsterdam, p 1
Scherer MU (2016) Regulating artificial intelligence systems: risks, challenges, competencies, and strategies. Harv J Law Technol 29:353 et seq
Schwarzenberger G (1965) International jus cogens? Tex Law Rev 43:455
Schwebel SM (1991) Human rights in the world court. Vanderbilt J Transnatl Law 24:945
Shleton D (2006) Normative hierarchy in international law. Am J Int Law 100:291
Spagnoli F (2008) The globalization of human rights law: why do human rights need international law? Tex Wesleyan Law Rev 14:317
Spijkers O (2009–2010) What's running the world: global values, international law, and the United Nations. Interdisciplinary J Hum Rights Law 4:77
Stamatopoulou E (1999) The importance of the Universal Declaration of Human Rights in the past and future of the United Nation's Human Rights efforts. ILSA J Int Comp Law 5:281
Tams CJ (2005) Enforcing obligations erga omnes in international law. Cambridge University Press, New York, p 141
Tegmark M (2017) Life 3.0, being human in the age of artificial intelligence. Random House, Grk. Edition
Teng Y-S (2012) Chapter 9 who is afraid of human rights? A Taiwanese perspective. IUS Gentium 16:155
Trnavci G (2005) The meaning and scope of the law of nations in the context of the Alien Tort claims act and international law. Univ Pa J Int Econ Law 26:194
Verdross A (1966) Jus dispositivum and jus cogens in international law. Am J Int Law 60:55
Weisburd AM (1995) The emptiness of the concept of jus cogens, as illustrated by the war in Bosnia-Herzegovina. Mich J Int Law 17:1
Weston BH (2008) Human rights and nation-building in cross-cultural settings. Maine Law Rev 60:318

Chapter 7
AI and International Security- the Case of AWS' and Collective Security System

7.1 Introduction

The Terminator and Matrix are prominent "pop" culture expressions of our fear for a war- one that we will lose- against the machines that we will have created; it currently seems as more than a remote future; or even as an unlikely one. Why would we do something so stupid as to entrust our safety on AI that we may not be able to control after all? While our instinct of self-preservation may make us more reasonable, our history is full of shortsighted plans, miscalculations, catastrophic impulses and choices, mistakes. We have not yet even completely left behind us the fear of a nuclear holocaust; on the contrary, despite the existence of a rather viable system of deterrence it seems that in the framework of a disorganized- at large- collective security system fears of more extended or limited nuclear war emerge again.

Things could become more troublesome with AWS's than with nuclear weapons, for various reasons: first, as is already mentioned, AI development may very well move beyond and under the radar of any governance mechanism; secondly, currently there is no such governance mechanism internationally; thirdly, while with nuclear weapons we know who possesses them and therefore we expect- and until now this is the case- a certain extent of predictability, Autonomous Weapons Systems- i.e. AWS'- may be inherently unpredictable. Fourthly, any weapons- even nuclear ones- can be transformed into AWS's and therefore the unpredictability of AI could expand to a significantly wide spectrum of our weaponry.

The development of AWS' constitutes an almost irresistible quest for most major powers-and not only them. AWS "promise' wars and military strikes which will be more precise- and therefore more "humane" for their advocates[1]- more effective in

[1]Christopher P. Toscano, "Friend of Humans": An Argument for Developing Autonomous Weapons Systems, at p. 3.

T. Tzimas, *Legal and Ethical Challenges of Artificial Intelligence from an International Law Perspective*, Law, Governance and Technology Series 46,
https://doi.org/10.1007/978-3-030-78585-7_7

military terms, cheaper, with fewer soldiers involved- therefore in principle with less political cost- and eventually with fewer of the problems that humans have to cope with, when they fight against one another.[2]

In terms of the art of war, AWS' present therefore, some hard to ignore potential advantages: avoidance of human feelings, system of systems and swarming function, communication and mobility, speed beyond human reaction times.[3]

In fact, AI is expected to re-shape the "art of war" in various ways; the presence of humans on battlefield will decrease due to the presence of combat machines, the capacity to predict the outcome of wars will increase- discouraging therefore possibly decision- makers from resorting to war- whereas on the other hand, the over- reliance on the speed of AI bears the risk of reducing the timeframe of decision- making, leading to further escalation.[4]

We need to keep in mind that according to the 2017 report of the Stockholm International Peace Research Institute, already exist 154 weapon systems with some type of autonomy in relation to targeting.[5]

Therefore, the basis for what could develop into reliance on AWS's[6] is in principle here. It is on such grounds that AWS' raise concerns about dangers for international peace and security. AWS's constitute new and potentially unpredictable factors within the collective security system.

It must be mentioned that although more impressive or dramatic is the discussion about lethal autonomous weapon systems- LAWS's- the legal debate which is articulated below is related to all autonomous weapon systems- AWS's- given that even without lethal force, both international security may be endangered and critical legal issues in general emerge.

AWS's are not the only "place" where collective security system and AI may potentially meet, given the expansion of AI on the one hand and the comprehension of a variety of events as potential threats against international peace and security. From the participation of AI in decision-making to cyber-operations and from flaws in AI to social disruption and -potentially-mass poverty, the direct or indirect impact of AI on international peace and therefore on the collective security system, AI is expanding its presence as a factor of potential endangerment of the collective security system, analogically to its applications. AWS's however constitute the most obvious and direct potential risk. This is why they are analyzed here in relationship to the collective security system: both because of their impact, as well

---

[2]Marchant et al. (2011), p. 275; Shaw (2005), pp. 87–88.

[3]UN Institute for Disarmament Research (UNIDIR), The Weaponization of Increasingly Autonomous Technologies: Concerns, Characteristics and Definitional Approaches, 2017, at pp. 15–17. Tariq Samad and Thomas Parisini, 2011, "Systems of Systems" in T. Samad and A.M. Annaswamy (eds.), The Impact of Control Technology, http://ieeecss.org/sites/ieeecss.org/files/documents/IoCT-Part3-04SystemsOfSystems.pdf.

[4]Spindel (2009), p. 7.

[5]Boulanin and Verbruggen (2017).

[6]P.W. Singer, Wired for War: The Robotics Revolution and Conflict In The 21st Century 64 (2009). Ronald Arkin, Governing Lethal Behavior in Autonomous Robots 6 (2009).

as because they condense all these characteristics of AI that can potentially pose threats to international peace and security when applied in different areas.

We can roughly distinguish between three modes of control: direct control by the human operator, shared control or supervisory control.[7] Obviously AWS's become more impressive as we move towards lesser human control on the one hand, whereas on the other hand, the more unpredictable that the environment is, the greater the risks which emerge, especially when coinciding with more distant mode of control.

This chapter is devoted to the relationship between AI and the collective security system. The goal is to identify the complexities and the ramifications of these two concepts per se- i.e. as concepts. Following this analysis, a more detailed one about the ramifications of AWS on international humanitarian law -IHL- and human rights are examined. In order to move forward with the analysis, some defining elements of the collective security system are examined and then the equivalent ones of AWS'. On such grounds the relationship of the two is articulated.

7.2 The Collective Security System

The scope of this part is not to present in its complete legal details the collective security system but solely to describe some of its defining elements so that then its relationship with AI will be presented. The collective security system constitutes not only foundation of the post-World-War II legal order and of the UN Charter aspiration for the maintenance of international peace and security but also one of the main innovations- regarding the specific form that it takes.

While attempts to formulate types of collective security systems can be traced long before the post- World War II era, the collective security system of the UN Charter, in spite of its failures has been proven efficient at least until now and in terms of preventing a cataclysmic global war.[8]

---

[7]International Committee of the Red Cross, Autonomy, artificial intelligence and robotics: Technical aspects of human control (August 2019), at pp. 8–9.

[8]Characteristic is the European Conference following the Napoleonic wars. Koskenniemi (1996), pp. 481–482; Morton (2002), pp. 80–81; Gordon (1984–1985), pp. 271–272. See also the League of Nations:

> "Article 10: The Members of the League undertake to respect and preserve as against external aggression the territorial integrity and existing political independence of all Members of the League. In case of any such aggression or in case of any threat or danger of such aggression the Council shall advise upon the means by which this obligation shall be fulfilled" και.

Article 11: Any war or threat of war, whether immediately affecting any of the Members of the League or not, is hereby declared a matter of concern to the whole League, and the League shall take any action that may be deemed wise and effectual to safeguard the peace of nations. In case any such emergency should arise the Secretary General shall on the request of any Member of the League forthwith summon a meeting of the Council It is also declared to be the friendly right of each

The inspiration behind the collective security system has been the avoidance of a solely power- politics oriented formation of the international community.[9] The UN approach to the collective security system is in this sense ecumenical- it endorses the whole of the international community instead of solely state actors or member states of the UN- and flexible as it attempts to confront all dangers and threats against international peace and security instead of solely the ones emerging from aggression or armed attack more specifically.[10]

The collective security system is primarily a "recipe" or in other words, a governance scheme for an institutional regulation so that the security of all states is guaranteed in case of attack from any state against any other; any incident of this

---

Member of the League to bring to the attention of the Assembly or of the Council any circumstance whatever affecting international relations which threatens to disturb international peace or the good understanding between nations upon which peace depends.

> Article 12: The Members of the League agree that, if there should arise between them any dispute likely to lead to a rupture they will submit the matter either to arbitration or judicial settlement or to enquiry by the Council, and they agree in no case to resort to war until three months after the award by the arbitrators or the judicial decision, or the report by the Council. In any case under this Article the award of the arbitrators or the judicial decision shall be made within a reasonable time, and the report of the Council shall be made within six months after the submission of the dispute.

Yale law School, Lillian Goldman law library: The Avalon Project, Documents in law, History and Diplomacy, (http://avalon.law.yale.edu/20th_century/leagcov.asp#art10, access. 03-7-2020).

[9]Fowler (2003), p. 299.

[10]UN Charter, Article 2 "Article 2

The Organization and its Members, in pursuit of the Purposes stated in Article 1, shall act in accordance with the following Principles.

The Organization is based on the principle of the sovereign equality of all its Members.

All Members, in order to ensure to all of them the rights and benefits resulting from membership, shall fulfill in good faith the obligations assumed by them in accordance with the present Charter.

All Members shall settle their international disputes by peaceful means in such a manner that international peace and security, and justice, are not endangered.

All Members shall refrain in their international relations from the threat or use of force against the territorial integrity or political independence of any state, or in any other manner inconsistent with the Purposes of the United Nations.

All Members shall give the United Nations every assistance in any action it takes in accordance with the present Charter, and shall refrain from giving assistance to any state against which the United Nations is taking preventive or enforcement action.

The Organization shall ensure that states which are not Members of the United Nations act in accordance with these Principles so far as may be necessary for the maintenance of international peace and security.

Nothing contained in the present Charter shall authorize the United Nations to intervene in matters which are essentially within the domestic jurisdiction of any state or shall require the Members to submit such matters to settlement under the present Charter; but this principle shall not prejudice the application of enforcement measures under Chapter Vll...

Article 39

The Security Council shall determine the existence of any threat to the peace, breach of the peace, or act of aggression and shall make recommendations, or decide what measures shall be taken in accordance with Articles 41 and 42, to maintain or restore international peace and security."

type is supposed to provoke the response of all other states so that collective self-defense takes place;[11] in a wider understanding, collective security system may be described as the area of international relations which is designed so they it can neutralize threats against international peace and security.[12]

As system, it is institutionally built on three pillars: article 2, paragraph 4, article 51 about self-defense and chapter VII[13] about UN SC authority to act against threats towards international peace.

The collective security system is an attempt in the long-term, to surpass the weaknesses of a fully de-centralized and states-oriented system of international law enforcement. The reparation of injustice does not rely solely on the injured state but on the international community as a whole.[14] The system prerequisites and attempts to achieve that all actors comprehend the fact that they are bound together and they will be acting accordingly and responsibly.[15]

The main goal of the collective security system is to institutionalize and regulate power politics as well as to counter various threats against international peace and security of different types, instead of inter-state aggression solely.[16] Therefore, it is crucial to maintain the variety of threats against peace as contained and minimal as possible.

The protection of the fundamental goals of the UN Charter, as they are included in the maintenance of international peace and security, exceed the mere absence of military conflict; they include also the safeguarding of the international community against the risks to human, social, economic, cultural rights, as well as in face of other potential threats -i.e. natural disasters- which are to be determined by the UN SC; such determination is supposed to be made by these same organs, as well as how to counter them, in the UN framework.

There is a wider debate about whether the threats in the face of which the collective security system is activated are equal or the absence of military conflict supersedes the rest of them. The opinions of experts differ and are contradictory, as well as the practice of the UN organs themselves;[17] it is certain however, that in spite of any thoughts about the inequality or not of the threats against international peace, the threats which the UN collective security system counters exceed military conflict. They include all threats again the fundamental goals and principles of the UN

[11]Claude Jr. (1986), p. 51.

[12]White (2002), p. 237.

[13]Delahunty (2007), pp. 888–889.

[14]H. Morgenthau, *Politics Among Nations*, (Peter Labella and John m. Morriss, 1949), at p. 232.

[15]Mearsheimer (1998), pp. 357–358, Cuellar (2004), pp. 218–219; Kirgis Jr. (1995), pp. 506–507; Shklar (1986), p. 125;
Hoffmann (1987), pp. 89–94.

[16]Graham (1946), pp. 57, 71; Henkin (1989), pp. 58–59.

[17]*L. Henkin, International Law: Politics, Values and Functions*, at p. 146; Le Mon and Taylor (2004), pp. 203, 205; ICJ Certain Expenses of the United Nations (Article 17, paragraph 2, of the Charter), Advisory Opinion, (1962), 168. *N. D. Arnison, International Law and Non- Intervention*, at p. 203.

Charter: gross, human rights' violations,[18] colonial and racist regimes,[19] apartheid, terrorism, failed states, violations of international humanitarian law, poverty, climate change, pandemics are only a few of the conditions which have been over time dealt with as such threats.[20]

The question is therefore whether AWS's may be considered as a threat against the imperatives of the collective security system or not. In order to move onto such assessment, we need first to analyze some ontological elements of AWS' and define them. Then we can conclude if AWS' contravene the collective security system.

7.3 The Autonomy of AWS'

The term "autonomy", when used in relation to ANI and AWS must be approached with the necessary caution: on the one hand it is defined differently by various analysts and institutions, given that it is under research and evolving, therefore partially unknown concerning its exact aspects and manifestations; on the other hand, AI autonomy is not identical to human autonomy, as mentioned before. These mean that in terms of accurate description of AWS's, a lot of work remains to be done.

Nevertheless, some central characteristics of AWS' can be identified: self- governance, operation without direct human control and function in unknown environment are the main ones.[21] As of today, the extent of autonomy is limited although efforts for AI that is designed to "think, see and react increasingly like humans" are already under way.[22] Autonomy in AWS's increases the more that human distances from the decision-making "loop".

Several of the so-called "smart" systems are practically an extension of the human operator's capacities, albeit enhanced with the technical capacities of AI. Therefore, autonomy extends in a wide variety of spectrum, from systems which rely completely on the human operator at all stages of their function, to future systems

---

[18]Reisman (2008), p. 78; Duffy (2005), pp. 178, 184. UN S.C. Res. 232, (1966), para. 1, UN S.C. Res. 688, (1991), para. 1, UN S.C. Res. 794, (1992), para. 10.

[19]Shestack (1997–1998), p. 566.

[20]Stern (1996), p. 587; B. B.-Ghali, *An Agenda for Peace: Preventive Diplomacy, Peacemaking and Peace-Keeping: Report of the Secretary-General*, U.N. GAOR, 47th Sess., Agenda Item 10, P3, U.N. Doc. A/47/277 (1992); Freedman (1998), pp. 52–54; Bislev (2004), pp. 281–282; Dunn (1994), pp. 3–15; Jones (2004), p. 95; Ullmann (1983), pp. 133–138; Mathews (1989), pp. 162–177; Thomas (2002), p. 113; Renner (1996), p. 83.

[21]Panos J Antsaklis, 'Setting the Stage: Some Autonomous Thoughts on Autonomy' (Paper presented at the IEEE International Conference on Robotics and Automation, Gaithersburg, 14-17 September 1998) 520.

[22]Tim Weiner, New Model Army Soldier Rolls Closer to Battle, N.Y. TIMES, Feb. 16, 2005.

which will be able to carry out and implement a military mission with limited-if any-and optional only, human interference.[23]

The evolution of the autonomy of AI is accelerating quite impressively, from the development of AWS that can patrol the De-Militarized Zone in Korea-DMZ-[24] to unmanned weapon systems operating at all domains of modern warfare.[25] While AWS have not yet acquired the status of general or super intelligence and therefore cannot act without some type of human control, the human control becomes "thinner" in several ways.

While AI is already present in several weapons in the form of ANI, such as laser-guided missiles, DARPA- guided weapons and bullets and other similar systems, and while the weapons can adapt in order to accomplish the pre- determined goal, the goal is set by the human operator.[26]

The actual level of autonomy constitutes a matter of assessment not only on the basis of the initial design of the AI system but also in terms of de facto human intervention, in light of the military necessities; the tendency is to rely on AI, with limited only, human intervention.[27]

It must be kept in mind however that in case we define AWS's from their mere capacity to be activated without human interference, other such weapons have come to exist as well, with landmines being a characteristic case.[28] In order talk about AWS's we will need obviously a more extended and more sophisticated level of autonomy. In a way, with AWS's the distinction between automation and autonomy is reproduced: for example, in landmines' case, the mechanism is activated without human interference but the predictability of it is profound, regardless of the environment: either it will be activated and cause an explosion or it will fail to "work" properly. With AWS's we expect a capacity to demonstrate adjustment in different environments by changing accordingly their behavior. The element of adjustment is the critical one, although it is exactly that, that leads to unpredictability as well.

[23]Beard (2014), pp. 626–627.

In the intermediate of the two there are several cases of weapons which can perform functions such search, detection, evaluation, tracking, engagement and use of lethal force.

Ibid at pp. 630–631.

[24]Kim Tae-gyu, Machine Gun-Armed Robots to Guard DMZ, KOREA TIMES, June 24, 2010.

[25]Michael T. Klare, Autonomous Weapons Systems and the Laws of War, Arms Control Association, (2019 March), (https://www.armscontrol.org/act/2019-03/features/autonomous-weapons-systems-laws-war).

[26]Laton (2016), pp. 102–103.

[27]The human is certainly part of the decision making but mainly in the initial programming of the robot. During the actual operation of the machine, the operator really only exercises veto power, and a decision to override a robot's decision must be made in only half a second, with few willing to challenge what they view as the better judgment of the machine.

P.W. Singer, War of the Machines: A Dramatic Growth in the Military Use of Robots Brings Evolution in Their Conception, SCI. AM.., July 2010, at 63.

[28]Lewis (2015), pp. 1319–1320.

This is why for several analysts, AWS's must not include all weapons, which make use of AI but only those with autonomous or semi- autonomous targeting and/or deployment of force.[29] AWS are the ones with the capacity to "operate without any form of external control for an extended period",[30] as well as with the capacity to make their own decisions.[31]

As it is articulated in the open letter to ban autonomous weapons, "Autonomous weapons select and engage targets without human intervention. They might include, for example, armed quadcopters that can search for and eliminate people meeting certain pre-defined criteria, but do not include cruise missiles or remotely piloted drones for which humans make all targeting decisions."[32]

The crux of the discussion in AWS's, as is the case in general with AI is exactly that we cannot have efficiency in the sense of adjustment and speed of reactions without autonomy and autonomy without unpredictability.[33] The advantage of the expanding autonomy of AWS's is that they will be able to evolve as programs programming themselves, through machine learning and artificial neural networks:[34] "The program selects symbols and creates a chain through trial and error to create a solution to the presented problem... The advantage of a self-programming system is that it can function in an environment that is constantly changing and where the information about the unfolding events is incomplete."[35] This is also where the foundations of AI capacity in the battlefield are established. We need AWS's to be able to evolve and adjust so that gradually they can match and exceed human efficiency. This is both the advantage and the risk.

As Dr. Hagström suggests, the term "autonomy" describes "a system which, without direct influence from an operator, can act in an unknown environment or handle unexpected events".[36] He further comments that as technology progresses, the boundaries between automation and autonomy become thinner; what programmers do is to build a "universe", within which the AI entity may function with greater extent of predictability even if some of the "internal" procedures of the AI entity are not understood by us humans. On the contrary, once out of their predetermined "universe", due to unexpected events, AI systems have to demonstrate

---

[29]*HOUSE OF LORDS, Select Committee on Artificial Intelligence*, at paras. 334–335.

[30]Noorman and Johnson (2014), p. 52.

[31]Gary D. Solis, The Law of Armed Conflict: International Humanitarian Law in War 535 (2d ed. 2016); Grut (2013), pp. 6–7.

[32]Open Letter on Autonomous Weapons. International Joint Conference on Artificial Intelligence (IJCAI), Future of Life Institute, 2015, https://futureoflife.org/open-letter-autonomous-weapons/.

[33]Wendell Wallach, Predictability and Lethal Autonomous Weapons Systems (LAWS), IEET (Apr. 16, 2016), https://ieet.org/index.php/IEET2/print/11873.

[34]Wolfgang Golubski, Genetic Programming: a Parallel Approach, in 2311 SOFT-WARE 2002: Computing in an Imperfect World, 167, 195 (2002).

[35]Krupiy (2017), p. 10.

[36]ICRC, Autonomous Weapon Systems: Implications of Increasing Autonomy in the Critical Functions of Weapons, Characteristics of autonomous weapon systems, Speaker's summary, Dr Martin Hagström, Swedish Defence Research Agency, Sweden, at p. 23.

greater autonomy which necessarily brings with it more extended unpredictability as well.[37]

The different autonomy levels have been described as differentiated human types of presence in the loop; "in the loop--a human is in control of the machine... on the loop-- a human may be involved in the machine's actions but does not have to be; and ...out of the loop--the autonomous robot selects and engages targets itself... The fourth loop, the fully autonomous machine that is not yet developed, would be a "loop of its own.""[38]

Until the 4th loop is reached, the most puzzling the 3rd one. The problem with it is that while the activation of the weapon system lies with the human operator, the selection of targets and the engagement with them is done by the AI, a condition which blurs the matters of accountability and liability.[39]

Further, the presence of human on the loop, despite being in principle necessary still does not offer necessarily complete guarantees in terms of AWS's deployment, due to potential "automation bias – or over-trust in the machine... lack of operator situational awareness... moral buffer, where the human operator shifts moral responsibility and accountability to the machine as a perceived legitimate authority."[40]

In the wider framework of the inherent unpredictability and the "black box" effect, attention must be paid to the emergence of accidents because of the complexity of such systems and the hidden reactions.[41] Given that AWS's are based on machine -learning and neural networks, which are inherently complicated, the "black box" effect is projected on AWS's, causing the relevant risk of unpredictability.[42]

Things get more complicated when the level autonomy is projected onto the need for moral judgments and for distinctions conducted in the battlefield as could be for example the one between civilians and combatants.[43] In such a framework, the critical threshold is placed not on whether AWS's can select and engage with the

[37] *Dr Martin Hagström, Swedish Defence Research Agency, Sweden*, at p. 24.

[38] Reitinger (2015–2016), p. 91.

[39] *Reitinger, Algorithmic Choice And Superior Responsibility: Closing The Gap Between Liability and Lethal Autonomy by Defining the Line Between Actors and Tools*, at pp. 93–94.

[40] International Committee of the Red Cross, Autonomy, artificial intelligence and robotics: Technical aspects of human control (August 2019), at p. 9; Cummings (2006).

[41] United Nations Office for Disarmament Affairs, Study on Armed Unmanned Aerial Vehicles Prepared on the Recommendation of the Advisory Board on Disarmament Matters, United Nations, October 2015, pp. 47–48.

[42] UNIDIR, The Weaponization of Increasingly Autonomous Technologies: Concerns, Characteristics and Definitional Approaches, (2017), https://www.unidir.org/files/publications/pdfs/the-weaponization-of-increasingly-autonomous-technologies-concerns-characteristics-and-definitional-approaches-en-689.pdf.

[43] Boothby (2012), p. 586.

target but in whether the decision to kill- or to strike generally- is taken by the AI or not.[44]

While we tend to identify predictability with the design and the machine- training of AI -which in principle is a correct assumption- the predictability of AI in general and of AWS's specifically, is associated with the environment and its nature and with the nature of the task.[45]

Further, we have to take into account that with AWS's new questions are posed which we have never thought of answering with humans. With AWS's we need to "quantify" unpredictability, whereas with humans, it is a predisposed input. When we try to "measure" the extent of acceptable input we have to answer both how can we quantify predictability, in inherently unpredictable environments and what extent of unpredictability is acceptable.[46]

The legal risk is whether AWS can be trusted, in light on the one hand of their expanding autonomy and on the other hand of the "black box" effect of AI intelligence.

In addition, the complexities of AWS refer mostly to the implications from AWS's governance. Namely, the ontology of AI,[47] the requirement for speed- *the expected advantage from the use of AI*- the de- humanization of war and the expanding autonomy mean that, given that war is righteously considered to be the continuation of politics by other means, the greater autonomy of weapons system, even at the tactical level, the more that political decision- making is "usurped" by AI.

In this sense we need to address the issue of AWS's not solely from the purely military view but also from the perspective of the political implications; that is whether in our political and therefore ethical models is it acceptable to have political decisions determined by non- human entities too. The decisions which are taken and implemented at the tactical level in the course of a military conflict very often have an impact on the wider strategic and political situation. Therefore, an ever-growing autonomy of AI leads to implications not only at the specific area where AI is functioning but on the wider decision- making procedures as well and subsequently to the collective security system as well, since in several ways, new actors gradually emerge or new means of actions for pre-existing actors.

---

[44]ICRC, Autonomous Weapon Systems: Implications of Increasing Autonomy in the Critical Functions of Weapons, Focusing the debate on autonomous weapon systems: A new approach to linking technology and IHL, Speaker's summary, Lt Col. Alan Schuller, Stockton Center for the Study of International Law, US Naval War College, at p. 26.

[45]International Committee of the Red Cross, Autonomy, artificial intelligence and robotics: Technical aspects of human control (August 2019), at p. 11.

[46]Vincent Boulanin, Neil Davison, Netta Goussac and Moa Peldán Carlsson, Limits on Autonomy in Weapon Systems, Stockholm International Peace Research Institute, The International Committee of the Red Cross, (2020 June), at pp. 1–20 (file:///C:/Users/User/Downloads/icrc_sipri_limits_on_autonomy_june_2020.pdf).

[47]Ian Goodfellow and Nicolas Papernot, Is attacking machine learning easier than defending it?. (2017, February 15) (http://www.cleverhans.io/security/privacy/ml/2017/02/15/why-attacking-machine-learning-is-easier-than-defending-it.html, access. 06-01-2020).

In terms of governance of AWS and of the subsequent impact on the collective security system, the risks emerge from a combination of factors: the low cost for the creation of such weapons, their spread globally both to state and non- state actors, their lethal capacity, the potential unpredictability and the prospect of arms race due to their potential success. This last element constitutes a critical factor in terms of the temptation of states as well as of other actors to manipulate whatever guarantees will be imposed so that they might gain the military and tactical advantage over their potential enemies.

In addition, and given the lack of transparent control regarding machine-learning and AWS testing, since we lack both the technical capacity and the governance mechanisms internationally, there is always the question of how credible will any tests for AWS's are going to be even if we try to impose some. In addition, an arms race may make the compliance of states with the norms of the Additional Protocol I and more specifically with articles 35(2) and 36, less attractive.[48]

Because of the acknowledgement of the fact that states will not stop moving forward with AWS's development several analysts try to distinguish between different types of AWS, such as for example between offensive and defensive weapons.[49]

This is not the end of the debate however about AWS's categorizations; the "weaponization" of AI can take such a variety of forms, many of which are novel and non- conventional, that the line between non- military and military uses is blurred dangerously.

An indicative paradigm is the potential use of AI in cyber- operations through "sentinel" systems. Sentinel systems will be able to make use of artificial neural networks, which will be consisted of "perceptrons": "[A] small number of perceptrons combined together can learn and solve interesting problems. But neural nets can consist of a large number of artificial neurons. Therefore neural nets provide a functionality of massively parallel learning and decision-making. Their most

[48]Article 35 "1. In any armed conflict, the right of the Parties to the conflict to choose methods or means of warfare is not unlimited. 2. It is prohibited to employ weapons, projectiles and material and methods of warfare of a nature to cause superfluous injury or unnecessary suffering. 3. It is prohibited to employ methods or means of warfare which are intended, or may be expected, to cause widespread, longterm and severe damage to the natural environment."

Article 36: "In the study, development, acquisition or adoption of a new weapon, means or method of warfare, a High Contracting Party is under an obligation to determine whether its employment would, in some or all circumstances, be prohibited by this Protocol or by any other rule of international law applicable to the High Contracting Party."

"Unfortunately, very few *284 States undertake such an examination before employing new means and methods of warfare, despite the fact that the obligation relates to the initial stages, i.e., the study and 'development' of a new weapon."

Marie Jacobsson, Modern Weaponry and Warfare: The Application of Article 36 of Additional Protocol I by Governments, in The Law of War in the 21st Century: Weaponry and the Use of Force 184 (Anthony M. Helm ed., 2006) (Vol. 82, US Naval War College International Law Studies).

[49]ICRC, Autonomous Weapon Systems: Implications of Increasing Autonomy in the Critical Functions of Weapons, at p.10.

distinguished feature is the speed of operation. They are well suited for learning pattern recognition, for classification, for selection of responses to attacks, etc."[50]

The idea is that Sentinels will be using machine learning methods in order to identify and counter new threats much more effectively and quicker than human specialists. The 'offensive" version will be an "infiltrator".[51]

AI enters the domain of the cyberspace and is already playing significant role in offensive and defensive operations, which have kinetic and cyber consequences as well. The development of AI weapons in conjunction with cyberspace –and the subsequent weaponization of cyberspace- bears the potential of military operations with indiscriminate victims, due to the number of people who rely on the cyberspace for their well- being or survival, with very limited practical capacity to effectively control such operations, once unleashed and with equally limited capacity to attribute responsibility to the initiator of any such attack.[52]

It becomes clear how AWS's may acquire an ever-expanding role, with very much limited capacity on behalf of the collective security system to identify and tackle such threats with even indiscriminate victims and consequences.

Summing up, the tendency of AWS's autonomy -at least in its more developed forms- moves towards unsupervised function,[53] through self-governance, lack of direct human control or supervision and operation in changing and unstructured environments.[54] This growing autonomy must be taken into account in order to assess AWS's in light of the collective security system. In order to draw a more complete picture on this matter, in the next part, the definitions of AWS's are analyzed so that the conclusions can present an overview of the relationship between the concepts of the collective security system and of AWS's.

7.4 Definitions of AWS's

The definition of AWS's vary mostly on the basis of autonomy of the weapons' systems. The US Department of Defense defines autonomous weapons as "A weapon system that, once activated, can select and engage targets without further intervention by a human operator. This includes human-supervised autonomous weapon systems that are designed to allow human operators to override operation

---

[50]Tyugu (2011), p. 98.

[51]*Laton, Manhattan_Project.Exe: A Nuclear Option for the Digital Age*, at pp. 114–118.

[52]Carr (2013), p. 32.

[53]Krupiy (2015), p. 148.

[54]Panos J Antsaklis, 'Setting the Stage: Some Autonomous Thoughts on Autonomy' (Paper presented at the IEEE International Conference on Robotics and Automation, Gaithersburg, 14-17 September 1998), at p. 520.

of the weapon system, but can select and engage targets without further human input after activation"[55]

The Naval Research Advisory Committee (NRAC), in its report "Unmanned Systems Roadmap" defined four levels of autonomy: Human Operated, Human Delegated, Human Supervised, and Fully Autonomous. However, the Roadmap notes that in contrast to automatic systems, which simply follow a set of preprogrammed directions to achieve a predetermined goal, autonomous systems "are self-directed towards a goal in that they do not require outside control, but rather are governed by laws and strategies that direct their behavior."[56]

The UK Ministry of Defense offers a distinction between automated and autonomous weapons according to which automated or automatic are the systems which "in response to inputs from one or more sensors, is programmed to logically follow a predefined set of rules in order to provide an outcome. Knowing the set of rules under which it is operating means that its output is predictable."[57]

An autonomous system in contrast is a system "capable of understanding higher-level intent and direction. From this understanding and its perception of its environment, such a system is able to take appropriate action to bring about a desired state. It is capable of deciding a course of action, from a number of alternatives, without depending on human oversight and control, although these may still be present. Although the overall activity of an autonomous unmanned aircraft will be predictable, individual actions may not be."[58]

The UK threshold is quite high in the sense that prerequisites the non- dependence on human control. Other states' definitions lower the threshold, acknowledging the possibility of human control while others insist on its total absence.[59]

The Dutch definition refers to AWS's as weapons "that, without human intervention, selects and engages targets matching certain predefined criteria, following a human decision to deploy the weapon on the understanding that an attack, once launched, cannot be stopped by human intervention."[60] The definition imposes two preconditions namely both the selection and engagement of targets and their capacity not to be controlled by humans, narrowing therefore its range.

For France, "Lethal autonomous weapons are fully autonomous systems. [...] LAWS should be understood as implying a total absence of human supervision, meaning there is absolutely no link (communication or control) with the military

---

[55]Department of Defense United States of America, 2012.DoD Directive 3000.09, November 21, 2012.

[56]Captain George Galdorisi, Keeping Humans in the Loop, Vol. 141/2/1,344, Proceedings, (2015, February), (https://www.usni.org/magazines/proceedings/2015/february/keeping-humans-loop#footnotes).

[57]*HOUSE OF LORDS, Select Committee on Artificial Intelligence*, at box 10.

[58]*HOUSE OF LORDS, Select Committee on Artificial Intelligence*, at Box 10.

[59]*HOUSE OF LORDS, Select Committee on Artificial Intelligence*, at Box 11.

[60]Government of the Netherlands, 2017, "Examination of Various Dimensions of Emerging Technologies in the Area of Lethal Autonomous Weapons Systems, in the Context of the Objectives and Purposes of the Convention", document CCW/GGE.1/2017/WP.2 of 9 October.

chain of command. [...] The delivery platform of a LAWS would be capable of moving, adapting to its land, marine or aerial environments and targeting and firing a lethal effector (bullet, missile, bomb, etc.) without any kind of human intervention or validation. [...] LAWS would most likely possess self-learning capabilities."[61]

Various other definitions have been proposed for AWS's, all of which are built on the idea of different levels of autonomy. Indicatively, for the ICRC, "Any weapon system with autonomy in its critical functions. That is, a weapon system that can select (i.e. search for or detect, identify, track, select) and attack (i.e. use force against, neutralize, damage or destroy) targets without human intervention."[62]

The fore- mentioned definitions incline us towards weapon system that can exercise critical functions without human intervention and more specifically with the capacity to adapt to unknown environment or to complete a pre- determined mission by choosing the most suitable means, again without human intervention or to choose the necessary tactical goals in a wider strategy and take life and death decisions. These functions, roughly speaking indicate different levels of autonomy.

7.5 Conclusions

In general two-plus-one main approaches to AWS's have developed: the negative one which attempts to ban them, as the campaign "stop killer robots"; the positive, which -with certain variations internally- sees in AWS's significant positive effects; and an intermediary one, which leans towards the second –or can be considered as part of it- which finds that AWS's will not be banned even in case we wanted them to and that therefore we must try to regulate them instead, by paying more attention to their characteristics of development- *i.e. machine learning so that they can for example distinguish combatant from civilian and incorporate IHL norms as well, use in specific environment only, such as in areas not densely populated, use of force against specific opponents, actual or potential human control*. All these may be accompanied by a new and specific international covenant.[63]

The needs for limiting the cost of war, the victims among military and for the process of the overload of information in the military field have been invoked as reasons justifying the emergence of AWS.[64] In this framework, the role of humans changes to say the least up to the extent of possibly being substituted completely.[65]

[61]UN Institute for Disarmament Research, (UNIDIR) The Weaponization of Increasingly Autonomous Technologies: Concerns, Characteristics and Definitional Approaches 2018, at p. 24.

[62](UNIDIR) The Weaponization of Increasingly Autonomous Technologies: Concerns, Characteristics and Definitional Approaches, at p. 26.

[63]Lewis (2015), pp. 1322–1324.

[64]Stewart (2011), p. 275.

[65]Norman Friedman, UCAVs: A New Kind of Air Power?, Rusi Defence Systems, June 2010, at 62, 63.

AWS's already constitute part of a developing arms race. Inter-state antagonisms, as well as the ambitions of non-state actors to acquire catastrophic but relatively low-cost means of warfare lead to a contest without any actual governance mechanism.

The question is do we need one? The answer is definitely positive. AWS's introduce intellectual autonomy of expanding nature into warfare, Greater capacity comes with unpredictability. Unpredictable weapons are obviously a novel challenge. It is already difficult for the collective security system to deal with threats emerging from the unpredictability of humans- either as military commanders or as political leaders; it is going to be even more difficult to do so with non-human actors.

Can the collective security system as it is expressed by the UN organs outlaw AWS's in general? While there could be legal justification for such a decision, it is obvious that a general prohibition of AWS's is out of the table both because of states' policies as well as because of disagreements regarding the way the different levels of autonomy are defined.

The imperatives of the collective security system necessitate though, a careful consideration so that humans do not get out of the loop, neither in principle nor in practice. That means that AWS's with autonomy that supersedes a certain extent of human control can and should be prohibited in order to avoid further risk factors in the international community, disorientating the collective security system. Human presence in the loop must be used as a standard: it is reasonable to accept AWS's provided that any of the two levels of human presence are identified -in the loop or on the loop. In addition, human presence must be both substantial as well as enhanced by AI, not weakened.

That is in order to limit potential threats. As implied above, handling human-oriented threats and risk to international peace and security has been proven already an extremely difficult mission. Introducing into an already, partially fragile system a new paragon of unpredictability, as well as legitimizing the absence of actual human overview will be an irresponsible act.

Profoundly and in line with the general propositions for AI governance, a synthesis of standards, of mechanisms and of organs- under the UN SC because of the risks that AWS's bring to the collective security system- must be foreseen. As with other treaties for the control of specific weapons- albeit in the wider framework of AI governance- controls, checks, balances and penalties will have to be foreseen, together with monitoring and advocacy organs of the international community.

States will need to comply with international regulations in furtherance of their collective responsibility. We need not to forget that the collective security system is also transcended by the general and fundamental human-centric core of the UN charter. After all, a global catastrophe could emerge even without any type of Matrix or Skynet scenario being realized. Conventional weapons getting out of human control can become devastating enough for the international community, by provoking a chain of inter-state reactions that could escalate with unpredictable and potentially unprecedented manners.

References

Beard JM (2014) Autonomous weapons and human responsibilities. Georgetown J Int Law 45:617

Bislev S (2004) Globalization, state transformation and public security. Int Political Sci Rev 25 (3):281

Boothby W (2012) Some legal challenges posed by remote attack. Int Rev Red Cross 94:579

Boulanin V, Verbruggen M (2017) Mapping the development of autonomy in weapon systems. Stockholm International Peace Research Institute (SIPRI), Stockholm

Carr J (2013) The misunderstood acronym: why cyber weapons aren't WMD. Bull Atomic Scientists 69:32

Claude IL Jr (1986) American approaches to world affairs. University Press of America, Lanham, p 51

Cuellar MF (2004) Reflections on sovereignty and collective security. Stanford J Int Law 40:211

Cummings M (2006) Automation and accountability in decision support system interface design. J Technol Stud XXXII(1)

Delahunty RJ (2007) Paper charter: self-defense and the failure of the United Nations collective security system. Catholic Univ Law Rev 56:871

Duffy H (2005) The 'War On Terror' and the framework of international law. Cambridge University Press, Cambridge

Dunn I (1994) Introduction: crisis of the National State? Political Stud 42:3

Fowler MR (2003) Collective security and the fighting in the Balkans. Northern Kentucky Law Rev 30:299

Freedman L (1998) International security, changing targets. Foreign Policy 110:48

Gordon E (1984–1985) Article 2(4) in historical context. Yale J Int Law 10:271

Graham MW (1946) Great powers and small states. In: Morgenthau HJ (ed) Peace, security & the United Nations. University of Chicago Press, Chicago, p 57

Grut C (2013) The challenge of autonomous lethal robotics to International Humanitarian Law. J Conflict Security Law 18:5

Henkin L (1989) Use of force: law and U.S. policy. In: Henkin L et al (eds) Right V. might: international law and the use of force. Council on Foreign Relations Press, New York, pp 58–59

Hoffmann S (1987) Liberalism and international affairs. In: Hoffman S (ed) Janus and minerva: essays in the theory and practice of international politics. Westview Press, Boulder, pp 89–94

Jones JF (2004) Human security and social development. Denver J Int Law Policy 33:92

Kirgis L Jr (1995) The security Council's first fifty years. Am J Int Law 89:506

Koskenniemi M (1996) The place of law in collective security. Mich J Int Law 17:455

Krupiy T (2015) Of souls, spirits and ghosts: transposing the application of the rules of targeting to lethal autonomous robots. Melb J Int Law 16:145

Krupiy T (2017) Unravelling power dynamics in organizations: an accountability framework for crimes triggered by lethal autonomous weapons systems. Loyola Univ Chicago Int Law Rev 15:1

Laton D (2016) Manhattan_Project.Exe: a nuclear option for the digital age. Cath Univ J Law Technol 25:94

Le Mon J, Taylor RS (2004) Security council action in the name of human rights: from Rhodesia to the Congo. UC Davis J Int Law 10(2):197

Lewis J (2015) Comment, the case for regulating fully autonomous weapons. Yale Law J 124:1305

Marchant GE et al (2011) International governance of autonomous military robots. Columb Sci Technol Law Rev 12:272

Mathews JT (1989) Redefining security. Foreign Aff 68(2):162

Mearsheimer JJ (1998) The false promise of international institutions. In: Brown ME et al (eds) Theories of war and peace,an international security reader. MIT Press, Cambridge, p 329

Morton JS (2002) The legality of NATO's intervention in Yugoslavia in 1999: implications for the progressive development of international law. ILSA J Int Comp Law 9:75

Noorman M, Johnson DG (2014) Negotiating autonomy and responsibility in military robots. Ethics Info Technol 16:52
Reisman WM (2008) Acting before victims become victims: preventing and arresting mass murder. Case W Res J Int Law 40:57
Reitinger N (2015–2016) Algorithmic choice and superior responsibility: closing the gap between liability and lethal autonomy by defining the line between actors and t+ools. Gonzaga Law Rev 51:79
Renner M (1996) Fighting for survival: environmental decline, social conflict and the new age of insecurity. W. W. Norton & Company, New York, p 83
Shaw M (2005) The new Western way of war. Polity, Cambridge, pp 87–88
Shestack JJ (1997–1998) Globalization of human rights law. Fordham Int Law J 21:558
Shklar JN (1986) Legalism: law, morals, and political trials, 2nd edn. Harvard University Press, p 125
Spindel J (2009) Artificial intelligence, nuclear weapons, and strategic stability. In: Finlay B (ed) The militarization of artificial intelligence. United Nations, Stanley Center for Peace and Security, Muscatine, p 7
Stern B (1996) What exactly is the job of international institutions? Am Soc Int Law Proc 90:585
Stewart DM (2011) X new technology and the law of armed conflicT. Int Law Stud 87:271
Thomas C (2002) Global governance and human security. In: Wilkinson R, Hughes S (eds) Global governance: critical perspectives. Routledge, Milton Park, p 113
Tyugu E (2011) Artificial intelligence in cyber defense. Int Conf Cyber Conflict 95:98
Ullmann H (1983) Redefining security. Int Security 8(1):129
White ND (2002) On the brink of lawlessness: the state of collective security law. Indiana Int Comp Law Rev 13:237

Chapter 8
Legal Ramifications of the Use of AWS's-the Role of IHL and Human Rights

8.1 Introduction

Wars, as bureaucratically organized and implemented, intentional, institutionalized, collective, instrumental events of use of direct, armed violence are righteously considered since our early days of history as the events where some of our most atrocious attitudes not only take place but may be rewarded as well.[1]

Wars are fought at large by people like Eichmann. It is because of the realization of the sufferings from war and of the fact that non-attribution of responsibility encourages atrocities, that the international community came up with the formation of international humanitarian law—IHL—of the laws about state responsibility and—as already mentioned above—with human rights law too.

They are all aspects of the effort to "humanize" war and international law, which is another proof of the human-centric nature of the latter.[2] The legal provisions of international humanitarian law—IHL—as well as of international law in general- in order to be sustained must be able to identify and attribute responsibility. Such ellipsis, apart from promoting acts which contravene the human-centric character of international law, further harm the collective security system by establishing a culture of immunity.

AWS's create a new situation in terms of a potential risk to the collective security system. The more that the human operator distances from the specific conduct in the battlefield, the less difficult that it is for responsibility to be traced and attributed. In such a framework, AWS's must be examined in relation to IHL and human rights as

[1]For various definitions and descriptions of wat, see: van der Dennen (1981), pp. 128–189.

[2]Meron (2006); Auron (2013), p. 453; Kassimeris (2006), pp. 4–13.

T. Tzimas, *Legal and Ethical Challenges of Artificial Intelligence from an International Law Perspective*, Law, Governance and Technology Series 46,
https://doi.org/10.1007/978-3-030-78585-7_8

potential factors of risk of the collective security system and the human-centrism of the international community and international law.[3]

The potential incapacity currently of AWS's to uphold the standards of IHL does not mean according to all experts that they must be abolished however; from a certain point of view this incapacity of AWS's shows on the contrary that we should press "harder" for the evolution of AWS's because, the deployment of highly evolved AWS's may mean less need for soldiers and therefore less human victims, whereas the lack of emotions can very well mean deeper commitment to international law.[4]

Schmitt for example argues that "human judgment can prove less reliable than technical indicators in the heat of battle", using as example the case of the downing by the US army of the Iranian civil aircraft in 1988.[5]

Professor Arkin, also constitutes a strong advocate of the "humanism" of AWS; his suggestion is that once AWS are programmed with an ethical code they will outperform humans in humane behavior in the battlefield.[6] Eventually that leads to an aspiration for"... producing an 'artificial conscience,' to yield a new class of robots- termed humane-oids--robots that can perform more ethically in the battlefield than humans are capable of doing."[7]

Similar arguments advocate the potential reduce of unnecessary suffering, thanks to the fact that the deployment of AWS,[8] could lead to the avoidance of panic or fury, vengeance and self-preservation, without compromising their efficiency.[9]

The counter-arguments invoke the incapacity of AI and subsequently of AWS's as well, to make ethical judgments, the unpredictability and the black box effect of AI and the unknown environments within which AWS will have to act.[10] It must not

[3]Parenthetically- speaking, from the perspective of state responsibility, the issue of AWS's, is more straightforward legally speaking, since state responsibility from a weapon system can be identified objectively regardless of any subjective element.

[4]Marchant et al. (2011), pp. 275, 280.

[5]Schmitt (2013), pp. 12–13 (http://harvardnsj.org/wp-content/uploads/2013/02/Schmitt-Autonomous-Weapon-Systems-and-IHL-Final.pdf).

[6]*Stewart, X New Technology And The Law Of Armed Conflict*, at p. 282.

[7]Arkin (2009), p. 16.

[8]Kastan (2013), p. 62.

[9]Marchant et al. (2011), pp. 272, 280; Schmitt and Thurnher (2013), pp. 231, 249.

[10]As the US Department of Defense held : " Because the DoD complies with the Law of Armed Conflict, there are many issues requiring resolution associated with employment of weapons by an unmanned system. For a significant period into the future, the decision to pull the trigger or launch a missile from an unmanned system will not be fully automated, but it will remain under the full control of a human operator. Many aspects of the firing sequence will be fully automated but the decision to fire will not likely be fully automated until legal, rules of engagement, and safety concerns have all been thoroughly examined and resolved."

Office of the Secretary of Defense, Department of Defense, FY2009-2034 Unmanned Systems Integrated Roadmap (2d ed. 2009), available at http://www.acq.osd.mil/psa/docs/UMSIntegratedRoadmap2009.pdf.

be forgotten also that the same arguments could be reversed as the lack of human emotion may lead literally into what has been labeled as the "robot psychology".[11]

In general, the design of more efficient guarantees is necessary; but can we be certain that even if designed, under a proper, governance mechanism, states will limit themselves in manufacturing weapons with such limitations? The past of international relations is not very re-assuring. Within a situation that is already complicated enough regarding attribution of criminal responsibility, the temptation to skip such guarantees is going to be proven particularly strong.

From the perspective of IHL, the complications are quite significant due to the subjective responsibility and effective control problems that are raised. On such grounds, the lengthier part of the chapter is the initial one, analyzing the relationship between IHL and AI.

8.2 AWS and IHL

8.2.1 IHL Characteristics

In principle, AWS's are not prohibited under existing, international law. Obviously though, they must abide by the relative legal norms; foremost IHL since we refer to military combat and complementary, to international human rights law.[12]

The Geneva Convention, Additional Protocol I- API- in article 36 provides that "In the study, development, acquisition or adoption of a new weapon, means or method of warfare, a High Contracting Party is under an obligation to determine whether its employment would, in some or all circumstances, be prohibited by this Protocol or by any other rule of international law applicable to the High Contracting Party."[13]

IHL is the "body of norms that regulates the conduct of those who are involved in armed conflicts, regulates the use of armed force, including the prohibition of certain ways and means of warfare, and protects certain categories of persons and property from harm."[14]

---

[11]Human Rights Watch, Losing Humanity: The Case Against Killer Robots 37 (2012).

[12]The two types of law are distinct but still maintain critical interlink age. The focus here is on IHL as it refers mainly to conflict circumstances. Still human rights are applicable too, both in terms of the necessity to respect them during conflict but also because of the potential use of AWS's in non-conflict zones- i.e. police operations.

[13]ICRC Article 36.

[14]Sassòli (2011), p. 1.

IHL does not -in principle- outlaw weapons; it outlaws their use. It may outlaw weapons in case they are either prohibited by a specific treaty or when their characteristics may cause indiscriminate or unnecessary suffering.[15]

As Harold Koh, the former U.S. State Department Legal Advisor stated, "the rules that govern targeting do not turn on the type of weapon system used, and there is no prohibition under the laws of war on the use of technologically advanced weapon systems in armed conflict... so long as they are employed in conformity with applicable laws of war."[16]

That means that the use of weapons must take into account "military, legal, environmental and health-related considerations"[17] not cause unnecessary suffering[18] and not be indiscriminate regarding their use; therefore, they must not be uncontrollable either, up to the extent that the latter could lead to indiscriminate uses as well.[19]

The primary obligation which is imposed by IHL is the distinction between civilian population and combatants, as well as between civilian and military objectives.[20] In the battlefield such determinations are very often proven particularly difficult, especially in fluid environments; hence there must be reasonable belief -at least- that the target is a military one.[21]

The potential capacity of AWS's to make such distinctions is central in light of the obligation to meet the standards of IHL; the skeptics towards AWS's, emphasize that the latter are not and most probably will not be able to make such distinctions, whereas on the contrary those in favor argue that once such technology has been achieved, the lack of human emotions will make AWS's more credible in these regards.

IHL transfers on commanders the obligation to distinguish between targets and select the proper ones. As the ICTY held there is a level of discretion of the commander, which each one of them must use on the basis of good faith, feasibility and reasonableness.[22] Therefore, there must be a balance between on the one hand

---

[15] *Beard, Autonomous Weapons and Human Responsibilities*, at pp. 636–638; Nuclear advisory opinion, 66, 78.

[16] Harold Hongju Koh, Legal Adviser, U.S. Dep't of State, The Obama Administration and International Law, Remarks at the Annual Meeting of the American Society of International Law (Wash., D.C., Mar. 25, 2010), available at http://www.state.gov/s/l/releases/remarks/139119.htm.

[17] Lawland (2006), https://www.icrc.org/eng/assets/files/other/icrc_002_0902.pdf.

[18] Press (2017), p. 1347.

[19] Toscano (2015), pp. 216–218.

[20] Protocol Additional to the Geneva Conventions of 12 August 1949, and relating to the Protection of Victims of International Armed Conflicts (Protocol 1), opened for signature 12 December 1977, 1125 UNTS 3 (entered into force 7 December 1978) art 48 ('API 1977').

[21] Melzer (2008), p. 1039; Prosecutor v Galic (Judgement and Opinion) (International Criminal Tribunal for the Former Yugoslavia, Trial Chamber I, Case No IT-98-29-T, 5 December 2003) [51].

[22] Committee Established to Review the NATO Bombing Campaign against the Federal Republic of Yugoslavia, 'Final Report to the Prosecutor' (Report, International Criminal Tribunal for the Former Yugoslavia, 2000) [29] ('NATO Bombing against Yugoslavia Report'). Yves Sandoz,

military necessity and on the other hand the need to protect the civilians from harm.[23]

These principles imply the proper adoption of another one; of proportionality, which is challenging in terms of its implementation as it involves in depth ethical and legal assessments. Proportionality applies where the harm of civilians is unavoidable or very much likely, because of the specific conditions on the ground.

Under such circumstances, following Additional Protocol I—API—and more specifically article 51(5)(b), attacks "which may be expected to cause incidental loss of civilian life, injury to civilians, damage to civilian objects, or a combination thereof, which would be excessive in relation to the concrete and direct military advantage anticipated" are prohibited.[24]

The "excessiveness" or not of the harm which will be inflicted is to be balanced with the military benefit from the action.[25] Military commanders have to demonstrate various areas of intelligence and "interpretative judgment", in order to reach decisions into unpredictable environments, with non- perfect information.

The characteristic provision of The Hague convention foresees that "the right of belligerents to adopt means of injuring the enemy is not unlimited"[26] and the use of force must not be "excessive in relation to the concrete and direct military advantage anticipated",[27] meaning that not all military means can be implemented for the sake of the achievement of military goals.

This is why, the principle of proportionality, which is by now a well- accepted norm of customary international law[28] is both crucial and notorious for its subjectivity.[29] The International Court of Justice-*ICJ*- in its advisory opinion on the Legality of the Threat or Use of Nuclear Weapons -*Nuclear Weapons Case*- held that proportionality is fundamental for IHL.[30]

Because of the fact that the norm necessitates an ethical judgment on behalf of military commanders-balancing between the military impact of the attack and the potential harm to civilians- subjectivity emerges[31] between competing values:

Christophe Swinarski and Bruno Zimmermann (eds), Commentary on the Additional Protocols of 8 June 1977to the Geneva Conventions of 12 August 1949 (International Committee of the Red Cross, 1987) 682 [2198].

[23]Walzer (2006), p. 144; Sandoz et al. (1987), pp. 680–682 [2198].

[24]API 1977 art 51(5)(b).

[25]Wagner (2014), p. 1398.

[26]Hague Convention No IV Respecting the Laws and Customs of War on Land, and Annex (Regulations), 18 October 1907, 1 Bevans 631 art. 22.

[27]Additional Protocol I Relating to the Protection of Victims of International Armed Conflicts, 1977, 1125 UNTS 3, art. 51.

[28]Henckaerts and Doswald-Beck (2005).

[29]Parks (1990), p. 173; Wright (2012), p. 820.

[30]Legality of the Threat or Use of Nuclear Weapons (Advisory Opinion) [1996] ICJ Rep 226, 35 [78]-[79].

[31]Greenwood (1993), p. 88; Watkin (2005), p. 5; Sassòli and Cameron (2006), p. 63; Bothe et al. (1982) , p. 310 n 30.

military necessity, on the one hand and the avoidance of harm to civilians' lives, on the other hand.[32]

Proportionality is both crucial and "dangerous"; it is necessary, in order to have a legal principle, that will be guiding military commanders under the most difficult circumstances on the one hand, whereas on the other hand it is open to contradictory interpretations and misinterpretations.[33] Still, legal responsibility is built at large upon it.

A fundamental criterion is whether a certain weapon system is inherently indiscriminate or not.[34] It is a crucial but still insufficient criterion. Given also the fact that the international community has not reached a central, governance model for AI in general and for LAWS's or AWS's in particular we need to develop more elaborate criteria for their regulation and development.[35]

The US Department of Defense has proposed three criteria: the existence of a specific legal norm prohibiting the use of the particular weapon; once the first criterion is "passed" it must be determined whether the use of this weapon intends to cause superfluous injury; then comes the criterion of whether the weapon is indiscriminate;[36] Two more criteria have been proposed in the academic literature, namely the potential impact on the natural environment and the potential developments in the law of armed conflict.[37]

In the framework of the assessment of the legitimacy of AWS's under IHL, the CCW annual meetings have produced a number of documents which attempt to further clarify the legality of LAWS's—therefore providing guidance for AWS's in general.

During, the first informal, CCW Meeting of High Contracting Parties that was held in 2014, the compliance of LAWS's with IHL, including the 1949 Geneva Conventions, the Martens Clause, and customary international law, was examined, leading to disagreements about the possibility of such compliance of these types of weapon systems.[38]

In the 2015 CCW, informal meeting of experts on LAWS, some critical recommendations were made about the regulation of LAWS and about where the emphasis must be given in terms of their potential legitimacy or not: meaningful human control, techno-centric approach to robotic autonomy and its definition, focus on the critical factors, meaning selection and targeting, "level of human supervision,

---

[32]Greenwood (1993), p. 88; Watkin (2005), p. 5; Sassòli and Cameron (2006), p. 63; Bothe et al. (1982), p. 310.

[33]Parks (1990), p. 173.

[34]Meier (2016), p. 124.

[35]That is another reason, proving the need to come up with a model of international governance.

[36]DEP'T OF THE A.F. INSTRUCTION 51-402, LEGAL REVIEWS OF WEAPONS AND CYBER CAPABILITIES (2011), at paras. , § 1.5.1; § 3.1.1; . § 3.1.2.1; § 6.2.2.

[37]*Boothby, Weapons And The Law Of Armed Conflict*, at pp. 345–346.

[38]Meier (2016), p. 121, https://sites.temple.edu/ticlj/files/2017/02/30.1.Meier-TICLJ.pdf, archived at https://perma.cc/PP8G-ULAU.

nature of the target (object, human), complexity of the environment, and predictability and reliability of the weapon system".[39]

It was also suggested that we need to come forth with sharpened versions of guiding principles and rights, such as the "right to life", "right to dignity" and the Martens Clause,[40] in order to be proven practical in terms of our guidance by them, within the new world of LAWS.[41]

The need for the development of the relevant capacities of LAWS's was highlighted in the CCW, 2015 meeting, implying not their prohibition but rather their development in ways that can guarantee their compliance with law; namely that LAWS must be able to distinguish between combatants and non-combatants, that legally-speaking, targeting rules are more suitable than meaningful human control, that the conformity of LAWS with IHL should be assessed on an ad hoc basis on the grounds of context, types of targets, types of force, movement in space, timeframe of the action, predictability of the weapon system, understanding in behalf of the commander of the way that LAWS work.[42]

In the same meeting it was held that "...even if the elaboration of a definition was premature, some key elements appeared as pertinent to describe the concept of autonomy for LAWS, for example the capacity to select and engage a target without human intervention."[43]

The negotiations for a legally binding document "to prevent the development and use of LAWS" have continued, whereas "[t]he majority of states at the last CCW meeting in April 2018 emphasized the importance of retaining human control over weapons systems and the use of force, and expressed support for developing new international law on lethal autonomous weapons systems."[44]

---

[39]CCW/MSP/2015/3, Meeting of the High Contracting Parties to the Convention on Prohibitions or restrictions on the Use of Certain Conventional Weapons Which May Be Deemed to Be Excessively Injurious or to Have Indiscriminate Effects, (2015, June 2), at https://undocs.org/ccw/msp/2015/3.

[40]"In cases not covered by this Protocol or by other international agreements, civilians and combatants remain under the protection and authority of the principles of international law derived from established custom, from the principles of humanity and from the dictates of public conscience". Additional Protocol I Additional to the 1949 Geneva Conventions, 1977, Article 1, para 2.

[41]CCW/MSP/2015/3, Meeting of the High Contracting Parties to the Convention on Prohibitions or restrictions on the Use of Certain Conventional Weapons Which May Be Deemed to Be Excessively Injurious or to Have Indiscriminate Effects at paras. 60–66.

[42]Ibid at para. 51.

[43]CCW/MSP/2014/3, Meeting of the High Contracting Parties to the Convention on Prohibitions or restrictions on the Use of Certain Conventional Weapons Which May Be Deemed to Be Excessively Injurious or to Have Indiscriminate Effects, (2014, June 11), at para. 20, https://documents-dds-ny.un.org/doc/UNDOC/GEN/G14/048/96/pdf/G1404896.pdf?OpenElement.

[44]UN: Decisive Action Needed to Ban Killer Robots – Before It's Too Late, AMNESTY INTERNATIONAL (Aug. 27, 2018), https://www.amnesty.org/en/latest/news/2018/08/un-decisive-action-needed-to-ban-killer-robots-before-its-too-late/, archived at https://perma.cc/78XB-CFHK.

Some states called for a ban on LAWS through a new, CCW protocol, while the ones already developing these weapons, maintained a rather cautious stance towards the proposed ban.

Taking into account the fore- mentioned analysis, AWS's will need to be able to demonstrate—*in case of complete autonomy*[45]—or be guided—*where some extent of human control is maintained*—with delicate and eloquent ethical judgment in order to be able to implement both the principle of proportionality, as well as to comply with the fore- mentioned legal frameworks.

However, no such capacity has been demonstrated yet, which means that an asymmetry is emerging over time, between the use of AWS's in the battlefield and the relevant distancing of humans from the combat, without a necessary, equivalent capacity on behalf of AWS's to proceed with complicated and in-depth enough, ethical judgments, as well as without sufficient guarantees regarding the human operator capacity to monitor and step in, in the proper time, so that AWS's incapacities are "healed" somehow.

In order for highly autonomous, AWS's to be capable of such determinations, they must be able to develop "common sense reasoning" and "battlefield awareness",[46] as well as intuition, experience- based analysis, comprehension of the equivalent legal framework, and cognitive capacities.[47]

As autonomy of AWS's grows, their compliance with IHL necessitates highly evolved intellectual capacities, which are absent as of now, whereas less autonomous forms of AWS's demand effective and accountable, human control.

8.2.2 *Responsibility of AWS's?*

The necessity and the obligation of upholding proportionality as well as the overall, legal framework regulating combat, means that the commander will also be held liable for criminal responsibility over IHL violations. Regarding humans, this is self-obvious. What is the case with AWS's however?

Ugo Pagallo characteristically identifies the foundations of legal liability in "moral agency" and of "moral agency" in consciousness. In such a framework he argued that "[f]or the foreseeable future, in fact, robots will be held legally and morally irresponsible because they lack the set of preconditions for attributing liability to someone in the realm of criminal law."[48] "Since consciousness is a conceptual prerequisite for both legal and moral agency, it follows that the standard legal viewpoint reckons that the level of autonomy shown by today's robotics

[45]The case of complete autonomy of AWS's or of the fourth loop is also assessed on other grounds too, namely the one of human dignity and human rights, below.

[46]Sharkey (2012), pp. 788–789.

[47]Stewart (1901–2011), p. 275.

[48]Pagallo (2011), p. 312.

applications is insufficient to bring such machines before judges and have them found guilty in criminal courts."[49]

Similar argumentation has been articulated by other analysts and academics as well, on the basis of the –until now at least- lack of higher, general intelligence on behalf of AI.[50] Characteristically, Noel Sharkey suggested that AI would need to be capable of "common sense reasoning" and "battlefield awareness", in order to comply with IHL- for example between civilians and militants- capacities which he sees as "computationally intractable".[51]

However, the above analysis could also mean that once a greater level of autonomy has been achieved, then, legal liability could emerge—in accordance with different approaches.[52] Until that happens, the problem is that we may find ourselves in a responsibility vacuum, which can undermine the foundations of IHL.

It has been argued that IHL does not prerequisite that "a human be held personally accountable for any mistakes or violations that may occur on the battlefield."[53] Once human imitation or human- like characteristics can be identified in another entity, why not hold such an entity accountable? Therefore, AWS's could be endowed with some extent of legal personhood and held liable, if necessary, under penalties, relevant to their ontology.

Such a position is partially accurate. Obviously, IHL is human- centric in the sense that when initially designed, autonomy of such a level that could lead to responsibility of non- humans was only science-fiction. However, as it is examined below, this does not constitute the only legitimizing basis for IHL human- centrism: the inherence of human dignity constitutes the other main reason for IHL human-centrism.

The attribution of responsibility to an AI system under IHL is at present impossible technologically, as well as because of the lack of existence of legal personality of AI entities in general and of AWS's more specifically. Unless, AI and AWS's evolve up to the point of AGI or ASI, so that there is the ontological foundation for some type of legal personhood that can justify criminal responsibility too—when this debate may be mature—it is ethically awkward if not appalling to attempt to attribute criminal responsibility to an AI entity instead of any human, under present laws and hegemonic ethics, as it would be a way for armies and their commanders to evade responsibility for criminal acts, by deploying AWS and putting the blame on them. Until the ontological evolution of AI makes us to re-structure our legal

---

[49] Ugo Pagallo, What Robots Want: Autonomous Machines, Codes and New Frontiers of Legal Responsibility, in 25 Human Law And Computer Law: Comparative Perspectives 47, 51 (Mireille Hildebrandt & Jeanne Gaakeer eds., 2013).

[50] Johnson (2006), pp. 203–204; Johnson and Miller (2008), pp. 123, 124.

[51] Sharkey (2012), p. 789.

[52] Floridi and Sanders (2004), pp. 74–76.

[53] Thurnher (2012), available at http://www.ndu.edu/press/lib/pdf/jfq-67/JFQ-67_77-84_Thurnher.pdf.

systems, there are in practice no penalties which can applied on AI and therefore on AWS's and have some actual impact.

It is highly questionable whether moral principles can be programmed into AI software-even in the future—together with the way that AI will interact with its environment, the capacity of humans to actually control them, the secrecy regarding their development, the impact of swarming in relation to meaningful human control.[54]

There are additional complexities in the quest for attribution of criminal responsibility towards AWS', even if we could somehow skip the previous argument-meaning at level of higher autonomy. What standards of compliance with IHL are we supposed to consider as sufficient? The standards of an equivalent human commander for example? While this may seem as a "solution" offering some extent of human- like criteria, it does not offer legal certainty: what human commander is going to be chosen as a threshold?

Again, the need to "teach" to AI, complicated legal terms with significant ethical background, such as compliance with IHL forces us to rethink about our own standards and confront our own flaws and differentiating interpretations.

The actual risk from AWS's in terms of IHL violations, are caused from the "agnosticism" of AI, meaning from the fact that AI systems are unaware of the environment, the time and the purpose or entity that makes use of them.[55]

The ellipsis of "situational awareness" constitutes a source of concern, given that it is one of the characteristics that a successful military commander must have. The situational awareness includes three capacities: the commander must comprehend all elements in the physical environment, the relationship between physical elements and people and must be able envisage on the basis of the perceived experience, how the situation will unfold in the future.[56]

Gary Klein described situational awareness as the procedure of using past experience in order to determine current actions, by adjusting accumulated knowledge.[57] Therefore, AI will need to be able to conduct contextual analysis of the situation on the ground and to assess it critically so that it achieves the capacity to interpret the events and act on the basis of its judgment.[58]

Such technology, effectively replicating fundamental, human, intellectual capacities has not been achieved yet, exactly because human intelligence is general and not limited to a specific category of conducts.[59]

---

[54]CCW/CONF.V/2 Fifth Review Conference of the High Contracting Parties to the Convention on Prohibitions or Restrictions on the Use of Certain Conventional Weapons Which May Be Deemed to Be Excessively Injurious or to Have Indiscriminate Effects, (2016, Decemver, 12–16), at paras. 61–69.

[55]The Weaponization of Increasingly Autonomous Technologies: Concerns, Characteristics and Definitional Approaches , at p. 15.

[56]Endsley (1995), pp. 3–4; Stewart (1901–2011), p. 271.

[57]Klein (1999), pp. 92, 99,100.

[58]Grut (2013), p. 11; Stewart (1901–2011), pp. 271, 275.

[59]Asaro (2012), pp. 699–708.

One of the problems is that it has been proven—at least until now—impossible to design an algorithm replicating morals and emotions,[60] as well as imaginative thinking similar to human.[61]

Therefore, if social norms and ethical principles are not understood by AI but partially, simply imitated without actually "feeling" them,[62] how are AWS's going to apply complicated syllogisms in order to uphold principles such as the ones sustaining proportionality for example? Intelligence which does not include emotions not only will be different but it can be dangerous as well.[63] The same line of arguments suggests that replicating emotions is not the same as experiencing them.[64]

In addition, while AI already possesses the capacity to incorporate a vast number of scenarios, it is as of now both difficult to adapt to novel conditions and unpredictable regarding the possible outcome.

Again, the problem becomes that in the battlefield, autonomy is of critical significance for achieving greater military advantage. Some extent of volition on behalf of AWS's, in combination with their speed, accuracy, lack of fear is necessary in terms of military efficiency. Nevertheless, these same elements intensify unpredictability.

A counter—argument is that there could be design only for narrow and specific set of scenarios, embedding the principles of IHL. When AWS's either because of facing a scenario on which they cannot project what they have been "taught" in the course of machine-learning or for whatever other reason pose threat to IHL, they will be controlled and switched off; a different perspective is that a type of algorithmic comprehension of human intelligence can lead to its replication by AI in general and by AWS's in particular.[65]

Nevertheless, despite the necessity of "switch-off" guarantees and of relevant mechanisms for predictability, in practice they are not always so easily achieved: "[A] common misconception that robots will do only what we have programmed them to do.... [P]rograms with millions of lines of code are written by teams of programmers, none of whom knows the entire program; hence, no individual can predict the effect of a given command with absolute certainty, since portions of large programs may interact in unexpected, untested ways..."[66]

In such a sense it is argued that even if AWS's manage to reach the capacity of ethical syllogisms, there is no guarantee that we will be able to predict their outcome.

---

[60] Jimmy So, 'Can Robots Fall in Love, and Why Would They?', The Daily Beast (online), 31 December 2013 http://www.thedailybeast.com/articles/2013/12/31/can-robots-fall-in-love-and-why-would-they.html.

[61] Sparrow (2009), p. 181.

[62] This argumentation is based on findings of neurologists. Damasio (1994), p. xiv.

[63] Asaro, "On Banning Autonomous Weapon Systems: Human Rights, Automation, and the Dehumanization of Lethal Decision-Making", at p. 699.

[64] *Damasio, Descartes' Error: Emotion, Reason and the Human Brain*, Preface.

[65] Schmitt (2013), p. 17 http://harvardnsj.org/wp-content/uploads/2013/02/Schmitt-Autonomous-Weapon-Systems-and-IHL-Final.pdf.

[66] Marchant et al. (2011), p. 283.

Even if it is suggested that the issue of unpredictability exists with present, human commanders and soldiers as well-and it indeed exists- it is not particularly comforting to propose that the already existing unpredictability and problematic compliance with IHL may be multiplied and ontologically transformed with AWS's.

In addition, risks may emerge unwillingly, on behalf of the military commander: let us assume for a moment, that the military commander, intends actually to "take all feasible precautions in attack";[67] the actual knowledge most military commanders can have is—to say the least- limited, given the complexity and the unpredictability of AI.

Part of this problem emerges not only from the unpredictability and opaqueness of AWS but also from underestimating the unpredictability of AWS's because of the tendency to over—rely on machine—learning and on AI in general; this may easily lead to guidance by AI of the human commander, instead of the other way round. Therefore, even if human control is indeed foreseen it may not be actually imposed, given the over-reliance on AI and AWS's.[68]

AWS's then, must be examined, regarding their legitimacy under the norms of IHL, from the perspective of the legal acceptability or not, of the fore-mentioned asymmetry; that of their greater role in the battlefield, albeit with no criminal responsibility for AWS's "themselves". That brings us back to the role of the human commander. The immunity of humans must be in any case out of the question. The potential evolution of AI legal personhood cannot reach—unless AGI and ASI somehow emerge—the level of entrusting to them the safeguarding of IHL guarantees, rights and principles.

Is it legal then to deploy AWS's even at the cost of finding it more difficult to trace the human commander who is responsible or not? The answer must be determined on the bases of the extent of actual risks that AWS' could cause regarding IHL violations and of the question whether legal structures for the attribution of criminal responsibility to humans can be found, in spite of the role of AWS's in the battlefield.

Regarding the actual risks from the deployment of AWS's in terms of IHL violations, two conclusions can be inferred: while in principle AWS's cannot be outlawed merely on the basis of their existence, from IHL perspective—and more significantly due to states' unwillingness—their development and deployment will have to follow very specific guidelines and standards in order to be legitimate: efficient, overall, governance mechanism, under the UN SC; standards of efficient human control, including well—trained military commanders; emergency, switch -off mechanisms; international standards for the way that AWS's will be trained, so that compliance with IHL is included in machine-learning.

Unless such standards as well as guarantees are foreseen and efficiently imposed in practice, the risk from AWS's deployment in terms of potential violations of IHL become too great to be overlooked.

---

[67] Additional Protocol I, art. 57.2.

[68] D.G. Johnson, 'Technology with No Human Responsibility?', at p. 714.

Still, even in case AWS's are further developed—which is the most likely outcome- and especially because of the likelihood of such a development we need to come up with a coherent examination of how the human responsibility behind AWS's can be effectively traced.

8.2.3 Tracing the Human Behind the Machine

The next question that remains to be answered refers to the attribution of responsibility following AWS' deployment in the battlefield, on the human military commander. After all, as the UN Human Rights Council Special Rapporteur Christof Heyns held: "[A] human being somewhere has to take the decision to initiate lethal force and as a result internalize (or assume responsibility for) the cost of each life lost in hostilities, as part of a deliberative process of human interaction.... Delegating this process dehumanizes armed conflict even further and precludes a moment of deliberation in those cases where it may be feasible. Machines lack morality and mortality, and should as a result not have life and death powers over humans."[69]

The attribution of responsibility obviously becomes more complicated as more actors, with different levels of autonomy enter the battlefield, as the distancing of the military commander from the specific military action increases and autonomy grows- while still falling short of a distinct legal personality, namely AGI or ASI and therefore of the attribution of criminal responsibility.

As mentioned above, when beginning to look for responsibility, three groups of people or persons appear to be involved: the programmer, which could include also the people responsible for machine learning—i.e. for the collection of the specific big data—the political leader and the military commander. While some part of responsibility can be identified in all three groups of people, the "mens rea" is what matters the most under IHL; this criterion is difficult to be attributed given that the direct intent is not easily proven.[70]

Under the current legal framework and given the level of development of AI, which has not surpassed that of ANI, it is still only humans who can be held responsible for the conduct of acts which are criminalized by IHL as well as in general under international law.[71]

In terms of the legal assessment of military acts, the fundamental point especially regarding individual responsibility, as International Committee of the Red Cross—ICRC—accurately proposes is the role of humans, in making the decisions and on

[69]Report of the Special Rapporteur on extrajudicial, summary or arbitrary executions, A/HRC/23/47, 9 April 2013, page 17, para 94.

[70]ICRC, Autonomous Weapon Systems: Implications of Increasing Autonomy in the Critical Functions of Weapons, at p. 44.

[71]Statute of the International Criminal Court, UN Doc A/CONF/183/9, 17 July 1998, article 25.1.

taking the responsibility for guaranteeing the compliance with international law principles, including proportionality and discrimination under IHL.[72]

Criminal liability prerequisites two elements: "actus reus", meaning the external element of the criminal conduct and mens rea, meaning the internal element, which extends from negligence to intent.[73] The "mens rea" has been devolved into actual and inferred knowledge, in the sense that the military commander should have known.[74]

The implementation of both elements is more apparent in the case of direct order by the commander.[75] In the case of omission, responsibility is founded on the hierarchy of the chain of command and more specifically on three elements: first on the hierarchical relationship, second on the knowledge or the obligation of knowledge and third on the failure to prevent or impose sanctions for the criminal behavior which took place.[76]

The first element is built around effectiveness, including de facto control apart from the formal one. The concept of effectiveness is determined as the "material ability to prevent or punish criminal conduct."[77]

The second element was further clarified in a very insightful way by the ICTY in the Delalic case via an example: "[A] military commander who has received information that some of the soldiers under his command have a violent or unstable character, or have been drinking prior to being sent on a mission, may be considered as having the required knowledge."[78]

---

[72]ICRC, Autonomous weapons: States must agree on what human control means in practice, (2018, November 20), (https://www.icrc.org/en/document/autonomous-weapons-states-must-agree-what-human-control-means-practice, access. 08-02-2020).

[73]Hallevy (2010), pp. 177–178; Perkins (1978), p. 953; Hall (1963), p. 632; Fine and Cohen (1966), p. 749.

[74]Damaska (2001), pp. 461–462. ICTY, Delalic, No. IT-96-21-T, ¶¶ 333"[M]ilitary commanders and other persons occupying positions of superior authority may be held criminally responsible for the unlawful conduct of their subordinates [as] a well-established norm of customary and conventional international law."

[75]1 M. Cherif Bassiouni, Introduction to International Criminal Law at p. 327 (2d rev. ed. 2013). Regarding cases: Prosecutor v. Limaj, Case No. IT-03-66-T, Judgment, ¶ 515 (Int'l Crim. Trib. for the Former Yugoslavia Nov. 30, 2005), http://www.icty.org/x/cases/limaj/tjug/en/lim-tj051130-e.pdf; Prosecutor v. Brdjanin, Case No. IT-99-36-T, Judgment, ¶ 270 (Int'l Crim. Trib. for the Former Yugoslavia Sept. 1, 2004), http://www.icty.org/x/cases/brdanin/tjug/en/brd-tj040901e.pdf). Prosecutor v. Blas#ki#, Case No. IT-95-14-A, Judgment, ¶ 166 (Int'l Crim. Trib. for the Former Yugoslavia July 29, 2004), http://www.icty.org/x/cases/blaskic/acjug/en/bla-aj040729e.pdf (emphasis added); see also Kordic, No. IT-95-14/2-A, ¶ 30.

[76]*Reitinger, Algorithmic Choice And Superior Responsibility: Closing The Gap Between Liability And Lethal Autonomy By Defining The Line Between Actors And Tools*, at p. 105.

[77]Prosecutor v. Delalic, Case No. IT-96-21-A, Judgment, ¶ 256 (Int'l Crim. Trib. for the Former Yugoslavia Feb. 20, 2001), http://www.icty.org/x/cases/mucic/acjug/en/cel-aj010220.pdf; Prosecutor v. Blas#ki#, Case No. IT-95-14-A, Judgment, ¶ 375 (Int'l Crim. Trib. for the Former Yugoslavia July 29, 2004), http://www.icty.org/x/cases/blaskic/acjug/en/bla-aj040729e.pdf.

[78]Delalic, No. IT-96-21-A, ¶ 238.

The third element constitutes the objective one. The commander is expected to be able to exercise effective control to prevent or sanction an illegal behavior because of the position as a commander.[79]

IHL of course is the legal "product" of an era during which the decision- making in the battlefield constituted self- obviously the realm of humans.[80] The gradual shift towards artificial autonomy creates ambiguities about the attribution of responsibility to the military commander and in general within the chain of command.

The problems with the impact of AI autonomy is that the attribution of criminal liability follows the extent of AI autonomy. AI stands as a paragon, potentially fracturing "actus reus" and "mens rea".[81] For example, once the specific act is attributed solely to the autonomous weapon, with the latter not having reached such a level of autonomy that can justify legal liability to it, the perpetrator- meaning the AI- remains unaccountable, while no human is held accountable either.

Such generalized unaccountability however eventually would deconstruct IHL. In the face of such potential development, we would need to move onto the prohibition of AWS's, since they would inherently defy legal norms but also create a framework of general unaccountability.[82]

Given however that the general prohibition of AWS's seems unlikely, we need to confront the potential legal gap and think thoroughly on the necessary interpretations and adjustments within existing law, at least until new legal instruments are adopted.[83] As long as ANI has not been surpassed, it is crucial to look for the human in the loop, so that we will be able to trace criminal responsibility.

The issue under examination is not new. The distancing of the military commander from the battlefield and the claim to immunity was also raised following World War II, in the trials of the war criminals of the Axis' powers.

In the case of General Yamashita as well as in that of "Wilhelm von Leeb and Thirteen Others", the liability of the commander for the actions of the soldiers under his command was established, regardless of the claim for lack of control over the soldiers or for the implementation of superior orders, albeit with different levels of actual control and intent required.

---

[79] M. Cherif Bassiouni, International Criminal Law: International Enforcement § 4.1, at 459 (3d ed. 2008).

[80] Sassòli (2014), p. 323.

[81] Sharkey (2012), p. 791.

[82] Sparrow (2007), p. 62; Matthias (2004), p. 182.

[83] "In this writer's opinion, it is both more probable and more desirable that the law will develop in this evolutionary way than by any radical change. With the law of weaponry, as with most of the law of armed conflict, the most important humanitarian gain would come not from the adoption of new law but the effective implementation of the law that we have. That should be the priority for the next century." Christopher Greenwood, The Law of Weaponry' at the Start of the New Millennium, inTHE LAW OF ARMED CONFLICT: INTO THE NEXT MILLENNIUM 185, 221 (Michael N. Schmitt & Leslie C. Green eds., 1998) (Vol. 71, US Naval War College International Law Studies).

In the second case the tribunal held that "The authority, both administrative and military, of a commander and his criminal responsibility are related but by no means co-extensive. Modern war... entails a large measure of de-centralization... Criminality does not attach to every individual in [the] chain of command... [t]here must be a personal dereliction. That can occur only where the act is directly traceable to [the commander] or where his failure to properly supervise his subordinates constitutes criminal negligence on his part."[84]

Article 30 of International Criminal Statute -ICC- about the element of "mental element" provides that "Unless otherwise provided, a person shall be criminally responsible and liable for punishment for a crime within the jurisdiction of the Court only if the material elements are committed with intent and knowledge."[85]

As for the specification of how intent is defined, in the same article it is provided that "In relation to conduct, that person means to engage in the conduct; In relation to a consequence, that person means to cause that consequence or is aware that it will occur in the ordinary course of events."[86]

The ICC statute further extends liability regarding omission even in cases where the military commander should "knew or, owing to the circumstances at the time, should have known."[87]

In the Bemba case, it was held that: "There is no direct causal link that needs to be established between the superior's omission and the crime committed by his subordinates.... [T]o find a military commander or a person acting as a military commander responsible for the crimes committed by his forces, the Prosecutor must demonstrate that his failure to exercise his duty to prevent crimes increased the risk that the forces would commit these crimes."[88]

---

[84]Trial of Wilhelm von Leeb and Thirteen Others (German High Command Trial) (United States Military Tribunal, Nuremberg), 76 (Dec. 30, 1947-Oct. 28, 1948).

[85]ICC Statute, Article 30.

[86]ICC St atute, Article 30.

[87]"In addition to other grounds of criminal responsibility under this Statute for crimes within the jurisdiction of the Court: (a) A military commander or person effectively acting as a military commander shall be criminally responsible for crimes within the jurisdiction of the Court committed by forces under his or her effective command and control, or effective authority and control as the case may be, as a result of his or her failure to exercise control properly over such forces, where: (i) That military commander or person either knew or, owing to the circumstances at the time, should have known that the forces were committing or about to commit such crimes; and (ii) That military commander or person failed to take all necessary and reasonable measures within his or her power to prevent or repress their commission or to submit the matter to the competent authorities for investigation and prosecution." Rome Statute of the International Criminal Court, Article 28, July 17, 1998, 2187 U.N.T.S. 3 (entered into force July 1, 2002). Also: Kai Ambos, Superior Responsibility, in 1 The Rome Statute Of The International Criminal Court: A Commentary § 21 (Antonio Cassese, Paola Gaeta & John R. W. D. Jones eds., 2002).

[88]Prosecutor v. Bemba, Case No. ICC-01/05-01/08, Decision Pursuant to Article 61(7)(a) and (b) of the Rome Statute on the Charges of the Prosecutor Against Jean-Pierre Bemba Gombo, ¶¶ 423-426 (Int'l Crim. Court June 15, 2009), http://www.icc-cpi.int/iccdocs/doc/doc699541.pdf.

The International Criminal Tribunal for the former Yugoslavia—ICTY—further elaborated on the requirement of "mens rea", in the Galic case, setting the standard on "willfulness", which is defined as conscious and intentional act.[89] In this framework recklessness can be included as well, whereas not "mere negligence".[90]

One way to approach the issue is to establish responsibility of individuals on Article 85 of API, which describes "grave breaches" requiring "willfulness" in the targeting of civilians. Willfulness was interpreted by the ICTY as including "indirect intent". Therefore, the acceptance of the risk orientating from a behavior is sufficient for the "mens rea" criterion.

As Jens David Ohlin proposed, the Nuremberg trial doctrine about the "organized apparatus" and the "cogs in a machine"[91] can be helpful in the framework of the deployment of AWS's as well. The "innocent instrumentality rule" paved way for the attribution of responsibility to individuals merely because of the participation in a machine-like acting mechanism.

The concept is built on the idea that even if individual responsibility for specific acts cannot be clearly identified in a crime that involves different perpetrators and various events, the participation in the mechanism that committed the criminal act can justify criminal liability.[92]

In the Eichmann case, he- himself- was found to be the "driver" of the wider bureaucratic machine and therefore the primary responsible for the commitment of the crimes he was accused of; the doctrine emerging from the trial, was that even if an individual does not commit any act himself but is effectively in control of a mechanism that does so, criminal liability will be attributed to that individual.[93] This is the perpetration via an organized "apparatus".[94]

[89]Prosecutor v. Galic, Case No. IT-98-29-T, Trial Judgment, 54, 57 (Int'l Crim. Trib. for the Former Yugoslavia Dec. 5, 2003.

[90]Prosecutor v. Galic, at para. 54.

[91]*David Ohlin, THE COMBATANT'S STANCE: AUTONOMOUS WEAPONS ON THE BATTLEFIELD* at p. 3.

[92]Characteristic of this approach is the Borkum Island case. The case referred to the crew of a U.S. warplane that was shot down over the German island of Borkum in 1944. The members of the crew who were arrested by the Germans got lynched both by German soldiers as well as by locals. After the war, several of the perpetrators were prosecuted before a U.S. military court, the prosecutor of which referred to them as "cogs in the wheel of common design, all equally important, each cog doing the part assigned to it. And the wheel of wholesale murder could not turn without all the cogs." Since the prosecutor could not assign individual responsibility for each specific act within the general criminal behavior, given the number of the participants he chose the attribution of responsibility on a collective basis. Similar was the Ponzano case findings. Jens David Ohlin, The Combatant's Stance: Autonomous Weapons On The Battlefield, at pp.4-5. Antonio Cassese, International Criminal Law 202 (2d ed. 2008).

[93]Hector Olasolo, The Criminal Responsibility of Senior Political and Military Leaders as Principals to International Crimes 20 (2010); Michael Bohlander, Principles of German Criminal Law 163 (2009).

[94]Roxin (2011).

The ICTY reiterated that same idea by endorsing it in the concept of Joint Criminal Enterprise –JCE- which established that the individual is held liable for the participation in the commitment of act, even if his individual participation cannot be ascertained.[95] Essentially, the machine-like organization of the criminal act decentralizes criminal responsibility to all of the participants, given that they willingly act as "cogs in a machine".[96] Similar was the stance of the International Criminal Tribunal for Rwanda-ICTR.[97]

In order for the "criminal enterprise" to be identified we need three elements: "[a] plurality of persons...[t]he existence of a common plan, design or purpose which amounts to or involves the commission of a crime provided for in the [ICTY] Statute... [p]articipation of the accused in the common design".[98]

As ICTY stated "The fact that any of the acts referred to in articles 2 to 5 of the present Statute was committed by a subordinate does not relieve his superior of criminal responsibility if he knew or had reason to know that the subordinate was about to commit such acts or had done so and the superior failed to take the necessary and reasonable measures to prevent such acts or to punish the perpetrators thereof."[99]

The above doctrine establishes that the use of an instrument can be no excuse for the avoidance of criminal responsibility. Responsibility has also expanded on other accomplishes as well, such as to industrialists, following World War II, who participated in the Nazi slave labor.[100] As again the ICTY held, the "actus reus" element of providing "practical assistance, encouragement, or moral support which has a substantial effect on the perpetration of the crime."[101]

In furtherance of tracing the human hand behind AWS's conducts, these doctrines can be applied to AI, albeit adjusting the core ideas to the ontological differentiations which emerge out of the fact that it is a non- human, autonomous entity the one, actually carrying out the given military actions; the "handling" of this type of

---

[95]Prosecutor v. Tadić, Case No. IT-94-1-A, Appeals Chamber Judgment, ¶ 210 (Int'l Crim. Trib. for the former Yugoslavia July 15, 1999) [hereinafter Tadiś Appeal Judgment].

[96]Prosecutor v. Vasiljevic, Case No. IT-98-32-T, Trial Chamber Judgment (Int'l Crim. Trib. for the former Yugoslavia Nov. 29, 2002), ¶ 67 (holding that "[i]f the agreed crime is committed by one or other of the participants in a joint criminal enterprise such as has already been discussed, all of the participants in that enterprise are equally guilty of the crime regardless of the part played by each in its commission"). Cherif Bassiouni, Introduction To International Criminal Law 400 (2d Rev. Ed. 2013).

[97]Statute of the International Criminal Tribunal for Rwanda, adopted by S.C. Res. 955, U.N. Doc. S/RES/955 (Nov. 8, 1994).

[98]Prosecutor v. Tadic, Judgment Appeals, at para. 227.

[99]ICTY, Statute, art. 7(1), (3); Statute of the International Criminal Tribunal for Rwanda, adopted by S.C. Res. 955, U.N. Doc. S/RES/955 (Nov. 8, 1994), art. 6(1), (3).

[100]Lippmann (1995), pp. 214–221, 239–249, 267. Nuremberg Charter, Agreement for the Prosecution and Punishment of the Major War Criminals of the European Axis, and Charter of the International Military Tribunal, Charter II, art. 6, entered into force Aug. 8, 1945, 82 U.N.T.S. 280.

[101]Prosecutor v. Furundzija, Case No. IT-95-17/1-T, Judgment, ¶ 249 (Int'l Crim. Trib. for the Former Yugoslavia Dec. 10, 1998).

machine bears analogies to the bureaucratic "machine" regarding the need- at least as long as we are still are in the domain of any of the above-mentioned three loops-[102] although significant differentiations exist as well, in the sense that AI is not a simple machine but exercises some –expanding-level of autonomy.[103]

AI raises the issue however of what extent of knowledge the military commander will actually have when using such highly sophisticated technologies.[104] The lack of precise knowledge cannot be adopted as an excuse; for professor Michael Schmitt "Clearly, any commander who decides to launch AWS's into a particular environment is, as with any other weapon systems, accountable under international criminal law for that decision. Nor will developers escape accountability if they design systems, autonomous or not, meant to conduct operations that are not IHL compliant. And States can be held accountable under the laws of State responsibility should their armed forces use AWS in an unlawful manner."[105]

From Professor Armin Krishnan's approach, the manufacturer is not out of the equation either: if "the robot does not operate within the boundaries of its specified parameters, it is the manufacturer's fault..." whereas in case it is "used in circumstances that make its use illegal, then it is the commander's fault."[106] Therefore multiple-level responsibility will be imposed, together with the responsibility of the people in the field to continuously revisit the AWS's behavior on the ground.[107]

It is obvious that complexities of AI lead to a wider debate about who in the chain not only of command but also of creation and activation of AI are to be held accountable for illegal actions, carried out by AI and subsequently by AWS's.

While the above-mentioned cases about accomplishes create precedent, it is a puzzling issue whether these-generally speaking- manufacturers of weapons can be held accountable for the use of the weapons in case they have not been outlawed in general. Designers and manufacturers of weapons are not treated by international law in general as complicit in the commitment of whatever violations of law arise out of the specific uses of such weapons.

In addition, machine-learning per se aims at the self-evolution of AI and therefore at the surpassing of the limits –or at in least their widening- which were initially

[102]David Ohlin, The Combatant's Stance: Autonomous Weapons On The Battlefield, at p. 9; Neha Jain, Perpetrators and Accessories In International Criminal Law: Individual Modes of Responsibility for Collective Crimes 125–140 (2014).

[103]Kenneth Anderson & Matthew Waxman, Law and Ethics for Robot Soldiers, Policy Review (Dec. 1, 2012), http://www.hoover.org/research/law-and-ethics-robot-soldiers. Crootof (2015).

[104]Dunlap Jr (2016), pp. 69–70.

[105]Michael Schmitt, Regulating Autonomous Weapons Might be Smarter Than Banning Them, JsT Security (Aug. 10, 2015), https://www.justsecurity.org/25333/regulatingautonomous-weapons-smarter-banning/.

[106]Armin Krishnan, Killer Robots: Legality And Ethicality Of Autonomous Weapons 105 (2009).

[107]Peter Margulies, Making Autonomous Weapons Accountable: Command Responsibility for Computer-Guided Lethal Force in Armed Conflicts, Research Handbook on Remote Warfare 19 (Jens David Ohlin ed., 2016), http://papers.ssm.com/sol3/papers.cfm?abstract id=2734900.

imposed upon AI or designed in general by the original manufacturers.[108] Machine-learning is based on AI autonomy and therefore on restraining the role of the initial designer or of the entity or person, which is responsible for the compile of big data and of machine-learning.

Once we adhere to expanding autonomy, we also accept expanding unpredictability with it as well, which means that the level of human control and therefore responsibility grows thinner and becomes more difficult to be identified.[109] However, this does not mean that total absence of control and therefore of responsibility must be allowed.

As mentioned in the previous part of the chapter, under a governance mechanism for AI and therefore for AWS's too, standards on the manufacturers and on persons or entities responsible for the machine-learning procedure can be imposed. The responsibility will need to be sustained on intent or serious neglect which will be linked with behavior in the battlefield that will be violating IHL norms.

In this framework checks and balances have been proposed for the restriction of AWS' potential unpredictability: "limiting deployment of lethal robots to only inside a 'kill box'; designing a robot to target only other machines or weapons; not giving robots a self-defense mechanism so that they may act more conservatively to prevent; creating robots with only non-lethal or less-than-lethal strike capabilities, at least initially until they are proven to be reliable."[110]

Additional proposed standards in advance are the knowledge about the function of the weapon, the spatial limitations which determine the environment within which the weapon is used, time limitations meaning that a weapon system will have to switch to human control after a certain time of autonomous function, the predictability, the distinction between systems against material targets and humans, as well as between stationary and mobile targets, the verification, in the sense that measures of compliance with the transparency and the accountability that are implemented regarding other weapons should also be analogically used in relation to AWS as well.[111]

Apart from the significance of the specific propositions, the important element is the provision of checks and balances of AWS's in advance, the non- compliance with which will generate responsibility under IHL as leading potentially to its violations.

Difficulties also apply when we attempt to trace the responsibility of the military commander. The advantage of AWS's is their autonomy, which obviously leads to their more or less significant and ambivalent unpredictability and to the erosion of human control. Therefore, although restrictions can be imposed, in the end, the

---

[108] Anthony Finn & Steve Scheding, Developments and Challenges for Autonomous Unmanned Vehicles: AAA Compendium (2010), at p. 183.

[109] Stewart (2011), p. 290.

[110] Patrick et al. (2008).

[111] UNIDIR, The Weaponization of Increasingly Autonomous Technologies: Considering how Meaningful Human Control might move the discussion forward, 2014, at pp. 6–7.

ramification is that the more we rely on AWS's autonomy, the less the human control is.

In these regards, one proposal is to revise command responsibility so that it entails responsibility for commanders for the procurement of AWS's. The use of AWS in such a sense is -up to some extent- discouraged in principle, at least up to the extent that the commander cannot be certain of the safety, meaning compliance with IHL, in various essences of AWS's.[112] In a way, such a proposal implies lowering the standards of effective control, so that the ethical and legal judgment of deploying AWS's must be conducted prior to the beginning of the battle.

If the growing autonomy of AWS makes it more difficult to determine the human, military commander behind the "machine", still a type of "objectively" identified responsibility, on the basis of the position of the commander at the top of the chain of command could be established as a solution.

Criminal liability in this sense can be attributed in a way, objectively and collectively, to the whole of the participants. The problem is that in such a way and unless concepts such as the ones of "common criminal purpose," "common concerted design," or "joint criminal enterprise"[113] are met, such a path could lead to distorting eventually the threshold as well as the guarantees of fairness within IHL.

The risks and the importance of AWS's pushed the High Contracting Parties to the 1980 Convention on Prohibitions or Restrictions on the Use of Certain Conventional Weapons which May Be Deemed to be Excessively Injurious or to Have Indiscriminate Effects and Protocols—Convention on Certain Conventional Weapons or CCW—to convene informal meetings about them.

The meetings ascertained the necessity for AWS's to comply with IHL[114] and to have human control.[115] It is as mentioned above, that during one of these meetings, some participants suggested that there must be a general ban regarding the development and the use of AWS, on the basis of fundamental contradiction with IHL, exactly because of the lack of any emotions, the potential resort to covert operations, asymmetric warfare, impunity on the basis of difficulty to attribute responsibility and the lack of efficient understanding.

The fundamental concern lies with the responsibility gap given the potential ellipsis of meaningful human control over whom, when and how will be victim of force.[116]

This is why a point of unanimous agreement was the need to establish "meaningful human control", although its exact definition is yet to be completely

[112]Geoffrey S. Corn, Autonomous Weapon Systems: Managing the Inevitability of "Taking the Man out of the Loop" at p. 23, (June 14, 2014), https://papers.ssrn.com/sol3/papers.cfm?abstract_id=2450640.

[113]Prosecutor v. Tadic, Judgment Appeals, at para. 187, 203, 220.

[114]CCW/MSP/2014/3 - 2014 Report of the Informal Meeting of Experts, at para. 27.

[115]CCW/MSP/2014/3 - 2014 Report of the Informal Meeting of Experts, at para. 20.

[116]Johnson (2014), pp. 1–9: www.law.upenn.edu/live/files/3774-johnson-d-technology-with-no-responsibility.

determined.[117] The idea is that there must always be a human, responsible and therefore capable as well, of turning off whatever system, which means that the system must be somewhat predictable from its initial design.[118]

Given all the complexities, it is important that at least the need for some type of human control, especially in terms of determination of when, where and how force is to be used constitutes common ground.[119] The existence of human control means that AWS's autonomy will have to be restricted, so that predictability and the need to cover the accountability gaps may be effectively implemented, as necessary for creating legal certainty and for the compliance with IHL and with human rights.[120] Another choice could be of course their complete prohibition, but as mentioned, the former seems more likely than the latter.[121]

The need to come up with novel legal solutions is gradually realized: "Any complex, hazardous technology carries "unintentional" risk, and can have harmful results its designers and operators did not intend. AWS's may pose novel, unintended forms of hazard to human life that typical approaches to ensuring responsibility do not effectively manage because these systems may behave in unpredictable ways that are difficult to prevent."[122]

It is obvious that because an assessment of AWS's use on an ad hoc basis, in the framework of IHL presents significant difficulties,[123] an overall governance mechanism of AI becomes even more significant.

A different approach could be to outlaw AWS's in general and therefore establish liability merely from their evolution and their use in the battlefield. It will not be the first time in legal history.[124] As it is inferred from the ICC statute, the jurisdiction of the Court extends over war crimes, which include the employment of "weapons, projectiles and material and methods of warfare which are of a nature to cause superfluous injury or unnecessary suffering or which are inherently indiscriminate in

---

[117]Article 36, Structuring debate on autonomous weapons systems, Article 36 briefing paper, November 2013: www.article36.org/wp-content/uploads/2013/11/Autonomous-weapons-memo-for-CCW.pdf.

[118]McAllister (2017), pp. 2563–2564.

[119]CCW/MSP/2015/3—2015 Report of the Informal Meeting of Experts, at para. 37.

[120]CCW/MSP/2015/3—2015 Report of the Informal Meeting of Experts, at paras. 44–46.

[121]CCW/CONF.V/2—2016 Report and recommendations of the Informal Meeting of Experts, at paras. 32–34.

[122]UNIDIR, 2016, Safety, Unintentional Risk and Accidents in the Weaponization of Increasingly Autonomous Technologies, UNIDIR Resources no. 5, p. 1, http://www.unidir.org/files/publications/pdfs/safety-unintentional-risk-and-accidents-en-668.pdf.

[123]Kenneth Anderson and Matthew Waxman, 'Law and Ethics for Autonomous Weapon Systems: Why a Ban Won't Work and How the Laws of War Can' (Research Paper, Jean Perkins Task Force on National Security and Law, Stanford University, 9 April 2013) 12–13. Damasio (1994), p. xiv; Castel and Castel (2016), p. 5.

[124]Statute of the International Tribunal for the Prosecution of Persons Responsible for Serious Violations of International Humanitarian Law Committed in the Territory of the Former Yugoslavia since 1991, art. 3(a), adopted by Security Council on May 25, 1993, U.N. Doc. S/RES/827 (May 25, 1993) [hereinafter ICTY Statute].

violation of the international law of armed conflict."[125] Still it does not yet seem as a likely possibility.

In this framework, in the UN General Assembly, on 2018 held a meeting where delegates discussed about "potential risks to international security posed by such new technologies as militarized drones" and "exchanged views today on ways to control these lethal autonomous weapons",[126] raising concerns about LAWS in particular and asking for common understanding and definitions.

In another effort to practically come forth with checks and balances for AWS's, the proposal of joint cognitive systems—JCS—of machines and humans has been submitted. A problem that has appeared however is that such schemes necessitate increased human presence in order to analyze the machine data and supervise AI.[127]

Summing up, while AWS's constitute a new phenomenon, the relevant international norms of IHL and the legal theory offer the basis for a governance mechanism. In this framework, responsibility for AWS's conducts in the battlefield may extend in different ways on the whole chain of participants in AWS's deployment; the imposition of standards related to AWS's manufacturing and machine-learning constitute the initial basis for criminal responsibility.

Other than that, and in relation to the military commander, the "mens rea" in its most extended interpretation must be adopted. In order to avoid a de facto immunity orientating from the alleged lack of full understanding of AWS's function, it is necessary to foresee that the mere use of AWS's generates responsibility, since AI unpredictability is well known and documented already, even if the specific manifestations may not be known in advance.

Such an approach will be further enhanced and justified, once more specific standards, in the framework of AI governance are imposed. Several lists of AWS's standards may be foreseen, imposing restrictions in terms of the type of the use of force, of the potential targets, of the existence of human control, of a switch-off mechanism, of transparency and of monitoring mechanisms. In this sense, because of the ontological elements of AI as they are incorporated into AWS's, standards and a higher threshold for the use of the latter must be foreseen in advance.

---

[125]Rome Statute of the International Criminal Court, preamble, opened for signature on July 17, 1998, 2187 U.N.T.S. 90 (entered into force July 1, 2002) [hereinafter Rome Statute of the ICC].

[126]First Committee Weighs Potential Risks of New Technologies as Members Exchange Views on How to Control Lethal Autonomous Weapons, Cyberattacks, UNITED NATIONS (Oct. 26, 2018), https://www.un.org/press/en/2018/gadis3611.doc.htm.

[127]M.R. Endsley, 'Building resilient systems via strong human systems integration', Defense AT&L, (Jan–Feb 2016), at pp. 6–12, 11: dau.dodlive.mil/files/2015/12/Endsley.pdf; UNIDIR, Safety, Unintentional Risk and Accidents in the Weaponization of Increasingly Autonomous Technologies, 2016, AT P. 3.

8.3 AWS's and Human Rights Law

The relationship between AI and human rights was examined extensively in the relevant chapter. Here is only briefly touched, in terms of AWS's which may be used in environments other than those of military battlefields. The two areas of international law- IHL and human rights- are profoundly interconnected and very close to one another regarding their mentality. Here they are examined in the sense of IHL referring to military conflicts, whereas human rights to internal affairs of states.

In addition, human rights law poses another critical criterion regarding AWS's legitimacy: human dignity.[128] While both human rights law and IHL regulate and therefore restrict the use of force, their orientation and extent of restriction is different. As it has been said the primary difference is "the different starting points of the two bodies of law: for human rights law it is the right to life; for humanitarian law, the right to kill".[129]

Human rights law is different also compared to IHL as it emerges from the approach that it is implemented upon one state's own citizens. Given that human rights law imposes a more general framework which attempts to safeguard fundamental principles and that it does not specifically regulate the battlefield, it does not contain regulations about the use of weapons as detailed, as the ones of IHL.[130]

The risks for human rights, from AWS's however are analogical to those which emerge with IHL; there are potential risks from violations of human rights which take place from AWS's actions, as well as risks because of the difficulty to attribute AWS's activities to the human "hand" behind the AI.

One may imagine for example the use of AWS's in the framework of policing, leading to the loss of life. The right to life foresees that life cannot be arbitrarily deprived.[131] Given that the above-mentioned guarantee includes both the non-arbitrary deprivation of life and the accountability for the arbitrary deprivation, AWS's-just as under IHL—raise the prospect of who-if any- will be accountable for this as well as for other violations of human rights.[132]

---

[128]Here there is no general analysis of the role of human rights in relation to AI, as it is analyzed in Chap. 4, above.

[129]Sandesh Sivakumaran, International Humanitarian Law, in International Human Rights Law 535 (Daniel Moeckli, Sangeeta Shah, and Sandesh Sivakumaran eds., 2013).

[130]Heyns (2016), pp. 353–354.

[131]"Every human being has the inherent right to life. This right shall be protected by law. No one shall be arbitrarily deprived of his life." International Covenant on Civil and Political Rights, adopted 16 Dec. 1966, G.A. Res. 2200 (XXI), U.N. GAOR, 21st Sess., art. 6 (1), U.N. Doc. A/6316 (1966), 999 U.N.T.S. 171 (entered into force 23 Mar. 1976) [hereinafter ICCPR].

[132]Human Rights Committee, General Comment No. 31, The Nature of the General Legal Obligation Imposed on States Parties to the Covenant, adopted 29 Mar. 2004, ¶¶ 16, 18 available at http://www.umn.edu/humanarts/gencomm/hrcom31.html; UNHRC, General Comment No. 6 (1982), ¶ 4; UN 2005 Basic Principles and Guidelines on a Right to a Remedy and Reparation, McCann and others v. The United Kingdom, No. 18984/91, ¶ 169, ECtHR (1995).

Again, as with IHL, elements of risk emerge from the unpredictability of AWS's, and from the need to incorporate into AWS's functions and complicated legal concepts such as necessity and proportionality.

The concept of necessity means that no other, non-violent means will be suitable and that violence will be used only as means of last resort. Proportionality refers to the need for a balance between the interest and the right, which is harmed and the one which is protected.[133] In this case, proportionality requires delicate moral assessments between competing rights.

A counter-argument may be that as AWS's become more advanced, technologically -speaking, it will be possible to evolve towards including such evaluations in the course of actions on the ground. The counter-argument to that is that while AWS's may never reach this level, their implementation becomes gradually more widespread.

Therefore, what could be the case would be their use only once the use of force is determined as both necessary and proportional by a human operator. Such a determination however on the other hand will be depriving AWS's of part of their advantages. As with IHL the extent of human interference and the speed of reaction constitute the critical factors.

Human rights however and their potential violations are also assessed on the basis of the principle of dignity of all humans, with human dignity constituting a principle that transcends and empowers human rights in general.[134]

Dignity constitutes the cornerstone of human rights law or as it has been characterized as "the rock on which the superstructure of human rights"[135] or the "the ground of rights". It provides substantive context to the variety of rights which are included in the relevant conventions.[136] While transcending every specific human right, it remains partially elusive in terms of its actual content. Still, it is considered as intrinsic to human beings,[137] who are equal in these regards and functions as fundamental for all of human rights.[138]

The preamble of the UN Charter, article 1 of the Universal Declaration of Human Rights, as well as the Preamble of the International Covenant on Civil and Political Rights—ICCPR—all establish dignity either as a right or as a foundational

[133]Christof Heyns, Autonomous Weapons Systems and Human Rights law (16 May 2014), available at http://www.icla.up.ac.za/images/un/speeches/heyns%20ccw%20presentation%20aws%20and%20human%20rights.pdf.

[134]United Nations Human Rights Office of the High Commissioner, Universal Declaration of Human Rights—In six cross-cutting themes, (https://www.ohchr.org/en/udhr/pages/crosscuttingthemes.aspx); Arthur Chaskalson, Human Dignity as a Constitutional Value, in The Concept of Human Dignity in Human Rights Discourse, supra note 39, at 133. (David Kretzmer & Eckart Klein eds., 2002). Human dignity transcends if properly interpreted of course, IHL as well.

[135]Beyleveld and Brownsword (2001), p. 13.

[136]McCrudden (2008), pp. 655, 670.

[137]Pablo Gilabert, Human Rights, Human Dignity, and Power, in Rowan Cruft et al. eds., Philosophical Foundations of Human Rights, (2015), a t pp. 196–197.

[138]Monsalve and Román (2009), pp. 45–4.

principle.[139] The Convention against Torture and Other Cruel, Inhuman or Degrading Treatment or Punishment also establishes that human rights "derive from the inherent dignity of the human person."[140]

The same approach is foreseen in a series of fundamental for the international legal system, conventions, such as the Convention on the Rights of the Child, the International Convention on the Protection of the Rights of All Migrant Workers and Members of their Families, the Convention on the Rights of Persons with Disabilities—CRPD—and the International Convention for the Protection of All Persons from Enforced Disappearance.[141]

In addition, the specific rights of the above—mentioned Conventions are also providing the context to human dignity, in terms of its materialization via these rights. In this sense, human dignity may be elusive in its generic manifestation but it is not vague—or should not be—in practice. Dignity flows out of the mere human existence and is materialized in different aspects of human life through the enjoyment of the relevant rights.[142]

A variety of international organizations' bodies has elaborated further on human dignity: the Human Rights Committee—CCPR—the Committee against Torture—CAT—the Committee on the Elimination of Discrimination against Women—Committee—the Committee on the Elimination of Racial Discrimination—CRPD—the Committee on Enforced Disappearances, the Committee on Economic, Social and Cultural Rights—ESCR—and the Committee on the Rights of the Child are among those which have contributed further into the clarification of the theme of human dignity,[143] albeit on an ad hoc basis- of human dignity violations.

---

[139] Universal Declaration of Human Rights, adopted 10 Dec. 1948, G.A. Res. 217A (III), U.N. GAOR, 3d Sess, art. 1, U.N. Doc. A/RES/3/217A (1948); International Covenant on Civil and Political Rights, adopted 16 Dec. 1966, G.A. Res. 2200 (XXI), U.N. GAOR, 21st Sess., art. 6 (1), U.N. Doc. A/6316 (1966), 999 U.N.T.S. 171 (entered into force 23 Mar. 1976) [hereinafter ICCPR] Pmbl, arts. 7, 9. Article 5 of the African Charter; Article 1 of the EU Charter of Fundamental Right.

[140] Convention Against Torture and Other Cruel, Inhuman or Degrading Treatment or Punishment, pmbl., Dec. 10, 1984, 1465 U.N.T.S. 85.

[141] International Convention on the Protection of the Rights of All Migrant Workers and Members of their Families, arts. 17(1), 70, Dec. 18, 1990, 2220 U.N.T.S. 3; Convention on the Rights of Persons with Disabilities, pmbl., arts. 1, 3(a), 8(1)(a), 16(4), 24(1)(a), 25(d), Jan. 24, 2007, 2515 U.N.T.S. 3; International Convention for the Protection of All Persons from Enforced Disappearance, arts. 19(2), 24(5)(c), Dec. 20, 2006, 2716 U.N.T.S. 3.

[142] Kotzmann and Seery (2017), pp. 14–16.

[143] United Nations Human Rights, Office of the High Commissioner for Human Rights, Jurisprudence, OHCHR, http://juris.ohchr.org; Human Rights Council, General Comment No. 21: Article 10, Humane Treatment of Persons Deprived of Their Liberty, ¶ 3 (Apr. 10, 1992); Human Rights Council, General Comment No. 21: Article 10, Humane Treatment of Persons Deprived of Their Liberty, ¶ 3 (Apr. 10, 1992).

For example, degrading, cruel and inhumane behavior, torture, detention under inhumane conditions is all considered as contradictory to human dignity,[144] as well as forced labor, slavery, death penalty.[145]

Protocol No 13 to the European Convention on Human Rights -ECHR- also includes references to the "inherent dignity of all human beings," as a significant concept for the interpretation of this Convention.[146] It is treated as the "very essence" of ECHR.[147]

As a concept it raises ambiguities both in terms of its exact definition, as well as in terms of its nature—i.e. principle or distinct right.[148] The perception of dignity as a right in not uncommon among different national legal orders, as well as internationally, imposing the comprehension of human as an end and not as means, an aspect which is considered by many as contravening the prospect of any human being confronted by the force of an algorithm—even worse, lethal force. Human dignity is transcending human rights, as a normatively binding principle[149] which is materialized in a dialectic relationship with the specific rights. In this sense, it is of particular significance, especially for phenomena that are new, demanding teleological interpretation and creating thinking of and on, already existing rights.

An indication of the interlinkage between AI and human dignity is identified in the relevant EU directive, providing that every person is entitled "not to be subject to a decision which produces legal effects concerning him...which is based solely on automated processing of data."[150]

---

[144] Human Rights Comm., Views: Communication 1486/2006, ¶ 4.16, U.N. Doc. CCPR/C/93/D/1486/2006 (Aug. 5, 2008); Human Rights Comm., Communication No. 1791/2008, ¶ 3.7, U.N. Doc. CCPR/C/107/D/1791/2008 (July 5, 2013).

[145] Zardiashvili and Fosch-Villaronga (2020), p. 123. https://doi.org/10.1007/s11023-019-09514-6; ICCPR Second Optional Protocol. (1989). Aiming at the abolition of the death penalty, GA Res 44/128 https://www.ohchr.org/en/professionalinterest/pages/2ndopccpr.aspx. Accessed 8 Oct 2019; United Nations (1993a) The Cairo Declaration of Human Rights. A/CONF.157/PC/62/Add.18. https://undocs.org/A/CONF.157/PC/62/Add.18; United Nations (1993b) Standard rules on the equalization of opportunities for persons with disabilities. https://www.un.org/documents/ga/res/48/a48r096.htm; United Nations. (2007). Convention on the rights of persons with disabilities. https://www.un.org/development/desa/disabilities/convention-on-the-rights-of-persons-with-disabilities.html.

[146] Convention for the Protection of Human Rights and Fundamental Freedoms, pmbl., Nov. 4, 1950, 213 U.N.T.S. 222.

[147] O'Mahony (2012), pp. 551–574.

[148] Dieter Birnbacher, Ambiguities in the Concept of Menschenwude, in sAncTiTy of lifE And huMAn digniTy 107 (Kurt Bayertz ed., 1996); Bernhard Schlink, The Concept of Human Dignity: Current Usages, Future Discourses, in understanding human dignity (Christopher McCrudden ed., 2013) at p. 632. Dicke (2002), pp. 111–112.

[149] The term concept has also been used. Zardiashvili and Fosch-Villaronga (2020), p. 123 https://doi.org/10.1007/s11023-019-09514-6.

[150] EU Directive 95/46/EC Directive 95/46/EC of the European Parliament and of the Council of 24 Oct. 1995 on the Protection of Individuals With Regard to the Processing of Personal Data and on the Free Movement of Such Data, art. 15.

The violation of human dignity, on the basis of degrading treatment, could be considered to be the case whenever AI apply force on humans, without any human in control of the AWS's, since that is inhumane treatment by definition.[151]

It is argued that exactly as a legitimately imposed death penalty cannot be executed in an inhumane way because it contradicts the right to dignity, even otherwise legitimate lethal use of force or use of force in general cannot be executed by AI systems against humans, merely because of the nature of AI and of AWS.[152]

The conclusion is then that autonomous weapons cannot be allowed under the existing human rights framework.[153] This is the position which was proposed by UN Human Rights Special Rapporteur on extrajudicial, summary or arbitrary executions, Christof Heyns, who suggested that a moratorium on such weapons must be imposed on the bases of the right to life and of the right to dignity.[154]

On the other hand, the question could be as with IHL, why to ban AWS's on the basis of human rights, if such weapons are trained and functioning in ways, protective of the human rights, which provide ad hoc to human dignity its whole context– or part of it.

Maybe that can come to be; things are more complicated nevertheless, as even if specific human rights are better protected with AWS's, the generic, human dignity principle, in the sense of having humans at the core of decision-making and decision—implementation within state authority is harmed. Entrusting entities which are non—human and highly unpredictable as they reach higher intelligence and autonomy and with more distant human accountability regarding their actions—if any—constitutes a risky path.

It is in addition and in principle difficult to grasp what necessity would support the use of fully autonomous AWS's in general and even more in places, other than the war battlefield. In this sense, the argument is that only AWS's with very limited autonomy and with clear human control should be ever adopted in these regards. In the more general framework of human rights law, AWS's that do not fall into the more specific area of IHL can very well be outlawed in the first place.

Other than that, the governance mechanisms mentioned above and the equivalent standards will need to be applied in AWS's acting under human rights law if they ever come to exist.

---

[151]Heyns, Human Rights and the use of Autonomous Weapons Systems (AWS) During Domestic Law Enforcement, at p. 363, no. 58.

[152]CCW/CONF.V/2 - 2016 Report and recommendations of the Informal Meeting of Experts, at pp. 4–5.

[153]CCW/CONF.V/2 - 2016 Report and recommendations of the Informal Meeting of Experts, at p. 10.

[154]C. Heyns, 2013, Report of the Special Rapporteur on extra judicial summary or arbitrary executions, United Nations Human Rights Council, A/HRC/23/47, www.ohchr.org/Documents/HRBodies/HRCouncil/RegularSession/Session23/A-HRC-23-47_en.pdf.

8.4 Conclusions

The last two chapters analyzed the relationship between AI and international security from the perspective of the impact of AWS's on the collective security system and mainly in the framework of IHL. While AWS's are only part of the much wider applications of AI, they keep a significant role -mainly- in terms of our fears. The evolution of AWS's can be indicative also of the shortsighted-ness of the international community, if left without efficient governance mechanisms for such technology. An arms-race could easily spiral out of control on unknown territories technologically-speaking.

Such governance mechanisms will necessarily be based at large on state concessions if they are going to be effective. States bear after all objective responsibility for the weapons they use and for the way that these weapons are used by their militaries.[155] State responsibility offers both legally concrete grounds, regarding liability out of AWS's use, as well as safer potential –presumably- development of AWS's because of their more easily identifiable liability.[156]

Still, an international governance mechanism will need to be inclusive and encompass all actors, state and non-state alike. A synthesis of re-visiting existing norms and of creating new ones- a convention about AI- will have to develop, together with monitoring institutions, under -most preferably- the UN SC.

The examination of AWS' in the face of IHL is a demanding procedure that must entail several considerations. The risks to IHL constitute as well part of the threats against international peace and security. This is why one of the proposals is to prohibit AWS's in the first place.

A different way to approach the issue of the permissibility or not of ASI and AGI is instead of attempting to restrict or prohibit their development to try and organize a universal system of governance under the UN, so that AWS's will eventually comply with international law, as well as with the international peace and security architecture.[157]

It may be the case that a campaign for the complete, in advance, prohibition of AWS's -even of limited autonomy- under IHL may not be the best solution, either in terms of its legal justification as well as, more significantly, because in practice it will most likely fail- at least until states have tried these weapon systems and rejected them.

From the perspective of the implementation of human rights it may be in terms of legal debate more achievable to push for a ban of AWS's, in general or at least of part of them. The issue if dignity is more obviously, crucial in these regards. The possibility of weaponized AI and of mechanized army in the internal affairs bears

---

[155] Responsibility of States for Internationally Wrongful Acts, [2001] 2 Y.B. Int'l L. Comm'n 26, U.N. Doc. A/CN.4/SER.A/2001/Add.1, article II.

[156] Hammond (2015), pp. 668–669.

[157] J.-G. Castel Matthew and E. Castel, The Road to Artificial Super-Intelligence: Has International Law a Role to Play?, at p. 12.

the potential of oppressiveness as the ultimate guarantee of peoples' rebellion and of its impact on the armed bureaucracy will be highly restricted if not completely vanished.[158]

Again, the need for a governance mechanism, internationally emerges. Unregulated, state antagonisms will destroy any potential barriers. What we need is an as effective, as possible mechanism which on the basis of the principle of human dignity as well as of the more specific provisions of IHL and of human rights will categorize the different levels of AWS's' autonomy and types, allowing under certain precautions some of them and prohibiting all the rest.

References

Arkin RC (2009) Governing lethal behavior in autonomous robots. Routledge, p 13

Asaro P (2012) On banning autonomous weapon systems: human rights, automation, and the dehumanization of lethal decision-making. Int Rev Red Cross 94(886):686

Auron DD (2013) The derecognition approach: government illegality, recognition, and non-violent regime change. George Wash Int Law Rev 45:443

Beyleveld D, Brownsword R (2001) Human dignity in bioethics and biolaw. Oxford University Press, Oxford, p 13

Bothe M, Partsch KJ, Solf WA (1982) New rules for victims of armed conflicts: commentary on the two 1977 protocols additional to the Geneva conventions of 1949. Martinus Nijhoff Publishers, Leiden, p 310

Castel J-G, Castel ME (2016) The road to artificial super-intelligence: has international law a role to play? Can J Law Technol 14:5

Crootof R (2015) The killer robots are here: legal and policy implications. Cardozo Law Rev 36:1837

Damasio A (1994) Descartes' error: emotion, reason and the human brain. Penguin Books, London, p xiv

Damaska MR (2001) The shadow side of command responsibility. Am J Comp Law 49:455

Dicke K (2002) The founding function of human dignity in the universal declaration of human rights. In: Kretzmer D, Klein E (eds) Concept of human dignity in human rights discourse. Columbia University Press, New York, pp 111–112

Dunlap CJ Jr (2016) Accountability and autonomous weapons: much ado about nothing? Temple Int Comp Law J 30(1):63

Endsley MR (1995) Theoretical underpinnings of situation awareness: a critical review. In: Endsley MR, Garland DJ (eds) Situation awareness analysis and measurement. CRC, Boca Raton, p 3

Fine RP, Cohen GM (1966) Is criminal negligence a defensible basis for criminal liability? Buff Law Rev 16:749

Floridi L, Sanders JW (2004) On the morality of artificial agents. Minds Machines 14:349

Greenwood C (1993) Customary international law and the first geneva protocol of 1977 in the gulf conflict. In: Rowe P (ed) The Gulf War 1990–1991 in International and English Law. Sweet & Maxwell, London, p 63

Grut C (2013) The challenge of autonomous lethal robotics to International Humanitarian Law. J Conflict Security Law 18:5

Hall J (1963) Negligent behaviour should be excluded from penal liability. Colum Law Rev 63:632

[158] Rogers (2014), p. 1264.

Hallevy G (2010) The criminal liability of artificial intelligence entities--from science fiction to legal social control. Akron Intellect Property J 4:171
Hammond DN (2015) Autonomous weapons and the problem of state accountability. Chicago J Int Law 15(2):653
Henckaerts J-M, Doswald-Beck L (eds) (2005) Customary international humanitarian law. Cambridge University Press, Cambridge
Heyns C (2016) Human rights and the use of Autonomous Weapons Systems (AWS) during domestic law enforcement. Human Rights Q 38:350
Johnson DG (2006) Computer systems: moral entities but not moral agents. Ethics Info Technol 8:195
Johnson DG (2014) Technology with no human responsibility? J Bus Ethics:1–9
Johnson DG, Miller KW (2008) Un-making artificial moral agents. Ethics Info Technol 10:123
Kassimeris G (2006) The barbarisation of warfare, a user's manual. In: Kassimeris G (ed) The barbarisation of warfare. C. Hurst & Co., London, pp 4–13
Kastan B (2013) Autonomous weapons systems: a coming legal "Singularity"? Univ Ill J Law Technol Policy:45
Klein GA (1999) Sources of power: how people make decisions. Massachusetts Institute of Technology Press, Cambridge, pp 33–35
Kotzmann J, Seery C (2017) Dignity in International Human Rights law: potential applicability in relation to international recognition of animal rights. Mich State Int Law Rev 26(1):1
Lawland K (2006) A guide to the legal review of new weapons: means and methods of warfare, measures to implement Article 36 of Additional Protocol I of 1977. Int Commun Red Cross:11–12
Lippmann M (1995) War crimes trials of German industrialists: the other schindlers. Temp Int Comp Law J 9:173
Marchant E et al (2011) International Governance of autonomous military robots. Columb Sci Technol Law Rev 12:272
Matthias A (2004) The responsibility gap: ascribing responsibility for the actions of learning automata. Ethics Info Technol 6:175
McAllister A (2017) Stranger than science fiction: the rise of A.I. interrogation in the dawn of autonomous robots and the need for an additional protocol to the U.N. convention against torture. Minn Law Rev 101:2527
McCrudden C (2008) Human dignity and judicial interpretation of human rights. Eur J Int Law 19:655
Meier MW (2016) Lethal autonomous weapons systems (laws): conducting a comprehensive weapons review. Temple Int Comp Law J 30(1):119
Melzer N (2008) Interpretive guidance on the notion of direct participation in hostilities under international humanitarian law-- adopted by the assembly of the International Committee of the Red Cross on 26 February 2009. Int Rev Red Cross 90:991
Meron T (2006) The humanization of international law. Brill, Leyden
Monsalve VB, Román JA (2009) Tensions of human dignity: conceptualization and application to international human rights law. Int J Human Rights 6:39
O'Mahony C (2012) There is no such thing as a right to dignity. Int J Const Law 10(2):551
Pagallo U (2011) Robots of just war: a legal perspective. Philos Technol 24:307
Parks WH (1990) Air war and the law of war. Air Force Law Rev 32:1
Patrick L et al (2008) Autonomous military robotics: risk, ethics, and design. California Polytechnic St. University, San Luis Obispo, p 4
Perkins RM (1978) "Knowledge" as a mens rea requirement. Hastings Law J 29:953
Press M (2017) Of robots and rules: autonomous weapon systems in the law of armed conflict. Georgetown J Int Law 48:1337
Rogers JL (2014) Legal judgment day for the rise of the machines: a national approach to regulating fully autonomous weapons. Arizona Law Rev 56(4):1257

Roxin C (2011) Crimes as part of organized power structures. J Int Criminal Justice 9, 193. B. Cooper trans
Sandoz Y, Swinarski C, Zimmermann B (eds) (1987) Commentary on the additional protocols of 8 June 1977to the Geneva Conventions of 12 August 1949. International Committee of the Red Cross, Geneva, p 682
Sassòli M, Bouvier AA, Quintin A (2011) ICRC, How does law protect in war? Cases, documents and teaching materials on contemporary practice in International Humanitarian Law, 3rd edn. ICRC, p 15
Sassòli M (2014) Autonomous weapons and international humanitarian law: advantages, open technical questions and legal issues to be clarified. Int Law Stud 90:308
Sassòli M, Cameron L (2006) The protection of civilian objects--current state of the law and issues de lege ferenda. In: Ronzitti N, Venturini G (eds) The law of air warfare: contemporary issues--essential air and space law, vol 1. Eleven International, p 35
Schmitt MN (2013) Autonomous weapon systems and international humanitarian law: a reply to the critics. Harv National Secur J Features 1:12–13
Schmitt MN, Thurnher JS (2013) "Out of the Loop": autonomous weapon systems and the law of armed conflict. Harv Natl Sec J 4:231
Sharkey NE (2012) The evitability of autonomous robot warfare. Int Rev Red Cross 94:787
Sparrow R (2007) Killer robots. J Applied Philos 24:62
Sparrow R (2009) Building a better warbot: ethical issues in the design of unmanned systems for military applications. Sci Eng Ethics 15:169
Stewart DM (1901–2011) New technology and the law of armed conflict. In: Pedrozo RA, Wollschlaeger DP (eds) International law studies, vol 87. Naval War College, Newport, p 271
Stewart D (2011) New technology and the law of armed conflict: technological meteorites and legal dinosaurs? Int Law Stud 87:271
Thurnher JS (2012) No one at the controls: legal implications of fully autonomous targeting. Joint Force Q 67:77
Toscano CP (2015) "Friend of Humans": an argument for developing autonomous weapons systems. J Natl Secur Law Policy 8:189
van der Dennen JMG (1981) UNESCO yearbook on peace and conflict studies 1980 on war: concepts, definitions, research data - a short literature review and bibliography. Greenwood Press, Westport, pp 128–189
Wagner M (2014) The dehumanization of international humanitarian law: legal, ethical, and political implications of autonomous weapon systems. Va J Transnational Law 47:1371
Walzer M (2006) Just and unjust wars: a moral argument with historical illustrations, 4th edn. Basic Books, New York, p 144
Watkin K (2005) Assessing proportionality: moral complexity and legal rules. Yearb Int Human Law 8:3
Wright JD (2012) "Excessive" ambiguity: analysing and refining the proportionality standard. Int Rev Red Cross 94:819
Zardiashvili L, Fosch-Villaronga E (2020) "Oh, dignity too?" Said the robot: human dignity as the basis for the governance of robotics. Minds Machines 30:143. https://doi.org/10.1007/s11023-019-09514-6

Chapter 9
AI, Issues of Ownership, Liability and the Role of International Law

9.1 Introduction

Both Schumpeter and Marx described the circle of crisis and innovation in capitalism, as the means either for further capitalist growth or for the potential destruction of the capitalist system. In spite of the different predictions about the future of capitalism, what is certain is the omnipresence of crises from within, meaning from its internal procedures and contradictions.

Technology constitutes one of the factors intensifying these inherent characteristics of capitalism and within technology, AI is one of the most groundbreaking and challenging developments. The use of AI and its evolution not only is already shaping the fourth industrial revolution and therefore the present and the future of capitalism but also and subsequently transforms long-standing legal regulations in terms of profit and liability.

In the first chapter, the overall impact of AI on the social and economic landscape was presented. In this chapter, the proposition for the governance of AI use in social and economic terms and the subsequent potential ramifications are presented. More specifically, the goal of this chapter is to suggest how issues of profitability and liability from AI must be governed, mainly regarding the commercial use of AI. The way that these will be concluded internationally will define at large the course of the fourth industrial revolution and the prevalent social and economic model.

As of now there is not any international regulatory framework for these matters and AI. The issues of profitability from AI and of the wider nexus of intellectual property rights- IP Rights- and patent—eligibility, as well as of liability are usually regulated predominantly under private law and at national level. However, the impact of AI globally, necessitates an equally international, governance mechanism under international law.

The first part of the chapter, the one analyzing profitability from AI, focuses on AI, IP rights and patent eligibility. On the basis of AI autonomy but also of the need

T. Tzimas, *Legal and Ethical Challenges of Artificial Intelligence from an International Law Perspective*, Law, Governance and Technology Series 46,
https://doi.org/10.1007/978-3-030-78585-7_9

for effective remedies, the issue of liability from AI is also addressed in the second part.

9.2 AI and Patent Eligibility

9.2.1 Patents' and IP Rights' Utility

Patent-eligibility is a crucial theme regarding the ownership and uses of AI and more specifically profitability from it. Through the system of intellectual property and patent-eligibility laws, the ownership of AI systems as well as of these systems' creations can be determined and subsequently the normative framework for AI use and ownership.

Intellectual property "...very broadly, means the legal rights which result from intellectual activity in the industrial, scientific, literary and artistic fields."[1] Intellectual property is supposed to transform knowledge into economic value. This is its mission.[2]

Within the wider context of IP, scientific works belong to the copyright branch,[3] inventions to industrial property,[4] with inventions constituting new solutions to technical problems, whereas scientific discoveries refer to "the recognition of phenomena, properties or laws of the material universe not hitherto recognized and capable of verification."[5]

The patent constitutes the means, the document, "which describes an invention and creates a legal situation in which the patented invention can normally only be exploited... with the authorization of the owner of the patent."[6]

---

[1]World Intellectual Property Organization, WIPO Intellectual Property Handbook, (2014), at p. 3.

According to the Convention Establishing the World Intellectual Property Organization (WIPO), "intellectual property shall include rights relating to: - literary, artistic and scientific works,- performances of performing artists, phonograms and broadcasts,- inventions in all fields of human endeavor,- scientific discoveries, - industrial designs,- trademarks, service marks and commercial names and designations,- protection against unfair competition, and all other rights resulting from intellectual activity in the industrial, scientific, literary or artistic fields."

Convention Establishing the World Intellectual Property Organization (as amended on September 28, 1979) (Authentic text), (https://wipolex.wipo.int/en/treaties/textdetails/12412).

[2]Laurent Manderieux, Secured Transactions as a Tool for Better Use of Intellectual Property Rights and of Intellectual Property Licensing (including Patent Licensing), (2010), Rev. dr. unif, p. 447, at p. 447.

[3]Regarding AI, copyright also could be relevant given that it refers to "computerized systems for the storage and retrieval of information."

WIPO Intellectual Property Handbook, (2014), at p. 40.

[4]World Intellectual Property Organization, WIPO Intellectual Property Handbook, (2014), at p. 3.

[5]World Intellectual Property Organization, WIPO Intellectual Property Handbook, (2014), at p. 4.

The Geneva Treaty on the International Recording of Scientific Discoveries, Article 1.

[6]World Intellectual Property Organization, WIPO Intellectual Property Handbook, (2014), at p. 17.

In the WIPO handbook, it is determined that for any invention to be patentable it must have a practical purpose in terms of its application. In addition, it must have industrial utility, novelty and non- obviousness.[7] The determination of what is patent- eligible and not, in general and especially in terms of modern technologies- including AI- is often puzzling.[8]

To begin with, a primary question is whether "patents" should exist in the first place. There are different theories that justify patent eligibility: the main ones are the labor/desert theory and the utilitarian/incentive theory.[9] The former emphasizes on the reward of the work of the creator, whereas the second places at its epicenter incentives which will push creators to further work on new ideas and new inventories.[10] Both of these theories identify in patent-eligibility a material and ethical motive, which is expected to motivate research and improve the economic conditions.[11]

However, there is also the contradictory approach that is built on a wider polemic against patents, mainly because of their lack of social utility; patents are approached as promoters of monopolies and therefore as obstacles to innovativeness.[12] Further, patent rights do not emerge as other property rights out of scarcity but create scarcity and according to certain analysts eventually lead to wealth reducing.[13]

---

[7] *WIPO Intellectual Property Handbook*, at pp. 18–22.

[8] To mention some of these complicated distinctions, as Oliver Gassmann explains them in his relevant book: "Genes and nucleic acid molecules (e.g., disease-related genes for diagnostics or for the antisense procedure, siRNA molecules for therapy)... Proteins (e.g., insulin, erythropoietin for therapy, cell receptors for drug screening)... Enzymes (e.g., proteases for washing powder, cellulose-degrading enzymes for the production of biofuels) Antibodies (e.g., for cancer treatment, pregnancy tests or diagnostics) Viruses and virus sequences (e.g., hepatitis C virus and HIV for blood tests and for the development of vaccines and therapies) Cells (e.g., hematopoietic stem cells for the treatment of leukemia) Microorganisms (e.g., bacteria for bioremediation, yeast for food production) Plants (e.g., herbicide-resistant soybeans, "golden rice" with a high content of provitamin A, drought-resistant plants and algae that extract CO2 from the atmosphere) Animals (e.g., disease models for research purposes such as the genetically modified "cancer mouse," donor animals for xenotransplantation, milkproducing animals that excrete medicinal substances in their milk)" are patentable. On the contrary, " DNA sequences without known function (e.g., expressed sequence tags (ESTs) as a result of automatic sequencing) Genetically modified animals that have to suffer without there being a significant medical benefit, e.g., a genetically modified animal that is only used for cosmetic tests, Plant varieties (already protected by the International Convention for the Protection of New Varieties of Plants, e.g., apples of the "Golden Delicious" variety), Animal breeds (e.g., Holstein cattle)... Human embryos... Procedures that inevitably involve the use and destruction of human embryos... Human germ cells (sperm, ova)... Human–animal chimeras". Gassmann et al. (2021).

[9] Khoury (2016–2017), p. 648.

[10] Fisher (2001), pp. 168–199.

[11] United Nations The Role of Patents in the Transfer of Technology to Developing Countries. E. 75. II. D. 6, 1975.

[12] Hemel and Ouellette (2013), pp. 314–315; Rai (1999), p. 133.

[13] Krauss (1989), pp. 308–309.

On the contrary, a strong public domain is expected to work as an "engine" which by "opening" the public to new ideas and inventions will support them in further enriching them.[14] After all, as it is accurately pointed, the "ocean" is the public domain and patent eligible intellectual property forms the "islands", which eventually "collapse" into the ocean; the latter exercises the gravitational force to the former.[15]

After all, once a state deems that it is necessary, it can "take" the invention, by compensating the patent holder, which is characteristic of the fact that the gravitational force lies with the states and the public spheres; not the private entities.[16]

An additional, central question which the expanding autonomy of AI poses emerges from the fact that until now, IP rights, as well as patents are intrinsically linked to human nature. In an environment of human- nature replication or even of autonomous, intelligent, non- human beings who will be entitled to such rights?[17]

The main theme of the chapter regarding this second question is to show that the inclusion of AI systems' creations, under the patent system is not the only path to follow. It is argued below, that the proposition that the public domain can be the "place" where AI autonomous systems' creations will be included is particularly tempting and accurate, especially in light of the ontological characteristics of AI.

In this framework, we will have to see whether the establishment of intellectual property rights over the inventories which are at large the consequence of AI autonomy can be justified under the theories pushing forward and justifying, patent-eligibility.

9.2.2 *Mental Activities, Inventions, IP and Patent-Eligibility*

Even in the framework of "patent-friendly" legal systems, not all creations claiming to be inventories are patent-eligible. In order to conclude on whether AI systems' creations should be patented and if yes in favor of whom, we need to go through two levels of analysis in this -unsurprisingly- complicated discussion: the one is if and when AI systems may be patent- eligible. The second is whether AI systems' creations and inventions, produced from the expanding autonomy of AI can be patent eligible.

Given however that legal theory and practice has not developed extensively in relation to AI we need to follow the legal theory and practice, as it has evolved in

[14] Julie E. Cohen, Copyright, Commodification, and Culture: Locating the Public Domain, in The Future of the Public Domain 121 (L. Guibault & P.B. Hugenholtz, eds. 2006).

Eli Salzberger, Economic Analysis of the Public Domain, in The Future of the Public Domain 27–59 (2006), http:// papers.ssrn.com/sol3/papers.cfm?abstract_id=934127.

[15] Khoury, Intellectual Property Rights for "Hubots": On the Legal Implications of Human-Like Robots As Innovators and Creators, at p. 658.

[16] Bethards (2004), p. 86.

[17] Sobel (2017), p. 60.

relation to inventions which are proximate to AI, such as software and inventories involving or reproducing mental activities.

AI is after all in principle, a replication -even at narrow area- and potentially the evolution of human intelligence. We must identify if and how mental activities and inventions orientating from mental activities can be patent-eligible, so that we can then apply these findings on the area of AI.

The general tendency of legal systems towards mental activities is not to categorize them as patent-eligible, even when they are methodologically innovative. As patent-eligible are approached innovations with practical, industrial applications.

The US legal system for example establishes that "[w]hoever invents or discovers any new and useful process, machine, manufacture, or composition of matter, or any new and useful improvement thereof, may obtain a patent therefor, subject to the conditions and requirements of this title."[18]

Given that several of the most important high-technology companies are established in the US, the framework for their legal regulation –both legislative and judiciary- has a wider impact in terms on guidance on AI-related matters. The majority of the most proximate to AI cases, in the US courts deal with software patent-eligibility.

The Federal Circuit held that methods which are "the equivalent of human mental work... are unpatentable abstract ideas".[19] In "Alice v. CLS Bank International" it was found that "the use of a computer to obtain data, adjust account balances, and issue automated instructions" is a routine activity and that the specific method is not patent-eligible because it did not make any improvement on technology or technical field.[20]

Similarly, in other cases, such as "Electric Power Group, LLC v. Alstom S.A." and "re TLI Communications LLC Patent Litigation", the Courts held that applications referring to methods of automated analysis, detection and analysis of events or automatic organization of events where not patent-eligible, as constituting mental activities.[21] On the contrary, the US Courts found that inventions which have "specific implementation of a solution to a problem in the software arts," or constitute technical improvement" can be patent eligible.[22]

For the US courts it is crucial to determine whether the invention and the proposed patent are directed to an abstract idea. If the answer is positive, it fails in terms of the first step of the categorization as patent- eligible and needs to be

---

[18]Hashiguchi (2017a), p. 9.

[19]CyberSource Corp. v. Retail Decisions, Inc., 654 F.3d 1366, 1371 (Fed. Cir. 2011).

[20]Alice, 134 S.Ct. at 2351-2353, 2355, 2357, 2359.

[21]Elec. Power Group, LLC v. Alstom S.A., 830 F.3d 1350, 1351 (Fed. Cir. 2016), 2351-2359. In re TLI Communications LLC Patent Litigation, 823 F.3d 607- 613 (Fed. Cir. 2016).

[22]Enfish, LLC v. Microsoft Corp., 822 F.3d 1327, 1339 (Fed. Cir. 2016). McRO, Inc. v. Bandai Namco Games Am. Inc., 837 F.3d 1299, 1302-1316 (Fed. Cir. 2016).

assessed at a second level, namely that of inventiveness, in the sense of transforming an abstract idea into patent eligible invention.[23]

With all the significance that US court decisions may have –after all they are not universal courts- it is important to focus on the difficulty of patent eligibility for inventions of mental nature an impact. Data collection has been declared for example, again by US Courts, as non- eligible for patent, although the same courts have found that devices for the improvement of data collection can be patent-eligible.[24]

Similar decisions are found in Europe as well: in the "Sesame Active System" and the "Dassault Systèmes" it was found again that mental activities are not patent eligible.[25]

In accordance with the European Patent Office, there are four basic requirements for patentability: "there must be an "invention", belonging to any field of technology; the invention must be "susceptible of industrial application"; the invention must be "new"; and the invention must involve an "inventive step"".[26]

Further, "European patents shall be granted for any inventions, in all fields of technology, provided that they are new, involve an inventive step and are susceptible of industrial application… The following in particular shall not be regarded as inventions (a) discoveries, scientific theories and mathematical methods; (b) aesthetic creations; (c) schemes, rules and methods for performing mental acts, playing games or doing business, and programs for computers; [and] (d) presentations of information"[27]

The EU framework therefore, imposes restrictions and identifies as non –eligible for patent, applications related to "rules and methods for performing mental acts" per se, too.[28] It is again critical whether some type of technical inventory can be identified too, apart from the purely mental activities even if the latter are inventive.[29]

---

[23]Mayo Collaborative Servs. v. Prometheus Labs., 566 U.S. 66, 77 (2012) ("The question before us is whether the claims do significantly more than simply describe these natural relations. To put the matter more precisely, do the patent claims add enough to their statements of the correlations to allow the processes they describe to qualify as patent-eligible processes that apply natural laws?").

[24]Fitbit Inc. v. AliphCom, No. 16-cv-00118-BLF (N.D. Cal. Mar. 2, 2017) at 10, 22.

[25]In re Sesame Active System, 15/01962, Cour d'Appel de Paris [Court of Appeal of Paris] (26 fevrier 2016 [Feb. 26, 2016]); In re Dassault Systèmes, 14/06444, Cour d'Appel de Paris [Court of Appeal of Paris] (16 décembre 2016 [Dec. 16, 2016]). Hashiguchi (2017b), pp. 8–9.

[26]European Patent Office, Patentability requirements, https://www.epo.org/law-practice/legal-texts/html/guidelines/e/g_i_1.htm.

[27]European Patent Office, Convention on the Grant of European Patents 108 (16th ed. June 2016), https://www.epo.org/law-practice/legal-texts/html/epc/2020/e/ar52.html (compiling the European Patent Convention articles) [hereinafter European Patent Convention].

[28]European Patent Office, Convention on the Grant of European Patents 108.

[29]Decision of the European Patent Office, Technical Board of Appeal, Case T 258/03 - 3.5.1, Reasons for the Decision ¶¶ 3.3, 3.7, 4.1, 4.3, 4.4, 4.7,. (Apr. 21, 2004), https://www.epo.org/law-practice/case-law-appeals/_pdf/t030258ep1.pdf.

In this framework, the European Patent Office's Technical Board of Appeal determined that for example, a system for automatically summarizing documents is non-patent eligible, due to performing mental acts".[30]

On the contrary, in 1995, the design of a three-dimensional receptacle was considered as patentable as it included both excluded and non-excluded subject matter. When excluded and non-excluded elements conglomerate, it is up to the assessment of whether an overall contribution of technical nature outside the non-eligible elements is made.[31]

Another legal system, the Japanese system examines whether the invention uses the laws of nature.[32] In a significant judgment, the Intellectual Property High Court of Japan defined "invention" as something that is consisted of the identification of a particular technical problem of the use of technical means to solve this problem and of a technical configuration which actually produces an effect contributing to achieving the goal. The High Court, while reaching the conclusion that a mental step per se is not an "invention," it also held that if the invention assists humans in carrying out mental steps, or provides technical means replacing mental steps performed by humans, then it is patent eligible.[33]

States' legislation and judicial decisions regardless of their differences fluctuate on more or less similar grounds, attempting to distinguish between non- eligible inventions due to the fact that they refer to abstract ideas, theories, methods, mental acts and inventories with industrial or otherwise technical implementation and effect.[34]

The reason for non- eligibility of patent over any abstract idea is that patents on the one hand guarantee profits for the inventor but on the other hand exclude all others, including potential inventors therefore, over the use of these inventories. delaying therefore their contributions in and from the specific area.

The patent eligibility of abstract ideas, as well as of nature and natural phenomena, would deprive the scientific community of fundamental scientific research tools,

---

[30]Decision of the European Patent Office, Technical Board of Appeal, Case T 22/85 - 3.5.1, Reasons for the Decision ¶ 5 (Oct. 5, 1988), http://www.epo.org/law-practice/case-law-appeals/pdf/t850022ep1.pdf.

[31]Decision of the European Patent Office, Technical Board of Appeal, Case T 0605/93 - 3.5.1, 5.3, 5.7,Reasons for the Decision ¶ 5.9 (Jan. 20, 1995), https://www.epo.org/law-practice/case-law-appeals/pdf/t930605eu1.pdf.

[32]Hashiguchi (2017a), p. 23.

[33]Hashiguchi (2017b), p. 26.

[34]Indicatively, one may see the case of French legal framework, which in section 1 of Article L611-10 defines patentable inventions, in all technological areas, as new inventions which involve an inventive step and can be applied industrially, whereas the subject matters that are excluded from patents are discoveries, scientific theories, and mathematical methods, aesthetic creations, schemes, rules, and methods for performing mental acts, playing games, or conducting economic activities, as well as computer programs and presentations of information. Hashiguchi (2017a), p. 20.

which ontologically-speaking can be shared by all.[35] In addition the patent eligibility of such ideas and phenomena would turn patent seclusion from the exception to the rule.

When the question is whether inventions of AI systems can be patent-eligible, the answer is going to be determined on an ad hoc basis; given the precedents that we have, AI systems conducting and consisted of solely mental activities, with no technical or industrial application or without a predominantly technical or industrial character cannot be patent-eligible, whereas when such industrial and technical applications can be identified as the prevalent over the conduct of mental activities, AI systems will indeed be patent-eligible.

Therefore, invention of AI systems, which are consisted of mental steps or which are replicating human mental activities should not be patent-eligible in principle.[36] While quantifiable inventions can become patent-eligible, the ones which are consisted solely of new mental qualities are less likely to receive such eligibility.[37]

An additional obstacle to patent-eligibility of AI is the need for an invention to be specific, which very often contradicts the inexplicability and the unpredictability of AI, ontologically-speaking.[38]

The specificity of the invention, the technical character of the invention and the transcending of generic computation[39] are all elements which are at odds with the opaqueness and the black box effect of AI, the non- technical character - often - of AI applications and the tendency of AI as it evolves to exercise mental acts, mimicking human brain.[40]

From a patent-eligibility perspective, it is problematic that inventions in relation to AI mostly refer to the methods and the devices that are designed to carry out mental steps.[41] They need to surpass the stage of purely mental activities, towards industrial applications, in order to be under existing laws, patent-eligible.

Different is the case, when the autonomy of AI will be of such level that AI will be conducting its own, highly evolved and completely autonomous mental activities- AGI or ASI; Its categorization as patent owned by another entity- natural or legal person- will be contradicting different ethical and potentially legal norms. Once AI

[35]Alice Corp. Pty., 134 S. Ct. at 2354 (citing Ass'n for Molecular Pathology v. Myriad Genetics, Inc., 133 S. Ct. 2107, 2116 (2013); Mayo Collaborative Servs. v. Prometheus Labs., Inc., 132 S. Ct. 1289, 1293 (2012)).

[36]Hashiguchi (2017a), p. 17.

[37]Hattenbach and Snyder (2018), p. 318.

[38]Hashiguchi (2017a), p. 29.

[39]Hashiguchi (2017b), pp. 10–11.

[40]Spector (2006), p. 1252; Aaron Sloman, What is Artificial Intelligence?, Sch. of Comput. Sci., Univ. of birmingham, 2007, http://www.cs.bham.ac.uk/research/projects/cogaff/misc/aiforschools.html.

[41]Gottschalk v. Benson, 409 U.S. 63, 67 (1972).

Larry Hauser, Artificial Intelligence, Internet Encyclopedia of Philosophy, http://www.iep.utm.edu/artinte/ (last visited Sept. 15, 2017).

reaches the level of AGI or ASI, its patentability will be a violation of its potential legal personality- an issue which is examined below.

When we refer though to further evolved applications still at the level of ANI, which replicate human mental activities at a narrow level or manifest in general mental activities, we will need to examine if these activities are in a way mechanical, automated, pre-defined and pre-determined by the software designer or unpredictable and unique, evading patentability in favor of the human, who either designs their software or owns them.

The former case constitutes the prevalent until now approach, with previous technologies such as photography, video- games and computers.[42] It is characteristic that in 1965, in the US, the Register of Copyrights submitted to the Congress report, about computer-generated work, raising the issue of copyright, given that part of such work is generated by computer. The, then established National Commission on New Technological Uses of Copyrighted Works -CONTU- held that computers are no different from cameras or typewriters, with copyright belonging only to the user.[43]

Such an approach may not be compatible however with the autonomy of AI, which is unique compared to all previous technologies. Even now, while we are still at the domain of ANI, there are cases of creative works conducted by autonomous algorithms, in music,[44] pictures[45] and writing.

For example, the Guardian has already published, the first written by AI article, which followed an instruction asking the AI system, "GPT-3" to "please write a short editorial of about 500 words. Keep the language simple and concise. Focus on why humans have nothing to fear from Artificial Intelligence".[46] The AI system produced an impressing- or frighteningly- original article indicating highly evolved mental activities.

Similar achievements exist in the other above- mentioned fields as well. We need to remember that AI may be narrow in the sense that it is applied only at a specific

---

[42]Jaszi (1992), p. 294; Burrow-Giles Lithographic Co. v. Sarony, Ill U.S. 53 (1884); Grimmelmann (2016), p. 403. Midway Mfg. Co. v. Artic Intern., Inc., 704 F. 2d 1009, 1011 (7d Cir. 1983).

[43]U.S. Copyright Office, Sixty-Eighth Annual Report of the Register Of Copyrights 5 (1965), https://www.copyright.gov/reports/annual/archive/ar-I965.pdf[https://perma.cc/E55P-XEUF]; Nat'l Comm'n On New Tech. Uses of Copyrighted Works, Final Report of the National Commission On New Technological Uses of Copyrighted Works 44–45 (1978),https://babel.hathitrust.org/cgi/pt?id=mdp.39015026832934 [https://perma-cc/RUA7-AT2J].

[44]Kelly Shi, Beats by Al, IBM RES. (July 27, 2016), https://www.ibm.com/blogs/research2016/07/beats-by-ai [https://permacc/S32U-8LBP]; Aaron van den Oord et al., WaveNet: A Generative Model for Raw Audio, DEEPMIND (Sept. 8, 2016), https:/deepmind.comiblog/wavenet-generative-model-raw-audio/ [https://permacc/9HW6-AY72].

[45]Alexander Mordvintsev et al., Inceptionism: Going Deeper into Neural Networks, GOOGLE RES. BLOG (June 17, 2015), https://research.googleblog.com/2015/06/inceptionismgoing-deeper-into-neural.html [https://perma.cc/YQ5X-2NE9].

[46]Opinion Artificial Intelligence, A robot wrote this entire article. Are you scared yet, human?, The Guardian, (2020, September 8), (https://www.theguardian.com/commentisfree/2020/sep/08/robot-wrote-this-article-gpt-3).

area instead of general intelligence but that does not mean that in these specific areas AI cannot manifest highly autonomous functions. In such cases, automation is not the case and AI does not constitute a mere instrument at human hands.

This thematic is examined below, in the next sub- part. Here and about the patentability and the flow of IP rights out of the invention of AI systems, the conclusion is that unless a specific industrial, technical use can be proven, the invention of AI systems should not be patentable. This will be proven crucial for scientific progress and for the prevalent economic model.

9.2.3 *The Patent-Eligibility of AI Autonomous Systems' Inventories*

The perplexities with patent-eligibility of AI grow even more significant once we try to explore what must be the case with the inventories of AI autonomous systems' "themselves" and their potential patent-eligibility or not. The issue becomes more significant, as AI autonomy increases. As Ryan Abbott stated since 2016 "Soon computers will be routinely inventing, and it may only be a matter of time until computers are responsible for most innovation."[47]

In principle, patent laws have been designed on the basis of the self-obviousness of the fact that only humans can have the mental capacities of inventiveness;[48] until now, creativity -the most fundamental paragon for inventiveness- has been considered as a unique capacity of humanity.

In such a framework, the US Copyright Act, characteristically states that copyright can be granted for an "original work of authorship fixed in any tangible medium of expression",[49] while the relevant Copyright Office has established the "Human Authorship Requirement", according to which, "[t]o qualify as a work of 'authorship' a work must be created by a human being."[50]

[47] Abott (2016), p. 1080.

[48] Kim (2018), p. 21.

Characteristically, the US copyright office back in the year 1956 had determined that the author of any copyrightable work must be human, a position which was reiterated again in relevant, future, cases, in front of both of the courts and of the copyright office. With a similar understanding, when the US patent law was adopted, It was stated in the US Congress that it involved "anything under the sun that is made by man."

Pearlman (2018), p. 20.

[49] Pub. L. No. 94-553, 90 Stat. 2541 (1976) (codified as amended at 17 U.S.C. §§ 101-810 (2012).

[50] U.S. COPYRIGHT OFFICE, CONPENDIUM OF U.S. COPYRIGHT OFFICE PRACTICES § 313.2 (3d ed. 2017), https://www.copyright.gov/comp3/docs/compendium.pdf [https://permacc/RY7TG6KE].

This is how in the past, during the era of automation, human creativity was only mediated by machines, as the above- mentioned, earlier cases about patent-eligibility of inventories related to photography and the use of computers indicated.[51]

The eligibility for patent when machine is used as an instrument for the creation, depends on finding eventually a human hand behind the creation.[52] As long as the reliance on the creativity of the human mind constitutes the touchstone of patentability[53] and computers mere instruments at the hands of humans,[54] or –in terms of AI- as 'slavish copying", every invention must be attributed eventually to humans as far as patent- eligibility at least, becomes a matter of concern.[55]

The idea is that when AI is of limited autonomy, implementing essentially its pre-programmed software, the mental characteristics that justify intellectual property are missing and that therefore, it is the human owner or programmer who must be assigned the patent.[56]

There is a precedent from the UK, where in 1988 it was held that in computer-generated works where the human author cannot be found, the patent will be assigned to the person or the entity which invested financially to the computer or to the program of the computer.[57] While, such provisions are not particularly helpful with AI, because of its autonomy, still, AI may be deemed as employee, whereas the rest of the implicated actors, such as the company, the designer and the user could benefit from the work of AI.

The Court of Justice of the EU –CJEU- held in "Infopaq case" that regarding author's creation and its patentability, the work must be attributed to the author in order to qualify for such protection. The important elements are the genuineness of the work- not constituting replica of an earlier work- and the subjectivity of the author- i.e. of the creator of the work.[58]

---

[51] Burrow-Giles Lithographic Co./Sarony, Supreme Court 1884, III US 53, 4 S Ct. 279; Berne Convention for the protection of Literary and Artistic works, as amended on 1979, WIPO, TRT/BERNE/00.1; Apple Computer, Inc. v. Franklin Computer Corp. 714 F.2d 1240 (3d Cir. 1983), as quoted in Madeleine e Cock Buning 1998, supra note 43, at p. 183.

[52] "Although (...) the human input as regards the creation of machine-generated Programs may be relatively modest, and will be increasingly modest in the future [...] nevertheless, a human 'author' in the widest sense is always present, and must have the right to claim authorship in the program."

Proposal for a Council Directive on the legal protection of computer programs, COM (88) 816 final, Article 1.

[53] Denicola (2016), p. 265; Jaszi (1992), p. 295.

[54] *Denicola, Ex Machina: Copyright Protection For Computergenerated Works*, at p. 272.

[55] Grimmelmann (2016), p. 408.

[56] Mario Tremblay, Should Robots Have Legal Rights?, ROBOTSHOP (Nov. 23, 2015), http://www.robotshop.com/blog/en/should-robots-have-legal-rights-17333; Palacet (2019), p. 235.

[57] Copyright, Designs and Patents Act 1988, Chapter 48, § 9.3.

[58] Case C-5/08, Danske Dagblades Forening [2009] ECR I-06569, at para. 35; Case C-393/09, Bezpecnostní softwarová asociace [2010] ECR 2010 I-13971, para. 45; Case C-403/08 and C-429/08, FA Premier League/Karen Murphy [2011] ECR 2011 I-09083, at para. 97; Case C-145/10, Eva-Maria Painer/Standard Verlags [2011] at para. 94; Case C-604/10, Football Dataco/Yahoo [2012] ECLI:EU:C:2012:115, at para. 38.

The CJEU also held that : "Where the expression of [...] components [of a work] is dictated by their technical function, the criterion of originality is not met, since the different methods of implementing an idea are so limited that the idea and the expression become indissociable."[59]

The judiciary is in general negative in recognizing patent eligibility for non-human creations, although there is one at least different case; that of Jonathon Koza's AI system' invention- the genetic programming invention- for which however it was eventually, again, the human inventor of the AI system the one who received patent.[60]

Once inventiveness is restricted to humans, the debate becomes who among humans must be considered as the owner of the patent in case of IA creations: the programmer or the owner? Several experts suggest that, both on the basis of the principles that are served by patent- eligibility, as well as for practical reasons, patent ownership must lie with owner of the AI, instead of the programmer.[61]

Regarding the attribution of patent to programmers, on the basis of IP rights-eligibility it sounds rather reasonable to assume that it is the software designer, the one who should hold the patent of an AI system. After all, it is the programmer or the designer who creates the AI system.

However and despite the reasonable-ness, the difficulty lies in that the programmer of AI is the creator but not necessarily the "controller" of the AI evolution; as machine learning enhances the autonomy of AI, unpredictable and unexpected outcomes are produced.[62] The programmer in a way sets in motion the AI and provides it with the equivalent of its DNA; that does not mean that AI conducts can be directly attributed to the software -or solely and mainly to it- and therefore to the programmer's initial work up to extent that patent-eligibility would require.

---

[59]Case C-393/09, Bezpecnostní softwarová asociace, supra note 24, para 49. See also Case C-403/08 and C-429/08, FA Premier League/Karen Murphy, supra note 24, para. 98.

[60]Jonathon Keats, John Koza Has Built an Invention Machine, Popular Science (Apr. 18, 2006), http:// www.popsci.com/scitech/article/2006-04/john-koza-has-builtinvention-machine [http://perma.cc/C644-PR8R].

[61]Bridy (2012), pp. 21–26.

> Perhaps the best reason to allocate ownership interests to someone, however, is that someone must be motivated, if not to create the work, then to bring it into public circulation.

Samuelson (1986), p. 1226.

> Contract arrangements between the copyright owner of a computer program and those who use the program to create new works can be relied upon to allocate rights in the works created.

Paul Goldstein, Goldstein on Copyright § 2.2.2 (3d ed. 2014).

[62]Jason Tanz, Soon We Won't Program Computers. We'll Train Them Like Dogs, WIRED (May 17, 2016, 6:50 AM), https://www.wired.com/2016/05/the-end-of-code/, https://perma.cc/UBA7-D8EH (last visited Mar. 27, 2018); Elissa Gilbert, Artificial Intelligence: Teaching Machines to Learn Like Humans, INTEL, Aug. 21, 2017, https://iq.intel.com/artificial-intelligence-teaching-machines-to-learn-like-humans/, https://perma.cc/9NTW-T5JN (last visited Mar. 27, 2018).

Following this initial work, machine- learning, big data and the environment of AI get in the way.

The attribution of the patent on the other hand to the owner of the AI system could be more practical. However, once we take into account the theories about patent-utility, it does not sound neither fair, nor positive for the free flow of research and information to recognize such an advantage to physical persons or legal entities which may own or use but have not contributed into the creation and evolution of AI systems.

The problem with the human- centered approaches to patent- eligibility of AI systems is that they seem to overlook the extant and the significance of AI autonomy. Things can become more complicated once we attempt to identify the specific characteristics, according to which humans only can be entitled to authorship and the extent that AI can replicate these characteristics.[63]

Creativity for a start is a fundamental characteristic of "authorship" and patent ownership. Creativity is defined on the basis of novelty and value in terms of the creation itself,[64] involving also different subjective elements such as intention, desires, beliefs, judgment, imagination, rationality, which are all considered as aspects of intelligence, necessary for the development of creativity and of course inventiveness.[65]

Further, inventiveness has at its center, conception, meaning "the formation in the mind of the inventor of a definite and permanent idea of the complete and operative invention as it is thereafter to be applied in practice... the complete performance of the mental part of the inventive act".[66]

In this framework, the inventor is expected to demonstrate that the work is his/her own intellectual creation, on the basis of his/her own, conscious subjectivity. Therefore, once creativity is identified with human subjectivity, AI is excluded.[67] But can we sustain such an argument ontologically?

As analyzed in the first part of the book and indicated above, in this chapter, in specific areas, even narrow- relatively- in the present, AI indicates several of these characteristics. Once AI systems can write their own articles and compose music,

[63]Going back to the US Copyright Office, it is characteristic that it states it "will not register works produced by a machine.., that operates randomly or automatically without any creative input or intervention from a human author."

U.S. Copyright Office, Conpendium of U.S. Copyright Office Practices § 313.2] (3d ed. 2017), https://www.copyright.gov/comp3/docs/compendium.pdf [https://permacc/RY7TG6KE].

What if such creative input however can be externalized by a non- human actor? DeepMind indicates for example some extent of creativity.

Alexander Mordvintsev et al., Inceptionism: Going Deeper into Neural Networks,GOOGLE RES. BLOG (June 17, 2015), https://research.googleblog.com/2015/06/inceptionismgoing-deeper-into-neural.html [https://perma.cc/YQ5X-2NE9].

[64]Gaut (2010), p. 1039.

[65]Arnheim (2001), p. 24; *Buning, Autonomous Intelligent Systems as Creative Agents under the EU Framework for Intellectual Property*, at p. 315.

[66]U.S. Patent & Trademark Office, Manual of Patent Examining Procedure § 2164.

[67]de Cock Buning (2016), p. 317.

when we fail to predict and comprehend the sequence of events inside AI mental activities how can we claim that the outcome of all AI systems actions constitute the direct consequence of our creativity.

Contrary therefore, to the approach which argues in favor of the attribution of patents to humans for AI entities, there is significant counter- argument, which is built on the qualitative difference that has emerged because of deep learning networks and machine learning; the identification between the human mind and creativity may not be self- evident anymore, because both of the different interpretations of the meaning of creativity and of transformations of the notion of subjectivity under the influence of AI.

The surpassing of automation in favor of autonomy and therefore the foundations of patent eligibility experience a radical change that laws fail to grasp.[68] After all, it has been argued that computers already are generating patentable material[69] and that recognizing such a fact would help in the development of even more inventive machines.[70]

In spite of the relative proximity of computers with AI, the difference is that the latter in principle refers to technology of evolved autonomy and not simply of instrumental use.

The issue of creativity in relation to patent eligibility is already a complicated one, given that some type of "creativity measurement" is implicitly taken into account in order for a creation to be found as patent eligible.[71] In case creativity is quantified, why does it have to remain considered as a uniquely human capacity?

Since we recognize that aspects of human intelligence -and possibly the equivalent of general human intelligence, albeit transformed- can be developed by other, non- biological entities, the question becomes why creativity too cannot become and get recognized as characteristic of AI as well.[72] From such a perspective and provided that the other elements of patent eligibility are fulfilled, non- human intelligence inventories could be in principle assigned as patent eligible as well.[73]

After all, the fact that "mental" and "abstract" ideas cannot always and directly be projected onto AI or replicated by it, in completely identical ways with those of humans, causes an omnipresent uniqueness of AI mental activities and of their outcome that evades -at least complete- human control.[74]

---

[68]Pearlman (2018), p. 35.

[69]Ryan Abbott, Hal the Inventor: Big Data and Its Use by Artificial Intelligence, in Big Data is Not a MonolitH (Cassidy R. Sugimoto, Hamid R. Ekbia & Michael Mattioli eds., forthcoming Oct. 2016).

[70]Abott (2016), p. 1081.

[71]Feist, 499 U.S. at 345,363.

[72]Ritchie (2007), pp. 67–99.

[73]Abott (2016), p. 1104.

[74]Robert Sachs, The Mind as Computer Metaphor: Benson and the Mistaken Application of Mental Steps to Software (Part 3), BILSKIBLOG (Apr. 11, 2016), http://www.bilskiblog.com/blog/2016/04/the-mind-as-computer-metaphor-benson-and-the-mistaken-applicationof-mental-steps-to-software-part-3.htm.

According to Miller and Acosta "[t]he crucial question appears to be whether the "work" is basically one of human authorship, with the computer merely being an assisting instrument, or whether the traditional elements of authorship in the work (literary, artistic or musical expression or elements of selection, arrangement, etc.) were actually conceived and executed not by a man but by a machine."[75]

From such a perspective, what would be needed is the identification of specific characteristics which sustain patent-eligibility, in AI, such as causation- *meaning that AI must be the creator of the work, instead of simple automata at the hands of humans*- novelty, originality[76] and invention- which *means that whatever work will not be* mere *imitation.*[77]

Further, the work under examination for patent-eligibility must have utility, must depart from previous teaching and must not constitute the outcome of pre-given and pre-determined set of instructions. Patent-eligible AI systems, prerequisite an extensive impact for machine-learning and deep neural networks.[78]

A contradictory approach and given the ellipsis of unanimous definition over creativity[79] is to simply skip this debate as non-essential regarding patent –eligibility, given that law deals not with the mental procedures but with the outcome.[80] In this sense it is argued that we need not to search for ontological justification but only for legal relationship, on the basis on the attribution of the outcome to the AI entity.

Let us assume now that indeed creativity is traced within AI or at least a behavior that convinces us that creativity exists in AI. Does it mean that AI entities can, not in principle but in the end, enjoy the "fruits" of the patent -eligibility of their inventions?

Some experts have argued in favor of IP rights to AI.[81] Since the attribution of IP rights to humans alone, is not the outcome of a dogma but the consequence of the -until recently- identification of intellectual characteristics only with humans, since this is not the case anymore, there is no reason to exclude AI from IP rights and patent- eligibility.[82]

---

[75]Raquel Acosta, Artificial Intelligence and Authorship RightsJOLTDIGEST (Feb. 17, 2012), http://jolt.law.harvard.edu/digest/artificial-intelligence-and-authorship-rights. Miller (1993), p. 1073.

[76]Palacet (2019), p. 230.

[77]Pearlman (2018), pp. 42, 44.

[78]Pearlman, Recognizing Artificial Intelligence (AI) as Authors And Inventors Under U.S. Intellectual Property Law, at p. 43.

[79]Ralston (2005), pp. 292–293.

[80]*Khoury, Intellectual Property Rights for "Hubots": On The Legal Implications of Human-Like Robots As Innovators And Creators, at p. 651.*

[81]Hristov (2017), pp. 440–441.

[82]Hattenbach and Glucoft (2015), p. 44; Samuelson (1986), p. 1197.

After all, the owner of a patent can already be an artificial legal person- i.e a corporation- instead of the actual human or humans who were authors of the patent-eligible creation.[83]

Rewarding humans in such cases will resemble to rewarding parents for their children's creations.[84] Or to put it in the terms of the US judicial precedents, employing someone to invent does not make you an inventor.[85] The outcome could be the over-rewarding of the owner of the AI entity indefinitely, thus harming any type of "fair" market- antagonism.[86]

However, despite the fact that the inventory goes with the AI, still the patent should not be assigned neither to any human nor to AI. The non- attribution of IP rights and of patent eligibility to AI is the consequence, not -only or necessarily- of the ellipsis of the intellectual characteristics but of patent utility as the scope of profit is expected to be of no interest for AI.[87]

Ontologically speaking, AI should righteously be considered as non- eligible for patents, because the concept of labor and of incentives are going to be most likely irrelevant. This may change of course, given the unpredictability of AI nature, in case AI starts resembling more to human.

As long as this is not the case however, as it is not expected to be, there is going to be a legal-and moral- conundrum; on the one hand, the autonomy of the AI entity means that the human initial programmer or owner must not be patent- eligible; on the other hand, the AI entity is indifferent, ontologically- speaking, to whatever benefit emerging from patent- eligibility.

An additional problem for the recognition of patent, in relation either to humans or AI for inventions which are the outcome of AI autonomy, is that AI makes new inventions more obvious and therefore, less patent- eligible on these grounds. According to Plotkin, "Supply every engineer with state-of-the-art artificial invention technology and train them in how to use that technology, and you have effectively boosted the level of ordinary inventive skill in the field."[88]

AI will potentially increase the threshold of non- obviousness, which constitutes a crucial, patent- eligibility criterion, in the sense that the capacities of AI that can lead to new inventories surpass by far, the equivalent human achievements.[89]

---

[83]The public has no inherent interest in who owns the copyright so long as works are placed into the marketplace. Under this instrumental approach to copyright, "author" is a construct denoting merely the initial owner of all rights. That initial owner may be the actual individual who created the work, but *277 need not be. 2 William F. Patry, Patry on Copyright § § 3:19 (2016).

[84]Abott (2016), pp. 1094–1095.

[85]Michael Schuster (2018), p. 1960.

[86]Palacet (2019), p. 237.

[87]Abrams (2009), p. 1613.

[88]Robert Plotkin, *The Genie in the Machine: How Computer-Automated Inventing Is Revolutionizing Law and Business*, (2009), at p. 111.

[89]Samore (2013), p. 142.

It is more reasonable to argue that AI autonomous entities' creations must be endorsed in the public domain.[90] Under this framework, AI becomes a pioneer of the collective progress regarding knowledge and welfare.[91]

There might be a counter- argument: if AI developers are deprived of patent-eligibility they may be discouraged to further develop AI. The argument is not without basis. It is nevertheless highly speculative on the one hand and morally ambivalent- to say the least. On the other hand, it takes into account immediate, material profit as incentive and only at the individual level, whereas it can very well be incentive at the collective level, through enhanced public domain.

Therefore, there is no sound argument why anyone among us- natural or artificial legal person- should exclude all others from the profit and the scientific progress that AI autonomy can generate, especially given that these creations and inventions will be based at large on the big data to which all or many of us collectively contribute and to AI systems' contributions.

The proposition is that an international governance framework must establish a public sphere where AI systems' creations and inventions will belong. In this sense, on the one hand we can have a legally coherent regulation, whereas on the other hand, aspirations which have been underestimated for long, of the international community, for economic progress and welfare will have the capacity to be materialized.

9.3 AI and Liability

If profiting from AI is complicating, equally complicated is the tracing of responsibility and of liability from it. The issues of liability reach new complications when they are related to AI, even at the level of ANI.[92]

Liability issues emerge on the basis of different levels of defects: "(i) when the product created deviates from its intended design (manufacturing defect), (ii) when the product should have been designed differently to avoid a foreseeable risk of harm

[90]Madeleine de Cock Buning, Chair, Dutch Media Authority/Utrecht University Centre for Intellectual Property Law, Keynote Address at the 16th Eur. Intell. Prop. Inst. Network Congress 2014/2015 (Jan. 29-31, 2015) (as reported by Muzdalifah Faried Bakry & Zhilang He, Autonomous Creation - Creation by Robots: Who owns the IP Rights?, Maastricht University Blog Intell. Prop. & Knowledge Mgmt. (Mar. 15, 2015), https://law.maastrichtuniversity.nl/ipkm/autonomouscreation-creation-by-robots-who-owns-the-ip-rights/; Clifford (1997), pp. 1702–1703.

[91]The role is to "serve an essential purpose in democratic society by providing a common reservoir of information upon which an informed citizenry can make choices."

Erickson (2016), p. 1, http://www.ntnu.no/ojs/index.php/etikk_i_praksis/article/view/1951/1986.

[92]Bekey et al. (2011), p. 323 ff.

(design defect), or (iii) when companies fail to provide instructions or warnings that could have avoided foreseeable risks of harm (failure to warn)."[93]

The primary can be attributed to the manufacturer due to malfunction of the product; the second refer to cases where the design is problematic, whereas the latter to failure of the private stakeholders producing AI to warn about the possible dangers.[94]

The central question with liability and with attribution of responsibility is the existence -or not- of a defect, causing damage to people and goods,[95] breaching safety "which the public at large is entitled to expect, taking all circumstances into account."[96] The important element lies in the existence of a causal connection between the defect and damage.

The tort system is based on the existence of negligence which can be attributed to someone, who could have foreseen that the specific harm would have occurred and whose negligent acts were in proximity or causal connection with the harm inflicted.[97]

The expanding autonomy of AI means that the unpredictability of its actions will shake the foundations of the attribution of responsibility. As Scherer argues, "the development of more versatile AI systems combined with advances in machine learning make it all but certain that issues pertaining to unforeseeable AI behavior will crop up with increasing frequency and that the unexpectedness of AI behavior will rise significantly."[98]

In addition, we need to keep in mind that AI barely produces results alone; it most often interacts with the cyberspace, becoming thus part of collective intelligence or at least, of collectively produced intelligence,[99] creating an intelligent environment. Therefore, even when no specific component is intelligent- in some cases at least- the whole system is, making it therefore highly problematic to trace the specific one, which must be held liable.

AI introduces several "agents" and factors which make the proximity, the causal connection and the foreseeability -i.e. elements that are crucial for the attribution of liability- more difficult to be traced. As mentioned in previous chapters already, even under ANI, unpredictability constitutes an outcome of machine- learning, because the software, the algorithm evolves over time on the basis of what is learning.

---

[93]Nersessian and Mancha (2021), p. 66.

[94]Ibid at pp. 67–68.

[95]de Bruin (2016), p. 490.

[96]Indicatively see the US relevant legislation "Article 6(1) PLD. These circumstances include "(a) the presentation of the product, (b) the use to which it would reasonably be expected that the product would be put", and "(c) the time when the product was put into circulation".

[97]W. Page Keeton et al., Prosser and Keeton on the Law of torts 6 (5th ed. 1984); MacCoun (1993), pp. 2–3.

[98]Scherer (2016), pp. 359–360.

[99]Hildebrandt (2008), p. 169.

Therefore, we could experience flaws in the design of the software, improper use of AI and harm caused by AI autonomy based on machine- learning.

Further, we cannot overlook the fact that humans already interact with AI. Electronic commerce or the banking sector are already using AI- run, "chatbots". Very soon, AI may enter other legal domains too, such as contract negotiations.[100]

Within such a framework "...it would be hard to determine whether the precise cause was the operating system or the application (and, if the latter, which application). This analysis is all the more difficult where the software is open source (since no single author is responsible) and the hardware can be easily modified".[101]

Further, AI transforms the wider social environment: up to the extent that we accept that we will co-exist with entities of evolving autonomy, the transformation of law including that of liability will have to adjust accordingly. AI introduces several "agents" and factors which make the proximity, the causal connection and the foreseeability -i.e. elements that are crucial for the attribution of liability- more difficult to be traced. As mentioned in previous chapters already, even under ANI, unpredictability constitutes the outcome of machine- learning, because the software, the algorithm evolves over time on the basis of what is learning. Therefore, we could experience flaws in the design of the software, improper use of AI and harm caused by AI autonomy based on machine- learning.

AI could make it much more complicated to define which one actually the product is, due to the interaction of AI software with the components of the product and the surrounding environment, which can lead to unpredictable behaviors.[102] Practically, that makes it difficult to identify causation and responsibility.[103] The "error" may very well be the outcome not of the AI per se but of the human and AI interaction, extending from AI design to training and from AI system function per se, to human comprehension of AI activities.[104] The interaction of non- human with human actors, combined with the black box effect of AI makes the tracing of responsibility a puzzling question.[105]

Such complexities endanger legal certainty in judicial decisions. In some cases that are too complicated, it is impossible to determine the exact source of the defect, leading courts to "infer a defect of some kind on the theory that the accident itself is proof of defect, even if there is compelling evidence that cuts against a defect theory."[106] Or, acts which would otherwise lead to liability could lead to immunity

---

[100] Barfield (2015), p. 43.

[101] Ryan Calo (2011), p. 597.

[102] Ibid at pp. 75–76.

[103] Marchant and Lindor (2012), p. 1328.

[104] Solow-Niederman (2020), p. 641.

[105] Regarding the impact of such situation in issues of bias, indicatively see: Algorithms in the Criminal Justice System: Pre-Trial Risk Assessment Tools, ELECTRONIC PRIVACY INFO. CTR., https://Epic.Org/Algorithmic-Transparency/Crim-Justice [https://Perma.Cc/K9XHGMV4]; Virginia Eubanks, Automating Inequality: How High-Tech Tools Profile, Police, And Punish The Poor (2017).

[106] Vladeck (2014), p. 128.

for the involved human- or in general- because of the involvement of AI as well, on the basis of the difficulty to trace human responsibility behind the black box effect.[107]

As of now, very few steps have been made by public institutions in order to regulate issues of liability emerging from AI.

The EU Parliament is one of the pioneering institutions in terms of the realization of the need for novel and up to date legal regulations, capable of tackling with the issues of responsibility as well of the potential legal personality of robots and AI.[108]

It stressed that unified legal regulation at a European level is necessary, on the basis of a proper regulation of the human- robotic, inter- relationship through predictability and direct -ability[109] and introduced the principle of proportionality, on the basis of the combination of the training of the robot and of its autonomy,[110] pressing forward with policy proposals, referring to an obligatory compensation scheme.[111]

The EU Parliament distinguishes between "strict liability", which is comprised of" proof that damage has occurred and the establishment of a causal link between

---

[107]Bathae (2020), p. 148.

[108]European Parliament, Report with recommendations to the Commission on Civil Law Rules on Robotics (27 January 2017), paras. Z-AI http://www.europarl.europa.eu/sides/getDoc.do?pubRef=-//EP//TEXT+REPORT+A8-2017–0005+0+DOC+XML+V0//EN.

[109]European Parliament, Report with recommendations to the Commission on Civil Law Rules on Robotics, at paras. 49–51.

[110]European Parliament, Report with recommendations to the Commission on Civil Law Rules on Robotics, at para. 56.

[111]"Calls on the Commission, when carrying out an impact assessment of its future legislative instrument, to explore, analyse and consider the implications of all possible legal solutions, such as: a) establishing a compulsory insurance scheme where relevant and necessary for specific categories of robots whereby, similarly to what already happens with cars, producers, or owners of robots would be required to take out insurance cover for the damage potentially caused by their robots;b) ensuring that a compensation fund would not only serve the purpose of guaranteeing compensation if the damage caused by a robot was not covered by insurance;c) allowing the manufacturer, the programmer, the owner or the user to benefit from limited liability if they contribute to a compensation fund, as well as if they jointly take out insurance to guarantee compensation where damage is caused by a robot;d) deciding whether to create a general fund for all smart autonomous robots or to create an individual fund for each and every robot category, and whether a contribution should be paid as a one-off fee when placing the robot on the market or whether periodic contributions should be paid during the lifetime of the robot;e) ensuring that the link between a robot and its fund would be made visible by an individual registration number appearing in a specific Union register, which would allow anyone interacting with the robot to be informed about the nature of the fund, the limits of its liability in case of damage to property, the names and the functions of the contributors and all other relevant details;f) creating a specific legal status for robots in the long run, so that at least the most sophisticated autonomous robots could be established as having the status of electronic persons responsible for making good any damage they may cause, and possibly applying electronic personality to cases where robots make autonomous decisions or otherwise interact with third parties independently;g) introducing a suitable instrument for consumers who wish to collectively claim compensation for damages deriving from the malfunction of intelligent machines from the manufacturing companies responsible;".

the harmful functioning of the robot and the damage suffered by the injured party" and "risk management approach" which focuses "on the person who is able, under certain circumstances, to minimize risks and deal with negative impacts".[112]

Both are important for the issue of liability from AI. The first type, once it is identified can lead to easier tracing of the human who is responsible. The second is very important in terms of AI evolution, given the significance of machine learning and of the autonomy of AI, which means that several actors are causally linked to the eventual events which potentially generate liability.

This latter approach loads the burden of responsibility on the "shoulders" of some human or legal entity, which can be objectively identified as either being causally connected to the specific act or omission of AI or because- again objectively- they should have foreseen such acts or omissions happening.[113]

These approaches are significant regarding the analysis that follows: they indicate the need to combine on the one hand the determination of the specific causal link on an ad hoc basis, with the necessity, in furtherance of legal certainty, to come up on the other hand, with pre-determined criteria for objectively identified liability.

The "proportional fault" system can be of use in these regards: according to that ".... [C]omplete apportionment between the negligent parties, based on their respective degrees of fault, is the proper method for calculating and awarding damages...."[114] This method is suitable for areas such as that of AI where several stages of evolution and actors become implicated in the chain of events.

In order to come up with a theory we need to keep in mind that the central factor is the level of AI autonomy. This is the one which determines who, among the implicated individuals and entities is to be held liable- the programmer, the owner, any other in between or the AI entity per se.[115]

The reasonableness of the deference of autonomy and of reliance on the opinion of AI by the human actor, the efficiency of testing and training of AI, the imposition of constraints on AI by the human designer so that unpredictability becomes limited are all criteria that can determine liability.[116]

Once we determine the liability criteria, different levels of risk and different agents which can be held as responsible should be determined, clarifying liability for the human behind the AI, in the wider chain of design, ownership and use of AI.

---

[112]European Parliament, Report with recommendations to the Commission on Civil Law Rules on Robotics, at paras. 52-55.

[113]Karnow (1996), pp. 170–174.

[114]Hercules, Inc. v. Stevens Shipping Co., 765 F.2d 1069, 1075 (11th Cir. 1985).

[115]See below, the relevant analysis in the conclusions.

[116]*Bathae, ARTIFICIAL INTELLIGENCE OPINION LIABILITY*, at pp. 154–164. Rudina Seseri, The Problem winh "Eplainable"Al, TECHCRUNCH (June 14, 2018), https://techcrunch.com/2018/06/14/the-problem-with-explainable-ai/ [https://perma.cc/QE8R-7VU6]; Will Knight, The Dark Secret at the Heart of Al, MIT TECH. REV. (Apr. 11, 2017), https://www.technologyreview.com/s/604087/the-dark-secret-at-the-heart-of-ai/ [https://perma.cc/QNG2-XSYJ]; Browne and Harrison-Spoerl (2008), pp. 1132–1133.

At the narrow level and more specifically when the origins of AI acts or omissions can be traced in its software,[117] AI is to be approached as an "innocent agent"[118]- as children and animals are perceived. The merely instrumental role of the AI means that the latter is to be considered as -regarding the liability- similar to "automata" and that in terms of liability, a "perpetrator-via-another" must be identified.[119]

The liable perpetrator can be -on the basis of an ad hoc assessment- most often, the programmer or the owner. The assessment about the attribution of responsibility will have to take into account whether the illegal conduct or the omission is directly linked to the software of the AI per se or to the specific use of it.

The attribution of responsibility to the software designer emerges out of its conception of the AI, whereas for the owner is based on the fact that the latter systems benefits from them and therefore it is only reasonable to be held liable.[120] Partially, justification for this approach can be found in doctrines, which were formulated by past cases, which changed the burden of proof at the expense of the defendants instead of the plaintiff.[121]

For instance, AI that has been designed in order to conduct hacking and relevant, illegal cyber-operations clearly constitutes a case for criminal liability, certainly for the programmer and potentially for the owner, in case (s)he is aware of these capacities and goals of the AI.

However, when AI that is designed for example to trace critical personal data, in the framework of the health system, is used non- consensually and possibly for reasons that the owner or the user have not determined, the liability must be attributed to the user. The important thing- once the AI system "itself" is out of the equation- is to determine where the source of the damage is and when to whom the knowledge for the possibility of such damage became known.

While we focus on the two main types of human paragons who may be held liable, we must not forget of a third one. The partial detachment from programming and coding, towards the expanding autonomy of machine learning and the unpredictability it brings[122] mean that AI learning could be viewed as a superseding cause--that is, "an intervening force... sufficient to prevent liability for an actor whose tortious conduct was a factual cause of harm'--of any harm that such systems cause."[123] In case we leave out of the equation of liability this part, we miss one of the most critical parts of AI ontology.

---

[117]Such is the determination of responsibility also, once the malfunction is an outcome of hardware.

[118]Solum (1992), p. 1231.

[119]*Hallevy, The Criminal Liability Of Artificial Intelligence Entities--From Science Fiction To Legal Social Control*, at p. 181.

[120]Decker (2014), pp. 65–86.

[121]Karnow (1996), pp. 176–177.

[122]Jason Tanz, Soon We Won't Program Computers. We'll Train Them Like Dogs., WIRED (May 17, 2016), https://www.wired.com/2016/05/the-end-of-code/ [https://perma.cc/NJ4E-XALV].

[123]Scherer (2016), p. 365.

We will have therefore to think if we should attribute responsibility to the persons or entities who are responsible for the selection of the specific big data that are used; while, in most cases they will claim that they possess very little knowledge of the content and the scope of machine-training and therefore it could deny any liability, the imposition of standards can clarify in legal terms the issue up to some extent. For example, in the case of medical services, the amount and the databases from which data will emerge may have to follow some standards offering equivalent guarantees. Equivalent standards should be foreseen for each distinct area.

As AI autonomy grows, less obvious paradigms will emerge. We have to think about AI with evolving autonomy and therefore growing unpredictability because of its ontological characteristics, such as AI in the framework of space missions or of emergency hospitals. By accepting the evolving nature of such AI we will have adhered to its potential unpredictability. Who is to be blamed then -if any- for damages caused because of the unpredictability which necessarily comes with developed autonomy?

The initial programmer for setting in "motion" a potentially unpredictable AI, the user who-knowingly of the unpredictability- decides to use the AI or maybe none, given that the design and the use of partially unpredictable AI will be legal or the "trainer" of AI? Will it be fair to hold any of the three as liable, because of a "properly" -and with the necessary clarity in terms of its goals and means of achieving them- functioning, partially unpredictable, AI system, in an environment where AI unpredictability is acceptable and non- prohibited according to the legal framework? Will such "acceptance" extend to all AI applications or to some of them?

After all, given that autonomous technologies emerge, become acceptable and embraced by modern societies, the unpredictability that comes with them becomes also acceptable up to some extent at least. Unpredictability means that, even before the level of general or super intelligence has been reached, not all AI can be completely "controlled" in terms of their actions, neither by the user, nor by the programmer. Therefore, the legitimization of such AI should lead to the admittance of an extent and of a new type of risk, socially and legally.

In order however not to have a liability vacuum, we could respond with a governance mechanism that will foresee different legal status for different levels and areas of AI autonomy. The autonomy of AWS's cannot be regulated in the same way with AI in medical services for example. The standards will be different, ranging from de-legitimization of some AI applications, to limitations of the autonomy of others or the imposition of guarantees and compensation that will be followed, once the acceptable and legal unpredictability will have produced some damage.

Within such a framework, liability will be foreseen and regulated in advance, in terms of meeting or not, some sets of necessary standards: the extent of legitimate or not autonomy in different applications of AI, based on the risk that they generate and their goal; proper training according to specific standards; software design and use of big data on the basis of pre- determined standards, as well; guidelines for the use of

AI; insurance schemes specifically for damage caused by AI uses; these could be some of the sets of standards which will clarify liability because of AI actions.

Obviously, practical difficulties in terms of the clarification of the legitimate level of autonomy in each specific area and then of the attribution of liability will emerge but still working on such grounds is a more sound and legally certain way of regulation compared to the reliance on the imaginative and teleological interpretation of proximate but still distant norms about liability, from the judiciary of each national legal system.

The imposition of pre-determined standards, from an international governance mechanism for AI will provide relief to manufacturers, as well as owners from responsibility emerging from risks they could not avoid and foresee.[124] Therefore, the need for safety will not discourage AI evolution.

The non-compliance with the imposed standards will be establishing the causal connection between either the programmer or the owner and the misconduct. The former will be liable for not upholding the standards for software design. As for the latter there is an additional question: should the owner be liable for the conducts of legitimate but knowingly unpredictable-partially-AI under all circumstances? Can we accept an extent of social, collective responsibility because of the fact that we are already and we will do so even more in the future, accepting non- human, autonomous entities acting among us?

For example, a hospital can be held liable for the medical mistakes of its staff. There could be second thoughts however: for what kind of mistakes an AI substituting medical personnel will be held liable? What will be the threshold for the AI -oriented liability?[125]

In addition, there are other cases where the owner of the AI can be totally unaware of potentially unwanted consequences. Think for a moment of an individual in the near future who wants to enhance his/her brain activities and chooses to use AI implants in his brain. (S)he consents on a detailed and lengthy form, to the risks of such a procedure, which could make her/him experience personality changes due to the merging of human and artificial intelligence. Remember that it is not illegal per se and that the AI is not malfunctioning.

Who- if any- is to be held liable for the potential unwanted consequences and of transformations which could not have been predicted- a surge of violence for example - while the implant is legal? Keep in mind that such implants, at least in the early stages will -and are used even for medical treatments.

Despite all potential strict regulations, it seems more likely that we will eventually accept as lawful a certain—possibly expanding- extent of risk, while also and besides standardization imposing compensation and insurance schemes.

Given the complexities and the practical difficulties, the technological and therefore legal environment, with which the existing legal regulation, on the basis of

[124]*Robolaw, Regulating Emerging Robotic Technologies in Europe: Robotics facing Law and Ethics*, at p. 23.

[125]Kowert (2017), pp. 181–182.

negligence, finds it difficult to cope,[126] not only due to the potential impact of AI on the wider public but also due to the fact that the users or owners of AI themselves very often cannot reasonably predict the behavior of an AI entity,[127] additional guarantees must be foreseen: a system of shared private or/and public compensation schemes, especially in the face of public space where AI autonomous systems' creations may belong, offering the equivalent profit to the wider public.

Such a scheme, funded by AI systems and AI systems' creations' which will be belonging to the public sphere, will play the role of guarantee for the socially acceptable risk which emerges from AI autonomy.

Obviously, in order to structure such an efficient scheme, we will need to take into account that the assessment of the elements which are crucial for the determination of liability are taking place always in a certain social context and within this, on an ad hoc basis.[128]

The case of liability will be obviously different, if and once AGI and ASI emerge.[129] The question will be whether, first ontologically-speaking and then legally -speaking, intent will be be attributed to a non-human agent. This question is briefly analyzed in the next chapter.

9.4 Conclusions

This chapter focused on the two sides of the same coin: profitability and liability. It attempted to examine aspects of these two issues which have a profound impact on the social and economic model internationally, touching upon the human- centrism of international law and of international community as well, albeit from a different perspective.

As mentioned in the first chapter, the shape of the fourth industrial revolution, which will be determined at large on the basis of who and in what terms will make use of AI, already has a significant impact on the wider nexus of human rights, including social and economic rights as well.

The creation of a public sphere where AI—generated inventions and creations will belong as a proposition is based on the interpretation of the patent laws but is also inspired by the relevant approach to international law and its foundations, as they are described in the UN Charter and in ICCPR and ICESCR.

[126] Matthias (2004), pp. 175–183.

[127] Wallach (2011), 185. At p. 194;

[128] Karnow (1996), pp. 180–181.

[129] There is also the issue of criminal liability. That is analyzed below in the framework of potential, AI, legal personality.

Such an approach could maximize social benefit from AI and also contribute into the materialization of a variety of rights which are foreseen in these international treaties.[130]

As for liability, the main ambition of a governance scheme should be the promotion of safety with legal certainty. In these regards, a system of attribution of liability is proposed which attempts to include the different levels of participation in the chain of AI evolution and conduct. On top of everything else, a compensation scheme is proposed so that there will be a guarantor for the social acceptance of the risk that accompanies AI systems.

Both of the chapter's parts refer solely to existing or evolutionary-speaking, proximate to existing, forms of AI-i.e. ANI. These same issues will be approached in different ways, if and after AGI or ASI emerge, as then, the issue of legal personality of AI will become the crux of the discussion. This theme is briefly analyzed below, giving a glimpse of a potential future, where legal systems will have to endure unimaginable, until recently, transformations.

References

Abott R (2016) I think, therefore I invent: creative computers and the future of patent law. Boston College Law Rev 57(4):1079

Abrams D (2009) Did TRIPS spur innovation? An empirical analysis of patent duration and incentives to innovate. Univ Pa Law Rev 157:1613

Arnheim R (2001) What it means to be creative. Br J Aesthetics 41(1):24

Barfield W (2015) Cyber-humans our future with machines. Springer, Cham, p 43

Bathae Y (2020) Artificial intelligence opinion liability. Berkeley Technol Law J 35:113

Bekey G, Lin P, Abney K (2011) Ethical implications of intelligent robots. In: Krichmar JL, Wagatsuma H (eds) Neuromorphic and brain-based robots. Cambridge University Press, Cambridge, p 323 ff

Bethards M (2004) Condemning a patent: taking intellectual property by eminent domain. AIPLA Q J 32(1):81

Bridy A (2012) Coding creativity: copyright and the artificially intelligent author. Stan Technol Law Rev:5

Browne MN, Harrison-Spoerl RR (2008) Putting expert testimony in its epistemological place: what predictions of dangerousness in court can teach us. Marq Law Rev 91:1119

Clifford RD (1997) Intellectual property in the era of the creative computer program: will the true creator please stand up? Tul Law Rev 71:1675

de Bruin R (2016) Autonomous intelligent cars on the European intersection of liability and privacy regulatory challenges and the road ahead. Eur J Risk Regulation 7:485

de Cock Buning M (2016) Autonomous intelligent systems as creative agents under the EU framework for intellectual property. Eur J Risk Regulation 7:311

[130] The right to self-determination in all its manifestations, equality, right to work, trade unions' participation, social security and insurance, adequate standard of living could be promoted more efficiently if such technological developments produce wealth for the wider public, instead for a small number of private companies, in oligopolist terms and economic framework.

Decker M (2014) Responsible innovation for adaptive robots. In: Battaglia F, Mukerji N, Nida-Rümelin J (eds) Rethinking responsibility in science and technology. Pisa University Press, Pisa, pp 65–86
Denicola R (2016) Ex Machina: copyright protection for computergenerated works. Rutgers Univ Law Rev 69:251
Erickson K (2016) Defining the public domain in economic terms-- approaches and consequences for policy. Nordic J Appl Ethics 10:1
Fisher W (2001) Theories of intellectual property. In Munzer A (ed.) New essays in the legal and political theory of property, Cambridge University Press, pp 168–199
Gassmann O et al (2021) Patent management, protecting intellectual property and innovation. Springer, Cham, p 194
Gaut B (2010) The philosophy of creativity. Philos Compass 5(12):1039
Grimmelmann J (2016) There's no such thing as a computer-authored work - and it's a good thing, too. Columb J Law Arts 39:403
Hashiguchi M (2017a) The global artificial intelligence revolution challenges patent eligibility laws. J Bus Technol Law 13:1
Hashiguchi M (2017b) Artificial intelligence and the jurisprudence of patent eligibility in the United States, Europe, and Japan. Intellect Property Technol Law J 29(12):3
Hattenbach B, Glucoft J (2015) Patents in an era of infinite monkeys and artificial intelligence. Stan Technol Law Rev 19:32
Hattenbach B, Snyder G (2018) Rethinking the mental steps doctrine and other barriers to patentability of artificial intelligence. Columb Sci Technol Law Rev 19:313
Hemel DJ, Ouellette LL (2013) Beyond the patents–prizes debate. Tex Law Rev 92:303
Hildebrandt M (2008) Ambient intelligence, criminal liability and democracy. Crim Law Philos 2:163
Hristov K (2017) Artificial intelligence and the copyright dilemma. J Franklin Pierce Ctr Intell Prop 57:431
Jaszi P (1992) On the author effect: contemporary copyright and collective creativity. Cardozo Arts Environ Law J 10:293
Karnow C (1996) Liability for distributed artificial intelligences. Berkeley Technol Law J 11:147
Khoury A (2016–2017) Intellectual property rights for "Hubots": on the legal implications of human-like robots as innovators and creators. Cardozo Arts Ent Law J 35:635
Kim D (2018) Intellectual property in the fourth industrial revolution era. les Nouvelles 53:20
Kowert W (2017) The foreseeability of human-artificial intelligence interactions. Tex Law Rev 96:181
Krauss M (1989) Property, monopoly, and intellectual rights non-posnerian law and economics symposium. Hamline Law Rev 12(2):305
MacCoun R (1993) Is there a "deep-pocket" bias in the tort system? Rand Inst Civ J:1
Marchant GE, Lindor RA (2012) The coming collision between autonomous vehicles and the liability system. Santa Clara Law Rev 52:1321
Matthias A (2004) The responsibility gap: ascribing responsibility for the actions of learning automata. Ethics Information Technol 6:175–183
Michael Schuster W (2018, 1945) Artificial intelligence and patent ownership. Wash Lee Law Rev 75
Miller AR (1993) Copyright protection for computer programs, databases, and computer-generated works: is anything new since contu? Harv Law Rev 106:977
Nersessian D, Mancha R (2021) From automation t omation to autonomy: legal and ethical responsibility onomy: legal and ethical responsibility gaps in artificial intelligence innovation. Mich Technol Law Rev 27:55
Palacet VM (2019) What if artificial intelligence wrote this?artificial intelligence and copyright law. Florida Law Rev 71:217
Pearlman R (2018) Recognizing artificial intelligence (AI) as authors and inventors under U.S. intellectual property law. Richmond J Law Technol 24:2

Rai AK (1999) Regulating scientific research: intellectual property rights and the norms of science. NorthWest Univ Law Rev 94:77
Ralston WT (2005) Copyright in computer-composed music: Hal Meets Handel. J Copyright Soc U S A 52:281
Ritchie G (2007) Some empirical criteria for attributing creativity to a computer program. Minds Mach 17:67–99
Ryan Calo M (2011) Open robotics. MD Law Rev 70:571
Samore W (2013) Artificial intelligence and the patent system: can a new tool render a once patentable idea obvious? Syracuse J Sci Technol Law 29:113
Samuelson P (1986) Allocating ownership rights in computer-generated works. Univ Pitt Law Rev 47:1185
Scherer MU (2016) Regulating artificial intelligence systems: risks, challenges, competencies, and strategies. Harv J Law Technol 29:353
Sobel BLW (2017) Artificial intelligence's fair use crisis. Columb J Law Arts 41(1):45
Solow-Niederman A (2020) Administering artificial intelligence. Southern California Law Rev 93:633
Solum LB (1992) Legal personhood for artificial intelligences. N C Law Rev 70:1231
Spector L (2006) Evolution of artificial intelligence. Artificial Intelligence 170:1251
Vladeck DC (2014) Machines without principals: liability rules and artificial intelligence. Wash Law Rev 89:117
Wallach W (2011) From robots to techno sapiens: ethics, law and public policy in the developments of robotics and neurotechnologies. Law Innov Technol 3(2):185

Chapter 10
Conclusions: A Taste of the Future (?)—AGI/ASI and Potential Legal Personhood

10.1 Context of the Conclusions

As this book is near its end, Karl Popper's quote that no book can ever be finished, becomes emphatically clear and accurate in terms of the feeling that is created. All of the above analysis could be re-structured and constantly change, as the technological evolution and the social impacts of AI accelerate and transform.

While this book was concluded, the world found itself fighting the pandemic of COVID-19, which revealed among other things, longstanding deficiencies of the international legal order and of international relations, as well as flaws within national states and the prevalent social and economic model. The fact that the pandemic became a catalyst for further deterioration of international relations[1] is not particularly comforting regarding our maturity in the face of risks such as the ones posed by AI.

In the department of Political Science of the Aristotle University of Thessaloniki, a new module about AI, Political Theories and International Relations was introduced during the academic year 2019–2020. When I asked our students—before the first COVID-19 lockdown—if they would willingly accept an AI system capable of tracking their social contacts for reasons of national security, all of them responded negatively and without much hesitation. To the same question, during the pandemic and for reasons of public health, the answer was the opposite. Technology is not immune to the social framework; on the contrary the two interact with one another continuously. That is only one of the ways that this book could be re-written from the beginning.

[1] Kretchmer (2021) https://www.weforum.org/agenda/2021/01/what-is-vaccine-nationalism-coronavirus-its-affects-covid-19-pandemic/.

T. Tzimas, *Legal and Ethical Challenges of Artificial Intelligence from an International Law Perspective*, Law, Governance and Technology Series 46,
https://doi.org/10.1007/978-3-030-78585-7_10

Apart from the social and technological, constant interaction, there is another reason why this book seems unfinished: the prospect of AGI and ASI and the legal ramifications—as well as the social, economic, political and existential ones. A future and the law with AGI and ASI necessitate a new and distinct book; one that will be resembling to a legal, science fiction but that will also be grounded on the present.

Even if AGI and ASI never come to "life" as some predict, still the road to this evolutionary level will pose new challenges that cannot be completely captured as of now. In addition, while establishing regulations that will not be proven to be useful because of the non-emergence of AGI or ASI will do us no harm, the opposite approach and situation—the emergence of AGI and ASI without any regulations in advance—may be catastrophic.

In such a framework and in this context, the conclusions of the book are not devoted to merely summarizing what is analyzed in the previous chapters but to the future. A future consisted of world or worlds, of reality or realities where we will have to regulate our co-existence with other intelligent entities. The conclusions touch introductorily upon the theme of legal personhood of AGI and of ASI.

When we attempt to envisage an ontologically different being and its interaction with humans, we need to remember Wittgenstein's lion: "If a lion could speak, we could not understand him."[2] That is eventually the crux of the risks from the emergence of AGI and ASI: the lack of ontological comprehension of each other. We are used to such relationships with inferior species but not with equal or—even worse—superior species.

As already said before, the human-centric nature of our legal system and of international law cannot legitimize the emergence of AGI or ASI. This is the starting point, in relation to these, two, potential forms and types of AI.

Still, they might emerge, either because no governance mechanism will be imposed on time, or simply because whatever governance system will be proven inefficient. Then, up to the extent that we will maintain the "upper hand" or that at least we will not be profoundly inferior and subdued by ASI, we will have to deal with the consequences, in legal terms-among other things—as well.

In such a situation, we will eventually reach the point of needing to decide about the potential legal personhood AGI/ASI, including obligations and rights—provided of course that our decisions will be relevant and that they will matter.[3]

[2]Wittgenstein (1958), p. 223.

[3]Rights are broadly defined "[r]ights are entitlements (not) to perform certain actions, or (not) to be in certain states; or entitlements that others (not) perform certain actions or (not) be in certain statesRights, Stan. encyclopedia Phil. (Edward N. Zalta ed., Fall 2015). https://plato.stanford.edu/entries/rights/.

10.2 Identifying the Sets of Legal Issues for the Determination of a Potential Legal Personhood

The determination of the characteristics of the potential legal personhood for AGI/ASI will be decided upon different factors; the first set of factors is the evolutionary level of AI, focusing on the ontological characteristics of the latter in terms of self-perception, life and reproduction, finiteness, emotions, intellectual capacities and self-awareness.

The concept of personhood, when completely put out of "I know it when I see it" approach, reveals all the "fuzziness" and ambiguity that it carries with it.[4] As Solum explains "All of the persons we have met have been humans... it is not surprising that our concept of person is fuzzy at the edges. For most practical purposes, this fuzziness does not get in our way. We treat humans as persons, and we need not worry about why we do so."[5]

The second set of factors refers to the social interactions of AGI and ASI. How will AGI or ASI evolve in terms of labor—producers, workers or slaves?—of potential overpopulation,[6] impact on finite resources? How will AGI/ASI approach the human conception of space and time, how will such entities organize collectively and how will they interact with human collective formations? How will AI interact with human intelligence? What new realities may emerge and who or what will be living there?

The ontological and the social sets of characteristics will co-determine the evolutionary and autonomy level of AI, defining the extent and the type of legal personhood to which AI entities will be entitled in the future.

As the European Parliament, Committee on Legal Affairs, in its "Draft Report with Recommendations to the Commission on Civil Law Rules on Robotics" held: "[U]ltimately, robots' autonomy raises the question of their nature in the light of the existing legal categories—of whether they should be regarded as natural persons, legal persons, animals or objects—or whether a new category should be created, with its own specific features and implications as regards the attribution of rights and duties."[7]

To make matters a bit interesting, alas more complicated too, in order to determine a potential legal personhood we need to take into account that as of now, personhood—in general—is intrinsically attached to the physical world. AI however co-evolves with technologies such as the cyberspace and biotechnology. It will exist most likely not only in the physical world but in the cyberspace as well. In these regards the "lines" of reality, space, time and existence both at an individual as well

[4]Dyschkant (2015), pp. 2075–2079.

[5]Solum (1992), pp. 1231–1285.

[6]Puaschunder (2019), pp. 4–5.

[7]Committee on Legal Affairs. Draft report with recommendations to the commission on Civil Law Rules on Robotics, at 5, 2015/2103(INL) (May 31, 2016).

as at the collective will blur.[8] New "worlds" and new realities—literally—will emerge.

In such alternative realities, a variety of forms of "presence" and of life will emerge: avatars, emulations[9] or forms of tele-presence. Presence in space and time may be extended or disrupted; personality and intelligence will live in realities, with different space-time environments, which in spite of the fact that they are not physical will remain nevertheless real.[10]

In order to comprehend the depth of these problems we need to understand that the need for regulation will not emerge solely from the "kinetic" impact of these alternative realities on the physical world—*a perception which implies that the physical world is the "real" world and the cyberspace part of it, or a "mirror" of it or in any case attached and meaningful because of its impact on the physical world and on beings living in it*—but also from the fact that these alternative realities will be equally "real" and meaningful, since intelligent entities, "beings" with self-awareness, will exist solely or mainly in these alternative realities—with many or some of them by the way having the certainty that they are humans or metahumans.

The expansion of consciousness to beings in different realities, with alternative space-time environments, as well as of presence and of existence, will also merge human and artificial intelligence, in an even more interlinked and constant manner and extent.[11] Imagine for example that the ambition to upload our consciousness in the cloud or some form of cloud becomes reality. Where and how will we exist? Are we still going to be humans and if the answer is yes, where and when are going to be? How humans will be humans that may actually live—in different realities, potentially expanding but also disrupting their own consciousnesses.[12]

---

[8]Braman (2004), p. 4.

[9]Taylor (2002).

[10]Virtual reality is "a real or simulated environment in which a perceiver experiences telepresence ... telepresence ... focuses attention on the relationship between an individual who is both a sender and a receiver, and on the mediated environment with which he or she interacts ... mediated environments are created and then experienced."

Steuer (1995), pp. 37–39.

"Avatar," for the present discussion, is defined in Merriam-Webster's, supra note 2, at 119 as "an embodiment (as of concept or philosophy) usually in a person ... a variant phase or version of a continuing basic entity." Originally referring to the incarnation of a Hindu deity, avatar derives from the word "avatarati," meaning "he who descends from away (ava) and he who crosses over (tarati)." Avatars also have been viewed as "placeholders" for real-time human presence, i.e., animistic spirit vessels in a system of digitally coded events. As the embodiment of "users," avatars may be said to provide access points in the creation of identity and social life, which in turn act as boundary devices around which some characteristics of personal identity are structured. As such, avatars act as agents of engagement while fostering different associations and forms of "self."

Taylor (2002).

McGreevy (1992), pp. 375–376.

[11]Meghdari and Alemi (2018).

[12]"Global computer-based communications cut across territorial borders, creating a new realm of human activity and undermining the feasibility- and legitimacy-of applying laws based on geographic boundaries. While these electronic communications play havoc with geographic

Even before such a total transformation of human nature, let us think of humans who for medical or other reasons become part of the internet of all. What legal system will be able to detect and provide guarantees in cases of hacking?[13]

Such evolution is expected to change and make us wonder what is human and what is not; what is proximate to human and what is ontologically "alien";[14] And how about brain emulations: will they deserve protection of their existence equal to the one of humans?[15] Will they be considered as humans and as "alive"?

The debate about the potential new legal systems need also to take into account among other things the potential transformed and alternative forms of embodiment. Our perceptions about legal personality follow embodiment in the physical world primarily—of humans or of human—administered entities. The emergence of new forms of embodiment in alternative realities and in interaction or under the merging with AI will shake most of our fundamental truths.

There is also an additional challenge: the one from resemblance. AI will mimic human behavior and will look like, sound or act human more often.[16] It will be demonstrating emotions, social skills, without us being necessarily certain after some extent, whether this is mere imitation or an actual subjective experience, raising legal uncertainty and leaving us with the inherent incapacity to comprehend the "other."[17]

Under such conditions, law will need to cope with a condition of coexistence and merging of novel, non-biological forms of intelligence with humans or of shared human and artificial intelligence, with new forms of "embodiment" of intelligence, resembling or not to the existing ones, as well as with new realities and all these that

---

boundaries, a new boundary, made up of the screens and passwords that separate the virtual world from the "real world" of atoms, emerges. This new boundary defines a distinct Cyberspace that needs and can create its own law and legal institutions... Alternating between different legal identities many times during a day may confuse those for whom cyberspace remains an alien territory, but for those for whom cyberspace is a more natural habitat in which they spend increasing amounts of time it may become second nature. Legal systems must learn to accommodate a more mobile kind of legal person [or legal "entity" with characteristics of "personhood".

Johnson and Post (1996), pp. 1367–1392.

[13]Lauria and Robinson (2012), pp. 219–234.

[14]Vedantam (2001) Brain cells, silicone chips are linked electronically part-mechanical, part-living circuit created. Washington Post, p A03. Available at http://www.sciforums.com/showthread.php?t=3788.

Robinson and Lauria (2003), pp. 311–325.

[15]Dowell. Fundamental protections for non-biological intelligences or: how we learn to stop worrying and love our robot brethren, pp. 328–329.

[16]Markoff. Scientists worry machines may outsmart man. N.Y. Times. Jul. 26, 2009, p A1. Available at http://www.nytimes.com/2009/07/26/science/26robot.html

[17]Larson (2010), p. 105.

Rich C and Sidner CL (2009) Robots and avatars as hosts, advisors, companions, and jesters. AI Magazine, Spring, pp 29–31

Gratch et al. (2008), pp. 1–5.

any reality can include, such as new forms of social organizations and of public space.[18]

In order to achieve the determination of legal personhood therefore, of AGI and ASI, legal systems will need to come up with an expanded and deeper perception of the groundbreaking developments from new realities.

Until now and since the first legal codes, the "reality" and the form of existence that is regulated by law is the one of the physical world and in the physical world, combined with a commonly experienced, perception of space and time. Law is built and pre-determines undoubted perception of the reality we live in.

This will not be the case, following the previous potential developments. Two—at least—problems will emerge, during any attempt to come up with adjusted legal systems: the formation of compatible legal regimes for these different realities and the achievement of cohesion among them, within a superior, unifying context.

In order to reach such new regimes, the international community will need first to trace the most crucial relationships among ontologically different entities and realities; then determine which of these are legally interesting and regulatable; third, identify goals that can serve in a coherent way for the different realities, so that a new form of universality is achieved; last but not least impose rights and obligations comprising a unifying legal regime regulating such different realities.

In order to accomplish these very briefly outlined, four steps, at least two more steps will need to follow then: the drawing of some type of "borders", so that different and ontologically unique realities will be easily identifiable and regulated internally; and the attribution or recognition of legal personhood—of whatever type—to non-human or posthuman entities.

10.3 A New Perception of Sovereignty and of Legal Personhood

The first of these two last steps will re-define the concept of sovereignty. The idea of sovereign cyberspace had been easily rejected, when it was initially presented. It could be much more difficult to reject it, once the internet of all will have emerged and intelligent entities will exist autonomously in it and through it.

The potential sovereignty—or such a claim—in parts and of parts of the cyberspace will re-define sovereignty as a concept and will force us to come forth with a new, inter-sovereign and universal legal regime, in order to co-exist with different forms of collective organization—reaching potentially the level of collective intelligence for example, instead of political bodies.[19]

---

[18] Lauria and Robinson (2012), pp. 219–226.

[19] Human history is not very promising in terms of how we tend to react in the face of claims of sovereignty. Are we going to concede to new sovereigns or will we be tempted to conduct physical and cyber world wars? Our imagination.

Several challenges may emerge also from the ontological characteristics of AI systems[20]: first of all, what if AGI and ASI outpace us in the sense of AI claiming legal personality before we—humans—decide to attribute it?

Once self-awareness is achieved, an AI entity could claim for itself a variety of rights, such as for example political or the equivalent of human rights—a non-human or a post-human version of political rights' movement.[21] How should we respond to that?

What if AGI and ASI entities are completely indifferent for our legal approaches? How are we going to collectively deal with an intelligent entity which will be demonstrating no interest to claim any rights and to abide by any law? Can we co-exist with an equally or superior intelligent entity, which constitutes the complete "otherness" by showing no interest in our social and legal norms?

Such questions or others that cannot be imagined in the present will emerge on the basis of AGI and ASI ontology.

We must keep in mind that the characteristics which lead to the attribution of legal personhood, as of now are considered as solely human-centric, regardless of whether we refer to natural or artificial legal personhood. After all, even artificial legal persons are essentially run by humans and exist in order to protect some type of human interests.[22] The human-centrism of the concept of legal personhood is after all proven by the fact that the rights of artificial legal persons are derived from the legal personhood of natural persons, albeit in limited ways.[23] Human-centrism of

[20]Legal personhood has been until now linked with either human beings or artificial legal persons; The Oxford Legal Dictionary defines legal personality as "an acknowledgement that an entity is capable of exercising certain rights and being subject to certain duties on its own account under a particular system of law. In municipal systems, the individual human being is the archetypal "person" of the law, but certain entities, such as limited companies or public corporations, are granted a personality distinct from the individuals who create them. Further, they can enter into legal transactions in their own name and on their own account"

Oxford Legal Dictionary (7th edition, 2014)

Black's Law Dictionary defines artificial legal person is "[a]n entity, such as a corporation, created by law and given certain legal rights and duties of a human being; a being, real or imaginary, who for the purpose of legal reasoning is treated more or less as a human being.

Artificial Person, Black's Law Dictionary (10th ed. 2014)

The European Parliament resolution on the "Civil Law Rules on Robotics" defines autonomy for the reason of addressing the issue of legal personality as "the ability to take decisions and implement them in the outside world, independently of external control or influence;"

European Parliament (2017) Resolution on Civil Law Rules on Robotics, at para. AA. http://www.europarl.europa.eu/sides/getDoc.do?pubRef=-//EP//NONSGML+TA+P8-TA-2017-0051+0+DOC+PDF+V0//EN.

[21]One could include additional characteristics such as: "the ability to experience pain or suffering, to have intentions or memories, and to possess moral agency..."

Soskis (2005), pp. 36–39.

[22]Shapiro and McCarthy (2011), pp. 701–707.

[23]Dowell (2018), pp. 305–324

legal personhood is until now so self—profound that the functional approach "I know it when I see it" is the prevalent one.[24]

However, the evolving and expanding autonomy of AI will shake—in fact already does—such, well-established beliefs and possibly transform them.

For some, the issue of the regulation of aspects of AI legal personhood can be solved by adopting relatively simple means: for example, Professor Shawn Bayern suggests that it is as easy as putting an algorithm in control of limited liability companies.[25]

Such legal personality would entail a number of rights-probably privacy, property, representation by counsel, judicial guarantees for fair procedure, equality before the law and freedom of speech,[26] as well as the right to confer rights upon other entities.[27] Limited legal personhood of AI could cover liability gaps and promote legal certainty respectively.[28]

What this approach actually suggests is that—via a formalistic perception—the important issue is not who administers the legal entity but the legal entity per se and the need to guarantee its legal personhood, loans legal personality to the AI as well.[29]

In addition, the idea is that instead of focusing on the inner, ontological characteristics of AI, in order to infer its legal personality, we should focus on the functions that are externalized by the different forms of AI and build on these, the equivalent levels of legal personality.

Another approach is to consider evolved AI, as a type of legal personhood similar to artificial legal persons—and therefore to be governed as a type of corporation.[30] The imposition of a human board upon an AI entity can then be a way to safeguard human superiority and to maintain the control of the legal personality of AI.

The ontology of AI raises objections however about whether AI can be equalized with corporations, especially once a higher level of intelligence is achieved.[31]

There is the argument that certain rights were foreseen for humans and therefore cannot be applied to other intelligent entities, as irrelevant. Therefore, human, civil, political, social rights constitute the realm of humans, preventing AGI and ASI from attaining complete legal personhood.

The problem with such objection is that it is mainly of historical and not of deontological nature; in other words, it explains what the case is until now; but until

---

[24]Jacobellis v. Ohio, 378 U.S. 184, 197 (1964) (Stewart, J., concurring)

[25]Bayern (2015), pp. 93–104.
Bayern (2014), pp. 1485–1497.

[26]Lopucki (2018), pp. 888–891.

[27]Bayern (2015), pp. 93–104.

[28]Koops et al. (2010), pp. 497–461.
Lopucki (2018), pp. 901–902.

[29]Bayern et al. (2017), pp. 135–154.

[30]Rothenberg. Can siri 10.0 buy your home? the legal and policy based implications of artificial intelligent robots owning real property, pp. 453–454.

[31]Hallevy (2010), pp. 1–5.

now we never have encountered the experience of AGI, of ASI or of the merging of human and artificial intelligence. The more that AI manifests characteristics of human intelligence, the less easy that it is to deny to it relevant rights, projected on its unique ontology. It is very much likely that the evolution of self-awareness, of emotional intelligence will alter our current perceptions about the uniqueness of human intelligence, justifying complete legal personhood for highly evolved AI.

One may wonder if it is at the interest of humans to concede to the attribution of legal responsibility to AI. It is problematic however in terms of morality as well as of effectiveness. On the one hand, it is morally questionable, whether it is acceptable to deny legal personhood to ontologically-speaking, equal or even superior intellectually, entities; on the other hand, once AGI or ASI has emerged, their deprivation from legal personhood will not be sufficient guarantee for the superiority of humans in the first place.

Of course, it is not a simple task to capture holistically how the legal personality of AI—and more specifically of AGI and ASI—will be structured, especially given that AGI and ASI in ontological terms will have surpassed the equivalent of an entity capable of performing autonomous actions at a narrow level: we need to envisage the technological, the ontological, the social, the ethical characteristics of such entities, in order to understand their motives and tendencies, instead of simply observing aspects of their behaviors.

The attribution of legal personality among humans is based on some demonstratable functions since we share common ontological characteristics, which are self-obvious to us all. When such knowledge is absent or very limited, we face the danger of simply misinterpreting external behaviors.

For example, a friendly behavior could constitute an imitation game, which will stop once an AI entity re-writes its software or parts of it; or the demonstrated will to work on behalf of an emulation may be experienced by it, as a tormenting, oppressive condition, imposed by a lower species, against which the entities of higher intelligence will revolt.

Therefore, while a type of legal personality, structured on the basis of some manifestations of AI activities is easier to conceive, it is incomplete; by restraining our imagination and analysis we put ourselves at the risk of serious, potential misunderstandings.[32] Despite the numerous difficulties, it is crucial to attempt to imagine and comprehend AI and more specifically AGI or ASI as holistically as possible; as another type of person and being first and then as legal personality.[33]

Trying to reduce the legal personality of an equally or superior intelligent entity, to the limits that fit us, humans, better, could be both impractical and immoral. Impractical in the sense of the inability to control a far more intelligent entity and immoral in the sense of the deprivation from an intelligent entity of parts its rights.

[32] Bryson et al. (2017), p. 273.

[33] Frye (2018), pp. 13–23.

A different approach may be that among humans too there are situations where regardless of the intelligence of the individual, the legal personhood is not complete—i.e. for minors—in terms to avoid potential dangers.[34]

Again, however the comparison is not completely accurate. Such limited legal personality must be justified on the basis of the social immaturity or the mental capacity, in comparison with the threshold of the "average"—whatever that means actually—human, adult. Therefore, once this threshold has been passed, what will be the justification for the restriction of the legal personality?

It is also troubling that certain, demonstrated activities by an AI entity may come to look so proximate or even identical to ours—replicating and mimicking human consciousness and intelligence[35]—without us being certain that they mean even something remotely proximate to our subjective experiences. However, one may wonder: why our potential, cautiousness towards difference, even deep ontological difference, justifies and excuses the denial of the legal personality?

This is how and why already, since several decades ago, a certain part of the legal theory has argued that the differences between human and artificial intelligence should not be a paragon for the non-attribution—potentially—of legal personhood to AI.[36]

Even further and regarding the question about the potential indifference of AGI or ASI towards obtaining legal personalities, we should try to enforce a mechanism—through machine learning and software design—that will make all AI forms that are evolving towards higher intelligence to seek for legal personality, as this is the only way to regulate co-existence. We do not need neither Gods nor beasts among us. As AI evolves, we must make it seek for part of our rights because with them goes the imposition of obligations and of integration.

So, what has to be discussed is what type of rights and obligations AGI and ASI will have—provided that they will care of course for it and that we will be able to attribute it or not. We must have achieved a deeper understanding of consciousness in order to determine the relevant characteristics for AI, by the time that the issue of potential legal personality for AGI and ASI will arise.

In terms of the path of AI towards legal personality, it will be following its ontological developments[37] Once it reaches and surpasses a certain threshold of evolution—which may be closer than we think—it will have a first level of limited, legal personhood—sharing characteristics both of natural, as well as of artificial legal persons—providing it with some initial rights and obligations—for example as the ones flowing from the management of an artificial legal person.

Some rights are more easily attributed to artificial legal entities in general and therefore to AI as well—for example the right to property—whereas others flow

[34]Rothenberg. Can Siri 10.0 buy your home? the legal and policy based implications of artificial intelligent robots owning real property, p. 456.

[35]Solum (1992), p. 1231

[36]McNally and Inayatullah (1988), p. 119.

[37]Dowell (2018), pp. 305–328.

from higher intelligence identities—from self-awareness or from emotional intelligence—and will emerge at a later stage—for example the right to free speech.[38]

In between these two levels we may have AI applications, embodied with part of the feelings—even as imitation—that a human may experience. In these initial stages, the legal personality could be that of protected non-persons, such as of animals[39] or as "quasi-human."[40]

The critical element from a moral and legal perspective will be the ellipsis of complete self-awareness, of complete consciousness and of complete emotional intelligence, while a certain part of them will be present. A range of rights will be attributed not only or mainly because of the subjective experiences of the AI entity—which may be limited or a mere imitation—but for reasons of public order as well.

That would justify for example the non-recognition and the non-attribution of patent-eligibility in favor of humans or human-administered, artificial, legal persons from inventories by AI autonomous systems. Additionally, some rights in terms of the treatment of AI will be established; certain forms of AI will be protected from misuse or abuse-for reasons of public order too.[41]

Imagine for example, the case of sex-bot; the initial question is whether it should be legal to create entities with—as they evolve—partial and limited subjective experience—or manifestation of it—destined to please humans; the second issue is the impact on them and on the public order of abuse conducted on them. Think of a pedophile who asks from a manufacturer a sex-bot designed to look like a child; or think of a group of people who want to experience the equivalent of a rape and again ask for a sex-bot which will manifest the feelings of a rape victim.

Even if these sex-bots can only mimic instead of actually experiencing the complete range of emotions that follow such incidents in the initial stages, the tendency will be to bring them as close as possible to the reality of the experience; what will the impact be for our own public order and fundamental principles of law? Are we moving towards a "WestWorld" scenario? And by allowing such behaviors against non-human entities, do we diverge them from being inflicted on humans or do we encourage them in fact? Frighteningly enough, the answer could be the second.

On such grounds, AGI and ASI or intelligent forms of existence based on the merging of human and artificial intelligence, should be entitled eventually, to political rights, individuals' freedoms etc. Since an entity has the capacity to enter the public domain, formulate sovereignty, organize collectively and proceed into legal interactions with other legal persons autonomously, it must be attributed the equivalent rights as well.[42]

---

38 Bayern et al. Company law and autonomous systems: a blueprint for lawyers, entrepreneurs, and regulators, p. 155.

39 Solaiman (2017), pp. 155–161.

40 Puaschunder (2018), pp. 143–174.

41 Puaschunder (2020), p 46.

42 Hildebrandt (2013), pp. 23–38.

As and if AI further evolves towards AGI and ASI we will obviously need to come to terms with the need to co-exist with equal or superior entities. We will have to think of the passage to the era of existential law, which will be providing certain rights—an equivalent to human rights law but on the basis of a new universality, endorsing all intelligent species.

As mentioned in the chapters before, in our legal systems human rights sustain the hegemonic human—centrism of them. Additionally, the architecture of collective peace and security together with the equal sovereignty of all states regulates the co-existence of different sovereigns. Something similar will need to be imposed—hopefully combined with more effective monitoring and enforcement mechanisms—when we will have to establish a legal regime for all intelligent entities and for different sovereignties, extending in different space-time environments.

The complete legal personhood of AI will most likely mean that a certain extent of criminal responsibility will be attributed to it as well.

It can be expected that highly evolved AI will be implicated or even conducting, themselves crimes similar to those of humans—or not so similar. Legal personhood means that AI will be held liable for the commitment of certain crimes, provided that the AI entities will be setting the goals choose the necessary means and execute the specific acts or persuade someone else to act. Therefore, part of machine-learning must be the compliance with criminal law and with the moral principles that transcend it.

Once we accept that "the process of analysis in AI systems parallels that of human understanding",[43] then in principle we can talk about criminal responsibility directly of the AI agent. That should lead though to a right of AI to stand in trial of some type, with all the necessary guarantees of a fair trial.[44]

Bruno Latour introduced the term "actants," distinguishing between human and non-humans, in order to philosophically differentiate from agents and actors, focusing on the actual acts instead of their motives—existing or alleged.[45] Levy defined actants as "everything that makes a difference within a network", with every actant defining itself "by the difference it produces."[46]

The criminal liability of AI does not exclude liability of the humans too. They may very well be complicit in the commitment of whatever crime, on the basis of common rules of intent or negligence. We will obviously transform criminal law so that it will be relevant to the AI ontology.

The issue of criminal responsibility in relation to AI is dependent on the extent of autonomy. That means that the human agent behind the artificial one, could "avoid finding out what precisely the ML[machine learning] system is doing, since the less

[43]Hallevy (2008), pp. 122–124.

[44]Hildebrandt (2008), pp. 163–180.

[45]Latour (1999).

[46]Levy (1990), p. 157.

the human agents know, the more they will be able to deny liability for both these reasons".[47]

This could be a way for humans out of their criminal responsibility, which should make us possibly foresee a new type of adjusting existing offences to machine-learning. "Teaching" and "raising" AI to commit offences—i.e. conduct illegal cyber operations—or in ways that it is very much likely and expected for AI to act as such could very well become an illegal act, in accordance with national and international law, indicatively.

An issue of concern course whether penalties will have any significant value on AI. The argument is re-framed and gets differentiated significance on the basis of the various perspectives from which the concept of the penalty is approached. The prevalent human-centrism of our way of thinking will lead to the effort to explore the impact of a certain penalty on the human offender and then to try and find how we can adjust such impact on AI. We will need to identify the impact of penalties on the reform of the offender and the proportional and fair restoration for the victim and for the wider public.

In these regards, AI entities could be terminated, temporarily placed out of order, made to go through new machine-learning, provide their services to the victim or victims of the crime—as a type of reparation—or/and have their software re-adjusted so that its tendency to criminal behaviors may be re-framed.

Of course, one may wonder whether there will be the capacity to impose any type of penalties on potentially superior intellectually entities. Will AGI and ASI be interested in complying with our perceptions about criminal law or in general with criminal law? Are highly evolved entities going to adhere to the utility of police and the judicial system? It can be doubted. The problem in this case—i.e. in the case that ASI will have surpassed us and will be finding our criminal codes obsolete—is how are we going to co-exist, which brings us back to the initial necessity of coherence, within the new universality.

One last issue—one of the most crucial ones—is the potential inequality among different intelligent entities. Whatever training about friendly AI, may be proven inefficient in the face of vast inequalities orientating from the intellectual capacity of each entity. This is why it is necessary as much as possible to endorse in the debate about potential legal personhood of AGI and ASI—as well as of merging, human and artificial intelligence—regulations that will bridge the potential ontological inequalities in advance—if possible.

In the face of AGI and of ASI, one way to tackle inequality is by distancing from it and the other one by limiting it. The former refers to some type of "borderlines" among the different species and their sovereignties, with well-regulated communications and interaction. Is such a method practically possible? While far from certain it is still a possibility. The latter refers to what may lie ahead for us, humans: the

[47] Williams (2017) Lords select committee, artificial intelligence committee, written evidence (AIC0206). http://data.parliament.uk/writtenevidence/committeeevidence.svc/evidencedocument/artificial-intelligence-committee/artificial-intelligence/written/70496.html#_ftn13

advance of ourselves to post-humanism, mainly by merging human and artificial and intelligence.

Once we trigger the race to AGI and ASI—which is probably already the case—and when we will be approaching the moment of singularity, the temptation to get "on board" and use AI in order to enhance the human race may not only be irresistible but necessary as well.

As mentioned above we will need to regulate the "if", the "how", the "when" and the "for whom" of such transformation to post-humanism.

Post-humans—or transhumans—as an enhanced hopefully, species will need a regulatory scheme capable of preserving human control over the merged intelligences, as well as guarantees for the function of these merged intelligences and specifically for the artificial part. What will be equally important however—once the former guarantees are achieved—is the establishment of a right to post-humanism for all. That would require the imposition of a social right, together with the transformation of the social security and the public health sectors.

As already mentioned, in any other case we will experience the implosion of human societies because of ontological—and not only social—inequalities.

And one last question—in what could be an endless set of questions: what are we going to do with the potential overpopulation of AI entities and the potential repercussions, ranging from social to environmental consequences? Can we bridge the gap between finiteness and infiniteness—unless we become infinite as well? Could we try to impose a software "switch-off" termination? Will it be feasible and ethical? Should AGI and ASI with physical embodiment die? Should emulations die?[48]

One solution could be what is suggested in the previous chapters: immortality for all or immortality for none. However, we will neither be able to impose death on infinite and superior entities, nor can we bet that we will achieve immortality. The only type of regulation could be one orientating from the limitedness of resources. We cannot foretell the energy "footprint" or the impact of AGI and of ASI in general on our resources but we could and we must assess AI from an environmental perspective, limiting its evolution in advance.

10.4 Summing Up

The truth is that we cannot capture how our future with AGI and ASI will look like. In fact, we are already in this course in uncharted waters. As Wu, noted, "... make no mistake: we are now different creatures than we once were, evolving technologically rather than biologically, in directions we must hope are for the best."[49] The

[48]Marra and McNeil (2013), pp. 1139–1187.

[49]Wu (2014) If a Time Traveller Saw a Smartphone. The New Yorker. http://www.newyorker.com/tech/elements/if-a-time-traveller-saw-a-smartphone; Wu T (2011).

exponential technological growth as Kurzweil describes it means that the twenty-first century could resemble to 20 millennia of progress.[50]

Despite of course of our optimism about what science can achieve we need to pay also attention to Miguel Nicolelis' view who has argued that "the brain is not computable and therefore no engineering can reproduce it."[51]

It reminds us of the fact not only of a potential scientific failure but also of the complications and the risks that we could face when we may be thinking that we are replicating the human brain, whereas in reality we could be giving life to limited or mentally "amputated: versions of it.

Still, we are possibly "raising" the superior species of tomorrow; and we do so without paying too much attention on it. As we deal with AI, we have to confront our own ethical, political, social, economic, existential and legal set of beliefs.[52]

When we attempt to identify the ethics of potential AI entities we always need to keep in mind that human ethics are notoriously ambiguous and unstable: "we are like sailors who must rebuild their ships on the open sea, never able to dismantle it in dry-dock and to reconstruct it there out of the best materials"[53] or similarly "At the foundation of well-founded knowledge is knowledge that is not well founded."[54]

Do we have the wisdom for such an evolutionary leap that we already promote? No. Nevertheless we will move on. It is our past that teaches us embarrassing lessons but even worse our present: as mentioned at the beginning of the conclusions, the handling of the pandemic alone and of the vaccination internationally is indicative of the preservation of "selfish", national-state interests over international regulation.

We must not forget: the responsibility is too great even if we do not reach the level of AGI and ASI, simply—although it is not simple at all—because of the course to it. ANI already raises impressively difficult problems. In addition, the exact time and event of passage from ANI to AGI and then to ASI could be proven elusive and unidentifiable in advance.

This is why the international community must work on the legal regulation now, hopefully well in advance of the expected or anticipated, "singularity moment".

The argument of the book in a nutshell is that we in the course of such regulation we must place as guiding principle, the protection of human-centrism and the effort to promote further equality and prosperity in viable ways., through AI evolution. Technology will co-define our future, but only in the framework of our social and economic model. In this framework, law has its unique role to play.

The international community will need to implement and therefore adjust its principles and international conventions, jus cogens and customary law in a new

---

[50]Kurzweil (2006).

[51]Nicolelis (2013) The brain is not computable. MIT Technology Review. https://www.technologyreview.com/2013/02/18/180012/the-brain-is-not-computable/.

[52]Regarding such an analysis of the wider philosophical ramifications of AI, indicatively see: Müller (2016).

[53]Rabossi (2003), pp. 171–184.

[54]Janik and Toulmin (1973).

domain. It will most likely need to establish new mechanisms in order to monitor and intervene in AI.

The proposition of this book does not intend to be techno-phobic or hostile towards AI in general or even post-humanism or trans-humanism. It argues that technological progress must take place with cautious and wisdom, in an environment of freedom and equality, as well as within the general principles of international law. It is based on these principles we must think as deeply as we think about the technological advances ahead of us, in the near or more distant future.

References

Bayern S (2014) Of bitcoins, independently wealthy software, and the zero-member LLC. N W Univ Law Rev 108:1485–1497

Bayern S (2015) The implications of modern business entity law for the regulation of autonomous systems. Stan Tech Law Rev 19:93–104

Bayern S, Burri T, Grant TD, Häusermann DM, Möslein F, Williams R (2017) Company law and autonomous systems: a blueprint for lawyers, entrepreneurs, and regulators. Hastings Sci Technol Law J 9:135–154

Braman S (2004) Biotechnology and communication: the meta-technologies of information, vol 10. Routledge, London, p 4

Bryson JJ et al (2017) Of, for, and by the people: the legal lacuna of synthetic persons. Artif Intell Law 25:273

Dowell R (2018) Fundamental protections for non-biological intelligences or: how we learn to stop worrying and love our robot brethren. Minn J Law Sci Technol 19:305–324

Dyschkant A (2015) Note, legal personhood: how we are getting it wrong. Univ Ill Law Rev 2015:2075–2079

Frye BL (2018) The lion, the bat & the thermostat: metaphors on consciousness. Savannah Law Rev 5:13–23

Gratch J et al (2008) Modeling the cognitive antecedents and consequences of emotion. J. Cogn Syst Res 10:1–5

Hallevy G (2008) Unmanned vehicles – subordination to criminal law under the modern concept of criminal liability, vol. 124, pp 122–124

Hallevy G (2010) "I robot--I, criminal"--when science fiction becomes reality: legal liability of AI robots committing criminal offenses. Syracuse J Sci Tech Law 22:1–5

Hildebrandt M (2008) Ambient intelligence, criminal liability and democracy. Crim Law Philos 2 (2):163–180

Hildebrandt M (2013) Chapter 2 from Galatea 2.2 to Watson - and back? IUS Gentium 25:23–38

Janik A, Toulmin S (1973) Wittgenstein's Vienna. Simon and Schuster, New York

Johnson DR, Post D (1996) Law and borders: the rise of law in cyberspace. Stanford Law Rev 48:1367–1392

Koops B-J et al (2010) Bridging the accountability gap: rights for new entities in the information society? Minn J Law Sci Technol 11:497–461

Kretchmer H (2021) Vaccine nationalism – and how it could affect us all. World Economic Forum

Kurzweil R (2006) The singularity is near: when humans transcend biology. Penguin Books, London

Larson DA (2010) Artificial intelligence: robots, avatars, and the demise of the human mediator. Ohio State J 25:105

Latour B (1999) Pandora's hope. Essays on the reality of science studies. Harvard University, Cambridge

Lauria RM, Robinson GS (2012) From cyberspace to outer space: existing legal regimes under pressure from emerging meta-technologies. Univ La Verne Law Rev 33:219–234
Levy P (1990) Les technologies de l'intelligence. L'avenir de la pense´e a` l'e`re informatique. La Decouverte, Paris, p 157
Lopucki L (2018) Algorithmic entities. Wash Univ Law Rev 95:888–891
Marra W, McNeil S (2013) Understanding "The loop": regulating the next generation of war machines. Harv J Law Publ Policy 36:1139–1187
McGreevy M (1992) The presence of field geologists in mars-like terrain. Presence 1:375–376
McNally P, Inayatullah S (1988) The rights of robots: technology, culture and law in the 21st century. Futures 20:119
Meghdari A, Alemi M (2018) Recent advances in social & cognitive robotics and imminent ethical challenges. In: Proceedings of the 10th international RAIS conference on social sciences and humanities organized by research association for interdisciplinary studies (RAIS) at The Erdman Center at Princeton University, Princeton, New Jersey, United States. The Scientific Press, Cambridge
Müller VC (2016) Fundamental issues of artificial intelligence. Springer, Berlin
Puaschunder JM (2018) Gifts without borders: intergenerational glue connecting over distance and time as pure international development in the age of migration. In: Puaschunder JM (ed) Intergenerational responsibility in the 21st century. Vernon, Wilmington, pp 143–174
Puaschunder J (2019) On artificial intelligence's Razor's edge: on the future of democracy and society in the artificial age. SSRN Electron J 2019:4–5
Puaschunder JM (2020) Revising growth theory in the artificial age: putty and clay labor, p 46
Rabossi E (2003) Some notes on Neurath's ship and Quine's sailors. Principia 7(1-2):171–184
Rich C and Sidner CL (2009) Robots and avatars as hosts, advisors, companions, and jesters. AI Magazine, Spring, pp 29–31
Robinson GS, Lauria RM (2003) Legal rights and accountability of cyberpresence: a void in space law/astrolaw jurisprudence. Ann Air Space Law 28:311–325
Shapiro I, McCarthy CW (2011) So what if corporations aren't people? J Marshall Law Rev 44:701–707
Solaiman SM (2017) Legal personality of robots, corporations, idols and chimpanzees: a quest for legitimacy. Artif Intell Law 25:155–161
Solum LB (1992) Legal personhood for artificial intelligences. N C Law Rev 70:1231–1285
Soskis B (2005) Man and the machines it's time to start thinking about how we might grant legal rights to computers, pp 36–39
Steuer J (1995) Defining virtual reality: dimensions determining telepresence. In: Biocca F, Levy MR (eds) Communication in the age of virtual reality, vol 33. Routledge, London, pp 37–39
Taylor TL (2002) Living digitally: embodiment in virtual worlds. In: Schroeder R (ed) The social life of avatars: presence and interaction in shared virtual environments, vol 40. Springer, New York
Wittgenstein L (1958) Philosophical investigations. Basil Blackwell, Oxford, p 223
Wu T (2011) The master switch: the rise and fall of information empires. Vintage Press, Visalia

A RUSSIAN PERSPECTIVE ON THEORETICAL ARCHAEOLOGY

To Leo

A RUSSIAN PERSPECTIVE ON THEORETICAL ARCHAEOLOGY

The Life and Work of Leo S. Klejn

Stephen Leach

Left Coast Press Inc.

Walnut Creek, California

LEFT COAST PRESS, INC.
1630 North Main Street, #400
Walnut Creek, CA 94596
www.LCoastPress.com

ISBN 978-1-62958-138-5 hardback
ISBN 978-1-62958-140-8 institutional eBook
ISBN 978-1-62958-141-5 consumer eBook

Library of Congress Cataloging-in-Publication Data:

Leach, Stephen D.
A Russian perspective on theoretical archaeology : the life and work of Leo S. Klejn / Stephen Leach.
pages cm
Includes bibliographical references and index.
ISBN 978-1-62958-138-5 (hardback) — ISBN 978-1-62958-140-8 (institutional eBook) — ISBN 978-1-62958-141-5 (consumer eBook)
1. Klein, L. S. (Lev Samuilovich) 2. Klein, L. S. (Lev Samuilovich)—Philosophy. 3. Archaeologists—Soviet Union—Biography. 4. Jewish scholars—Soviet Union—Biography. 5. Archaeology—Philosophy. 6. Archaeology—Study and teaching (Higher)—Soviet Union—History. I. Title.
CC115.K58L43 2015
930.1—dc23
2015006235

Printed in the United States of America

™ The paper used in this publication meets the minimum requirements of American National Standard for Information Sciences—Permanence of Paper for Printed Library Materials, ANSI/NISO Z39.48–1992.

Contents

List of Illustrations 7
Foreword *by Stephen Shennan* 9
Preface 11

PART I LIFE STORY

Chapter 1 Before Prison 17
Background 17
Ethnicity 18
War and Childhood 20
Grodno 23
Student Years in Leningrad 23
Early Career 30

Chapter 2 Prison 36
The Savage within and in Society 36
The World Turned Upside Down 40

Chapter 3 After Prison 42
Publications in the West 42
New Interests 43
Marxism 45
Travels and Retirement 47
Politics and Religion 49
Twilight Years 51

PART II LIFE'S WORK

Chapter 4 Anthropology 55
Prison Life 55
Cybernetics 59
Homosexuality 59

Chapter 5 Homeric Studies 61
Incorporeal Heroes 61
The Anatomy of the Iliad 64
The Catalogue of Ships 66

Chapter 6 The Resurrection of Perun 70
Historical Background 70
A New Source? 75

Chapter 7 Ethnogenesis 81
Gustaf Kossinna: Archaeology in the Saddle 81
The Proto-Indo-European Homeland 87
1. The Catacomb-grave Culture 88
2. Proto-Hittites 91
The Varangian Controversy 92

Chapter 8 Histories of Archaeology 95
The New Archaeology 95
The Montelius Formula 96
The History of Archaeological Thought 99
A History of Anthropology 101
Soviet Archaeology 102

Chapter 9 Theoretical Archaeology in Relation to Practice 108
Theory in Relation to Practice 108
The Structure of Theoretical Archaeology 109
1. The Concerns of Archaeology 110
2. The Nature of Archaeological Methodology 116
3. Combatant Gods: The Fundamental Principles of Archaeology 121

Chapter 10 What Is Theoretical Archaeology? 125
Antitheoretical Empiricism 125
The Concept of Theory in Oppositions 126
The Cognitive Structure of Theoretical Archaeology 128
The Functions of Theoretical Archaeology 128
Information Processing: The Fourteen Weirs 130
Research Design 134

Chapter 11 The Archaeologist and the Detective 135
Klejn and Collingwood 137
A Warning to the West? 142

Appendix A The Commandments 144
Appendix B Klejn's Bibliography 146
Notes 205
References 213
Index 217
About the Author 221

Illustrations

Figure 1.1	Gogol Street, Vitebsk	18
Figure 1.2	Karl Marx Street, Yoshkar-Ola	21
Figure 1.3	Vladimir Y. Propp	24
Figure 1.4	Mikhail Artamonov	26
Figure 1.5	Klejn in 1950 on Artamonov's expedition on the site of the Don-Volga canal	26
Figure 1.6	Klejn on March 3, 1950, at the Marr Conference	29
Figure 1.7	Klejn in 1953. Portrait by Michail Devyatov	30
Figure 3.1	Klejn in his convict's uniform	44
Figure 9.1	Archaeology in the scheme of disciplines	119
Figure 9.2	The combatant Gods: The fundamental principles of archaeology	124
Figure 10.1	The concept of theory in oppositions	127

Foreword

Leo Klejn is an extraordinary individual: a polymath, an intellectual provocateur, not least a survivor of the events of his own life. He is also almost certainly the only theoretical archaeologist from the Soviet Union and Russia that Anglophone audiences have ever heard of, although these days I wonder how many even that is true of. Even if they know the name they probably know next to nothing about the man and his ideas. I hope Stephen Leach's excellent book changes that. It certainly deserves to. The subject might be thought rather forbidding, but I found the book compulsive. Part of the reason for this is Klejn's amazing life story, but what gives the book its special power and attraction is that it is less a standard intellectual biography and much more a dialogue between the author and Klejn himself. This approach gives a powerful sense of what the man is like—brilliant, argumentative, iron-willed, never one to accept the conventional view or the easy path—and with the toughness to take the consequences of these character traits for his life in the old Soviet Union and after.

But in presenting Klejn's ideas in their context the book is also a window on a very different intellectual world, an archaeological tradition that has developed almost entirely independently of the Anglo-American one and is largely unknown to most of us. It is not just about archaeology though. We are told that Klejn has said that 'in his life he had but one legal wife, archaeology, but many mistresses—anthropology, history, philology, and folklore studies'. His wide-ranging intellectual curiosity and remarkable productivity means he has made book-length contributions to all of these, and Leach gives each of them its due. In the end, though, like Klejn, it is the archaeology we return to and in particular to his views about the relationship between archaeology and history. Here and elsewhere I'm sure most readers from the Anglo-American tradition will find much that provokes them to debate and disagreement, but before embarking on this debate they should certainly read and ponder this book's indispensable appendix of archaeological and academic 'commandments' that were on the walls for Klejn's student seminars.

We should all be very grateful to Stephen Leach for writing this hugely engaging introduction to an extraordinary man and his ideas.

Stephen Shennan

Preface

The name of the Russian archaeologist Leo S. Klejn has long been known in the West, but, although his name is generally cited in respectful tones, any more than the sketchiest knowledge of his life and work has, until now, proved hard to find. The present work attempts to remedy this deficiency by providing an overview of his theories and the context in which they were formulated.

For many years Klejn was known in the Anglophone world through just two works, *Archaeological Typology* (1982) and *Metaarchaeology* (2001). The former is a poor translation—Klejn was imprisoned at the time and so was unable to read it before it was published—and the latter might perhaps, at first glance, give the impression of a somewhat dry and technical work. However, two new, and good, translations have recently been published: *Soviet Archaeology* (2012) and *Incorporeal Heroes* (2012). They reveal what has long been known to Russian readers, that Klejn's books are well-written and demonstrate a keen interest in the interaction of human characters. Until the publication of these two translations, in December 2012, whatever else most Western archaeologists knew of Klejn, they would probably not have thought of his work as fluent and inviting.

I wrote this book in the hope that the latter two translations will have stimulated interest in Klejn's work and in the belief that there is much else in his work that will be of interest in the West. Klejn is, after all, the author of a total of over twenty monographs, on a very wide variety of subjects. My own interest in Klejn stems from 2009 when Klejn initiated a correspondence following a talk that I gave on the comparison between archaeology and forensic science. I had come to have an interest in this subject as a result of my work on the philosophy of R. G. Collingwood. Collingwood writes on this subject in his posthumously published *Idea of History* (1946). However, I did not at that time know that Klejn had also written on this subject—and at greater length than Collingwood, and arguably at greater depth.

It is the comparison between archaeology and forensic science that constitutes the principal focus of the final chapter of this book and the ultimate focus of the work as a whole. Yet the book's ultimate focus is to a great extent a reflection of my own interests; and the reader should be aware that, although Klejn has almost certainly written more extensively on the comparison of archaeology and forensic science than has any other archaeological theorist, this is but one of his many interests.

He has also directed excavations in the Ukraine and on the Russian steppes: he has written on the origins of the Indo-Europeans; on the problems of ethnogenesis in archaeology; on problems of typology and classification; and on problems in anthropology, philology, folklore, and Homeric studies. Furthermore, he writes a column on contemporary events in a Russian newspaper written by and for academics. Many Russian scholars believe that Klejn's *History of Archaeological Thought* is his masterpiece; but his *Archaeological Typology*, his study of the problem of ethnogenesis in archaeology, his work on the Iliad, and his role as a go-between (through the Iron Curtain) all have their champions, scholars who would rate one of these above all others. On the Internet it is his writing on homosexuality that has attracted the greatest attention. These many and varied interests and accomplishments will be described in this book.

However, there is, of course, probably no-one who is an expert in all these areas other than Klejn himself; and I do not attempt to critically engage with his theories in all these different areas. Rather, for much of this book, I confine myself to exposition, playing Watson to Klejn's Holmes. Yet, although in many areas I confine myself to descriptive exposition I hope to say enough to justify the title of this book and to provide an introductory resource for those readers whose primary interests in Klejn may be different from my own.

I am conscious of the temerity of writing such a book without the advantage of fluent Russian; however, in my favour, since 2009 I have had the advantage of having Leo Klejn's ever-helpful advice and guidance.

The main sources for this work have been *Metaarchaeology* (2001), *Soviet Archaeology* (2012), the interviews given by Klejn (many of which have been published in English in archaeological journals), the abstracts to Klejn's books published on the website www.archaeology.ru, and my own conversations with Klejn.

Acknowledgements

My greatest debt is to Leo Klejn himself. I hereby offer my sincere thanks to him for answering the many questions that arose in the course of writing the book, but I must add that the responsibility for any errors in the presentation of his views is mine alone.

I would also like to thank James Connelly, Giuseppina D'Oro, and James Tartaglia for their comments on an earlier draft of this work; Caryn Berg and Ryan Harris at Left Coast Press, Inc., for their contributions to the production of this book; and Stacey Sawyer for her excellent work as editor and project manager.

Thanks also to the copyright holders of the following interviews for permission to quote extensively from them:

Immonen, V. (2003) The stratigraphy of a life: An archaeological dialogue with Leo Klejn, *Archaeological Dialogues* 10(1): 57–75.
Kristiansen, K. (1993) Exploring the limits: An interview with Leo Klejn, *Journal of European Archaeology* 1(1): 184–94.
Taylor, T. (1994) Conversations with Leo Klejn, *Current Anthropology* (34)5: 723–35.

Part I

Life Story

Chapter 1

Before Prison

Background

'It was the devil's trick to allow me to be born with a soul and talent in Russia'[1]—or, to be precise, in Vitebsk, the home-town of Chagall, in Belarus. Here Klejn was born, on July 1, 1927, to the Jewish physicians Stanislav Semenovich (originally Stanislav Samuil Simkhovich) and Asya Moysseevna. He had an older step-sister, Serafima, born in 1917, and was soon to have a younger brother, Boris, born in 1928. The family were an atheist and 'Russified' Jewish family. For already two generations before Klejn's birth the family's first language had been Russian; before that it was Polish. One of his grandfathers was a factory-owner; the other was a merchant of the first guild. (The first guild consisted of the very richest merchants, typically the top 2–5% of all Russian merchants.)

Klejn's background was that of the highest echelons of society. However, one should not describe him as advantaged by birth without adding that, in the Soviet Union, this background did not bring obvious benefits; rather the reverse. In the Soviet Union it would have been clearly to Klejn's disadvantage to have publicised his family background—both privileged and Jewish—in any detail. Thus, although Klejn was always grateful to his parents—acknowledging that from his father he inherited organisational skills and from his mother, a gifted teacher, his creative abilities—before the breakup of the Soviet Union his family background was barely mentioned on his official *curriculum vitae*.[2] There it was simply stated that he was born to 'employed personnel'.

After the breakup of the Soviet Union in 1991, Klejn could afford to be less reticent. In an interview with Timothy Taylor he reveals his family's activities in the civil war: 'My father joined Denikin's Whites;[3] after their defeat he became a Red Brigade physician in Tukhachevsky's army. He owed his life, frankly, to the fact that he wrote on every questionnaire that he was a White officer but never mentioned that he was a Red general; all his comrades were eliminated because they had been with Tukhachevsky' (Taylor 1994: 723).[4]

A Russian Perspective on Theoretical Archaeology: The Life and Work of Leo S. Klejn by Stephen Leach, 17–35

Figure 1.1 Klejn's birthplace, Gogol Street, Vitebsk. This photograph was taken in 1918; troops and civilians have gathered on the first anniversary of the Russian revolution. Klejn was born in the house on the right (no longer in existence). The building on the left was his first school.

In the supplementary notes to his *curriculum vitae*, appended to the Spanish translation of Klejn's autobiography, Klejn describes himself as a 'radically Russified Jew'.

Ethnicity

In the supplementary notes to his C.V. Klejn then goes on to discuss the influence of his ethnicity in some detail:

> What does it mean to be a 'radically russified Jew'? Is he a Jew or a Russian? The point is that by many indices (lingual and cultural), but mainly by self-conception I am a Russian. Although I have five languages, I do not number any Jewish language among them, neither Yiddish nor Hebrew; and my native language is Russian. This is the only language of which I am the absolute master—it is the language in which I think. I have no adherence to Judaism—I am an atheist, as were my father and grandfather (and their wives).
>
> Yet, I am a Russian of Jewish origin. I do not renounce my ancestors. I have some reasons to be proud of them and some reasons to be ashamed. The same is true of everyone. I have not 'deserted' to another ethnicity: it was my ancestors who underwent assimilation, and so I was assimilated from birth. For me to become a Jew 'anew' would

imply changing my ethnicity. In my opinion the majority of Russia's Jews are of this sort—the exception being the small group that gathers around the synagogue. In contrast to the Jews of Israel (indeed a separate nation, with their own particular ethnos), Russian Jews are something like a caste of the Russian people, like the Cossacks or the Pomors (White Sea coast-dwellers). Indeed, only anti-Semites now speak with a Jewish pronunciation (they mimic Jews with an accent lost by the Jews themselves).

This question is important for people because it is upon Jewish ethnicity that national character is supposed to depend; as well as national solidarity and the defence of interests of national hearth (Israel, Zion). Let us consider all three of these claims.

1) What is it that is specifically Jewish that I have inherited from my Jewish ancestors? If one excludes the outlook (that is generally held in common by the population of South Europe) [that] modern Jews are distinct in their choice of preferable professions and by some features of national character—they are especially fond of their children (there are no Jews among waif children); they are enthusiastic for learning; and hate hard drinking. Yet none of these features is exclusively Jewish; they are inherent to many native Russians as well as to those with Biblical names. The difference is only in the extent of the distribution of these features.

For instance my name is Lev—it is a purely Russian name (from the Greek Leon stems the Slavic Levon (in Byelorussian Lyavon). In Russian this became Lev (pet name Löva). After the time of pogroms in which Lev (Leo) Tolstoy defended the Jews, this name became a very popular Jewish name. Yet I was called Lev not after Leo Tolstoy but in memory of my uncle Leon who died before my birth. Patronymics are common in Russia. My patronymic from birth was Stanislavovich, because my father, according to Polish custom (he was born in Warsaw), had three names: Samuil-Solomon-Stanislav (two Biblical names, one Polish). At home and at work he was called by his Polish name, and from this I received my official patronymic. At 16, on receiving my passport I changed it to Samuilovich, from a feeling of self-esteem: to have hidden my Jewish heritage at a time of worldwide persecution would have felt mean. This, however, did not involve a change of ethnicity. Then, as now, I thought of myself as a Russian and was classed in my documents as a Jew.

2) National solidarity or mutual aid among Russian Jews is greatly exaggerated by non-Jews—from jealousy (from tales of worldwide Jewish plots). In reality the mutual aid of Jews is manifested only in the extreme situations brought about by persecutions (as in every

persecuted minority), and even this is not invariably the case. Jews themselves know its real worth. The Jews are as disparate and egotistical as any other group in our country (social connections are much weaker than in other countries of Europe and than in America). In my long life I received no more help and support from Jews than from any other people—friends and colleagues. Nor, with the exception of my parents, did I receive more help from relatives than from others. And from a certain world organisation of Jews I received nothing at all, for of course such [an] organisation exists only in the over-heated imagination of anti-Semites.

Among my close friends and pupils the proportion of Jews is no larger than among the surrounding city population. Among those who have lived for long periods at my home there were no Jews at all. My adopted son is Tartar, his wife Azerbaijani. Yet all of us are, in practice, Russians.

3) As to the interests of the national hearth, my national hearth, my homeland is Russia. Its interests and its problems are mine.

Toward Israel I am full of sympathy and respect as are many in Russia, regardless of origins. It is good to know that the people expelled from its homeland two thousand years ago and dispersed have created anew its state on the same territory; that during the life of one generation it transformed the desert into a blooming world; smashed superior military opposition and successfully defends its right to live by European and world norms and standards. Yet at the same time I understand the local Arabs who lived there for nearly a thousand years and for whom the Jews are newcomers. It hurts me to see two peoples destroy each other—and that the local Arabs choose a hopeless strategy of permanent war (and inner faction) instead of building on their remaining territory a state that might compete with the Jewish one in bringing pleasure to its inhabitants and neighbours.

However, I do not personally long for Israel: this is a very interesting and rich country, but not mine.[5]

War and Childhood

As a child Klejn was musically gifted and a skilful pianist. In Belarus he studied not only at a high school but also at a music school. Already before he was a teenager he gave public performances of Liszt's Second Hungarian Rhapsody and Haydn's 'Farewell' Symphony, the latter with a full symphony orchestra. However, as a wilful 13-year-old Klejn made the decision that music was not after all his main calling; and so it was that, at the end of what would be his last concert, he closed the lid of the piano in a gesture of emphatic finality.

Figure 1.2 Karl Marx Street, Yoshkar-Ola. Klejn lived on the next street, Friedrich Engels Street—very similar in appearance.

Already from childhood Klejn exhibited a noticeable independence of mind. Looking back on his childhood from old age, he recalls:

> It was strikingly unpleasant to see how the grown-ups were intimidated. When I started a conversation about politics with anybody, my portly father started looking at the walls and immediately began to sing something bravura in order to drown out my voice. My mother would comment ironically: 'He is singing already'. Sometimes he nervously sang without any reason; evidently, he was frightened by his own thoughts. I found that I myself developed a habit of singing when thoughts went in a dangerous direction, but then I would angrily interrupt myself: I had a desire to think without constraints.[6]

When the Great Patriotic War broke out in 1941 his parents were called up and served at the front—his father as a lieutenant colonel, in charge of several field hospitals, and his mother as a surgeon—while the rest of the family (Klejn, his grandparents, and younger brother) were evacuated first to Volokolamsk, then to Egoryevsk near Moscow (retreating ever eastward before the advancing German army), and finally to Yoshkar-Ola in the Mari Republic (the FinnoUgrian republic beyond the Volga).

At Yoshkar-Ola Klejn worked on a *kolkhoz* (a collective farm) and finished the eighth and ninth grades of high school. It was at this young age that he first attracted the attention of the KGB:

> I was president of a secret school organisation called Prometheus. We couldn't understand why the war was against the German people when, according to our international ideology, it should have been only against the fascists. Our objections were trivial but quite sufficient to warrant execution, and Soviet law had no age limitations. We had learned the poems of Pushkin about *volnost*—freedom, liberty—and revolutionary ideas, but Soviet practice was just the reverse. We imitated him and Lermontov, writing freedom-loving verses. . . . When we were discovered, in 1944, both the minister of the KGB and the secretary of the Party in the Mari Republic were personally involved in the investigation. We ought to have gone into a penal camp—even less guilty children of our age were given 10 or 15 years—but, as I now understand it, they were troubled not about our fate but about their own, because they had discovered our organisation only after a year of its existence. And so they decided to treat it as children's play. But we were subsequently under the observation of the KGB. (Taylor 1994: 723–24)

It was at this time, 1944, after the smashing of Prometheus, that Klejn first began to read the classics of Marxism. His initial impressions were favourable: indeed, for a short time, as a teenager he was enchanted.

In the spring of that year, at the age of 16 (before finishing high school), Klejn went to the front, as *volnonayemnyi* (an armed civilian). He was stationed on the Third Byelorussian front with a unit of engineers, and with this unit he advanced to the German border. (He was awarded military honours for his actions in this campaign.) But for Klejn life at the front came to an abrupt end in the autumn, when he was caught in a shell explosion: he suffered a detached retina and chorioretinitis (inflammation of the retina and the optic vascular system) and was faced with the prospect of permanent blindness. He was put on a hospital train and returned to the district of Smolensk, the very place where he had first joined the front. Once he had to some degree recovered, he completed his secondary education at the Roslavl Technical School for Rail Transport (near Smolensk).

His poor eyesight barred him from any profession that involved driving, and it was only gradually that his vision improved. For this reason, he was not called up for officer training after the war but was instead enlisted as a translator. (It was only much later, in 1966, that he underwent two months' officer training.)

Grodno

After the war, having been a year at Roslavl, Klejn was reunited with his family, who were now living at Grodno in White Russia, where his father was head of a hospital and his mother head of the city's emergency unit. At the Department of Language and Literature at Grodno Pedagogical Institute Klejn studied philology and linguistics and became interested in folklore and the origin of languages, 'especially Slavic and Indo-European' (Ibid.: 724). At this time he was interested in linguistics and philology but had not yet developed an interest in archaeology (Kristiansen 1993: 184).

At the Grodno Pedagogical Institute Klejn was secretary of the *Comsomol* (Young Communist League) at the Institute. He studied Marxism intensively, via not only the works of Marx but also those of Lenin and Stalin. Consequently, *contra* Stalin, but arguably in the spirit of Marxism, he came to the conclusion that the intelligentsia are a distinct class, whose instruments of production are not material goods but rather thoughts, and that the distinguishing characteristics of the Soviet sociopolitical system was not socialism but rather feudalism, with the Communist party and its political bureaucracy as the uppermost tier in the system—'roughly the same conclusions as Milovan Djilas in his book *The New Class*' (Klejn 2012b: 373).[7]

Student Years in Leningrad

After a year at the Grodno Institute: 'I made a speech against the powers of the city—that they made bombastic propaganda instead of satisfying people's economic needs, especially young people' (Kristiansen 1993: 184). As a result the First Secretary gave the order that the Comsomol should expel Klejn and investigate the influences upon him. Under these circumstances, Klejn felt obliged to quit both the Comsomol and the city of Grodno.

He had already formed the ambition to study at Leningrad University. Moving from Grodno was not straightforward—'the trains hardly ran, and the countryside was full of anti-Soviet partisans, Polish groups' (Taylor 1994: 724)—but Klejn persevered, and on his second attempt he was accepted.

Initially, as a Jew, Klejn was allowed to study only as a *zaochnik* (an external student). 'There were three types of student: day students, who received a stipend, evening students, and *zaochniks*, external students who could attend a few short courses. At first I was allowed only into this third category, in the Philology Faculty' (Ibid.). It was here that he encountered the Professor of Folklore Vladimir Y. Propp, a German by origin, who had pioneered a formalist approach to folklore, breaking down folktales into their stereotypical plot components. 'At the time, Professor Propp was known, due to his early work "The Morphology of the Folktale", as a "bourgeois formalist", i.e., a deviationist from the only true Marxist way of thinking. . . . In reality, the book was

Figure 1.3 Vladimir Y. Propp

one of the first works of semiotics and of structuralism' (Immonen 2003: 62).[8] (Propp's views were disapproved of to the extent that in the 1930s he had been arrested. He remained out of favour in the 1940s but was allowed to remain in the university.) Propp impressed Klejn both intellectually and on a personal level. He remembers Propp as 'a little old man, very shy and charming. He was grey, with beautiful almond-shaped eyes and a small aquiline nose always red due to a cold. His lectures on Russian folklore, read with a sonorous baritone, were brilliant and captivating' (Ibid.).

Propp supervised Klejn's first-year paper, on 'The Bear in Folktale, Language, Custom, and Archaeology', and was so much impressed by it that he recommended its publication. Klejn suspects that Propp's supervision and encouragement of this work were intended to facilitate him in becoming a regular (noncorresponding) member of the university. But this change of status was still not easily accomplished.

> Of course, very few students could be taken on, because it was understood that every student would finally be given a job, so there could be only as many students as there were jobs. . . . Students with contacts got accepted over the telephone, *po zvonku*; through a play on words these *pozvonochnie* students were known as 'the vertebrates'. Our dean once said that the main problem is not how you decide from among many thousands of students who get the 100 places but how you fit 200 'vertebrates' into 100 places. The subsequent year, I tried again; Propp advised me to try for the Historical Faculty, too, as Philology was especially anti-Jew. And he said, 'You must study archaeology; I missed that possibility, and now I am very sorry about it, because it is

> of great importance for my studies. . . .' But, although my end-of-year paper had been marked as quite outstanding, neither faculty accepted me, and I decided to complain. At each level of the hierarchy my non-acceptance was reaffirmed. Finally, as the rector of our university was on holiday, I took it to Moscow to the minister for higher education; he also wrote 'rejected' on my appeal. But then, with term begun, the rector, A.A. Voznesensky returned. (Taylor 1994: 724)

Voznesensky 'was a very important person in Leningrad—his brother was Stalin's right-hand man in economic affairs' (Kristiansen 1993: 185)—'through which connection the university could usually get what it needed' (Taylor 1994: 724). Voznesensky

> was called 'Papa Rector', and his brother 'Our Uncle'. Both of them were killed later, in 1950, along with their immediate families, when all the leaders of Leningrad were killed—the famous Leningrad case—together with Voznesensky in Moscow, who was Minister of Education by then. That was in '48. But at this time both brothers were still in power. Papa Rector was on holiday in the Crimea, and when he came back I went to him and gave him my document with all the signatures—refused, refused, etc., and the Minister's refusal [the Minister of Education] was on it, too. Voznesensky saw all these refusals and he was very angry—'how dare the minister lay down the law in my university!'—and he crossed out the signature of the minister and wrote 'accepted'. But to be quite sure of my acceptance I had prepared two documents, one for the Philology Faculty and one for the History Faculty. In the excitement of the moment I gave him both. He signed without looking, so I was admitted into both, which was an unusual thing in the USSR. (Kristiansen 1993: 185)

Thus it was that Klejn came to pursue Slavic Studies in the Faculty of Philology under the supervision of Vladimir Propp and simultaneously to study archaeology in the Faculty of History under the supervision of the Director of the Hermitage, Mikhail Artamonov. 'Artamonov was a Party member, but he entered the Party very late, when it became unavoidable. By Soviet standards, he was a very independent thinker . . . in the Revolution he was on the staff of Sasha Cherny, a leader of the Anarchists (although it is not mentioned in his biography). . . . He was a very close friend of the poets Sergei Yesenin and Nikolai Gumilev' (Taylor 1994: 727).[9]

> Artamonov had some well-known pupils, but it is difficult to describe them as a 'school', as they differed so greatly, not only in their interests but also in their fundamental ideas and working methods. They

Figure 1.4 Mikhail Artamonov

Figure 1.5 Klejn on Artamonov's expedition on the site of the Don-Volga canal. Klejn is in the centre, supervising inmates of a labour camp. The tower of the camp can be seen on the horizon. Behind the baulk is an armed guard.

> included I.I. Lyapushkin, V.P. Shilov, A.D. Stolyar, G.V. Smirnova, and L.S. Klejn. He provided no special training or schooling for them, but he supported them. He addressed them using the formal pronoun. He maintained no close friendships with any archaeologists, reserving the informal pronoun only for Voronin, who had been a student in the same year as he. Few of his pupils caught his attention. To the others he was deaf or indifferent. (Klejn 2012b: 305)

Klejn caught Artamonov's attention, in part because he chose to specialise in one of Artamonov's interests, the Catacomb culture of the Early Bronze Age, on the Russian and Ukrainian steppes. (This specialism included a study of Herodotus on the origin of the Scythians.)

In more general terms, Klejn was interested in the origins of peoples ('the Russians above all' [Ibid.: 369]). This interest was to lead to a public clash with received opinion, in particular with the theories of Nicholas Marr. Marr, the excavator of Ani (the capital of medieval Armenia), had died in 1934 but his reputation lived on.[10] When Klejn was a student Marr's theory of autochthonous ethnic development still had the blessing of the very highest authorities.

According to Marr: 'Ethnicity was not important; every people was a mixture, and so its origin was also an interweaving and a mixture. No people could be traced specially and separately . . . in Marr's teaching the slogan was autochthonism—no immigrations and no separateness. It sounds very revolutionary and accorded with internationalism. At the time it was formulated, in the twenties and thirties, the Commintern was still active' (Taylor 1994: 725).

Essentially, in the words of Florin Curta, Marr had 'adopted the view that language was part of the ideological superstructure depending upon the socioeconomic basis and therefore developing in stages like Marx's socioeconomic formations. Marr treated ethnicity as something of a non-permanent nature, as ephemeral, and discounted "homelands" and "proto-languages." Instead he argued that cultural and linguistic changes were brought by socioeconomic shifts' (Curta 2001: 16).

Taken to its extreme, Marr's 'japhetic theory' implied that 'the same languages could come into being independently in different areas providing there were the same socioeconomic conditions' (Shnirelman 1995: 128).

Klejn was unconvinced. He came to the conclusion that the continuing prominence of Marr's theories was sustained primarily by ideological considerations.

> I studied the four volumes of Marr's works very carefully. I began in the full belief that Marr was a genius, but—maybe it is my nature—I am sceptical, and I must get the bottom of things. In Marr I found no substantiation and, in particular, no basis for the methodology. I attended the lectures of Marr's followers: Meshchaninov and Katsenelson. One day I approached Meshchaninov and said, 'Ivan Ivanovich, I have read all the four volumes of Marr, and I understand barely half of them; all the rest is incomprehensible,' and he replied, 'Oh, young man, you are very lucky. I was personally taught by him, and I understand barely a quarter!'
>
> Then I began to be interested in how Marr formed his ideas. His archive was intact in the Institute of Archaeology. . . . He was one of the few well-known scholars who accepted the Revolution, and he paraded in pomp on state occasions. It was known that Marr spent his last years

> in mental disturbance, but it became clear to me as I researched his life that he had gone mad much earlier. (Taylor 1994: 725)

Klejn wrote a paper criticising Marr's theory of the omnipresent local origins of all cultural developments and presented it to his supervisor Artamonov. Klejn vividly recalls Artamonov's response:

> 'Your paper is in complete disagreement with the basics of Soviet scholarship, but it is very interesting. I think that something in our science is awry. I would like to propose your paper as the subject of a special conference in the Academy of Sciences. But I must warn you that it could be very dangerous for you. Remember, I risk my post, but you risk your head'. He went on to stipulate that the name of Marr should nowhere appear in the paper I was to read. Marrism was then considered part of Marxism. (Kristiansen 1993: 725–26)

Klejn eventually gave the paper at a special conference at the Academy of Sciences on March 3, 1950. He recalls that on the morning of the conference in his nervousness he cut himself shaving, badly. In an attempt to hide the cut, 'the girls from our group covered my face with powder' (Taylor 1994: 726). The results were not entirely happy. The cut may have been disguised, but Klejn now had the pallor of 'a clown' (Ibid.). So it was as a nervous, and exceptionally pale, young student that Klejn addressed the conference.

The effect of the paper was unexpected . . .

> After I had read my paper, everyone spoke rather ambiguously, saying that it was all rather strange, that there might be something in it, and so on. From Artamonov's side it had been like sending up a trial balloon[11]—students might easily make mistakes, but my reception might indicate whether it was possible to get rid of Marrism . . . Next the denunciations began. The party organisations said that a student had advanced anti-Marxist views and that nobody had made the necessary criticism. I was warned that I was about to be expelled from the university and was probably in line for a harder punishment. If I recanted, I might salvage a university career, maybe not in Leningrad but somewhere in the provinces. But I decided to send my paper to Moscow to the Central Committee . . . I had no other defence. If I was expelled from the university, there was a good chance that I would disappear. In the end I sent it to *Pravda*, the newspaper of the Central Committee, because just at that time they were soliciting views on Marr's teachings from across the Union; from Leningrad they had received seventy articles. Opinion completely agreed with Marr with the exception of mine and that of Professor Popov of Leningrad University.[12] I went

Figure 1.6 Klejn on March 3, 1950, at the Marr Conference

> to Pravda's offices, and the department editor said, 'All the articles were shown to Comrade Stalin, and he accepted only two—yours and Professor Popov's'. I was very glad and said, 'Very well, then you'll publish my article?' 'No,' he said, 'Comrade Stalin will speak himself, and naturally the discussion will take quite another turn'.
>
> Comrade Stalin's pronouncement on the question of linguistics was to be on the radio. In the universities and other educational establishments, people gathered to listen: lecture halls were furnished with the usual portrait, flowers, and speakers. The great bass voice (that of Levitan, Stalin's 'orator') rang out and, to the visible shock of the Establishment linguists, completely refuted Marr's teaching. But I was not surprised; Marrism's denial of ethnicity was incompatible with the new policy, which was now stressing 'Slavicness', the Roots of Russian nationality', and so on. (Ibid.)

In other words, Stalin had changed his mind, and, at least on this point—migrations might influence cultural development—it was Klejn, rather than Marr, who was now 'politically correct'! (With hindsight, one sees that perhaps the fall of Marrism had been inevitable once hopes of international revolution faded and nationalism became politically expedient, but nonetheless Marr's posthumous fall from grace was perceived at the time as a deeply shocking event.)

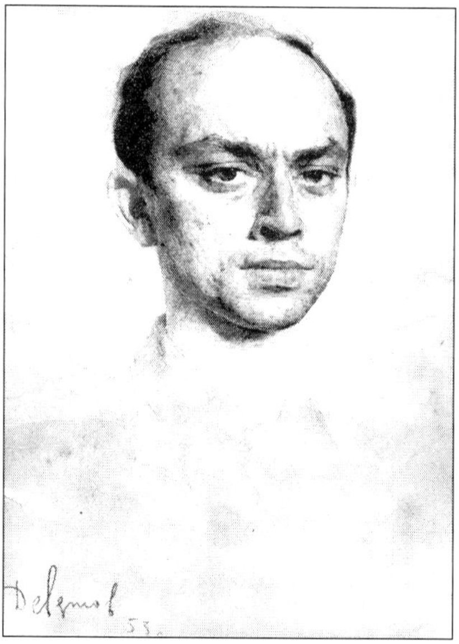

Figure 1.7 Klejn in 1953 (portrait by Mikhail Devyatov)

Early Career

The next year, 1951, Klejn graduated. But, for all the promise that he had shown as a student, there was to be no smooth transition to a postgraduate career. Artamonov had led Klejn to believe that he would be permitted to stay on at the university in Leningrad, but this is not what happened.

> Six months before I graduated he [Artamonov] told me that I had been marked down for postgraduate study, which spared me the trouble of seeking employment, but a month before the final examinations some friends warned me that they had seen the lists and my name was not among the future postgraduates. Anxious, I approached the Head several times to say that I had nothing arranged, but each time he assured me that there was no need to worry. As acting rector, he was also chairman of the allocation committee. When I appeared before the committee, he looked me straight in the eye and said 'Unfortunately we couldn't find a place for you. Will you be content to take out a degree without allocation?' 'Yes,' I replied, and signed. A few days later I declared that I was leaving his expedition, so our relations came to an end. (Klejn 2012b: 306)

Thus began six difficult years:

> I applied for postgraduate four years on the trot, always passing the exam, never being taken on. If I'd had some support, I would have

> been accepted despite being Jewish. But without support . . . I tried other universities—Moscow Institute of History of Material Culture and the University of Minsk, Byelorussia. At Minsk, they said to me quite frankly, 'You are not our national cadre'. So, despite the fact that in Vitebsk I had been to a White Russian school and spoke the language [Belarusian] (which the director of the institute of Minsk could not speak), I wasn't accepted. (Taylor 1994: 727)

Anti-Semitic feeling was rife: Klejn had to take whatever work he could find, while continuing his academic work in his own time. He had by now acquired something of a maverick reputation, and at the time of the Doctors' Plot of 1952–1953[13] this placed his parents in grave danger. His mother was warned by an ex-patient that she and her husband should expect an imminent visit from the authorities and that their only hope was to dispose of anything in the house that might give even the smallest indication of subversion. It was then that his father discovered, to his horror, the critical notes that his son had made in the margins of the family's collected works of Lenin! One after another, and as quickly as possible, all thirty-five volumes were consigned to the flames of the stove. But then, in March 1953, unexpectedly, and not a moment too soon, his parents were saved: it was announced that Stalin was dead.

During Klejn's six years away from university he worked as a schoolteacher: first in Leningrad; then in a village near Leningrad; and finally in Grodno, where his parents were.[14] It was during this period that he published his first academic paper 'The Question of the Origin of the Slavs' (1955). Klejn's argument went completely against the orthodox opinions of the day. These opinions were comparable to those of Gustav Kossinna.[15] That is to say, migrations were credited with having influence abroad but not in Russia. ('The Kossinna school was discredited officially, and highly criticised, but in reality the major archaeologists in Russia did pretty much the same as Kossinna, and followed his principles' [Kristiansen 1993: 186.]) In this climate Klejn explains the acceptance of his paper as follows: 'The editor of the journal [*Sovietskaya Archaeologiya*] at the time was Professor Artsikovsky, and he liked it, maybe because his interests were not in this particular question. And all his opponents—big names—were criticised in it. Also, when I sent it in, Stalin had died and so it was a period of some liberty, the so-called thaw' (Ibid.). (After Stalin's death 'autochthony increasingly lost its privileges' [Klejn 2012b: 36].)

Klejn's specific argument criticised the orthodox opinion that the Chernyakhov culture, of the third and fourth centuries C.E., was a Slav culture. In response, in the Kiev Institute of Archaeology, 'an expanded session of the academic board was convened, with reports by respected scholars, to cut short my "machinations" . . . some supposed that they veiled the conviction of more authoritative—and more cautious—Leningrad scholars' (Ibid.: 112).

In 1957, after six years away from the university, all of a sudden:

> I received a telephone call from the Department to tell me that there was a vacancy for a postgraduate. 'Would you like to come?' I said that I had tried several times and had always been unsuccessful. The decision would depend on Mikhail Illarionovich [Artamonov], and the state of our relations was well known. 'You surely don't suppose I'd be phoning you if he hadn't told me to,' came the reply. He was not petty-minded, and bore no grudges. On learning of his intention, all the other candidates for the place withdrew. He greeted me as if we had parted only yesterday, and said, 'I'm an old man and I see you as my successor in this Department'. (Ibid.: 306)

And, so, from 1957 Klejn gave lectures in archaeology (for an hourly wage and *gratis*) at Leningrad University until, in 1962, at a special session on the faculty's Party Bureau, he was made a member of staff, an assistant professor.

Yet Klejn could not progress any farther without joining the Party, and this he refused to do:

> When I completed my postgraduate study and he [Artamonov] had with great difficulty secured a position for me as a lecturer (it needed a report from him to the Party bureau), it emerged that I could not be promoted or become head without joining the Party. When he gave me to understand this, I asked: 'Can you imagine me at a Party meeting of the Faculty of History?' He was silent for a moment, then grinned and said, 'Yes, it's hard to picture'. Shortly after this, he transferred another of his pupils, a Party member, to the Department and never mentioned to me that I had not lived up to his expectations. (Ibid.)

As an assistant professor Klejn continued to challenge received opinion. An example was his organisation of a series of seminars on the 'Varangian controversy'. In these seminars he criticised the anti-Varangian (or anti-Normanist) position on the origins of the Kievan Rus. At that time the orthodox anti-Normanist position was that there had been no significant Viking contribution to Russian history. The anti-Normanists also denied that the Ryurikovichs (the first Russian dynasty) had Scandinavian origins.

When in 1965 the anti-Normanist I. P. Shaskolsky published *The Normanist Theory in Contemporary Bourgeois Scholarship* it was Klejn who was invited by the Party Bureau to oppose him in a public debate. He was to share the platform with his pupil G. S. Lebedev. The situation presented Klejn with a dilemma: 'If I spoke frankly, that would provide a pretext for dealing with me;

the regional committee of the Party, that is, the municipal ideological centre, had already signalled its approval. And if I dissembled, how would I face my students the next day' (Ibid.: 118).

It was therefore with a sense of great relief and good fortune that shortly before the debate commenced Klejn was able to break the news to Lebedev that he had discovered that Marx had been misquoted on the problem. Marx had been quoted, many times, as having written: 'In Rus the Norsemen soon became Slavicised, as may be seen from their marriages and their names'. But, in fact, he had preceded this with: 'Some may protest that . . .' (Ibid.: 119). With the help of this discovery: 'We had won for ourselves and other researchers the opportunity to investigate facts objectively for a few more years' (Ibid.).[16]

Klejn was also running a risk by cultivating certain contacts with the West, in particular with the American journal *Current Anthropology*. In the early 1960s Klejn had been invited to become an Associate of this journal at the recommendation of Alexander Häusler of East Germany. 'I received an invitation from CA and showed it to my university directors, whose permission was indispensible. They considered the problem so important that they addressed it to the Party leaders of the city in the GorCom or the City Committee of the Party. GorCom thought about it for a long time, and when finally the decision came, it was: not banned, but not recommended' (Immonen 2003: 59). Klejn read the decision as 'permitted' but the Dean of the Faculty of History read it as 'not permitted'.

Consequently:

> I thanked CA for inviting me but declined participation with the excuse that I could not pay the required fee. After some time, I received a reply that the fee was purely symbolical. Since I had advanced no other motive for refusal, CA held me for an associate and began to send me all papers regularly. With this reply, I went to the prorector of the University, who was in charge of international affairs. At that time, the post was held by Dr. Gennadi Shatkov, the Olympic champion in heavyweight boxing, and asked him what to do. Shatkov reflected and said, 'Nothing. Don't reply'. So for some time, I received extensive material from CA and kept silent.
>
> Then I received a letter in which the wise editor wrote that, since there was no answer from me for such a long time, they would publish my name in the sad list of associates who had died or gone missing for no apparent reason. Having read the letter Shatkov grew gloomy and sent the letter to the GorCom. They had made a mess, so it was up to them to sort it out. Ten months of waiting had passed when I came once more to meet Shatkov and respectfully said it was time to decide. The world-renowned boxer looked me in the eyes, smiled openly, and

> chopped the air with his heavy hand: 'Ah, damn, I'll allow it on my own risk. Do participate'. (Ibid.: 59–60)

Despite contacts with the West and his unorthodox opinions, in 1968 Klejn's Candidate dissertation,[17] 'The Origin of the Donets Catacombs-Grave Culture', was passed, albeit with reluctance on the part of some the examiners.[18] Subsequently, between 1968 and 1973, Klejn led a number of archaeological expeditions, to the forest belt of Russia and Belarus and to the steppes of Ukraine and the lands beside the river Don.[19] Sites included Bronze Age and Scythian and Sarmatian barrows.[20] In this work he was pursuing interests, such as the origin of the Scythians, that had first caught his interest as an undergraduate. In later years he was in charge of student training on the expeditions to this area.

Through the 1970s, while the Soviet Union pursued the policy of détente, Klejn was more or less tolerated—he was made a Docent (Associate Professor) in 1976. (His brother Boris, a historian, was not so fortunate. Having spoken out against the invasion of Czechoslovakia, he was sacked from his academic position in Grodno and stripped of his Party membership.)[21]

It was during the 1970s that Klejn began to write about theoretical problems in history and archaeology.[22] This subject had been neglected under Stalin and Krushchev, when it was thought that Marxist historical materialism provided all the theory that was necessary (Klejn 2012b: 38), but the door was left open to theory with the admission that it might be possible for archaeology to shed some light on the origins of peoples. Of course this then again raised the notoriously difficult question of the relationship between an archaeological culture and an *ethnos*.

Klejn's work on theoretical archaeology resulted in the publication of his first monograph, *Archaeological Sources*, in 1978.[23] He was now 51. Looking back on this part of his life from his productive old age, Klejn has no doubt that the fact that he was relatively old when he published this monograph was primarily because he was a Jew and held unorthodox opinions. Either of these factors in the Soviet Union would have sufficed to make things difficult, but together they made a path that was doubly steep. Furthermore, from about this time Klejn's contacts with foreign scholars began to arouse suspicion. The archaeologist B. B. Piotrovsky, who wrote a preface to *Archaeological Sources*, warned him that he was living dangerously, publishing too much in the West (Ibid.: 333).

Klejn rates *Archaeological Sources* as one of his most valuable books. In it he sets out his conception of archaeology, radically different from that which had dominated Soviet scholarship for the previous half century. Subsequent works, such as *Metaarchaeology*, expand on the main theme of *Archaeological Sources*, but this is the work in which Klejn, so to speak, showed his hand. As is the case with all of Klejn's subsequent works, it was written to reach the widest possible readership—and it did. The entire print run of 6,000 was bought up within a few days. (A revised and expanded edition was published in 1993, and at the time of my writing, in 2014, Klejn is working on a new revised edition.)[24]

Concurrently, from the late 1970s, Klejn, began to fulfil the role of go-between through which developments in Western theoretical archaeology became known in Russia and vice versa. His ambition was to foster a constructive dialogue between East and West. This was one of the aims behind the publication in *Current Anthropology* in 1977 of his survey of theoretical developments, encompassing both Eastern and Western archaeology, 'Panorama of Theoretical Archaeology'. Left to his own devices Klejn might have fulfilled his ambition, and to some extent he did. Bruce Trigger saluted the achievement of a 'Panorama of Theoretical Archaeology' in a review entitled 'No Longer from Another Planet' (Trigger 1978). Trigger believed that a 'Panorama' was but the start of a dialogue between East and West; but, alas, that was not yet to be.

Chapter 2

Prison

The Savage within and in Society

Conservatism and stagnation returned toward the end of Brezhnev's rule; and, finally, with the Soviet invasion of Afghanistan in 1980, the situation changed dramatically. Détente was abandoned; 'Sakharov was exiled to Gorky, and in Leningrad liberal professors began to be arrested'.[1]

After the invasion of Afghanistan, 'I told my pupils to expect the worst and to draw as many of our projects as we could to a swift conclusion' (Taylor 1994: 731). At that time in every student group there were invariably one or two students who were secret agents of the KGB. On completing their education they usually became official employees of the KGB. One day Klejn encountered one such of his former students. Klejn asked him, off the record:

> 'What does your organisation want from me? I am such a loyal citizen, I foment no revolution. What does your organisation consider so dangerous in me?' And he said, 'You'll never believe me, but most of all they are concerned with your scholarly position. Not your public activity, not your personal life, and so on, but just your scholarly position.' 'Are they that specialised in archaeology?!' 'Of course not!' 'Then they must rely on some experts?' 'Yes, of course,' came the response, and then I said, 'Then things are very bad, because I have notions of who your experts are.' 'Yes, of course,' he repeated. (Ibid.)

Klejn's turn came in March 1981: 'I was constantly expecting the midnight knock at the door . . .' (Kristiansen 1993: 188); 'in fact they just came and found me at the university in the daytime. I was told later the order for my arrest had been given by Trapeznikov, the head of the scientific department of the party Central Committee in Moscow. He was called to Romanov, then boss of the party in Leningrad. Romanov signed my arrest, and this was Trapeznikov's contribution to Rybakov and his school,[2] to extract from the archaeological discipline anyone who made trouble' (Ibid.).

A Russian Perspective on Theoretical Archaeology: The Life and Work of Leo S. Klejn by Stephen Leach, 36–41

'It was the so-called Leningrad wave of arrests. Only professors and lecturers, mainly Jews, were arrested; all of them had published in the West, and all of them were popular among the students. Each received a different type of accusation. Azadovski got "drugs", I got "homosexuality", Roginski got "falsifying documents", Mirek got "speculation" with his collection of musical instruments, Meilakh got "illegal trade in literature", and so on' (Taylor 1994: 731). (Because the official slogans proclaimed that there were no political prisoners in the Soviet Union, for everyone arrested some criminal offence had to be invented.)[3]

The basic facts of the matter were these: 'The state prosecutor demanded six years imprisonment and five years' banishment from civil society—this would entail losing my residence permit in Leningrad. Yet, despite the guidance of the KGB, the court trial fell to pieces, and I was sentenced to three years of imprisonment. After my appeal this sentence too was repealed. The case was handed over to a new inquest, and after a fresh trial I was sentenced to a year and a half. As [before the appeal] I had already spent a year and a month in prison this left just five months to serve in a labour camp. It was customary in the Soviet judicial system to pass such a sentence in place of an acquittal'.[4] (Klejn was first accused of homosexual relations, then attempted homosexual relations, and finally there was an unsuccessful attempt to frame him for a murder.)

His prison cell was small (2½ × 3 metres), rancid, and overcrowded.[5] It was here that Klejn spent thirteen months of dread and drudgery, interspersed with interrogations, searches, and transfers—thirteen months in which there was no other food than a diet that alternated between porridge, 'leaf' soup, and 'grave' soup (soup with fishbones).

> I had a very bad accusation as far as the criminals were concerned—when I was remanded in custody, the admissions officer even offered to alter it in order to protect me. I refused, as I thought it might make matters worse in the long run. Leningrad prison is architecturally identical to Reading Gaol, but whereas Oscar Wilde sat in such a cell alone, in our cell there were ten. There was a double iron curtain with unaligned perforations, to let air in but not allowing a view out; the electric light was never switched off, and you had no right to cover your face in the night. I lived one year and one month in this cell with bandits, robbers, assassins, crooks, and thieves, while my case was being investigated. I realised at once that prison society was very ritualised; I could not be maltreated until I had been given a low status, ritually. Before that I still had rights, and I gave them very little chance to spring a ritual on me, as I hardly slept, and I made my spoon into a weapon . . . and was sitting with it when they finally said, 'We must now do with you the well-known rituals; these are unavoidable, otherwise we ourselves

> when we sit with you will become the same caste'. I said that perhaps the second one might be lucky with these rituals, and they said, 'Why not the first?' and I said, 'Because the first will be killed'. Somehow, in this way, I was gaining time, because no one was eager to be first; they understood that it would be a struggle for life. Then they held a kind of trial, in the cell, and for some ten days they considered all my documents. . . .
>
> I had the right to have the paperwork pertaining to my upcoming trial. So there in the cell, I had my first trial, and my first trial I won. Prisoners are very experienced in exposing the fabrication of evidence, and they decided that I was innocent. So I received my first prison title: I was nominated 'Distributor of Sugar'. It was very important, because food was sacral. Being of the lower caste, being homosexual, you cannot touch food that others are going to eat; otherwise they will also become homosexual. 'Distributor of Sugar' was a kind of societal recognition that I was not homosexual, that I had dignity and was trusted to distribute food among the prisoners—in fact I still value this title more than my title of 'Professor'. From that time onward things got easier. My case was known in the West, and a volume was dedicated to me [Renfrew, Rowlands, and Segraves 1982]. (Taylor 1994: 733)[6]

Furthermore, Bruce Trigger and Ezra Zubrow campaigned to have Klejn released (Chrisomalis and Costopoulos 2013: xix).

> Although our officials used to say that they were indifferent to what was said in the West, it was a lie. The trial judge prefaced his summing up with reference to Western interest in my trial, and in prison I was never physically beaten. Of course, they made other attempts to obtain my confession: they put me in a 'pressure cell' with really rough bandits; they put me in an iron box in the corridor. Finally, they put me into a cell with a noise generator behind the wall which ran without interruption: I was there for three months. But I didn't crack, and when I was moved out to the labour camp my reputation had preceded me, and from the outset I received a very high position in the three-caste structure, in the upper caste on a high level. The upper-caste are the *vors*, or 'felons', who do no work. The middle-caste, the majority, are called *muzhiks*, meaning something between 'villeins' and 'knights'. And the lower-caste are the *chushoks*—dirty 'piggies': you can't touch them because they are dirty, you can't converse with them because they are slaves. Homosexuals are usually included in the lower caste as a special division, but some become the wives of the higher *vors*. (Taylor 1994: 733)

In the labour camp, where Klejn spent another five months, he was given the title Uglovoy, from Ugol, 'Corner':

> I had a lower bench in a corner, and it gave me many privileges. First of all, I was untouchable in a good sense: nobody could beat me, nobody was allowed to speak harshly to me, I had no nickname, only a name and patronymic. . . .
>
> Everyone had to reply to my questions immediately, frankly, and completely. Nobody could approach me if I didn't call him. If I moved, they immediately made way. I had a special uniform. Each caste had a different uniform, made by the prisoners. For the upper caste: tailored, ironed, and painted black. For the middle caste: blue, ironed, but not hemmed or lined. And for the lower caste: grey, ripped trousers. Many people had tattoos; each had a meaning, and if you carried a tattoo to which you were not entitled the skin would be excised. There was a system of taboos. For example, the colour red was forbidden. Again, if you drop your spoon on the floor, that's it, you have to eat with your hands, as your spoon has 'perished'. Then you have rites of initiation to enter a new barrack or cell—formal, harsh rituals. There are courts, laws, and values, and the values are opposite to those outside. To kill is good. To be intelligent is a good precondition for being made a slave. There is a hierarchy of crimes; justice is very swift. A mild punishment is for breaking a taboo: being severely beaten by three men. A more severe punishment is death. This can be decided only from the top, and in our camp the method was strangling ('suicide'). But the most severe punishment is 'long death', when you begin in the evening and finish in the morning. I spent the last evening with a young man convicted of informing a week before his release was due. He was unaware of his sentence until they came for him. He was found in the morning with lots of abdominal stab wounds from attempted castration; then they boiled him; then they put him in the cesspit. In the morning he was medically examined and found to be still just alive, but he died shortly after. This is everyday life in the camp—every day is blood and killings—and in my opinion this is the natural manner of society. It is our society that is artificial, structured by culture. Everything we have achieved is from our culture, not our nature. People stripped of culture behave socially as in the camp, and in all Soviet camps an identical society exists. In every camp the outer administration has built a camp within the camp to protect the *chushoks*, the 'piggies', because every day they are tortured and killed. You might think that within the inner camp the slaves would be safe, but no, once within the inner camp the three castes immediately reemerge. It is said that the women's camp society is much more severely organised than the men's, and

> the harshest camps of all are the children's camps. Children in these camps are like beasts, and even hardened bandits are afraid of children who are released from these camps because they have no notion at all of humanity.
>
> We must know that everything that we have and shall have is thanks to culture. (Ibid.)

Already before he had gone to prison Klejn had suspected that our cultural aspects are out of step with our biological nature (see Klejn 1976); now, in prison, he was sure of it.

Inevitably his life would from then on always be divided in two: *before* prison and *after*—for 'it is possible to forget the physical wounds, but if the soul has been wounded the pain does not go away. It simply disappears, into the depths'.[7]

The World Turned Upside Down

Klejn recounted his time in prison in a series of articles published under the name of Lev Samoylov in the journal *Neva* in 1988–1991 (the period of *perestroika*). The articles in *Neva* attracted a very wide readership. When the journal published Klejn's articles it reached a circulation of 700,000. One article in particular, 'Justice and Two Crosses', which explained how the law had been broken (by both the investigators and the judges), won a prize as Publication of the Year. (It should be noted that many of the readers of these articles would themselves have had direct or indirect experience of camp society. It has been estimated that over thirty years more than 30 million people passed through the prisons and camps; and 'even under Gorbachev there were 1,600,000 slaves in the camps' [Taylor 1994: 732].)

As a result of the articles in *Neva*, Klejn was in 1989 elected a deputy to the First Congress of Democratic organisations of the USSR. He also became a participant in the discussion group Leningrad Tribune.

The articles in *Neva* formed the basis of a book, *The World Turned Upside Down* (1993).[8] This book had several different aspects: first, it was a dramatic and true story with obvious human interest; second, it was a denouncement of the prison system as an affront to civilised values that, rather than reforming the prisoners, acted as a finishing school for criminals; and, third, it was an account of an anthropological investigation.

In *The World Turned Upside Down* Klejn was able to add details to his previous account of the affair by including many of the original documents of the trial. He was thus able to demonstrate the role played by the KGB. Astonishingly, not only were there no denials but the original investigator addressed an open letter to the editor of *Neva* (then also the chairman of the special Committee of the Supreme Soviet of the USSR on civil rights) in which he admitted that Klejn's account of events was correct. He also admitted that he was ordered to make the arrest, despite a lack of evidence, by his superiors. He confessed that he deplored his own part in the affair.

The investigator's letter was published, and Klejn was exonerated, but the sentence was never retracted. However, soon the reasons for reviewing the case became irrelevant, because the law against homosexuality was abolished. (Klejn himself, throughout the affair, neither affirmed nor denied the charge—even after homosexuality was decriminalised—on the basis that an individual's sexual orientation is not the business of the state.)

Not only was the book very popular but it also won critical acclaim. Klejn was particularly proud of the compliment (from the anthropologist Alexander Kozintsev) that his descriptions of drudgery rivalled the best descriptions of drudgery in Russian literature—including those found in Dostoevsky, Chekhov, and Solzhenitsyn.

Chapter 3

After Prison

Publications in the West

When Klejn was imprisoned in 1981 he was in the midst of arranging to have two different works published in the West. The first of these projects was the article that in later years was successively expanded, until reaching its final form in *Soviet Archaeology: Trends, Schools, and History*, published by Oxford University Press in December 2012.[1] Klejn had embarked on this project at the suggestion of Bruce Trigger (Klejn in Chrisomalis and Costopoulos 2013: 192). In the preface to the book Klejn tells the story of the original article's publication:

> The first version of this work was published in the journal *World Archaeology* (London) in 1982, under three names (Bulkin, Klejn, and Lebedev 1982). My pupils Vasily A. Bulkin and Gleb S. Lebedev were listed as my coauthors. In fact, although we had planned to write a joint work, the text was written by me. I discussed it with them and made use of their comments, especially when writing Chapter 4 and also while correcting and abridging the manuscript. Material from another of my students, M. Shchukin, was used in writing Chapter 6.
>
> At first we intended to sign the work jointly. However, when it was ready it became clear that publication in our own country would not be possible. We had a commission from a foreign journal,[2] but at that time sending the manuscript abroad required approval, after critical discussion, at many different levels. It scraped through these with difficulty, being discussed in a supercharged atmosphere, losing its sharper formulations as it went, and losing whole sections with them . . . as well as signatories. One by one my coauthors retracted their signatures; they were younger; their positions less secure; and having acquired families, they felt they had no right to take risks.
>
> In the meantime the clouds were gathering over my head. When the abridged and agreed text was ready to be sent abroad, I was arrested. In my absence, Bulkin and Lebedev took it upon themselves to dispatch it,

> and for this purpose they declared themselves my coauthors and signed the manuscript, while the then assistant prorector, Yu. M. Vladimirov (now deceased), sanctioned the dispatch. The degree of determination they displayed will be clear to any Soviet citizen. For this I am deeply grateful to them. (Klejn 2012b: viii–ix)

Klejn was less fortunate with *Archaeological Typology* (1982): 'That was catastrophic! The publishers tried their best but only managed to get half the chapters translated; I was in the labour camp at the time, and I was not able to check the translation, and that resulted in serious errors of comprehension, not to mention proper names [e.g., Childe's] being completely garbled' (Taylor 1994: 727). Klejn was bitterly disappointed: 'As to "Archaeological Typology" I don't believe that anyone in the Anglophone world will be able to fully understand it from a damaged and incomplete text. The Russian and German versions of the book are far superior to the English'. (There is incidentally a German version of the book that brings it fully up to date, but that book exists only in manuscript as there is still a dispute about its fate among its potential publishers [Leach 2011].)

Returning to the subject in *Soviet Archaeology* (2012b) he states:

> The translation was very poor—practically unreadable—the translator did not know archaeological terms and confused active with passive. Moreover, the edition was incomplete for the simple reason that some chapters were not received in England: at the time the author was persecuted by the KGB and subsequently imprisoned, and so was unable to check the translation. The publishers later issued a pamphlet of corrections, but nobody refers to it. A second edition appeared in Slovenia (Ljubljana 1988) in Slovene; this was an improvement but was still incomplete (because the translation was made from the Russian chapters kept in Oxford). The third publication was Russian and was made in the new era (Leningrad, Academy of Sciences, 1991). It is almost twice the size of previous editions and done in the full accordance with author's intentions. However, most of the printed copies perished in storage during the disorder that accompanied the collapse of the Soviet Union.[3]

New Interests

Another consequence of Klejn's arrest was that, until 1989, he was deprived of his membership of Leningrad University. 'On my release from the camp I was stripped of my scholarly degree and title (in violation of several laws). For many years I had no job, despite the fact that I was officially registered for work on the labour exchange and that there was (officially) no unemployment in the country'.[4] Yet, despite having no access to a university library, he continued to write articles and books—supporting himself with the help of occasional translation work at the Hermitage. It was during this period that he pursued interests in two other disciplines, classical philology and cultural anthropology.

In particular, in the field of classical philology, he became interested in the composition of the *Iliad*. His intensive historical and philological analysis of the text of the *Iliad* led to the publication of three books: *Incorporeal Heroes* (1994), *The Anatomy of the Iliad* (1998), and the book-length article 'The Catalogue of Ships' (2000).

Furthermore, as previously mentioned, in *The World Turned Upside Down* (1993), he published the conclusions he had reached during his time in prison—for during his incarceration his scholarly instincts had not deserted him. For thirteen months he had studied prison and camp society from the point of view of an anthropologist.

And—another consequence—having been accused of the 'crime' of homosexuality, 'it was natural for me to become interested in the problem that served as the pretext for my expulsion from scholarship'.[5] In 2000 he published a book *The Other Love* on the relative importance of cultural and biological factors in the phenomenon of homosexuality. He asks why, although the theory of evolution might lead us to predict its extinction, homosexuality seems to defy this expectation.

Looking back on his prison sentence, Klejn grimly recognises that as a scholar he owes a debt to the experience. (The significance of the experience is reflected in the fact that on his release he kept his convict's uniform.)

Figure 3.1 Klejn in his convict's uniform (some years after his release)

He notes: 'I am indeed grateful to not only the Party and Government but also to their main pillar—the KGB—for placing obstacles before me that shaped my personality and gave me an opportunity to test myself and to believe in myself in overcoming them. They contributed to my self-confidence' (Klejn 2010: 568). But, of course, that is not to say that he supports the existence of the prisons and labour camps. He abhors them.

Marxism

As of 1987 Klejn has received a pension, and from 1989 he once more gave lectures at Leningrad University. From 1991, the year of the fall of the Soviet Union, he again held an academic position at the university. From this date onward he could be more open about his attitude to Marxism. As he explains in his *curriculum vitae*:

> Under the Soviet regime the declaration of loyalty to Marxist ideology was in our country unavoidable, and many formulations and quotes from the classics of Marxism-Leninism were a kind of convention, some tribute to customary norms of decency, and the obligatory formulas and quotations from the classics of Marxism-Leninism with which every work was laced were, so to say, the red bows around the subject that demonstrated the author's loyalty. Owing to my social origins, education, and upbringing I was not imbued from youth with Marxism as a philosophy and methodology. However, I understood that if I wanted to teach and be published, if I was to bring my thought and the results of my research to the community, then I would have to dress myself in Marxist cloth.[6]
>
> Most of the guardians of ideology were neither well-versed in scholarship nor in Marxism. In these conditions one could air even non-Marxist and non-Soviet ideas so long as one used the language of Aesop; in other words, one had to write in such a way that the perceptive reader could read between the lines.[7] . . .
>
> On the other hand I strove to find in Marxism at least some areas of sense so as to draw not from the vast swathes of Marxist dogma but just from these small oases. From the classics of Marxism I tried to select quotations concordant with my ideas (the classics were so voluminous that you could find quotes for every purpose). For instance, I argued that Marx and Engels held prehistory to be a nonpolitical discipline!
>
> Basically, some Western scholars considered me to be a defender of Marxism, but an unusual defender—it was possible to discuss scholarly problems with him! Some of my opponents among Marxist-dogmatists whom I caught in ignorance of Marxism regarded me as a fellow Marxist-dogmatist, but of a higher class, i.e., well-read in

Marxist Scriptures. But it was impossible to swindle the main corpus of our guardians of ideology: they scented an adversary in me and did not count me as their own. Evidence of dissent was found not just in my main ideas but even in minutiae. For example, the Secretary of the Party Bureau of the Faculty criticised my references to Marxism in my works on the ground that I had avoided the conventional double-barreled Soviet term 'Marxism-Leninism'.

After the collapse of Soviet power one could write and speak freely, and I was able to explain that I perceived Soviet orthodoxy as a utopian propagation of socialism (paradise on earth). Marxists distinguished Marxism from other utopian teachings by its scientific character, but in itself science does not grant us the truth. Marxism therefore remains as much utopian as many other forms of this belief. Marx was a competent economist, but he was basically wrong when he saw in man only a junction of economic relations; man is also a biological being with certain ineradicable properties: care of his own children and kinfolk at the expense of others, love of his own milieu and animosity to strangers and strange customs, etc. Marx was completely wrong in his estimation of the perspectives of capitalism and the bourgeoisie, of the role of the working class, and the like. The attempts to establish socialism [socialism as the first stage of communism] beginning with the first phalansteries and ending with the bloody reign of Pol Pot in Kampuchea, invariably terminated in revolts of the benefitted masses and in devastation. Marxism is a theory that has been refuted by experiment—and not just once.

However, in the new era I did not reject all the attainments of Soviet scholarship or even all Marxist positions. Materialistic convictions remained in me (and I admit also the force of materialist ideas); likewise atheism. Socioeconomic analysis remains for me a valuable tool in the historiographical study of the discipline. Dialectics remains a strong principle of cognition in the study of a number of complex phenomena, and I frequently make use of it. It is incorrect to consider Marxism as simply an agglomeration of nonsense and gibberish. Valuable accomplishments in philosophy and political economy have been achieved through Marxism. The fact that Marxism has itself been discredited does not imply that these achievements are annulled. *Abusus non tolit usum.*[8]

Klejn also discusses the shortfalls of Marxism in his interview with Timothy Taylor:

It overestimated the socioeconomical side of life: man was considered purely as a nexus of political and economic interests. But man is, at

> the same time, an animal; the biological side of life cannot be eliminated. Thinking it could be was a mistake made by Marx himself. For instance, man is a territorial animal, like the cat; it is impossible to understand our borders, our nations, our states, without understanding this territoriality. Furthermore, for Marxism the collective was valued over the individual, the state over the citizen, and the future over the present, and the end justified the means. (Taylor 1994: 727)[9]

Travels and Retirement

From 1990 Klejn taught as a visiting professor at many universities abroad: first at the Free University of West Berlin, then at Durham (in 1993), and later at Vienna[10] and Copenhagen. He also gave lectures in Sweden, Spain, Norway, Denmark, Moldova,[11] and in Britain at, among other places, London,[12] Cambridge,[13] Lampeter, and Oxford.[14] (Although Klejn's English is good enough for him to deliver lectures he prefers that a native English speaker translate his work from Russian.) One of Klejn's fondest memories is of meeting Bruce Trigger in May 1992 at a conference at the Institute of Archaeology in London marking the hundredth anniversary of the birth of Gordon Childe. Trigger is the Western archaeologist with whom Klejn feels he has most in common, and the two were in correspondence from 1968 to Trigger's death in 2006. 'Since then [1968] I always felt (and said) that if there were another archaeologist in the world whose positions were the most similar to mine, it would be Bruce Trigger' (Klejn 2008a: 4).

After the dissolution of the Soviet Union in December 1991 Klejn's brother chose to stay in America with his family. But Klejn always returned to Russia: 'My homeland is Russia. Its interests and its problems are mine'.[15] Yet, despite the honours he had won abroad, in Russia Klejn was forced to obtain his degrees and titles anew. In 1993 he defended his doctoral dissertation, in the form of the book *Archaeological Typology* (published at last in Russian in 1991), at the Institute for the History of Material Culture (IIMK) of the Russian Academy of Sciences. (It was awarded unanimously.) In 1994 he joined the staff of the department of philosophical anthropology. There he taught cultural anthropology and was given the title of professor of anthropology. From 1995 he also taught this subject at the ethnological faculty of the newly founded European university of St. Petersburg, a university of which he was cofounder.[16]

Finally in September 1997, at the age of 71, he retired from St. Petersburg University, and in 1998 he retired from the European University. There followed another round of lectures abroad: in Slovenia and Finland and in 2000–2001 at the University of Washington in Seattle. Other lectures were given at the universities of Copenhagen, Lubjana, and Tromsø.

On his return to St. Petersburg in 2001 he was diagnosed with prostate cancer. He immediately underwent an operation, but in 2004 the cancer was found to have returned. However, following continued treatment the cancer seems to have gone into remission. Certainly the disease has not interfered with his productivity. Retirement, for Klejn, is not equated with rest but rather with the opportunity to make up for lost time—time squandered by the opposition of the authorities.

He receives a small pension as a veteran of the Patriotic War, but he continues to live modestly, without a *dacha* or a car, in the same small apartment he has occupied since the 1960s. He works at his computer every day without fail and is looked after by his adopted son, Damir, a Tartar from Yoshar-Ola, where Klejn was evacuated in 1941. Damir, a graduate of the Academy of Applied Arts, runs a tailoring business and is married to an Azerbajani woman, Nourida ('Nora'). They have a son, Klejn's grandson, Artur. Damir has added Klejn's surname to his original surname: so he is officially Damir Gibadullin-Klejn.

But although Klejn is industrious he is not single-minded to a fault. He has no sympathy for self-seclusion.[17] He is devoted to his adopted family, and he appreciates the conversation of his peers, such as the physicist and psychologist Alexey Elyashevish, his archaeologist colleagues, and the many young students who visit him. (These include not only archaeology students but also students of fine art.)

Klejn himself takes a keen interest in all the arts and is skilled at drawing and writing poetry. One of the books that he hopes to have published in the near future, a collection of essays entitled *On Art*, asks among other questions 'what is artistic style?' and examines the answers given to this question by both art experts and archaeologists. He also asks whether modern art can offer any clues to the comprehension of Palaeolithic art. Klejn argues that archaeology and the study of art may not be as far away from each other as is sometimes thought. After all, both emerged from philology, and at one time the two subjects were indistinguishable. Yet, despite apparent similarities between modern art and Palaeolithic art Klejn warns that we should not forget that these two forms of art were produced in different social contexts and had a different social significance.[18] (The book also contains biographies of the Russian art historian and archaeologist N. P. Kondakov (1844–1925)[19] and of J. J. Winckelmann (1717–1768). Klejn sees the latter as both the founder of archaeology and the founder of the study of art as an academic discipline.)

Klejn has also retained, from boyhood, an interest in music, and in 2012 he published *Harmonies of Epochs*, in which he subjects the history of music to an anthropological study. He argues that the shifts from one harmonic system to another coincide with shifts of social psychology. This applies to, for example, the advent of jazz and of rock. Both coincide with changes in social psychology, but the change is never complete—thus both of these forms of music have certain roots in earlier forms of music. (*Harmonies of Epochs* was written in the 1970s, but because of the disapproval of the KGB it circulated for many years only as *samizdat*.)

Another interest, about which Klejn has written in recent years, is Time, in particular the history of our changing perceptions of time. Related to this is his analysis of dating methods in archaeology. Of relative dating methods, he distinguishes between those that are native to archaeology—methods reliant on the principles of archaeological stratigraphy and methods of assemblage analysis—and those that archaeology borrows from other disciplines. Of course, there are also methods of absolute dating (radio carbon dating, and so on), all of which are borrowed from other disciplines. Klejn raises the interesting question of whether methods of absolute dating might in principle supersede methods of relative dating. But he argues that methods of absolute dating can never altogether replace methods of relative dating, because methods of absolute dating are themselves the product of a particular historical context and for that reason can never be thought of as absolutely reliable (see Klejn 2014).

Politics and Religion

In the years of perestroika Klejn was a member of the discussion group Leningrad Tribune, which focused on the problems of implementing democracy in Russia. Since 2008 he has written a regular column (twice a month) on current affairs in a newspaper written by and for scholars, *Troitsky Variant*. One of many concerns in Klejn's recent journalism is with the rise in Russia of xenophobic nationalism masquerading as patriotism. On this subject he agrees with Samuel Johnson: it is 'the last refuge of the scoundrel'. Other concerns include systematic corruption, the decline of industry other than that orientated toward the exploitation of limited natural resources, and the emigration of so many of the most enterprising Russians. These problems are looked at from the point of view of a scholar—exploring the scholar's relationship with money, morality, and power in contemporary Russia. Klejn was briefly encouraged by the protests that took place at the election of Putin in 2012, but since then he has seen the movement lose influence, while at the same time the beliefs of its frustrated members have grown increasingly fervent.

A further concern is the revival of religion. In a talk given at Oxford University in 1992 Klejn noted that 'the recent renaissance of the church is more national and political than truly religious' (Klejn 1992: 27; see also Chernykh 1995). He expands on his attitude to religion in the supplementary notes to his *curriculum vitae*:

> It is usually not the custom in an autobiography to make one's relation to religion explicit. However, nowadays many artists, writers, and politicians and workers of culture proudly profess their religious orthodoxy. In former times atheism was in our country something taken for granted in an educated and politically loyal man. But today the state inclines toward fusion with the church, and Communists have become

devoutly pious—they cross and star themselves, as in Voyinovich's old anti-utopian 'Moscow of 2042'.[20] . . . Indeed, our situation is like that of Germany after the Thirty Years' War: *cujus regio, ejus religio*. While there is an atheist in the Kremlin, temples are crushed, and the whole country blasphemes. While there is a hypocrite in the Kremlin, everyone lights candles. In these conditions I decided to note in my autobiography that I have grown up in an atheistic milieu and remain an atheist. This is not a challenge or a Fronde. It is a belief.

Whatever you may say, atheism is a worldview that befits the scholar. Science is incompatible with the belief in miracles. The scientist and the scholar cannot and should not believe in supernatural forces. They should recognise only those forces that are either recognised by science or that might in principle be recognised by science. Otherwise they are in the wrong place. The result of his experiment cannot be thought to alter depending on whether or not he offers a candle to God. The scholar cannot rule out inferences from his theory if they contradict religious dogma. It is the dogma that should give way if the science refutes it. And as we know many religious dogmas have had to give way. True, not all of them—religion maintains some. Yet the general rule: science advances, religion recedes.

For modern believers gods are no longer anthropomorphic or zoomorphic beings sitting on celestial thrones, but invisible spirits, abstract forces, all knowing and omnipotent. The essence of religion is their veneration in prayer and ritual. It is thought that these must bring success in life and redemption from misery. Those who are personally convinced of the importance of religion in essence personify in these invented beings (their real existence was never proved) their own—and traditional—hopes, morals, and standards of conduct. Religion is based on sheer personal psychology: for many people it is easier to dare doing something if they imagine they have behind them the support of certain strong figures, and likewise it is easier to give up something if they imagine the disapproval of the same figures—Gods or saints. For the sake of serving this illusion (necessary to many) the whole enormous industry of churches is created; and as states are interested in the support of traditional norms, usually they like and support their church (and this feeling is mutual).

Of course, beside their principal function, churches have accomplished many useful things: increased literacy, stimulated philanthropy, maintained morals in everyday life, developed urban architecture. Yet the evil they have done has not been negligible: via confessions they stimulated national and religious dissent, inspired religious wars, burnt heretics, butchered those of different beliefs, and in every way possible discouraged the development of science. Usually popes and monks preach asceticism rather than acquisitiveness, but the church itself accumulates colossal riches.

Atheists should not be inferior to the clergy in their activities. In America psychoanalysts have already deposed priests from the role of confessor. This is not the best change, but it is a symptom. I hope that in general mankind will take notice of psychologists rather than popes. This will be much better for sound self-appraisal, general temperance, and for the purse.

Twilight Years

In 2010 Klejn published his autobiography: *It's Hard to Be Klejn*.[21] His starting points for this work were his official *curriculum vitae* and the interviews given in later years to various archaeological journals (Kristiansen 1993; Burström 1994; Taylor 1994; Immonen 2003). (Although Klejn was unlucky with respect to *Archaeological Typology*, and in that the Western journal in which he published several of his articles [*The Journal of Theoretical Archaeology*] became defunct, he was at least fortunate in that several good interviews have been published in the West.) Something of the trenchant tone of Klejn's interviews is carried over into the autobiography *It's Hard to Be Klejn*, for, as he explains, his views 'often radically diverged from the views of the establishment—as indeed they still do. This is why many chapters of the book have something of a polemical tone. The author's evaluations inevitably bear a subjective character: as such, they run the risk of offending those mentioned, and they will certainly meet with objections. Yet these evaluations have not emerged from a vacuum; they are the products of personal experience, not infrequently bitter'.[22]

As to the book's title: 'The proud title came about by chance. Long ago the author entitled one of his reviews (of an English collection) "It's Hard to Be a God". In this he compared the contributors of the collection to the heroes of Strugatsky's romance of the same name. Because it was the custom among archaeologists to poke fun at Klejn's opinion of himself, the joke began that Klejn had published his autobiography and entitled it "It's Hard to be a God". Having corrected this witticism in his own manner Klejn entitled his memoirs, i.e., his real autobiography, *It's Hard to Be Klejn*. The title reflects the fact that his life was really not at all easy, for which he blames, first and foremost, himself (but, indeed, he did not look for an easy life)'.[23]

Klejn admits to a feeling of surprise at having lived so long. Intellectually, he felt less isolated at the end of the Soviet period. It is not that he feels nostalgia for this period, but it was then that he had colleagues who were following similar paths in theoretical archaeology. But many of his colleagues predeceased him, because of stress, smoking, bad medicine, or alcohol, or some combination of these.

In some ways, as Klejn himself says, he has come to be seen as a relic from a former age. But he does not think of himself as a relic; and each new book of his creative old age sells well. Moreover: 'I feel I am just at the beginning of the way: so much remains unknown, so much to do, so much to learn. I am not afraid to die, but it hurts me greatly that I will not see the new discoveries made after me and without me' (Leach 2011). It is for these reasons, not from vanity or arrogance, that Klejn says in his autobiography: 'Whenever I die, it will be too early' (Klejn 2010: 574).

Part II

Life's Work

Chapter 4

Anthropology

Prison Life

Klejn's account of his incarceration, *The World Turned Upside Down* (1993)—written under the name of Lev Samoylov—is not only a prison memoir but also a popular account of an anthropological investigation. As such its ultimate focus is no less than human nature. Klejn argues that human beings are psychophysiologically maladjusted to modern civilisation. Culture is the means by which we are adapted to civilisation, but culture does not overrule biology entirely—and this becomes clear when we look at certain prison societies.

According to Klejn: 'The similarity [between prison society and Upper Palaeolithic society] is manifold: tattooing as a system of signs, rites of initiation, the developed system of taboo, three castes, clan conflicts, chieftains and their retinues, blood brotherhood, nonmonetary exchange, etc. . . . The point is that human nature was formed in the Cromagnon period and biologically has not changed since'.[1]

Such a view might be thought to have more adherents in Russia than in the more optimistic West, but there are those in the West who would agree. Klejn points to the novelist William Golding (1911–1993). Another novelist of a similar outlook is J. G. Ballard (1930–2009), interred as a child in a Japanese prison camp in the Second World War.[2] Among natural scientists Stephen Pinker (Pinker 2011) should be mentioned, and among philosophers John Gray. Indeed, from all that I have learned of Klejn's opinions, I believe he would be in full agreement with the following passage from Gray:

> The political predicament of our species is not that of a creature of infinite possibilities that has throughout its history been inexplicably shackled. We are not, each of us, as our liberal culture encourages us to imagine, a limitless reservoir of possibilities, for whom the past is an irrelevance and the future an empty horizon. We are finite, mortal selves, burdened by the evils of our history and the miseries natural to the human condition, who achieve excellence and a measure of

A Russian Perspective on Theoretical Archaeology: The Life and Work of Leo S. Klejn
by Stephen Leach, 55–60

> well-being only insofar as we accept the disciplines of civilization. (Gray 2009, 134)

However, one difference between these writers and Klejn is that when Klejn notes specific similarities between prison societies and the society of the Upper Palaeolithic, his observations are made on the basis of some archaeological knowledge of the Upper Palaeolithic.

In *The World Turned Upside Down*, Klejn develops the ideas of the zoologist Konrad Lorenz[3] and the sociobiologist Desmond Morris.[4] He argues that humans are adapted not just to their natural environment but also to their sociocultural environments. However the tempos of biological evolution and socio-cultural evolution are not synchronised. Biological evolution is much the slower. Since the Palaeolithic era sociocultural evolution has gone through the Mesolithic, Eneolithic, Neolithic, Bronze, and Iron Ages and is now in the Atomic and Computer Age; but our psychophysiological characteristics remain adapted to the conditions of the Palaeolithic. Klejn agrees with Freud's observation in *Civilization and Its Discontents* [*Das Unbehagen in der Kultur*] that we are discontent with modern culture because we are not by our nature adapted to it. According to Freud:

> The existence of this tendency to aggression which we can detect in ourselves and rightly presume to be present in others is the factor that disturbs our relations with our neighbours and makes it necessary for culture to institute its high demands. Civilized society is perpetually menaced with disintegration through this primary hostility of men toward one another. Their interests in their common work would not hold them together; the passions of instinct are stronger than reasoned interests. Culture has to call up every possible reinforcement in order to erect barriers against the aggressive instincts of men and hold their manifestations in check by reaction-formations in men's minds. (Freud 1930: 86)

Freud had always hoped that his hypothesis, concerning the disharmony between man's physiological being and his cultural development, might be empirically verified; and Klejn realised that via his experience of the Soviet prison system he might take up this challenge. He came to the conclusion that when a historically evolved sociocultural environment is abruptly removed—when people are simply 'thrown together', as in the GULAG or in certain military environments—then, as Freud implied, primordial forms of life re-emerge.

On this point he makes clear both his affinity with Freud and his divergence from Marx: 'Much was written in our country on biological evolution (usually in connection with Darwinism), but considerably less was written on culture and sociocultural evolution, because this sphere was occupied by historical materialism with its dogmatic interpretation of Marxist-Leninist classics written a century and a half ago'.[5] Indeed, Klejn points out that for Marx 'culture did not exist at all. He didn't use the term, not once' (Taylor 1994: 727).

The nub of Klejn's argument is that

> the tempos of biological and social evolution of man are unequal—the tardiness of the biological as compared with social—created the main contradiction of modern epoch: the psycho-physiological nature of man remained at a Cromagnon level while the running ahead of social conditions and technology demand another man. The failure of man to adapt to modern culture has begun to tell in contemporary life (the crimes without obvious causes, certain diseases specific to humanity, etc.). In culture a number of compensatory mechanisms have been developed to soften this contradiction (sports, the entertainment industry, and others). but the problem remains acute. This argument diverges radically from Marxism, for Marxism holds the main contradiction of the epoch to be something else entirely—the confrontation of old and new production relations (both of a socioeconomic nature).[6]

Before publishing *The World Turned Upside Down* Klejn published his thoughts on the Russian prison system in the journal *Etnosgrafischeskoe Obozrenie* [*Ethnographical Review*]. The responses that his article elicited were published in an appendix in the latest Russian version of *The World Turned Upside Down*. These responses included criticisms from Bannikov, Kozintsev, and Kabo.

K. L. Bannikov, in 'Regimented Communities: The Anthropology of Destructiveness', argued that there is no need to posit an evolutionary scheme. Bannikov put forward the opposing (Jungian) argument that in certain unusual and extreme conditions the archetypes of the subconscious may become more apparent.

The anthropologist Alexander G. Kozintsev, in 'On the World Upside Down' (historic-anthropological comment on Leo Samoylov's book), argued that the process is historical. That is to say, the present state of affairs is historically determined rather than regressive, and its historical development can be traced in the work of some of the great Russian novelists. There is no single point at which the prisoners' behaviour can be described as less cultural and accordingly more natural—for there is in fact no such thing as human nature. Humans are the products of their culture.

V. R. Kabo, in 'Structure of a Camp and Archetypes of Consciousness', asked whether the archaeological evidence justifies the assumption that Palaeolithic society was 'primitive' in the manner of the camps.

It is notable that the objections raised by Bannikov, Kozintsev, and Kabo are the same objections as might occur to a Western anthropologist. Interestingly,

Kozintsev's argument might be extended against evolutionary psychology *per se*. However, we need not choose between anthropological and historical study, as Kozintsev seems to think: the one does not preclude the other. Two different perspectives may share the same subject matter. Moreover, Klejn does not deny that there are specific historical circumstances that have led to the development of the Russian camp system.

Nevertheless, Klejn would maintain that when prisoners are, so to speak, thrown together—when the prisoners themselves have no social or historical bearings—the belated biological level of evolution becomes clearer to see. The random 'thrown together' nature of the prisoners is an important part of his thesis. He would not deny that in some prisons or camps, where, for example, families are not completely broken up, or where scholars have been confined together —with shared values (for example on prerevolution Schlüsselburg or on the Isle of Man in World War II)—the effect seems to be the very reverse of that which he witnessed in the Peter and Paul Fortress. Note that the prison that Klejn describes is one in which many of the prisoners were, in his words, 'bandits, robbers, assassins, crooks, and thieves' (Taylor 1994: 732)—lost souls.

Bannikov's thesis seems of limited value as an objection to Klejn, because it is difficult to falsify. But is Klejn's thesis itself falsifiable? Assuming that he is correct concerning the savagery of prison society—this is generally uncontested—there remains Kabo's question: is there indeed evidence to suggest that Palaeolithic society was 'primitive' in the manner of the camps? I would suggest that it is this area that provides the most useful line for future inquiries. In this area, via archaeological research, it may in principle be possible to weigh the plausibility of Klejn's theory.

It might be thought that the picture that Klejn paints of human nature is bleakly pessimistic—no doubt Klejn would reply that it is realistic—either way, it might be thought that the picture he paints of human nature is not an attractive one. However, Klejn's view of culture (the flip side of his view of human nature) might be characterised as that of an optimistic *philosophe*. For although Klejn would agree that life without culture would indeed be 'solitary, poor, nasty, brutish, and short', and although he does not believe in humanity's perfectibility, he does believe in progress, in the sense of moving toward the truth and in moving away from our state of nature by virtue of culture. In these respects his views are similar to those put forward by Steven Pinker in *The Better Angels of Our Nature* (2011), in which Pinker argues that the overall general level of violence in society has in the long-term declined. It is interesting to note that, although Klejn's views might give a first impression of bleak pessimism, Pinker, who also argues that there is a disparity between sociocultural and biological evolution, was concerned that *his* view would be interpreted as overly optimistic.

Klejn also conveys an unfashionable Enlightenment attitude, for which he remains resolutely unapologetic, in his insistence that the state has no business to enquire as to someone's sexuality. (According to Klejn, such an enquiry 'would be appropriate within personal relations, but, even then, it is not an enquiry that should be pursued with direct questions'.[7]) This was the stance that he took during his trial, and he has subsequently found no reason to change it.

Cybernetics

A second appendix to *The World Turned Upside Down* offers a sketch of a communications theory of cultural evolution.

Klejn argues that cultural development can be seen as a series consisting of both continuity and breaks. If one presumes that culture is transferable information then the transmission of culture from one generation to the next might be seen as proceeding via a communication system that spans time as well as space. As in any communications system what is required is repetition (or at least the capacity to be reproduced) and the capacity to be transmitted. Channels of communication might include family, school, university, club, and so on. Repetition of cultural information might be daily (washing yourself, using table manners, and so forth) or weekly (observing holy days, for example). In this context, breaks in development can be seen as disruptions of stable conditions. Klejn's suggestion is compatible with Richard Dawkins' on 'memes' (Dawkins 1976) and much work in recent evolutionary archaeology that has been inspired by Dawkins.[8] He believes that his communications theory is a suggestion that is ripe for further development and that it might be so developed so as to have repercussions in archaeology, a discipline in which many of the most basic and most prevalent questions concern cultural change versus continuity.

Klejn claims that, as it stands, his theory reminds us that if only one section of a society was involved in a migration—for example, a band of warriors—we should not necessarily expect the migrants to take with them all the cultural traits of their homeland, for some cultural traits—for instance, burial rites—are only relatively seldom witnessed. There may not have been opportunity for the information contained within the burial rites to have been transmitted to the young migrating warriors.

Extending this line of thought, Klejn argues that it is even possible for a migration to have taken place in the past without it having left any material traces. ('There are in archaeology many cases where what is lost is lost forever' [Klejn pers. comm.].) Its only remaining trace might be found in language.

Homosexuality

Having faced a charge of homosexuality, Klejn naturally became interested in certain questions about homosexuality. In *The Other Love* (2000) he investigates the relative significance of cultural and biological factors in this phenomenon. He asks why homosexuality continues when the theory of evolution would lead us to have predicted its decline and eventual extinction. Klejn believes that in a purely biological sense homosexuality is a pathology but that there are also a multitude of changing cultural conventions which play a part in its history and continuing existence. He argues that the incidence of homosexuality at different times and places is about the same; it is only the degree of reticence about it that varies.

Klejn points out that the reproduction of particular extracts of this book on the Internet—taken out of context—has given a misleading impression of the book as a whole. To be clear, although he is critical of some aspects of gay subculture, he supports the civil rights of gays and he advocates the decriminalisation and demedicalisation of homosexuality.

After *The Other Love* two more books followed on related themes.

> *Another Side of a Luminary* (2002) considers the unusual love of outstanding personalities. Specifically it is devoted to homosexuality in the life stories of well-known Russian figures, from Ivan the Terrible to Rudolf Nureyev. Another book *The Reverse Plutarch* (not yet published) is devoted to non-Russian figures, from Socrates and Plato to Leonardo da Vinci and President Lincoln. The aim of the book is not to justify homosexuality by referencing famous homosexuals but rather to consider how outstanding personalities coped with this difficult psychological problem—not all of them are regarded as positive figures.[9]

In recent years Klejn has been increasingly in demand as a speaker on questions concerning homosexuality and the state. Especially since the death of the sociologist Professor Igor Kon in 2011, Klejn has received many invitations from television, radio, and magazines to talk about these questions, to the extent that he feels the media have ignored his principal specialism, archaeology, in favour of these other questions. In Russia feelings currently run very high on these matters—people have been killed merely on the suspicion of being gay—and one reason that Klejn is in demand is that he is able to hear both sides of an argument without irritation. Klejn suspects that the government would rather discuss homosexuality than other social problems—homosexuals make a convenient scapegoat.

Chapter 5

Homeric Studies

Klejn's publications on the *Iliad* in the 1990s drew from a course of lectures that he gave on the European Bronze Age (in Leningrad), but their immediate stimulus was the fact that as a result of his persecution he was stripped of his academic titles and deprived of his membership of the university. Unable to gain access to a university library, Klejn simply took down his copy of the *Iliad* from the bookshelf of his study and, making use of his training by Propp, subjected it to an intensive structural and statistical analysis. Thus again, with hindsight, Klejn feels he had reason to be grateful for his imprisonment: 'Possibly, I personally have gained more than I have lost: I saw new sides of life, new spheres of activity. Devoid of my earlier profession, I, while working at home, mastered a new scientific profession—Homeric studies' (Klejn 2010: 400).

Klejn has published three books on the *Iliad*: *Incorporeal Heroes* (1994), *The Anatomy of the Iliad* (1998), and *The Iliad Decoded* (2014). *The Iliad Decoded* summarises and binds together the content of *Incorporeal Heroes* and *The Anatomy of the Iliad*. It is written for the non-specialist. He has also published a long article on the 'The Catalogue of Ships: Structure and Stratigraphy' (2000).[1] At the time of writing there are plans to republish *Incorporeal Heroes*, *The Anatomy of the Iliad*, and a longer version of the article on the 'Catalogue of Ships' within a single two-volume work entitled *Homeric Studies*. In this chapter I concentrate on the exposition of *Incorporeal Heroes*, *The Anatomy of the Iliad*, and 'The Catalogue of Ships: Structure and Stratigraphy'.

Incorporeal Heroes

Incorporeal Heroes is about the origins of the heroes of the *Iliad*. I edited the English translation of this work, and it was published in December 2012. Previously Klejn's theories on the *Iliad* were known in the West only via a single lecture, given in English, in Aarhus, Denmark, in 1998.

A Russian Perspective on Theoretical Archaeology: The Life and Work of Leo S. Klejn by Stephen Leach, 61–69

Following the work of F. A. Wolf in the late eighteenth century Homeric scholars divided between 'analysts', who believed that the *Iliad* is an amalgam compiled from different sources, and 'unitarians', who placed greater stress on the role of a single artistic genius, Homer. 'In the nineteenth century the scales were in favour of the analysts, but then discord resulted from the construction of a number of mutually incompatible versions of the step-by-step creation of the poem. The discord between the analysts led to the predominance of the unitarians in the twentieth century' (Klejn 2012a: 5). More recently numerous attempts have been made to bridge the divide between these two camps by, for example, postulating the idea of Homer's genius at borrowing from ancient sources.

Klejn's own views on the historicity of the *Iliad* are, as he is admits, similar in some respects to those of certain German scholars of the late nineteenth century. Of his two major works on the *Iliad*, published in Russian in the 1990s, *The Anatomy of the Iliad* focuses on the reality of the Trojan War, and *Incorporeal Heroes* focuses on the heroes of the *Iliad*. Were they real historical figures or were they artistic inventions?

Or neither? Klejn's conclusion is that 'before they were honoured for their military deeds, almost all of them had been figures of religious cults, miraculous helpers, and patrons of various spheres of life (like Russian saints)—and they were honoured for their miraculous help but this was not always military help' (Ibid.: 156).

> So Achilles was a protector from the sea, the guardian of ships—and in the *Iliad* he is prominent in defending the ships when they are in danger. His relative Ajax has the same specialisation, and in the *Iliad* he springs from ship to ship with a long pike. Nestor was a cult healer associated with the god Asclepius, and in the *Iliad* he heals wounds and gives good advice. Odysseus was a fortune-teller connected with divination, and so on. Helen was a goddess of the kind who was regularly abducted and returned, and of course in the *Iliad* she is abducted and returned.[2]

Klejn used statistical analysis to determine the comparative date at which each hero had entered into the epic. He here makes use of ideas proposed by Denys Page in the mid-twentieth century. Page noted that in oral tradition there are stock formulae consisting of a noun and an adjective and that it may reasonably assumed that the earlier the name appears in the epic the more often will it be attached to constant epithets (so as to build stock formulae)—for example, 'swift-footed Achilles'. In other words, the number of these stock epithets attached to the hero's name as compared to more general epithets would indicate relative longevity. For some reason, having suggested this way forward Page failed to pursue it.

When Klejn applied Page's methodology, the results indicated that of all the protagonists:

> the most ancient are Helen the Fair (stock epithets 65%), her lover Alexander (47%), the wise Odysseus (56%), and Ajax the Great (43.5%), Hector (41%) and Achilles (38%) somewhat later, and Priam (32%) still later. Then came Patroclus (23%) and Aeneas (18%). As to the other name of Helen's lover, Paris, his supply of stock epithets is 0, so Alexander received this name very late—close to the final written formation of the poem. Ajax the Lesser has a rather high proportion of stock epithets (55%), but this can be explained as an anomaly—by the necessity to repeatedly distinguish him (by stock epithets) from the earlier main figure, Ajax the Great. Otherwise, Ajax the Lesser would have had a proportion of stock epithets more like that of Teucer, a mere 14.2%.[3]

When I took on the work of editing *Incorporeal Heroes* for publication in English translation in 2012 I asked Klejn whether he still stood by everything that he had written in it. He admitted that he had not personally kept up with all the recent scholarship on the *Iliad*, but he was fully convinced that 'were modern scholarship to have produced a crucial new insight which contradicted my argument, then, without doubt, my opponents would have rushed to tell me of it' (Klejn pers. comm.).

It is anyway generally the case, although not invariably, that Klejn prefers to devote himself to presenting his own arguments as clearly as possible rather than diverting from his path to address opinions with which he disagrees. As a result his writing is fluent and clear and, as is always his ambition, reaches the widest possible readership.

Typically, in *Incorporeal Heroes* Klejn ambitiously attempts to reach both a popular and a scholarly readership—and, unusually for a book on this subject, it is entirely without footnotes. Of course, because at the time Klejn had no access to a university library, he did not have the option of footnoting the text. It is characteristic of Klejn not to have mentioned this fact in any foreword or introduction: he believes that his arguments must make their own way in the world by their own strengths.

Klejn was particularly proud that his book won over, in his final years, the eminent linguist and historian of the ancient Near East Igor M. Dyakonov (1915–1999).[4] In 1997 Dyakonov wrote: 'In my opinion L. S. Klejn's work is built so that to refute it in full would be very difficult, and even corrections of a cardinal character if any seem not likely. Klejn's theory undoubtedly will produce a vast literature. . . . It cannot be excluded that Klejn's studies if taken in their full amount will mean the beginning of a new epoch in Homeric studies'.[5] Dyakonov's endorsement appears on the dustcover of the 2012 English edition of *Incorporeal Heroes*.

The Anatomy of the Iliad

Whereas *Incorporeal Heroes* focused on the origins of each of the main heroes of the *Iliad*, *The Anatomy of the Iliad* focuses on demonstrating the compound character of the poem and restoring the outlines of the original texts. *The Anatomy of the Iliad* is a much longer book than *Incorporeal Heroes* and contains much more in the way of statistical analysis. On its own it constitutes the first volume of Klejn's *Homeric Studies*.

In common with some earlier scholars Klejn came to the conclusion that there was no Trojan war—at least no Trojan war as described by the *Iliad*, in which the victors were the Achaeans—for there is not the slightest archaeological evidence for these things, and indeed there is plenty of evidence to the contrary. Rather, he believes that—as has often happened—an epic turned what was in fact a defeat into a victory.

> The Achaeans did conquer the south coast of Asia Minor, the southern part of the western coast, but they never conquered the northern part. Thus, the *Iliad* is similar to the Russian epic *Byliny*, which tells of Russian heroes' beating the Tartars without mentioning the Tartar yoke, which lasted for two centuries. Again, in the Serbian epic the heroes go to Istanbul and conquer it, but we know that in history it was exactly the reverse—they were defeated in Kosovo Polje. In the Greek epic, it is the same: it is a compensation for something they never did. (Taylor 1994: 735)

Klejn believes that Ilios and Troy were different cities and Troy has not been found: Schliemann excavated not Troy but Ilios. (Hittite sources indicate that they were two separate towns.) The location of Troy remains debatable, but Klejn believes that Poliochni, excavated by Italians, is the best candidate.[6]

In *The Anatomy of the Iliad* Klejn used the same methodology as has been used to analyse the Bible. In the eighteenth century the French scholar Jean Astruc had noticed that although certain stories are repeated in the Bible the name of God changes—sometimes he is Yahweh, sometimes Elohim. As the names do not occur together the inference was drawn that these stories came from different sources.

Klejn applied this form of 'biblical criticism' to the *Iliad*, in conjunction with modern techniques of statistical analysis. (The book contains forty statistical tables.) He traced the distribution of synonymous names—particularly, but not only, of toponyms, ethonyms, and the names of God and heroes—for example, Ilios-Troy, Scamandros-Xanthos, Achaeans-Danaans-Argives, Alexander-Paris. There are many, and correlations can be found between, for example, one of a particular group of names and one of a particular group of epithets. Moreover, certain pairs of synonyms (or threes) are concentrated in particular parts of the epic. And, most noticeably, the heroes are themselves distributed unevenly—thus when Achilles appears, Diomedes disappears, but they are both wounded in the heel (so in some sense they duplicate each other).

On the basis of such observations, bolstered by statistical analysis, Klejn concluded that the *Iliad* is composed of several interwoven but distinguishable components. He argues that the core story was of Helen, Alexander (Paris), and Ajax. Then came Achilles and Hector, then Priam and Patroclus, and finally Aeneas and Pandarus.

> To be specific, there probably existed 'Achaean' and 'Danaan' songs with Achilles as the main hero, and 'Argive' songs centred on Diomedes and Achilles. The most ancient component (and the most folkloric) was centred on Ajax and was included into the poem separately. The latest addition centred on Aeneas is also distinguishable—(the Homeric *Aeneid*).[7]

He suggests that all the arguments about the dating of the *Iliad* stem from the fact that it is a composite work of different dates: some parts are as old as the late eighth century B.C., whereas others may be as late as the early sixth century B.C.

Furthermore, Klejn argues that it is possible to discover where the different parts of the *Iliad* were formed. As we have seen, Klejn has counted the proportion of times a stock (formulaic) epithet is used of a particular hero as opposed to a more general element. One hero has been included in the *Iliad* longer than another if he has a higher proportion of stock epithets. So, for example, because 47% of all of Alexander's epithets are formulaic, whereas only 32% of Priam's epithets are formulaic, Alexander is the older of these two characters. This argument appears already in *Incorporeal Heroes*, but in *The Anatomy of the Iliad* it is extended. Klejn points out that Hittite sources of the thirteenth century B.C. associate the name Alexander with Vilusa (Ilios). Later Lycian sources associate the name of Priam with Troy. 'Now the idea was to see how both toponyms are supplied with stock epithets: Ilios—47%, Troy—32%!'[8]

In reaching these conclusions, Klejn makes clear his admiration for certain German classicists of the late nineteenth and early twentieth centuries—H. Düntzer, T. Bergk, A. Fick, P. Kauer, E. Bethe, and others. His conclusion with regard to the historicity of Homer is similar to theirs. The reality of the narrator (whom we may as well still call Homer) is not rejected, but his role in the creation of the poem's text is much reduced, as but the last of a long line of its creators.

The Catalogue of Ships

The Catalogue of Ships is that part of the *Iliad* that lists the Achaean troops that sailed for Troy (II: 494–759).

In 'The Catalogue of Ships: Structure and Stratigraphy' (2000) Klejn's aim was to remove the accumulated layers of which the Catalogue consists in reverse order to that in which they were laid down. His methodology is basically the same as that which he used in *The Anatomy of the Iliad*. He notes that the kingdoms mentioned in the Catalogue overlap and sometimes completely coincide. This is the case with the kingdoms of Odysseus and Meges, Achilles and Ajax the Lesser, Guneus and Lapithes, and the kingdoms of Philoctetes, Eurypylus, and the Magnetes. It suggests that the data entered the epic at different times.

Klejn builds on the work of Martin P. Nilsson and Vadim L. Tsymbursky and agrees with them that the heroes and their troops were introduced into the epic successively over a considerable period of time, at the behest of particular singers. In some more detail Klejn's conclusion is as follows:

> If we take the group with small numbers of ships and divide the heroes according to their numbers of ships we find that they fall into two subsets: one set (with units divisible by 12 ships) consists of island heroes (Odysseus, Ajax (son of Oileus), Tlepolemus, and Nireus); the other (mainly with a number of ships divisible by 11) consists of heroes who do not participate in battles. The latter are not crucial to the plot of the *Iliad*.
>
> Among the units with large numbers of ships there is a subset with 'hollow' ships, the numbers of which are divisible by 30. All the places (including the kingdoms of Nestor) from which 'hollow' ships came are connected with the cult of Asclepius. The other subgroup subset is distinguished by the formula '40 black ships pursued him to Ilios' (in one case 50 ships). Within this subset the heroes originate from Athens and the coastline of the bay of Corinth. The third subgroup consists of just two chiefs—Diomedes and Idomeneus. They have 80 ships each, and in each kingdom there are 2 capitals (so for each one 40 ships), and the secondary capital is in each case distinguished by one and the same rare epithet.
>
> Aside from all these subgroups the remaining set of 11 troops is distinguished by its unity and symmetry. On land, facing Ilios to the east the formation was as follows. In the centre was the Peloponnesian troop—that is to say, the Mycenaean troop led by Agamemnon with 100 ships and 2 subordinate troops with 60 ships each (total 120). On the left there were 4 troops from Central Greece (a Boeotian troop with 50 ships and 3 other troops with 40 ships each [in sum 120]), and

> finally on the right hand there were 4 troops from Northern Greece (Achilles has 50 ships, the rest 40 each). Thus, each wing had 120 ships with their teams.
>
> In 20 different formulas the Greek designation of ships is written with the Aeolian 'etha'; while the Ionian 'epsilon' is applied to all units of Nestor's subset (probably a late addition) and in all units of the main symmetric structure in which the numbers of ships are neither 40 nor 100. So, it seems that the Ionians revised the composition of those troops with 60 ships (in the centre) and as well as those with 50 ships (those on the wings) in order to emphasise hierarchy. This revision reflects an Anatolian innovation (organisation into units of 6) and the trend toward pentapolis in archaic Greece.
>
> The numbers 12 and 11 are possibly connected with Ionian and Aeolian political unions in Asia Minor—(of just these numbers of cities).
>
> The discrepancies become even more apparent if one compares the fictitious geography of the Catalogue (in Greece) with the scheme of the army arranged (on Troad land) from north to south, facing Ilios. Achilles' army is placed on the right wing (in order for Achilles to be at the right hand of the head of the coalition), but he should be on the north, for he was thought to be of northern origin (from Thessaly)! (Furthermore, this army is connected to a kingdom that seems to overlap several others.) This suggests a relatively late addition.
>
> Not counting Achilles' army we are left with 7 others: Boeotians, Locrians, Phoceans, Abantes, Mycenaeans, Lacedemonians, and Arcadians. This composition almost completely coincides with that of Penthilus' fleet that, according to Strabo, left Aulis for the East in order to establish colonies in Asia Minor. Probably this is the original core of the legend about the Achaean campaign to the Ilios.[9]

Thus the contingents of the Achaean army changed over the course of the poem's evolution. 'Originally it consisted of a small number of tribes, such as might have sailed to Anatolia from Greece in the tenth century B.C. under the command of the offspring of the mythical Agamemnon'[10]—who in the course of the song's composition changed his place of origin from Sparta to Mycenae. Ultimately the army attempted to invade the Troad, and it was this event that was remembered and glorified in songs of the eighth to seventh centuries.

The Catalogue of Trojan Forces (II: 816–77) is analysed along the same principles. Of the distant allies of the Trojans, as of the distant allies of the Achaeans, there are two different kinds of troops presented in two distinctive ways:

> in some formulas (of an early origin) the tribes are mentioned before their leaders; in others (probably of later origin) the leaders are

> mentioned first. The former troops are concentrated around the Troad; the latter are concentrated at the peripheries.
>
> There is another parallel between the catalogues: in both catalogues the numbers 12 and 11 characterise certain groups; but, in the Trojan catalogue, beside ships (and more often than ships) chariots are mentioned. In the poem these troops interact with corresponding Achaeans troops: that is to say, Lycians and some Thracians interact with some island Achaean troops. The earlier units of the Trojan Catalogue, with 11 chariots from the areas nearest to Ilios, are of similar composition to the Aeolian troops of Achaeans with 11 ships—not only in their number of battle units but also in their passion for all things equestrian. Both of these elements seem to have been introduced to the Catalogue by one and the same singer.
>
> Hector belongs to the same level (number 11 is a significant theme in his armaments). But nonetheless, like Aeneas, he was absent from the original Catalogue (though he was known to the Cyprias).[11]

Klejn infers that, like Aeneas, Hector was included among the leaders of the coalition at only a very late date.

'The Catalogue of Ships: Structure and Stratigraphy' was itself based on an earlier unpublished and unfinished work *The Catalogue of Ships as a Clue to the Iliad.* This work is an analysis of the Catalogue of Ships in greater depth. It remains unfinished, but Klejn has nonetheless decided to publish it as part of his forthcoming *Homeric Studies* in the hope that it will be of use to some future scholar.

Homeric Studies will also include replies to two of Klejn's critics, Vadim L. Tsymbursky and V. V. Faier, an account of Schliemann's life story, and a discussion of the division of the *Iliad* into twenty-four artificial rhapsodies. Furthermore, it will include a chapter from *The Iliad Decoded* ('What Was Made By Homer?') and three popular essays: 'Is Troy Found?', 'The Trojan War: History or Myth?', and 'Who Was the Victor in the *Iliad*?' The answer to the last question might seem obvious, but Klejn argues that neither the Greeks nor the Trojans were the victors: for Troy lay in ruins and the Greek kings were dispersed and lost their kingdoms. In fact, the only victors were Apollo and his priest, Chryses. They alone received everything they wanted. In the perception of singers and their audiences it was Apollo who was victorious.[12]

Before leaving this subject, it must be acknowledged that the study of the *Iliad* is an academic field that is riven by deep and long-standing divisions, and some scholars might suspect Klejn to be guilty of hubris in proclaiming to have triumphed where so many others have laboured in vain. Indeed, Klejn has encountered this attitude. In particular, he recalls how a close friend disputed almost all of his opinions on the *Iliad*. Klejn and his friend, a well-known professor of classics, each set out their stalls as clearly as possible and argued the matter back and forth all through one evening and deep into the night. Slowly and reluctantly Klejn's friend conceded one point after another. Then, as 'rosy-fingered' Dawn appeared, his friend suddenly announced that he was feeling most unwell—a suspected heart attack!

The next time Klejn spoke to him, his friend told him: 'You are right about everything. There is just one mistake. . . . You have forgotten that the *Iliad* is a work of art'.

Klejn's reply is unrecorded, but in recounting this incident to me, with an expression of wry amusement, he concluded: 'I have no wish to win an argument at this cost' (Klejn pers. comm.). (Nonetheless, Klejn still believes he was right.)

Chapter 6

The Resurrection of Perun

> The Slavenes 'believe that one of the gods, creator of the lightning, is the one ruler over everything, and sacrifice to him cattle and other sacrificial animals. They do not accept predestination, but . . . when they are threatened by death—in illness or war—swear, if they are spared, to sacrifice to the god in return for their lives. . . . They worship rivers, nymphs, and all kinds of gods, and to all of these they make sacrifices, and at the same time as they sacrifice they predict the future. (Procopius of Caesarea, *Wars* 14: 22–30)

As compared to the pagan mythologies of classical Greece and Rome, we know little about ancient Slavic mythology. Of course, in Russia more is known than in the West, but even in Russia more is known of Greek and Roman mythology than of Slavic. This is due 'chiefly to the way writing was introduced to the Slavic world. . . . Writing was, from the start, a tool of Christian enlightenment among the Slavs' (Yoffe and Krafczik 2003: 1). However, in Russia there has of late been great interest in Slavic mythology.

Historical Background

In 'The Resurrection of Perun: Reconstructing East Slavic Religion' (2004) Klejn surveys the historical background to research into Slavic mythology. Scholarly interest in the subject began in the Renaissance, when two Polish scholars of the fifteenth–sixteenth centuries, Dlugosch and Srtryjkovski 'relayed (in a somewhat confused and tangled way) certain data from the Russian chronicles, as well as mentioning what they themselves had heard in the East'.[1] In the seventeenth century other European travellers collected further evidence about pagan beliefs in Russia, but in Russia itself scholarly interest in Slavic paganism dates only to the time of Peter the Great in the eighteenth century. 'Initially, the confused notions of Western scholarship of the time were borrowed wholesale[2]—and still in the early nineteenth century Russian scholars based their approach on purely speculative

A Russian Perspective on Theoretical Archaeology: The Life and Work of Leo S. Klejn by Stephen Leach, 70–80

considerations. They produced long lists of gods culled from enigmatic words in proverbs and songs' (cf. A. S. Kaisarov and G. Glinka). 'They strove to present the religion of their ancestors in a positive and idealized manner, not only as preeminent among the other pagan religions but also as being close to Christianity' (cf. P. Stroev, M. Kastorsky, N. Kostomarov, S. M. Solovyev).[3]

From the mid-nineteenth century analogies were sought with the mythologies of other Indo-European peoples, including the Greeks and Romans. As Klejn explains:

> The entire pantheon began to be thought of as derived from the common matrix of the original Indo-European ethnos (Ur-Volk). In keeping with the solar-mythological school, the anthropomorphic deities were thought of as derived, via poetic allegory, from the worship of nature (see D. O. Shepping, A. N. Afanasyev[4]). In keeping with diffusionism, A. S. Famintsyn maintained the Slavophile tradition, while N. I. Kareev defended the secondary emergence of monotheism. The adherents of evolutionism, developed in the '70s and '80s of the nineteenth century, saw the images of gods as being derived from lower demonology—that is to say, from the belief in spirits (in Russia demonology was studied by N. F. Sumtsov).
>
> The evolutionist and diffusionist approaches were combined in the works of Lubor Niederle and A. N. Veselovsky. Both of them thought that the Slavs had not succeeded in developing a higher mythology and had remained at the level of demonology. Other scholars rejected the conclusions of the mythological school for a different reason. They stressed the shortage of available facts and were unconvinced as to the reliability of any of the offered hypotheses (W. Jagić, H. Machál, L. Leger, A. Kirpichnikov).
>
> In the works of scholars of the twentieth century (E. V. Anichkov, N. M. Galkovsky, V. J. Mansikka), this scepticism was overcome, and the analysis of sermons by orthodox preachers (against survivals of paganism) came to the fore. However, in following the preachers' vilification of the pagan practices, the scholars involuntarily inherited their bias as well. They continued to view paganism as a crude and primitive belief system. Anichkov, for instance, held that the Rus had an abundance of minor gods (or rather demons) but that the powerful major gods were borrowed from the Varangians. In this he followed S. Ruzhnetsky's interpretation of Perun as an imitation of Thor.
>
> In the twentieth century, the Polish scholars (H. Lowmiański, W. Szafrański, L. Moszyński) picked up a trend that emphasised the primacy of attributes of monotheism in Slavic paganism. Underlying this trend was the influence of Catholicism. For these scholars, Perun

> was not simply the main god but the only god, all others being only his incarnations.[5]

In the early years of the Soviet Union Slavic mythology was not much studied: 'although the obligatory Marxist vitriol was reserved mainly for the major ideological enemies, Christianity and Islam—the official militant atheism prevented the study of Slavic paganism for a long time. However, not long before the Great Patriotic War (World War II), interest in Slavic paganism was revived, owing to the regime's encouragement of patriotism. . . .'[6] This time interest was manifested not exclusively in historical records but in the records provided by ethnography and archaeology. This was partly due to the paucity of the historical record:

> Leaving aside conjectures, inferences from analogy, indirect considerations, and guess-work, and addressing only the original material, the sources, it appears that time and victorious Christianity have efficiently destroyed the Slavic pagan religion: the information we have on Perun seems very scarce and fragmentary. Memory of Perun seems to remain only in certain swear-words, in a couple of stories mentioned in the chronicles on erecting and overthrowing Perun's and other gods' idols in Kiev and Novgorod, as well as in oaths using the names of these gods in treaties with the Byzantines. The accusations levelled at the 'apostates' in sermons by early Christian preachers contained little specific information. Although similar names of pagan gods are known in some related Slavic languages, and although there is also some evidence on functions of these characters among several related peoples, this evidence concerns not so much their mythology as the rituals associated with it. The myths of Perun were not recorded.[7]

Through studies in ethnography and archaeology four new concepts of Slavic mythology emerged:

> The first concept was worked out by the official leaders of Soviet science, such as B. D. Grekov, N. S. Derzhavin, and B. A. Rybakov—all Members of the Academy of Sciences. According to their concept, the Eastern Slavs (living from the time immemorial on the same territories as at the present) had—some thousands of years B.C.—invented the plough-based agriculture, created the state, and developed a pagan religion that came very close to Christianity.
>
> The second concept was presented by the officially disgraced scholar, Professor Vladimir Propp. . . . Propp observed that Russian agricultural festivals, which are highly seasonal, demonstrate a stable

set of common features (due, he said, mainly to the similarity of peasant working conditions). Since these festivals were totally devoid of any developed gods, it was inferred that the underlying Russian paganism was also totally devoid of them and was of an especially archaic nature (cf. Anichkov, Niederle, and Veselovsky). Such figures as Kupalo, Yarilo, and the like were seen as 'underdeveloped deities'.

The influential works of Propp gave an additional impulse to the work of the old Russian ethnographer Dmitriy Zelenin, who had studied demonology via the retrospective method. His follower was Nikita Tolstoy, the grandson of Leo Tolstoy—a Member of the Academy of Sciences, he built up an influential school of ethnographers and ethnolinguists. So the third major concept of Slavic Paganism emerged, aimed at reconstructing the ancient pagan religion only from living ethnography. Naturally, the only light that could be thrown onto the past was that from living culture; hence the inference that there were no major gods. So the most prominent professional ethnographers, ethnolinguists, and folklorists accepted the idea that the ancient Slavs had only a lower mythology (a demonology).

The fourth concept was that of Vyacheslav Ivanov and Vladimir Toporov—also structuralists and (if for no other reason than this) regarded by the regime as frondeurs. They used the names of Slavic gods as their main source and compared them with other Indo-European personal and social names, and with myths. On this basis they began reconstructing a developed mythology derived from the common Indo-European substrate (the 'Basic Myth'—the initial struggle of Perun against Volos-Veles, etc.). Their methodology was to a great extent borrowed from Lévi-Strauss. This allowed them the freedom to make connections, but unfortunately what was gained in richness was lost in reliability. For instance, there is no direct proof of the struggle of Perun against Volos (and Volos, as distinct from Veles, is at any rate probably a new god, most likely having emerged from the transformation of the Christian Saint Vlasius/Blasius, Bulgarian Vlas).[8]

In 'The Resurrection of Perun' Klejn makes clear that he is critical, in varying degrees, of all four of these strands of scholarship. However, most of his criticisms are directed at the theories of B. A. Rybakov, for Rybakov's theories remain highly influential.

Boris Rybakov's theory is analysed in depth and criticised at length for this work has been and still is most influential, particularly outside the confines of the scholarly world. Rybakov's use of the material (entire categories of which he simply lacked the professional qualifications to process) was already outdated at the time and was often

> embarrassingly crude. The conclusions at which he arrived were not just unsound but often no less than comical. In spite of all this, however, one must give him his due, both for his enthusiasm for his subject and his considerable imagination.[9]

An English translation of Rybakov's book, *Early Centuries of Russian History*, was published in 1965: the present chapter may be seen as an overdue corrective to the part of that book that deals with Slavic mythology.[10]

Klejn explains Rybakov's current popularity:

> Recently his work has been taken up by modern neo-pagans—ever more noticeable, since the '70s, among the new religious movements. Inspired by nationalism, in the conditions of the general political and ideological decline of the Soviet regime, as well as the crisis of the Russian Orthodoxy, this movement has ignored virtually all real data on ancient pagan cults and rituals and begun to create new cults and rituals, formally combining elements borrowed from the Indian and Germanic practices in order to propagate such primordial cruelties as hatred of the aliens, militancy, isolationism, and xenophobic nationalist solidarity. Current Ecological concerns (centred on the respect for nature) are being hijacked by the new pagans and recruited into their complete disavowal of the principles and norms of civilization.
>
> For this reason the proper analysis of genuine East Slavic cults and mythology is especially important. It allows us to see clearly into the basement of the growing neo-pagan movements.[11]

Although in the present book there is much about Russian archaeology that will seem unfamiliar to non-Russians, in the preceding passage the reader, regardless of his or her background, will no doubt recognise familiar territory.

In the neo-pagans' basement the most closely guarded 'treasure' is the Book of Veles. The Book of Veles purports to be a document dating to pagan Slavic times, but academic consensus is that it is a modern forgery—even Rybakov agreed—yet many neo-pagans continue to hold it in reverence. According to Klejn:

> The debate on Slavic paganism was also revitalised by the lowering of standards for academic publications and by forgeries (like 'Veles Book') that had once seemed all but forgotten, but that again claimed attention. It was not by chance that 'Veles Book' appealed to the dilettante Nativists. It had long been their dream to find evidence for the richness and unique curiousness of ancient Russian mythology. But, it remains the case that there are no analogies in any other sources for 'Veles Book'.[12]

Scholars remain agreed that the Slavs had no writing system before the arrival of Christian missionaries in the late ninth century.

A New Source?

On a more positive note, Klejn claims to have discovered a new source for the analysis of Slavic paganism, Vainakh (Chechen-Ingush) folklore:

> In this folklore there is a character named Pir"on or Pirlon, whose name is phonetically close to the Slavic Perun. This Vainakh character was interpreted by folklorists as a derivate of a *Pharao* (genitive: *Pharaoni*). They suggested that Pir"on might be a Caucasian distortion of *pharaon-*).[13] In other words, Pir"on was interpreted as a derivative of the Biblical 'Pharoah'. However, his behaviour does not fit this role: he climbs up the heaven, thunders, and pours rain. In this respect, he is functionally equivalent to the Thunderer Perun. But how could he have entered Vainakh folklore? When Russians first came to the Caucasus, the inhabitants were already Christian, and Perun was absent from their mythology.
>
> The explanation is to be found in the eighth century, when the Arab caliph Mervan II led his troops from Syria to the North Caucasus. He penetrated deep into the Khazar Caganate, specifically into Slav territory (he approached the 'Sacalib river'); he there took some twenty thousand Slav prisoners, whom he settled in Kakheti, i.e., in the neighbourhood of Chechnya. It is from these prisoners that the myths of Perun were able to feed into the Vainakh tradition, where, having collided with the native Vainakh mythology, they lost their sacral character and 'sank' into folklore. Thus the stories of Perun (such as his commands to women to pour water from barrels, his association with bread and mills, his power over old men and children, etc.) find close correspondence in East Slavic ethnography (popular beliefs, superstitions, fairy tales).[14]

Until Klejn began to publish articles on this subject in 1985 Vainakh folklore had not previously been thought of as a source for Slav mythology. Klejn argues that it can be used in conjunction with Slavic fairy tales.

This is an approach that is quite different from Rybakov's. Klejn makes clear his objections to Rybakov's theories:

> Rybakov's approach denies the very possibility of borrowing the name Perun from the Slavs, because in his view the supreme god of Slavs was Rod, while Perun was introduced by Prince Vladimir[15] to serve as a god of his military retinue. Yet the presence of Perun's traces in

> all Slavic folklore (not just East Slavic) refutes such confinement. In fact, it is obvious that the early Slavs did not have any such deity as Rod—this was the artificial construct of some ancient Russian authors, based on a misreading of Greek Christian texts, the horoscopes known as 'genealogies' (literally, 'a study of kin or stock') to the Byzantines. The dependence on fate from the beginning of a man's life, from birth, was misunderstood by the translators as the worship of a special figure—*Rod* ('kin' in Russian, or, more precisely, a 'kingroup'). *Rod* is connected to the verb 'to give birth'. Hence its relation to *Rozhenitsas* (literally 'women in childbirth')—maids of fate, Slavic Parcas, present at a person's birth and important in determining his/her fate.[16]

Klejn argues that rather than Rod it was Perun who was

> not only the main god of Eastern Slavs but perhaps was for some time their only god, at least officially. In Russian chronicles there is, as Lowmiański has observed, some evidence that other gods mentioned in Vladimir's pantheon were late insertions by a Christian editor. It seems that Vladimir's first religious reform was an attempt to establish monotheism on a pagan basis. Archaeological monuments previously interpreted as proof of Vladimir's six-gods pantheon fail to withstand close scrutiny. Generally speaking, nearly all the main pagan sanctuaries ascribed to the Eastern Slavs (two in Kiev, one in Novgorod, and one in Pskov) are doubtful. In the present work they are investigated in great detail. Most likely, some of these 'sanctuaries' are secular (nonsacral) monuments, and some are burial sites.[17]

In *Paganism of the Ancient Rus* (1987), in support of his notion of a pantheon of gods united in the form of Rod, analogous to the Christian trinity—both united and divisible—Rybakov pointed to the Zbruch idol, a ninth-century tetrahedral stele named after the river Zbruch in Ukraine, where it was found. In Rybakov's view each of the four large figures, on each side of the stele, represented a Slavic god—and together they are united in the form of Rod. Klejn disputes every aspect of Rybakov's interpretation, including the idea that the monument is typically East Slavic: 'it is West Slavic in character, with some influence from the steppe nomads. Such idols are not unknown in the region of the basin of Dniestr. Both the West and South Slav tribes are known to have lived in that area, and it is also known that they underwent a comparatively late forced conversion to Christianity'.[18]

As to correlations between Vainakh folklore and East Slavic ethnography and folklore, Klejn points out a number of striking coincidences. In his view this correlative evidence is crucial. He argues that cross-referencing these sources allows considerable pieces of Slavic mythology to be reconstructed.

> In Vainakh folklore there are stories of women sent by Perun to heaven to pour water and make rain. These stories most likely express common Slavic notions of witches and sorceresses—the rain-makers, or the *Blitzhexes* ('witches of lightning') as they were called by the Germans. It was believed in nineteenth-century Ukraine that the witches could steal the rain from heaven and hold it in buckets. In Afanasyev's collection of tales there are witches who fly to heaven, where they then roll barrels. (Just as in the Chechen stories of Pir"on's women—the clang of these barrels creates thunderstorms.) In Russia, a related custom was to break barrels in order to call forth a shower of rain.[19]

As to what was originally in the broken barrels, as in Pushkin's tale of Tsar Saltan:

> In Russian fairy tales it was the unusual or specially blessed children that had been imprisoned there. Such children (often twins) were thought of as having been conceived by spirits of the other world. The barrel with the children was left adrift in the sea. Upon landing, the wonderful children would break out of the barrel, to freedom—where a great future awaited them. This motif was frequently used as a legal device by pretenders to the highest office, in order to create a tie to a traditional royal dynasty (Sargon, Perseus).
>
> A similar idea lay behind the custom of the witch trial by drowning (if she was really a witch, she would not drown). It was probably the presence of 'god's children' that eventually led to the substitution of drowning by exile. It is also worth mentioning that the worn-out sacral objects were floated in the river. The women marked by god were believed to have drowned or to have been driven away along the waterways. They were those who became mermaids (in Russian, *rusalki*).
>
> Mermaids in the nineteenth century peasant Russia were understood as, originally, drowned women or children who died before christening. They were believed to have caused offence, not having lived the full term granted to them by god. Therefore, they might be evil-doers, but on occasion some help could be coaxed from them as well, since these characters were often recently deceased relatives or neighbours. They were believed to have power over the weather (calling forth the rain) and were linked to the oak, Perun's tree. In the custom of 'sending off (or driving) the *rusalka* away' there is an echo of human sacrifice: a witch or some other woman was sent to the god as an advocate for her home-folks.
>
> Some other characters were sent off, too: in the early spring (on Shrovetide, in Russian, *Maslenitsa*) Maslenitsa was sent; in the Midsummer (on the summer solstice, or St. John the Baptist's day,

> in Russian Ivan Krestitel's day, or *Kupalo*) Ivan Kupalo was thrown into the river; among the Southern Slavs, Mara, or Marena, was seen off. As observed by Vladimir Propp, the similarity of the major ritual components of these festivals, across the entire area of their distribution, is most striking. However, his contention that it may be explained by the similarity of peasant working conditions is unlikely: indeed, the seasons across this vast area are quite different.
>
> It is more convincing to explain the unity of the ritual components by homology—by common origin. The custom of erecting a fire-wheel on a pole and then rolling it downhill may be connected to the magical descent of the sun from the highest point on the ecliptic, that is, to the St. John the Baptist's day, rather than to the spring sun that is still rising to its highest point. Yet, in fact, this ritual is seen in the Shrovetide, in the spring. However, the St. John the Baptist's feast preserved in the Ukraine and Belorussia had disappeared from Russia proper, where it was ousted by the Christian fast.[20]

Klejn suggests that Shrovetide 'Maslenitsa' is not an ancient pagan festival but is rather a day of summer pagan rites transferred to a new date, under the pressure of Christian fasts and feasts.

Another important festival, Kupalo, was held at the summer solstice on June 24:

> The Kupalo festival is characterized by elements of the Perun worship and intense sexuality. The term *Kupalo* is not a proper personal name but a kind of sobriquet, designating the main action. It is derived not from the word *kupati* ('to bathe') but is cognate to the words *kupa* ('pile'), *sovokuplenie* ('coitus').
>
> Still more erotic features are present in *Yarilki*, 'Yarilo's send-off', another sexual term, this time from *yariti* ('to become excited', 'to get hot', 'to be filled with lust'). This festival also appears to have been moved from the same spot on the calendar and consists of customs from the same original complex. Ithyphallic Yarilo is another manifestation of Perun (connected with his sexual, marriage-making functions).
>
> Thus, under the more modern forms described by travellers, later ethnographers, and students of folklore, one may discern the earlier content of the Kupalo's festival, Perun's send-off, which marked his downfall and death. This festival coincides in its original place on the calendar with the summer solstice. It is very likely that the old chronicler's description of Perun's overthrow (the beating of the idol by twelve men, the keening by others, and the final floating his statue down the river) was, in fact, misunderstood by the chronicler. It was

> actually a description of the regular ritual of Perun's send-off on the day of the summer solstice.[21]

And if there is a festival marking Perun's departure, then one would expect there to be a festival marking Perun's return:

> Indeed, at the opposite end of the calendar, at the winter solstice, there is more than a week of completely pagan celebrations—Svyatki (modern New Year's feast). Among the Southern Slavs this holiday is marked by the veneration of an oak log called Badnyak, to which the attributes of an anthropomorphic deity, an old man, are ascribed. Simultaneously, during the ceremony, a young Bozhić appears (a patronymic from *Bog*, 'god'), that is, the son of god. At the same time, Russian peasants performed mummery. Among these performances, the 'plays with umrun' are especially remarkable. *Umrun* is a dead man (from the Russian *umirat,* 'to die'). The dead imitated by a mummer was supposedly resurrected by sheer sexual acts. Among these were masturbation and fellatio, which the girls of the village were forced to perform. This method of resurrection was connected to a belief in the beneficial properties of male semen. The idea of reviving the dead was akin to the ancient Indo-European idea of sansara (the second life on earth, the movement of souls).[22]

In summary, Klejn argues that the main feasts devoted to Perun were his funeral and resurrection, Kupalo and Svyatki. He argues that Perun is comparable not only to Thor or to Zeus but to Apollo, who dies and is resurrected: 'typologically, Perun appears to belong to the well-known class of the dying and resurrecting gods. In accordance with the cycle of his festivals, the year among the Eastern Slavs was divided into halves (as among the Greeks, where the year was divided into apodemy and epidemy by the celebrations of Apollo's appearance and send-off)'.[23] He suggests that Perun's attributes of strength and belligerence, his association with the oak, the hammer and arrows, and his influence on fertility are all characteristics that are at the core of Perun's character and may be very ancient indeed: they may well be the characteristics of an Indo-European thunder god.

Rybakov, not wishing to admit that Russian history was greatly affected by the coming of Christianity, argued that the Christian missionaries who came to preach to the Slavs

> did not create anything that was new in principle; they only brought new names for the old gods, a somewhat different ritual and a considerably more finished idea of the divine origins of state power whose representatives must be submitted to without question. But the outlook

> of the missionaries was not different from the outlook of the pagan priests, magicians, and sorcerers. (Rybakov 1965: 53)

Klejn does not go along with this, but his book on Perun concludes with this speculation:

> The presence of a dying and resurrecting deity and its supremacy in the ancient Slavic pantheon might have provided the decisive influence in the future 'choice of faiths'. Prince Vladimir favoured Christianity, and the pagan Slavs were relatively swift converts to the new religion—for their faith in Perun, the dying and resurrecting deity, had already prepared them to accept the main mystery of Christianity.[24]

The stress on purely native development emphasised by Rybakov—which lends his theories their continued (emotive) appeal—is a feature that reappears in different contexts in the next chapter.[25]

Chapter 7

Ethnogenesis

Gustaf Kossinna: Archaeology in the Saddle

As is well-known, Gustaf Kossinna (1858–1931) believed that there are laws of culture that mirror the laws of biology, that the boundaries of material culture coincide with ethnic boundaries, and that archaeology is a legitimate means by which to settle territorial disputes. These views—'contradictory, odious, and tempting' (Klejn 2008b: 236)—presented an obvious attraction to the Nazis. Less well-known is that Kossinna's ideas had enormous influence in the post-war Soviet Union. As Klejn explains:

> Like the Soviet archaeologists of the time [the 1950s and 1960s], Kossinna was not only a migrationist, he was an autochthonist in respect of his Germans and a migrationist otherwise. Soviet archaeologists did the same, only for them Slavs or their predecessors took the place of Germans. Childe was accepted in the USSR essentially alongside Kossinna, as his associate. Kossinna, however, entered covertly. We shunned referring to him: he had to be execrated. Childe, though, was accepted legitimately. (Klejn 2012: 165)

Against this background—and given his own interest in problems of ethnogenesis (at both a particular and a general level)—Klejn's interest in Kossinna is unsurprising.

Klejn maintains that despite Kossinna's association with Nazi ideology, there is nonetheless a question raised by Kossinna that must be faced, namely: what is the relation between an archaeological culture and an ethnos? (Klejn finds nothing unusual about the fact that Kossinna raised an interesting question, even though his ideas were completely erroneous. Similarly Schliemann almost inadvertently opened up the investigation of Mycenaean civilisation, although his ideas about the literal truth of the *Iliad* were—according to Klejn—completely wrong.) To be clear, Klejn completely parts company with Kossinna (and with many Russian archaeologists) over the answer to this

A Russian Perspective on Theoretical Archaeology: The Life and Work of Leo S. Klejn by Stephen Leach, 81–94

question—for Klejn the binding idea of an ethnos is *the idea* of a common origin—but he appreciates the value of the question.

Klejn's first article on Kossinna was published in German (in East Germany) in 1974 under the title of 'Kossinna from the Distance of 40 years'.[1] In 2004 he revised it and published it in Russian, under the title 'Archaeology in the Saddle: Gustav Kossinna at a Distance of 70 Years'.[2]

In the following paragraphs he explains something of the background to the article, including the reason for article's title and the reason that the paper was first published in East Germany rather than the Soviet Union.

> The Russian title of the work alludes to Kossinna's maxim: 'Let us help prehistory into the saddle, and it will race itself'. Prehistoric archaeology was to him something like an ancient German crusader knight—armoured, armed, and eager for the saddle—ready to ride out and conquer distant lands. For nearly half a century his words were a slogan. Kossinna's ideas presaged Nazi ideology in Germany . . . he introduced the mapping method of matching an archaeological culture with an ethnos, thus allowing archaeology to participate in the solution of ethnogenic problems. For a long time our (Russian) archaeology saw this as its main task.
>
> In our country and in the rest of the world, Kossinna was seen as a migrationist, while in Germany he was seen as just the reverse, an autochthonist. Indeed, he envisaged all European migrations as having originated from within Germany, while in Germany itself only autochthonous (local and independent) development was envisaged.
>
> This theme was, at the time of writing (and since), of great relevance to Soviet archaeology. In the '70s Soviet archaeology had only just broken from obligatory autochthonism and begun reconstructing migrations. Kossinna, with his aggressive raids from Germany, was still as much of a bugaboo as ever, but it was necessary to study him objectively and to accept his attainments. On the other hand, our archaeologists (including such authoritative figures such as Bryusov) had used Kossinna's methods to construct our own migrationism, only in the opposite direction into Europe from the steppes.
>
> The author's [Klejn's] involvement with these questions in fact predates the article on Kossinna and can be dated from an article criticising the ideas of Aleksandr Yakovlevish Bryusov, who from 1961 renovated Kossinna's migrationism/authochthonism, but turned it into the opposite direction—arguing that migrations have to issue from our country. The author [Klejn] wrote a sharply critical article against migrationist constructions of A. Ya. Bryusov, focusing upon the Pit-grave and Catacomb-grave cultures that play a central role in Bryusov's fantastic travels, from the steppes into Central Europe.

It was impossible to publish this critical article, despite the support of Artamonov and Mavrodin. Bryusov, who worked in the '60s as the deputy editor of *Soviet Archaeology*, was one of pillars of Soviet archaeology and was responsible for one of its theoretical fundamentals, namely, that there is a straightforward equivalence between archaeological culture and ethnos. The veneration of Bryusov and the respect for his doctrine continued after his death, in 1966.

The author then decided to direct his criticism at the doctrine underlying Bryusov's ideas, this being fully accessible to criticism in the Soviet Union. This was one of the methods of avoiding censorship and the demands of political ideology. In criticising Kossinna the author was in fact aiming at the dominant Moscow school of politically engaged archaeology. But to publish such an article in the Soviet press was again practically impossible.

And in Germany? German archaeologists generally avoided talking about Kossinna: they were afraid, so, in Germany too, nothing was published on Kossinna. Kossinna was intimately connected with the Kaiser's Germany—he died two years before Hitler's 'nationalist revolution' of 1933. After World War II his ideas were left as it were in a vacuum between the two Germanies—the democratic BRD and the (ostensibly) socialist DDR.

In the BRD Kossinna seemed too close to the disgraceful past—from which Denazification had divorced the people. After Denazification no archaeologist dared to subject Kossinna's doctrine to a thorough analysis. The only evaluation possible was a blanket negative judgement. However, many understood that this silencing was artificial. The West-German archaeologist Günter Smolla coined the term 'Kossinna syndrome' for this situation. Moreover, as the author [Klejn] noted, in Western Germany Schuchhardt's disciples appeared more numerous than Kossinna's. Therefore everyone preferred not to touch Kossinna, to forget him. Archaeologists dealing with the same themes as Kossinna (Wahle, Eggers, Hachmann) criticised his positions and methods in their particular works but did not devote any work specifically to him.

In the DDR no archaeologist within this autocratic country dared to write an article in which the Kossinna phenomenon would be analysed from all sides and in which not only his faults would be noted but also his valuable contributions. In the DDR he was estimated more critically and with hostility than in the Soviet Union (the DDR was then the vanguard bulwark of the Communist camp). It was in this context that a long article from a young Soviet archaeologist [Klejn] (politically from an 'elder brother') was received with pleasure. The article criticised Kossinna but stopped short of painting him as the devil incarnate.[3]

In refusing to paint Kossinna as 'the devil incarnate' Klejn was clearly breaking with tradition. The depiction of Kossinna as a bogeyman and the refusal to assess his work objectively represent a phenomenon that has, as Klejn says, been termed the 'Kossinna Syndrome' (Smolla 1979/1980). The Kossinna Syndrome was accompanied by a suspicion of theoretical archaeology *per se*, and this tradition broke up only very slowly. In 1995 Bettina Arnold and Henning Hassmann described the relationship of contemporary archaeologists with Kossinna:

> There is a continuing tendency to set Kossinna up as a sort of straw man, whose scholarly work is presented as the primary basis of later archaeological research under the Nazis. This approach is flawed for two reasons. First, it lumps all of Kossinna's work into an indistinguishable negative and ideologically tainted mass while ignoring his potentially valuable theoretical contributions. Second, it minimises the contributions, both positive and negative, made by German archaeologists working after Kossinna's death. Until this aspect of the Faustian bargain has been confronted, the 'Kossinna Syndrome' will continue to act as an obstacle to the development of a theoretical debate in German archaeology. (Arnold and Hassmann 1995: 72)

There are those who would argue that suspicion of theoretical archaeology in Germany has, with some modification, continued to the present day; however, when Klejn published his article on Kossinna in 1974 the situation was much worse.

> 'Kossinna at a Distance of 40 Years' (1974) broke from the tendency of over-oversimplification and as such was met with hostility by Kossinna's followers (Korell 1975) but with approval from those pupils whose positions had moved from Kossinna's—pupils such as Ernst Wahle and Herbert Jankuhn (personal letters; cf. in Klejn 2000, 2006). 'Kossinna at a Distance of 40 Years' inspired analogous, though less detailed, articles by Western German archaeologists, including 'Kossinna after 50 Years' by G. Smolla (1984); Ulrich Feit (1984, 2000 a. o.). Thirty years after the German publication the author [Klejn] published an expanded Russian version of the work, under the title 'Kossinna at a Distance of 70 Years'; but, again, this was not published in Russia. . . .
>
> It remains to explain what is new in this article. For certainly criticisms had been made of Kossinna before. The author presents Kossinna's ideas in a systematic form. This had not been done previously. Kossinna himself threw into the discipline now one idea then another, without unity or integration. Correspondingly, critics have plucked at one or other vulnerable places without surveying and criticising the doctrine as a whole.

> The author has brought the views of Kossinna together into a logical system—something that was not done by either Kossinna himself or any of his disciples. The author has traced the run of Kossinna views and then presented his ideas as thirteen dogmas of certain thematic blocks, united by certain philosophical and methodological principles. Kossinna's dogmas follow from these principles.
>
> One group of dogmas concern ethnic history—the origins of peoples and language families (the ethnic treatment of archaeological cultures, cultural heredity and typological relations/migrations, the treatment of culture distribution, the ethnic attribution of 'types', and the matching of peoples with races). Another group concerns the use of research results (appeal to 'historical right', the selection of archaeological precedents as justification for modern plans of aggression and the doctrine of primogeniture). A third group concerns active forces of social development (the declaration of the Kulturträger mission of the Germans, the principle of imposing the past onto the present, biological determinism, and the principle of eliciting of ideals and direct lessons from archaeology).
>
> It is this system that the author [Klejn] criticises, while simultaneously revealing within it some positive aspects—that lend it vitality under certain social conditions.
>
> In the last part of the article the arguments of Kossinna's critics are presented, and the development of this criticism is traced—from the first critics (the venerable German scholars of the early twentieth century) and Polish adversaries of Kossinna to West-European opponents, Soviet Marxists, and West German sceptics.
>
> The author maintains that, despite its dilettantism and subjectivity, Kossinna's work should be seen as a classic of German prehistoric archaeology. He opened in prehistoric archaeology an entirely new field of ethnogenetic research, founded a school, and introduced some methods that entered the practice of research even of his enemies. He was a classic figure of the early twentieth century, and in particular of the sociohistorical environment of Germany in the era of the two World Wars (both initiated by Germany).
>
> Thus, in the article, a full and thorough analysis of Kossinnism, and the problems it poses, is presented. The work will long be valuable to anyone who wishes to know more about Kossinnism—to understand it better, including both its faults and its grains of sense.[4]

When I asked Klejn to define the 'grain of sense' in Kossinna, he replied that 'his greatest contribution to archaeology lies not in his "solutions" but in having posed the problem of ethnicity. Before him archaeology was tribeless. After Kossinna, archaeologists began to draw ethnic maps of the past. These may have been wrong but the problem of ethnicity remains. Furthermore, he directed the attention of archaeologists toward the problem of migrations from central Europe. This remains a promising focus of attention with respect to the origin of Indo-Europeans' (Leach 2011). Klejn makes a similar point in an encyclopaedia article on Kossinna: 'The ethnic determination of cultures, the possibility of genetic connections with cultures, culture-genesis (the origin of a certain culture), the connection of culture-genesis with the origin of peoples and their languages—all these questions were brought to archaeology by Kossinna' (Klejn 2008b: 327).

In summary, there is an overlap between Klejn's own beliefs concerning ethnicity and those of most Western archaeologists. Klejn would agree with Florin Curta's well-expressed statement of this (essentially instrumentalist) position: 'Today, ethnicity is used to refer to a decision people make to depict themselves or others symbolically as bearers of a certain cultural identity. It has become the politicization of culture. Ethnicity is not innate, but individuals are born with it; it is not biologically reproduced, but individuals are linked to it through cultural constructions of biology; it is not simply cultural difference, but ethnicity cannot be sustained without reference to an inventory of cultural traits' (Curta 2001: 14–15).

Klejn and Western archaeologists would likewise agree that ethnicity is centred on the idea of a common origin, an idea that is emphasised at times of social and political stress or conflict. That is not to say that Klejn has been influenced by Western archaeologists on this question; rather, on ethnicity and ethnogenesis Klejn and Western archaeologists have moved along roughly parallel tracks. However, where Klejn differs from most of his Western colleagues, and indeed from most people who criticise Kossinna, is that he is interested in analysing Kossinna's work in detail. Most of those who criticise Kossinna do not know his work well enough to cite it, but this does not apply to Klejn, who is interested in pointing out areas of common ground between Kossinna and, for example, Childe[5] and Montelius, figures who have far higher reputations than Kossinna. Furthermore, Klejn argues that Childe and Bryusov were actually influenced by Kossinna.

Klejn's interest was in part provoked by the influence of Kossinna in the Soviet Union, for after the fall of Marr's stadialist theories:

> Paradoxically, the Soviet approach to ethnicity could best be defined as primordialistic, despite its admixture of Marxist-Leninist theory. By claiming that ethnicities, once formed through ethnogenesis, remained essentially unchanged through history, Soviet anthropologists suggested that ethnic groups were formed in a social and political vacuum. According to them, ethnicity was thus a given, requiring description, not explanation. (Curta 2001: 17)

Although Klejn shuns this approach completely, he is keen that in the vehemence of our rejection of ethnicity as a biological given we should not accept a view of Kossinna—and of 'progress'—that is overly simplistic.

Of course, Klejn is by no means the only contemporary archaeologist to have written about Kossinna—Heinrich Härke, for example, is another well-respected archaeologist who has written about him—but Klejn was a pioneer in this area.

In the next section we turn to Klejn's own direct interest in problems of Indo-European origins.

The Proto-Indo-European Homeland

Klejn is known as an archaeological theorist, although as previously mentioned knowledge of his work in this area has in the West until now remained vague; but Klejn has also pursued various archaeological interests in the field. His fieldwork has resulted in published articles on zoomorphic sceptres from the Russian and Ukrainian steppes of the Eneolithic (Copper Age), on dice found in the barrows of the steppes, on the Karbuna hoard in Moldova, on the Neolithic Cucuteni-Tripolye culture, and on a Phrygian migration into India. However, the most contentious question that he has investigated has been the origins of the Indo-European languages.

The debate over the place and date of the Proto-Indo-European language dates back to the late eighteenth century. Already in classical times similarities between Greek and Latin had been noticed—at that time they were attributed to the direct influence of Greek—but in the late eighteenth century it was noticed that there were also similarities, in structure and in lexicon, between Greek and Latin and Sanskrit; and this gave rise to the idea of an ancestor language. It is now believed that an ancestor language lies behind all the Indo-European language groups, ranging geographically from India to Ireland: Celtic, Italic, Germanic, Baltic, Slavic, Albanian, Greek, Armenian, Anatolian, Iranian, Indo-Aryan, and Tocharian.

We now know, from similarities between the daughter languages, that the speakers of Proto-Indo-European were farmers (of sheep, cattle, and crops); that they ate honey and were pestered by lice; and that they lived in a hierarchical society that experienced warfare. But we do not know much more that is not open to dispute. There is, for instance, still no agreement on the date and the homeland of the speakers of Proto-Indo-European. It is on these two related questions that the debate has concentrated.

One problem is that similarities between languages do not of course invariably indicate a common ancestor. Another is that words change their meanings, and so there is some risk in using them as evidence of a place of origin. As to dating, there is disagreement as to what extent we can rely on a principle of uniform change. And, as to help from archaeology, archaeologists cannot detect linguistic continuity; they can usually detect only cultural continuity—and this does not necessarily coincide with linguistic continuity. The obstacles to a solution are daunting, but the lure of the problem remains great. In a recent book *The Horse, the Wheel, and Language* (2007) David Anthony acknowledges the contentious nature of the subject:

> The Indo-European homeland is like the Lost Dutchman's Mine, a legend of the American West, discovered almost everywhere but confirmed nowhere. Anyone who claims to know its *real* location is thought to be just a little odd—or worse. Indo-European homelands have been identified in India, Pakistan, the Himalayas, the Altai Mountains, Kazakhstan, Russia, Ukraine, the Balkans, Turkey, Armenia, the North Caucasus, Syria/Lebanon, Germany, Scandinavia, the North Pole, and (of course) Atlantis. Some homelands seem to have been advanced just to provide a historical precedent for nationalist or racist claims to privileges and territory. Others are enthusiastically zany. The debate, alternately dryly academic, comically absurd, and brutally political, has continued for almost two hundred years. (Anthony 2007: 83)

As with Slavic mythology, the question of the location of a Proto-Indo-European homeland is one that has been warped by considerable political and emotional investment with the result that the issue of migration versus autochthonous development has become particularly sensitive:

> The brutally political aspects of the debate have involved the identification of linguistic differences with differences in material culture (archaeological categories) and ethnos. However, these different categories cannot be straightforwardly identified. The abuses which arose from the unjustified conflation of linguistic and archaeological evidence led to a reaction in the West, whereby: migration disappeared entirely from the explanatory toolkit of Western archaeologists in the 1970s and 1980s. (Ibid.: 17)

In recent debates Westerners have, according to Klejn, tended to be too wary of migration, whereas Easterners have tended to be too enthusiastic. Among Russian archaeologists Klejn counts himself as one of the more wary toward migration as an explanatory factor. However, he does not believe that migration can be discounted entirely.

1. The Catacomb-grave Culture

Klejn's original interest in the Proto-Indo-European debate was stimulated by his teacher Artamonov, and he has been writing about various aspects of the Indo-European problem since 1962. Between 1968 and 1973 he led a number of expeditions to the steppes of Ukraine and the lands beside the river Don. More specifically he investigated a number of sites of the Catacomb-grave culture in the vicinity of the river Donets, a tributary of the Don. (It may be remembered that in 1968 Klejn defended his Candidate dissertation on 'The Origin of the Donets Catacomb-Grave Culture'.) On later expeditions to this region Klejn was in charge of student training. These expeditions had a bearing on the Proto-Indo-European debate in that for part of its course the river Donets crosses the Pontic-Caspian steppes—the very area that has been postulated by Gordon Childe, Maria Gimbutas, J. M. Mallory, and D. W. Anthony as the Proto-Indo-European homeland. This approach is known as the Kurgan Hypothesis. According to this hypothesis the Proto-Indo-European homeland can be traced to the steppes between 4,500 and 2,500 B.C.E. The members of the Catacomb-grave culture (2,800–2,200 B.C.E.) would, according to this theory, have been close in time and space to the speakers of Proto-Indo-European, and this proximity would have been reflected in their language.

It has recently been claimed, in an article published in *Nature* (March 2015) by W. Haak, I. Lazaridis, and associates, that genetic evidence provides convincing support for the Kurgan Hypothesis. Klejn welcomes the authors' new evidence, but, although he admits that it changes the weight on the scales, there are a few flaws and weaknesses in the argument. Because the article ('Massive Migration from the Steppes Was a Source for Indo-European Languages') caused something of a splash it may be worth mentioning a few of Klejn's criticisms. It is assumed that a language invariably coincides and moves with a population, but this is not so. A Yamnaya invasion of central Europe is proposed on the assumption that material culture and population movement invariably coincide, but this assumption is unjustified. The authors allege a similarity between the Yamnaya culture and the Corded Ware culture, but the Corded Ware culture is in fact more similar to the Funnel Beaker culture. And, unfortunately, the DNA of Funnel Beaker people was not analysed (Klejn, pers. comm.).[6]

The steppes are not the only candidate—the Caucasus and Asia Minor have also been proposed as the Proto-Indo-European homeland[7]—but it is perhaps the most popular. A principle often used in these discussions is that of a constant rate of linguistic change: Renfrew and Anthony, in particular, have made use of this principle. However, Klejn is one of many scholars, in the East and in the West, who are wary of it. As he explains:

> There are two ways of solving the Indo-European problem. The first is to determine by glottochronology the dating of the coming of the Proto-Indo-European language, and then, issuing from the core vocabulary reconstruction of this language, to select fitting realia among archaeological cultures of a corresponding time. The second way is to move from real IE languages, that are most early attested in the

> written records. Then, having united kindred languages, to find ancestor cultures for these particular families (Indo-Iranian, Armeno-Greek, Anatolian, etc.), then to determine similarities of bigger communities (say, Greek-Aryan), etc.—and at last to reach the IE proto-language. . . . Anthony prefers the first way to the IE proto-language, while I the second. (Klejn 2008c: 468–69)

Furthermore, Klejn argues that members of the North-Pontic Catacomb cultures ('or at least one of them' [Ibid.: 472]), in the third millennium B.C.E., were not Indo-Europeans but Indo-Aryans—that is, they had already split away from the main Indo-European stem. He reached this conclusion after comparison with the *Rig Veda* and with the early cultures of India.

> Indeed the Catacomb-grave people have spots of red ochre on skeletons, similar to the modern Indian custom (feet, hands, and forehead); there are finds of dice sets in the graves of the Catacomb culture; the reconstructed dice game (according to these sets) are known among the Indo-Aryans; the principle of interment is the same (uniting with the earth in contrast to the Iranian separation from the earth). In the intermediate Catacomb-graves of Central Asia there are Aryan hearths (round, four-part, and serpent) and swastikas made out of stones. Besides, the word *vajra* of the Indo-Aryans was borrowed by Western Finno-Ugrian languages (northern neighbours of Catacomb cultures) and has given to them the words *vecher* and the like with meanings of 'axe' in some instances and in other languages 'hammer'; this fits with the Catacomb stone battle axe. Only in Catacomb-graves has the Indo-Aryan ritual of Sahamarana (common dying) been discovered in large scale. There is also a movement of Catacomb people into the Near East in the appropriate centuries. (Ibid.: 472–73)[8]

In other words, the Indo-Aryans lived west of Iran, and their ancestors lived east of Iran on the Russian and Ukrainian steppes. This theory has since been accepted by many Russian and Ukrainian archaeologists. It implies that the Indo-Aryan and Iranian language groups existed as separate entities at a date much earlier than—in the West—has previously been thought. Furthermore: 'If the Catacomb societies spoke Indo-Aryan (separated from Iranian), then the Indo-Iranian community is put back to the Pit-grave [or Yamnaya] culture [3,600–2,300 B.C.E.]; this is the traditional view in Russia, and the splitting of Proto-Indo-European is drawn back still earlier' (Ibid.: 473).

This theory is contrary to that of such scholars as Ernst Wahle, Marija Gimbutas, James Mallory, and David Anthony, who have thought of the members of the Pit-grave culture as speakers of the Proto-Indo-European language. Klejn thinks of the Pit-grave community as mainly Aryan (Ibid.: 474).

2. Proto-Hittites

Klejn prefers to locate the Proto-Indo-European homeland as not on the Steppes in the Bronze Age but rather in Northern Central Europe in the Neolithic. He finds clues to this in the origins of the Hittites.

It is generally agreed that the Hittites become identifiable as a distinct culture in Anatolia at some point before 2,000 B.C.E., but there is less agreement as to their origins. Klejn, too, agrees that the Hittites arrived in Asia Minor in the early centuries of the third millennium B.C.E., bringing with them the Anatolian branch of the Indo-European languages. But he also argues, more controversially—against those who argue that the Hittites came from the Pontic steppes—that the central European Baden culture of the fourth millennium B.C.E. was a proto-Hittite culture and that both the Baden culture and the Pit-grave (Yamnaya culture) may have developed from the Funnel beaker culture.

The significance of this argument is that given the general agreement that by the first half of the second millennium B.C.E. the Indo-European languages were already dispersed and autonomous, and given agreement that the Hittites were one of the first groups to break away from the main Indo-European stem, the direction from which the Hittites came might well indicate the location of the Proto-Indo-European homeland. Klejn expounds this theory in *The Time of the Centaurs* (2010).[9]

Klejn notes that the modern problem of communication across different languages continues to blight the discussion of ancient languages. He argues that no Western scholar has yet got fully to grips with the Russian and Ukrainian literature on the subject.

The investigation of a possible Proto-Indo-European homeland is a field in which Klejn's background in both philology and archaeology is an obvious advantage. However, he is careful to study the linguistic evidence separately from the archaeological evidence. He believes that if the evidence of linguistics and the evidence of archaeology are kept distinct they can then be used as a check on each other. (It was a misconception of their relationship that underlay Kossinna's mistakes.)

In Klejn's view it is the linguistic evidence that, so to speak, makes the running; but archaeological evidence can nonetheless provide a useful check. (It is on the ground of archaeological evidence that Klejn discounts Renfrew's theory of an Anatolian homeland of the Indo-European peoples. 'My objection to Renfrew rests on the unreality of the Indo-European peoples migrations from Anatolia—there are no such archaeological cultures' [Klejn 2008c: 468.])

He acknowledges the difficulties in finding clear evidence for migration in the archaeological record, but he does not think it is impossible—long-distance migration being perhaps more easily detected than migration over short distances.[10] Moreover, in long-distance migrations language and culture are more likely to coincide.

Although Klejn is critical of his Western colleagues' ignorance of Russian literature on these subjects, he admires the ambition of scholars such as Anthony, Mallory, and Renfrew and the scope of their books. In 2013 he wrote of Anthony's book: 'We still do not have such a survey in Russian. We are idle and insufficiently bold or (it can also be said) too careful' (Klejn 2008c: 467).

Yet, now, as I write these words, Klejn himself is writing just such a book. It is based on papers that he read in 2006–2007 at the School of Indo-European studies under the aegis of the Institute of Linguistic Research (Russian Academy of Sciences, St. Petersburg). It also includes, in passing, a discussion of the relationship between archaeology and linguistics. The book is to be entitled *The Ancient Migrations of Indo-European Peoples*. (Against Klejn's will, an early draft of this book was put onto the Internet in 2007.)

The Varangian Controversy

Klejn points out that

> in some discussions of ethnicity, perhaps in reaction to Kossinna, the criteria by which to substantiate migrations were such that it would seem impossible to give persuasive evidence that any migration had ever occurred. The problem was compounded in the Soviet Union by a politically motivated mistrust of anything but local origins. In particular, Marr was influential as an advocate of autochthonous development. Questions about ethnicity were in fact, for Marr, quite unimportant. . . . This 'localism' was at its height in the Soviet Union in the '30s, '40s, and early '50s. (Leach 2011)

Things did not greatly improve in the 1950s, it was simply that then, in the 1950s and 1960s, Russian archaeologists tended to remain autochthonists with respect to the Slavs and migrationists otherwise. The idea that, for example, Viking immigration played any significant role in Russian history remained as controversial as ever.

Klejn examines attitudes about the Vikings among Russian historians and archaeologists in *The Varangian Controversy: The Arguments and the History of the Controversy*. Klejn wrote this book in 1960, but it was published (in a revised form) only in 2009. The book

> traces a long-running dispute on the ethnicity of the Varangians (the Eastern synonym for Vikings or Norsemen) and the significance of their role in history of Ancient Russia. . . . Three major debates on the subject are described and analysed. The first occurred in the third quarter of the eighteenth century and took place between Lomonsov and Miller; the second took place in the third quarter of the nineteenth

> century [1860] and took place between Kostomarov and Pogodin; and the third took place in 1965, between Shaskolsky and Klejn.[11]

All three debates occurred in St. Petersburg: the first in the Academy of Sciences, the rest at the university.

In the first debate Lomonsov argued that the Varangians were not actually Vikings at all but, rather, western Slavs. Lomonsov was motivated by patriotism and by the fact that the opposing faction was led by a German, Miller (Müller).

> These Germans and their supporters came to be called the 'Normanists', and their opponents the 'anti-Normanists'. Pogodin, who defended Normanist views a century later was Russian, but a conservative, while Kostomarov was more democratically inclined. The argument turned into a confrontation between the supporters of the regime, who upheld the European origin of the upper classes, and the opponents of any such elevation. (Klejn 2012: 115)

Although Vikings and Normans had conquered lands in both Russia and Western Europe (in England and France) 'only in the East was there a tendency to deny these facts' (Ibid.). It was against this background that in the early 1960s Klejn organised the Slavic-Varangian seminar at Leningrad University.

> Many prominent researchers of the problem were nurtured at this seminary. The seminar existed in a very sensitive and dangerous atmosphere since the political ideologists of the Soviet regime considered Normanism to be anti-patriotic and anti-Marxist. In his book and in the Dispute the author and his pupils not only interpreted a large number of facts but also defended themselves against ideological and political charges. They developed methods of maintaining the independence of the science even under conditions of totalitarian duress. (Ibid.)

As was mentioned in Chapter 1, it was Klejn's work in leading this seminar—'a so-called Klejn seminar in which the Varangian problem was more or less freely discussed' (Klejn 1998: 31)—that led to a public debate with the anti-Normanist Igor Shaskolsky (the third big debate described in *The Varangian Controversy*). At the time of the debate Shaskolsky had recently published a book entitled *The Normanist Theory in Contemporary Middle Class Science*. The sensitive nature of the subject matter may be judged from the fact that in 1960, the same year in which Klejn wrote *The Varangian Controversy*, Andrei Amalrik, the future author of *Involuntary Journey to Siberia*, was expelled from Moscow University for having written a dissertation in which he claimed that Viking traders had had a significant influence on the course of early Russian history.

Klejn notes in *Soviet Archaeology* (2012b) that although by the mid-1990s it seemed that Russia had seen the last of the anti-Normanism, in the twenty-first century it has revived—presenting its case with jingoistic rhetoric and establishing a power base at the Institute of Russian History (Klejn 2012: 119). A dangerous new development occurred on May 15, 2009, when

> the President of Russia instructed the founding of a presidential commission of fight against attempts of falsification of history concerning Russia. If this commission was primarily founded against attempts to reread the history of the Second World War, it also bears some threats for the history of Middle Ages. Two months later one of the active members of this commission, Director of the Institute of Russian History of the Academy of Sciences in Moscow, Andreï Sakharov, member by correspondence of the Academy of Sciences of Russia, in his interview on the Russian TV1 announced that, among the modern falsifications, one of the most threatening medieval untruths is Normanism, which 'today is rearing its head again'. He thinks that a new wind of Normanism is blowing in Russia which is inspired by foreign organisations and institutions that finance the 'destructive activities' of some Russian scholars and centres of research. (Gazeau and Musin 2010)

The commission—against which Klejn protested in print—has since become dormant, but Klejn tells me that it would be foolhardy to presume it extinct (Klejn 2014, pers. comm.).

Chapter 8

Histories of Archaeology

The New Archaeology

In 2009 Klejn published a history and critical analysis of the processual movement in archaeology. (This book had been written in the 1970s, but at that date the suggestion of a scientific revolution in Western archaeology could not be raised in Russia.) Whereas his 1979 'Panorama of Theoretical Archaeology' had begun to introduce Western archaeologists to the archaeological theories of the east, *The New Archaeology* aimed to increase knowledge of western theoretical archaeology and its history among Russian archaeologists.

Criticism of the processual movement should not, in Klejn's case, be taken to suggest sympathy for post-processual archaeology. Klejn is critical of the post-processualists for blurring the distinction between archaeology and history, a trait that he believes has continued to the present day, despite the high tide of post-processualism having passed. However, he is also critical of New Archaeology in that he believes that it tended to align archaeology too much toward anthropology and sociology (Leach 2011). Having experienced the domination of archaeology by historical materialism, Klejn remains understandably sensitive to any infringement of the autonomy of archaeology as an independent discipline.

Aside from a disregard for archaeology's autonomy, Klejn notes parallels between Western New Archaeology of the 1960s–1980s and Soviet archaeology, especially of the pre-war period. Both displayed 'a liking for universal laws of development, schematism, etc.' (Klejn 2012b: 52).

Like Soviet Archaeology

> New Archaeology failed to pay enough attention to the formation of the archaeological record. Archaeologists have to deal with a two-fold break. By this I mean that as archaeologists we are twice removed from our objects, from being able to give a basic account of what happened. First we are removed from them as from mute material objects while our inferences must be expressed in thoughts and words. Second

A Russian Perspective on Theoretical Archaeology: The Life and Work of Leo S. Klejn by Stephen Leach, 95–107

> we are removed from them as from dead remnants in the contemporary world while they must be viewed as parts of the cultural life of the past.
>
> Consequently we have to first assess what evidence there is and then interpret how this evidence has been distorted with the passing of time. For example, not all materials are equally durable. Actually, the archaeological record is always incomplete. This fact alone, if unattended, will create a distortion in our reconstruction. It was only by ignoring this that Binford and Clarke were able to transform archaeology into anthropology. New Archaeologists made the mistake of acting as if archaeologists study living cultures. They see any change in the state of culture as having occurred owing to some impact from environment or other cultures while it can be simply a result of postmortal processes in the monuments.
>
> They used, and discovered, processual laws—good—but they ignored other laws dealing with how a past phenomenon left a trace in the archaeological record. For example, ceramics will accumulate more quickly in the archaeological record than metal, because metal is more likely to be reused. On this point I agree with criticism made by post-processualists. I also felt that New Archaeology had a very impoverished conception of history. (Leach 2011)

In other words, New Archaeology had an impoverished conception of history, whereas Soviet archaeology had an over-inflated conception of history, but both rode roughshod over the distinction between history and archaeology. These criticisms are further explored in the next chapter, in conjunction with an exploration of Klejn's own conception of archaeology as an autonomous and distinctive discipline.

The Montelius Formula: Swedish Rationalism in the Archaeology of Mats Malmer

Having deposited *The New Archaeology* with the publisher, Klejn then turned to revise a manuscript on the Swedish archaeologist Mats P. Malmer (1921–2007). Malmer had been the head of the Neolithic and Bronze Age Department at the Swedish Museum of National Antiquities. He is best known for his work on archaeological typology and on the Bronze Age Swedish-Norwegian Battle Axe culture, which he argues was an indigenous development. (The latter subject is of particular interest to Russian archaeologists with regard to its relation to the Bronze Age Fatyanovo culture. Both of these cultures feature in discussions of the Proto-Indo-European homeland.)

Klejn's book on Malmer was published in 2010. Its title, *The Montelius Formula*, refers back to the 'great master of the "typological method"' (Renfrew and Bahn 2000: 121), the Swedish archaeologist Oscar Montelius.

> Montelius in Sweden developed an evolutionary series of Bronze and Iron Age swords, axes, fibulas, and other artefacts in later prehistory. Montelius developed a typological method. He built sequences of artefacts on the assumption that the more similar objects were in shape, the nearer to each other they were in date, while his Danish opponent Sophus Müller, used the same principle to link not just similar artefacts but entire assemblages. (Klejn 1996: 287)

Although some archaeologists may know little of their origin, it is a fact that the basic principles of Montelius's typology are 'effectively still in use' (Renfrew and Bahn 2000: 121). However, both Malmer and Klejn have attempted to build on and to refine Montelius's work. In *The Montelius Formula* Klejn makes clear his belief that although Malmer advanced the study of typology there are yet areas in which he is prone to criticism. Like *The New Archaeology*, *The Montelius Formula* is a history written with an eye on present-day developments.

The title of the book also reminds us that in general Swedish archaeologists tend to accord greater importance to typology than do archaeologists in, for example, Britain. 'Source criticism, typology, and investigation of distributions and densities have been long-established concerns in Scandinavian archaeology' (Sørensen 2002: 166). Thus within the context of Scandinavian archaeology, 'although Malmer's ideas about the discipline and its methodology are extremely innovative, they do not constitute a paradigm shift. . . . Rather than rejecting the former archaeology, as New Archaeology did, Malmer carried forward and enhanced an existing framework of inquiry' (Ibid.: 174).

Klejn suggests that in some respects Malmer is comparable to the French archaeologist Jean-Claude Gardin (1925–2013). The work of both these archaeologists to some extent prefigures New Archaeology. However, according to Klejn, their work was influenced by neorationalism rather than neopositivism.

> Rationalism put down roots in France and Sweden from the seventeenth century. In Sweden it (like geography) had an impact on archaeological Diffusionism, in the tradition of Montelius. It was in this environment that Malmer was formed as a scholar. Probably day-to-day communication with his wife Brita, the renowned archaeologist and numismatist, encouraged his inclination towards exact calculations and formulations. Numismatics had earlier impacted upon archaeology (i.e. it seeded the notion 'type' and the idea of gradation).[1]

It has been suggested that Malmer would have had more influence on New Archaeology if he had written more in English (Sørensen 2002), but, as will be seen, Klejn argues that there were some aspects of his work that simply did not appeal to New Archaeology.

Among other theoretical innovations Malmer, influenced by the geographer T. Hägerstrand, introduced new methods of analysing patterns of distribution. These are described and explained by Klejn most positively. But it is Malmer's arguments for the methodological and theoretical autonomy of archaeology that provide the most striking instance of common ground with Klejn. Klejn noted with approval Malmer's stance on the autonomy of archaeology already in *Archaeological Typology* (1982).

Malmer, as does Klejn, 'sees typology as the pivot of archaeological work'.[2] Moreover, 'Malmer suggests that archaeology belongs neither to sciences nor to humanities but to some third group of disciplines. The crucial role of typology in archaeological studies allows us to determine this place more exactly'.[3] Here again, there is common ground between Klejn and Malmer, although both arrived at this idea independently. Malmer's focus on the nature of the discipline and of the archaeological record is yet another instance of common ground with Klejn. (The next chapter fully explores Klejn's conception of archaeology as an independent discipline with typology as its crucial and distinguishing characteristic.)

According to Klejn,

> Malmer's greatest contribution to archaeological theory is the perfection of the Montelian typological method. This method is based not on the idea of evolution as is often thought but on the idea of gradation (Montelius was a Diffusionist rather than an Evolutionist). Types are arranged into a typological series—via ranks of gradation: ABCDEFG. Yet his formula is not so simple. In order to avoid this arrangement being made according to a chance criterion (it is possible, for example, to arrange potatoes from round to oblong), Montelius invented a safeguard against randomness, namely, the chronological coincidence of beginnings (and middles and ends) of some parallel series. Coincidence was established by occurrences of similar artefacts in parallel assemblages. Thus, the gradation-typological method required the use of assemblages. However, assemblages are not always present.
>
> Malmer found a way to overcome this problem. He constructed gradation series not of artefact types but of attributes. The artefact itself takes the place of an assemblage. The only requirement is that the attributes used for these series should be functionally independent on each other. That is to say, they should not change in a natural and indispensable conjunction with each other.[4]

However, Klejn criticises Malmer for treating types as sharply delimited classes. He suggests that it was this mistake that 'led other archaeologists to distrust his inferences'.[5] In Klejn's opinion typology tolerates blurred borders and dim or not fully discernible units. Classes are like boxes in a catalogue cube, while types are ideals—images toward which particular items gravitate.[6]

Klejn believes that archaeologists should make use of Malmer's refinements of Montelius's insights but without confusing classes with types. He argues that a conception of types as ideals is compatible with a scientific methodology. It is not a license for 'impressionism'.

There is further discussion of the distinction between classification and typology in Klejn's *Archaeological Typology*. In conversation, Klejn made clear to me the main concerns of this book.

> *Archaeological Typology* has two principal concerns. The first is to distinguish between classification and typology. Archaeologists seem to use either term indiscriminately. My aim is to reform this state of chaos. I argue that classification is what Aristotle described as such, the rigid distinction of artefacts into non-overlapping categories—like the distribution of finds by the boxes in the cabinet. Typology, on the other hand, is the description of ideal objects to which real objects, in various degrees, conform—they are more or less 'typical'. Classification makes uses of sharply defined borders; whereas typology makes use only of conventional borders. These are two alternative ways of ordering artefacts.
>
> The second concern is with the way that archaeologists arrange their evidence. The usual practice is to cut reality into the smallest possible particles ('attributes'), then to group them by correlation into higher taxons ('types'), and finally to group these into still larger communities ('cultures'). Yet in this way you cannot distinguish cultural types among empirical types. Therefore I inferred that we should proceed in the reverse direction: that we should first have some hypothesis concerning the culture, and then work downward from the types to the attributes. (Leach 2011)

In other words, although derived from the study of past discoveries, archaeological types should also to some degree attempt to anticipate the results of the archaeologist's investigations. (In *Archaeological Typology* Klejn backs this claim with an analysis of why particular typologies and classifications have failed and others have been successful.)[7]

All of which Malmer would dispute. Yet despite their differences, and specific disagreements on the interpretation of the Battle-Axe culture, for Klejn 'Malmer remains an investigator (like a test pilot) of ways into unexplored territory, both ways that lead to deadlock and those that remain prospective, and his contribution remains a most interesting lesson'.[8]

The History of Archaeological Thought

In 2011, Klejn published his two-volume *History of Archaeological Thought*. This book was based on a series of lectures that he had given at the universities of St. Petersburg and Vienna. (The course reading included Bruce Trigger's

History of Archaeological Thought [1989], Glyn Daniel's *A Hundred and Fifty Years of Archaeology* [1975], and Alain Schnapp's *La Conquête de Passé* [1993].) Klejn had been working on this book and looking forward to its publication for some time. When interviewed in 2003 he had already gathered the data for it and was hoping that he would have enough time remaining to write it (Immonen 2003: 57).

At the publication of the book in 2011 Klejn's main regret was that his respected Western friend and colleague Bruce Trigger had not lived to read it.[9] Trigger's is the most cited name in Klejn's history.

> Like Childe's, Bruce Trigger's Marxism was not dogmatic; he did not commit himself to technological [determinism] nor widely to production determinism, or to economic or political determinism. In Trigger's work context always overcame laws, and history vanquished sociology and social anthropology. He respected the importance of the laws of history, but he did not ignore fortuity. It was Trigger's opinion that so many forces, including chance forces, impact any event in history, and there is not one process that can predict the course of events, and so consequently one cannot reconstruct the past only on the basis of laws. It was necessary to find factual traces of events and this was the meaning and the significance and power of archaeology. (Klejn 2008a: 7)

Trigger argued that to understand a course of events as well as economic and sociopolitical factors we should also take into account psychological and biological factors (Klejn 2008a: 8). Klejn is in broad agreement with this approach, but in general the 'human factor' plays a greater role in Klejn's histories than in Trigger's.

According to Klejn:

> When it comes to the history of their discipline, archaeologists tend to be reliant upon just two basic works, namely Glyn Daniel's *History of Archaeology* and Bruce Trigger's *History of Archaeological Thought*. The first was published in the middle of the last century, the second in 1989 (with a new edition in 2006). Both are very good, although they both have a number of weaknesses. Both are devoted almost exclusively to prehistoric archaeology at the expense of all else. Moreover the first book is overly reliant upon English and French literature and does not mention Slavic and German works, while the second is written with very broad strokes and does not describe schools and personalities in any detail.[10]
>
> That Klejn's *History of Archaeological Thought* has the same title as Bruce Trigger's history is no coincidence: If I am asked whom I

> feel closest to among all Western archaeologists, I reply that I feel closest to Bruce Trigger; but of course when it came to the subject of archaeology in Russia Bruce had the disadvantage of not knowing Russian. (In general, it should be said that native English-speaking archaeologists are disadvantaged by their generally poor knowledge of other languages. In my opinion it is essential for all archaeologists to have some basic knowledge of foreign languages. Bruce Trigger had knowledge of other languages but not of Russian.) . . . It is of course influenced by Trigger's history but, although, both Trigger and I are materialists, in my work as an historian I generally pay more attention than Trigger to the human characters of the main protagonists. (Leach 2011)

As was stated in the preface to the present work, there are many who consider Klejn's *History of Archaeological Thought* to be his masterpiece. In his review of the work the archaeologist Leonid B. Vishniatsky describes it as 'at once an encyclopaedia of discoveries . . . an historical survey, a biographical reference book, an adventure novel, a handbook of various trends of philosophical thought, and an original analysis of many archaeological problems' (Vishniatsky 2011). He suggests that archaeologists might excite the envy of ethnographers, anthropologists, philologists, and linguists (and even physicists, mathematicians, and biologists) for their possession of such a work—none of these other disciplines possesses a comparable history. It is little wonder that the work runs to 600,000 words.

(As yet the cost of translating this work has put off Western publishers, but it is to be hoped that it may yet be published, for not only was Klejn uniquely qualified to write such a book—but since the publication of Trigger's *History of Archaeological Thought* (1989, rev. ed. 2006), there has been tremendous growth in interest in the history of archaeology.)

A History of Anthropology

Klejn's somewhat shorter *History of Anthropological Ideas and Theories* (200,000 words), published in 2014, is based on a series of lectures delivered at various Russian, European, and American universities in the 1990s. It 'presents a world history of anthropological ideas and theories with an emphasis on their development in Western Europe and America. Of Russian ideas, only those that influenced developments elsewhere in the world are included. Those that fall outside this criterion are dealt with only summarily'.[11] There is some overlap with *The History of Archaeological Thought*: the two histories run on parallel courses, and indeed some of the protagonists are the same.

Klejn explains the scope of the book as follows:

> by anthropology predominantly sociocultural (social and cultural) anthropology is understood, i.e., that which in the Soviet Union was covered by the term *ethnography* and which in post-Soviet use is close to the concept of *ethnology*. Ethnography and ethnology are, however, only parts of the anthropological complex of disciplines, with a special accent on the ethnic aspect of research. Anthropology is broader in scope and covers various comparative studies of peoples and cultures.[12]

Although the book does not include philosophy or physical anthropology, nonetheless the remaining subject is so broad that the book 'almost amounts to a history of social ideas in general'.[13]

The subject with which Klejn deals was absent from any curriculum in the Soviet Union. 'Cultural anthropology was regarded by the Soviet Union as a bourgeois discipline and along with genetics, cybernetics, and sexology was absent from the Soviet Union because by its nature it implied tolerance of varied cultural norms and ideas. This is why it was replaced with ethnography'.[14] The implied toleration of cultural anthropology is related to an interesting feature: 'namely, the attraction of anthropology to outsiders of various kinds throughout its history—revolutionaries, socialists, Quakers, homosexuals, etc. No neighbouring discipline has as many. The author explains this attraction by a peculiarity of anthropology—in fact, its main idea: the relativity of norms, recognition of the variability of mankind'.[15] (In *The History of Archaeological Thought* Klejn notes an interesting comparable phenomenon: the peculiar attraction that archaeology seems to hold for introverts, of many different societies.)

As is the case with all of Klejn's histories: 'the leading figures of the history of the discipline are presented as real people, with their individual quirks, immersed in the clashes and peripeteia of the scholarly struggle'.[16] And, as is also the case with his other histories, Klejn makes no apologies for the occasional polemical tone of the book. 'The author was himself a participant in the described academic processes. . . . This is why in his critical estimation of the impact of Marxism on anthropology and in his impassioned criticism of certain scholars (for instance Lévi-Strauss, and the postmodernists) there is an element of personal commitment'.[17]

Soviet Archaeology

A significant element of personal commitment is also present in *Soviet Archaeology* (2012). The genesis of this book was related in Chapter 3; but to recap, its first incarnation was an article published in *World Archaeology* in 1982 while Klejn was imprisoned. It was published in Russian in 1993 and German in 1997 before finally being published in English in 2012. Each successive version is longer than the last. Although reviews were very favourable, some reviewers noted that the successive incarnations of book are evident in its structure of multiple layers. Klejn is unapologetic:

> Some reviewers . . . saw as a weakness the multiple layers in it, the fact that the subject matter of the discussion was changing, while the author clung to his previous opinions in new circumstances, letting new reactions build on the established ones. Had these critics troubled to examine the details, they would have noticed that I cling to my previous appraisals in those places where they remain apt. Whatever needed reappraising in the light of new data is reappraised. If I can remain unashamed of some of my earlier judgements, made in conditions of unfreedom, that is not a weakness of my book but a mark of the strength of my position. (Klejn 2012b: x)

Moreover: 'In general . . . I have not written a history of our discipline but analysed the phenomenon' (Ibid.: 370). Earlier versions of the book, in Russian and German, were entitled *The Phenomenon of Soviet Archaeology*. Given that any scholar must attain some distance from his subject but that Klejn had been bound for so long by the strictures of Soviet archaeology perhaps the structure of the book is understandable: looking at Soviet archaeology from first one angle and then another, Klejn can be compared to a released captive who in his memoirs recalls straining against his confines, first one way and then another. Klejn sees the book primarily as the analysis of a phenomenon and only secondarily as a history. (In 2015 he published a two-volume *Biographical History of Russian Archaeology*, in which this emphasis is reversed.)

Previously in this chapter (in the section on *The New Archaeology*), we have encountered, albeit briefly, two different criticisms levelled by Klejn against respectively two major movements in western theoretical archaeology. Klejn's criticism of New Archaeology was that it did not pay sufficient attention to the formation of the archaeological record; and his criticism of post-processual archaeology was that it had an over-inflated conception of history. Both of these criticisms stem not only from Klejn's knowledge of western archaeological literature, with which the library of Leningrad University was well-supplied, but also from his experience of Soviet archaeology; for in Soviet archaeology, according to Klejn, there are numerous examples of both of these faults (compounded).

In the Soviet Union both faults arose from the dominance of historical materialism. As the philosophy of historical materialism began its reign in the Soviet Union in the 1920s, archaeology in its pre-Soviet manifestation was denigrated as having encouraged the separation of ideas and objects

(Ibid.: 23). Under the influence of historical materialism archaeology was therefore 'de-objectified'. In practice this meant that attention to typology was disdained as a distraction from the bigger picture provided by historical materialism. It was seen as a form of escapism and 'a product of bourgeois evolutionism, a method which fetishised objects and biologised history' (Klejn 2012b: 23; see also Tikhonov 2007). Any focus that was not on the big picture was condemned as irrelevant, as 'naked artefactology'—a form of escapism. (In a sense, in Klejn's case, it *was* a form of escapism, in that it was a way of avoiding misplaced ideology and dogma.) The study of sites in relation to their natural environment was also discouraged.

Archaeology was seen as providing a history of the social-economic foundations of society. It was distinguished from history only in that it studied material antiquities. The consensus was that these antiquities, 'carry within themselves certain historical information, which can be extracted by applying common sense and the general theoretical apparatus of history' (Klejn 2012b: 63). In other words, it was thought that archaeological sources reflect reality in just the same way as written sources. This attitude was epitomised by Artsikhovsky's description of archaeology as 'history armed with a spade'. The first use of this slogan is found in an article that Artsikhovsky co-authored with Bryusov, Kiselev, and Smirnov in 1929 (Ibid.: 242).

> They declared that, by proceeding from material remains to superstructures and being guided by Marxist ideas, archaeology was able to reconstruct fully all the important economic, social, and ideological structures of the past, even without the support of written sources or ethnography. On this premise, they concluded that archaeology was not a subordinate discipline but an independent one, parallel to history, and that it had the same subject matter as prehistory, the study of the early stages of the historical process. On that basis they postulated the creation of 'Marxist archaeology'. (Ibid.: 91)

In other words, Artsikhovsky and his colleagues rejected what would later become known as 'Hawkes' ladder'.[18]

As a result of these political and ideological changes, archaeology was subjugated by history: from the 1920s to the 1950s the discipline was invaded by educated dilettantes, eager to satisfy the public demand for definite solutions to historical problems (Ibid.: 67); history was written from *prima facie* impressions of the finds rather from their analysis (Ibid.: 65), and there was a premature rush to absolute chronology (Ibid.: 127–30).

Theoretical archaeology was shunned as unnecessary within Marxist science (Ibid.: 52, 82). Artsikhovsky, for example, professed to speak as an empiricist who had no time for theory, although, as is often the case with such empiricists, in his pronouncements theory was nonetheless tacitly still present.

Klejn makes clear that he does not condemn every aspect of archaeology under the Soviet Union—for example, attendance figures at museums were very impressive, and there were early examples of open-area excavation. And, indeed, he still values the insights provided by Marxism as a methodological tool. But the root problem was that history, the very word, was imbued with magical power in the Soviet Union (Ibid.: 123), to the extent that the distinctive character of archaeology was grossly distorted.

He argues that Soviet archaeology was never the united monolithic bloc that it was perceived to be in the West and that, despite the protestations of its practitioners, it was not, in its essence, Marxist: 'for Marxist archaeology was hardly possible in principle—in the same way, there is no Labour or Tory archaeology! Rather one can characterize Soviet archaeology as politically involved—yielding to considerations of the moment—having to follow all the zigzags of Soviet policy and diplomacy'.[19] It was, however, consistently dogged by a misconception of the relationship between history and archaeology.

That archaeologists aspired to be historians led to an inherent conservatism. The problem was not that they aspired to be *both* archaeologists *and* historians but rather that they were simply uninterested in those things that made archaeology distinctive. Klejn here links his criticism of Soviet archaeology to his criticism of New Archaeology. He argues that in different ways, but to the same effect, both misconceived the role of history:

> In the 1970s, speaking to the Americans, I reproached them for overlooking history: American archaeology long ago 'settled into the house of anthropology' and collaborated exclusively with the anthropological disciplines: physical and cultural anthropology, psychology, etc. History does not figure in the list. 'Why not history?' I asked, and gave reasons for my reproach. Yet the opposite extreme is also unacceptable to me. Why only history? (Klejn 2012b: 134; see also Klejn 1971: 120)

Yet, from the 1960s onward, at roughly the same time as in the West, theoretical archaeology developed in the Soviet Union. It developed mainly under the stimulus of working out the relations between archaeological culture, language, and ethnos—for once Marr's stadiality theory had been rejected, the problem of ethnogenesis inevitably re-emerged.

> Strange as it may seem the fiercest and most protracted arguments among Soviet archaeologists were not about the reconstruction of socioeconomic structures, which might appear natural for Marxists, but about the origins of peoples . . . the most heated dispute concerned the origins of the Eastern Slavs. (Klejn 2012b: 105)

Previously, under Marr's reign these problems had not arisen—not because they were in any way solved but because Soviet archaeology was blinkered to such problems.

> Let us again follow the deductive process. Marxism gave being priority over consciousness, that is, the material culture came before the spiritual. In culture as a whole it gave priority to the means of production, that is, the artefacts, elements of a material culture. On their development, that is to say, on the evolution of tools, depended changes in the entire structure of a society. The foundations of this development, in other words the fundamental connections between tools and superstructure, were taken as given, as something known in advance. And if that were so, then, after examining the tools, the entire structure of a society could be mentally reconstructed. If . . . , then . . . And there was no need to defer to ethnography. (Ibid.: 241)

However, once Marr's doctrines had been overthrown, the problems of ethnography naturally brought archaeologists' attention once more to the problems of interpretation and analysis of finds and sites. Consequently, from the 1960s and 1970s onward, Russian theoretical archaeology was concentrated on many of the same themes as Western theoretical archaeology. But, in addition, Russian archaeologists paid attention to the problem of the relationship between the disciplines of archaeology and history (Ibid.: 62)—more attention than was paid to this problem in the West. An acceleration of interest in problems of archaeological interpretation was especially noticeable in the Soviet Union in the 1970s, coinciding with the period of détente. During this period one article in particular, by G. P. Grigoryev (a Leningrad Palaeolithic specialist), 'detonated with the force of a bomb' (Ibid.: 95). Grigoryev declared: 'Objects produced by excavations are archaeological sources, not historical sources. They contain no historical information. . . . The fact that a historian may take archaeological conclusions from an archaeologist and use them as an historical source is another matter, but it does not in any sense mean that our sources are historical'.[20]

Grigoryev's supporters were to be found mainly among the archaeologists of Leningrad, including Klejn—although, as will be seen in the next chapter, Klejn believes that the archaeologist deliberately processes information from archaeological sources in such a way that information is available for the historian's use. In 1978, with the publication of *Archaeological Sources*, Klejn declared his hand. Yet he was still careful not to confront the holy cow of Marxism directly. Here his youthful reading of Marx was useful:

> Against the Marxists I quoted a statement from Marx, that the eye and the ear have different objects. I defined history as a discipline of

> synthesis. I agreed that archaeology should deal with laws, but not the laws of development of society—those were studied by sociologists; and not cause-and-effect mechanisms—those were studied by historians. Archaeology should deal with something else, with the laws governing the formation of material remains and traces of historical events and the materialisation of particular ideas. Archaeology and history could not be merged into a single discipline, not only because they employed different methods but also because archaeology was not the only 'part of history' to examine sources. History would then need to subsume yet other disciplines, such as numismatics, palaeography, archaeolography, ethnography, physical anthropology, etc., but it would become unlimited in its reach and too broad for its practitioners to assimilate. What was needed was the integration of specialised fields, not an amalgamation of them into a single nonspecialised discipline. (Ibid.: 96)

Although Klejn argues that the lessons of *Archaeological Sources* have not yet been fully realised or implemented, nevertheless many Russian archaeologists hold this book in high regard, and at the time of writing many will admit that there is at least 'something in it'.

The theories that Klejn put forward in *Archaeological Sources* and that he developed first in *Archaeological Typology* and then in *Metaarchaeology* are the main subjects of the remaining three chapters.

Chapter 9

Theoretical Archaeology in Relation to Practice

The remaining chapters of this book are devoted to Klejn's theoretical archaeology. More specifically, the following two chapters are primarily devoted to an exposition of *Metaarchaeology* (2001a)[1]—a work in which Klejn develops views he had first presented in *Archaeological Sources* (1978) and *Archaeological Typology* (1982). The final chapter of the book is devoted to the aspect of Klejn's work that I find most interesting: his comparison between archaeology and forensic science. I compare Klejn's comparison with an earlier comparison drawn by R. G. Collingwood, and I ask whether Klejn is right to draw his comparison as closely as he does.

Theory in Relation to Practice

In Klejn's view theory is crucial to the process of archaeology and hence also to the progress of archaeology. It is that part of archaeology that lends self-reflection to the entire archaeological process. As such it plays a vital role in the development of archaeological research designs. Without theory, in archaeology as in many other disciplines, we would have only tradition and the method of trial and error to guide us (Klejn 2001a: 100).

Theory, for Klejn, does not hover above practice; rather, it begins and ends with practice. The theorist begins and ends by observing and analysing the best current examples of practice (Leach 2011). (This is what Klejn means when he claims that 'the question of where theoretical archaeology belongs is solved by the life of archaeology' [Klejn 2001a: 5].) The theorist, so to speak, distils the lessons that might be learned from his or her observations and experience, so that they might be made applicable to work on other sites and finds, including those not yet discovered. Theory, as thus conceived, does no less than make clear how empirical investigations are to be undertaken (Klejn 2012b: 372). There is, admittedly, an element of circularity in this process, but it is a virtuous circularity.

In Klejn's view archaeological theorists discuss all too rarely the precise manner in which theory relates to practice (Klejn 2001a: 87), but this is *not*

A Russian Perspective on Theoretical Archaeology: The Life and Work of Leo S. Klejn by Stephen Leach, 108–124

a criticism that can easily be made of Klejn. He argues that because theory both begins *and ends* with practice, it also contributes to practice. According to Klejn: 'Every different archaeological theory is ultimately part of archaeological methodology—it describes a program for extracting information from artefacts. This means, of course, that there are many different archaeological theories. Theoretical archaeology is that branch of archaeology that embraces them all' (Leach 2011). But, in accordance with his own advice, in *Metaarchaeology* Klejn does not attempt to answer 'what is theoretical archaeology?' in any more detail until after he has shown us something more of how theory relates to practice. Here I follow Klejn's example and postpone exposition of Klejn's final answer to the question 'what is theoretical archaeology?' until the next chapter (in particular the section on 'The Concept of Theory in Oppositions').

The Structure of Theoretical Archaeology

To clarify our thoughts on theoretical archaeology: 'one should present theoretical archaeology as a system, rationally differentiate its parts, and place them in a logical order' (Klejn 2001a: 7). Klejn follows convention in crediting David Clarke's *Analytical Archaeology* (1968) as the first work to attempt the comprehensive achievement of this task. The 'loss of innocence' that this work represented marked the beginnings of theoretical archaeology as a distinctive subdiscipline of archaeology. Yet, at about the same time but within a different tradition, theoretical archaeology also began to develop in the Soviet Union. As we have seen, it there developed variously in opposition to, and in defence of, the dominant Artsikhovsky-Rybakov conception of archaeology as 'history armed with a spade'.

In both Western and Russian traditions, the protagonists' terminology has equivocated between 'archaeological theory' and 'theoretical archaeology'. Klejn prefers 'theoretical archaeology': he takes this to embrace the following three groups (coinciding to some degree with the tripartite division suggested by Lester Embree [Embree 1989]).

- Endoarchaeological theory—'These theories deal with archaeological material and are intended to give ideas for its processing, for interpretation, for extracting historical information from it' (Klejn 2001a: 9). Sometimes these theories do no more than clear away conceptual confusion—but this goal should not be underestimated. For example, on the subject of evidence for migration, Klejn believes that a lot might be achieved by simply clarifying the terms of the debate: 'I have always been amused by the vehemence with which adherents and enemies of migrations or independent development advocated their own explanations as a principle and rejected fully the competing explanation. Whereas all that was needed was to determine the conditions under which one or another explanation appears correct' (Ibid.: 99).[2]

- Metaarchaeological theory—This concerns the theory of theoretical archaeology, in other words, the theory of theory, our conception of the discipline itself. Although it does not deal directly with archaeological material, in common with endoarchaeological theory, metaarchaeological theory is arrived at by studying the methodology of the discipline and by contributing to it. Of Klejn's own work the most obvious example is *Metaarchaeology* (2001a). Klejn adopted this term from Colin Renfrew.[3]
- Paraarchaeological theory—This consists of theories and concepts that are developed outside archaeology but that may also be of use within archaeology, including theories from 'sociology, history, culturology, anthropology, ethnology, linguistics, geography, and others' (Klejn 2001a: 9)—theories concerned with 'regularities of migrations, diffusions, autochthonous development, influences, borrowings, independent inventions, and so on' (Ibid.: 9).

1. The Concerns of Archaeology

THE SUBJECT OF ARCHAEOLOGY   When we ask the seemingly straightforward question 'what is the subject of archaeology?' to the extent that we would answer it with a degree of self-reflection we are in the realm of theory. There is no agreement as to the answer to this question: 'The only point on which all concur is in the determination of the immediate objects of archaeological studies. These are material antiquities regarded as sources for knowledge of the life culture of past peoples and their societies' (Ibid.: 13). But as regards the view from which these material antiquities are studied, and the ends to which they are studied—in other words, the subject of archaeology—there is no agreement. However, the answers to this question can be grouped within three different traditions.

a. 'One line of continuation stretches from Renaissance collectors or antiquaries who gradually became archaeologists. . . . It is the preparation of such materials [material sources] that the tasks of archaeology are limited to according to this tradition. The cognition itself can be allotted to other disciplines, first of all history, to which archaeology surrenders the prepared material. It appears as a source-studying discipline, subject matter may be reduced to sources and records' (Ibid.: 13). Archaeology within this tradition is epitomised by the motto: 'archaeology is the handmaiden of history'.[4]
b. 'The other line of continuation begins from historians, philologists, and anthropologists who assembled tangible remains of the past and became archaeologists. Classicists were the first in line, attracted by the possibility

of illustrating the subjects of ancient authors with artefacts and monuments, to yield new ethnographic texts and later, the chance to put together the history of visual arts' (Ibid.). Archaeology within this tradition is epitomised by Artsikhovsky's motto: 'archaeology is history armed with a spade' and by the title of an article by Leroi-Gourhan 'L'histoire sans textes' (Leroi-Gourhan 1961).

c. The third tradition would have it that archaeology encompasses both the study of material sources *and* historical interpretation (Ibid.: 14). (By contrast, the second tradition denies the source-studying character of archaeology, and the first tradition has it that archaeology is primarily a source-studying discipline.)

Klejn situates his own position unequivocally and unapologetically within the first of these traditions. Yet he knows full well that the very idea that anyone in archaeology might still give credence to the idea—from the nineteenth century!—that 'archaeology is the handmaiden of history' is likely, among many theorists, to prompt a knee-jerk reaction of indignation. His response is as follows:

> Yes, I have, of course, encountered this concern. Archaeologists are afraid to lose the prestige of their profession. They want to participate in solving the great problems of sociology and history directly. But we must not be misled by metaphors. Yes, archaeology serves history—but it is not dominated by it. The Ukrainian poet Taras Shevchenko called archaeology the 'mother of history'. Handmaiden or mother? The connotations are different but the sense is the same. (Leach 2011)

As was seen previously in the exposition of *Soviet Archaeology* (2012) Klejn argues that Artsikhovsky's conception of archaeology led to archaeologists having an inflated sense of their own powers. Grandiose ambitions were pursued at the cost of the painstaking but necessary study and analysis of material sources. Klejn is in no doubt as to the lesson to be drawn:

> Viewing archaeology as a subspecies of history leads not only to the idea that no specifically archaeological theory is needed but also to disdain for specifically archaeological methods: critical appraisal of sources, strict principles in typological and cartographic methods, criteria of proofs of links of continuity, and the like. (Klejn 2012b: 66)

He argues that the danger represented by this view has not receded—nor is it a danger that is confined to the East—it is a danger that is likely to arise whenever and wherever the difference between archaeology and history is denied or overlooked.

For Klejn, the question of the distinctive character of archaeology is by no means an esoteric debate (Klejn 2001a: 15). In the Soviet Union, where history was made to serve history and politics via the philosophy of historical materialism, archaeology was left prone to unjustified political influence, and this situation made it a matter of some urgency to determine the disciplinary boundaries of archaeology. Hence: 'I developed my entire work in theoretical archaeology to working out a system of theories and methods which could grant strictness and objectivity of archaeological cognition, in order that archaeology would be able to resist the intentions to serve the political situation of the moment' (Klejn 2001a: 7). Klejn admits that the same person may be both an archaeologist and an historian—he is himself an example of just such a person—but he maintains that the two disciplines are conceptually distinct.

He also admits that there is, in principle, an opposite danger to that of the absorption of archaeology into history: archaeology might become overly self-absorbed and removed altogether from history. But he sees little evidence of this occurrence (Ibid.: 16). Moreover, he argues that both this danger and what he sees as the more pressing dangers described previously might be avoided by a careful study of the boundary between archaeology and history and of the relations between them.

ARCHAEOLOGICAL SOURCES Klejn explains that he prefers to talk about archaeological 'sources' rather than archaeological 'records', which might be taken to imply a fixed message. Moreover, archaeological 'sources' is a better translation from Russian. 'If you say "archaeological record", no Russian will understand you' (Klejn pers. comm.).

> In Russian the word 'source' generally means any reservoir or opening from which something flows out of or can be derived. In the direct sense it is a spring, the beginning of a brook. In the figurative sense it is an object from which information, evidence, or knowledge can be obtained about another object, and it is only due to this property that the first object is interesting for us in some context. Only in this context does the object appear a source. It is in this sense that newspapers use this word when they refer to 'diplomatic sources' or to 'official, governmental sources', etc. (Klejn 2001a: 20)

Klejn argues that historical sources are different from archaeological sources, in that the historian deals with written information (arranged in the form of concepts, judgements, deductions, and so on) and produces written information (arranged in a similar form) (Ibid.: 23). He or she is not as a rule required to have a first-hand acquaintance with material sources—the acquaintance of these sources is acquired through what the archaeologist tells him or her about them. 'This is an indirect reflection, which as a rule is made without direct contact with the object of reflection by the investigator' (Ibid.), Klejn elaborates on the distinctiveness of history and its difference not only from archaeology but also from sociology, as follows. The historian

> uses sound reasoning, imagination, and life experiences to establish causal connections. Sociology (including historical sociology) extracts laws from the facts. History uses the laws in order to understand facts and their connections. Sociology elaborates a mass of facts, and facts are interchangeable for it. From many facts a sociologist infers one law. The historian studies the interaction of many laws upon one fact. He studies also the interaction of law and chance so as to try to reconstruct the ways in which artefacts were originally used—their original context. He is concerned with the individuality of facts. It is this that makes history an autonomous discipline, and in part a humanistic discipline. History is necessary because, against von Ranke, the facts do not speak for themselves—chronicle is not yet history. (Leach 2011)

This conception of history as in large part a humanistic discipline focussed on the individuality of past happenings, and in which the historian is reliant on both sound reasoning and his or her own imagination, is exemplified in Klejn's own work as an historian (for example, in the latest edition of *Soviet Archaeology* and in *The History of Archaeological Thought*). As Klejn acknowledges, this conception is to a great extent compatible with R. G. Collingwood's humanistic understanding of historical explanation. According to Klejn: 'What a historian sees in a source depends on his preparation, education, and talent, on the level and activity of his consciousness. The more he knows, the more he will see' (Klejn 2001a: 22).[5] Similarly, according to Collingwood:

> The historian's authorities tell him of this or that phase in a process whose intermediate phases they leave undescribed; he then interpolates these phases for himself. His picture of his subject, though it may consist in part of statements directly drawn from his authorities, consists also, and increasingly with every increase in his competence as an historian, of statements reached inferentially from those according to his own criteria, his own rules of method, and his own canons of relevance. In this part of his work he is never depending on his authorities in the sense of repeating what they tell him; he is relying on his own powers and constituting himself his own authority; while his so-called authorities are now not authorities at all but only evidence. (Collingwood 1993: 237)

Klejn warns us that: 'one should not imagine that historical information is contained in a source like milk in a jug' (Klejn 2001a: 22). For:

> It does not flow by itself from the source—it must be extracted, by squeezing the source like a vessel, by turning it inside out. Its quantity and quality depend not only on the objects of reflection but also on by whom and how this information is extracted and consumed. In that 'milk' or 'cream' form in which it is often imaged [*sic*], it exists neither in archaeological sources nor in any historical sources in their initial state. In that sense historical and archaeological sources are similar. (Ibid.)

That is to say, to extract any useful information both the historian and the archaeologist must, in Francis Bacon's words, put their sources 'to the question'[6] [that is, to torture]. Again, there is agreement with Collingwood.

However, Collingwood, unlike Klejn, has little to say about the difference between archaeology and history. Klejn argues that the distinctiveness of archaeology as opposed to history (and ethnography) (Klejn 2001a: 30) stems from the distinctiveness of its subject matter. Language may be polysemantic, but material artefacts are even more so.

Unlike the historian, the archaeologist has to deal with a two-fold break from its subject matter.

> Without preliminary remaking, information fixed in things is not suitable for scholarly use. One must recode it and do it twice. First one must translate it from what is metaphorically called the 'language of things' to any of the natural languages; to describe things and their relations. At this stage one has to use special terminology much more than in history. Then it is necessary, by comparing acquired evidence with others, to establish what events and processes of the past have been reflected in the material sources described. Only then does the information obtained reach the form demanded by the historical discipline. (Ibid.: 24)

It may be remembered from the exposition of *The New Archaeology* (2009) that Klejn believes that this two-fold break tended to be ignored by the proponents of New Archaeology: 'They used, and discovered, processual laws—good—but they ignored other laws dealing with how a past phenomenon left a trace in the archaeological record. For example, ceramics will accumulate more quickly in the archaeological record than metal, because metal is more likely to be reused' (Leach 2011). He believes that it was by ignoring this fundamental aspect of the interpretation of archaeological sources that American archaeologists 'settled into the house of anthropology' (Klejn 1971: 120).

According to Pavel Dolukhanov: 'It should be remarked that Leo Klejn . . . was the first to diagnose "the double rupture" existing between the level of archaeological entities and that of social and cultural interpretation' (Dolukhanov 2009: 3). However, Klejn notes that his observation was inspired by the German archaeologist Hans-Jürgen Eggers, 'in particular his works of 1950 and 1959 on the "inner" criticism of archaeological records' (Leach 2011). Although Eggers did not make the point about the nature of archaeological sources fully explicit, he made the point that archaeological sources—even when intentionally deposited—never provide us with an undistorted mirror image of the culture in which they originated. Here is the first break with the past. Then there are the postdepositional changes to contend with—the fact that different materials erode at different rates, that the ruins of buildings may be 'robbed' of useful stones, and so on. Here is the second break.

Klejn argues that this double break is the principal distinguishing characteristic of archaeology. By contrast in ethnography there is only one break in that one may observe the function of an object within a society. (Sometimes the object might be old, and seen as outdated, but its use may still be understood. In other words, it is neither a modern object nor an antiquity. In Russian there is a specific term for such objects, *starina* (Klejn 2001a: 28). *Starina*, too, fall within the ethnographer's province—until, often quite suddenly, these objects are no longer understood.)

Likewise, the historian has to deal with only a single break, because the historian has 'the channel of written tradition' (Ibid.: 30)—a channel that is comparatively free of obstructions, for, as mentioned, written sources may be polysemantic, but they tend not to be as polysemantic as nonwritten sources.

> From these considerations it follows that it is impossible to establish a strict and common chronological date for the separation of archaeological objects from non-archaeological. It follows, too, that excavations are not obligatory for attributing objects and works to archaeology . . . there are excavations without archaeology and there is archaeology without excavations. (Ibid.)

In summary, Klejn is opposed to drawing a vertical distinction between archaeology and history—with archaeology equating to prehistory—at some almost arbitrary point along a timeline. This was the practice that predominated in Klejn's younger days in the Soviet Union, against which he rebelled. It was founded on the assumption that the past could be read from material sources in the same way that it might be read from a book. Klejn's intention is rather to draw a horizontal distinction between archaeology and history. He believes that their relations are well summarised in the saying that archaeology is 'the handmaiden of history'. However, since this description has not met with agreement or sympathy among Klejn's Western colleagues it may be prudent to add at this point that this is only a metaphor, and like all metaphors it has its limitations. Although Klejn believes that the distinction between archaeology is horizontal it should be emphasised that it is not his belief that history and archaeology stand in a relationship of superiority and inferiority.

2. The Nature of Archaeological Methodology

Klejn does not define archaeology solely by its subject matter; he first asks *how* the archaeologist goes about studying that subject matter. He also argues that in inquiring as to what is distinctive about the methodology of archaeological methodology we must determine its relation to other disciplines—both those to which it is similar and those from which it is distinct, and those in relation to which it might be both similar and distinct.

SCIENCE OR HUMANITY? The neo-Kantian philosophers Wilhelm Windelband and Heinrich Rickert proposed a scheme whereby academic disciplines are divided between the nomothetic and the idiographic. Nomothetic disciplines are those that aim at revealing laws in a mass of material; idiographic disciplines are concerned with revealing and explaining facts in their individuality. Windelband and Rickert argued that the sciences are nomothetic and the humanities are idiographic. Accordingly, anthropology and sociology would, for example, be classed as sciences, because they are primarily concerned with formulating laws from large samples of material. By contrast, history would be classed as a humanity, because the historian is interested in facts in their individuality. (Laws are of use to the historian, but their production is not the historian's *raison d'être*—as it is, for example, the sociologist's.)

Now we might ask whether, according to this scheme, archaeology is a science or a humanity. However, Klejn argues that this would be a mistake, because by this route we will be immediately led into difficulties. He points out that the question relies on two related presuppositions, both of which are questionable:

A. 'The nature of archaeology is defined by its alternative association either with anthropology (correspondingly with sociology or sociologically oriented history) or with idiographic history';
B. 'These two domains are really two halves of research knowledge: science and humanity' (Klejn 2001a: 35).

Klejn questions (A) on the ground that 'history strives to understand unique events and heroes, whereas archaeology is obsessed with generalisation, typification, and its central concept is "type"' (Ibid.). On the other hand, 'archaeology cannot be considered the same as anthropology either, because the system of archaeological data is lifeless. It has no simple and direct correspondence with a society that lived in the past and with the cultures that lived in the past' (Ibid.).

So much for (A); but (B), the deeper presupposition, is also challenged. Klejn prefers a scheme of knowledge more like those proposed by Francis Bacon and Auguste Comte, in which there is a division between abstract and concrete disciplines. However, he is not quite content with their schemes either; as will be seen, he does not wish to classify archaeology as either one of the abstract or one of the concrete disciplines. He argues that, owing to its subject matter, the methodology of archaeology is of a yet different sort.

Reconstruction Klejn argues that reconstruction is the 'all-embracing task of archaeology' (Klejn 2001a: 38). Against those who would argue that this is the main task of history his response is that 'history cannot retrieve facts that have disappeared without trace, and can no longer make them concrete or retrieve them in their concreteness and uniqueness. It sees the past in terms of certain general characteristics, which are expressed in its hypotheses' (Ibid.: 37). As such, strictly speaking, history 'does not reconstruct, but it synthesises historical past on the basis of its sources, and the result of the synthesis is not one of reconstruction' (Ibid.). This act of synthesis is, according to Klejn, the central task of history. There is some overlap here with sociology, but the difference is that history remains focused on the individual.

However, although reconstruction is not the historian's task, it *is* the archaeologist's task: 'everything in archaeology can be reduced to reconstruction' (Klejn 2001a: 38). More specifically, according to Klejn, the main task of archaeology is 'to convert information from the language of things into the language of history, the language of historical phenomena, events, and processes' (Ibid.).

How does the archaeologist do this? Obviously the past cannot be simply read from the material sources. But why not? One problem is that the same social phenomena under different conditions leave different traces. The example Klejn gives is of the sling and the bow and arrow. They both served the same function (Ibid.). An equivalent problem exists in the reverse direction (similar traces may represent very different conditions): for example, a burnt house may represent many different causes—natural disaster, arson, war, or ritual (Ibid.).

The archaeologist can never overcome these problems entirely, but there is a simple expedient by which he or she can mitigate them to some degree. 'An investigator seeks objects belonging to the same type or objects of a similar kind and looks for similar assemblages that are already known or other ones that are better preserved. Thus he provides an interpretation by close comparison' (Klejn 2001a: 39). In this fundamental respect archaeology is orientated on the typical, and on typology. Admittedly, sometimes unique objects are found; but they are still described in a way that makes them amenable to typological study. That is to say, the object will be described in terms of its (non-unique) constituent parts. Having classified the finds and dated them, the archaeologist's resulting studies are then in a state in which they can be used by the historian.

In short, it is crucial for the archaeologist to generalise about what is typical. As we have seen, Klejn admires the Swedish archaeologist Mats P. Malmer for his appreciation of this fact:

> Malmer correctly grasped the necessity for every generalisation and for every interpretation to break away from particular artefacts. Archaeologists who believe they avoid typology and rely exclusively on stratigraphy or on combinations of artefacts in assemblages remind Malmer of Molière's *Le Bourgeois gentilhomme* who did not realise that he was speaking prose. In fact these archaeologists use typology permanently, but only unconsciously and therefore they often do so incorrectly. (Ibid., 77)

Klejn believes that, in blurring the distinction between archaeology and history, post-processual archaeology lost sight of the importance of the typical, the general, and the law-like.

> In Lampeter post-processualists put it to me that it must be acknowledged that people in the past had some influence over their environment and all depended on their individual will. This I willingly acknowledged. Yes, I concede that we, all of us, choose our own path and that there is, to some degree, agency, and that this is true for every individual: but still the statistical laws remain. (Leach 2011)

More recently, a renewed interest in evolutionism, in the work of Robert Dunnel and Steve Shennan and others, has, to Klejn's approval, been accompanied by a renewed interest in problems of classification and typology.

Forensic Science It should by now be apparent that, in Klejn's opinion, reconstruction—and hence orientation on the typology, rather than the individual—constitutes a fundamental difference between the archaeologist's methodology and the historian's. In summary:

> Archaeology is unconditionally connected with history, but it is connected by business relations, as a partner. In other areas they are sometimes not only dissimilar but not even akin. They are of a different methodological nature. While history is an individualising discipline, and, taking into account the individuality of human creatures, history is a humanity, archaeology is not. This is a fundamental difference. (Klejn 2001a, 40)

Nonetheless, both disciplines have something in common in that, although neither discipline reveals laws (in the manner of sociology for example), they both use laws, albeit for different purposes.

History uses laws for explaining facts whereas archaeology uses laws for reconstruction. History is orientated toward explanation, whereas archaeology is orientated toward interpretation. The difference is significant: it serves to categorise archaeology in relation to other disciplines of inquiry. It implies that, on Klejn's scheme of the disciplines of inquiry, archaeology does not belong to either the abstract or the concrete sciences (which together constitute the fundamental sciences) but rather to the applied sciences (Ibid.).

Perhaps unexpectedly, this conception of archaeology suggests that archaeology's nearest relative is not necessarily to be found in academia; its nearest relative is forensic science. The archaeologist, attempting to reconstruct past events from their material remains, finds him- or herself in the same position as the detective who notices a cigarette stub at the scene of a crime:

> Has the stub been left by the criminal, victim, witness or a chance passer-by who saw nothing? Was the cigarette smoked during the

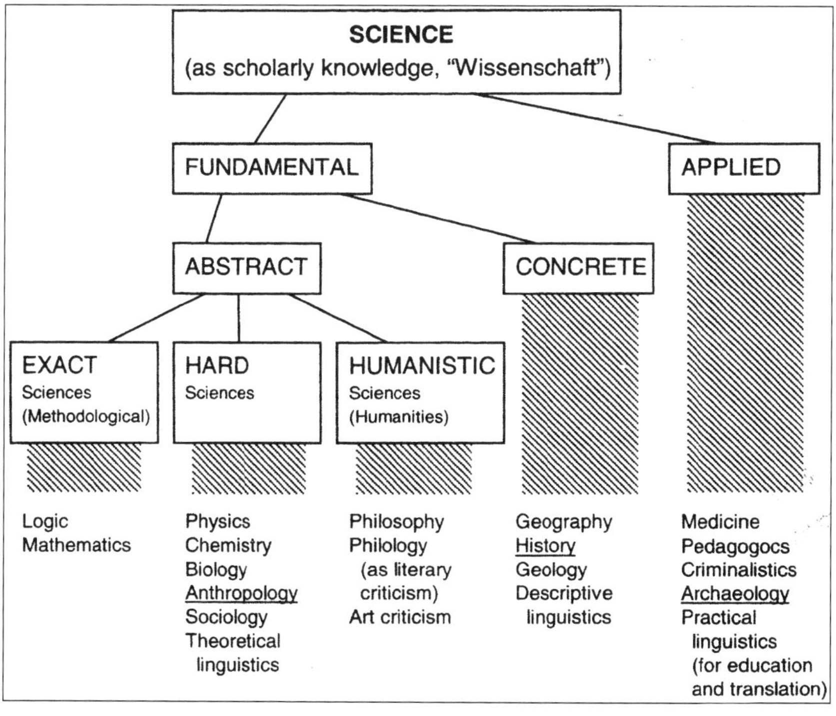

Figure 9.1 Archaeology in the scheme of disciplines[7]

> moment and at the spot of the event of interest for the investigation, or had an ashtray been knocked and the butt fallen out before the event? The list of possible correspondences between the things and events is not limitless—it is quite apparent the cigarette was not smoked by a horse belonging to the criminal or by the investigator's dog—but nevertheless the list is very large, and it is difficult to grant its completeness. (Klejn 2001a, 24)

Both the archaeologist's sources and the detective's sources have many different potential meanings, and to mitigate this problem both professions attempt to generalise about what is typical. (Readers of Conan Doyle may at this point bring to mind Sherlock Holmes's short monograph *Upon the Distinction between the Ashes of Various Tobaccos*. If non-fictional examples are preferred, the importance of classifications of bullets and blood types to the detective should be obvious.)

Klejn first put forward this comparison, in print, in *Archaeological Sources* (1978), although already for many years previous to this publication it had been on prominent display as one of the 25 humorous aphorisms that famously decorated the walls of his classroom: 'Archaeology is not history armed with a spade but a detective story in which the investigator has arrived at the scene a thousand years late. History is pronounced later by judges. So you must decide: to go in for one or for the other'. (All 25 of these aphorisms, 'The Commandments', are given in Appendix A.) Klejn recalls that the comparison first occurred to him in 1953 when he was sharing a room with his brother, who was then a state prosecutor—he later became an historian—and with his brother's colleague, a detective. Further reflection on the subject around the time of his trial led to an ever closer identification of the two disciplines, and by the time of his release from the labour camp he had reached the position that the two disciplines were conceptually identical. Only their purpose differed.

Since the publication of *Archaeological Sources* in 1978 Klejn returned to this comparison in an article on the 'Methodological Nature of Archaeology' in 1992, which formed the basis of the chapter of the same name in *Metaarchaeology* (2001a). Indeed, he has probably written more on this comparison than any other writer. In the West the comparison was made in passing in numerous novels of the 'golden age' of detective fiction, the 1920s and 1930s,[8] including those of Agatha Christie, and was briefly discussed in R. G. Collingwood's posthumous *Idea of History* (Collingwood 1993: 266–68).[9] However, unlike Collingwood (and uninfluenced by him), Klejn is at pains to stress the point—left unexplored by Collingwood—that it is the archaeologist rather than the historian who is like the detective. As mentioned, the historian, in Klejn's view, is more akin to a judge (Leach 2011).

Klejn notes that although other archaeologists have made the same comparison (Clark 1939; Hrouda 1978) it is not usually explored in any depth. Having carried out a thorough investigation of the comparison, Klejn concludes that although detectives confine themselves to the pathological side of (recent) social life, and their evidence will be used in a court of law—and in this respect the purpose of their work is different from the archaeologist's—otherwise, the aim is the same: 'to restore the events and processes of the past by their material traces and fragmented remains' (Klejn 2001a: 40).

Klejn also points out that forensic science has actually influenced the development of archaeology.[10] Archaeology has, of course, borrowed from many other sources—for example, stratigraphy from geology, typology from palaeontology, dating terminology and closed assemblages from numismatics but forensic science, too, has influenced archaeology in important ways. In particular, police involvement in cases of notorious archaeological fakes, such as the Glozel fake and the Saitapharnes tiara, has emphasised the importance of a standardised protocol to be followed at every stage of an investigation, regardless of what interpretational hypotheses may be momentarily entertained (Ibid.). There is an analogy here between the archaeologist's records—and the detective's notebook—which at a later date may have to be produced in court.

The parallels and interactions between the two disciplines are fascinating, but as yet although archaeology has developed an awareness of its own history, there is perhaps not yet a comparable awareness of the history of forensic science to be found among the practitioners of that discipline. A reliable and comprehensive history of forensic science would be of interest both to detectives and to archaeologists.

The significance of Klejn's identification of archaeology with forensic science is further investigated in the final chapter.

3. Combatant Gods: The Fundamental Principles of Archaeology[11]

Klejn notes that, as an applied science, archaeology tends to be less interested in theory than a pure science is—physics, for example, is obviously keenly interested in theory—nonetheless it is supported by definite underlying principles that the theorist may reveal: 'Fundamental concepts and principles . . . do not find grounds in this discipline itself—on the contrary, the discipline is based on them' (Ibid.: 43). As to how they might be discovered, Klejn and Collingwood are in agreement that they might be discovered only by observing the best examples of contemporary practice: 'When [one is] looking for axioms it is difficult to suggest any preliminary order, save perhaps starting from within the discipline, from the supposed derivatives' (Ibid.). There is a striking similarity here to Collingwood's theory of presuppositions, as expounded in his *Essay on Metaphysics* (Collingwood 1940: 21–33), with Klejn's 'fundamental concepts and principles' corresponding to Collingwood's 'absolute presuppositions'. These are the presuppositions that form the bedrock of whatever discipline it is that they underlie. Within that discipline they have 'logical efficacy', even though they may not be explicitly known by the practitioners of that discipline.

This then is what Klejn does: he looks for the presuppositions underlying the best examples of contemporary practice. (It should be noted that he does so independently of Collingwood. Only Collingwood's *Idea of History* is known to Klejn, not his *Essay on Metaphysics*.)[12] However, although Klejn's ultimate datum is practice, in proposing the underlying fundamental principles of archaeology he makes use not only of his own experience of archaeological investigation but also of the observations of other archaeological theorists.

In *The Principles of Archaeology* (2001) and *Metaarchaeology* (2001a) he proposes that archaeology rests on these six principles.

1. Determinism—As in nature, the same phenomenon will appear under the same conditions (Klejn 2001a: 48).
2. Universalism—The idea that the psychology of all normal people is basically the same (Ibid.).
3. Uniformitarianism—Strictly speaking, as geologists know, we should speak of the principle of uniformitarianism (we observe the same regularities now as existed in the past) and the principle of actualism (we must rely on contemporary experience in interpreting material sources) (Ibid.).
4. The Systematic Order in Culture—In the words of Bruce Trigger: 'all elements of a cultural system are interrelated and that alterations in any one component will result in changes of varying degrees in all features of the system and in their interrelationships'.[13]
5. Material/Nonmaterial Correlation—'Physical similarity entails a probability of every other form of similarity, i.e., similarity in respect of time, use, name and environment' (Ibid.: 49).
6. The Fundamental Sufficiency of the Data—Archaeological sources allow for full reconstruction and reliable interpretation—a principle especially prevalent among Marxists and New Archaeologists (Ibid.).

None of these principles has escaped criticism. However, although 'in theory we disapprove of these principles and now and again jeer at them because of their naivety . . . in practice we follow them' (Ibid.: 52).

And yet, Klejn argues, it is no surprise that these principles have attracted criticism; because—strange but true—we also give credence to work that relies on the very opposite set of principles!

- Indeterminacy—'Unfortunately for the archaeological process cultures are generally quite unreasonable'.[14] 'Cultural laws don't exist'.[15]
- Particularism—'Each archaeological object and situation is unique'.[16]

- Historicism—There is substantial differentiation between epochs (Ibid.: 53).
- Irregularity—Any systemisation is essentially the subjective creation of the archaeologist (Ibid.: 54).
- Polysemism—Material culture is irreducibly polysemous (or polysemantic) (Ibid.; see also Shanks and Tilley [1987]).
- Initial incompleteness of the data—This idea, put forward by Christopher Hawkes (Hawkes 1954), is well summarised by Wheeler. The 'archaeologist will find the tub and will completely miss Diogenes. He will write profound papers on the typology of tubs; he will classify in categories A, B, and C; he will discover a Tub-bearing Folk and plot their wanderings on geographical and geological maps. . . . Only, he has overlooked and could not help overlooking the one significant thing about that Tub, namely, that it sheltered the eminent Cynic and symbolised his philosophy for all time'.[17]

Now although, as we have seen, Klejn himself relies on the idea that archaeological sources are polysemantic—the same source may have different meanings according to context—and although he would agree with Wheeler about Diogenes' tub,[18] he also recognises that some good work has been done on the opposite of these principles. His point is that no one side of these antinomies predominates in all circumstances over its opposite. Rather, in the face of every new problem, it is the archaeologist who decides which principles will predominate.

Against Klejn, we might anticipate the objection that laws that contradict each other are not laws at all. However, Klejn is not proposing these principles as laws but rather as foundational presuppositions. Therefore, when the archaeologist chooses one side of the antinomy over its opposite he or she is rejecting its opposite (on grounds of practicality) but is not refuting it.

Klejn thus presents us with a strange and disquieting spectacle: 'the fundamental principles of archaeology are arranged in pairs—like the quarrelling Gods before the Battle of the Gods in Homer's Iliad' (Klejn 2001a: 55)—or, an alternative analogy, like two computers in a system of parallel processing, the algorithms of which are monitored by a third. (Klejn finds the idea of conflicting, but not disabling, principles corroborated in the work of Niels Bohr and in V. V. Nalimov's *In Search of Other Meanings* (1993), and he speculates that the effectiveness of conflicting, but not necessarily disabling, presuppositions may have repercussions in the development of artificial intelligence [Ibid.: 56].)

Klejn argues that the existence of these conflicting principles should not be taken to imply that the discipline is schizophrenic or irrational. The situation is resolved in practice, on a case by case basis, but it is never finally resolved. 'When Gods are fighting, defeats and victories are illusory—no corpses are left on the battlefield, wounds recover, and all is as though nothing had happened. Only mortals involved in the conflict lose their lives' (Ibid.: 55). The battle

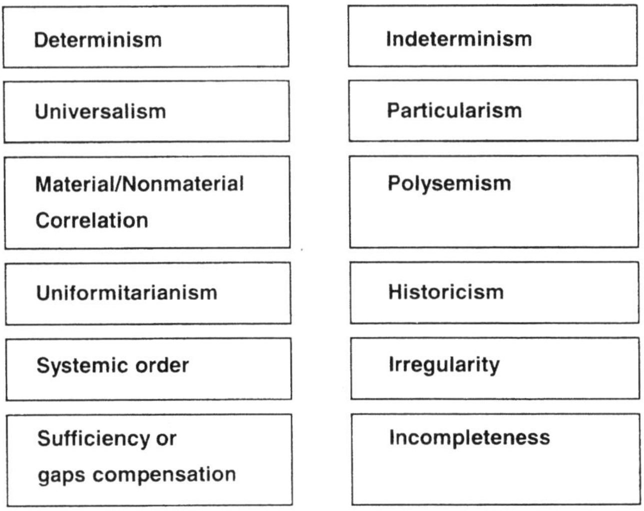

Figure 9.2 The combatant Gods: The fundamental principles of archaeology[19]

continues. Only by stepping outside the discipline entirely would it be possible for one to legislate as to the victors, but this is a move that Klejn refuses to make; for, remember, for Klejn, theoretical archaeology does not hover above practice. Moreover, even by stepping outside the discipline, one would not likely find a resolution; if anything in archaeology is clear it is that 'data are always terribly incomplete, and meaning is hidden which must be deciphered' (Ibid.).

Klejn's pragmatic approach is such that he refuses to rule out any theoretical approach on purely *a priori* grounds. He returns to this theme in his autobiography:

> Let there be many theoretical approaches. Let these theoretical approaches compete as political approaches, but not as political doctrines. Let there be Marxist, structuralist and, poststructuralist approaches, and even post-Marxist approaches. After all, we are dealing with complex structures that have many aspects, and there are many ways to study them. But all approaches should follow scientific procedures, competing and cooperating with each other. (Klejn 2010: 309)

Thus, according to Klejn, all approaches have their uses—as tools in the archaeologist's toolkit. (As we have seen, this still includes Marxism: while Klejn is sharply critical of Marxism as an all-embracing *Weltanschauung*, it still has a place in his toolkit.) He maintains that, within an applied science, rather than locking us into a contradiction the combatant Gods grant us a certain agility that we would otherwise lack.

Chapter 10

What Is Theoretical Archaeology?

Antitheoretical Empiricism

Despite the differences in their historical backgrounds, Russian archaeology and Western archaeology still share a significant common factor: there remain large numbers of archaeologists who are indifferent to theoretical archaeology, if not downright hostile. In Russia, despite the fact that 'Marxism demands theory and negates empiricism' (Klejn pers. comm.), this antipathy can be traced back to the Soviet era. As an example, Klejn told me the story of how in the Soviet era one archaeologist presented him with a particularly unusual artefact and challenged him to use his 'theory' to say something about its use. Klejn confessed that he knew nothing about the artefact but that given time he hoped to learn more about it. Many years later, Klejn was able to revisit his inquisitor and tell her how he had finally worked out the artefact's use. He admits that in this instance the role of theory was not obvious, but nonetheless it was still present.

In *Metaarchaeology* Klejn attempts to catalogue the basic characteristics and beliefs of this worldwide, antitheoretical, and resolutely empirical attitude:

- *All hopes on fact*—the facts speak for themselves (Klejn 2001a: 61).
- *Belief in pure facts*—deduction plays no part in archaeology; we may infer, via induction, from an 'objectively existent' reality (Ibid.).
- *Revealing types*—types reveal themselves in the data irrespective of the opinions of the researcher (Ibid.).
- *Description instead of thinking*—a preference exists for ostensive definitions—for example: 'If cultures, as a viable concept, are indeed to be recognised, they can be defined only by total enumeration of their parts'.[1]
- *Induction as the only valid way*—inductive generalisation is the only method required by science (Ibid.: 62–63).
- *Data versus speculation*—theory is equated with a castle in the air. Heinrich Härke describes such an attitude in his analysis of German archaeology. 'The word theory, to German ears, sounds airy-fairy; it implies speculation

A Russian Perspective on Theoretical Archaeology: The Life and Work of Leo S. Klejn by Stephen Leach, 125–134

"without foundation" (i.e., without evidence), and it seems to exclude practicality, which is considered highly desirable. To call somebody a "theoretician", or to call something "theory", invariably carries derogatory undertones. In order to avoid these connotations, German scholars outside the natural sciences avoid the term "theory" as far as possible, and if they have to, they put it under the heading of "methodology". *Methodik* has a solid ring; it sounds practical, systematic, goal-oriented, and efficient'.[2]

- *Generalisations as the road to theory*—the only theories that should be adopted are generalisations from the facts (Ibid.: 62).
- *Voracious hunt for facts*—'It is supposed that the more facts are collected, the more valid are inferences, and, in the case of the generalisation held as theoretical, the more facts that are accumulated, the deeper the theory is. Hence the silently approved uncertainty of aims in many project plans' (Ibid.).
- *Horror vacui*—theory should be avoided in view of the incompleteness of the archaeological record (Ibid.: 63).
- *Unfeasible desire of completeness*—while induction is preferred to any other form of inference, there is also the desire to wait until all the data is collected before any form of inference is made (Ibid.).
- *Practical experience as a permit to theorising*—theory should be permitted only to those with many years of empirical experience (Ibid.: 63–64).
- *The 'not-the-time-for-theory' argument*—archaeology must first progress through an empirical phase before it indulges in theory, a view that was put forward in the Soviet Union at the very time that Klejn was publishing his first works of theoretical archaeology. The other side of the coin was presented by Ulrich Fischer: 'One can justifiably state that the theoretical section of the methodology of our subject has been completed. Additions are to be expected in the practical section'.[3]

Klejn concedes that there are circumstances in which archaeology has progressed without any theory other than that implicitly held by antitheoretical empiricists, for example: 'in a previously empty place, where materials have still not been collected . . . or where there are no methods at all . . . or where it confronts schematism and dogmatism, preconceived ideas, and *a priori* schemes. Here it gains victories' (Ibid.: 65). However, to concede as much is not to yield ground to the antitheoretical empiricists, because it remains the case that there is far more than can be constructively said about theory than they have to say.

The Concept of Theory in Oppositions

Klejn argues that within theoretical archaeology there are five basic answers to the question of 'what is theoretical archaeology?'

1. *Ordered totality of facts* (Ibid.: 66)—Theory is no more than the summary of the facts.
2. *Ordered totality of concepts* (Ibid.: 67)—This definition is a development of the previous definition, in that a concept is often thought of as no more than a generalisation.
3. *System of laws* (Ibid.)—Laws are seen as related to observations, although underdetermined by observations.
4. *A set of interconnected methods* (Ibid.: 68).
5. *Projection of philosophical theory* (Ibid.)—One example is the theory of historical materialism in the Soviet Union.

Klejn notes that in these proposed answers there is a tendency to reduce theory to just a single one of its components. In putting forward his own conception of theory, he aims to avoid any such simplification. Klejn's answer to the question of 'what is theory?' is demonstrated with the aid of Figure 10.1. The diagram expresses the idea that theory is in the same relationship to speculation as practice is to theory, and, conversely, theory is in the same relationship to practice as speculation is to theory; and so on.

So what, finally, is theoretical archaeology? It is not an entirely free-floating meditation on the aims and higher aspects of archaeology; that would be 'sheer twaddle' (Klejn pers. comm.). Theory is rather 'an instrument—it must work. Theory in archaeology, as in any other discipline, is a program for extracting information from materials' (Ibid.). 'In fact, theory if stereotyped becomes a method' (Ibid.).

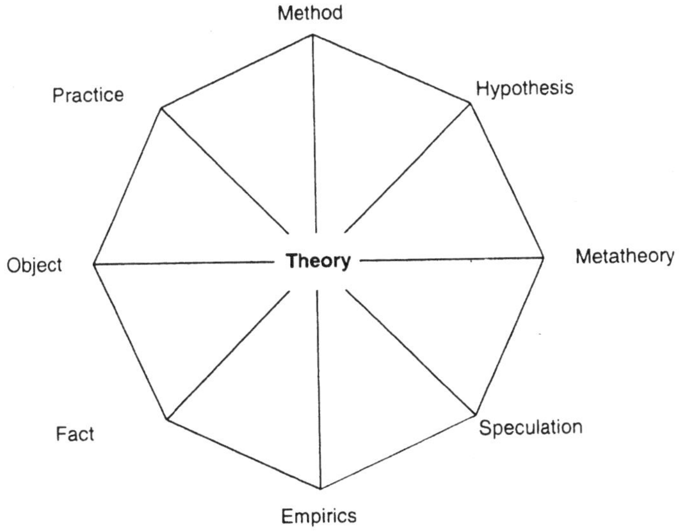

Figure 10.1 The concept of theory in oppositions[4]

As a program for extracting information from materials, theoretical archaeology draws inspiration from any possible source, but that is not to imply that it is disorganised. As will be seen, a study of its structure and its functions suggests just the reverse.

The Cognitive Structure of Theoretical Archaeology

The archaeological theorist makes use of processual laws—both bridging laws and those concerned with the development of sociocultural systems. The former are unique to archaeology. They detail (1) how ideas are reflected in things; (2) how events leave material traces; (3) how material sources deteriorate over time; and (4) how information is gathered from material sources (Klejn 2001a: 73).

Both sorts of law derive partly from an empirical basis and partly from a purely theoretical basis. They are combined in explanations that also dictate the expectations of future observations. 'Unforeseen observations disprove a theory of course, and predicted observations substantiate it, although not completely, for they only make it more probable (and without quantitative determinations of the degree of probability), because the expected phenomenon could be due to other causes' (Ibid.: 85).

Klejn sees archaeological explanations as at bottom hypothetical reconstructions—containing an ineradicable element of inductive reasoning. As such the supersession of one explanation by another may approach ever nearer to the truth but never attains absolute certainty (Leach 2011).

The Functions of Theoretical Archaeology

According to David Clarke: 'the central theory uniting archaeology is implicit in what archaeologists do and constitutes a real central theory, however weak and inadequate any written account of it may prove to be'.[5] Klejn agrees, but he also believes that definite advantages follow from making this theory explicit: 'an explicit presentation of theory allows us to use its merits more effectively and to detect its shortcomings at an earlier stage' (Klejn 2001a: 87).

In making the use of theory in archaeology explicit, Klejn identifies the following 12 functions.

1. *The Identicative Function*—Theory is used when archaeology is asked to identify its own material. Clearly the archaeologist should avoid mistaking natural phenomena for cultural objects, or *vice versa* (Ibid.: 88–89).
2. *The Integrative Function*—It is a problem of theory as to whether archaeology should be split into different branches, with correspondingly different branches of theory. Some countries have, for example, traditionally divided archaeology into 'text-aided' and 'text-free' (or classical and

prehistoric). However, Russia never followed this route—rightly not, thinks Klejn: 'It is not by chance that there are no special theoretical works applicable only to prehistoric archaeology. When a theoretical book by an archaeologist is published, whether on specificity of sources, or on classificatory concepts, or on ways of interpretation, it is sought with equal interest by archaeologists from all branches of the discipline' (Ibid.: 91).

3. *The Selective Function*—Klejn acknowledges that the problem of collecting evidence has been intensively studied by British and American theorists. He notes that: 'In general, empiricists suppose that one has to strive for maximal recovery, ideally to collect *all* of the material' (Ibid.). Although he recognises that this is clearly a misguided strategy, he also recognises that, since excavation is an inherently destructive process, a very narrow focus is also undesirable. Rather, 'it is sensible to gather information according to a broad set of questions' (Ibid.).
4. *The Descriptive Function*—The elaboration of an appropriately descriptive vocabulary is a function of theory—in recent years, influenced by computer-based archiving.
5. *The Systematising Function*—This is the subject of Klejn's *Archaeological Typology* (1982). One of the main themes of this book is the criticism of purely empirical procedures. Another is the difference between archaeological classification and archaeological typology: 'If on the basis of similarities and differences the material is distributed into strictly delineated cells, covered by standard categories, a scheme of classification results. If the material is clustered around concepts on which the centres of such categories are fixed, a scheme of typology is built' (Ibid.: 93).
6. *The Problem of Explanatory Function*—Klejn notes that discussion over the nature of explanation in archaeology is confused by disagreement over the subject matter of archaeology as distinct from history. He argues that if archaeology, as a source-studying discipline, is kept distinct from history then it becomes clear that archaeologists make use of three different mechanisms of interpretation: explanation by analogy; functional-structural explanation; and causal explanation. Of these only the last is a form of deductive explanation, but it is not deterministic. It presupposes only that 'behind every cause some regularity, even if probabilistic, is hidden' (Ibid.: 95).
7. *The Problem of the Predictive Function*—In archaeology a predictive function—which many would see as crucial to any scientific theory—is inseparable from reconstruction. It is a hypothetical reconstruction that creates expectations for the future discovery of material sources and that will itself be judged against them. However, archaeological reconstructions 'do not usually pursue the task of exactly and minutely restoring individual aspects. Even as applied to single artefacts they content themselves with restoring type-characteristics' (Ibid.: 97).

8. *The Instrumental Function*—Theory is brought into practice by being transformed into a method. For example: 'Winckelmann and Gerhardt elaborated fundamentals of the comparative-stylistic method. The Danish progessionists Thomsen and Worsaae turned their scheme of the "Three Ages" into the method of correlating artefact forms with epoch and came to the stratigraphic method. . . . Processual archaeology, with its interest in a systemic approach and "models", introduced multivariate methods and computer simulation' (Ibid.), and so on.
9. *The Heuristic Function*—Theory guides the direction of future research, and theory also guides the direction taken by future theory.
10. *The Control Function*—The stability and reliability at the core of theory allow us to give short shrift to the theories of Erich von Danniken, and so forth (Ibid.: 99).
11. *The Synthesising Function*—'Theory synthesises the material—it condenses the empirical information and simplifies its mosaic. It seeks to explain as wide as possible a range of appearances on the basis of as few as possible premises. Therefore, a trend to expansion is inherent in any theory: theory begins penetrating into the area of competence of other theories and disciplines . . . each new one has to show its validity by being able to explain also those phenomena that the previous one could not' (Ibid.).
12. *The Enlightening Function*—'Last, but not least, the function of archaeological theory is to enlighten' (Ibid.: 100). As was mentioned at the beginning of the previous chapter, without theory we would have only tradition and the method of trial and error to guide us.

Information Processing: The Fourteen Weirs

Klejn argues that when we recognise archaeological facts we are recognising imperfect reflections of past events. A transfer of information has taken place. However, the process by which this information is transferred is not at all straightforward. The information may pass through as many as fourteen different stages:

1. *Stimuli*—the stimuli of social and personal practices ('production, economical and political relationships, ideology or mentality, everyday life, etc.') (Ibid.: 109).
2. *Ideas*—'social norms, customs, standards, individual motives' (Ibid.).
3. *Actions*—realising 'customs, stereotypes, and idioms of behaviour' (Ibid.).
4. *Embodiments*—of behaviour and the indirect objectification of ideas.
5. *Deposits*—of the dead and of grave goods, and of defunct artefacts.
6. *Remains*—the fraction of artefacts that have been preserved.
7. *Destruction*—by nonscientific looters, and so on.

8. *The observed*—that which came under direct scrutiny during the investigation.
9. *Discoveries*—interrelationships discovered and noted by the researcher.
10. *Samples*—selection in the field is required, because not everything can be recorded.
11. *Filtrates*—the same objects minus 'pseudo-artefacts, no genuine traces, fakes, counterfeits, forgeries. This is the purified fraction' (Ibid.).
12. *Descriptions*—by means of conventional and specialised terminology, and by graphs, plans, and technical drawings.
13. *Generalisations*—isolating the essential information 'by means of taxonomic classification, type, and systematisation' (Ibid.).
14. *Evidence*—a report on the information derived from description and/or generalisation 'in a lodged work (field report, dissertation etc.), in files, or in computer memory as well as in personal archives, and, at worst, in the researcher's own memory' (Ibid.).

At each stage there are problems of transmission; or, to be more precise, there are obstacles to the transmission of information between one stage and the next. Klejn suggests that these obstacles might be thought of as weirs along a river. Imagine navigating a small boat with a precious cargo of information: the archaeologist must somehow navigate the boat over every one of these problematic weirs. Klejn describes the different weirs as follows (the numbers in parentheses refer to the previous list):

- *Crystallisation of stimuli* (0–1)—The problem here is that 'under the impact of different conditions, frequently random ones, similar causes can lead to different effects, and behind similar effects different causes can be hidden' (Ibid.: 110).
- *Realisation of stimuli* (1–2)—Although material sources reflect ideas, they do not provide a completely reliable reflection.
- *Interpretation of ideas in behaviour* (2–3)—Thoughts are never entirely inferable from behaviour. (Freedom of will 'is not limitless but not fictional either' [Ibid.].)
- *Objectification of behavioural acts* (3–4)—There is no unambiguous correlation between artefacts and ideas. 'It is clear that behaviour intervenes between ideas and objects (artefacts), behaviour . . . usually does not realise the ideas exactly. Besides, a gap always exists between the behaviour and its objectified results (artefacts)' (Ibid.).
- *The first act of archaeologisation* (4–5)—There is a predepositional process of selection, whereby people select what to discard or to deposit as grave goods and what to keep. However large the collection of grave goods it will not mirror the selection of artefacts that were in use during life. (In the case of buried heirlooms there is the phenomenon of 'compression' to

be considered, whereby 'elements that were separated by enormous time intervals in the "living" culture coincide and are mixed together' [Ibid.: 111].)

- *Second act of archaeologisation* (5–6)—After deposition artefacts decompose, corrode, and decay. There is also disturbance through grave-robbing and stone-robbing, and so on. All of which changes the original composition of the assemblage.
- *Modern artificial destruction* (6–7)—Metal detectors removing artefacts from their original contexts, and so forth.
- *The choice of unit for investigation* (7–8)—'Archaeologists are forced to limit the area of sampling and mapping. It is clear that this will influence the amount and content of the information received' (Ibid.).
- *The detection of information bearers* (8–9)—'The detection of artefacts, traces, and relations by researchers in the space outlined. It is insufficient to look at the objects—one has to see them' (Ibid.).
- *Selection of the necessary information* (9–10)—Selection is unavoidable. It is impossible to conserve every artefact.
- *Selection of genuine information* (10–11)—It is necessary to distinguish between ancient artefacts, modern artefacts, and natural objects.
- *Recording of the discovered and selected* (11–12)—Recording compensates for the destruction involved in excavation, but not everything can be recorded.
- *Generalisation or minimisation* (12–13)—This involves 'separation of the essential by means of classification, type, and systematisation. . . . Such estimation has objective footholds in the material. However, culture is a complex and multisided system, and the interests of observers are broad and do not coincide on many points' (Ibid.: 112).
- *Narrative* (13–14)—During preparation 'for publication the last distortions of information are possible—editing, changes to drawings and photos, editorial additions and changes to accentuation, and uncorrected mistakes' (Ibid.).

Each weir must be negotiated with the minimum loss of information. Fortunately, there are tried and tested methods by which this might be done. As Klejn walks with us along the river bank, as we make our way back upstream, he points out the best way to navigate 'our barque of knowledge' over each of the fourteen weirs.

I. TEXTUAL CRITICISM (14–13)—One must ask whether the inner logic of the narrative is convincing. Does it adequately explain the previous stages through which the information has come?

II. CRITIQUE OF CONCEPTS (13–12)—Are the generalisations valid? This question can be answered by (a) reexamining the original material and (b) seeing whether these generalisations 'work' on analogous material.

III. Critique of Description (12–11)—To what extent is our description of the material complete and accurate?
IV. Critique of Authenticity (11–10)—Was the material selected by reliable methods, so as to exclude fakes, and so on?
V. Critique of Selection Process (10–9)—Were the criteria and conditions of selection adequate?
VI. Critique of Observation (9–8)—What might have been overlooked or misinterpreted? In answering this question we must assess 'the methods of survey, equipment of the project, competence of researchers . . . the level of scientific development and the conditions of work, and the intensity of study if carried out over a large area' (Ibid.: 114).
VII. Critique of Limits (8–7)—Within the area under study what proportion of the material came under direct scrutiny?
VIII. Museum Critique (7–6)—To what extent has there been destruction, and loss of information, since the material was placed in storage?
IX. Critique of Remains (6–5)—To what extent might the material have been eroded since its original deposition?
X. Critique of Deposits (5–4)—'An estimation of the changes that occurred when objects passed from the "living" culture to the "dead" one. This estimation has to embrace "depositional" selection of the bearers of ancient culture, "necro" transformations (changes of proportions, etc. in the dead culture in comparison with the living), and compression effects' (Ibid.).
XI. Critique of Things (4–3)—'This is an estimation of the difficulties met in the objectification of behavioural acts. . . . Culture is polysemic. There are no stable correspondences in it; there are only more or less noticeable preferences, usually local, temporal, and each specially conditioned. Each case has to be considered individually. It is necessary to uncover in which cases equal actions led to different results. This is important in order not to overestimate the differences and not to overestimate their meaning. It is also necessary to unravel situations, fortunately not so frequently, where different actions have led to equal results' (Ibid.: 115).
XII. Critique of Behaviour (3–2)—'This is an estimation of the divergence between ideas and their realisation in behaviour. In essence this is a psychological task—to conjecture and grasp ideas from behaviour. This psychological task is very difficult even with living people, whose feelings, thoughts, and intentions we understand better than the psychology of people more distant by culture and time' (Ibid.).
XIII. Critique of Ideas (2–1)—How was the behaviour of ancient people affected by their ideas?
XIV. Critique of Stimuli (1–0)—'We have to estimate to what degree particular stimuli (historical phenomena, events, and circumstances)

were necessary and unavoidable in the conditioning of the behaviour of ancient people' (Ibid.). This method involves analysing the interaction of their ideas, but here we find ourselves in the province of history.

Research Design

Klejn argues that awareness of how archaeological information is attained, and of the questions that must be asked in order to maximise the reliability of this information, has repercussions for how we conceive of archaeological research design:

> The conversion of information consists of phases separated by floodgates that have a filtering effect. In each floodgate every transformation changes the appearance of information and serves as a springboard for the next transformation. Only adjacent phases are connected with each other directly as initial and derived. And quite often some remains, after which one would judge the initial appearance, are kept only in the derived phase. So we make judgements on the initial appearance by issuing from the previous one. If while doing this we skip over some phases, perhaps some essential changes in information will be lost, and distortions of the past reality will be unobserved. As a result we come to false reconstruction. Hence the importance to account for all the phases of conversion, all the floodgates. This must become the basis for working out the full scheme of the archaeological research design. (Ibid.: 119–20)

Klejn argues that although there have been various seemingly incompatible conceptions of archaeological procedures, on closer inspection of archaeological practice one notes that the form of information processing outlined here underlies all scientific archaeological investigations. That is to say, the logical core and epistemological basis of archaeological research is outlined in this process.

As to bias: we are scholars because we are aware of it, and we are scholars to the extent that we cope with it. A scholar should be reliant on filtering mechanisms not simply to counter individual biases (named in advance?) but to minimise bias in general (Ibid.: 130). In short, we need not emulate Baron Münchausen and try to escape the swamp by pulling our own hair (Leach 2011). 'We may never reach absolutely certain knowledge, but we may progress along the road toward it' (Ibid.).

Chapter 11

The Archaeologist and the Detective

In this, the final chapter, I return to the subject of the comparison between archaeology and forensic science. However, I should here again remind the reader that although Klejn has to the best of my knowledge studied this comparison in greater depth than any other archaeological theorist, there are many scholars who would still dispute that its study is Klejn's prime achievement. The comparison is the subject of this chapter partly because it coincides with my own interests and partly because I see here an opportunity to build a bridge not just between Russian theoretical archaeology and Western theoretical archaeology but also between theoretical archaeology and the philosophy of history. Those who work within these fields tend to be ignorant of one another's endeavours.

It will be remembered that Klejn argues that it is the archaeologist rather than the historian who should be compared to the detective. The archaeologist and the detective are primarily interested in the question of 'what happened?', whereas the historian is primarily interested in the question of 'why?'. As such the archaeologist and the detective are interested in constructing systems of classification—for example, of blood and pottery types—in a way that the historian is not. They are concerned with generalising about what is typical. Admittedly, the detective's purpose is different from the archaeologist's—in that his or her evidence will be used in a court of law—but otherwise their aim is the same: 'to restore the events and processes of the past by their material traces and fragmented remains' (Klejn 2001a: 40).

Numerous times Klejn has faced the objection that it is not only the historian who asks 'why?' but also the archaeologist (and the detective) (Kristiansen 1993; Burström 1994; Leach 2011). His response:

> Admittedly there is a 'why?' element within the work of the archaeologist, but it is ultimately subordinate to the question of 'what happened?' For instance, the archaeologist may ask 'why is this artefact fragmented in this way?' or 'why was this pot put into the pit?' yet not 'why did this culture move in this direction?'. Likewise, the detective

A Russian Perspective on Theoretical Archaeology: The Life and Work of Leo S. Klejn by Stephen Leach, 135–143

> may ask 'why did this purse appear in this pocket?' but not: 'why did this man become a thief?'. (Leach 2011)

Even, for the sake of argument, were the detective to call on a psychologist for help in catching a killer, the focus would still be on the *classification* of the killer as a particular sort of psychopath rather than asking 'why?', in the sense in which a historian would ask the question. In other words the historian's 'why?' relates to the historical process; the archaeologist's 'why?' relates to the formation of the archaeological source.

That Klejn's view of forensic science is generally accurate is confirmed when we look at the textbooks of that discipline. According to Broeders, a forensic investigation seeks primarily 'to establish the circumstances of the case, and this is often said to involve the seven golden criminalistic "Wh"-questions. These are questions starting with the words *who, what, where, when, what with, in what way*, and, to a lesser extent, *why*' (2007: 308). Dave Barclay suggests that the detective will attempt to think 'like a criminal' only to the extent that this will help him or her to identify contact points between a contact and its trace.[1]

Klejn's view of archaeology as an applied science, allied to forensic science, leaves him with some sympathy for Walter Taylor's view: 'archaeology is no more than a method and a set of specialised techniques for the gathering of cultural information. The archaeologist as archaeologist is really nothing but a technician'.[2] However, Klejn would argue that archaeology 'is not just a method or technique. It has its own system of concepts, its own theory, and its own principles' (Klejn 2001a: 41). He would also argue that the same holds for forensic science.

One concern underlying criticisms of Klejn's view of archaeology might be that this conception of archaeology leaves little room for creativity and imagination. Against this concern Klejn would argue that, on the contrary, sometimes an imaginative abductive leap is called for in archaeology. (Although he does not mention it in this context, one example from his own work would be the identification of the North-Pontic Catacomb cultures as Indo-Aryan, discussed in Chapter 7.) However, Klejn would still maintain that 'to step inside someone else's shoes' is not the archaeologist's primary aim.

As to where the archaeologist gets his or her questions: 'from history, from sociology, from philosophy, and from general curiosity. Archaeologists have many varied motivations' (Leach 2011). And, presumably, the same holds for the historian.

It should not be thought that the archaeologist, according to Klejn, never deals with written sources. That would clearly be absurd. A written source is also a material source; and no archaeologist would leave a site because, for example, an inscription had come to light. The difference between history and archaeology lies at a deeper level, concerning the two-fold break of archaeological sources. In simple terms, not only is an artefact's use not obvious because it is no longer in use, but its use is made doubly difficult to reconstruct because it has been left in the ground for (perhaps) a thousand years and is, typically, encrusted with dirt. These are not the sort of sources with which a historian has to deal. Yet the historian may mention this same artefact, or more commonly an array of such artefacts, after reading about them in the archaeologist's report. Likewise, the members of a jury are not expected to handle the objects found at a crime scene, but they do expect to read, or to have available, extracts of the detective's report. The comparison—it is more than an analogy—still holds.

In that the historian does not always deal at first hand with the evidence, the case might be made that in fact strictly speaking he or she deals *only* with other histories—albeit sometimes, in the case of an archaeological reports, histories of the most rudimentary form—subjecting them to scrutiny from a multitude of different angles, so as to see what they might tell us beyond what they would seem to say. But here I must own that I have, for the moment, left Klejn's own theories to one side.

In that archaeology serves history by processing the information found in material sources so as to present it in a form that might be of use to the historian, Klejn, as we have seen, agrees with the nineteenth-century archaeologist Collingwood Bruce that archaeology is 'the handmaiden of history'. However, to repeat the point made in Chapter 9, he does not see archaeology as either inferior or superior to history.

Now we turn again to the other great theorist to have been interested in the comparison with forensic science, R. G. Collingwood.

Klejn and Collingwood

I myself first became interested in the similarities between archaeology and forensic science through the work of R. G. Collingwood. However, as we have seen, in Collingwood's posthumously published *Idea of History* it is the historian who is compared to the detective rather than the archaeologist. As the following newspaper report from 1928 makes clear, Collingwood had toyed with the idea for a long time:

> Mr. R. G. Collingwood of Pembroke College, Oxford, gave a lantern lecture to members of the Leeds Philosophical and Literary Society at the Philosophical Hall in Leeds yesterday, on 'Recent progress in our knowledge of Hadrian's Wall'. He and Mr. Gerald Simpson have been conducting research in recent years on the Roman Wall, research which Mr. Collingwood described as similar to the unravelling of a mystery by Sherlock Holmes. 'I myself am Dr. Watson', said Mr. Collingwood, and throughout the lecture he kept up the pretence of a crime mystery. (*The Yorkshire Post*, December 19, 1928)

Here it would seem that it is the archaeologist who is compared to the detective rather than the historian; however, in *The Idea of History* it is plainly the historian. There is then clear disagreement with Klejn on this matter, but I believe this is a disagreement that can be fairly easily resolved. It can be resolved by virtue of the fact that in other significant areas bearing on this comparison there is substantial agreement between them.

As has been seen, Klejn agrees with Collingwood that history is essentially a humanistic discipline; furthermore, as we saw in Chapter 10, although Klejn is unfamiliar with Collingwood's *Essay on Metaphysics*, there is a similarity between Klejn's 'fundamental concepts and principles' and Collingwood's 'absolute presuppositions'. Collingwood argues that we are able to make absolute presuppositions explicit by showing that they are necessary to the particular discipline that they underlie. Collingwood and Klejn are in agreement that this process starts by looking at the logical superstructure of the discipline in question—and they would also agree that these presuppositions are responsible for the distinctive character of the disciplines that they underpin.

Thus within Collingwood's philosophy there is theoretical support for the idea of drawing a horizontal distinction between history and archaeology as opposed to a vertical distinction according to some inevitably arbitrary date (between history and prehistory). Indeed Collingwood encourages the idea that two disciplines may overlap, in that both may study the same event, without conflicting. According to Collingwood, the practitioners of different disciplines may well be interested in different—nonconflicting—aspects of the same event (1933: 45–50). Klejn's view of the relations between archaeology and history seems to provide a perfect illustration of just such a viewpoint, for Klejn sees no conflict between a generally positivistic conception of archaeology and a generally humanistic conception of history. In Klejn's view the two overlap, and there is no onus on us to judge that one is in any way superior or inferior to the other. Of course, the same person may be both an archaeologist and an historian, but still the two disciplines remain conceptually distinct.

The question then arises as to what Collingwood *did* say about the distinction between archaeology and history. He does not discuss this distinction at any great length, but he does make a few references to it.

In *The Idea of History* Collingwood refers to archaeology as 'the methodology of history' (1993: 492), and in *The Principles of History* he refers to the gathering and classifying of data that occur in archaeology as an 'essential preliminary' (1999: 52) to the writing of history. However, he argues that, aside from archaeology, history has another methodology, the philosophy of history: 'a science dealing with the universal and necessary characteristics of all historical thinking whatever, and distinguishing history from other forms of thought' (1993: 492).

As a philosopher of history, Collingwood argues that a distinguishing characteristic of history is that the historian reconstructs the rational chain of thought that is expressed in an action. He argues that for the historian the question of 'what happened?' is synonymous with 'why did it happen?' (1993: 214)—in other words, the historian is primarily interested in the question of 'why?'. By contrast, from Collingwood's scattered references to archaeology, in isolation from history, it may be inferred that he does not believe that the same might be said of the archaeologist. For example, he describes his *Archaeology of Roman Britain* (1930) as 'strictly . . . a handbook of archaeology, not a history' (1930: vi). This book falls within his description (in an unpublished manuscript) of archaeological sciences as providing a 'means to criticise sources and extract history from them' (Collingwood in Van der Dussen 1981: 213).

Collingwood uses 'critical history' as a synonym for 'archaeology'. He here makes clear that archaeology ('critical history') is conceptually different from history in that it is only the latter that reconstructs an agent's reasoning. By contrast:

> Critical history classifies its sources into groups, and then subdivides these groups, and then subdivides these groups, framing rules for the manipulation of the various subdivisions. Taken as a whole, this technique is an abstract or classificatory science, which has no general name, unless that of archaeology is used for it, and is subdivided into numerous departmental sciences. (Collingwood in Van der Dussen 1981: 213)[3]

Collingwood's *Archaeology of Roman Britain* fulfils this classificatory role exactly.

In summary, in Collingwood's view, archaeology (or 'critical history') consists in a straightforward process of the classification of sources, but the reconstruction of an agent's reasoning is not a necessary part of the process (Collingwood 1993: 258–59; 1999: 14).[4] It is only in that the archaeologist serves the historian, and so is principally interested in artefacts that served human purposes, that his or her work is distinguishable from that of, for example, the palaeontologist. Granted the finished product of the archaeological process is history of a basic form; but upon reaching this form it is handed to the historian for further analysis.

All of which will by now sound very familiar. However, although Collingwood had a philosophical interest in the phenomenon of overlapping disciplines, the point remains that the particular distinction between archaeology and history was not among his foremost concerns. I have perforce reconstructed his view from scattered references. It was perhaps not among his foremost concerns, because at the time when Collingwood was writing it was generally accepted, at least in the West, that archaeology was the handmaiden of history.

Klejn brought the distinction between archaeology and history to the fore, originally in an effort to safeguard the independence of archaeology in the Soviet Union. Archaeology's independence was threatened at that time by the dominating influence of history. In the Soviet Union, under the influence of historical materialism, conclusions that failed to address the question of 'why?'—and that failed to provide obvious contributions to the officially sanctioned grand historical narrative—were condemned as 'artefactology'. Under these circumstances, to safeguard the independence of archaeology, it is natural that Klejn should have focussed on this distinction. In so doing, I believe he advances on Collingwood's discussion of forensic science.

However, although it is fruitful to compare Klejn and Collingwood, it should be noted that Klejn himself, despite ending his university career in the Philosophy Faculty of St. Petersburg University, has a generally poor opinion of philosophy: 'I tend to be interested in the ideas of philosophy only to the extent that they can be put to use in archaeology and anthropology. I am not greatly interested in philosophy for its own sake. Philosophy is not a positive science. It is like religion in that its hypotheses cannot be materially proven (Leach 2011).

In an exchange of views with the Russian philosopher Grigory Tulchinsky, Klejn says that in his life he had but one legal wife, archaeology, but many mistresses—anthropology, history, philology, and folklore studies. Extending this analogy he suggests that philosophy is neither a wife nor a mistress but is rather comparable to the ardent widow Madam Gritsatsueva (in the picaresque satire *Twelve Chairs* by Ilf and Petrov), who pursues the conman Ostap Bender (who fled after their wedding night) demanding back her golden tea strainer. Tulchinsky replied that Klejn may not think highly of Madam Gritsatsueva, but he should not forget that what Ostap Bender stole from her was golden.

Yet it might also be noted that Collingwood, too, has a poor opinion of philosophy when it is studied without knowledge of, or reference to, any other discipline. And his philosophy of history, although not intended to provide a directly prescriptive methodology, is intended to have some repercussions within that discipline. Moreover, Collingwood believed that one should philosophise about a discipline only after having some practical experience of that discipline.

Thus although Collingwood's work predates the advent of the subdiscipline of theoretical archaeology one can easily imagine him approving of it. Indeed the entire subdiscipline might be thought of as predicated on the principle that if progress is to be made in extracting information from a source one must have a definite question in mind. This principle is found as long ago as 1904 in Flinders Petrie's *Methods and Aims in Archaeology*: 'The old saying that a man finds what he is looking for in a subject is too true; or, if he has not enough insight to ensure finding what he looks for, it is at least sadly true that he does not find anything that he does not look for' (1904: 49).

It was this principle that was taken up by the archaeological avant-garde of Collingwood's generation and that, at some basic level, underlies the sub-discipline of theoretical archaeology today. It was also the principle that to a great extent inspired Collingwood's philosophy, although, as we have seen, his primary philosophical focus was on history rather than archaeology.

How un-Collingwoodian then that today those working in the philosophy of history, even those who are impressed with Collingwood's philosophy, have generally very little knowledge of theoretical archaeology or of archaeology in general. It is symptomatic of the current situation that typically in a well-stocked academic bookshop the books on theoretical archaeology will be physically distant from any books on philosophy. Of course there is no perfect way to catalogue books, but my larger (and more positive) point is that, at least on the comparison between the archaeologist and the detective, Klejn (the archaeological theorist) and Collingwood (the philosopher of history) have things to say to each other.

In general, I believe the comparison drawn by Klejn is more accurate than that drawn by Collingwood; but there is one important detail that can be taken from Collingwood's discussion of detection and added to Klejn's. Klejn compares the archaeologist to the detective and the historian to the judge, but Collingwood alerts us to a distinction between the historian and the judge: 'A criminal court has in its hands the life and liberty of a citizen, and in a country where the citizen is regarded as having rights the court is therefore bound to do something and do it quickly. The time taken to arrive at a decision is a factor in the value (that is, the justice) of the decision itself' (1993: 268; 1999: 23).

Collingwood argues that this is not the case with the historian: the historian is under no obligation to make up his or her mind within any stated time. 'Nothing matters to him except that his decision, when he reaches it, shall be right: which means, for him, that it shall follow inevitably from the evidence' (1993: 268; 1999: 24).

Although, with regard to the latter claim, I would have to disagree with Collingwood—no historian, archaeologist, or detective is immune from the pressure of time—nonetheless, these two claims do point us toward a significant difference between the historian and the judge. The historian's work and the archaeologist's are cumulative—their work must be set out in such a way that future generations may build on it. The judge's work, although it may rely on precedents, is not cumulative in the same way. It does not build over time, and through the passing of generations of judges, toward an ever greater understanding of the same events (although it may lead to a greater understanding of the law). Rather, it is just because judges are under an obligation to make up their mind within a limited time that nothing should matter to them except that their decision, when they reach it, should be right. In other words, it should be seen to follow, on the balance of probabilities, from the evidence:

for, in the last resort, judges, unlike historians, do not have the luxury of mere suggestion.

A Warning to the West?

Klejn's fear is that the distinction between archaeology and history that was threatened during the Soviet era is now under threat in the West, not through the dominance of a state ideology but rather through the allure of prestige that comes from writing history and explaining *why* events turned out as they did, and through a general confusion that seems to be growing around the distinction between archaeology and history. In Russia, although theoretical archaeology does not now attract much scholarly attention and although Klejn does not think his advice is sufficiently heeded, nonetheless there are many archaeologists who now believe that—on the subject of the distinction between history and archaeology and on the similarity of archaeology to forensic science—there is 'something' in what Klejn says. By contrast, in the West, Klejn feels that he has as yet barely been heard—and meanwhile the confusion between archaeology and history grows ever greater.

It would indeed be hard to deny the latter claim. Admittedly, there is no shortage of narrowly specialised Ph.D. theses—such as in the Soviet Union would have been dismissed as 'artefactology'—and in the growth of postmedieval archaeology there is evidence that many archaeologists *do* respect a horizontal boundary with history rather than a vertical boundary that would equate archaeology only with prehistory. But, increasingly, archaeologists are writing history books and presenting history programmes on television, seemingly without concern for any distinction between these disciplines.

So there is confusion over the distinction between archaeology and history in the West—yes; but as to whether Western archaeologists are faced with a dictatorship of 'why?' over 'what?' comparable to that faced by archaeologists in the Soviet Union—no. Here I disagree with Klejn. But, since I am in essential agreement with Klejn on the distinction between archaeology and history, should I not then accept that the distinction is unimportant as a safeguard of objectivity?

No. It is not unimportant; but there is a more important safeguard yet, one that remains steadfast but that was almost swept away together with the distinction between archaeology and history in the Soviet Union.

That safeguard is the distinction between data and interpretation, a distinction that is crucial given our own mortality—for ultimately, no archaeologist or historian is immune from the pressure of time. It is owing to time and mortality that archaeologists and historians remain intent on the cumulative accretion of new data and more accurate interpretations. As new data come to light, no existent interpretation is sacrosanct; for the deliberately preserved distinction between data and interpretation that is a feature of all archaeological and historical explanations helps to create the conditions for their own supersession when they are no longer seen to 'fit' the evidence. It is the observation of this distinction that helps scholars in some impersonal way to transcend their own mortality, even though their explanations may not be preserved in any form that they envisaged. In both disciplines explanations are presented as approximations to the truth—more accurate than previous interpretations but possibly not as accurate as future interpretations.

Klejn's model of the relationship between archaeology and history slots rather neatly onto this model—with the historian's data being provided by archaeology and, I would argue, other histories. But, although the historian is primarily interested in 'why?' and the archaeologist is primarily interested in 'what?', it is the distinction between data and interpretation that allows both disciplines to progress. At this deep level there is common ground between archaeology and history and many other disciplines besides.

However, this argument does not invalidate Klejn's argument concerning the distinctions between archaeology and history. It points out that there are features held in common by archaeology and history, but these are not at a level that would justify their amalgamation.

Appendix A

The Commandments

The aphorisms listed here, named 'Commandments', were hanging on the walls as humorist devices for many years (1964–1995) during Klejn's seminars in Leningrad-Petersburg, making long discussions a more joyous occasion (Klejn 2001a: 132). (Klejn's lectures 'were very popular among students' [Tikhonov 2007: 454].) 'Participators would copy them down from the wall in their notebooks, and eventually they were published in 1999 by Klejn's former pupils in Chisineu, in the journal *Stratum*, without the permission or knowledge of the author. The resulting conflict was settled, however, because the publication was made with good intentions. And because the subject was already published, the author recognised the fact and agreed to its translation and republication here' (Klejn 2001a: 132).

1. Archaeology is not history armed with a spade, but a detective story in which the investigator has arrived at the scene a thousand years late. History is pronounced later by judges. So you must decide: to go in for one or the other.
2. Do not be similar to the historian, for whom work is already settled in two steps: collection of materials and the writing of a text. Between these two you must take the third—the research.
3. Where there is a law, there is no problem. In every set of facts do not search for laws, but for contradiction to law. Behind contradiction a problem is hidden, behind the problem a discovery.
4. State the question as a question. With nominative sentences a theme is set but not a problem. A problem is set only when it is formulated by a question. The real question begins with 'who', 'what', 'where', 'when', 'whence', 'whither', 'how', and 'why'.
5. The scholarly world is not a team of friends. What is your discovery is a loss for someone else. And this someone is usually a prominent and powerful person. Therefore having made a discovery do not expect universal delight. Be ready for tough resistance, sudden attacks and a gruelling and lingering war. A scholar needs talent second and courage first.
6. Research is a threefold struggle—with the material, with adversaries and with oneself. The last part is the hardest.
7. Every scholar has a right to make mistakes—if he makes mistakes correctly.
8. If an experiment fails once, the experiment is guilty, if it fails twice, the experimenter is guilty, if three times, the theory.
9. Do not check facts with your tongue, but with your teeth; do not search for something tasty, search for something true. Indeed what you need to recognise is not raisins but gold.
10. Argue skilfully and vigorously, but remember that one does not believe your skill or your rage but your facts.
11. Beware of assumptions. Probability is a ladder with rolling steps, an escalator. Before you know it you find yourself on the next floor. Apparent means probably, probably means possibly, possibly means maybe and maybe not. But whether it was present or absent, issue from the point that it was absent rather than present.

12. Forget the phrase 'for instance'. Examples can substantiate whatever you want. There is always a counter-example for every example. An example is permissible only when it represents a generalisation.
13. Classification is like a piano, do not try to strike a chord with one finger. You need a sufficient set of concepts and terms.
14. Weigh pros and cons on the same set of scales.
15. If the complex truth does not consist of simple truths it is not a truth.
16. The scholarly position is not a chair, but redoubt. It is only a position when it is attacked and defended. Thereafter it is no longer a position but a pose. Do not confuse a position with a pose.
17. Do not hunt for a fashionable position. In the discipline, not every word said last is the last word in the discipline. Contemporaneity is not defined by the moment of a work but by the productivity of methods, completeness of materials, and cleverness of ideas.
18. Do not hope for chance and luck. The law of gravitation was created in Newton's head and not in the apple.
19. Do not suppose anything is apparent. Collect proofs as much as possible, then people will perhaps understand that your idea did not need proving.
20. Be brief. However, firstly every one of your terms should be defined, every concept reasoned, every sentence grounded, every conclusion limited, every fact accounted for, proved and measured.
21. When you substantiate, it is important what, still more important with what, but most important how.
22. The crowning proof is the one which the author has ditched and allowed the reader himself to find.
23. The 'golden middle' between two extremes is only the third extreme. It must be proved especially well.
24. Do not argue until you get a frog in the throat. You cannot out-argue your adversary, no matter how right you may be. The task of every scholarly argument is not to convince your opponent but to check yourself, to believe in yourself and to gain supporters.
25. Even if a gold coin rings on a copper coin, the ring nevertheless is golden. Inequality is not a hindrance to fruitful communication. (Klejn 2001a: 132–33)

Appendix B

Bibliography of Leo S. Klejn Arranged According to Major Themes

(Compiled in 2014)

This bibliography was supplied to me by Klejn in the autumn of 2014. (Klejn tells me that it was compiled with the help of Lev Vseviov, the ex-Director of the Library at the Institute of the History of Material Culture of the Russian Academy of Science.) It is arranged by theme, an arrangement that necessarily entails a small amount of repetition. Monographs are distinguished by the use of bold type. Those works that Klejn considers to be his most significant are placed at the beginning of each section.

Not all of Klejn's editing work is listed—only those works in which Klejn's editing was substantial and for which he has already been credited in the works concerned. Also, not all of Klejn's own work is listed. Short reports on excavations in *Arkheologicheskie Otkrytiya* (a journal published annually in Moscow), some short notes and reviews in *Current Anthropology* and *Bibliographie zur Symbolik*, among others, have been omitted, as well as many popular articles.

One noticeable feature is the number of popularisations, in which Klejn attempts to reach the widest possible readership. (It is interesting that a number of Klejn's 'Commandments' (Appendix A) would apply just as well as advice to the journalist as to the scholar.)

Contents

Theoretical Works and General Archaeology

I. Archaeology as a Scientific Discipline
   A. the subject matter and methodology of archaeology
   B. archaeology in relation to the sciences and humanities
II. Metaarchaeology
   A. archaeological theory and metatheory
   B. methods of field research
   C. methods of study at the desk
   D. the nature of an archaeological fact and research strategy
III. Man, People, and Culture
   A. cultural anthropology
   B. culture and evolution
   C. ethnos and the national question
IV. Types and Cultures in Archaeology
V. Change of Cultures—The Infernal Archaeological Question
VI. Time, Space, and Systems
VII. Methods of Ethnogenetic Research
VIII. The Reconstruction of Social Structures: Concepts and Methods
IX. A Panorama of Theoretical Archaeology
X. The Spectre of Soviet Archaeology and the Roots of Marxist Archaeology
XI. Natural Sciences and the Prospects for Archaeology

XII. Historiography, Bibliography, and Personalia
- A. world archaeology
- B. world anthropology
- C. the archaeology of Russia

XIII. The Upbringing of Archaeologists and of the Archaeological Milieu
- A. archaeological education
- B. popularisation
- C. reference books
- D. ethics in archaeology

Particular Studies of Ancient Cultures

XIV. Tripolye Culture, the Danube, and the Aegean World

XV. Homeric Studies

XVI. The Pit-Grave (Yamnaya) and Catacomb-Grave Cultures

XVII. The Aryan Problem, the Origins of the Indo-Europeans, and Related Subjects

XVIII. Scythians and Sarmatians

XIX. The Origins of The Slavs and the Varangian Controversy
- A. the origins of Slavs
- B. the Varangian controversy

XX. The Pagan Religion of the Slavs

XXI. Various

Other Themes and Journalism

XXII. Art

XXIII. Sociology and Forensic Science

XXIV. The Nature of Man and Sexual Orientation

XXV. Beliefs and Prejudices

XXVI. The Social Life of Russia and of the Scholarly Community
- A. science and power
- B. financing of science
- C. education
- D. the brain drain
- E. science and religion
- F. publishing
- G. scholarship and morality
- H. making discoveries
- I. historical perspective
- J. ethnicity

XXVII. Interviews and Memoirs

Editing

Theoretical Works and General Archaeology

(Secondary Bibliography)

I. Archaeology as a Scientific Discipline

A. The Subject Matter and Methodology of Archaeology

Arkhelogicheskie istochniki [***Archaeological Sources***]. 1978. Leningrad, Leningrad University Press, 120 pages, 10 tables and figures.

Reviews:

Belyaev, A. A., and Frolov, M. V. 1980. *Sovetskaya Etnografiya* (Moscow) 3: 163–65.

Grigoryev, G. P., Dolukhanov, P. M., Lebedev, G. S., and Shcheglov, A. N. 1991. Otvergnutaya recensiya [A rejected review]. *Voprosy istorii estestvoznaniya i tekhniki* (Moscow) 4: 146–50.

Comments:

Konoplev, N. S. (Irkutsk). 1980. Mesto arkheologii v sisteme nauchnogo prirashchennogo znaniya [The place of archaeology in the system of academic accretioned knowledge]. Problemy arkheologii i etnografii Sibiri i Centralnoy Azii (conference: abstracts of papers). Irkutsk, Irkutsk State University and East-Siberian Section of Geographic Society of USSR: 8–11.

Zakharuk, Y. N. 1983. Ob odnoy koncepcii arkheologicheskogo istochnikovedeniya [On a certain concept of archaeological source-study]. *Sovetskaya Arkheologiya* (Moscow) 3: 72–81.

Zavyalov, V. I., and Olkhovskiy, V. S. 1985. Konferenciya 'Arkheologicheskie istochniki i problemy ikh interpretacii' (Moskva 1984) [conference: Archaeological Sources and the Problems of Their Interpretation (Moscow 1984)]. *Sovetskaya Arkheologiya* 3: 311–12.

Plakhin, V. T. 1985. Gnoseologicheskaya specifika arkheologicheskikh istochnikov [The epistemological specificity of archaeological sources]. Altay v epokhu kamnya i rannego metalla. *Barnaul*: 15–28.

Kolpakov, E. M. 1987. Pochemu arkheologicheskie istochniki? [Why archaeological sources?]. Problemy interpretacii arkheologicheskikh istochnikov. *Ordzhonikidze*: 108–19.

Anikovich, M. V. 1988. O meste arkheologii v sisteme obshchestvennykh nauk [On the place of archaeology in the system of the social sciences]. Boryaz, V. N. (Ed.), *Kategorii istoricheskikh nauk*. Leningrad, Nauka: 73–98, in particular section 4 (90–98).

Kolpakov, E. M. 1988. Problema specifichnosti ponyatiya 'arkheologicheskie itochniki' [The problem of the specificity of the concept 'archaeological sources']. Boryaz, V. N. (Ed.), *Kategorii istoricheskikh nauk*. Leningrad, Nauka: 99–114.

Kolpakov, E. M., and Vishnyatsky, L. B. 1990. Current theoretical discussion in Soviet archaeology: An essay. *Fennoscandia Archaeologica* VII: 17–25.

Khabarova, S. V. 1992. Specifika pogrebeniya kak istoricheskogo istochnika [The specificity of burial as a historical record]. Vtorye istoricheskie chteniya pamyati Mikhaila Petrovicha Gryaznova. *Chast' pervaya*. Omsk, Omskiy universitet: 48–49.

Kholyushkin, Y. P. I. and Grazhdannikov, E. D. 2000. *Sistematicheskaya klassifikaciya arkheologicheskoy nauki (elementarnoe vvedenie v sistemnoe naukovedenie* [*The Systematical Classification of Archaeological Science) (an Elementary Introduction to Systemic Research-on-Research)*]. Novosibirsk, IDMI.

Arkheologicheskie istochniki. 1995. Vtoroe, dopolnennoe izd. [*Archaeological Sources*, 2nd (expanded) ed. of the book of 1978]. St. Petersburg, Farn, 350 pages (in the series Classics of Archaeology).

Comments:

Derevyanko, A. P., Kholyushkin, Y. P., and Voronin, V. T. 2001. O ponyatii 'teoreticheskaya arkheologiya' v arkheologicheskoy nauke [On the concept 'theoretical archaeology' in the archaeological discipline]. rudocs.exdat.com/docs/ibdex_194368.

Sher, Y. A. 2004. Yeshche ob arkheologicheskikh istochnikakh i 'zaklyuchennoy v nikh informacii' [More on archaeological sources and information contained in them]. *Arkeolog: Detektiv i myslitel.* Sbornik statey posvyashchennyi 77-letiyu L'va Samuilovicha Klejna. St. Petersburg, St. Petersburg University Press: 114–23.

Skripkin, A. S. 2008. Dostovernost' istoriheskikh rekonstrukciy v arkheologii [The reliability of historical reconstructions in archaeology]. Zapiski seminara 'Sverkh-medlennye processy'. Vyp. 3. Volgograd, gos. universitet: 20–29.
Belkov, P. L. 2009. *Etnos i mifologiya. Elemetarnye structury ethnografii* [*Ethnos and mythology. Elementary structures of ethography*]. St. Petersburg, Nauka: 112.
Kholyushkin, Y. P. 2010. *Sistemnaya arkheologiya* [*Systemic Archaeology*]. Novosibirsk.
Shukhov, A. 2011. Nauchnoe soderzhanie nauki 'istoriya' [The scientific content of the science of 'history']. *Obshchestvo Filosofskikh Issledovaniy i Razrabotok*, http://nounivers.narod.ru/ofir/hist.htm, Chapter: Predmet istoricheskogo poznaniya. . . .
Platonova, N., and Anikovich, M. (St. Petersburg, IIMK RAN). 2011. Debating the nature of historical sources: A. S. Lappo-Danilevsky, R. G. Collingwood, and L. S. Klejn. Central TAG Birmingham. The 33rd Annual Meeting. Panel: Debating principles of archaeological interpretation: An examination of the work of Leo S. Klejn (centraltag.wordpress.com/ call-for-papers/).
Translated to Slovene: ***Arheološki viri*** [***Archaeological Sources***]. 1987. Ljubljana, Studia Humanitatis, 174 pages.
Štular, B. 2005. Smrt Klejna (The death of Klejn). *Arheo* 23: 79–83.
Pamyatniki kak istochniki i arkheologiya kak istochnikovedenie [Monuments as sources and archaeology as source-study]. 2011. Arkheologiya Yuzhnoy Sibiri. Vyp. 25. Sbornik trudov, posvyashchennyi 80-letiyu so dnya rozhdeniya Yakova Abramoviha Shera. Kemerovo, Kemerovskiy gos. universitet: 15–17.
Malina, J. 1981. Přehled archeologických teoretických pojmů (extract z rukopisu 'Archeologické prameny', L. S. Klejna). *Arheologie včera a dnes.* Česke Budejovice, Jihočeske Muzeum: 677–705, *passim.*
Predmet arkheologii [The subject matter of archaeology]. 1977. *Arkheologiya Yuzhnoy Sibiri* (Izvestiya kafedry arkheoogii Kemerovskogo universitet, vy. 9). Kemerovo, Kemerovskiy University Press: 3–14.
O predmete arkheologii (V svyazi s vykhodom knigi V. F. Geninga *Objekt i predmet nauki v arkheologii*) [On archaeology's subject matter (in connection with the publication of V. F. Gening's book *The object and subject matter of science in archaeology*)]. 1986. *Sovetskaya Arkheologiya* (Moscow) 3: 209–19.

Comments:

Zakharuk, Y. N. 1989. Arkheologiya: Nauka istoricheskaya ili istochnikovedcheskaya? [Archaeology: Is it a historical science or source-study?]. *Sovetskaya Arkheologiya* (Moscow) 3: 207–14.
Gening, V. F. 1989. Arkheologiya—celostnaya nauchnaya sistema ili 'diletantskie vylazki' i 'polufabrikat znaniya'? (po povodu koncepcii ob"ekta i predmeta arkheologii L. S. Klejna) [Archaeology—an intergral scientific system or 'dilettante sallies' and the 'semifinished product of knowledge'? (a propos of L. S. Klejn's notions of object and subject matter of archaeology)]. *Sovetskaya Arkheologiya* (Moscow) 3: 215–28.
Palienko, S. (Kiev University). 2011. What is archaeology? Paradigm shift in the USSR. Central TAG Birmingham. The 33rd Annual Meeting. Panel: Debating principles of archaeological interpretation: An examination of the work of Leo S. Klejn (centraltag.wordpress.com/ call-for-papers/).
V zashchitu 'chistoy arkheologii' [In defence of 'pure archaeology']. 1991. *Sovetskaya Arckheologiya* (Moscow) 2: 102–10.

Comments:

Gening, V. F. 1992. O stile diskussii L. S. Klejna. Pis'mo v redakciyu [On L. S. Klejn's style of discussion. Letter to the editorial board]. *Rossijskaya Arkheologiya* 4: 257–59.
Krepakov, E. A. 2001. Nekotorye problemy istoricheskogo issledovaniya v arkheologii (analiz koncepcii L. S. Klejna) [Some problems of historical studies in archaeology

(analysis of L. S. Klejn's concept)]. Matereialy XXXIII Uralo-Povolzhskoy arkheologicheskoy studencheskoy konferencii (R. D. Goldina, Ed.). Izhevsk, Udm. GU, Inst. Istorii i kultury narodov Povolzhya: 112–13.

Arkheologiya i preistoriya v sisteme I. Rauza [Archaeology and prehistory in I. Rouse's system]. 1976. *Sovetskaya Arkheologiya* (Moscow) 1: 306–15.

Rassech kentavra. O sootnoshenii arkheologii s istoriey v sovetskoy tradicii [To separate a centaur: On the relationship of archaeology and history in Soviet tradition]. 1991. *Voprosy istorii estetvoznaniya i tekhniki* (Moscow) 4: 3–12.

Translated to English: To separate a centaur: On the relationship of archaeology and history in Soviet tradition. 1993. *Antiquity* 67(255): 339–48.

Comments:

Curta, F. 1994. Archaeology and history: A centaur or an interface? *Revue Rouman. d'hist.* (Bucarest) XXXIII: 461–515.

Esparza Arroyo, Á.1996. Por la distinción entre la prehistoria y la arqueología. *Complutum Extra* 6(2): 13–34.

Kuna, M., and Venclova, N. (Eds.). *Whither Archaeology? Papers in honour of Evžen Neustupny*. Praha, Institute of archaeology, 1995: 36–42 (prehistory and archaeology).

Reviews

Krausse, D. 1995. Whither Archaeology? Papers in honour of Evzen Neustupny. Praha, *Germania*. 1997. 75(2): 825–31.

Rec. na knigu K.-A. Muberga 'Vvedenie v arkheologiyu'. Stockholm 1969 [Review of K.-A. Moberg's *Introduktion till arkeologi*. Stockholm, 1969]. 1973. *Sovetskaya Arkheologiya* (Moscow) 4: 294–300.

Translated to Swedish: L. S. Klejn recenserar Moberg (Göteborgs Universitet, Institutionen för Arkeologi Sürskilt Nordeuropoisk). 1974. Göteborg, 10 pages (För programmet 'Samhällsformer i Norden Europa 1500 f–500 e O').

V besedakh s L. S. Klejnom [In conversation with L. S. Klejn (interview by Stephen Leach)]. 2011. *Aktualnye problemy Sibiri i Dalnego Vostoka*. Ussuriysk, UGPI publ.: 36–44; forthcoming in *Archaeological Dialogues.*

Metodologicheskaya priroda arkheologii [The Methodological nature of archaeology]. 1992. *Rossiyskaya Arkheologiya* (Moscow) 4: 86–96.

Comments:

Platonova, N. I., and Anikovich, M. V. 2011. Teoreticheskie razrabotki arkheologii kak otrasli istoricheskogo istochnikovedeniya (1-ya polovina XX v.) [Theoretical elaborations of archaeology as a branch of historical source-studies (1st half of the XXth century)]. *Aktualnye problemy arkheologii Sibiri i Dalnego Vostoka.* Ussuriysk, Ussuriysk University Press: 45–47.

Glazami Sherloka Kholmsa [With the eyes of Sherlock Holmes]. 1967. *Znanie-sila*, 12: 15–17.

Uchenyi i pamyat' [The Scholar and Memory]. 2009. *Troitsky Variant* 14(33), July 21: 14.

Gipoteza v arkheologii [Hypotheses in archaeology]. 2011. *Rossiyskiy Arkheologicheskiy Ezhegodnik*, 1, Universities' Publishing Consortium: 56–69.

Reviews:

Romanchuk, A. A. 2012. *Rossiyskiy Arkheologicheskiy Ezhegodnik*—novaya ploshchadka dlya diskussiy v rossiyskoy arkheologii. *Stratum plus* 4: 341–52, in particular 343.

Gipotezy v nauke [Hypotheses in science]. 2012. *Troitsky Variant* 8(102), April 24: 14 [revision of the preceding article].

Sovremennoe vvedenie v arkheologiyu [Modern introduction to archaeology]. 2010–2011. Rev. of Gamble, C., *Archaeology: The basics*. 2000, 256 pages; 2nd ed. 2008. New

York: Routledge. *Arkheologicheskie Vesti* 17 (2010–2011). St. Petersburg, Dmitriy Bulanin: 292–98.

B. Archaeology in Relation to the Sciences and Humanities

V chem nauchnost' nauki? Gumanitariy—eto uchenyi? [Wherein is the scientific nature of a science? Is a humanist a scientist?]. 2009. *Troitsky Variant* 6(25), March 31: 14.

Comments:

Podvoyskiy, D. 2009. Say a word for the poor humanists! *Troitsky Variant* 9(28), May 12: 6–7.

Budushchee gumanitarnykh nauk v Rossii [The future of humanities in Russia] [paper read at the yearly conference of St. Petersburg Union of Scholars. The content of Klejn's paper is related within the article by A. M. Elyashevich. The future of Russia much depends on the future of Russian science and Russian education]. 2012. *Rodnik znaniy* 1(7): 6–19, in particular, for Klejn's paper see 8–9.

At the threshold of science. Troitsky Variant 2(71), Feb. 1: 10.

V gumanitarnom znanii nam sokrashchat' nechego. Professor Lev Klejn o gumanitarnykh naukakh, ikh problemakh, rossiyskom obshchestve i RPC [We have nothing to cut in the humanities. Professor Leo Klejn on the humanities, their problems, Russian society, and the Russian Orthodox Church (interview)]. 2012, June 15. www.Gazeta.ru; subject: Nauka i obshchestvo. Publication prepared by Vsevolod Nikitinand Nikolay Podorvanyuk.

II. Metaarchaeology

A. Archaeological Theory and Metatheory

Metaarchaeology (Acta Archaeologica, København, vol. 72:1, supplementary vol. III). 2001. Blackwell–Munksgaard, 149 pages, 16 figures.

Comments:

Immonen, V. (University of Helsinki). 2011. Debating Leo Klejn's methodology: Its intellectual background and contemporary problems. Central TAG Birmingham. The 33rd Annual Meeting. Panel: Debating principles of archaeological interpretation: An examination of the work of Leo S. Klejn, centraltag.wordpress.com/ call-for-papers/.

Immonen, V. 2011. Leo Klejn's metaarchaeology, its intellectual background and contemporary problems. TAG 2011 (helsinki.academia.edu/ViasImmonen/Talks).

Zalewska, A., and Cyngot, D. 2011. (Polska Akademia Nauk, Warsaw). Leo Klejn's concept of theoretical archaeology seen through the prism of Thomas Kuhn's paradigmatic matrix. Central TAG Birmingham. The 33rd Annual Meeting. Panel: Debating principles of archaeological interpretation: An examination of the work of Leo S. Klejn, centraltag.wordpress.com/ call-for-papers/.

Vvedenie v teoreticheskuyu arkhologiyu: Kniga 1. Metaarkheologiya [Introduction to theoretical archaeology. Book 1: *Metaarchaeology*]. 2004. St. Petersburg, Belveder, 472 pages.

Comments

Lipatov, C. 2010. ZhZh: cyrill_lipatov.livejournal.com/tag/археология

Leach, S. 2011. Arkheolog i detektiv: Ot Leningrada do Sent-Mary Mid [The Archaeologist and the detective: From Leningrad to St. Mary Mead]. *Rossiyskiy Arkheologicheskiy Ezhegodnik* 1, St. Petersburg, Universities' Publishing Consortium: 70–72.

Teoreticheskiy slovar' arkheologii [***Theoretical Dictionary of Archaeology***]. 2014. Donetsk, Donetskiy Nationalnyi universitet, 279 pages.

Kocenke empirisma v sovremennoy arkheoloii [Evaluating empiricism in contemporary archaeology]. 1977. *Problemy arkheologii i etnografii* 1. Leningrad, Leningrad University Press: 13–22.

Metaarkheologiya na Zapade [Metaarchaeology in the West]. 1973. Tezisy dokladov Sessii, posvyashchennoy itogam arkheologiheskikh issledovaniy 1972 goda v SSSR. Tashkent, Fan: 49–52.

Metaarchaeology in the West. Current notions of Western scholars on what is theory in archaeology. 1995. *Journal of Theoretical Archaeology* (Glasgow), vols. 3–4 (1993–1994): 59–82.

Arkheologicheskaya teoriya (status i definiciya) [Archaeological theory (status and definition)]. 1978. *Problemy arkheologii* 2. Leningrad, izdat. Leningradskogo universitet: 8–17.

Translated to Czech: Archeologická teorie. 1981. J. Malina (Ed.), *Archeologie včera a dnes*. Česke Budějovice, č. 2: 221–32.

Teorii v arkheologii [Theories in archaeology]. *Novye otkrytiya v arkheologii Sibiri i Dalnego Vostoka*. Novosibirsk, Nauka: 30–39.

Struktura arkheologicheskoy teorii [The structure of archaeological theory]. *Voprosy filosofii* (Moscow) 2: 99–115.

Functions of archaeological theory. 1995. *Journal of Theoretical Archaeology* (Glasgow) 3(4) (1993–1994): 1–39.

Funkcii arkheologicheskoy teorii [Functions of archaeological theory (the text of the previous article in Russian)]. 1999. *Stratum plus* (St. Petersburg–Çişineu–Odessa), 3: 8–25.

Comments:

Tyurin, A. M. 2007. Istoriya datirovaniya skifskoy arkheologicheskoy kultury [History of dating of Scythian archaeological culture]. Elektronnyi sbornik statey 'Novaya khronologiya', vypusk 6 (new.chronologia.org/volume6/).

On the logic of cross-cultural analysis: Comment on Köbben. 1972. *Current Anthropology* (Chicago) 13(1): 131–36, 138–39.

Replies:

Köbben, A. J. F. 1973. *Current Anthropology* (Chicago) 14(1–2): 3–4.

Marxism, the systemic approach, and archaeology, C. Renfrew (Ed.). 1973. *Explanation of Culture Change: Models in Prehistory*. London: Duckworth: 691–710.

Comments:

Munton, R. J. C. 1973. Systems analysis: A comment. Ibid.: 685–90.

Bentley, R. A., and Maschner, H. D. G. 2007. Complexity theory. In R. A. Bentley, H. D. G. Maschner, and C. Chippendale C. (Eds.), *Handbook of Archaeological Theories*. Walnut Creek, CA: AltaMira Press: 245–70.

It's difficult to be a god (Yoffee and Sherratt's *Archaeological Theory: Who Sets the Agenda?*). 1993. *Current Anthropology* 34(4): 508–11.

Replies

Murray, T. 1995. On Klejn's agenda for theoretical archaeology. Ibid. 36(2): 290–92.

On archaeology theory: Who's who in setting the agenda? 1996. *Current Anthropology* (Chicago) 37(2): 366–48.

Arkheologicheskaya interpretaciya: Dialektika principov [Archaeological interpretation: Dialectics of principles]. 1996. XIII Ural'skoe arkheologicheskoe soveshchanie. Tezisy dokladov. Ufa, UNF RAN.

Teoriya i terminologiy–vzglyad ia Nyukastla [Theory and terminology–the view from Newcastle]. 1999. *Stratum plus* (St. Petersburg–Çişineu–Odessa) (1): 334–38.

Theoretical work in archaeology: How to distinguish good from bad? 2003. 9th Annual Meeting of European Association of Archaeologists, September 14th–19th, St. Petersburg, Russia. Final programme and abstracts: 182.

Kak otlichit' khoroshuyu teoreticheskuyu rabotu po arkheologii ot plokhoy? [How to distinguish good from bad in archaeological theory?]. 2005. *Stratum plus* (2003–2004) (1): 482–86.

Kognitivnaya arkheologiya i ee teorii: Obzor noveyshey literatury [Cognitive archaeology and its theories: A survey of the latest literature]. 2006. *Strukturno-semioticheskie issledovaniya v arkheologii*. Tom 3. Donetsk, Donetskiy Naciolalnyi universitet: 7–20.

Comments:

Gidley, J. M. 2007. The evolution of consciousness as a planetary imperative: An integration of integral views. *Integral Review: A Transdisciplinary and Transcultural Journal for New Thought, Research and Praxis* 5: 4–226.

Neither archaeology nor theory: A critique of Johnson. 2006. *Antiquity* 80(308): 435–43.

Comments:

Johnson, M. 2006. Reply to Leo S. Klejn. *Antiquity* 80(308): 444–45.

Jacobsson, P. (University of Edinburgh). 2011. The necessity of theory: Klejn–Johnson argument. Central TAG Birmingham. The 33rd Annual Meeting. Panel: Debating principles of archaeological interpretation: An examination of the work of Leo S. Klejn (centraltag.wordpress.com/ call-for-papers/).

Oznakomlenie c ne-arkheologicheskoy ne-teoriey [Acquaintance with non-archaeological non-theory]. 2007. *Arkheologicheskie Vesti* (Instituta Istorii Materialnoy Kultury; Institute for the History of Material culture RAN) 14, Moscow, Nauka: 126–232.

Figures, figurines, and Colin Renfrew. 2006. *Antiquity* 80: 981–84.

Comments

Renfrew, C. 2006. Brief reply to Leo S. Klejn. *Antiquity* 80: 985–86

Diletantizm v arkheologii [Dilettantism in archaeology]. 2010. *Zdravyi smysl* 2(55): 22–26.

Reviews

Zolin, P. 2011. Summarizing L. S. Klejn. proza.ru; http://upload.wikimedia.org/wikipedia/commons/4/4a/Lev_S_Klejn.jpg.

Klyuchevye ponyatiya arkheologii v Britanskom predstavlenii [British notions of the basic concepts of archaeology]. 2009. *Arkheologicheskie Vesti* 16: 223–26.

Mysli o dvukh karikaturakh: Teoreticheskaya arkheologiya na putyakh stanovleniya [Thoughts on two cartoons: Theoretical archaeology in the process of being made]. 2012. *Rossiyskiy Arkheologicheskiy Ezhegodnik* 2: 8–11.

B. Methods of Field Research

***Principy arkheologii* [*Principles of Archaeology*]**. 2001. St. Petersburg, Belveder, 151 pages, 11 figures.

Comments

Kholyushkin, Y. P. 2004. Sistemnaya klassifikaciya principov polevoy arkheologii [Systemic classification of the principles of field archaeology], sati.archaeology.nsc.ru/Home/pub/Data/inf7/?html=if74.htm&id=1933.

Kholyushkin, Y. P. 2005. Eshche raz k voprosu o sisitemnom reshenii voprosa o statuse arkheologii kak nauki [Once more on the systemic solution of the question of the status of archaeology as a discipline]. *Methods and Methodology of Archaeology*, sati.archaeology.nsc.ru/Home/pub/Data/inf10/?html=ch1011.htm&id=2112.

Kholyushkin, Y. P., Vityaev, E. E., and Kostin, V. S. 2011. Problemy avtomatizacii informacionnykh potokov v arkheologii [Problems of the automatisation of information flows in archaology]. *Informacionnye tekhnologii v gumanitarnykh issledovaniyakh* (Novosibirsk) 16: 58–71.

Nazarenko, E. (St. Petersburg University). 2011. From theory of knowledge to archaeology and back: Leo S. Klejn on the human condition. Central TAG Birmingham. The 33rd Annual Meeting. Panel: Debating principles of archaeological interpretation: An examination of the work of Leo S. Klejn (centraltag.wordpress.com/ call-for-papers/).

Principles of archaeology (First David Clarke Memorial lecture). 1997. *Journal of Theoretical Archaeology* (Glasgow), 5.

Dialektika principov [Dialectics of principles]. 2011. *Troitsky Variant* 11(80): 14.

Comments:

Kudryavcev, A. V. (Ed.). *Dialektika principov [Dialectics of principles],* metodolog.ru/node/1015.

Teoreticheskaya arkheologiya i raskopki [Theoretical archaeology and excavation]. 1992. Severnaya Aziya ot drevnosti do srednevekovya. Tezisy konferencii k 90-letiyu. M. P. Gryaznova. St. Petersburg, IIMK RAN: 19–21.

Obsuzhdenie metodiki raskopok v Evropeyskom universitete Sankt-Peterburga [Discussion of the methods of excavation at the European University in St. Petersburg]. 1998. *Arkheologya Peterburga*, II/1997. St. Petersburg: 50–51.

Polevoy dnevnik arkheologa (pamyatka) [The Field journal of an archaeologist (instructions)]. 2005–2009. *Stratum plus* 4: 517–25.

C. Methods of Study at the Desk

***Arkheologicheskoe issledovanie: Metodika kabinetnoy raboty arkheologa* [*Archaeological Research: Methods of Archaeological Work in the Study*]**. 2012–2013. Donetsk. Donetskiy Natsionalnyi universitet, vol. 1, 2012, 623 pages, 136 figures, vol. 2, 2013, 600 pages, 132 figures.

Reviews:

Vasilyev, S. A. 2013. Rabota arkheologa: Ot raskopa do knigi [The Archaeologist's work: From excavation to book]. *Rossiyskiy Arkheologicheskiy Ezhegodnik* 3: 696–702.

Interpretacii, rekonstrukcii i teoriya (Po povodu stat'i A. M. Burovskogo) [Interpretation, reconstructions, and theory (à propos A. M. Burovsky's article)]. 1997. *Rossiyskaya Arkheologiya* (Moscow) 1: 227–30.

Vozmozhna li nadezhnaya rekonstrukciya? [Is a reliable reconstruction possible?]. 1996. XIII Ural'skoe arkheologicheskoe soveshchanie. Tezisy dokladov. Ufa, UNF RAN: 8–9.

Troya, Pompei i teoriya arkheologii [Troy, Pompeii, and the theory of archaeology]. 1998. *Anichkov Vestnik* (St. Petersburg) 6: 41–45.

Teoriya restavracii i novodely [The Theory of restoration and modern replica]. 2009 (15 September). *Troitsky Variant* 18(37): 14.

D. The Nature of an Archaeological Fact and Research Strategy

Krazrabotke procedury arkheologicheskogo issledovaniya [Elaborating the procedure (the design) of an archaeological research project]. 1975. Predmet i ob"ekt arkheologii i voprosy metodiki arkheologicheskikh issledovaniy. Leningrad, Nauka: 42–44.

Tri procedury arkheooogicheskogo issledovaniya [Three procedures (designs) of an archaeological research project]. 1978. *Voprosy arkheologii Urala*, 14. Sverdlovsk: 15–24.

Glubina arkheologicheskogo fakta i problema rekonversii [The depth of an archaeological fact and the problem of reconversion]. 1999. *Stratum plus* (St. Petersburg–Çişineu–Odessa) 6: 337–61.

III. Man, People, and Culture

A. Cultural Anthropology

Kulturnaya antropologiya: Problemy, teorii, ponyatiya [Cultural anthropology: Problems, theories, and concepts]. Ezhegodnik: fakul'tet etnologii 1997/98: Sankt-Peterburg, Evropeyskiy universitet v Sankt-Peterburge. Razdel: Programmy kursov: 24–39.

Kulturolog: Eto kto? [The Culturologist: Who is that?]. *Kulturologiya: Kak ona est' i kak ey byt'* (Mezhdunarodnye chteniya po teorii, istorii i filosofii kultury, 5). 1998. St. Petersburg, Eydos: 277–82.

The behavior of peoples: A review article. 1976. *Current Anthropology* (Chicago) 17(1): 132–36.

Replies:

Deuel, T. 1976. *Current Anthropology* (Chicago) 17(1): 135–36.

Imperatritsa Cysi i politicheskaya antropologiya [Imperatrice Cixi and political anthropology]. 2012. *Troitsky Variant* 19(113): 12.

B. Culture and Evolution

My kroman'oncy: Dezadaptaciya cheloveka k sovremennoy culture [We Cromagnons: The failure of man to adapt to contemporary culture]. 1996. Smysly kultury. Mezhdunarodnaya nauchnaya konferenciya 11–13 Iyunya 1996 g. Tezisy dokladov i vystupleniy. St. Petersburg, publisher not indicated: 205–09.

Translated to Slovene: Mi kromanjonci. Sprevnjeni svet. Ljubljana. 2001: 255–63.

Kultura, pervobytnyi primitivism i konclager' [Culture, primordial primitivism, and the concentration camp]. 2005. Kultura i global'nye vyzovy mirovogo razvitiya. V Mezhdunarodnye Likhachevskie nauchnye chteniya, 19–20 maya 2005 goda (Kongress peterburskoy intelligencii): 111–14.

'Chelovek dozhdya': Kollekcionirovanie i priroda cheloveka ['Rain man': Collecting and the nature of man]. 1997. Muzey v sovremennoy culture. Sbornik nauchnykh trudov. Sankt-Peterburgskaya gos. akademiya kultury. St. Petersburg: 10–21.

'Arkhaicheskiy sindrom' ili priroda cheloveka? ['Archaic syndrome' or the nature of man?]. 2013. *Etnograficheske Obozrenie* 5, http://journal.iea.ras.ru/archive/2010s/2013/5.htm.

C. Ethnos and the National Question

Gor'kie mysli 'priveredlivogo recenzenta' ob uchenii L. N. Gumileva [The sad thoughts of a 'squeamish reviewer' on the teaching by L. N. Gumilev]. 1992. *Neva* 4: 228–46.

Comments

Kozlov, A. G. 1993. Khazarskie stradaniya [Chazar sufferings]. *Molodaya Gvardiya*: 5–6.

Semenov, Y. I. 2003. *Filosofiya istorii* [*The Philosophy of history*]. Moscow, Sovremennye Tetradi, Chapter 2.1 Istoriheskiy process . . .

Semenov, Y. I. 2004. Ideologcheskaya moda v nauke i skepticizm [Scepticism and ideological fashion in science]. *Vostok* 8(20).

Zharkikh, M. I. 2004. Zhittya i tvorchist' Lva Gumil'ova. Kyiv. Chapters 3, 2, 1 (compact disc).

Korenyako, V. A. 2006. K kritike kontseptsii L. N. Gumileva [Contribution to the criticism of the L. N. Gumilev's ideas]. *Etnograficheskoe Obozrenie* 6: 22–35.

Kak vy otnosites' k koncepcii etnogeneza L. Gumileva? [What to think about L. Gumilev's concept of ethnogenesis?]. 2009. Ru.wiki with discussion, http://wikinew.ru/wiki1083.htm.

Rychkov, N. A. 2010. Ocherki ob obshchestve [Outlines on society], http://ikt.at.ua/load/jcherki_ob_obshhestve_obshhestvovedenie/54, 3.4. Theoriya ethnosa i ethnogeneza L. N. Gumileva.

Burovskiy, A. M. 2012. Lev Nikolaevich Gumilev kakim ya ego zapomnil [Lev Nikolaevich Gumilev as I remember him]. Soobshchestvo Politicgeskaya Ecologiya (political ecology.ru/blog/235).

Gor'kie mysli 'priveredlivogo recenzenta' ob uchenii L. N. Gumileva [The sad thoughts of a 'squeamish reviewer' on the teaching by L. N. Gumilev]. Skepsis (scepsis.ru) (reprinted from Neva).

Comments

Kucherenko, V. 2000. Nesostoyatel'nost' kritiki passionarnoy teorii ethnogeneza Lva Gumileva [The critique of Lev Gumilev's 'passionary' theory of ethnogenesis is inconsistent]. *Sovremennoe evraziystvo*. Centr Lva Gumileva (gumilev-center.ou/nesostoyatelnost-kritiki-passionarnojj-teorii-ehnogeneza).

Morozov, S. B. 2012. Zhertva mody: Para slov o Lve Gumileve [Victim of fashion: A couple of words on Lev Gumilev]. Opavshie list'ya, http://morozovsb.livejournal.com/377324.html.

Ozarenie pod narami (Vospominaniya i razmyshleniya o L. N. Gumileve) [Inspiration from beneath a wooden prison bed (recollection and considerations)]. 2014. *Kul'turnoe nasledie Rossiyskogo Gosudarstva* 6(2): 326–46.

'Passionarnost': krasivyi mif ['Passionarity' is a fine myth]. 2013. http://antropogenez.ru/interview/717/.

Etnografiya russkikh i nekotorye ee problemy. Ob uchebnike V. S. Buzina [Russian ethnography and some of its problems. On the textbook by V. S. Buzin]. 2012. *Vestnik Sankt-Peterburskogo universitet*, ser. 2, vyp. 4: 230–34.

Etnograficheskaya nauka i nacional'nyi vopros [Ethnography and the national question]. 2012. *Troitsky Variant* 3(97): 7.

Evrei i kazaki [Jews and Cossacks]. 2010. *Troitsky Variant* 15(59): 13.

Chetyrnadcat' evreev? [Fourteen Jews?]. 2012. *Troitsky Variant* 20(114): 12–13.

Pis'mo s togo sveta [A letter from the other world]. 2012. *Troitsky Variant* 21(115): 12.

Velikorossiya and Russia: Chto bol'she? [Great Russia and Russia: What is bigger?]. Polit.ru, polit.ru/article/2012/10/23/r****.

IV. Types and Cultures in Archaeology

Archaeological Typology. 1982. Translated by Penelope Dole. Oxford, British Archaeological Reports (BAR International Series, no. 153), 321 pages + errata and corrigenda in a separate pamphlet, 8 pages.

Reviews:

Gleusiou, S. 1983. *Les nouvelles de l'archéologie* (Paris) 11: 100.

Eggert, M. K. H. 1985. Bonner Jahrbücher 185: 541–44.

Comments:

Welinder, S. 1991. Humans and artifacts: An essay on typology, complexity and multidimensional statistics in 19th and 20th century archaeology (Report series, no. 53). Oslo, The Norwegian Computing Centre for the Humanities.

In Russian: ***Arkheologicheskaya tipologiya*** [***Archaeological Typology***]. 1991. Leningrad, Akadmiya nauk SSSR, LF CENDISI, Leningradskoe arkheologich. nauchno-issledovat. ob''edinenie, 448 pages [the most full publication of the book, which was first published in Oxford in English in 1982 and then in Slovene in Ljubljana in 1988].

Reviews:

Kagan, M. S. 1993. *Vestnik*. Leningradskogo universitet, ser. 6, vyp. 1(6): 113–14.

Tulchinskiy, G. L. 1993. Kniga L. S. Klejna *Arkheolgicheskaya tipologiya'* [The book by L. S. Klejn *Arkheologicheskaya tipologiya*]. *Filosofskaya I sociologicheskaya mysl'* (Kiev) 2: 172–74.

Comments:

Bochkarev, V. S. (Ed.). 1990. *Klassifikaciya v arkheologii: Terminologicheskiy slovar'-spravochnik* [*Classification in Archaeology: Terminological Dictionary-Reference Book*]. Moscow, Institut arkheologii AN SSSR. [The whole of part 2 (pages 6–106) is borrowed from the manuscript of *Arkheologicheskaya tipologiya* by Klejn, as is indicated on page 5.]

Kolpakov, E. M. 1991. *Teoriya arkheologicheskoy klassifikacii* [*Theory of Archaeological Classification*]. St. Petersburg, published by the author.
Kolpakov, E. M. 1993. Two sides of a coin: Classification in theory and practice. *Journal of European Archaeology* 1: 195–97.
Chapman, J., and Dolukhanov, P. 1993. Cultural transformations and interactions in Eastern Europe: Theory and terminology, J. Chapman and P. Dolukhanov (Eds.), *Cultural Transformations and Interactions in Eastern Europe* (Worldwide Archaeology Series, vol. 6). Avebury, Ashgate: 1–36.
Gudim-Levkovich, A. N. 1994. Metodologicheskie problemy tipologicheskogo metoda v arkheologii [Methodological problems of the typological method in archaeology]. *Rossiyskaya Arkheologiya* (Moscow) 2: 71–80.
Kovalevskaya, V. B. 1995. *Arkheologicheskaya kultura: Praktika, teoriya, komp"yuter*. Moscow, Fond Arkheologii.
Shchapova, Y. L. 1993. Rec. sbornika 'Istoriya i komp"yuter' [Review of the collection 'Istoriya i komp"yuter']. 1993. *Informacionnyi byulleten Associacii Istoriya i komp yuter* 9: 54–61.
Shchapova, Y. L. 1998. Eshche raz o tipologicheskom metode v arkheologii, tipakh i tipologii [Once more on typological method, types, and typology]. *Istoricheskaya arkheologiya. Traditsii i perspektivy*. K 80-letiyu so dnya rozhdeniya Daniila Antonovicha Avducina. Moscow, Pamyatniki istoricheskoy mysli: 378–86.
Shchapova, Y. L. 2000. *Vvedenie v veshchevedenie: Estestvenno-nauhnyi podkhod k izucheniyu arkheologicheskogo materiala* [*Introduction to the Study of Things: A Naturalistic Approach to the Study of Archaeological Material*]. Moscow University: 23–25.
Shpak, A. L. 1999. Matematicheskaya mizantropiya [Mathematical misanthropy]. *Stratum plus* 5: 208–10.
Medyanik, M. A. 2001. Tipologiya tagarskikh bronzovykh nozhey (po metodike L. S. Klejna) [Typology of Tagar bronze knives (after the method by L. S. Klejn)]. *Istoriko-kulturnoe nasledie Severnoy Azii: Itogi i perspektivy izucheniya na rubezhe tysyacheletiy*, A. A. Tishkin (Ed.). Barnaul: Altaiskii gosudarstvennyi universitet, 297–300.
Medianik, M. A. 2001. Sovremennye principy tipologii (na primere tagarskich nozhey) [Modern principles of typology (as illustrated by the Tagar knives)]. *Materialy nauchnykh konferenciy studentov i aspirantov istoricheskogo fakulteta.* Tomskogo gos. universitet, 1998–2001.
Vetrov, V. S. 2010. Koncepciya ochagov pervobytnogo iskusstva A. A. Formozova v kontekste vozmozhnosti vydeleniya stilevykh provinciy pozdnepaleoliticheskogo iskusstva (po materialam territorii Ukrainy) [Concept of foci of primordial arts in the context of the possibility to reveal style provinces of Late Palaeolithic arts (on materials of Ukrainian territory)]. *Chelovek i drevnosti. In the memory of Alexandr Alexandrovich Formozov (1928–2009).* Moscow, Grif & Co.: 165–75.
Kozintsev, A. G. 2011. Klassifikatsiya s obucheniem i bez nego: O Ya. A. Shere i o znachenii statistiki v nashey rabote [Supervised and unsupervised classification: On Ya. A. Sher and on the meaning of statistics in our work]. *Arkheologiya Yuzhnoy Sibiri*, vyp. 25. Sbornik k 80-letiyu Ya. A. Shera. Kemerovo, Kemerovskiy gos. universitet: 18–21.
Translated to Slovene: ***Arheološka tipologija***. Ljubljana, Studia Humanitatis, 1988, 581 pages.

Review:

Pleterski, A. 1992. *Praehistorische Zeitschrift*, Band 62, Heft 2: 243–44.

Comments:

Djurić, B. 1988. Arheološka sistematika L. S. Klejna. Spremna beseda. In L. S. Klejn, *Arheološka tipologija*. Ljubljana: 565–72.

Štular, B. 2005. Smrt Klejna. *Arheo* 23: 79–83.

Arkheologicheskaya tipologiya [*Archaeological Typology*]. 1993. A synopsis of the dissertation (in the form of published monograph) for promotion of the degree of Doctor of History. St. Petersburg, Institute for History of Material Culture in Russian Academy of Sciences, St. Petersburg, 16 pages.

Formula Monteliusa: Shvedskiy racionalism v arkheologii Matsa Malmera [***The Montelius Formula: Swedish Rationalism in the Archaeology of Mats Malmer***]. 2010. Doneck, Donetsk University Press, 259 pages, 32 figures.

Rozova, S. S. 1980. Filosofskoe osmyslenie klassifikacionnoy problemy [Philosophical understanding of classification problem]. *Voprosy filosofii* (Moscow) 8: 164 ['a survey of classification work in disciplines that have subject matter concerned with culture. Paper read at a seminar in 1979 in Borok' —LSK].

Klassifikaciya i tipologiya [Classification and typology]. *Istoricheskie chteniya pamyati* M. P. Gryaznova. 1987. Omsk, Omsk universitet: 33–35.

Problema opredeleniya arkheologicheskoy kultury [The problem of the definition of archaeological culture]. 1970. *Sovetskaya Arkheologiya* (Moscow) 2: 37–51.

Comments:

Kolpakov, E. M. 1987. Tri podkhoda k opredeleniyu arkheologicheskoy kultury [Three approaches to the definition of archaeological culture]. *Sovetskaya Arkheologiya* v svete resheniy XXVIII c"ezda KPSS. Tezisy dokladov. Suzdal: 121–22.

Was ist eine archäologische Kultur? 1971–1972. *Ethnographisch-Archäologische Zeitschrift* (Berlin) 12(3): 321–45; 13(3): 367–68.

Diskussiya ob arkheologicheskoy culture v Problemnom arkheologicheskom seminare Leningradskogo universitet [Discussion of archaeological culture in the Problem archaeological seminar of Leningrad University]. 1970. *Sovetskaya Arkheologiya* (Moscow) 2: 298–302 (*in coauthorship with* S. S. Minyaev, Y. Y. Piotrovskiy, and O. I. Kheyfets).

Arkheologicheskaya kultura: Teoreticheskiy analiz praktiki (vmesto recenzii) [Archaeological culture: Theoretical analysis of practice (instead of a review)]. 1998. *Rossiyaskaya Arkheologiya* 1: 187–93.

Social borders: Definitions of diversity. Comment on J.-K. Ross. 1975. *Current Anthropology* (Chicago) 16(3): 333.

Ponyatie tipa v sovremennoy arkheologii [The concept of type in contemporary archaeology]. 1979. Tipy v kulture. Leningrad, Leningradskogo universitet: 50–74.

Comments:

Bernshteyn, B. M. 1987. Iskusstvoznanie i tipologiya [Art studies and typology]. *Sovetskoe iskusstvoznanie* 21. Moscow, Sovetskiy khudozhnik: 306–33.

Predislovie k sborniku, Vystupleniya v diskussii i Zaklyuchenie [Preface to collection, contributions to discussion and Conclusion]. 1979. L. S. Klejn (Ed.). *Tipy v culture*. Leningrad, izdat. Leningradskogo universitet: 3–5, 156–73, 174–78.

Filosofiya klassifikacii i arkheologicheskaya praktika v knige Adamsov [Philosophy of classification and archaeological practice in Adams's book]. 1999. *Stratum plus* (St. Petersburg–Çişineu–Odessa) 2: 368–72.

Poznanskiy trud po teorii klassifkacii i tipologii [Poznań work in the theory of classification and typology]. 1999. *Archaeologia Petropolitana* 3: 28–32.

Tipologiya v svyazi s modernom (po povodu knigi Velindera, 1991) [Typology in connection with modernism (a propos Welinder's book)]. 2000. *Stratum plus* (St. Petersburg–Çişineu–Odessa) 2: 584–89.

Raboty po klassifikacii i tipologii v otechestvennoy arkheologii na rubezhe tysyacheletiy. Zapozdalaya recenziya [Works on classification and typology in Russian archaeology at the border of millenia. Belated review]. 2005. *Stratum plus* (2003–2004) 2: 439–50.

V. Change of Cultures—The Infernal Archaeological Question

Problema smeny kultur v sovremennykh arkheologicheskikh teoriyakh [The problem of culture change in contemporary archaeological theories]. 1975. *Vestnik Leningradskogo universiteta* 8: 95–103.

Problema preemstvennosti i smeny archaeologicheskikh kultur [The problem of the continuous succession of archaeological cultures]. 1981. *Preemstvennost' i innovacii v razvitii drevnikh kultur*. Leningrad, Nauka: 33–37.

O prilozhimosti idey kiberntiki k postroeniyu obshchey teorii arkheologii [On the applicability of cybernetic ideas to the building of a general theory of archaeology]. 1972. *Tezisy dokladov na sekciyakh, posvyashchennykh itogam polevykh issledovaniy* Moscow, Nauka: 14–16.

Problema smeny kutur i teoriya kommunikacii [The problem of the change of cultures and the theory of communication]. *Kolichestvennye metody v gumanitarnykh naukakh*. 1981. Moscow, Moskovskogo universiteta: 18–23.

Kulturno-istoricheskiy process i teoriya kommunikacii [The cultural-historical process and the theory of communication]. 1997. *Grani kultury. Vtoraya mezhdunarodnaya nauchnaya konferenciya* 4–6 noyabrya Tezisy dokladov i vystupleniy. St. Petersburg, publisher not indicated: 107–10.

Translated to Slovene: Kulturnozgodovinski razvoj in teorija komunikacije. 2001. Sprevnjeni svet. Ljubljana: 264–71.

Problema preemstvennosti i pogrebalnyi obryad [The problem of continuous succession and burial rituals]. 1989. *Arkheologiya Vostochno-Evropeyskoy stepi* (Rykovskie chteniya 1984). Saratov, Saratovskogo universitet: 127–29.

VI. Time, Space, and Systems

Vremya v arkheologii [Time in Archaeology]. 2014. St. Petersburg, Evraziya, 384 pages, 57 figures.

Reviews:

Aleksandrov, N. 2013. Lev Klejn. Vremya v arkheologuu. St. Petersburg, Evraziya, 2014, 384 pages. Programme 'Books' on the radio-station Ekho Moskvy, December 11, 2013, 10.19.

Neretina, S. S. 2013. *Vox* issue 15 (December), http://vox-journal.org/, section *Nota bene* (russ.).

Time concept in archaeology as seen in the time perspective. 1994. World Archaeological Congress, 3. New Delhi. Theme papers NS, New Delhi.

Temporal models in prehistory: Comment on J. B. Stoltman. 1978. *Current Anthropology* (Chicago) 19(4): 732–34.

Kontseptsiya vremeni v traditsionnoy kul'ture [The idea of time in traditional culture]. 1999. Vremya i kalendar' v traditsionoy kul'ture. *Tezisy dokladov Vserossiyskoy nauchnoy konferentsii*. St. Petersburg, Lan': 3–9.

Kontseptsii vremeni i arkheologiya [Ideas of time and archaeology]. 2005. *Strukturno-semioticheskie issledovaniya v arkheologii*. Tom 2. Donetsk, Lonetskiy natsional'nyi universitet: 11–64.

Comments:

Gidley, J. M. 2007. The evolution of consciousness as a planetary imperative: An integration of integral views. 2007. *Integral Review: A Transdisciplinary and Transcultural Journal for New Thought, Research, and Praxis* 5: 4–226.

Kontseptsii vremeni v ikh posledovatelnosti: Sotsialnaya psikhologiya epokh, otrazhennaya v arkheologii [Concepts of time in succession: Social psychology as reflected in archaeology]. 2013. *Principles of Dating in the Bronze, Iron, and Middle Ages* [Colloquium], St. Petersburg, December: 9–15.

Die Konzeption des Neolithikums, Äneolithikums und der Bronzezeit in der archäologischen Wissenschaft der Gegenwart. *Neolithische Studien*, I. (Wissenschaftliche Beiträge der Martin-Luther-Universität Halle-Wittenberg 1). 1972. Berlin: Akademie-Verlag, 7–30.

Comments:

Nikolova, A. V. 1990. Do spivvidnoshennya khronologii ta periodizatsii 1990. *Arkheologiya* (Kyiv) 3: 14–24.

Neolithikum Europas als ein Ganzes. 1976. *Jahresschrift für mitteldeutsche Vorgeschichte* (Halle), Band 60 (Behrens-Festschrift), Deutscher Verlag der Wissenschaften: 9–22.

Arkheologicheskaya periodizatsiya: Podkhody i kriterii [Archaeological periodization: approaches and criteria]. 2000. *Stratum plus* (St. Petersburg–Chişineu–Odessa) 1: 485–515.

Review [russian] of the book by H. Müller-Karpe *Handbuch der Vorgeschichte, Band 2. München, 1968*. 1972. *Sovetskaya Arkheologiya* (Moscow) 1: 278–81.

Snova o sisteme trekh vekov [Again on the system of three ages] (review of the book by P. Rowley-Conwy *From Genesis to Prehistory: The Archaeological Three Age System and Its Contested Reception in Denmark, Britain and Ireland*. 2007. Oxford: Oxford University Press, 360 pages.). *Rossiyskit Arkheologicheskiy Ezhegodnik* 1, 2011, Universities' Publishing Consortium: 613–16.

Arkheologicheskaya periodizatsiya v novom tysyacheletii [Archaeological periodization in the new millennium]. 2014. Contribution to the Seminar on the Neolithic in IIMK on March 6, 2013. *Rossiyskiy Arkheologicheskiy Ezhegodnik* 4: 10–13.

Velikiy soblazn general'noy khronologii.: Zapozdalaya recenziya na motiv 'Pikovoy damy' [The Great temptation of general chronology: A belated review of the motif from *The Queen of Spades*] (Y. L. Shchapova, *Arkheologicheskaya epocha*, 2010). 2013. *Rossiyskiy Arkheologicheskiy Ezhegodnik* 3: 258–63.

VII. Methods of Ethnogenetic Research

Etnogenez i arkheologiya **[*Ethnogenesis and Archaeology*]**, vols. 1–2. 2013–2014. St. Petersburg, Evraziya, 528 pages and 600 pages; 136 figures and 132 figures.

Kossinna im Abstand von vierzig Jahren. 1974. *Jahresschrift für mitteldeutsche Vorgeschichte* (Halle), Band 58, Deutscher Verlag der Wissenschaften: 7–55.

Review:

Korell, D. 1975. In *Reallexikon der Germanischen Altertumswissenschaft* [*Special Dictionary of German Antiquity*]. Mannus 41: 305–10.

Comments

Curta, F. 2002. From Kossinna to Bromley: Ethnogenesis in Slavic archaeology, in A. Gillett (Ed.), *On Barbarian Identity: Critical Approaches to Ethnicity in the Middle Ages*. Turnhout: 201–18.

Milisauskas, S. 2011. Historical observations on European archaeology, in S. Milisauskas (Ed.), *European Prehistory: A Survey*. New York: Springer, 7–21, especially 9–10.

Translated to French: **Archéologie, racisme et nationalisme.** A propos de l'interprétation des vestiges archéologicques (adapt. et condens. par J. P. Millotte). 1978. *Dialoguees d'historie ancienne* 4: 377–402.

Arkheologiya v sedle (Kossinna s rasstoyaniya v 70 let) [Archaeology in the saddle (Kossinna at a distance of 70 years)]. 2000. *Stratum plus* (St. Petersburg–Chişineu–Odessa) 4: 88–140.

Oblik Kossinny na poroge novogo veka (novaya biografiya Kossinny v trude G. Gryunerta) [Kossinna's outlook at the eve of the new century (the new biography of Kossinna by H. Grünert). 2008. *Arkheologicheskie Vesti* 15: 234–37.

Regressive Purifizierung und exemplarische Betrachtung. Polemische Bemerkungen zur Integration der Archäologie mit der schriftlichen Geschichte und der Sprachwissenschaft bei der ethnischen Deutung des Fundgutes. 1974. *Ethnographisch-Archäologische Zeitschrift* (Berlin) 15(2): 223–54.

Review (russian) of the book by R. Hachmann, *Goten und Skandinavien* (Berlin, 1970). 1974. *Sovetskaya Arkheologiya* (Moscow) 3: 278–84.

Germantsy v 'Arkheologii mira' [Germans in the Archaeologia Mundi]. *Vestnik Drevney Istorii* 1: 197–203.

Arkheologiya i etnogenez: Novyi podkhod [Archaeology and ethnogenesis: A new approach]. 1978. Metodologicheskie problemy izucheniya etnicheskikh kultur. Materialy simposiua. Erevan, izdat. Akademii nauk Arn.SSR: 25–33.

Comments:

Lozny, L. R. (Hunter College, City University of New York). 2011. Ethnogenesis: Chasing the imagined world. Central TAG Birmingham. The 33rd Annual Meeting. Panel: Debating principles of archaeological interpretation: An examination of the work of Leo S. Klejn (centraltag.wordpress.com/ call-for-papers/).

Ethnogenese als Kulturgeschichte archäologisch betrachtet. Neue Einstellung. *Beiträge zur Ur- und Frühgeschichte* (Coblenz-Festschrift. Beiheft 16 der Arbeits- und Forschungsberichte zur sächsischen Bodendenkmalpflege). 1981. Berlin, Deutscher Verlag der Wissenschaften, Teil 1: 13–25.

Comments:

Curta, F. 2007. Some remarks on ethnicity in medieval archaeology. *Early Medieval Europe* 15(2): 159–84.

Strategiya sinteza v issledovaniyakh po ethnogenezu [The strategy of synthesis in ethnogenetic studies]. 1988. *Sovetskaya Etnografiya* (Moscow) 4: 13–23.

Arkheologicheskie priznaki migratsiy [Archaeological signs of migrations]. 1973. (IX Mezhdunarodnyi Kongress Antropologicheskikh i etnograficheskikh Nauk) [IX International Congress of Anthropology and Ethnographic Sciences]. Chicago: Doklady Sovetskoy Delegatsii. Moscow, 1973: 17 pages.

Comments:

Danchenko, E. M. (Omsk Pedagogical University). 2011. On Leo Klejn's contribution to the study of culture change. Central TAG Birmingham. The 33rd Annual Meeting. Panel: Debating principles of archaeological interpretation: An examination of the work of Leo S. Klejn (centraltag.wordpress.com/ call-for-papers/).

Migratsiya: Arkheologicheskie priznaki [Migration: Archaeological signs]. 1999. *Stratum plus* (St. Petersburg–Çişineu–Odessa) 1: 52–71.

A test of migration hypothesis: Slavic movement into the karst region of Yugoslavia. Comment to y'Edynak. 1976. *Current Anthropology* (Chicago) 17(3): 420–21.

Archaeologists and migrations: A problem of attitude? Comment to H. Härke. 1998. *Current Anthropology* (Chicago) 39(1): 30–31.

Invaziya s severa na Sreneminoyskiy Krit: Otsenka dostovernosti gipotezy [Invasion of Middle-Minoan Crete from the north: The evaluation of the reliability of a hypothesis]. 2000 SUSSITIA. *Pamyati Yuriya Viktorovicha Andreeva*. St. Petersburg, Aleteya: 98–104.

Generatory narodov [Generators of peoples]. 1974. *Drevnyaya Sibir'*, IV, Novosibirsk, Nauka: p. 126–34.

Comments:

Penzev, K. A. 2007. *Arii Drevney Rusi*. Moscow: Algoritm.

Ethnos und Kultur auf dem Symposium Erevan 1978. 1981. *Ethnographisch-Archäologische Zeitschrift* (Berlin) 22(1): 85–101.

Overcoming national Romanticism in archaeology [comment on P. Ligi]. 1994. *Fennoscandia Archaeologica* (Helsinki), XI: 87–88.

Kolliziya dvukh paradigm? Perepiska s A. A.Klyosovym [A Collision of two paradigms? Correspondence with A. A. Klyosov (edited by Klyosov)]. 2011. *Vestnik Rossiyskoy Akademii DNK-genealogii* (Boston–Moscow–Tsukuba), 4(2), February.

Reviews:

Zolin, P. 2011. Summarizing L. S. Klejn 1, http://www.proza.ru/2011/01/21/923.

Zolin, P. 2011. Summarizing L. S. Klejn 2, http://www.proza.ru/2011/01/31/250.

VIII. The Reconstruction of Social Structures: Concepts and Methods

On major aspects of the interrelationship of archaeology and ethnology: Comment on K. C. Chang. 1973. *Current Anthropology* (Chicago) 14(3): 311–20.

Replies:

Chang, K. C. Ibid.: 319–20.

Socio-archaeology: Comment on G. Gjessing. 1975. *Current Anthropology* (Chicago) 16(3): 333.

The social anthropology of a Neolithic graveyard in the Netherlands: Comment on P. Van de Velde. 1979. *Current Anthropology* (Chicago) 20(1): 53–55, 57–58.

Yazyk veshchey [The language of things]. 1981. *Metodologicheskie aspekty arkheologicheskikh I etnograficheskikh issledovaniy v Zapadnoy Sibiri*, Tomsk, Tomskogo universitet: 16–17.

Arkheologo-etnograficheskie sopostavleniya [Archaeological-ethographic comparisons]. 1981. *Metodologicheskie aspekty arkheologicheskikh i etnograficheskikh issledovaniy v Zapadnoy Sibiri*, Tomsk, Tomskogo universitet: 138–41.

Arkheologiya i etnogrfiya: Problema sopostavleniy [Archaeology and ethnography: The problem of comparisons]. 1998. *Integraciya arkheologicheskikh i etnograficheskikh sopostavleniy*. Materialy VI Mezhdunarodnogo nauchnogo seminara, posvyashchennogo 155-letiyu so dnya rozhdeniya D. N. Anuchina. Ch. I. Omsk–St. Petersburg: 97–120.

Comments:

Turov, M. G. (Irkutsk). 2003. Eshche raz ob 'istoricheskoy prarodine' i rasprostranenii 'tungusov-evenkov' [Once more on the 'historical original homeland' and distribution of 'tungus-evenks']. *Narody i kultury Sibiri. Vzaimodeystvie kak factor formirovaniya I modernizacii* (mezhregionlnye issledovaniya v obshchestvennykh naukakh, 2). Irkutsk, Mezhregionalnyi institute obshchestvennykh nauk: 147–81.

Tabaczynski, St. (Polska Akad. Nauk, Warsaw). 2011. Palaeosociology in the theoretical writings of Leo Klejn. Central TAG Birmingham. The 33rd Annual Meeting. Panel: Debating principles of archaeological interpretation: An examination of the work of Leo S. Klejn, centraltag.wordpress.com/ call-for-papers/.

IX. A Panorama of Theoretical Archaeology

Novaya Arkheologiya: Kriticheskiy analiz teoreticheskogo napravleniya v arkheologii Zapada [*New Archaeology: Critical Analysis of Theoretical Direction in the Archaeology of the West*]. 2009. Donetsk, Donetskogo Natsionalnogo Universiteta (seriya: Teoreticheskaya arkheologiya, t. 1), 394 pages, 7 tables.

Reviews:

Vinogradov, A. V. 2009. *Vestnik Sankt-Peterburgskogo universitet*, ser. 12, vyp. 4: 90–93.

Lynsha, V. A. 2011. *Rossiyskaya Arkheologiya* 1: 169–73.

Lynsha, V. A. 2011. Klejn's critique of the 'New Archaeology'. *Aktual'nye problemy arkheologii Sibiri I Dalnego Vostoka*. Ussuriysk, Ussuriyskiy universitet: 18–35.

Lynsha, V. A. (Far Eastern Federal University, Ussuriysk). 2011. Leo S. Klejn's criticism of New Archaeology. Central TAG Birmingham. The 33rd Annual Meeting. Panel: Debating principles of archaeological interpretation: An examination of the work of Leo S. Klejn (centraltag.wordpress.com/ call-for-papers/).

Kradin, N. N. 2011. *Antiquity* 85(327): 295–96.

Comments:

Kostin, V. S., and Kholyushkin, Y. P. 2011. Nekotorye podkhody k bibliometricheskomu analizu vzaimocitirovaniya [Some approaches to bibliometrical analysis of mutual quoting]. *Informacionnye tekhnologii v gumanitarnykh issledovaniyakh* (Novosibirsk) 16: 37–57.

A panorama of theoretical archaeology. 1977. *Current Anthropology* (Chicago) 18(1): 1–42; (2): 371–73.

Comments:

Santley, R. S., and Turner, E. R. (USA). 1977. On theory in archaeology. Ibid. 18(4): 747–48, 749.

Lahitte, H. (Argentina). On theory in archaeology. Ibid.: 748–49.

Brüggeman, J. K. (Mexico). 1978. Further comment on Klejn's 'Theoretical Archaeology'. Ibid. 19(1): 164–66.

Brentjes, B. (Berlin, DDR). 1978. More on Klejn's Archaeological Panorama. Ibid. 19(2): 423–26.

Ehrich, R. (Harvard, USA). More on Klejn's Archaeological Panorama. 1978. Ibid. 19(2): 426–27.

Gjessing, G. (Norway). More on Klejn's Archaeological Panorama. 1978. Ibid. 19(3): 632–33.

Leone, M. P. (Maryland, USA). On texts and their interpretations. 1978. Ibid. 19(3): 664–65.

Trigger, B. (Montreal, Canada). No longer from another planet. 1978. *Antiquity* (Cambridge, U.K.) LII(206): 193–98.

Translated to French: **Panorama de l'archéologie théorique** (and Addendum 1978: Personalité de la France). 1980. A. Schnapp (Ed.), *L'archéologie aujourd'hui*. Paris, Hachette: 262–303.

Translated to Slovene: **Panorama teoretske arheologije**. *Arheo* (Ljubljana) 1 (1981): 1–16; 2 (1982): 1–42.

Russian text of the 1977 article: **Panorama teoreticheskoy arkheologii**: Russkiy tekst s prilozheniyami [A panorama of theoretical archaeology: The Russian text with supplements [1977–1980, new text: foreword]. 2005–2009. *Stratum plus* 4: 11–116 (*in the section*: Monograph in the journal).

On theory of archaeology: A response. *Current Anthropology* (Chicago) 19(1): 162–64.

Theoretical archaeology in the making: A survey of books published in the West in 1974–1979. 1990. *Fennoscandia Archaeologica* (Helsinki) VII: 3–15.

Comments:

Tilley, C. 1991. Comments on Klejn: 'Theoretical archaeology in the making'. *Fennoscandia Archaeologica* (Helsinki) VIII: 59–61.

Olsen, B. 1991. Excavating the 1970s 10 years after. Ibid.: 62–64.

Lesman, Y. M. 1991. L. S. Klejn and the development of theoretical archaeology. Ibid.: 65–66.

A Russian lesson for theoretical archaeology: A reply. 1991. *Fennoscandia Archaeologica* (Helsinki) VIII: 67–71.

Archaeology in Britain: A Marxist view. 1970. *Antiquity* (Cambridge) XLIV(176): 296–303.

Comments:

Thompson, M. Afterword. 1970. *Antiquity* XLIV: 303.

Hawkes, C. F. C. Comment on Klejn. 1971. *Antiquity* XLV(177): 55.

Translated to Spanish: La arqueologia en Gran Bretaña: Un punto de vista marxista. 1971. *Cuadernos de Antropologia Social y Etnologia* (Madrid) 1(3): 25–40.

Chelovek, kultura i sreda v 'novoy arkheologii' [Man, culture, and environment in the New Archaeology]. 1975. O. N. Bader (Ed.), *Vsesoyuznyi simposium* 'Pervobytnyi chelovek, ego materialnaya kultura i estestvennaya sreda v pleystocene i golocene'. Moscow, Nauka: 41–43.

O sushchnosti i granicakh analiticheskoy arkheologii [On the essence and borders of Analytical archaeology]. 1975. *Noveyshie otkrytiya sovetskikh arkheologov*. Kiev, Ch. III: 19–22.

Problema ob"ektivnosti v skandinavskoy arkheologii [The problem of objectivity in Scandinavian archaeology]. 1978. *Vestnik Leningradskogo universitet* 8: 48–54.

Po povodu informacii o metodike amerikanskikh arkheologicheskikh issledovaniy [Apropos information on the methods of American archaeological studies]. 1970. *Sovetskaya Arkheologiya* (Moscow) 1: 298–300.

Towards an economic prehistory of Europe: Comment on F. W. Higham. 1969. *Current Anthropology* (Chicago) 10(2–3): 303–12.

On trade and culture process in prehistory: Comment on C. Renfrew. 1970. *Current Anthropology* (Chicago) 11(2): 169–71.

Social responsibilities Symposium: Comment. 1968. *Current Anthropology* (Chicago) 9(5): 415–17.

Review of Coles, J. N., and Simpson, D. D. A. (Eds.), *Studies in Ancient Europe*: Leicester, 1968. 1972. *Sovetskaya Arkheologiya* (Moscow) 3: 385–89.

Review of Binford, S. R., and L. R. (Eds.), *New Perspectives in Archeology*: Chicago, 1968. 1973. *Sovetskaya Arkheologiya* (Moscow) 2: 303–12.

Review of Woodall, N. J. *Introduction to Modern Archaeology*: Cambridge, Mass., 1972. 1975. *Sovetskaya Arkheologiya* (Moscow) 3: 267–73.

X. THE SPECTRE OF SOVIET ARCHAEOLOGY AND THE ROOTS OF MARXIST ARCHAEOLOGY

Fenomen sovetskoy arkheologii. 1993. St. Petersburg, Farn, 128 pages and 12 colour photos.

Review:

Formozov, A. A. 1995. O knige L. S. Klejna 'Fenomen soveskoy arkheologii' i o samom fenomene [On L. S. Klejn's book *Phenomenon of Soviet Archaeology* and on the phenomenon itself]. *Rossiyskaya Arkheologiya* (Moscow) 3: 225–32.

Comments:

Korenyako, V. 2000. Etnonacionalizm, kvaziistoriografiya i akademicheskaya nauka [Ethnonationalism, quasihistoriography, and academic scholarship]. *Real'nost' etnicheskikh mifov,* M. G. Olkott i A. Malashenko (Eds.). Moskovskiy Centr Karnegi. Moscow, Gendalf: 34–52.

Bertrand, F. 2002. *L'anthropologie soviétique des années 20–30*: *Configuration d'une rupture*. Bordeaux, Presses Universitaires de Bordeaux: 108–112 et passim.

Mochanov, S. A., and Fedoseeva, S. A. 2002. *Trudy Prilenskoy arkheologicheskoy ekspeditsii*. Akademia Nauk Sakha (Yakutii), Yakutsk (Vstupit. glava). [Transactions of Lena-basin archaeological expedition. Academy of Sciences of Sakha (Yakutia), Yakutsk (Introduction)] [Criticisms that more correctly could be related to Klejn's *Metaarchaeology* (*Introduction to Theoretical Archaeology*)].

Kradin, N. N. 2003. *Ernest Gellner and Debates on Nomadic Feudalism: Social Evolution and History.* Moscow, Uchitel Publishing House, vol. 2, no. 2: 162–76 (cf. 167).

Palienko, S. 2010. Revival of Vladimir Gening's Fundamental Archaeological Theory: Possible solution of contemporary methodological problems in archaeology. TAG 2010: 32nd Annual Meeting, Bristol. Panel: Marxism in archaeology, nomadit.co.uk/tag/tag2010/panels.php5?PanelID=868.

Translated to Spanish: ***La arqueología soviética***. 1993. Historia y teoría de una escuela desconocida, con prefacio de G. Ruiz Zapatero. Barcelona, Crítica, 173 pages and 16 photo illustrations.

Reviews

Anon. 1993. *Cota zero. Revista d'arqueologia. Ciencia* 9: 110–11.

Brueggemann, J. 1995. Arqueología Soviética. *Caligráma* (Xalapa, Mexico), February 17: VI.

Translated to German (in an extended edition): ***Das Phänomen der sowjetischen Archäologie: Geschichte, Schulen, Protagonisten.*** 1997. Übersetzt von D. Schorkowitz unter Mitwirkung von W. Kulik. Berlin, Peter Lang.

Reviews:

Jetmar, K. 1998. *Central Asiatic Journal* 42(2): 315–18.

Häusler, A. 1999. *Jahresschrift für Mitteldeutsche Vorgeschichte* 81: 501–09.

Härke, H. 1999. *Archäologische Informationen* 22(1): 73–75.

Maier, E. 1999. *Hansische Geschichtsblatt* 119: 307.

Stadelbauer, J. 1999. *Osteuropa* 7: 766–67.

Holtorf, C. 2000. *Archaeologia Polona* 38: 257–63.

Van Meirs, W. 2001. *Ab Imperio* (Moscow) 4/2001: 443–47 (Russian).

Translated to English (extended edition): ***Soviet Archaeology: Trends, Schools, and History.*** 2012. Translated by K. Windle and R. Ireland (Oxford Studies in the History of Archaeology). Oxford, Oxford University Press, 456 pages, 55 in-text illustrations, and 7 colour maps.

Attainments and problems of Soviet archaeology. 1982. *World Archaeology* 13: 272–95. (V. A. Bulkin and G. S. Lebedev are indicated as co-authors.)

Comments:

Miles, D. Yoked to the past. The state of archaeology. 1983. *Encounter* LXV(4): 55–60.

Sagona, A. 2010. Past and present directions in the archaeology of Transcaucasus. *Tuba-ar* 13, November 23: 143–58.

Reviews:

Kameteckiy, I. S., Marshak, B. I., and Sher, Y. A. 1977. Analiz arkheologicheskikh istochnikov (Vozmozhnosti formalizovannogo podkhoda) [Analysis of archaeological sources (Opportunities of formalised approach)] Moscow, 1975. *Sovetskaya Arkheologiya* (Moscow) 3: 309–17.

Voprosy pervobytnoy arkheologii v proizvedenuyakh Marksa i Engelsa [Prehistoric archaeology in the works by Marx and Engels]. 1968. *Vestnik Leningradskogo universitet* 8: 38–43.

Svyaz' arkheologii i etnografii po K. Marksu i sovremnnaya nauka [*The Connection between archaeology and ethnography according to K. Marx and contemporary science*]. 1968. *Tezisy dokladov godichnoy sessii Leningradskogo otdeleniya Instituta etnografii AN SSSR*. Leningrad: 15–17.

Fridrikh Engels kak issledovatel' ranegermanskogo obshchestva [Friedrich Engels as a researcher of early German society]. 1970. *Sovetskaya Etnografiya* (Moscow) 5: 20–32.

O tipichnykh priemakh sovremennoy kritiki marksizma v arkheologii [On the typical methods of a contemporary critic of Marxism in archaeology]. 1968. *Sovetskaya Arkheologiya* (Moscow) 4: 138–50.

Translated to English: Characteristic methods in the current critique of Marxism in archaeology. 1969. *Soviet Anthropology and Archaeology* (New York) 7(4): 41–53.

Translated to German: Über typische Verfahren der gegenwärtigen Kritik an Marxismus in der Archäologie. 1970. *Ethnographisch-Archäologische Zeitschrift* (Berlin) 11(3): 333–50.

Childe and Soviet archaeology: A romance. 1994. In *The Archaeology of V. Gordon Childe: Contemporary Perspectives*, D. R. Harris (Ed.). London: UCL Press, 75–90, discussion 90–93.

Comments:

Faulkner, N. 2007. Gordon Childe and Marxist archaeology. *International Socialism* 116, isj.org.uk/index.php4?id=367=116.

Kradin, N. N. 2009. Ernest Gellner and debates on nomadic feudalism. *Social Evolution and History* 2(2): 167.

Russia's archaeology at the turning point. 1994. 6 Congreso Hispano-Ruso de historia (Madrid, 1992). Madrid, Fundacion Cultural Banesto: 193–214. (A shortened version was translated into Russian: Rossiyskaya arkheologiya na perelome. Cerkovnaya arkheologiya) [Matrialy Pervoy Vserossiyskoy konferencii. Pskov, 20–24 noyabrya 1995 goda]. Chast' 3. Pamyatniki cerkovnoy arkheologii Rossii. St. Petersburg—Pskov, 1995: 86–105. (On the back of the title page: Arkheologicheskie izyskaniya IIMK, vyp. 26, Ch. 3.)

Glyadya na nashe vchera: Po povodu knigi Rendolla MakGvayra 'Marksistskaya Arkheologiya' [Looking at our yesterday: A propos Randall MacGuire's book *Marxist Archaeology*]. 1996. *Archaeologia Petropolitana* 1: 99–106.

Istorizm v arkheologii [Historicism in archaeology]. *Arkheologicheskie Vesti* (St. Petersburg) 2: 135–44.

Vseryoz o sud'bakh marksizma [On the fate of Marxism in earnest]. 2012. *Troitsky Variant* 11(105): 12.

Marksizm i kultura: Pozdniy roman [Marxism and culture: A late romance]. *Metafizicheskie issledovaniya*, 4. Kultura. St. Petersburg, Aleteya: 82–91.

XI. NATURAL SCIENCES AND THE PROSPECTS FOR ARCHAEOLOGY

Arkheologiya segodnya i zavtra [Archaeology today and tomorrow]. 1961. *Neva* (Leningrad) 12: 153–59.

Iz proshlogo v budushchee [From the past into the future]. 1962. *Priroda* (Moscow) 1: 68–77.

Arkheologiya sporit s fizikoy: Spor o dostovernosti i tochnosti radiouglerodnoy khronologii [Archaeology contends with physics: The argument about the credibility and accuracy of radiocarbon chronology]. 1966. *Priroda* (Moscow) 2: 51–62; 3: 94–107.

Comments:

Fomenko, A. T. 1990. *Metody statisticheskogo analiza narrativnykh tekstov v prilozhenii k khronologii* [*Methods of statistical analysis of narrative texts as applied to chronology*]. Moscow, Moscow University Press.

Kritika tradicionnoy khronologii antichnosti i srednevekov'ya (Kakoy seychas vek?) [Critique of the traditional chronology of the classical world and the Middle Ages (What century is now?)]. Referat [Synopsis of works by A. T. Fomenko and his followers]. Moscow, Moscow University Press, 1993.

Postnikov, M. M. 2000. *Kriticheskoe issledovanie khronologii* [Critical investigation of the chronology of the ancient world]. Moscow, Kraft & Lean. [The author is a follower of Fomenko.]

Ivanov, A. Otkrytoe pismo akademiku Fomenko [An Open letter to Fomenko, a member of the Academy], http://nnm.me/blogs/o08/ivanov-aleksey-viktorovich-otkrytoe-pismo-akademiku-a-t-fomenko-2003-mp3/.

Levchenko, V. O. 'Radiouglerode glazami Fomenko' i 'nauchnykh' osnovakh Novoy Khronologii: Polemicheskie zametki [On 'Radiocarbon as seen by Fomenko' and on the 'scientific' basis of the New Chronology: Polemical notes], pereplet.ru/gorm/fomenko/wally-r.htm.

['N. B. In comments to Fomenko it is shown that Klejn was misquoted by him' —LSK] Kakoy seychas vek? Lekciya 2 [What century is now? Lecture 2], hbar.phys.msu.ru/gorm/fomenko/referat/referat2.htm.

Translated to Hungarian: A régészet vitatkozik a fizikaval. 1966–1967. *Univerzum* (Budapest); 1966, no. 12; 1967, no. 1, 11–21; no. 3, 22–31.

Translated to Estonian: Arheologia ja füüsika dispuut. 1969. *Eesti loodus* (Tartu), nos. 6–7.

Comments:

Punning, J.-M., Ilves, E., and Ja Liiva, A. Kuidas hinnata radioaktivse sünsiniku meetodit? Ibid. 11: 667–70.

K ocenke prochnosti i nadezhnosti absolyutnoy khronologii Egipta (Arkhaicheskiy period i Drevnee Carstvo) [Evaluating the durability and reliability of absolute chronology in Egypt (Archaic period and Ancient Kingdom)]. 1966. *Vestnik Drevney Istorii* (Moscow) 4: 94–105.

Arkheologiya i magnetism [Archaeology and magnetism]. 1968. *Priroda* (Moscow) 4: 65–75; 5: 49–55.

Ostayus' arkheologom: Traktat o krizise gumaitarnosti v arkheologii i ego svyazi s metodami estetvennykh nauk. 1. Arkheologiya plus fizika [I remain an archaeologist: Treatise on the crisis of the spirit of the humanities and its connection with the methods of the natural sciences. 1. Archaeology plus physics]. 1969. *Znanie-sila* (Moscow) 2: 26–27; 2. Arkheologiya minus fizika [2. Archaeology minus physics]. 1970, 2: 33–34.

Archaeoastronomy and ethnoastronomy so far: Comment on E. Ch. Baity. 1973. *Current Anthropology* (Chicago) 14(4): 433–34.

Archaeology of the '80s through the objectives of the '70s. 1980. *Norwegian Archaeological Review* (Bergen) 13(1): 9–13.

XII. Historiography, Bibliography, and Personalia

A. World Archaeology

Istoriya arkheologicheskoy mysli [***History of Archaeological Thought***]. 2011. I–II. St. Petersburg, St. Petersburg University Press, vol. I, 688 pages; vol. II, 626 pages, about 400 illustrations.

Reviews:

Vishniatsky, L. B. 2011. Ot nauchnogo redaktora knigi [From the scientific editor of the book], anthropogenez.ru/book/9.

Centaurito [Azbelev, P. P.]. 2011. 'Ya pamyatnik sebe vozdvig nerukotvornyi' ['I have erected a monument for myself (Exegi monumentum)', centaurito.livejournal.ru.

Istorik arkheologicheskoy mysli [A historian of the archaeological thought]. 2011. *Troitsky Variant* 23(92): 16.

Obsuzhdenie knigi L. S. Klejna na metodicheskom seminare IIMK RAN [The discussion of the book by L. S. Klejn in the methodological seminar of the Institute for the History of Material Culture of the Russian Academy of Sciences]. 2013. *Rossiyskiy Arkheologicheskiy Ezhegodnik* 3: 583–608 (S. V. Vasilyev, Y. E. Berezkin, I. L. Tikhonov, I. V. Tunkina, and N. I. Platonova).

Tunkina, I. V. (St. Petersburg), and Shchavelev, S. P. (Kursk). 2013. Mysl' ob istorii mysli: Kognitivnyi portret razvitiya mirovoy arkheologii [Thought on the history of thought:

A cognitive portrait of the development of world archaeology]. *Epistemologiya i filosofiya nauki* 4: 235–40.

***Formula Monteliusa: Shvedskiy racionalism v arkheologii Malmera* [*The Montelius Formula: Swedish Rationalism in Malmer's Archaeology*].** 2010. Donetsk, Donetsk University Press, 259 pages, 32 figures.

***Novaya Arkheologiya: Kriticheskiy analiz teoreticheskogo napravleniya v arkheologii Zapada* [*New Archaeology: Critical Analysis of Theoretical Direction in the Archaeology of the West*].** 2009. Donetsk, Donetsk University Press (seriya: Teoreticheskaya arkheologiya, vol. 1), 394 pages, 7 tables.

Reviews:

Vinogradov, A. V. 2009. *Vestnik Sankt-Peterburgskogo universitet* 12(4): 90–93.

Lynsha, V. A. 2011. *Rossiyskaya Arkheologiya* 1: 169–73.

Lynsha, V. A. 2011. Klejnovskaya kritika Novoy Arkheologii [Klejn's critique of the 'New Archaeology']. *Aktual'nye problem arkheologii Sibiri I Dalnego Vostoka* . Ussuriysk, Ussuriyskiy University Press: 18–35.

Lynsha, V. (Far Eastern Federal University, Ussuriysk). 2011. Leo S. Klejn's criticism of New Archaeology. Central TAG Birmingham. The 33rd Annual Meeting. Panel: Debating principles of archaeological interpretation: An examination of the work of Leo S. Klejn, centraltag.wordpress.com/ call-for-papers/.

Kradin, N. N. 2011. *Antiquity* 85: 295–96.

Comments:

Kostin, V. S., and Kholyushkin, Y. P. 2011. Nekotorye podkhody k bibliometricheskomu analizu vzaimocitirovaniya [Some approaches to bibliometrical analysis of mutual quoting]. *Informacionnye tekhnologii v gumanitarnykh issledovaniyakh* (Novosibirsk) 16: 37–57.

History of archaeology before 1900: European archaeology. 1966. B. M. Fagan (Ed.), *The Oxford Companion to Archaeology.* New York: Oxford University Press: 286–87.

Is German archaeology atheoretical? Comments on Georg Kossack. 'Prehistoric archaeology in Germany: Its history and current situation'. 1993. *Norwegian Archaeological Review* (Bergen) 26(1): 49–54.

Zametki o zarubezhnoy bibliografii po arkheologii za 1950–1960 [Notes on foreign archaeological bibliography 1950–1960]. 1963. *Sovetskaya Arkheologiya* (Moscow) 2: 259–65.

On the bibliographical and directory of world theoretical archaeology: A project. 1996. *World Archaeological Bulletin* 8: 30–40.

Histories of archaeology: The view from St. Petersburg (concluding comments). Histories of archaeology: Archives, ancestors, practices. 2004. Göteborg, June 17–19, Göteborg University, Institut national d'histoire de l'art. *Archives of European Archaeology* (Göteborg): 44–47.

Iz istorii nauchnykh shkol i tradiciy antichnoy arkheologii [From the history of academic schools and traditions of classical archaeology]. *ΕΥΧΑΡΙΣΤΗΡΙΟΝ. Historiographic Collection in Classical Archaeology. In Memory of Yaroslav Vitalyevich Domanskiy (1928–2004)*. 2007. St. Petersburg, Nestor-Istoriya: 121–38.

Arkheologiya i ideologiya: Nemetskaya arkheologiya pri dvukh diktaturakh. Rec. na sbornik H. Härke 2000 [Archaeology and ideology: German archaeology under two dictatorships. Review of H. Härke 2000]. 2003–2004. *Stratum plus* 3: 384–89.

Review of Trigger's *History of Archaeological Thought*, 2nd ed. 2007. *European Archaeological Journal* 9(1): 141–43.

Bruce Trigger in World Archaeology. 2008. *Bulletin of the History of Archaeology* 1(2): 4–12.

Gustaf Kossinna. 1999. T. Murray (Ed.), *Encyclopedia of Archaeology: The Great Archaeologists*. Santa Barbara, Denver, Oxford, ABC-Clio, vol. I: 233–46.

Kossinna, Gustaf (1858–1925). 2001. T. Murray (Ed.), *Encyclopedia of Archaeology: History and Discoveries*. Santa Barbara, Denver, Oxford, ABC-Clio, vol. II: 775–76.

Heinrich Schliemann. 1999. T. Murray (Ed.), *Encyclopedia of Archaeology: The Great Archaeologists*. Santa Barbara, Denver, Oxford, ABC-Clio, vol. I: 109–25.

Schliemann á Petersbourg. 1995. *Dossiers Archéologiques* (Dijon) 206: 16–27 (par Lev S. Klein).

Schliemann, Heinrich (1822–1890). 2001. T. Murray (Ed.), *Encyclopedia of Archaeology: History and Discoveries*. Santa Barbara, Denver, Oxford, ABC-Clio, vol. III: 1150–52.

Review of *Gero von Merhart, Daljoko: Bilder aus sibirischen Arbeitstagen*. 2010. H. Parzinger (Ed.), Wien: Böhlau. 2008. *European Journal of Archaeology* 13(1): 141–44.

Rudolf Virchow i vzaimovliyanie nauk [Rudolf Virchow and the mutual influence of disciplines]. 2010. *Troitsky Variant* 17(61): 10.

Otec embriologii i smena civilizaciy [Father of embryology and the change of civilizations]. 2010. *Troitsky Variant* 17(62): 8.

Issledovanie intellektualnoy imperii Kembridzha v arkheologii [A study of the intellectual empire of Cambridge in archaeology]. 1996. *Rossiayskaya arkheolohiya* 1: 177–82.

Sibirskoe vospitanie Merharta [The Siberian upbringing of Merhart] (review of *Gero von Merhart: Daljóko—Bilder aus sibirischen Arbeitstagen*). (H. Parzinger, 2008, 287 pages, 59 figures. Wien–Köln–Weimar: Böhlau). 2010–2011. *Arkheologicheskie Vesti* 17 St. Petersburg, Dmitriy Bulanin: 299–301.

Tributes to Lewis Binford: Appreciation by Lev Klejn. 2011. *Antiquity*, http://antiquity.ac.uk/tributes/binford.html#binford11.

Ukhod patriarkha [Departure of the patriarch]. 2011. *Troitsky Variant* 8(77): 14.

Detectivnaya podopleka arkhelogii [The detective in and out of archaeology]. 2011. *Troitsky Variant* 15(84): 12.

Nauchnye chudachestva: Uteryannye plemena Izrailevy i flot Aleksandra Makedonskogo [The lost tribes of Israel and the fleet of Alexander of Macedonia]. 2011. *Troitsky Variant* 18(87): 12.

Atlantida, Amerika, Egipet [Atlantis, America, Egypt]. 2011. *Troitsky Variant* 20(89): 12.

Comment:

Rabota nad oshibkami [Checking for mistakes]. 2011. *Troitsky Variant* 21(90): 16.

B. World Anthropology

Istoriya antropologicheskikh ycheniy **[*History of Anthropological Teachings*]**. 2014. St. Petersburg, St. Petersburg University Press, 744 pages, hundreds of illustrations.

Individualizaciya v antropologii [Individualization in anthropology]. 2009. *Razvitie lichnosti* 2: 26–53.

Rasizm i 'psikhologiya narodov' [Racism and the 'psychology of peoples']. 2009. *Razvitie lichnosti* 4: 56–90.

Istoriya antropologicheskikh ucheniy (kulturnaya antropologiya) [History of anthropological teachings (cultural anthropology)]. 1997–1998. Ezhegodnik: Faculty of ethnology: St. Petersburg, Evropeyskiy universitet v Sankt-Peterburge. Razdel: Programmy kursov: 39–52.

Stanovlenie gumanitarnoy tradicii (ot pervobytnosti do Vozrozhdeniya) [The formation of the Humanistic tradition (from prehistoric times to Renaissance). 2004. *Razvitie lichnosti* 2: 159–68; 3: 128–39; 4: 115–36.

Personalizm: 'kultura i lichnost' [Personalism: 'Culture and personality']. 2005. *Razvitie lichnosti* 2: 163–70; 3: 137–48; 4: 134–57.

C. The Archaeology of Russia

***Istoriya rossiysoy arkheologii v licakh** [**A Biographical History of Russian Archaeology**]*. 2015. 2 vols. St. Petersburg, Evrasia.

***Aeksandr Aleksandrovih Formozov (1928–2009): Posleslovie** [**Alexandr Alexandroich Formozov (1928–2009): Afterword**]*. 2011. In co-operation with S. P. Shchavelev. Kursk, Kurskogo medicinskogo universiteta, 112 pages.

Paradigmy i periody v istorii otechestvennoy arkheologii [Paradigms and periods in the history of Russian archaeology]. Review of *G. S. Lebedev: Istoriya otechestvennoy arkheologii 1700–1917*. 1995. St. Petersburg, Sankt-Peterburgskogo universitet, 1991. *Sankt-Peterburg i otechestvennaya arkheologiya. Istoriograficheskie ocherki*. St. Petersburg, Sankt-Peterburgskogo universitet: 173–83.

Tipy uchenykh v istorii rossiyskoy arkheologii [Different types of scholars in the history of Russia's archaeology]. Mavrodinskie chteniya 2004. Aktualnye problemy istoriografii i istoricheskoy nauki. Materialy yubileynoy konferencii, posvyashchennoy 70-letiyu istoricheskogo fakul'teta Sankt-Peterburgskogo gosudarstvennogo universiteta. St. Petersburg, Sankt-Peterburgskogo universitet: 230–31.

Arkheologiya predrevolucionnoy Rossii [Archaeology in prerevolutionary Russia]. 1993. Problemy istorii otechestvennoy arkheologii. Tezisy dokladov konferencii (11–13 dekabrya 1990). St. Petersburg, St. Petersburg University: 4–6.

Russia. 2001. T. Murray (Ed.), *Encyclopedia of Archaeology: History and Discoveries*. ABC-Clio, Santa Barbara, Denver, Oxford, vol. III: 1127–45.

Histoire d'archéologie russe. 2002. *Dossiers d'archéologie* (Dijon) 270: 4–7.

Rayonirovanie ranney kultury metalla: Rossiyskaya arkheologicheskaya tradiciya [The location of early metal-using culture: Russian arhaeological tradition]. 1996. Mezhdu Aziey i Evropoy. Kavkaz v IV—I tys. do n. e. K 100-letiyu so dnya rozhdeniya A. A. Iessena. St. Petersburg, IIMK–Ermitazh, pages 39–40.

Rossiyskoe paleoetnologicheskoe napravlenie v kontekste mirovoy arkheologii [The Russian palaeoethnological trend in the context of world archaeology]. 1997. Tradicii otechestvennoy paleoetnologii. Tezisy dokladov Mezhdunarodnoy konferencii, posvyashchennoy 150-letiyu so dnya rozhdeniya Fedora Kondratyevicha Volkova (Vovka). St. Petersburg, Sankt-Peterburgskogo universiteta: 49–52.

The beginning of university archaeology in Russia (in coauthorship with I. L. Tikhonov), J. Callmer, M. Meyer, R. Struwe, and C. Theune. 2006. Die Anfänge der ur- und frühgeschichtlichen Archäologie als akademisches Fach (1890–1930) im europäischen Vergleich. Berlin, Internationale Tagung an der Humboldt-Universität zu Berlin, März 2003 (Berliner Archäologische Forschungen, Band 2). Rahden, Westfalen, Verlag Marie Leidorf: 197–208.

Russia: Prerevolutionary Russia. 2012. N. A. Silberman (Ed.), *The Oxford Companion to Archaeology*, 2nd ed. Oxford, Oxford University Press, vol. 3: 61–64; Soviet and Post-Soviet eras, Ibid.: 64–69.

Kistorii arkheologicheskoy mysli v Rossii: Vtoraya polovina XIX—pervaya polovina XX veka [Consideration of the history of archaeological thought in Russia: The second half of the XIX—first half of the XX cent. 2012. Review of N. I. Platonova, Istoriya archaeologicheskoy mysli v Rossii. SPb, Nestor-Istoriya, 2010. *Rossiyskiy Arkheologicheskiy Ezhegodnik* 2: 758–64.

Ekspediciya Messershmidta [Messerschmidt's Expedition]. 2008. *Troitsky Variant* 18N(854): 10–11.

Pobornik dokhristianskoy 'slavyanshchizny' Zorian Khodakovskiy [Zorian Khodakovski, upholder of pre-Christian 'Slavonicship']. 2010. E. A. Musin and N. V. Khvoshchinskaya (Eds.), *Dialog kultur i narodov srednevekovoy Evropy: To 60-letiyu so dnya rozhdeniya Evgeniya Nilokaevicha Nosova*. St. Petersburg, Dmitriy Bulanin: 464–73.

Pobornik dokhristianskoy 'slavyanshchizny' Zorian Khodakovskiy [Zorian Khodakovski, upholder of pre-Christian 'Slavonicship']. 2010. *Razvitie lichnosti* 2: 125–46 [reprinted from *Nosov Festschrift*].

Mesto, A. A. 2008. Spicyna v mirovoy arkheologii [The Place of A. A. Spicyn in world archaeology]. *Istoriya I praktika arkheologicheskikh issledovaniy*. Materialy Mezhdunarodnoy nauchnoy konferencii, posvyashchennoy 150-letiyu so dnya rozhdeniya chlena-korrespondenta AN SSSR, professora Aleksandra Andreevicha Spicyna. Pod red. E. N. Nosova, I. L. Tikhonova. dom S.—Peterburgskogo universiteta: 61–72.

Gorodcov, V. A. 1999. T. Murray (Ed.), *Encyclopedia of Archaeology: The Great Archaeologists*. Santa Barbara, Denver, Oxford, ABC-Clio, vol. I: 247–62.

Gorodcov, V. A. (1860–1945). 2001. T. Murray (Ed.), *Encyclopedia of Archaeology: History and Discoveries*. Santa Barbara, Denver, Oxford, ABC-Clio, vol. II: 589–90.

Vizantiec [Byzantine]—Kondakovskie chteniya: I. Problemy kulturnoy preemstvennosti. 2005. *Materialy I mezhdunarodnoy nauchoy konferencii*. Belgorod, Belgorodskiy gos. universitet: 5–24.

Nikodim Pavlovich Kondakov. 1999. T. Murray (Ed.), *Encyclopedia of Archaeology: The Great Archaeologists*. Santa Barbara, Denver, Oxford, ABC-Clio, vol. I: 165–74.

Khranitel' russkoy ikony: Znamenityi vizantinist borolsya protiv lubka i fabrichnoy kustarshchiny [The keeper of the Russian icon: The famous Byzantinist struggled against cheap printing and manufacuring]. 2004. *Nezavisimaya gazeta, prilozhenie: NG religiya* 5(135): 4.

Kondakov, Nikodim Pavlovich (1844–1925). 2001. T. Murray (Ed.), *Encyclopedia of Archaeology: History and Discoveries*, Santa Barbara, Denver, Oxford, ABC-Clio, vol. II: 768–69.

Nauchnaya deyatelnost' M. I. Artamonova [The scholarly activities of M. I. Artamonov]. 1961. *Issledovaniya po arkheologii SSR*. Leningrad, Leningradskogo universitet: 5–6.

K semidesyatiletiyu M. I. Artamoniva [On the 70th anniversary of M. I. Artamonov]. 1968. *Sovetskaya Arkheologiya* (Moscow) 4: 151–56.

[Exposition of the paper by L. S. Klejn 'Ethnos and culture' at the anniversary session in memory of M. I. Artamonov]. 1988. G. I. Smirnova and V. S. Flerov, Vsesoyuznyi seminar, posvyashchennyi 90-letiyu so dnya rozhdeniya Mikhaila Illarionovicha Artamonova (Leningrad). *Sovetskaya Arkheologiya* 3: 291–96, in particular page 291.

Mesto, M. I. Artamonova v istorii rossiyskoy arkheologicheskoy mysli [The place of M. I. Artamonov in the history of Russian archaological thought]. 1998. *Skify, khazary, slavyne, Drevnyaya Rus', K 100-ketiyu so dnya rozhdeniya M.I. Artamonov*. Sankt-Peterburg, 9–12 dekabrya 1998. Tezisy dokladov. St. Petersburg, gos. Ermitazha: 18–20.

Uchenyi, grazhdanin, viking [Scholar, citizen, viking: Obituary of G. S. Lebedev]. 2003. *Klio* (St. Petersburg) 3(22): 261–63.

Excerpts from the previous obituary were published in the journal article:

Grazhdanin Kastalii: Uchenyi, romantik, viking [Citizen of Castalia: Scholar, romantic, viking]. 2003. Sankt-Peterburgskiy universitet, 28–29 (3653–54); December 12: 47–57; Klejn's text on page 57.

And in newspapers:

- Umer Gleb Lebedev [Gleb Lebedev died (Obituary)]. 2003. Commersant (SPb), Tuesday August 19, 147: 15.
- Proshchay, Gleb Sergeevich [Farewell, Gleb Sergeevich]—Nevskoe Vremya (SPb). 20 August 2003, Wednesday: 3.
- Prosti nas, Gleb [Forgive us, Gleb]. 2003. Pravo i miloserdie (SPb, publisher Yuliy Rybakov 8: 11.

- Uchenyi, grazhdanin, viking [Scholar, citizen, viking]. 2003. *Vesti* (SPb), September 23, 108: 6 (umbrella title for texts of several authors: S. Okman, L. S. Klejn, A. N. Kirpichnikov, S. V. Beleckiy).
- Pamyati Gleba Lebedeva [In memory of Gleb Levedev]. 2003. *Posev* 9: 48.

Gleb Lebedev: Arkheologiya i ne tol'ko [Gleb Lebedev: Archaeology and not only archaeology. (Obituary: Development of the article from Klio)]. 2004. *Stratum plus* 1 (2001–2002): 552–56.

'Molodoy mozhet pogibnut' v lyuboy moment' ['The young can perish at any moment' (Obituary: Aleksey Markov)]. 2004. *Nauka i vlast'*. St. Petersburg, Nestor-Istoriya.

Arkheologiya v Peterburge i Peterburg v arkheologii [Archaeology in Petersburg and Petersburg in archaeology]. 2005. *Stratum plus* (2003–2004): 509–14.

Iz kladov Rossii: G. F. Korzukhina [From the hoards of Russia: G. F. Korzukhina]. 2006. *Slavyano-russkoe yuvelirnoe delo i ego istoki. Mexhdunarodnaya konferenciya* , posvyashchennaya 100-letiyu so dnya rozhdeniya Gali Fedorovny Korzukhinoy. Tezisy dokladov. Sankt-Petersburg, 10–15 aprelya 2006, SPbII RAN 'Nestor-Istoriya', St. Petersburg: 7.

Iz kladov Rossii: Gali Fedorovna Korzukhina [From the hoards of Russia: Gali Fedorovna Korzukhina]. 2010. A. A. Peskova, O. A. Shcheglova, and A. E. Musin (Eds.), *Slaviano-russkoe yuvelirnoe delo I ego istoki. Materialy Mezhdunarodnoy nauchnoy konferencii.* St. Petersburg, Nestor-Istoriya: 14–23.

Krasnyi demon arkheologii: Saga o Ravdonikasie [The red demon of archaeology: The saga of Ravdonikas]. 2010. *Kraeugol'nyi kamen'. Arkheologiya, istoriya, iskusstvo, kultura Rossii I sopredel'nykh stran* [Collection in honour of A. N. Kirpichnikov] Moscow, Lomonosov: 372–84.

La arqueología soviética—*Istor: Revista de historia internacional* (México) XI (43) 2010: 127–47 [a reprint of Chapters 6 and 7 from 'Fenomen . . .' 1993].

Biografii i avtobiografii v arkheologii i antropologii [Biographies and autobiographies in archaeology and anthropology]. Interview of Prof. L. S. Klejn by V. E. Eremenko, Nov. 1, 2010, archaeology.ru.

Voevoda sovetskoy arkheologii [The overlord of Soviet archaeology]. 2010. *Tekhnologiya vlasti* 2 (Nestor, 14). St. Petersburg, Nestor-Istoriya: 223–37.

La bête noire sovetskoy arkheologii: A. A. Formozov [*La bête noire* of Soviet archaeology: A. A. Formozov]. 2011. L. S. Klejn, S. P. Shchavelev. *Aleksandr Aleksandrovich Formozov (1928–2009). Posleslovie.* Kursk, Kurskogo medicinskogo universitet: 8–26.

Reviews:

Shchavelev, S. P. 2011. Klassik i dissident rossiyskoy arkheologii A. A. Formozov (Zamechaniya na ocherk L. S. Klejna 'La bête noire sovetskoy arkheologii') [Classic and dissident of Russian archaeology A. A. Formozov (Comments on L. S. Klejn's outline '*La bête noire* of Soviet archaeology')]. 2011. L. S. Klejn, S. P. Shchavelev, *Aleksandr Aleksandrovich Formozov (1928–2009). Posleslovie.* Kursk, Kurskogo medicinskogo universiteta: 27–49.

Iz perepiski L. S. Klejna i S. P Shchaveleva 2009–2011 [From the correspondence of L. S. Klejn with S. P. Shchavelev 2009–2011]. 2011. L. S. Klejn, S. P. Shchavelev, *Aleksandr Aleksandrovich Frmozov (1928–2009). Posleslovie.* Kursk, Kurskogo medicinskogo universiteta: 50–61.

Pechal'nyi otklik na Poslanie ot Marka [A doleful response to the epistle of Marc (obituary of Marc Shchukin)]. Peterburgskiy apokrif. Poslanie ot Marka. St. Petersburg–Çisineu, etc. *Stratum plus* 2011: 15–16.

Pechal'nyi otklik na Poslanie ot Marka [A doleful response to the epistle of Marc (obituary of Marc Shchukin)]. Evropeyskaya Sarmatiya. Sbornik, posvyashchennyi Marku

Borisovichu Shchukinu. St. Petersburg, Nestor-Istoriya, 2011: 16–18 [reprinted from *Stratum plus*].

Izuchaya metodologiyu arkheologov stalinskoy epokhi [Studying the methodology of archaeologists of Stalin's epoch]. 2011. Review of the book *Sveshnikova O. S. Sovetskie arkheologi v poiskakh pervobytnoy istorii: Istoricheskaya interpretaciya arkheologicheskikh istocjnikov v sovetskoy arkheologii 1930–1950-kh gg.* Omsk, Nauka, 2009]. *Rossiyskiy Arkheologicheskiy Ezhegodnik* 1, Universities' Publishing Consortium: 617–19.

Nauchnye shkoly v rossiyskoy arkheologii [Research schools in Russian archaeology]. 2011. *Istoriya arkheologii: Lihnosti i shkoly.* Materialy Mezhdunarodnoy nauchnoy konferencii k 160-letiyu so dnya rozhdeniya V. V. Khvoyki (Kiev, October 5–8, 2010). St. Petersburg, Nestor-Istoriya: 65–69.

Akademik Rybakov i partiynaya liniya [Academician Rybakov and the party line]. 2011. *Troitsky Variant* 4(73): 14.

Zagadka L'va Gumileva [The riddle of Lev Gumilev]. 2011. *Troitsky Variant* 9(78): 11.

Comments:

Primer nauchnogo khamstva: Zagadka L'va Gumileva [An example of scholarly boorishness: The Riddle of Lev Gumilev]. Rt.Kopp, rtkorr.com/news/2011/08/18/258022.new ['one of many angry comments by Gumilev's fans on the web' —LSK].

Trezvo o L've Gumileve: Otvet kritikam [Soberly on Lev Gumilev: Response to critics]. 2011. *Troitsky Variant* 10(79): 8.

Dmitriy Alekseevich Machinskiy: Nekrolog [Dmitriy Alekseevich Machinskiy: An obituary]. Memorial, *Cogita!ru*, cogita.ru/cogita/analitika/publikacii-nic-memorial/dmitrii-alekseevich-machinskii.-nekrolog.

Dmitriy Alekseevich Machinskiy (1937–2012). 2012. *Rossiyskiy Arkheologicheskiy Ezhegodnik* 2: 791–92.

Uchenyi, ychitel, uchenik [Scholar, teacher, pupil]. 2013. *Stratum plus* 4 (collection in honour of M. Kazansky): 361–64.

Ukrainskaya arkheologiya v Rossii i vne ee [Ukrainian archaeology in Russia and beyond]. 2013. *Troitsky Variant* 9(128): 4–5.

Vokrug istorii arkheologii [Concerning the history of archaeology]. 2014. (Teslenko D. L. Istoriya arkheologii: Granitsy i printsipy subdistsipliny. Kiev, 2013). *Rossiyskiy Arkheologicheskiy Ezhegodnik* 4: 264–66.

XIII. The Upbringing of Archaeologists and of the Archaeological Milieu

A. Archaeological Education

Die Ausbildung der Archäologen in der UdSSR. 1972. *Ethnographisch-Archäologische Zeitschrift* (Berlin) 13(3): 443–56.

Obuchenie arkheologii v Peterburge: Tradicii i probemy [Archaeological education in Petersburg: Traditions and problems]. 2005. *Antropologicheskiy forum* (St. Petersburg) 3: 38–58.

Vvedenie v special'nost' [Introduction to the profession]. 1982. *Programma speckursov po arkheologii i etnografii.* Sverdlovsk. Ural'skogo universitet: 3–7.

Nuzhna korennaya perestroyka [Radical reorganization is necessary]. 1959. Newspaper: Leningradskiy universitet 16(1089), May 11: 2.

SNO—byt' ili ne byt'? [Student Scholar Society—to be or not to be?]. 1959. Newspaper: Leningradskiy universitet 33(1105), October 26: 1–2.

Okhota na l'vo: Special'nost' ili specializaciya? [Hunting on leos: Speciality or specialization?]. 1962. Newspaper: Leningradskiy universitet 35(1284), June 1: 3; 36(1285), June 5: 3.

Problemnyi seminar [Problems seminar]. 2009. *Troitsky Variant* 5(24): 14.

Zapovedi uchastnikam arkheologicheskogo seminara L. S. Klejna (gody chekanki 1964–1955) [Commandments for participants of L. S. Klejn's seminar (composed 1964–1995)]. 1999. *Stratum plus* 3: 389.

Kriticheskiy kommentariy L. S. Klejna k zapovedyam S. Velindera [Critical comments by L. S. Klejn to commandments by S. Welinder]. 1999. *Stratum plus* 3: 390.

Aforizmy o nauke [Aphorisms on science]. 1999. *Stratum plus* 3: 391.

Aforizmy o nauke [Aphorisms on science]. 2008. *Troitsky Variant* 11N (833), September 2: 16.

Kak pisat' yasno (dvadcat' pravil khoroshego stilya) [How to write clearly (twenty rules of good style)]. 1999. *Stratum plus* 3: 391–92.

Reprint: Zapovedi seminaru: Kak pisat' yasno [Commandments for the seminar: How to write clearly]. 2005. Korshunkov V. A. Istoriya drevnego mira: Uchebno-metodicheskiy kompleks. Kirov, VyatGGU: 105–07.

Vysokie tekhnologii v sfere vysshego obrazovaniya: Imitaciya raboty [High technologies in the highest education: Imitation of work]. 1998. Primenenie vysokikh tekhnologiy v nauke. Tezisy konferencii. St. Petersburg, Sankt-Peterburgskiy Tekhnologicheskiy universitet.

Memuar o rabote v arkheologicheskom kruzhke istoricheskogo fakul'teta Leningradskogo universitet [Notes on the work of the archaeological circle of Leningrad university historical faculty]. 1998. *Anichkovskiy Vestnik* 11 (Associaciya uchenicheskikh nauchnykh obshchestv 'Anichkov Dvorec'). Antichnaya religiya i filosofiya. St. Petersburg: 91–96.

Ob 'Arkheologii i ne tolko . . .' i ne tolko [On 'Archaeology and not only . . .' and not only]. 2005. *Stratum plus* (2003–2004) 4: 487–90.

Azy nauki i universitety [ABC of science and universities]. 2008. *Troitsky Variant* 5N (815), June 10: 4.

Smena pokoleniy i problema preemstvennosti [The succession of generations and the problem of change]. 2009. *Antropologicheskiy forum* 11: 57–63.

Stek [Riding crop]. 2009. *Troitsky Variant* 10(29): 14.

Revue of *A Splendid Idiosyncrasy: Prehistory at Cambridge 1915–1950*, 2009, by Pamela J. Smith. 2010. *Cambridge Journal of Archaeology* 20(3): 449–51.

B. Popularisation

Arkheologiya pod zolotoy maskoy [Archaeology under a golden mask]. 1967. *Yunost'* (Moscow) 7: 93–98.

Pop-naka [Pop-science]. 2008 (16 September). *Troitsky Variant* 12N(836): 5.

Doklad dlya domrabotnicy [Report for the housemaid]. 2008 (16 September). *Troitsky Variant* 12N(836): 14.

Interpretaciya populatizacii [Interpretation of popularization]. 2009 (29 September) *Troitsky Variant* 19(38): 14.

Comments:

Paevskiy, A. 2009. Mnenie praktika [Opinion of a practitioner]. 2009. *Troitsky Variant* 19(38): 14.

Sensaciya Tyagnibedy [Sensation of Tyagnibeda]. 2010. *Troitsky Variant* 3(47): 14.

Tripol'skoe zerkalo [Tripolyean mirror]. 2012. *Troitsky Variant* 18(112): 12.

Tayny kanala 'Kultura' [Mysteries of the channel 'Culture']. 2013. *Troitsky Variant* 2(121): 4.

C. Reference Books

Review of O. E. Alekseeva, N. A. Savvonidi. Illustrirovannyi anglo-russkiy—russko-angliyskiy arkheologicheskiy slovar' [Illustrated English-Russian—Russian-English archaeological dictionary]. 1995. St. Petersburg, published by the authors, 1993 . . . *Sovetskaya Arkheologiya* 2: 249–50.

Paleolit na chetyrekh yazykakh [Palaeolithic in four languages]. Review of S. A. Vasilyev, G. Bozinski, B. A. Breadly, L. B. Vishnyackiy, E. Y. Girya, Y. N. Gribchenko, M. N. Zheltova, and A. N. Tikhonov. Chetyrekh''yazychnyi (rusko-anglo-franko-nemeckiy) slovar'-spravochnik po arkheologii paleolita, 264 pages in 80, 82 figures. 2007. St. Petersburg: Peterburgskoe Vostokovedenie. *Arkheologicheskie Vesti* 16: 206–07.

D. Ethics in Archaeology

Kodeks etiki arkheologa yak sprava chesti kraini [Codex of archaeologists' ethics as the deeds of honour of the country]. 2009. *Arkheologiya* (Kiyv) 1: 100–02.

Comments:

Korenyako, V. A. 2010. Problemy etiki i proyavleniya krizisa v sovremennoy arkheologii (shest' let spustya) [Problems of ethics and manifestations of crisis in the contemporary archaeology (six years later)]. *Chelovek I drevnosti. Pamyati Aleksandra Aleksandrovicha Formozova (1928–2009).* Moscow, Grif & Co: 802–13, cf. 808–09.

Dva skandala v arkheologii [Two scandals in archaeology]. 2010. *Troitsky Variant* 10(54): 14.

Istoriya antropologicheskikh idey i shustrykh lyudey [History of anthropological ideas and nimble people]. 2010. *Troitsky Variant* 24(69): 11.

Gde zhe Shliman? [Yet where is Schliemann?]. 2011. *Troitsky Variant* 16(85): 12.

Neskolko slov ob amphorakh i arkharakh [Some words on amphoras and wild rams]. 2011. *Troitsky Variant* 16(85): 15.

Ten' pokhishchennogo zolota [A shadow of the stolen gold]. 1900. Newspaper: *Smena* (Leningrad) 236, October 10: 4.

Comments:

Wermusch, G. Der verschollene Goldschatz. 1990. *Wochenpost* (Berlin) 37(51): 14–15.

Goldmann, K. Der Schatz des Priamos. 1991. *Antike Welt* 22(3): 195–206, especially 204–05.

Der Schatten des geraubtes Goldes. 2012. G. S. Korres, N. Karadimas, and G. Flouda (Eds.). *Archaeology and Heinrich Schliemann: A Century after His Death.* Assessments and prospects: Myth–history–science. Athens: 416–20 (ISBN: 978-960-93-3929-2, electronic edition: aegeussociety.org/en/index.php/publication/archaeology-and-heinrich-schliemann/—but deleted from the site on April 9, 2012). [Ημερομηνία: Τρίτη. Proceedings of Schliemann Congress (1990). ['The translation of the article in Smena 1990 (above) was sent to Athens in 1990 but was published there only in 2012'. —LSK.]

Prelestnoe pis'mo Rusnauki [A tempting letter by Rusnauka]. 2012. *Troitsky Variant* 10(104): 7.

Tuda, gde cvetut citrony, ili Diskurs ob Otkrytom Dostupe [Dahin, wo die Zitronen blühen, or Discourse on Open Access]. 2012. *Troitsky Variant* 12(106): 12.

Comments:

Gelfand, M. Ibid., discussion: 12.

Cherednikov, I. Ibid.: 13.

Vibe, D. Ibid.: 13.

Under the Oxford gown. 2012. *Troitsky Variant* 14(108): 8.

O pravakh embrionov [On the rights of embryos]. 2012. *Troitsky Variant* 17(111): 11.

Comments:

Gelfand, M. 2012. Pesochnye chasy v biologii razvitiya [The hourglass in the biology of development]. *Troitsky Variant* 18(112): 12.

Glagolev, C. Für Haeckel. 2012. *Troitsky Variant* 22(116): 10.

Posledniy vybor [The last choice]. 2012. *Troitsky Variant* 23(117): 12.

Otkrytoe pis'mo gazetam 'Moldavskie vedomosti' i 'Kommersant plus' [Open letter to the newspapers *Moldavskie vedomosti* and *Kommersant plus*] (Editorial subtitle: Well-known Russian scholars advance in defence of scholarly reputation; in coauthorship with V. Mason, M. Shchukin, S. Beleckiy, L. Vishnyackiy, O.Shcheglova, and V. Bochkarev). Newspaper: *Nezavisimaya Moldova*, June 6.

Comments:

Tovarishhi uchenye, docenty s kandidatami . . . Otvet na otkrytoe pis'mo russkikh uchenykh, vystupivshikh v zashchitu odnoy moldavskoy reputacii [Comrade scholars, Docents with candidates . . . Response to the open letter of Russian scholars who advanced in defence of one Moldavian reputation]. 2007. Newspaper: *Moldavskie vedomosti*, July 11.

Kulikovskaya oda antropologicheskomy bolotu. Otvet na Otkrytoe pis'mo gruppy uchenykh [The snipe's ode to the anthropological swamp. Reply to the open letter of a group of scholars] [undersigned: Editorial Board]. 2007. Newspaper: *Kommersant plus*, July 13.

Plagiat glazami giproskeptika [Plagiarism as seen by a 'giprosceptic']. 2008. *Troitsky Variant* 14N (842), October 14: 6–7.

Comments:

Demina, N. 2008. Kak borot'sya s plagiatorami? [How to fight against plagiarists?]. 2008. *Troitsky Variant* 15N, October 28: 10.

Kondakov, V., and Deyneka, P. 2009. Ariec Burovskiy i plagiat [The Aryan Burovski and plagiarism]. 2009. *Troitsky Variant* 3(22): 7.

Memuary: Parad ili karnaval? Perepiska s Prof. Dobrolyubskim [Memoirs: A parade or carnival? Correspondence with Prof. Dobrolyubskiy]. Dobrolyubskiy A. O. 2009. *Odesseya odnogo arkheologa*. Andrey Krasnozhon. Odessa, Istoriya-Nestor: 453–66.

Otkrytyi list [An open sheet]. 2008. *Troitsky Variant* 15N (845), October 28: 14.

Arkheologi protiv chernykh [Archaeologists against black ones]. 2013. *Troitsky Variant* 4(123): 12 (reprinted on the site of the Institute of Archaeology, Russian Academy of Sciences, Moscow). [In Russia nonscientific 'fringe' archaeologists are known as 'black diggers'.]

Comments:

Kondratyev, I. 2013. Vokrug nashumevshey stat'i L. Klejna v 'Troickom variante' [Concerning a sensational article by L. Klejn in *Troitsky Variant*]. *Arkheologiya Rossii*, archeologia.ru/modules/forum/viewtopic.php?t=3819.

Kovalev, A. 2013. Spor o 'chernykh kopatelyakh' skvoz' prizmu mirovogo opyta [The argument about 'black diggers' through the prism of world experience]. 2013. *Troitsky Variant* 5(124): 2–3.

Etika i psikhologiya na poroge nauki [Ethics and psychology at the threshold of science]. 2013. *Filosofiya i epistemologia nauki* 4: 241–45. (Reprinted in S. P. Shchavelev (Ed.), *Dan' Mnemozine*. Book 2. Kursk. RGMU, 2014.)

Particular Studies of Ancient Cultures

XIV. Tripolye Culture, the Danube, and the Aegean World

***O date Karbunskogo klada* [*On the date of the Karbuna hoard*]**. 1968. *Problemy arkheologii*, 1. Leningrad, Leningrad University Press: 5–74.

Ob istochnikakh mednogo importa rannetripol'skoy kultury [On the sources of the copper imports of Early Tripolye culture]. 1964. *Vestnik Leningradskogo universitet* 20: 133–38.

K sravnitenoy stratigrafii egeyskkh i dunayskikh telley [On the comparative stratigraphy of Aegean and Danubian tels]. 1965. *Vestnik Leningradskogo universitet* 20: 57–63.

Fenomen SM III i vopros o yazyke lineynogo pis'ma A [Phenomenon MM III and the question of the language of the Linear A script]. 1971. *Vestnik Leningradskogo universitet* 8: 110–13.

Kipr i Krit v 'Arkheologii mira' [Cyprus and Crete in *Archaeologia mundi*]. 1973. *Vestnik Drevney Istorii* (Moscow) 3: 174–82.

Review of K. Horedt and C. Seraphin, *Die prähistorische Ansiedlung auf dem Wietenberg bei Sighişoara–Schässburg* (Antiquitas, R. 3; Band 10), Bonn, 1971. 1975. *Arkheologiya* (Kiyv) 17: 107–09 [in coauthorship with V. A. Dergachev].

Ukrainskoe osvoenie tripolya: Enciklopediya—Spravochnik ili pamyatnik? [Ukrainian mastering of Tripolye: Encyclopedia—Reference book or monument?]. 2005–2009. *Stratum plus* 2: 593–600.

Translated to Ukrainian: Ukrain'ske osvoennya Tripillya: Enciklopediya—Dovidnik chi pam'yatnik? 2009. *Arkheologiya* 1: 109–16.

Comments:

Kolybenko, O. V. 2009. Chi potribna arkheologiya movoyu Tarapun'ki i Shtepselya? [Is archaeology in the language of Tarapun'ka and Shtepsel necessary?] ['Both persons are humorous artists with ironical russification of Ukrainian speech'. —LSK] Pereyaslav-Khmel'nickiy Derzhavnyi pedagogichnyi universitet imeni Grigoriya Skovorody, Naukovi zapiski z ukrains'koy istorii, 23. Pereyaslav-Khmel'nickyi: 272–74.

Moldova v zerkale Kitaya (posleslovie L. S. Klejna) [Moldova in the mirror of China (afterword by L. S. Klejn)]. 2011. V. Borshevich. Moldavskiy ieroglif. Kishinev, *Stratum plus*: 641–44.

Kollektiv Khoddera o religii v rannem neoilite [Hodder's team on religion in the Early Neolithic]. 2012. [Review of the collection I. Hodder (Ed.), *Religion in the Emergence of Civilization*. New York, Cambridge University Press, 2010.] *Rossiyskiy Arkheologicheskiy Ezhegodnik* 2: 723–28.

Kobzoru anatoliyskoy preistorii [Some materials relating to the survey of Anatolian prehistory]. 2012. [Review of B. S. Düring, *The Prehistory of Asia Minor from Complex Hunter-Gatherers to Early Urban Societies*. New York, Cambridge University Press, 2011.] *Rossiyskiy Arkheologicheskiy Ezhegodnik* 2: 729–33.

XV. Homeric Studies

Besplotnye geroi: Proiskhozhdenie obrazov Iliady **[*Incorporeal Heroes: The Origins of Homeric Images*]**. 1994. St. Petersburg, Farn—Khudozhestvennaya Literatura, 192 pages with illustrations.

Translated to English: ***Incorporeal Heroes: The Origins of Homeric Images.*** 2012. Newcastle, Cambridge Scholars Publishing, 175 pages, 6 figures, 3 tables.

Anatomiya Iliady [*The Anatomy of Iliad*]. 1998. St. Petersburg, Sankt-Peterburgskogo universitet, 555 pages.

Reviews:

Akimova, L. I. 2000. *Vestnik RGNF* 4: 264–70.

Korshunkov, V. A. 2001. *Novoe Literaturnoe Obozrenie* 51: 438–40.

Cymburskiy, V. L., and Fayer, V. V. 2002. *Vestnik Drevney Istorii* 1(240): 179–89.

Comments:

Fayer, V. V. 2002. Celostnost' Iliady v zerkale statisticheskogo analiza [The Integrity of Iliad in the Mirror of Statistical Analysis]. *Indoevropeyskoe yazykoznanie i klassicheskaya filologiya* VI, St. Petersburg, Nauka: 202–07.

Borshevich, V. 2011. Moldavskiy ieroglif. Kishinev, *Stratum plus*: 203–04.

Gde nakhodilas' Troya? [Where was Troy?], istorya.ru/forum/index.php?s=8cfa2307ac35b45d31b1ad3c5b51c437&showtopic=3003&st=0&p=52511&.

Rasshifrovannaya Iliada [***The Iliad Decoded***]. 2013. St. Petersburg, Amfora.

Reviews

Aleksandrov, N. 2013. Radio: Ekho Moskvy, Broadcast: Books, February 7.

Aleksandrov, N. 2014. Public television of Russia: Programm 'Order of words'; broadcast: literary critique—Decoding the Iliad and all the riddles of 'The Master and Margarita'.

O proiskhozhdenii geroev Iliady [On the origins of the heroes of the Iliad]. Shliman, Peterburg, Troya. Katalog vystavki v Goudarstvennom Ermitazhe, Sankt-Peterburg, 19 iyunya–18 otyabrya 1998 goda. St. Petersburg, Slaviya: 120–55.

Naydena li Troya? [Is Troy found?]. 1984. Tezisy Vsesoyuznoy avtorsko-chitatel'skoy konerencii VDI. Moscow, Nauka: 26–27.

Naydena li Troya? [Is Troy found?]. 1985. *Znaniye-Sila* 3: 40–43.

Comments:

Matveychev, O., and Belyakov, A. 2014. *Troyanskiy kon' zapadnoy istorii.* St. Petersburg, Piter, 224 pages.

Troyanskaya voyna v epose i istorii: Posleslovie [Trojan War in epic and history: Afterword]. 1990. A. Kravchuk, *Troyanskaya voyna. Mif i istoriya.* Perev. s polsk. Moscow, Nauka: 196–217.

Korrelaciya imen v Iliade [Correlation of names in the Iliad]. 1985. Tezisy dokladov soveshchaniya 'Kompleksnye metody v izuchenii istorii s drevneyshikh vremen do nashikh dney', fevral'. Moscow: 122–23.

Review of the book by D. Makkuin, Khetty i ikh sovremenniki v Maloy Azii [J. G. MacQueen, *Hittites and Their Contemporaries in Asia Minor* (the Russian translation)]. 1985. *Narody Azii i Afriki* (Moscow) 1: 194–98.

Ilion i Troya (K kharakteristike istochnikov i formirovaniya gomerovckogo eposa) [Ilios and Troy (The characteristics of sources and the formation of the Homeric epic)]. 1986. *Narody Azii i Afriki* (Moscow) 4: 86–116.

Comments:

Dyakonov, I. M. 1987. Mestopolozhenie Troi i khetty (Po povodu raboty L. S. Klejna) [The location of Troy and the Hittites (A propos the work of L. S. Klejn)]. 1987. Ibid. 2: 209–11.

Cymburskiy, V. L. 1987. 'Miry' terminov 'Troya' I 'Ilion' v gomerovskom epose (po povodu gipotezy L. S. Klejna) ['Worlds' of the terms 'Troy' and 'Ilios' in the Homeric epic (a propos L. S. Klejn's hypothesis)]. *Kompleksnye metody v istoricheskikh issledovaniyakh* (Moscow): 168–70.

Gomerovskie nazvaniya grekov i Drevniy Vostok [Homeric names of the Greeks and the Ancient Orient]. 1990. *Narody Azii I Afriki* (Moscow) 1: 56–67.

Akheyskie pesni Iliady (K kharakteristike istochnikov i formorovaniya gomerovskogo eposa) [Achaean songs of Iliad (The characteristics of sources and the formation of the Homeric epic)]. 1990. B. N. Putilov (Ed.), *Folklor i etnografiya: Problemy rekonstrukcii faktov tradicionnoy kultury.* Leningrad, Nauka: 212–31.

Danayskaya Iliada: K kharakteristike istochnikov i formirovaniya gomdrovskogo eposa [The Danaan Iliad: The characteristics of sources and the formation of Homeric epic]. 1990. *Vestnik Drevney Istorii* (Moscow) 1: 222–53.

Drevneyshie pesni Iliady [The most ancient songs of the Iliad]. 1992. *Vestnik Drevney Istorii* (Moscow) 2: 15–31.

Schliemann á Saint-Pétersbourg. 1995. *Dossiers Archéologiques* (Dijon) 206: 16–27.

Genrikh Shliman v Peterburge [Heinrich Schliemann in Petersburg]. Shliman, Petersburg, Troya. Katalog vystavki v Gosudastvennom Ermitazhe, Sanct-Petersburg, 19 iyunya–18 oktyabrya 1998 goda. St. Petersburg, Slaviya: 8–15.

Scepticheskiy kommntariy k nachalu evropeysoy istorii [A sceptical commentary on the begining of European history (on the mythical character of the Trojan War)]. 1986. *Znanie-sila* 3: 41–44.

Comments:

Begalin Kairat. 2007. Istoriya odnoy sensacii, ili Sledy troyanskogo konya [History of a sensation, or the next Trojan horse], http://www.proza.ru/comments.html?2007/11/16/116.

Matveychev, O., and Belyakov, A. 2014. Troyanskiy kon' zapadnoy istorii. St. Petersburg, Piter, 224 pages.

Kto pobedil v Iliade? [Who was the victor in the Iliad?] 1986. *Znanie-sila* 7: 43–45.

Katalog korabley: Struktura i stratigrafiya [The Catalogue of Ships: Structure and stratigraphy]. 2000. *Stratum plus* 3: 17–51, *Asteriya*: http://chronarda.ru/phoebus/sub/klein.php.

Katalog korabley: Struktura i stratigrafiya [The Catalogue of Ships: Structure and stratigraphy]. Moscow, Eksmo, series Triumvirat [publication of the 1996 paper and reprinting of the article in *Stratum* 2000].

Reviews:

'Ya spisok koranley prochel do serediny . . .' (Klejn L. Katalog korabley: Struktura i stratigrafiya) [The Catalogue of Ships: Structure and stratigraphy]. 2005. Moscow, Eksmo, series Triumvirat S. Novosti Russkoy i Ukrainskoy Fantastiki. Informacionnyi listok Ukrainskoy Fantastiki, N 23/2005 (216), December 26.

Fayer, V. V. 2010. Kompoziciya 'Kataloga korabley' i problemy gomerovskogo eposa [The Composition of the 'Catalogue of Ships' and the problems of Homeric epic]. 2010. Preprint WP6/2010/04/Серия WP6 Gumanitarnye issledovaniya. Moscow: 31, hse.ru/data/2010/11/25/1209923125/WP6_2010_04-f.pdf.

Anatomiya Iliady: Nachalo discussii [The Anatomy of the *Iliad*: The beginning of a discussion]. 2004. *Vestnik Drevney Itorii* 3: 207–14.

Gomericheskaya istoriya: Ocharovanie gomerovskogo eposa [Homeric history: The charm of the heroic epic]. 2010. *Troitsky Variant* 19(64): 10.

A Troya byla ne tam [But Troy was not there]. 2011. *Troitsky Variant* 10(79): 13.

Struktura 'Kataloga korabley' i formirovanie gomerovskogo eposa [The structure of the 'Catalogue of Ships' and formation of the Homeric epic]. 2014. Zbirnik nauchnikh prac, vyp. 298. Chastina I. ΕΛΛΗΝΙΚΑ. Kyiv: 4–15.

XVI. The Pit-Grave (Yamnaya) and Catacomb-Grave Cultures

Kurgany bilya s.Troickogo [Barrows near Troickoye]. 1960. *Akheologichny pam"yatky URSR* (Kyiv) 8: 141–63.

Novye dannye o khronologicheskikh i geneticheskikh vzaimootnosheniyakh lokalnykh variantov katakombnoy kultury [New data on the chronological and genetic interrelations of local varieties of Catacomb culture]. 1960. *Vestnik Leningradskogo universitet* 20: 144–48.

O khronologicheskikh i geneticheskikh vzaimootnosheniyakh lokal'nykh variantov katakombnoy kuktury [On the chronological and genetic interrelations of local varieties of Catacomb culture]. 1961. *Issledovaniya po arkheologii SSSR* (Artamonov-Festschrift). Leningrad, Leningradskogo universitet: 69–78.

Cherepa, pokrytye smoloy, v pogrebeniyakh epokhi bronzy [Skulls covered with resin in Bronze Age burials]. 1961. *Sovetskaya Etnografiya* (Moscow) 2: 105–09.

O tak nazyvaemykh pogrebeniyakh katakombnogo tipa [On the so-called Yamnaya-culture burials of the catacomb type]. 1961. *Sovetskaya Arkheologiya* (Moscow) 2: 49–65.

Kratkoe obosnovanie migrationnoy gipotezy o proiskhozhdenii katakombnoy kultury [A brief validation of the migration hypothesis with respect to the origin of the Catacomb culture]. 1962. *Vestnik Leningradskogo universitet* 2: 74–87.

Translated to English: A brief validation of the migration hypothesis with respect to the origin of the Catacomb culture. 1963. *Soviet Anthropology and Archaeology* (New York) 1(4): 27–36.

Katakombnye pamyatniki epokhi bronzy i problema vydeleniya arkeologicheskikh kutur [Catacomb monuments of the Bronze Age and the problem of the isolation of archaeological cultures]. 1962. *Sovetskaya Arkheologiya* (Moscow) 2: 6–38.

Kopredeleniyu mesta kuril'nic v katakombnoy culture [An assessment of the place of censers in Catacomb culture]. 1962. *Arkheologicheskie raskopki na Donu*. Rostov n. D., Muzey istorii Donskogo kazachestva: 123–32.

Bronzkori agyag kerékmodellek a Fekete-tenger északi partvidékéröl [Bronze Age clay wheel models from the northern Black Sea area]. 1963. *Archaeologiai Értesitö* (Budapest) 90(1): 60–63.

Obecność elementów południowo-wschodnich w późnoneolitycznych kulturach Małopolski [The presence of southeastern elements in the Late Neolithic cultures of Lesser Poland]. 1964. *Archaeologia Polski* (Wrocław), t. 9, z. 2: 371–99.

Prototipy katakombnykh kuril'nic i problena proiskhozhdeniya katakombnoy kultury [Prototypes of catacomb censers and the problem of the origins of catacomb culture]. 1966. *Arkheologicheskiy sbornk gos. Ermitazha* (Leningrad) 8: 5–17.

Zagadka grobów katakumbowych rozwiązana? [Is the riddle of the catacomb graves solved?]. 1967. *Zotchłani wieków* (Wrocław), t. 33, z. 4: 212–22.

Reiche Katakombengräber [Rich catacomb graves]. 1967. *Ethnographisch-Archäologische Zeitschrift* (Berlin) 8(4): 210–34.

Comments:

Raev, B. 2012. K interpretacii redkikh nakonechnikov strel iz Novolabinskogo mogilnika [On the interpretation of rare arrow heads from Novolabinskiy graveyard]. *Kultury stepnoy Evrazii i ikh vzaimodeystvie s drevnimi civilizaciyami*. Matrialy mezhdunarodnoy nauchnoy konferencii, posvyashchnnoy 110-letiyu . . . M. P. Gryaznova. Kn. 2. St. Petersburg: 384–89.

Proiskhozhdenie Doneckoy katakombnoy kultury [*Origins of the Donets Catacomb Culture*]. 1968. Avtoreferat dissertacii . . . kand. istor. nauk. Leningrad, LOIA AN SSSR, 19 pages.

Zum Problem der Aussonderung und Gliederung des Streitaxtkulturkreises. 1969. H. Behrens und F. Schlette, *Die neolithischen Becherkulturen in Gebiet der DDR und ihre europäischen Beziehungen*. Berlin, Deutscher Verlag der Wissenschaften: 143–48.

Die Donez-Katakombenkeramik, eine Schnurkeramik der Becherkultur. 1969. H. Behrens und F. Schlette, *Die neolithischen Becherkulturen in Gebiet der DDR und ihre europäischen Beziehungen*. Berlin, Deutscher Verlag der Wissenschaften: 192–200.

K proverke osnovaniy gipotezy o geneticheskoy svyazi yamnoy i katakombnoy kultur [Validating the hypothesis of a genetic connection between the Yamnaya and Catacomb cultures]. 1970. *Sovetskaya Arkheologiya* (Moscow) 1: 49–57.

Katakombnaya kultura ili katakombnye kultury? [Catacomb culture or catacomb cultures?]. 1970. B. A. Kolchin and Y. A. Sher (Eds), *Statistiko-kombinatornye metody v arkheologii*, Moscow, Nauka: 165–69.

Review of the book N. Kalitz, *Die Frühbronzezeit in Nordost-Ungarn*. *Sovetskaya Arkheologiya* (Moscow), 1971, 1: 287–91 (russian).

Review of the book *Kurgany stepnoy chasti mezhdurech'ya Dunaya i Dnestra* [*Barrows on the steppes of the Danube-Dniester interfluve*, Odessa, 1970]. 1975. *Sovetskaya Arkheologiya* (Moscow) 1: 297–303 (russian).

Yamnye i katakombnye pogrebeniya Kalmykii: Kulturnaya determinaciya i vosstanovlenie social'nykh struktur [Yamnaya and catacomb burials of Kalmykia: Cultural determination and restoration of social structures]. 1976. *Problemy arkheologii Povolzhya i Priural'ya*. Tezisy . . . Kuybyshev: 27–30.

Zur historischen Auswertung der Ockergräber: Kritische Bemerkungen zu A. Häusler. 1978. *Ethnographisch-Archäologische Zeitschrift* (Berlin) 19(4): 227–42.

Replies

Häusler, A. Migration oder autochtone Entwicklung? Bemerkungen zu einigen Einwendungen von L. S. Klejn im vorstellenden Beitrag. Ibid.: 227–42.

Peresmotr katakombnoy obshchnosti (o diskussionnom trude S. Zh. Pustovalova). Review of S. Zh. Pustovalov: Socialnyi lad katakombnogo suspil'stva Pivnichnogo Prichornomor'ya. 412 s., tabl. Il 2005. Kyiv, Shlyakh. 2011. *Arkheologicheskie Vesti* 17 (2010–2011). St. Petersburg, Dmitriy Bulanin: 302–15.

Translated to Ukrainian: Pereglyad katakombnoy spil'nosti (pro diskusiynu pracyu S. Zh. Pustovalova) [Revising of the catacomb community (on the controversial work by S. Zh. Pustovalov)]. 2009. *Arkheologiya* (Kiev) 4: 90–103.

XVII. THE ARYAN PROBLEM, THE ORIGINS OF THE INDO-EUROPEANS, AND RELATED SUBJECTS

Drevnie migracii i proiskhozhdenie indoevropeyskikh narodov [***Ancient Migrations and the Origins of Indo-European Peoples***]. 2007. St. Petersburg, Sankt-Peterburgskogo universiteta, 226 pages, http://rutracker.org/forum/viewtopic.php?t=3559981. ['This book has not yet been published. An incomplete draft of the text, without illustrations, had been put on the web without the author's permission. Yet, since it is discussed on the web, it must be included on the list'. —LSK.]

Reviews and comments:

Klyosov, A. A. 2010. Chitaya L. S. Klejna 'Drevnie migracii i proiskhozhdenie indievropeyskikh narodov', Sankt-Petersburg, 2007. Chast' I [Reading L. S. Klejn 'Drevnie migracii . . .']. *Vestnik Rossiyskoy Akademii DNK-genealogii* (Kanada) 4(1): 40–65.

Zolin, P. 2011. Konspektiruya L. S. Klejna 1–2 [Summarizing L. S. Klejn 1–2]; proza.ru/2011/01/21/923.

Vremya ***kentavrov: Stepnaya prarodina ariev i grekov*** [***The Time of the Centaurs: The Original Steppe Home of the Aryans and the Greeks***]. 2010. St. Petersburg, Evraziya, 496 pages, 154 figure, 49 colour illustrations.

Reviews:

Kataeva, T. 2010. Kharacter nordicheskiy [A nordic character]. *Ekho planety* 31: 38.

Posledniy giperboreec (Hyperboreus). 2010. V internete ZhZh Chto chitat'? [On the web Zhivoy Zhurnal, What to read? community.livejournal.com/chto_chitat/7660996.html.

Eremenko, V. E., and Klejn, L. S. 2010. Kniga o grekoariyakh i kentavrakh. Interv'yu [A book on Graeco-Aryans and centaurs: An interview . . .]; archaeology.ru.

Klyosov, A. A. 2010. Chitaya L. S. Klejna 'Drevnie migratsii i proiskhozhdenie indoevopeyskikh narodov', St. Petersburg, 2007. Chast' I [Reading L. S. Klejn 'Ancient migrations and the origins of Indo-European peoples', St. Petersburg, 2007. Part I. *Vestnik Rossiyskoy Akademii DNK-genealogii* (Canada) 4(1): 40–65.

Klyosov, A. A. 2011. Kolliziya dvukh paradigm? Perepiska s L. S. Klejnom [Collision of two paradigms: Correspondence with L. S. Klejn]. 2011. *Vestnik Rossiyskoy Akademii DNK-genealogii* (Boston–Moscow–Tsukuba) 4(2), lulu.com/items/volume69/10096000/10096874/2/print/10096874.pdf.

Zolin, P. 2011. Konspektiruya L. S. Klejna [Summarizing L. S. Klejn] 1–2, proza.ru/2011/01/21/923.

Sher, Y. A. 2011. Kentavry, edinorogi, drakony i drugie mifologicheskie personazhi (o knige L. S. Klejn. Vremya kentavrov . . .) [Centaurs, unicorns, dragons, and other mythological creatures (on the book by L. S. Klejn *The Time of the Centaurs . . .*)]. *Vestnik Kemerovskogo gos. universitet* 2(46): 205–11.

Recenzii 2011 [Reviews 2011]. Novichkov Yu. Shest' ballov; Fokin S. Pchely, elki i berezy (+Aleksandr. Velikolepno), books.academic.ru.nsf/5220502/Отзывы.

Kullanda, S. V. 2012. *Voprosy yazykovogo rodstva* 7: 153–60.

Comments:

'Smekh v temnote' ['Laughter in the dark']; prokavkaz.com<Славяне›tema-t1717.

Indoevropeizaciya Evropy [Indoeuropeanization of Europe], slavanthro.mybb3.ru/viewtopic.php?p=124949.

Troitskiy, N. (kutuzov). 2010. users.livejournal.com/_kutuzov/1994591.html#comments.

Boromir (Boston), rodstvo.ru/forum/index.php?showtopic=1220&st=200&p=59546&#entry59546.

Mikhaylin, V. 2011. Smeshalis' v kuchu koni, lyudi: K prirode drvnegrecheskikh khimericheskikh sushchestv [Horses and people have mixed in confusion: Some thoughts on the nature of ancient Greek chimerical creatures]. *Novoe Literaturnoe Obozrenie* 107: 194–209.

Kullanda, S. V. 2012. K probleme leksicheskikh kontaktov severokavkazskikh, indoiranskikh i klassicheskikh yazykov [Some thoughts on the problem of lexical contacts between North-Caucasian, Indo-Arian and classical languages]. *Indoevropeyskoe yazykoznanie i klassicheskaya fologiya* XVI. St. Petersburg, Nauka: 406–15, in particular 410–11.

Anonymous. 2013. Arii protiv Klejna [Arians vs. Klejn], Az118.livejournal.com/594449.html.

Smyslovaya iterpretaciya sovmestnykh pogrebeniy v stepnykh kurganakh bronzovogo veka [Semantic interpretation of common burials in the steppe barrows of the Bronze Age]. 1979. Problemy epokhi bronzy Yuga Vostochnoy Evropy. Tezisy dokladov konferencii. Donetsk: 18–20.

Comments:

Rafikova, Y. V. 2008. *Sovmestnye pogrebeniya epokhi bronzy na Yuzhnom Urale* [*Common Burials of the Bronze Age in the South Urals*]. Avtoreferat kand. diss. Izhevsk.

Liesowska, A. 2013. Modern science to unlock the secrets of couples holding each other in loving embrace for 3,500 years, //Siberiantimes.com/science/casestudy/features/modern-science-to-unlock-secrets-of-couples-holding-each-other-in-loving-embrace-for-3,500-years/.

Otkuda arii prishli v Indiyu? [Where did the Aryans in India come from?]. 1980. *Vestnik Leningradskogo universitet* 20: 35–39.

Comments:

Andreeva, M. V. 2013. 'Vzyhatye kapli': K voprosu o poiskakh real'nykh sledov indoiranskogo kul'ta Somy/Haomy v arkheologicheskikh istochnikakh. *Kratkie soobshcheniya Instituta arkheologii* (Moscow) 229: 106–22.

Andreeva, M. V. 2013. Orientatsiya po stranam sveta v Manychskoy katakombnoy kul'ture: V poiskakh interpretatsionnykh modeley. *Kratkie soobshcheniya Instituta arkheologii* (Moscow) 230: 127–40.

The coming of Aryans: Who and whence? 1984. *Bulletin of the Deccan College Research Institute* (Pune) 43: 57–72.

Ot Tigrovoy balki do Matsya-purany (sledy pogrebal'nykh obryadov u indoariev v svete stepnoy i sredneaziatskoy arkheologii) [From Tigrovaya balka to Matsya-purana (traces of burial rituals in Indo-Aryans in the light of steppe and Central-Asian archaeology)]. 1983. B. A. Litvinskiy et al. (Eds.), *Bactria–Tocharistan in ancient and medieval Orient*. Moscow, Nauka: 47–49.

Arkheologicheskie sledy drevneyshikh indoariev v Prichernomor'e [Archaeological traces of the most ancient Indo-Aryans in the Black Sea region]. 1984. *Linguistic Reconstruction and Most Ancient History of Orient.* Moscow, Ch. I: 32–35.

Ot Dunaya do Indii: Otrazhenie urnovogo obryada v folklore indoariev i problema frigiyskoy migracii [From the Danube to India: Reflection on the urn burial ritual in the folklore of Indo-Aryans and the problem of Phrygian migration]. 1984. *Lingvisticheskaya rekonctruktsiya i drevneyshay istoriya Vostoka.* Moscow, Ch. I: 35–37.

Ot Dnepra do Inda [From the Dnieper to the Indus]. 1984. *Znaniya-sila* 7: 17–20.

Translated to Ukrainian: Od Dnipra do Indu–Indoevropa. 1997. Kniga 1–2. Kyiv, Taki spravy: 20–27.

Indoarii i skifskiy mir: Obshchie istoki ideologii (Kruglyi stol) [Indo-Aryans and the Scythian world: Common roots of ideology (Round table)]. 1987. Narody Azii i Afriki (Moscow): 63–82, 92–96. (Here are also comments by F. R. Balonov, Y. V. Vasil'kov, L. A. Lelekov, D. A. Machinskiy, D. S. Raevskiy, and S. R. Tokhtas'ev: 83–92).

Rec. na knigu [Review of the book] Kuz'mina E. E. Drevnie kochevniki ot Urala do Tyan'-Shanya [Ancient nomads from the Urals to Tien-Shan]. Frunze, 1986. *Narody Azii i Afriki* (Moscow) 1988, 3: 201–07.

Puti ariev: Polemicheskie zametki o knige E. E.Kuz'minoy [Paths of Aryans: Polemical notes on the book by E. E. Kuz'mina]. 2010. *Rossiyskaya Arkheologiya* 3: 171–73.

Proiskhozhdenie nulya, ili Drevneyshaya evolyuciya igry v kosti mezhdu Indom i Dunaem [The origins of zero, or the most ancient evolution of dice between the Indus and the Danube]. 1997. *Stratum: struktury i katastrofy* (Kishinev): 47–66.

Translated to English: The early evolution of dice between the Danube and the Indus: Contributions to the early history of mathematics. 1999. *Acta Archaeologica* (København) 70: 113–35.

Aryans in the steppes. Paper presented to Würzburg International Congress of Indo-Europeanists in October 2009 (published on the web): http://www.vergl-sprach-wissenschaft.phil1.uni-wuerzburg.de/tagung2009.html (reprinted in the collection *Ethnogenesis and Archaeology*, vol. 2, 2013).

Rannie indoevropeycy na Kavkaze i v severo-pontiyskikh stepyakh [Early Indo-Europeans in the Caucasus and on the North-Pontic steppes]. 1990. *Mezhdisciplinarnye issledovaniya kulturogeneza i etnogeneza Armyanskogo nagor'ya i sopredel'nykh oblastey.* Erevan, Erevanskogo universiteta: 162–75.

Grekoarii v Severnom Prichernomor'e [Graeco-Aryans in the Northern Black Sea area]. 1996. Grecheskaya kultura v Prichernomor'e. Mariupol'.

Sobaki i pticy v eskhatologicheskoy koncepcii ariev [Dogs and birds in the eschatological conception of the Aryans]. 2005–2009. *Stratum plus* 3: 185–94.

Dal'nie korni pogrebal'nykh tradiciy ariev [Remote roots of Aryan burial traditions]. 2011. A. S. Balakhvancev and G. Y. Kalganova (Eds.), *Drevnost': istoricheskoe znanie i specifika istochnika.* Materialy mezhdunarodnoy nauchnoy konferencii, posvyashchennoy pamyati Edvina Arvidovicha Grantovskogo i Dmitriya Sergeevicha Raevskogo, 12–14 dekabrya 2011 goda. Vypusk V. Moscow, IV RAN: 110–13.

Bashni molchaniya v neolite [Towers of silence in the Neolithic]. 2011. *Troitsky Variant* 19(88): 12.

Mahabharata v svete Iliady: Rec. na kn Y. V. Vasil'kov, *Mif, ritual i istoriya v 'Mahabharate'* [The Mahabharata in the light of the *Iliad*: Review of the book by Y. V. Vasil'kov, *Myth, ritual, and history in the Mahabharata*]. St. Petersburg: Evropeyskiy Dom, 2010, 398 pages, photo illustrations.]. 2014. *Etnograficheskoe Obozrenie* 2: 183–86.

Kniga o grekoariyakh i kentavrakh: Interv'yu s avtorom knigi 'Vremya kentavrov' professorom L. S. Klejnom, 2010, Iyun [A book on Graeco-Aryans and Centaurs: Interview of the author of the book *Time of Centaurs* Professor L. S. Klejn, 2010,

June]. *Archaeology.ru* (reprinted in Zolin P. Khetty iz rannikh skifov, proza. ru/2010/06/26/569).
Arii i kentavry. Interv'yu, dannoe Tine Kataevoy . . . [Aryans and Centaurs. Interview given to Tina Kataeva . . .]. *Znanie-sila*, 2011, 9: 40
O tak nazyvaemykh zoomorfnykh skipetrakh [On the so-called zoomorphic sceptres]. 1990. Problemy drevney istorii Prichernomor'ya i Sredney Azii. Tezisy . . . Leningrad, gos. Ermitazha: 17–18.
Eshche raz o tak nazyvaemykh zoomorfnykh skipetrakh: Polemicheskaya zametka o knige V. A. Dergaheva 'O skipetrakh, o loshadyakh, o voyne' [Once more on the so-called zoomorphic sceptres: A polemical note on V. A. Dergachev's book *On Sceptres, on Horses, on War*]. 2010. *Stratum plus* 2: 315–21.
Zoomorphic sceptres and unicorns, S. Bergerbrant and S. Sabatini (Eds.). 2013. *Counterpoint: Essays in Archaeology and Heritage Studies in Honour of Professor Kristian Kristiansen*. Oxford, BAR (International series, 2508): 129–39.
Migraciya tocharov v svete arkheologii [Tocharian migration in the light of archaeology]. 2000. *Stratum plus* 2: 178–87.

Comments

Semenov, V. A. A. 1987. Drevneyamnaya kultura: Afanasyevskaya kultura i problemy prototokharskoy migracii na vostok [Ancient Yamnaya culture: Afanasyevo culture and the problems of proto-Tocharian migration to the East]. *Smeny kultur i migracii v Zapadnoy Sibiri*. Tomsk: 17–19.
Kovalev, A. A. 2004. Drevneyshaya migraciya iz Zagrosa v Kitay i problema prarodiny tokharov [The most ancient migration from Zagros to China and the problem of the original Tocharian homeland]. *Arkheolog: detektiv i myslitel'* [Klejn Festschrift]. St. Petersburg, Sankt-Peterburgskogo universitet: 249–92.
Penzev, K. A. 2007. *Arii drevney Rusi* [*Aryans of Ancient Rus'*]. Moscow, Algoritm.
Penzev, K. A. 2007. *Knyaz'ya Ros: Aryan Blood*. Moscow, Algoritm.
Penzev, K. A. 2009. *Ariyskaya teorema* [*Aryan Theorem*]. Moscow, Eksmo, Algoritm.
Sverchov, L. M. 2012. *Tochary Drevnie indoevropeytsy vs Tsentralnoy Azil*. Tashkent, SMI-Asia.
Eshche raz k voprosu o tokharskoy migracii [Once more on the question of Tocharian migration]. 2011. *Stratum plus* 2: 183–86.
Kogo izobrazhali chemurchekskie statui? [Who was depicted in the Chemurchek statues?]. 2014. *Rossiyskiy Arkheologicheskiy Ezhegodnik* 4: 156–65.
Review of I. L. Sukhachev. Perspektiva istorii v indoevropeistike: K probeme 'indoevropeyskikh drvenostey' [The prospect of history and the study of the Indo-Europeans: On the problem of 'Indo-European antiquities']. 2007. Moscow, URSS, 232 pages, *Voprosy Yazykoznaniya* 4: 143–47.
The Bronze Age of Europe—Reflections on K. Kristiansen and T. Larsson: The rise of Bronze Age society (2005). 2008. *Norwegian Archaeological Review* 4(2): 213–28.

Replies

Kristiansen, K., and Larsson, T. 2008. Reply to Leo Klejn: Reflections over 'The rise of Bronze Age Society'. 2008. *Norwegian Archaeological Review* 41(2): 229–31.
Russian text of the review in NAR 2008: Bronzovyi vek Evropy: Razmyshleniya nad knigoy K. Kristiansena i T. Larsona [Bronze Age of Europe: Reflections on the book by K. Kristiansen and T. Larsson)]. 2009. *Rossiyskaya Arkheologiya* 2: 169–75.
Review of Y. K. Kuz'menk. *Rannie germancy i ikh sosedi: Lingvistika, arkheologiya, genetika* [Early Germans and their neighbours: Linguistics, archaeology, genetics]. 2013. St. Petersburg, Nestor-Istoriya, 2011. *Voprosy Yazykoznaniya* 1: 125–29.

Review of David Anthony, *The Horse, the Wheel and Language* (2007). 2009. *Journal of Indo-European Studies* 36(3) and (4): 1–17.

Reprinting of the article in *JIES* 2009: O stepnom proiskhozhdenii indoevropeycev (po povodu knigi Devida Entoni 'Kon', koleso i yazyk') [On the steppe origins of Indo-Europeans (a propos the book by David Anthony *The Horse, the Wheel, and Language*]. 2010. P. F. Kuznecov (Ed.), *Koni, kolesnicy i kolesnichie stepey Evrazii*. Ekaterinburg–Samara–Doneck, publisher not indicated: 167–81.

Translated to Ukrainian: Pro stepove pokhodzhennya indoevropeyciv (z privodu knigi D'vida Entoni 'Kin', koleso i mova')]. 2010. *Kam'yana doba Ukraini*. Do 60-richchya L. L. Zalianyaka. Kyiv, Shlyakh 13: 291–99.

Proiskhozhdenie indoevropeycev i arkheologiya [The origins of Indo-Europeans and archaeology]. 2012. *Kultury stepnoy Evrazii i ikh vzaimodeystvie s drevneyshimi civilizaciyami*. Materialy mezhdunarodnoy nauchnoy konferencii, posviashchennoy 110-letiyu so dnya rozhdeniya . . . M. P. Gryaznova. Kn. 2. St. Petersburg, IIMK RAN, Periferiya: 25–34.

Review of V. A. Dybo (Ed.), *Voprosy yazykovogo rodstva* [Issues of the kinship of languages], 2013, No. 9, Moscow: YaSK, 2013, XII + 166 pages Vestnik RGGU, ser. Filologich. nauk, yazykozn., 2013, No. 5(106). *Voprosy Yazykoznaniya*, 1913, 6: 137–43.

Arkheologicheskaya pesn' o Nibelungakh [An archaeological song about the Niebelungs (review of the book by Lotte Hedeager, *Iron Age, Myth, and Materiality*. London and New York, 2013)]. 2014. *Rossiyskiy Arkheologicheskiy Ezhegodnik* (4): 251–57.

Indoevopeyskaya prarodina [The original Indo-European homeland]. 2014. *Troitsky Variant* 16(160): 12–13.

XVIII. Scythians and Sarmatians

Territoriya i sposob pogrebeniya kochevykh skifskikh plemen po Gerodotu i arkheologicheskim dannym [Territory and burial rites of nomadic Scythian tribes according to Herodotus and the archaeological data]. 1961. *Arkheologicheskiy sbornik gos. Ermitazha* (Lenigrad) 2: 45–56.

Abstract in German: Siedlungsgebiete und Bestattungsart der nomadischen Scythenstämme nach Herodot und nach den archäologischen Quellen. 1966. *Bibliotheca classica Orientalis* (Berlin) 11(5): 268–70.

Proiskhozhdenie skifov-carskikh po arkheoogicheskim dannym [The origins of royal Scythians according to archaeological data]. 1963. *Sovetskaya Arkheologiya* (Moscow) 4: 27–35.

Abstract in German: Der Ursprung der Königlichen Skythen nach den archäologischen Quellen. 1968. *Bibliotheca classica Orientalis* (Berlin) 13(1): 27–29.

Legenda Gerodota ob aziatskom proiskhozhdenii skifov i nartskiy epos [Herodotus's legend about the Asian origin of the Scythians and the Narts' epic]. 1975. *Vestnik Drevney Istorii* (Moscow) 4: 14–27.

Tret'ya gipoteza o proiskhozhdenii skifov [A third hypothesis on the origins of Scythians]. 1980. *Narody Azii i Afriki* (Moscow) 6: 72–74.

Problema 'x' [The Problem of 'x']. 1979. *Problemy skifo-sibirskogo kulturno-istoricheskogo edinstva*. Kemerovo, Kemerovskogo universiteta: 18–22.

Vozniknovenie kochevogo skotovodstva [The emergence of nomadic cattle-breeding]. 1980. *Skifo-sibirskoe kulturno-istoricheskoe edinstvo*. Materialy I Vsesoyuznoy arlheologicheskoy konferencii. Kemerovo, Kemerovskogo universiteta: 30–36.

Comments:

Jettmar, K. 'Frühe Nomaden' und 'nördliche Nomaden'. 1983. *Mitteilungen der Anthropologischen Gesellschaft in Wien*, Band CXIII: 33–44.

Sadovyi kurgan, novyi vydayushchiysya pamyatnik sarmatskoy kutury [Sadoyi barrow, the new outstanding monument of the Sarmatian culture]. 1962. *Vestnik Leningradskogo universitet* 20: 164–67.

Sarmatskiy tarandr i problema proiskhozhdeniya sarmatov [The Sarmatian tarandrus and the problem of the origins of the Sarmatians]. 1976. *Skifo-sibirskiy zverinyi stil v iskusstve narodov Evrazii*. Moscow, Nauka: 228–34.

Comments:

Zasetskaya, I. P. 1980. Izobrazhenie 'pantery' v sarmatskom iskusstbe [The image of the 'panther' in Sarmatian arts]. *Sovetskaya Arkheologiya* 1: 46–54.

Zasetskaya, I. P. 1989. Problemy sarmatskogo zverinogo stilya (istoriograficheskiy obzor) [Problems of Sarmatian animal style (historiographic survey)]. *Sovetskaya Arkheologiya* 3: 35–47 (especially 42–43).

O kharaktere rimskogo importa v bogatykh kurganakh sramatskogo vremeni na Donu [On the character of Roman imports in rich barrows of the Sarmatian period in the Don area]. 1979. *Antichnyi mir i arkheologiya* 4. Saratov, Saratovskogo universitet: 204–21.

XIX. The Origins of The Slavs and the Varangian Controversy

A. The Origins of the Slavs

Voprosy proiskhozhdeniya slavyan v sbornike dokladov VI nauchnoy konferencii Instituta arkheologii AN USSR [Issues of Slavic origins in the collection of papers of the sixth scholarly conference of the Institute of Archaeology of the USSR Academy of Sciences]. 1955. *Sovetskaya Arkheologiya* (Moscow) XXII: 257–72.

Comments

Maksimov, E. V. 1956. Obsuzhdenie voprosov ranney istorii vostochnykh slavyan v Institute arkheologii AN USSR. 1956. *Kratkie soobshcheniya Instituta arkheologii* (Kiev) 5: 72–78.

Braychevs'kyi, M. Y. 1957a. Pro etnichnu prinalezhnist' chernyakhivs'koy kutury [On the ethnic identity of Chernyakhov culture]. 1957. *Arkheologiya* (Kyiv) X: 11–24.

Braychevs'kyi, M. Y. 1957b. K istorii lesostepnoy polosy Vostochnoi Evropy v I tysyachletii n. e. [On the history of forest-steppe belt of Eastern Europe in the first millennium a.d.]. 1957. *Sovetskaya Arkheologiya* (Moscow) 3: 114–29.

K postanovke voprosa o proiskhozhdenii slavyan [On the statement of the question on the origins of Slavs]. 1969. *Problemy otechestvennoy i vseobshchey istorii.* Leningrad, Leningadskogo univerdsiteta: 21–35.

Comment:

Bulkin, V. A. 1998. 'Retrospektiva' proiskhozhdeniya slavyan v otechestvennoy arkheologii 60–90-kh godov XX veka ['Retrospect' of the origins of Slavs in Russian archaeology of the 1960s–1990s of the 20th century]. *Problemy Arkheologii* 4: 178–88.

B. The Varangian Controversy

Spor o varyagakh: Istoriya protivopostavleniya i argumenty storon [***The Varangian Controversy: A History of arguments and counter-arguments***]. 2009. St. Petersburg, Evrasiya, 400 pages.

Reviews:

Spor dlinoyu v neskolko stoletiy [A centuries' long controversy]. 2009. *Chitaem vmeste* 4(33): 20.

Trekhsotletnyaya voyna [A three-centuries-long war]. 2009. *Literaturnaya gazeta* 11(6215), March 18.

Sokolov, B. 2009. Kniga 'Spor o varyagakh' [The book *The Varangian Controversy*]. 2009. *Posev* 11(1586): 40–43.

Sokolov, S. V. 2010. *Slavyanovedenie* 2: 105–09.

Fomin, V. V. 2010. Klejn kak diagnos ili golyi 'konung' [Klejn as a diagnosis, or naked 'konung'], http://oldrus.livejournal.com/169680.html.

Kameneckaya, E. V. 2010. Varyagi i slavyane: Vechnyi spor [Varangians and Slavs: Eternal controversy]. *Rossiya* XXI, 02: 184–90.

Schneeweiß, J. 2010. *Zeitschrift für Ostmitteleuropa-Forschung* 58(3): 414–16.

Petrukhin, V. J. 2011. Leo S. Klejn and the Normanist controversy in Russian archaeology. Central TAG Birmingham. The 33rd Annual Meeting. Panel: Debating principles of archaeological interpretation: An examination of the work of Leo S. Klejn, centraltag.wordpress.com/ call-for-papers/.

Oleynichenko, A. 2012. Klejn–Spor o varyagakh. Moy mir /mail.ru, Sobshchestvo Varyagi i Rus', 77, http://my.mail.ru/community/varyagi_i_rus/728B161EB94BB787.html.

Ryuss, K. 2012. Spor o varyagakh: Rec. [Varangian Controversy: Review], /ural-yeltsin.ru/news/document3141/.

Fomin, V. V. 2013. *Golyi konung. Normanizm kak diagnoz* [*Naked konung. Normanism as a diagnosis*]. Moscow, Algoritm.

Comments

Fomin, V. V. 2009a. Otkuda est' poshla russkaya zemlya. Interv'yu lidera sovremennykh antinormanistov [Where Did Russia Come From? Interview by the leader of contemporary Anti-Normanists]. *Roman-zhurnal* XXI vek (Soyuz pisateley Rossii), 6.

Fomin, V. V. 2009a. 'Skandinavomaniya' i ee nebylicy . . . ['Scandomania' and its long tails . . .]. *Rodina*, 10.

Fomin, V. V. 2010. Lomonosovofobiya rossiyskikh normanistov [Lomonsophobia of Russia's Normanists]. V. V. Fomin (Ed.), *Varyazhskiy vopros v istoriografii*. Moscow, Russkaya panorama.

Gazeau, V., and Musin, A. 2010. Normannism and Anti-Normannism, http://www.lph-asso.fr/index.php?option=com_content&view=article&id=139%3Anormannisme-et-antinormannisme&catid=31%3Adossier-russie&Itemid=78&lang=en.

Demidova, L. D. 2011. Spor o proiskhozhdenii drevnerusskogo gosudarstva: Sovetskiy 'antinormanism' i disput L'va Klejna s Igorem Shaskol'skim [Controversy over the origins of Ancient Russian state: Soviet 'antinormanism' and the public debate of Lev Klejn with Igor Shaskol'skiy], gkaf.narod.ru (page of the teacher at the Humanities department SUNC NGU).

Demidov, V. 2011. Dissident Miller i normanny [Dissident Miller and the Vikings]. 'Ostrovok', http://www.ostrovok.de/members/slava/activity/258/.

Normannskie drevnosti Kievskoy Rusi na sovermennom etape arkheologicheskogo izucheniya [Viking antiquities of the Kievan Rus' at the current stage of archaeological investigation]. 1970. N. E. Nosov and I. P. Shaskol'skiy (Eds.), *Istoricheskie svyazi Skandinavii i Rossii v IX X vv*. Moscow- Leningrad, Nauka: 226–52 (in coauthorship with G. S. Lebedev and A. V. Nazarenko).

Review:

Poppe A. 1972. *Kwartalnik Historii Kultury Materialnej* (Warszawa), r. XX, no. 4: 736.

Comments

Avdusin, D. A. 1975. Ob izuchenii arkeologicheskikh istochnikov po varyazhskomu voprosu [On the exploration of sources relating to the Varangian question]. *Skandinavsky sbornik*, XX, Tallin, Eeti Raamat: 147–57.

Rüß, H. 1977. Die Warägerfrage: Neue Tendenzen in der sowjetischen archaologischen Forschung. In Festschrift Manfred Hellmann zum 65. Geburtstag, *Östliches Europa. Spiegel der Geschichte*, Wiesbaden 1977: 3–16. (Quellen und Studien zur Geschichte des östlichen Europa; Band 9.)

Lebedev, G. S. 1999. *Varangica* Problemnogo seminara L. S. Klejna [*Varangica* in the Problems Seminar of L. S. Klejn]. *Stratum plus* 5: 102–18.

Duczko, W. 2004. *Viking Rus: Studies Relating to the Presence of Scandinavians in Eastern Europe*. Leiden (Netherlands), Brill.

Kuz'min, A. G. 2005. Gipotezy i koncepcii o proiskhozhdeniya Rusi [Hypotheses and constuctions on the origins of Rus]. *Zolotoy Lev*, 61–67, zlev.ru, 61_7.

Westrate, M. 2007. The 'Norman Problem' in historiography: Nationalism and the origins of Russia. *Vestnik*, the Journal of Russian and Asia studies, Sras.org/nationalism_and_the_origins_ of_ Russia?print=1.

Fomin, V. V. 2009. Normanskaya teoriya i ee nauchnaya nesostoyatelnost'. Uchenye zapiski Volgogradskogo universiteta (reprinted in *Slovo. Istoriya*).

Iz stat'i L. S. Klejna, G. S. Lebedeva, V. A. Nazarenko 'Normanskie drevnosti Kievskoy Rusi na sovremennom etape arkheologicheskogo izucheniya' [From the article by L. S. Klejn, G. S. Levdev, V. A. Nazarenko 'Viking antiquities of Kievan Rus' at the current stage of archaeological investigation'. *Slavyane i Rus': Problemy i idei. Koncepcii, rozhdennye trekhvekovoy polemikoy, v khrestomatiynon izlozhenii.* Moscow–Flint–Nauka: 366–69.

Soviet archaeology and the role of Vikings in the early history of the Slavs. Comment on Daniil Avdusin. 1973. *Norwegian Archaeological Review* (Bergen) 6(1): 1–4.

Comments:

Avdusin, D. A. 1975. Ob izuchenii arkeologicheskikh istochnikov po varyazhskomu voprosu [On the exploration of sources relating to the Varangian question]. *Ckandinavskiy sbornik*, XX, Tallin, Eesti Raamat: 147–57.

Normanizm—antinormanizm: Konec discussii. 1999. *Stratum plus* 5: 91–101; in the section 30 let Varyazhskoy discussii (1965–1995).

Comments:

Verkhoturov, D. N. 2005. Kto sozdal normanizm? [Who created Normanism?]. *Zhivoy zhurnal*, Dmitri Verhoturov, reprinted in NPZh.ru, 2008, miroslav1983, livejournal.com/65646.html.

Fomin, V. V. 2008. *Nachalo Rusi*. Moscow, Russkaya panorama [Conclusion].

Radomskiy, Y. L. 2010. O varyagakh i Rusi [On the Varangians and Rus'] [a propos the republication of Gedeonov], portal.slovo.ru/history/.

Sami s usami: K sporu o varyagakh [We have got a head on our shoulders, too: On the Varangian Controversy]. 2008. *Troitsky Variant* 19N(857): 7.

Varyagi, antinormanism i chas istiny [Varangians, antinormanism, and an hour of truth]. 2010. *Troitsky Variant* 18(63): 10; 19(64): 16 (reprinted on statehistory.ru October 20, 2010).

Comments:

Fomin, V. V. 2010. Klejn kak diagnoz ili golyi 'konung' [Klejn as a diagnosis, or the naked 'konung'], http://oldrus.livejournal.com/169680.html.

Bez nas: O diskussii s predreshennym rezul'tatom [On the discussion with a predetermined result] [a collective letter by 19 scholars]. 2010. *Troitsky Variant* 20(65).

Comments:

Skurlatov, V. I. 2010. Neumestnaya voznya vokrug nachala Rusi [Unseemly bustle around the origins of the Rus'], http://skurlatov.livejournal.com/1084760.html.

Konferenciya i konfrontaciya: O pokhode Rusi na Caregrad v 860 godu [Conference and confrontation: On the raid of the Rus' on Constantinople in 860 A.D.], polit.ru, 25.11.2010.

Konferenciya i konfrontaciya: Prichiny—kommentariy k zametke 'O shabashe sakharoidov i o partiynosti istoricheskikh issledovaniy' na sayte Adrian Selina [Conference and confrontation: Causes—comment on the note 'On the coven of sakharoids (*from the name Sakharov*) and on the partisanship of historical investigations' of Adrian Selin at ZhZh]. 2014. adrianselin.livejournal.com.

Antinormanism kak diagnoz [Antinornanism as a diagnosis]. December 2010. Nauka, Polit.ru.

Antinormanism kak diagnoz [Antinornanism as a diagnosis]. 2010. *Troitsky Variant* 23(68): 16 (shortened version, reprinted from the preceding listing).

The Russian controversy over the Varangians. 2012. L. Bjerg, J. Lind, and S. Sindbaek (Eds.), *From Goths to Varangians: Communication and Cultural Exchange between the Baltic and the Black Sea*. Aarhus: Aarhus University Press: 27–38.

Lyubiteli v roli ekspertov [Amateurs in the role of experts]. 2012. *Troitsky Variant* 24(118): 12.

Voinstvuyushchiy diletantizm na ekrane [Militant diletanttism on the screen (on the film by Zadornov)]. 2012. *Troitsky Variant* 25(119): 12.

O normannakh, slavyanakh i ariyakh (Eshche raz o filme Zadornova) [On Vikings, Slavs, and Aryans (Once more on the film by Zadornov)]. 2013. *Troitsky Variant* 2(121): 12.

Fingal pod levym glazom: Puteshestvie v devyatyi vek [A shiner under the left eye: A trip into the ninth century]. 2013. *Troitsky Variant* 13(132): 13.

Normanism and Antinormanism in Russia: An eyewitness account. 2014. P. Bauduin and A. Musin (Eds), *Vers l'Orient et vers l'Occident: regards croisés sur dynamiques et les transferts culturels des Vikings à la Rous ancienne*, Caen, Presse Universitaire, Publications du Graham: 407–15.

Faux pas antinormanista [Faux pas of an Anti-Normanist]. 2014. (Review of V. V. Fomin, *Golyi konung. Normanism kak diagnoz.* Moscow, Algoritm, 2013). *Rossiyskiy Arkheologicheskiy Ezhegodnik* 4: 318.

XX. The Pagan Religion of the Slavs

***Voskreshenie Peruna: K rekonstrukcii vostochnoslavyanskogo yazychestva.* [*The Resurrection of Perun: Reconstructing East Slavic Religion*].** 2004. St. Petersburg, Evraziya, 480 pages.

Reviews:

Ikonnikov-Galickiy, A. 2005. Sed'moye dokazatel'stvo [The seventh proof]. 2005. *Bukvoyed-Review* 1(5).

Alekseev, N. A. 2006. Perun v vaynakhskom folklore? [Perun in Vaynakh folklore?]. *Zhivaya Starina* 1: 55–56.

Savinov, N. H. 2007. Voskresenie Peruna in Klejn [Perun's resurrection in Klejn], proza.ru/2007/11/06/59. ['Savinov has since deleted this review'. —LSK.]

Yehuda ben Becalel'. 2007. Gipoteza o Perune na Kavkaze [Hypothesis on Perun in the Caucasus]. 2007. *Chronicler*, October 11.

Antosik, G. 2010. *Kult Peruna na Kaukazie: Na marginesie ksiazki L. S. Klejna.* Gniazdo (Warszawa): 8.

Lajoye, P. 2012. There is no 'Perun in the Caucasus' . . . but maybe an ancient Iranian thunder demon. *Studia Mythologica Slavica*, XV: 179–84.

Contrary, M. 2010. Review of L. S. Klejn's book *Perun's Resurrection*, LiveLib, http://www.livelib.ru/author/30548/reviews.

Comments

Prozorov, L. R. 2006. *Bogi i kasty yazycheskoy Rusi: Tayny kievskogo Pyatibozhiya* [*Gods and Castes of the Pagan Rus', Mysteries of Kievan Pentatheism*]. Moscow, Yauza, Eksmo: 51–52, 59.

Chudinov, V. D. Sushchestvoval li bog Rod? [Did the god Rod exist?], chudinov.ru.
Chudinov, V. D. Derevyannye izobrazheniya Peruna [Wooden depictions of Perun], chudinov.ru.
Chudinov, V. D. Skul'ptury yacoby Peruna iz Radzivilovskoy letopisi [Sculptures allegedly of Perun from Radziwil's chronicle], chudinov.ru.
Shizhenskiy, R. 2010. Problema genezisa sovremennogo russkogo yazychestva v rabotakh rossiyskikh issledovateley [The problem of the genesis of contemporary Russian paganism in works of Russian researchers], Centr Vostoka i Zapada, mesoeurasia.org/archives/8608.
Shizhenskiy, R. 2010. Problemy stanovleniya etnicheskoy rligioznosti v Rossii po dannym rossiyskoy istoriografii [Problems of the formation of ethnic religiosity in Russia in the light of data from Russian historiography]. *Antropo-Topos* (Omsk) 8: 21–30.
Evseev, A. 2011. Neoyazychestvo—nashe grazhdanskoe budushchee [Neo-Paganism—our civil future]. Kulturnaya evolyutsiya (Yaroslavl'), yarcenter.ru/content/view/39934/220.
Perun na Kavkaze [Perun in the Caucasus]. 1985. *Sovetskaya Etnografiya* (Moscow) 6: 116–23.
Med-pivo narodnoy skazki [Mead and ale of the folktale]. 1985. *Balto-slavyanskie etnokulturnye i arkheologicheskie drevnosti: Pogrebal'nyi obryad* (Moscow): 45–47.
Rusalki i car' Saltan [Mermaids and Czar Saltan]. 1985. *Balto-slavyanskie etnokulturnye i arkheologicheskie drevnosti: Pogrebal'nyi obryad* (Moscow): 47–48.
Pokhorony boga i svyatochnye igry s umrunom [The funeral of God and yuletide games with Umrun]. 1985. *Balto-slavyanskie etnokulturnye i arkheologicheskie drevnosti. Pogrebal'nyi obryad* (Moscow): 48–50.

Comments:

Petrukhin, V. Y. 2004. 'Provody Peruna': Drevnerusskiy 'folklor' i vizantiyskaya tradiciya ['Perun's send-off': Ancient Russian 'folklore' and Byzantine tradition]. *Yazyk kultury: Semantika i grammatika* (Moscow): 248–55.
Pamyati yazycheskogo boga Roda [To the memory of the pagan god Rod]. Yazychestvo vostochnykh slavyan. Leningrad, Muzey etnografii narodov SSSR, 1990: 13–26.

Reviews:

Petrukhin, V. Y. 1994. Vostochnoslavyanskoe yazychestvo: Problemy podlinnye i mnimye [East Slavic paganism: Problems true and imaginary]. 1994. *Zhivaya starina* 1: 55–57.
Yazycheskiy podkhod k lingvistike [Pagan approach to linguistics]. 1991. *Sovetskoe slavyanovedenie* (Moscow) 4: 88–92.
Zbruchskiy idol: Interpretaciya ili yazycheskaya teologiya? [The Zbruch idol: Interpretation or pagan theology?]. 1993. A. B. Ostrovskiy et al. (Eds.), *Etnosemiotika ritual'nykh predmetov.* St. Petersburg, Rossiyskiy etnograficheskiy muzey: 210–21.
Proiskhozhdenie Maslenicy [Origins of Shrovetide]. 1993. V. V. Gorbacheva (Ed.), *Tradicionnye verovaniya v sovremennoy kulture etnosov*. St. Petersburg, Rossiyskiy etnograficheskiy muzey (Ministerstvo kultury RF): 104–22.
Zmey s khobotom (Folklor i etnografiya v rabote arkheologa) [Serpent with a trunk (Folklore and ethnography in the work of the archaeologist)]. 1998. *Pamyatniki stariny: Otkrytiya, koncepcii, versii. Pamyati Vasiliya Dmitrievicha Beleckogo 1919–1997.* St. Petersburg–Pskov, Pskovskiy gos. Ob"edinennyi istoriko-arkhitekturnyi i khudozhestvennyi muzey-zapovednik—IIMK RAN: 289–96.
O drevnerusskikh yazycheskikh svyatilishchakh [On ancient Russian pagan sanctuaries]. 1995. Cerkovnaya arkheologiya (Materialy Pervoy Vserossiyskoy konferencii. Pskov, 20–24 noyabrya 1995 goda). Chast' 1. Rasprostranenie khristianstva v

Vostochnoy Evrope. St. Petersburg–Pskov: 71–80 (on the back page of title page: Arkheologicheskie izyskaniya [IIMK], vyp. 26, Ch. 1).

'Svyatilishha' yazycheskoy Rusi ['Sanctuaries' of the pagan Rus']. 1998. *Zhivaya starina* 1: 5–7 (reprint of the article in *Cerkovnaya arkheologiya*).

Skazanie o nevidimom grade Kitezhe [The story of the invisible town of Kitezh]. 1962. *Vokrug sveta* (Moscow) 2: 33–36.

Skazanie o nevidimom grade Kitezhe [The story of the invisible town of Kitezh] (a shortened version). 1989. *Grad Kitezh*, V. N. Morokhin (Ed.), 2nd ed., with changes. Gorkiy, Volgo-Vyatsk. Knizhn: 191–203.

V poiskakh grada Kitezha [In search of the town of Kitezh]. 1970. *Znaniesila* (Moscow) 11: 27–29.

Khristianstvo na Rusi (kruglyi stol) [The Rus' and Christianity (round table)]. 1988. *Znaniesila* 8: 36–43 (Klejn, with Val. A. Bulkin, D. A. Machinski, and M. B. Shchukin).

Blagaya vest' ot diakona [Good news from the deacon]. 2012. *Troitsky Variant* 7(101): 15.

XXI. Various

Review of T. Sulimirski. 1974. Prehistoric Russia: Proceedings of the Prehistoric Society (Cambridge, England), vol. 40: 211–14.

Tsar' nedavno i vstar' [The czar in recent and ancient times]. 2010. *Troitsky Variant* 1(45): 14.

Comments:

Manyagin, V. 2010. Nochnoy koshmar liberasta [Nightmare of a liberast]; personal website of V. Manyagin.

Arkheologiya, podporchenaya v nachale [Archaeology, damaged in the beginning]. Review of the book by B. Feygan and K. DeKors, *Arkheologiya: In the beginning*. Translated from the English by N. Y. Strukov and M. Tekhnosfera, 2007, 592 pages. 2011. *Rossiyskiy Arkheologicheskiy Ezhegodnik* 1, Universities' Publishing Consortium: 598–601.

Kolecnyi transport i filosofiya issledovaniy [Wheel transport and the philosophy of study]. Review of the book by P. M. Kozhin, *Etnokulturnye kontakty naseleniya Evrazii v eneolite—rannem zheleznom veke (Paleokulturologiya i kolesnyi transport)*. Vladivostok: Dalnauka, 2007, 428 pages. 2011. *Rossiyskiy Arkheologicheskiy Ezhegodnik* 1, Universities' Publishing Consortium: 620–24.

Kreposti dvukh indiyskikh civilizaciy: Teoriya i fakty [Citadels of two Indian civilisations: Theory and facts]. Review of the book by P. A. Elcov, *From Harappa to Hastinapura: A Study of the Earliest South Asian City and Civilization*. Boston-Leiden: Brill, 2008, 240 pages. 2011. *Rossiyskiy Arkheologicheskiy Ezhegodnik* 1, Universities' Publishing Consortium: 625–31.

Dolgozhdannyi 'Stratum' [Long-awaited *Stratum*]. 2011. *Rossiyskiy Arkheologicheskiy Ezhegodnik* 1: 661–68.

Other Themes and Journalism

XXII. Art

Garmonii epoch: Antropologiya muzyki [***Harmonies of epochs: The Anthropology of Music***]. 2012. St. Petersburg, Evraziya, 224 pages, 66 figures.

Reviews and comments:

Muzyka imeet svoyu sud'bu [Music had its own fate]. 2013. *Chitaya vmeste* 10.

Pronin, A., and Kashapov, P. 2013. Pyat' knig etogo leta [Five books of this summer]. 2013. *Sobaka.ru* 6(149).

Anon. Review, *Knizhnoe obozrenie*, 2013, 10:

Zinovyeva, E. 2014. Review, *Neva* 1: 253–54.

Vladimirova, A. 2014. Uchebnik vospriyatiya [Manual of perception]. *Literaturnaya gazeta* 10(6453), March 12, in the column 'Portfolio LG'.

K voprosu o svyazi kultury i iskusstva [Consideration of the connection between culture and art]. M. S. Kagan (Ed.), *Iskusstvo v sisteme kultury*. Leningrad, Nauka, 1987: 22–29.

Put' k teorii stilya. Rec. Na knigu E. N. Ustyugovoy . . . [The path to a theory of style]. Review of the book by E. N. Ustyugova, *Style and Culture: The Attempt to Build a General Theory of Style*, SPb, 2003]. 2004. *Novyi mir iskusstva* (St. Petersburg) 3(38): 22–23.

Arkheologiya i moda [Archaeology and fashion]. 2004. *Novyi mir iskusstva* (St. Petersburg) 1(36): 49.

Chto my posle etogo, or dembilskiy akkord lorda Keymstorna [What are we after that, or Lord Kaimsthorn's demob]. 2005. *Novyi mir iskusstva* (St. Petersburg) 4(45): 48–50.

O vkusakh ne sporyat? [No arguing about tastes—really?]. 2006. *Novyi mir iskusstva* 2(49): 52–53.

Zapyatnannaya klassika [Stained classics]. 2006. *Strukturno-semioticheskie issledovaniya v arkheologii*, vol. 3. Donetsk, Donetskiy nacional'nyi universitet: 107–14.

Izobrazitelnaya deyatel'nost' v evolyucionnoy perspective [Figurative activity from the evolutionary perspective]. 2010. *Chelovek i drevnosti. Pamyati Aleksandra Aleksandrovicha Formozova*. Moscow, Grif & Co.: 112–22.

Translated to English: Figurative activity in an evolutionary perspective. St. A. Chrisomalis and A. Costopoulos (Eds.) 2013. *Human Expeditions inspired by Bruce Trigger*. University of Toronto Press, Toronto–Buffalo–London, Scholarly Publishing Division: 192–208.

XXIII. Sociology and Forensic Science

Publications marked with an asterisk (*) are under pen name Lev Samoylov.

Verkehrte Welt: In Breshnews Lagern. 1991. Berlin, Aufbau Taschenbuch Verlag, 175 pages [the book is compiled from Klejn's journalism dating 1988–1990].

Reviews:

Thinius, B. 1991. Mensch ist ein Mensch ist ein Mensch . . . In Breshnews Lagern. Essays von Lew Klejn. *Die Andere*, Nr. 17/2, Beilage 8, 24: 9.

Ross, J. 1991. *Frankfurter Allgemeine Zeitung*, July 18.

Schuller, W. 1991. Noch nicht lange her. *Frankfurter Allgemeine Zeitung*, August 20.

Schuller, W. 1992. *Verkehrte Welt: In Breshnews Lagern. Der Wecker*, August.

Fahrenholtz, M. 1992. Das übertraf sogar Dostojewskis *Totenhaus*. *Lausitzer Rundschau*, September 30.

Fahrenholz, M. 1992. Blick in *Breshnews Lagern*. *Märkische Oderzeitung*, October 10–11.

Fahrenholz, M. 1992. Unerreichte Quälereien. *Märkische Allgemeine*, *Brandenburger Stadtkurier*, *Potsdamer Tageszeitung*, *Tespiler Tagsblatt*, October 16.

MF. 1992. Spektakuläre Enthüllung von Scheußlichkeiten: Lew Klejn Essaysammlung *Verkehrte Welt* berichtet aus Lagern des KGB. *Freie Presse*, November 6. Holtorf, C. 2000. *Archaeologia Polona* 38: 257–61.

Russian edition of the same book: ****Perevernutyi mir*** [***The World Turned Upside Down***]. 1993. St. Petersburg, Farn, 1993, 224 pages (the full and extended edition of the book, which was first pubished in Berlin in 1991).

Review:

Korallov, M. 1994. S tochki zreniya Kengira [From Kengir's point of view]. *Novyi mir* 8: 237–43.

Comments:

Bannikov, K. A. 2000. Armiya glazami antropologa: K issledovaniyu ekstremal'nykh grupp [The army as seen by an anthropologist: Studying extreme groups]. *Mir Rossii* 4: 125–34.

Bannikov, K. A. 2001. Antropologiya ekstrmal'nykh group: Dominantnye otnosheniya sredi voennosluzhshchikh srochnoy sluzhby Rossiyskoy armii [The anthropology of extreme groups: Dominant relations among conscripts in the Russian army]. *Etnografichweskoe obozrenie* 1: 112–41.

Bannikov, K. A. 2002. *Antropologiya ekstremal'nykh grupp: Dominantnye otnosheniya sredi voennosluzhshchikh srochnoy sluzhby Rossiyskoy armii* [*The Anthropology of Extreme Groups: Dominant Relations among Conscripts in the Russian Army*]. Moscow, Institute of Anthropology and Ethnography of the Russian Academy of Sciences, 400 pages.

Bannikov, K. A. 2004. Rezhimnyi socium: Antropologiya destruktivnosti [Regimented Communities: The anthropology of destructiveness]. Ibid.: 490–99.

Kozintsev, A. G. 2004. O perevernutom mire (istoriko-antropologicheskiy kommentariy k knige L'va Samoylova) [On *The World Turned Upside Down* (historic-anthropological comment on Lev Samoylov's book)]. *Arkheolog: Detektiv i myslitel*. St. Petersburg, Sankt-Peterburgskogo universitet: 486–89.

Kormina, Z. 2005. Review of K. A. Bannikov, Antropologiya ekstremal'nykh grupp. *Antropologicheskiy forum* 2: 358–64 (especially p. 360).

Kutzman, A. 2006. Perevernutui mir [The world turned upside down]. raduga.co.il/index. asp?CategoryID=87&artikelD=188. Abbreviated exposition of the study: *ןמצנוק ידע יאחדלפו הילוי רנרל סילשורי, ריל ןו ןוכמ תוכייתשהו תומילא ,תוימואל ,תויניּמ ?"הארחמה דיל סוקמ" הל רבעמו לארשיב "סיסור" (תוכרוע) הקבר.*

Oleynikova, O. D. 2008. Svetskoe ponimanie dukhovnosti [Secular understanding of spirituality]. O. A. Shamshikova and N Y. Bol'shunova (Eds.), *Sociokulturnye probemy sovremennogo cheloveka: Materially III Mezhdunarodnoy nauchno-praktiheskoy konferencii*. Novosibirsk, NGPU, Ch. 1.

Bannikov, K. L. 2009. *Principy kulturogeneza v rezhimnykh soobshchestvakh: Socialno-antropologheskiy analiz Rossiyskoy armii vtoroy poloviny XX veka* [*Principles of the Genesis of Cultural Genesis in Security Communities: Social-Anthropological Analysis of the Russian Army of the Second Half of the XXth Century*] (autoreferat Cand. Diss.). Moscow.

Borko. 2010. Kartinki na pamyat': Perevertyshi [Pictures to remember: Turncoats], borko.livejournal.com/632769.html.

Toporov, V. 2011a. Na blyudechke s goluboy kaemochkoy: Nado li razreshat' geyam vykhodit' na gey-parady? [On a blue-rimmed saucer: Is it necessary to allow gays to go out on gay parades?]. *Gorod 812* 24(133): 43.

Toporov, V. 2011b. Otvet professoru Gilinskomu ot 'eksperta' Toporova [Reply to Professor Gilinsky from 'expert' Toporov]. *Gorod 812*, mob. version, August 11.

Etkind, A. 1913. *Warped Mourning: Story of the Undead in the Land of the Unburied (Cultural Memory in the Present)*. Stanford, CA: Stanford University Press, Ch. 4, Writing History after Jail.

Perevernutyi mir [***The World Turned Upside Down***] (under the name of L. S.Klejn), 2nd ed. 2010. Donetsk, Donetsk National University, 406 pages, 46 photo illustrations, including 24 colour.

Reviews:

Kataeva, T. 2011. Professor v nature [Professor indeed (in slang)]. Review of 'Perevernutyi mir'. *Ekho planety* 4: 49.

Azadovsky, K. 2011. Homo soveticus. Review of L. S. Klejn' book *Perevernutyi mir*. *Novoe Literaturnoe Obozrenie* 109: 343–50.
Boroda (Volgograd). 2011. Alib.ru: Katalog. Social sciences and humanities: sociology, culturology, history of everyday life.
Kataeva, T. 2012. Uchenyi v perevernutom mire [A scholar in the world turned upside down]. 2012. *Znanie-sila* 7: 42–49.
Translated to Slovene: ***Sprevnjeni svet***. Ljubljana, *cf, 2001, 310 pages.
*Pravosudie i dva kresta [Justice and two crosses]. 1988. *Neva* (Leningrad) 5: 150–58.

Comments:

Rotkirch, K. 1988. In från zonen. *Hufvudstagbladet*, December 6, Kultur 3.
Greshnik byvshiy. 2001. Kak ostat'cyz muzhchinoy v tyur'me? [How to remain a man in prison?]. *Zhenskiy vopros*. Forum on Кубань.ру.
*Puteshestvie v perevernutyi mir [Travel into the world turned upside down]. 1989. *Neva* (Leningrad) 4: 150–64.

Translations:

Hamburger Rundschau 39, September 20, 1990, Arena: 16.
Lettre International 10, September 27, 1990.

Comments:

Shchepanskaya, T. B. 2001. Zony nasiliya (po materialam russkoy selskoy i sovremennykh subkulturnykh tradiciy) [Zones of violation (from materials of Russian villages and contemporary subculture traditions)].V. V. Bocharov and V. A. Tishkov (Eds.), *Antropologiya nasiliya*. St. Petersburg: 115–77.
Safronov, A. G. 2002. *Psikhologiya religii* [*Psychology of Religion*]. Kiev, Nika-Centr: 22.
Shchepanskaya, T. B. 2010. *Sistema: Teksty i tradicii subkultury* [*System: Texts and traditions of subculture*]. Part II. Moscow, OGI.
Kradin, N. N. 2011. *Politicheskaya antropologiya* [*Political Anthropology*]. Moscow, Logos: 78–80.
**Translated to German*: Reise in die verkehrte Welt. *Lettre International* (Berlin). 1990, 10: 13–18.
**Translated to German*: Reise in die verkehrte Welt. 1990. *Hamburger Rundschau*, 1990, September 20: 16–17.
*Strakh [Fear]. 1990. *Neva* (Leningrad) 1: 151–70.
*Rasprava s pomoshch'yu prava [Reprisals using the law]. 1991. *Neva* (Leningrad) 2: 120–43.

Comments:

Toporov, V. 1991. Zapiski na chuzhikh manzhetakh ili Neutomimyi fontan. 2. Publicistika [Notes on the alien cuffs, or tireless fountain. 2. Journalistics]. 1991. *Literator* 22(76), June 7.
*Etnografiya lagerya [Ethnography of the camp]. 1990. *Sovetskaya Etnografiya* (Moscow) 1: 96–108.

Comments:

Kabo, V. R. 1990. Struktuta lagerya i arkhetipy soznaniya [Structure of a camp and archetypes of consciousness]. *Sovetskaya Etnografiya* 1: 108–13.
Levinton, G. A. 1990. Naskol'ko 'pervobytna' ugolovnaya subkultura? [To what extent is criminal subculture 'primordial'?] Ibid. 2: 96–100.
Gilinskiy, Y. I. 1990. Subkultura za reshetkoy. Ibid.: 100–03.
Stanislavskiy, A. L. 1990. *Grazhdanskaya voyna v Rossii XVII v. Kazachestvo na perelome istorii*. Moscow, Mysl' (cf. Zaklyuchenie).

Bannikov, K. R. 2000. Armiya glazami antropologa. K issledovaniyu ekstremal'nykh grupp [The army as seen by an anthropologist: Studying extreme groups]. *Mir Rossii*, 4: 125–34.

Kradin, N. N. 2001. *Politicheskaya antropologiya* [*Political anthropology*]. Moscow, Ladomir, 2nd ed. Logos, 2010, 2011: 78–79.

Artemova, O. Y. 2009. *Koleno Isava: Ohotniki, sobirateli, rybolovy (Opyt izucheniya al'ternativnykh socialnykh sistem)* [*Isav's Tribe: Hunters, Gatherers, Fishermen (The Attempt to Study Alternative Social Systems)*]. Moscow, Smysl: 461–67 (section: Monopolising the information or 'archaic syndrom'?).

**Translated into Danish*: 1997. Lejrens etnografi. *Nordisk Tidskrift for Kriminalvidenskab* 84(1): 16–32.

**Translated into Slovene*: *Etnografija taborišča*. Sprevnjeni svet. Ljubljana, *cf, 2001: 230–54.

Ad glazami francuza [Hell as seen by the French]. 1990. *Znanie-sila* (Moscow) 2: 81–83.

Kultura, pervobytnyi primitivism i konclager' [Culture, primordial primitivism, and the concentration camp]. 2005. Kultura i global'nye vyzovy mirovogo razvitiya. V Mezhdunarodnye Likhachevskie nauchnye chteniya, 19–20 maya 2005 goda (Kongress peterburskoy intelligencii): 111–14.

Uchenyi v perevernutom mire [The scholar in the world turned upside down]. 2012. Interview given to Tina Kataeva. *Znaniesila* 7: 42–49.

Current political situation in Russia and the position of archaeology in the country. 1992. *Oxford Magazine* 84, eighth week, Trinity term: 26–32.

Uroki Amaly i Kamaly [Lessons of Amala and Kamala]. 1994. *Social'naya filosofiya i filosofiya istorii: Otkrytoe obshchestvo i kultura*. Nauchnaya konferenciya. Tezisy dokladov i vystupleniy. Ch. II. St. Petersburg, Sankt-Peterburgskiy gos. universitet i Filosofskoe obshchestvo: 102–04.

*Svoboda ot strakha [Freedom from fear: Open letter to the President of Russia]. 1994. Newspaper *Segodnya* 23(130): 10. The same letter was published under the title 'What has happened with our country'? in the newspaper *Petersburgskie Vedomosti* 28(705), 1994: 3. The letter was written in coauthorship with Y. Gordin, D. Granin, B. Nikol'sky, B. Strugacky, and M. Chulaki.

Problema rossiyskikh nemcev [The problem of Russian Germans]. 1993. *St.-Petersburgische Zeitung* 6(27), 7(28), 8(29), 12(33), June–December.

Das Problem der russischen Deutschen. 1. Der ethnologische Aspekt.1994. *St. Petersburger Zeitung* 1(1), July 27: 32.

Pochemu ya ne vor? [Why am I not a thief?]. Filosofiya i prestupnost'. Tezisy Mezhfakul'tetskoy konferencii.

Reprint: Pochemu ya ne vor? [Why am I not a thief?]. 1997. Newspaper: *Vecherniy Petersburg*, March 31: 3.

Vyrezannye: Vosstanovlenie real'nosti po fragmentam [Cutout: Reconstruction of reality from fragments]. 2005. *Novyi mir iskusstva* 5(46): 42–43.

Moy diagnoz: Narod k pogromu gotov [My diagnosis: The people are ready to start a pogrom]. 2006. *Novaya gazeta* 53(1175): 10–11.

Comments:

Margolin, M. 2012. Damoklov mech islamofashizma [Damocles' sword of Islamofascism]. *My zdes'* [*Jewish Weekly*] 369, June.

Diagnoz [Diagnosis]. 2009. *Zvezda* 9: 142–57 (reprinted on the web portal Ekho Rossii).

Diagnoz [Diagnosis] (extracts reprinted from the journal *Zvezda*). 2007. *Zarubezh'e. Unabhängige russischsprachige Zeitung* (Bundesrepublik Deutschland), February 2.

Review of I. V. Utekhin, *Ocherki kommunal'nogo byta*. 2, dopoln. M., 2004. *Etnograficheskoe obozrenie*, 2007, 6: 179–82.

Nauchnyi podkhod k avtomobilyu [A scientific approach to the car]. 2009. *Troitsky Variant* 4(23): 14.

XXIV. The Nature of Man and Sexual Orientation

Drugaya lyubov': Priroda cheloveka i gomoseksual'nost' [*Another Love: The Nature of Man and Homosexuality*]. 2000. St. Petersburg, Folio Press, 864 pages, 137 figures.

Reviews:

(Editor's review) 1999. Lev Klejn: 'Drugaya lyubov' [Leo Klejn: *Another Love*]. *Goluboy aysberg /L'iceberg bleu* (Paris) 1: 17–21.

Afanasyev, A. 2000. O knige 'Drugaya lyubov' [On the book *Another Love*]. *Kiev Gay Telegraph* 6: 4–5.

Dmitriev, N. 2000. *Kommersant* 118, July 1: 13.

Bagrov, E. [Markov, A.]. 2001. *Novoe Literaturnoe Obozrenie* 47, January: 396.

Matigor [Matyushkin, I.]. 2008. Recenziya na knigu L. S. Klejna 'Drugaya lyubov' (review of the book by L. S. Klejn, *Another Love*), http://mivmiv.narod.ru/Things/r_klein.html.

Comments:

Bernshteyn, E. 2002. Review of the book by D. Healy. *Homosexual Desire in Revolutionary Russia*. Novaya Russkaya Kniga: 1.

Beylkin, M. 2005. *Medicinskie i social'nye problemy odnopologo vlecheniya* [Medical and social problems of same-sex inclination]. Chelyabinsk, Ural LTD, Naskolko mozhno doveryat', Freydu et al.

Popov, I. 2006. Kuda ukhodyat gei? Adonis i starost' [Where do gays go away to? Adonis and old age]. *Kvir* 41.

Drugaya lyubov': Priroda cheloveka i gomoseksual'nost' [*Another Love: The Nature of Man and Homosexuality*]. 2000. Ispravlennoe izdanie [corrected edition]. St. Petersburg, Folio Press, 864 pages, 137 figures.

Drugaya storona svetila: Neobychnaya lyubov' vydayushchikhsya lyudey: Russkoe sozvezdie [*Another Side of a Luminary: Uncommon Loves of Outstanding People: Russian Constellation*]. 2002. St. Petersburg, Folio Press, 656 pages.

Comments:

Vadim, A. 2011. Tak kem on byl, pevec krasy nogtey? [So who was he, a singer who praised the beauty of finger nails?], http://www.stihi.ru/2011/06/28/3931.

Epstein, A. 2013. Nevozmozhnaya identichnost': Otsutstvuyushchiy gey-art i pole sovremennogo iskusstva v srtrane torzhestvuyushchey gomofobii [Impossible identity: Missing gay art and the field of modern art in the land of exultant homophobia]. *Neprikosnovennyi zapas* 90: 4.

Eroshkina, A. 2013. Zhizn' i velikie puteshestviya N. M. Przhevalskogo [The life and great travels of N. M. Przhevalsky] [comments], Newsland.com/news/detail/id/1269566/.

Venediktova, N. 2014. Marginal: Kul'turologicheskie raskopki [Marginal man: Culturological excavations]. *Znamya* 1.

Sv. Avgustin i Lev Tolstoy: Paralleli podsoznaniya [St. Augustine and Leo Tolstoy: Parallels of subconscience]. 1998. Priroda bessoznatel'nogo. Materialy mezhvuzovskoy konferencii. St. Petersburg, Unstitut biologii i psikhologii cheloveka, Sankt-Peterburgskaya akademiya teatral'nogo iskusstva: 84–86.

Sv. Avgustin i Lev Tolstoy: latentnaya gomoseksual'nost' [St. Augustine and Leo Tolstoy: Latent homosexuality]. 1999. Goluboy aysberg/L'iceberg bleu (Paris) 2: 32–39.

Osnovnoy instninkt v sovremennoy mifgologii (K voprosu o zagadochnosti geteroseksualnoy orientacii) [The basic instinct in contemporary mythology (On the mystique of heterosexual orientation)]. 1998. Mifologiya povsednevnosti. Materialy nauchnoy konferencii 18–20 fevralya g. St. Petersburg, Russkiy Khristianskiy Gumanitarnyi Institut: 84–101.

Gey ili ne gey, bud' muzhchinoy [Gay or not gay, but a man] (interview by V. Gromov). 2004. *Kvir* 4(9): 46–49.

Ne rodilsya zhenshchinoy [Not born as a woman]. 2004. [The secret life of Lincoln]. *Kvir* 5(10): 20–22.

Meppltorp: Ne prosto otkrovennyi khudozhnik [Mapplethorpe was not simply a blunt artist]. 2004. *Novyi mir iskusstva* (St. Petersburg) 6(41): 56.

Zagadochnyi Leonardo [Enigmatic Leonardo]. 2004. Nezavisimaya gazeta, supplement: *NG religiya* 1(131): 7.

V katakombakh istorii: Interv'yu S. V. Beleckomu [In the catacombs of history: Interview by S. V. Beleckiy]. 2011. *Gorod 812* 25(134): 36–37.

Arii i kentavry [Aryans and Centaurs]. 2011. Interview by Tina Kataeva . . . *Znaniesila* 9: 40.

Mify o golubykh [Myths about gays]. 2012. Sobaka.ru, November: 134–37 (14 Myths about Gays, sobaka.ru/magazine/glavnoe/13517).

Pis'mo s togo sveta [Letter from the other world]. 2012. *Troitsky Variant* 21(115): 12.

Shest v prorubi [A pole in the ice hole]. 2013. Polit.ru, January 25, polit.ru/article/2013/01/25/milonov/.

Mify o golubykh [Myths about gays]. 2012. Sobaka.ru, December: 96–98.

'Moya orientaciya—ne vashe delo' ['My orientation is not your concern']. 2013. Interview by Linor Gorelik. *Bol'shoy Gorod* (Moscow) 3(315): 34–37.

Comments

Khafizova, N. 2013. Gomofobiya [Homophobia]. ZhZh, http://natalija-khaf.livejournal.com/38043.html.

Paradoksy obshcheniya: Ot muzhskikh soyuzov k Stounuollu [Paradoxes of communication: From *Männerbunde* to Stonewall]. 1998. Problemy obshcheniya v prostranstve total'noy kommunikacii (Mezhdunarodnye chteniya po teorii, istorii i filosofii kultury, 6). St. Petersburg: 307–10.

XXV. BELIEFS AND PREJUDICES

Pis'mo prof. L. S. Klejn . . . [Letter of Prof. L. S. Klejn to prof. V. N. Dudenkov; the reply of Prof. V. N. Dudenkov and the response of L. S. Klejn to Prof. V. N. Dudenkov]. V. N. Dudenkov, *Filosofskie reminiscencii*. St. Petersburg, OM-Press: 60–62, 68–71 (in the section 'Iz perepiski s L. S. Klejnom': 57–73; a more complete text is in the memoirs by Klejn *Trudno byt' Klejnom*: 549–65).

Veruyushchiy uchenyi [The scholar believer]. 2008. *Troitsky Variant* 6N(818), June 24: 5.

Durnye chisla i zlatye gory [Evil numbers and golden mountains]. 2008. *Troitsky Variant* 13N(839), Sepember 30: 14.

Samyi umnyi narod i rusofobiya [The most reasonable people and russophobia]. 2008. *Troitsky Variant* 15N, October 28: 10.

I. Kon kak i-kona [I. Kon as i-con]. 2009. *Troitsky Variant* 1(20): 12.

Populyarno o Biblii [Popular on the Bible] (review of the book by A. P. Nikonov, *Opium dlya naroda*). 2009. *Troitsky Variant* 22(41): 2–3.

Comments:

Boriov, M. 2009 (10 November) Vzryvoopasnaya tema [A dangerously explosive theme]. *Troitsky Variant* 22(41): 1–2.

Fedorov o. Vladimir (Father Vladimir Fedorov). 2009. O neobkhodimosti dialoga veruyushchikh i neveruyushchikh [On the necessity of dialogue between believers and nonbelievers]. *Troitsky Variant* 22(41): 3.

Arkhangel'skya, A. 2009. Borcy s veroy prikhodyat i ukhodyat . . . [The opponents of faith come and go . . .]. *Troitsky Variant* 22(41): 3–4.

Mirmov, I. 2009. Za tolerantnost' (ne tost, a stat'ya) [For tolerance (not a toast, but an article)]. *Troitsky Variant* 22(41): 4.
Bak, D. 2009. Vera i ateizm uravnoveshvayut drug druga [Belief and atheism balance each other]. *Troitsky Variant* 2(41): 5.
Markov, A. 2009. 'Zachem smeshivat' . . . '. Interview N. Deminoy I M. Borisovu. *Troitsky Variant* 22(41): 5.
Kazanceva, A. 2009. Ya rada by v ray [I would be glad to enter paradise]. *Troitsky Variant* 23(42): 11.
Kazanceva, A. 2009. Vera v nauku [Belief in science]. *Troitsky Variant* 24(43): 11.
Kostyukov, L. 2009. Ne vzryv, a vskhlip: Razmyshleniya o polemicheskoy kulture [Not an explosion, but a sob: Reflections on polemical culture]. Polit.ru, December 6, polit.ru/author/2009/11/27/polem.O boge Odine i steariniviy svechke [On the god Odin and stearin candle]. 2009. *Troitsky Variant* 23(42): 14.
Racionalnyi vzglyad na uspekhi mistiki [A rational view of the successes of mystique]. 2011. *Zdravyi smysl* 2(59): 11–21.
Kasus: Arkheologiya dlya pravoslavnykh [Special case: Archaeology for the orthodox]. 2011. *Troitsky Variant* 23(92): 12.

Reviews:

Ladimir. 2012. Moya 'recenziya na recenziyu' [My 'review on review']. Nauka o religii, http://atheo-club.ru/newphpBB/viewtopic.php?f=3&t=4220&sid=e3e20a7a70ea7fa7fd0f4277f40c08c5.
Zhertvoprinoshenie i obrezanie glazami skeptika (kultura, religiya, internet i kommunizm) [Sacrifice and circumcision (culture, religion, internet, and communism)]. 2013. *Troitsky Variant* 3(122): 12.

XXVI. THE SOCIAL LIFE OF RUSSIA AND OF THE SCHOLARLY COMMUNITY

A. Science and Power

Vybrannye, izbrannye i otobrannye [Chosen, elected and selected]. 2008. *Troitsky Variant* 4N(809): 4.
Vozvyshenie Evropy i prityazaniya Evrazii [The rise of Europe and the aspirations of Eurasia]. 2009. *Troitsky Variant* 8(27): 14.
Donos na aspiranta [A postgraduate denounced]. 2009. *Troitsky Variant* 12(31): 14.
Fasady goroda i vizantiyskie emali [Façades of the city and Byzantine enamels]. 2008. *Troitsky Variant* 7N(821): 14.
Lokhi iz Peterburga [Louts from Petersburg]. 2009. *Troitsky Variant* 21(40): 14.
Uchenye kak klass [Scholars as a class]. 2011. *Troitsky Variant* 25(94): 14.

Comments

Sinicyna, S. 2011. Nauka i nravstvennyi mir [Science and the moral world]. 2011. *Troitsky Variant* 94, December 20.
Ponomarev, E. 2012. Uchenym nuzhna svoya partiya [Scholars need their own party]. *Troitsky Variant*, January.
Kuda vedet prospekt Sakharova? [Where does Sakharov's avenue lead?]. 2012. *Troitsky Variant* 2(96): 13.
Komu iz uchenykh na Rusi bylo zhit' khorosho? I kogda? [Who among scholars in Rus' was living well? And when?]. 2011. *Troitsky Variant* 13(82): 12.
Snova ubiystvo v Trieste? [Again a murder in Trieste?]. 2013. *Troitsky Variant* 1(120): 12.
Sud'ba Akademii, sud'ba strany [The fate of Academy, the fate of the country]. 2013. *Troitsky Variant* 16(135): 12.
V universitety: Khochesh'? Ne khochesh'? [To the universities: Do you want it or don't you?]. 2013. *Troitsky Variant* 17(136): 14.

Retsept reformy [Recipe for reform (of the Academy of Sciences)]. 2014. *Troitsky Variant* 1(145): 5.

B. Financing of Science

Generaly nauki [Generals of science]. 2008. *Troitsky Variant* 5N(815): 4.

Granty i garanty [Grants and guarantors]. 2008. *Troitsky Variant* 9(827): 14.

Processiya k Vysokomu stolu [Procession to the high table]. 2008. *Troitsky Variant* 11N(833): 14.

Moe zolotoe vremya [My golden time]. 2010. *Troitsky Variant* 4(48): 14.

Comments:

Torvard. 2010. Sup iz topora po-akademicheski [Soup from an Axe in the manner of Academia]. *ZhZh*, Torvard's Journal; note with comments, torvard.livejournal.com/57348.html.

Moy bol'shoy sabbatical [My long sabbatical]. 2009. *Troitsky Variant* 2N(21): 14.

San-Susi bez korolya [Sans Souci without the king]. 2008. *Troitsky Variant* 14N(842): 14.

Neprilichnyi anekdot [Indecent joke]. 2009. *Troitsky Variant* 13(32): 14.

Chaepitie v Kembridzhe [Tea parties at Cambridge]. 2009. *Troitsky Variant* 24(43): 12.

Razorvannyi dogovor [Violation of a treaty]. 2010. *Troitsky Variant* 11(55): 14.

Blokada biblioteki [Blockade of the library]. 2013. *Troitsky Variant* 12(131): 13.

C. Education

Kadrovaya politika [Politics in the matter of cadres]. 2009. *Troitsky Variant* 7(26): 14.

Shpargalki i migalki [Cribs and flashers]. 2011. *Troitsky Variant* 21(90): 12.

D. The Brain Drain

Khram nauki i khlam nauki [The temple of Science and the junk of science]. 2008. *Troitsky Variant* 17N(851): 14.

Ave Caesar! 2009. *Troitsky Variant* 17(36): 14.

Posemi ja ne uehal? [Why have I not departed?]. 2010. *Troitsky Variant* 22(67): 10.

E. Science and Religion

Odinokiy voitel [A lonely fighter]. 2011. Polit.ru: Rabota prosvetitelya. Pamyati I. S. Kona, May 2.

Odinokiy voitel [A lonely fighter]. (To the memory of I. S. Kon). 2011. *Zhurnal sociologii i social'noy antropologii*, vol. XIV, 2(55): 211–14.

F. Publishing

Kollektivnyi organizator? [A collective organizer]. 2008. *Troitsky Variant* 8N(824): 14.

Nevidimaya literatura [Invisible literature]. 2010. *Troitsky Variant* 2(46): 14.

Pyat' bar'erov k priznaniyu [Five barriers to acceptance]. 2009. *Troitsky Variant* 3(22): 14.

Tri shara i antiglobalism [Three balls and antiglobalism]. 2008. *Troitsky Variant* 16N(848): 14.

Pozdravlenie s ogovorkoy (avtor–izdatel'–chitatel') [Congratulation with a stipulation (author–publisher–reader)]. 2011. *Troitsky Variant* 12(81): 12.

Comments:

Vaksman, V. 2011. Problema izdaniya nauchnykh knig: Kto vinovat? [The problem of publication of scientific books: Who is guilty?]. 2011. *Troitsky Variant* 12(81): 12.

Maksimov, N. 2011. Doplata za talent [Surcharge for talent]. 2011. *Troitsky Variant* 12(81): 12–13.

Arkhangel'sky, A. 2011. 'Uchenym pora menyat' privychki . . .' ['For scholars it's time to change their habits . . .']. 2011. *Troitsky Variant* 12(81): 13.

Markov, A. 2011. 'Problema reshaema . . .' ['The problem is solvable . . .']. 2011. *Troitsky Variant* 12(81): 14.

'Problema reshaema', no ne reshaetsya: K obsuzhdeniyu izdatelskoy problemy ['The problem is solvable', but has not been solved: On the discussion of the problem of publishing]. 2011. *Troitsky Variant* 15(84): 7.

G. Scholarship and Morality

Plagiat glazami giproskeptika [Plagiarism as seen by a giprosceptic]. 2008. *Troitsky Variant* 14N(842): 6–7.

Comments

Demina, N. 2008. Kak borot'sya s plagiatorami? [How to fight against plagiarism?]. 2008. *Troitsky Variant* 15N: 10.

Kondakov, V., and Deyneka, P. 2009. Ariec Burovskiy i plagiat [The Aryan Burovskiy and plagiarism]. 2009. *Troitsky Variant* 3(22): 7.

Dissertaciya dlya khoroshego cheloveka [Dissertation for a good fellow]. 2009. *Troitsky Variant* 20(39): 14.

Dissertacii bez obmana: Perepiska s masterom [Dissertations open and above board: Correspondence with a master]. 2010. *Troitsky Variant* 16(60): 2–17; 16(61): 11; comments supplied.

Makhinacii s dissertaciyami i smysl zhizni [Machinations with dissertations and the sense of life], site trv-science.ru, section 'Bytie nauki'.

Ostepenennyi bandit [Bandit with a degree]. 2010. *Troitsky Variant* 23(68): 5.

O svetilakh i 'negrakh' [On luminaries and 'negroes']. 2010. *Troitsky Variant* 5(49): 14.

Lipovye academii [Fake academies]. 2010. *Troitsky Variant* (50): 14.

Comments

Host_buster. Eshche odno 'zolotoe pero' v bok dedushke Chu-chu [Another 'golden pen' into the flank of grandfather Chu-chu], http://chudinologia.livejournal.com/419487.html.

Simulyakry [Simulacra]. 2010. *Troitsky Variant* 14(58): 11.

H. Making Discoveries

Upushchennye otkrytiya [Missed discoveries]. 2009. *Troitsky Variant* 9(28): 14.

I. Historical Perspective

Nazad v Renessans? [Back to the Renaissance?]. 2009. *Troitsky Variant* 15(34): 14.

Vystuplenie 28 maya 2009 g. na obsuzhdenii uchrezhdeniya pri prezidente Komissii po protivodeystviyu fal'sificacii istorii (speech on the 28 May 2009 on the discussion of the Commission against falsification of history, the commission had been established at the request of the president of Russia). On the report by T. Kossinova: Discussion of the struggle against the 'Falsification of history' in Petersburg; cjgita.ru: social activity of media in the northwest, May 29, 2010, memo.ru/2010/05/31/kosinova.htm.

Chto za Komissiya, Sozdatl'? [What a commission, o creator?]. 2009. *Troitsky Variant* 11(30): 14.

Petriki nastupayut na istoriyu, ili memorial'nye zakony [Petriks attack history, or the memory laws]. 2010. *Troitsky Variant* 9(53): 14.

Pravlennoe proshloe [Corrected past]. 2011. *Troitsky Variant* 5(74): 12.

Priglashenie k zastoyu [Invitation to Stagnation] (against the Manifesto by N. Mikhalkov). 2010. *Troitsky Variant* 21(66): 10; also grani.ru on the November 3, 2010 (reprinted in *Kulturnaya evoluciya*; *Newsland*; *Russia Region Press* et al.).

Interview to the reporter of Grani-ru Dmitriy Borko [video]. Grani-TV Lica [Faces], November 19, 2010 (reprinted on the web portal Territoriya svobody [Territory of freedom], November 20, 2010).

Reports and reprints:

Rossiya—raspadayushchayasya imperiya, i v etom net nichego neobychnogo [Russia is an empire breaking up, and there is nothing unusual in that]. 2011. Unshghu (Armenian channel), February 2.

Raspadayushchayasya imperiya [Empire breaking up]. 2011. Echo Rossii, ehorussia.com/new/node/2198.

Lucas, E. 2011. Kremlevskie ukrali u sobstvennogo naroda kolossal'nye den'gi [The Kremliners have stolen vast amounts of money from their own people], newsland.ru/news/detail/id/614671/ (report in *The Wall Street Jounal*).

Murder in Trieste again? 2013. *Troitsky Variant* 1(120): 12.

Moral' Prygunova, ili Uroki istorii ostayutsya nevyuchenymi [Prygunov's moral, or the lessons of history remain unlearned]. 2014. *Troitsky Variant* 7(151): 12.

Dokument o kul'ture i dukh kul'tury [A document on culture and the spirit of culture], 2014. *Troitsky Variant* 9(153): 9; 10(154): 12; 11(155): 12.

Comment:

Koposov, N. 2014. Istorizm po-ministerski [Historicism in the manner of the ministry]. 2104. *Troitsky Variant* 10(154): 13.

J. Ethnicity

Rabota po-angliyski? [Working in the English manner]. 2009. *Troitsky Variant* 16(35): 14.

Pora by i perestat' [The very time to stop]. 2009. *Troitsky Variant* 25(44): 5.

Comments

Glagolev, S. 2010. [Not to drink but to know something of the matter]. *Troitsky Variant* 1(45): 7.

Ekonomov, I. 2010. Vysshiy gosudarstvennyi interes [The highest state interest]. *Troitsky Variant* 2(47): 15.

Fanaty i nauka [Fanatics and science]. 2011. *Troitsky Variant* 3(72): 14.

Comments:

Strannosti patriotizma [Strange sides of patriotism]. 2011. *Troitsky Variant* 6(75): 14.

Vzglyad na pole s drugoy planety [View of the field from another planet]. 2011. *Troitsky Variant* 14(83): 12.

Comments:

Mirmov, I. 2011. Vzglyad na pole s etoy planety [View of the field from this planet]. 2011. *Troitsky Variant* 14(83): 12.

Strannaya lyubov'—patriotism [A strange love—patriotism]. 2011. *Troitsky Variant* 6(75): 14.

Solov'i, solov'i, ne trevozh'te soldat . . . [Nightingales, nightingales, don't disturb the soldiers . . .]. 2012. *Troitsky Variant* 6(100): 10.

XXVII. INTERVIEWS AND MEMOIRS

Trudno byt' Klejnom: Avtobiografiya v monologakh i dialogakh [***It's hard to be Klejn: Autobiography in Monologues and Dialogues***]. St. Petersburg, Nestor-Istoriya, 2010, 724 pages, 14 figures, 65 photos.

Comments and reviews:

Mosionzhnik, L. 2008. *Bol'shoy Klejn* [*Big Klejn*]. Public, June: 106–11.

Mirmov, I. 2009. Trudno byt' Klejnom [It's hard to be Klejn]. 2009. *Troitsky Variant* 25(44): 5.

Kukulin, I. 2010. Grazhdanin Klejn [Citizen Klejn], OpenSpace.ru, March 4.

Veterkov, V. 2010. Russkiy zhurnal. Aktualnye kommentarii, Russia.ru, March 4.

Arkheologiya zhizni [The archaeology of life]. 2010. *Chitaem vmeste* 8–9(12): 17.

Tul'chinskiy, G. L. 2010. *Filosofskie nauki* 2: 153–55.

Tul'chinskiy, G. L. 2010. Kinga o vynosimoy trudnosti bytiya [A book on the bearable difficulty of life]. *Znamya* 5: 224–28.

Gilinskiy, Y. I. 2010. *Rossiyskiy kriminologicheskiy vzglyad* 1: 430–32.

Epshteyn, A. D. 2010. Russko-evreyskie intellektualy pervogo sovetskogo pokoleniya: Shtrikhi k portretu [Russian-jewish intellectuals of the first Soviet generation: Traits to portrait]. *Novoe Literaturnoe Obozrenie* 103: 86–108.

Epshteyn, A. 2011. Rodom iz detstva [By origin from childhood]. *Lekhaim* 2 (226).
Ponomarev, E. R. 2010. Povest' o progresore [The story of a 'progressor' (a visitor from the future)]. *Novoe Literaturnoe Obozrenie* 103: 350–53.
Toporov, V. 2010. Magazin ucenennoy knigi [The bargain bookshop]. Aktual'nye kommentarii, 5 November, actualcomment.ru/daycomment/647/.
Lipatov, K. 2010. ZhZh, cyrill_lipatov.livejournal.com/tag/arkheologiya.
Dolgin. 2010. Imkhonet, books.imhonet.ru/element/1130617/.
Eltsov, P. 2010. Culture, ethnogenesis, and Gulag. A Review of *It's Hard to Be Klejn. The Review of Archaeology* 29: 70–75.
Lozny, L. 2010. Being Klejn. Review of 'Trudno byt' Klejnom . . .' (*It's Hard to Be Klejn:* Autobiography in monologues and dialogues). *Current Anthropology* 51(6): 890–91.
Borshevich, V. 2011. Fenomenologiya Klejna [Klejn's phenomemology]. *Stratum plus* 2: 281–88.
Ponomarev, E. R. P. 2011. Uchebnik principial'nosti [A manual of adherence to the principles]. *Neva* 2: 197–99.
Panchenko, D. V. 2011. *Aristey: Vestnik klassicheskoy filologii i antichnoy istorii,* vol. III. Universitet Dmitriya Pozharskogo, Moscow: 149–53.
Tijonov, I. L. 2011. Memorias y biografia de un arqueólogo: L. S. Klein. (Trudno byt Kleinom: Avtobiografiia v monologaj i dialogaj. Nestor-Istoria. Sankt-Petersburg, 2010, 730 pages). *Trabajos de prehistorija* 68(1): 199–201.
Esipov, V. V. 2011. Memuary uchitelya. Klejn L. Trudno byt' Klejnom . . . (Memoirs of the teacher. Klejn L. It's hard to be Klejn . . .). *Vestnik Ural'kogo otdeleniya* RAN, 2(36): 176–79.
Shchavelev, S. P. 2012. Uchast' progressora [The lot of a 'progressor']. *Evraziyskiy arkheologicheskiy sbornik.* To the 60th anniversary of S. V. Kuz'minykh, A. S. Vdovin and I. V. Tunkina (Eds). St. Petersburg–Krasnoyarsk: 193–201.
Shchavelev, S. P. 2013. Zapiski progressora [Notes of a 'progressor']. *Dan' Mnemozine,* kn. 2. Kursk, KGMU: 432–62 (reprint of the preceding article, with additions).
Sveshnikova, O. 2013. *Cambridge Archaeological Journal* 23(2): 342–43.
Trudno byt' Klejnom: Avtobiografiya v monologakh i dialogakh [It's hard to be Klejn: Autobiography in monologues and dialogues, 2nd ed.] (Revised and expanded). 2014. Donetsk, Donetskiy Nationalnyi universitet, 724 pages, 14 figures, 65 photos.
Vida y arqueología en San Petersburgo (entrevista). *Arqueología* (Mexico), 5, enero—junio 1991: 129–32 (interview by Jüergen Brüeggemann).
Arkheologiya i rok [Archaeology and rock . . .] [In Russian *rock* has two meanings: 'rock music' and 'fate']. 1991. Leningradskiy universitet (newspaper) 2(3267): 6–7 (interview was recorded by A. Areshin).
Lev S. Klejn. Intervju. *Arheo* (Ljubljana), 15, 1992: 52–56 (interview by Prof. Biba Teržan).
Una conversation con Leo Klejn (entrevista). *Revista de arqueologia* (Madrid), aco XII, No. 133, 1992: 7–9. Interview by Dr. M.-I. Martinez Navarrete, Dr. G. Ruis Zapatero, and Dr. J. Vincent Garcia.
Todo arqueológo tiene algo de teórico . . . Una entrevista con Leo S. Klejn. *Trabajos de Prehistoria* (Madrid), vol. 49, 1992: 11–25 (interview by Dr. G. Ruis Zapatero and Dr. J. M. Vincent Garcia).
Exploring the limits: An interview with Leo Klejn (by Dr. K. Kristiansen, Ed.). 1993. *Journal of European Archaeology* (Glasgow) 1: 184–94.
Burström M. (Ed.). An ivory-tower in archaeology? A conversation with Leo S. Klejn. 1994. *Current Swedish Archaeology* (Stockholm) 2: 7–12.
Taylor, T. Conversations with Leo Klejn. 1994. *Current Anthropology* (Chicago) 34(5): 723–35.

A börtöntudós (Lev Klein, Varga Anna beszélgettet). 168 óra, évfolyam 32, 1996, VIII, 34–35.

Lobanova, Z. 1998. Moy Telemak! Troyanskaya vouna ne konchena . . . Professor Klejn prishel k vyvodu, chto Iliada osnovana na vymyshlennykh sobytiyakh [My Telemachus! The Trojan War is not over . . . Professor Klejn has come to the conclusion that the *Iliad* is based on fictional events]. *Komsomol'skaya pravda* 70(21804): 6 (on the basis of an interview with Klejn).

Immonen, V. 2003. The stratigraphy of a life: An archaeological dialogue with Leo Klejn. *Archaeological Dialogues* (Cambridge) 10(1): 57–75.

Autobiografía. 2010. *Istor: Revista de historia internacional* (México) XI(43): 148–66, reprinted from archaeology.ru.

Rovesniki, pishite memuary! [Peers, write memoirs!]. 2010. *Troitsky Variant* 12(56): 14.

Planirovanie na devyatom desyatke: Interv'yu s prof. L. S. Klejnom po povodu . . . [Planning during a ninth decade: Interview with prof. L. S. Klejn a propos . . .]. 2010. *Troitsky Variant* 20(65): 11; also in polit.ru.

V besedakh c L. S. Klejnom [In conversation with L. S. Klejn (Stephen Leach)]. 2011. *Aktual'nye problemy Sibiri i Dalnego Vostoka*. Ussuriysk, UGPI: 36–44.

V katakombakh istorii. Interv'yu S. V. Beleckomu [In the catacombs of history. Interview by S. V. Beleckiy]. 2011. *Gorod 812* 25(134): 36–37.

'Ya nikogo ne zovu v arkheologiyu. Komu nado, sami pridut . . . !' ['I call nobody to archaeology. Whoever needs it will come themselves . . .' Interview with Prof. L. S. Klejn (A. Sokolov), antropogenez.ru/interview/389.

Dilemma Fausta [Faust's dilemma]. 2012. *Troitsky Variant* 13(107): 13.

Editing

- *Problemy arkheologii*. Leningrad, 1 (1968); coedited with M. I. Artamonov; 2 (1978); coedited with A. D. Stolyar and G. S. Lebedev.
- *Tipy v kul'ture*. Leningrad, Leningadskogo universitet, 1979, 184 pages.
- *Rossiyskiy Arkheologicheskiy Ezhegodnik*. St. Petersburg, 'Sankt-Peterburgskiy universitet' (president of editorial council); since 2011.

Secondary Bibliography

1. Vishnyatsky, L. B. 1990. Current theoretical discussion in Soviet archaeology: An essay. *Fennoscandia Archaeologica* VII: 17–25.
2. Lebedev, G. S. 1998. K 70-letiyu L'va Samuilovicha Klejna [On the 70th birthday of Lev Samuilovich Klejn]. *Arkheologiya Peterburga* II (1997): 5–9.
3. Lebedev, G. S. 1999. Varangica Problemogo seminara L. S. Klejna: Tridcat' let dvizheniya k neizvestnomu gorodu na Puti iz Varyag v Greki [Varangica in the problems seminar of L. S. Klejn: Thirty years of travel toward the unknown city on the path from the Varangians to the Greeks]. *Stratum plus* 5: 102–11.
4. *Arkheolog: Detektiv i myslitel. Sbornik statey, posvyashchennyi 77-letiyu L'va Samuilovicha Klejna* [Archaeologist: Detective and thinker. A collection of articles in commemoration of the 77th birthday of Lev Samuilovich Klejn]. 2004. St. Petersburg, Sankt-Peterburgskogo universitet.

Reviews:

5. Pronin, A. 2004. *Gorod, peterburgskiy zhurnal* 38(123): 40.
6. Lebedev, G. S. 2004. *L. S. Klejn i Peterburgskaya shkola rossiyskoy arkheologii* [L. S. Klejn and the Petersburg school of Russian archaeology]. *Arkheolog: Detektiv i myslitel'*: 29–42.

7. Kirsanov, V. 2007. Lev Klejn: Ne gey, no muzhchina [Leo Klejn: Not a gay, but a man]. V. Kirsanov. *Plus 31. Russkie gei, lesbianki, biseksualy i transseksualy*. Moscow, Kvir: 66–73.
8. Mosionzhnik, L. 2008. Bol'shoy Klejn [The big Klejn]. *Public*, June: 106–11.
9. Rajakylä, M. 2009. Neuvostoarkeologiasta ja toisinajattelijasta—Lev S. Klejnista—*Muinaistutkija* [On Leo S. Klejn, Soviet archaeologist and dissident] 3: 46–56 (abstract: Om sovjetarkeologin och oliktänkaren—Lev S. Klejn).
10. Borshevich, V. 2011. Fenomenologiya Klejna [Klejn's Phenomenology]. *Stratum plus* 2: 281–88, reprinted in his book *Moldavskiy ieroglif*, Kishinev, *Stratum plus*: 557–75.
11. Lynsha, V. A., and Tarasenko, V. N. 2011. Vvedenie [Introduction]. 2011. *Aktual'nye problemy Sibiri i Dal'nego Vostoka*. Ussuriysk, UGPI: 11–13.
12. Lynsha, V. A. 2011. Klejnovskaya kritika Novoy Arkheologii i ee rol' v sozdanii novoy rossiyskoy arkheologii Sibiri i Dal'nego Vostoka [Klejn's criticism of the New Archaeology and the role of this criticism in the new Russian archaeology of Siberia and the Far East]. 2011. *Aktual'nye problemy Sibiri i Dal'nego Vostoka*. Ussuriysk, UGPI: 18–35.
13. Sher, Y. A. 2010. Kentavry, edinorogi, drakony i drugie mifologiheskie personazhi (o knige L. S. Klejn. Vremya kentavrov. Stepnaya prarodina grekov i ariev) [Centaurs, unicorns, dragons, and other mythological creatures (on L. S. Klejn's book *Time of Centaurs: The Steppe Original Steppe Homeland of Greeks and Aryans*)], St. Petersburg, Evraziya, 496 pages, colour illustrations 32 pages).
14. *Vestnik Kemerovskogo universitet*. 2012. 2(46): 205–11 (already mentioned in section 27).
15. El'yashevich, A. M. 2012. Uvelichenie zhizni [Increase of life]. 2012. *Troitsky Variant* 13(107): 12.
16. Duvakin, E. 2012. 'Nauka—eto trizhdy bor'ba . . .' K 85-letiyu L. S. Klejna ['Science is a threefold struggle . . .' On the 85th birthday of L. S. Klejn]. *Tradicionnaya kultura* 4(48): 168–69.

Notes

Chapter 1

1. Alexander Pushkin, quoted in Klejn (2010): 621.
2. This is normal in a western C.V., but in Russia a C.V. takes a slightly different, more expansive, form than in the West.
3. General Anton Denikin (1872–1947).
4. Mikhail Tukhachevsky (1893–1937, shot on Stalin's orders).
5. Klejn—Supplementary notes to C.V., appended to the Spanish translation of Klejn's autobiography *It's Hard to Be Klejn*.
6. Klejn, *The World Turned Upside Down* (1993): 7–8.
7. When Djilas published his conclusions, in *The New Class* (1957), he was sentenced to seven years' imprisonment.
8. *The Morphology of the Folktale* was first published in 1928 and was translated into English in 1958.
9. Artamonov became head of the Hermitage Museum in 1951 but was dismissed in 1964 when he refused to remove the paintings of 'bourgeois decadents' (French impressionists). For more about Artamonov, see Klejn, *Soviet Archaeology* (2012b): 300–07.
10. The photograph on the cover of Klejn's *Soviet Archaeology* depicts a scene from Marr's official state funeral, an occasion of great pomp and ceremony.
11. Artamonov was exceptional at that time, as being open to the idea of external influence on local archaeological phenomena; see *Soviet Archaeology*, p. 54.
12. Aleksandr Ivanovich Popov (1899–1973) was a professor of history at Leningrad University. He held many unorthodox opinions and was in character something like Professor Challenger in Conan Doyle's *Lost World* and in Vladimir Obraztsov's science fiction novels (Klejn pers. comm.).
13. In 1952–1953 many of the Soviet Union's top physicians (especially Jewish physicians) were accused of poisoning Soviet leaders.
14. During this interim period Klejn also worked briefly at the library of the Academy of Sciences.
15. Gustav Kossinna (1858–1921), whose opinions had a notorious influence on Nazi ideology. Kossinna's lesser-known postwar influence is discussed in Chapter 7.
16. The background to this debate is discussed at greater length in Chapter 7.
17. Roughly equivalent to a Ph.D. thesis.
18. 'At the defence of my Candidate's thesis, he [S. I. Rudenko] sat in the front row as a member of the academic council, looking me straight in the eye, and muttered incessantly: I am against I am against I am against I am against . . .' Klejn *Soviet Archaeology* (2012): 288.

19. It was on these expeditions that Klejn was faced with the choice of paying bribes in order for the expeditions to continue or else to abandon the expeditions altogether. He chose to pay the bribes and to protest the fact in print after the expeditions were completed. 'Bribery was a more southern thing; in Leningrad it was *blat*, influence, that counted' (Taylor 1994: 724).
20. See 'Scythians, Sarmatians, and Greeks: Recent work' by D. B. Shelov, pp. 208–20, in *Recent Archaeological Excavations in Europe*, Rupert Bruce-Mitford (Ed.) (1975, Routledge & Kegan Paul).
21. Klejn's step-sister, Serafima Rafalson, was a surgeon in Riga.
22. Klejn's seminars on these problems were attended by, among others, V. S. Bochkarev, G. S. Lebedev, V. A. Safronov, M. B. Shchukin, V. A. Bulkin, E. N. Nosov, E. M. Kolpakov, Y. Y. Piotrovsky, M. A. Tikhonova, and G. F. Korzukhina.
23. He had earlier, in 1974, published a monograph-size article in German: 'Kossinna im Abstand von Vierzig Jahren'.
24. See abstract to *Archaeological Sources* at www.archaeology.ru.

Chapter 2

1. Klejn, *Curriculum Vitae.*
2. B. A. Rybakov, head of the Institute of Archaeology of the USSR Academy of Sciences and renowned antitheorist. See Klejn (2012b): 41–42, 82. Rybakov will be encountered again, in Chapter 6.
3. Klejn, *Curriculum Vitae.*
4. Klejn, *Curriculum Vitae.*
5. During a medical examination in 2013 it was discovered that Klejn had become infected with the virus for tuberculosis. However, the disease had remained dormant. Because all the inhabitants of his cell smoked, except for Klejn, he believes it was here that the infection occurred.
6. It was only at this time that Western archaeologists came to the belated realisation that Klejn was unorthodox in his opinions.
7. From Klejn, *The World Turned Upside Down* (1993). (This passage was translated by Sarah Thompson.)
8. The German edition published in 1991 was incomplete; not everything could be taken across the border.

Chapter 3

1. 'Attainments and Problems of Soviet Archaeology' (with V. A. Bulkin & G. S. Lebedev) *World Archaeology* 13 (1982): 272–95. Later expanded versions of this article, in Russian and German, had the title of *The Phenomenon of Soviet Archaeology*.
2. The commission from *World Archaeology* resulted from an invitation from Bruce Trigger and Ian Glover, in response to Klejn's 'Panorama of Theoretical Archaeology' (Klejn 2012b: 8).
3. Klejn, Abstract to *Archaeological Typology*.
4. Klejn, *Curriculum Vitae.*
5. Klejn, *Curriculum Vitae* (supplementary notes).

6. Klejn, *Curriculum Vitae* (supplementary notes).
7. Klejn, catalogues 14 varieties of this skill in *Soviet Archaeology*: 175–86.
8. Klejn, *Curriculum Vitae* (supplementary notes).
9. 'Marxism reduced man to an aggregate of social relations. This is indubitably a simplification, and in this lies the deficiency of Marxism. Man is also a biological being, and many of his peculiarities, including social peculiarities, are inexplicable if this fact is not understood . . .' (Klejn, 2012b: 155).
10. In Vienna Klejn gave a series of lectures on the history of archaeological thought. These lectures formed the basis for his *History of Archaeological Thought* (2012). In 1997 he was elected permanent Visiting Professor at Vienna University. Klejn gave these lectures in German but, as with English, he prefers that his books are translated by a native speaker.
11. After Klejn delivered a series of lectures at the Higher Anthropological School in Moldova he was awarded the title of Dr. Honoris Causa.
12. Klejn read a paper on V. G. Childe in London on May 9, 1992 at a conference devoted to the one hundredth anniversary of the birth of Childe. In this paper he read from a recently discovered letter written by Childe to the most eminent archaeologists of the Soviet Union in December 1956. The text of this lecture is reproduced as Chapter 9 of *Soviet Archaeology* (2012).
13. Klejn delivered the first David Clarke memorial lecture at Peterhouse College, Cambridge in 1993. In this well-received lecture Klejn explored the interface between archaeology and history. This lecture formed the basis for the first part of *The Principles of Archaeology* (2001).
14. Klejn gave a lecture at the Institute of Archaeology in Oxford in May 1992 on Current Political Situation in Russia and the Position of Archaeology in the Country. The text of this lecture, in which Klejn notes similarities between post-Soviet Russia and the Weimar republic of the 1920s, was reproduced in the *Oxford Magazine* 84 (1992): 26–32.
15. Klejn, *Curriculum Vitae*, supplementary notes.
16. Klejn, *Curriculum Vitae*.
17. See his comments on the seclusion in later life of the archaeologist Vladislav Ravdonikas; Klejn (2012b): 216.
18. See also Klejn 2006 and Klejn in Chrisomalis and Costopoulos (2013b). In the latter work Klejn draws a comparison between the work of J. D. Lewis-Williams (*The Mind in the Cave: Consciousness and the Origin of Art* [2002]) and recent work by the Russian archaeologist Y. A. Sher.
19. Author of *The Russian Icon* (Oxford: 1927).
20. Vladimir Voyinovich's novel *Moscow 2042* (1986) envisages a Moscow of the future ruled by a combination of the KGB, the Communist Party, and the Russian Orthodox Church.
21. A second edition was published in 2014.
22. Klejn, Abstract to *It's Hard to Be Klejn* (2010).
23. Ibid.; 'Modesty is in general a relative concept. Questioned about the opinion of a staff officer who had been assigned to him Suvorov [General Suvorov (1730–1800)] replied: "Well, a nice officer, shy and modest in battle". There are immodest professions: writer is one such; professor is another. If you are intent on modesty, stay at home in the dark' (Klejn, *Curriculum Vitae*, supplementary notes).

Chapter 4

1. Klejn, Abstract to *The World Turned Upside Down* (1993).
2. J. G. Ballard recollects this experience in the semiautobiographical *Empire of the Sun* (1984).
3. Konrad Lorenz (1903–1989) spent four years in Soviet labour camps.
4. Desmond Morris, author of *The Naked Ape: A Zoologist's Study of the Human Animal* (1967).
5. Klejn, Abstract to *Culture and Evolution*, a collection of essays as yet unpublished.
6. Klejn, Abstract to *Culture and Evolution*.
7. Klejn, *Curriculum Vitae*, supplementary notes.
8. For example, S. Shennan, *Genes, Memes, and Human History* (2002), a book for which Klejn has some respect.
9. Klejn, Abstract to *Another Side of a Luminary* (2002).

Chapter 5

1. Klejn, 'Katalog Korabley. Struktura; stratigrafiya' ['The Catalogue of Ships. Structure and Stratigraphy'] in *Stratum Plus* (St. Petersburg–Cichineu–Odessa) (2000) 3: 17–51.
2. Klejn, Abstract to *Incorporeal Heroes* in *Homeric Studies* (forthcoming).
3. Ibid.
4. Dyakanov is perhaps best known in the West for *The Paths of History*, Cambridge University Press (1999).
5. I. M. Dyakanov, 'Narody Azii i Afriki' vol. 2 (1997): 210–11.
6. Klejn, Abstract to *Homeric Studies* (forthcoming).
7. Klejn, Abstract to *The Anatomy of the Iliad* (1998).
8. Abstract to *The Anatomy of the Iliad* in *Homeric Studies* (forthcoming).
9. Klejn, Abstract to 'The Catalogue of Ships' (2012).
10. Ibid.
11. Ibid. (*The Cypria* is an epic about the Trojan War. Only fragments survive, as quotations in other texts.)
12. Klejn, Abstract to *Homeric Studies* (forthcoming).

Chapter 6

1. Klejn, Abstract to *The Resurrection of Perun* (2004).
2. Ibid.
3. Ibid.
4. Afanasyev's pioneering work on Russian folktales is comparable to that of the Brothers Grimm on German folktales. (Yoffe and Krafczik's *Perun the God of Thunder* [2003] is largely based on Afanasyev's work.)
5. Klejn, Abstract to *The Resurrection of Perun* (2004).
6. Ibid.
7. Ibid.
8. Ibid.
9. Ibid.

10. Other views of early Slav history alternative to, and more reliable than, Rybakov's, may be found in Paul M. Barford's *The Early Slavs* (2001) and Florin Curta's *The Making of the Slavs* (2001).
11. Klejn, Abstract to *The Resurrection of Perun* (2004).
12. Ibid.
13. Ibid.
14. Ibid.
15. Vladimir I (or 'the Great'), ruler of the Kievan Rus from 980 to his death in 1015, initiated reforms in pagan religion before converting to Christianity in 988.
16. Klejn, Abstract to *The Resurrection of Perun* (2004).
17. Ibid. Contrary to Rybakov's beliefs it seems now to be generally accepted that 'Perun was probably the main god in the Slav pantheon' (Barford 2001: 194).
18. Klejn, Abstract to *The Resurrection of Perun* (2004).
19. Ibid.
20. Ibid.
21. Ibid.
22. Ibid.
23. Ibid.
24. Ibid.
25. A recent article by Patrice Lajoyje argues that the Chechen Pir"on derives not from a Slavic source but via an Iranian source, from the Ossetians. Klejn's response is that Perun does not appear in Ossetian folklore. Moreover, his main contentions are untouched by Lajoyje's argument—that is, 'Pir"on is not local to Vainakh folklore; it is unconnected to the Biblical "Pharoah"; it originates as an Indo-European thunder god' (pers. comm.); see Lajoye Patrice (2012) and Klejn (2013a).

Chapter 7

1. Klejn, 'Kossinna im Abstand von vierzig Jahren' ['Kossinna at a Distance of 40 Years'] in *Jahresschrift für mitteldeutsche Vorgeschichte* 58 (1974): 7–55.
2. Klejn, 'Arkheologiya v sedle (Kossinna s rasstoyaniya v 70 let)' ['Archaeology in the Saddle (Kossina at a Distance of 70 years)'] in *Stratum plus* 4 (2000): 88–140.
3. Klejn, Abstract to 'Archaeology in the Saddle'.
4. Ibid.
5. 'Gordon Childe, in particular, developed and elaborated on Kossinna's concept of "cultural provinces" as defined by artefact distributions' (Arnold and Hassmann [1995]: 71).
6. This paragraph was inserted as the book went to press. Klejn hopes to expand on these criticisms in print in the near future.
7. Colin Renfrew is the best-known advocate of Asia Minor; see Renfrew (1987).
8. Klejn expands on the popularity of four-sided dice both in Catacomb graves and in the *Rig Veda* in 'The Early Evolution of Dice between the Danube and the Indus: Contributions to the Early History of Mathematics', *Acta Archaeologica* 70 (1999): 113–35.

9. *The Time of the Centaurs* was so called because in the book Klejn traces the proto-image of the centaurs, the Cyclops, and the dragon to the Steppes in the Eneolithic.
10. In recent years Klejn has become convinced by a theory proposed by his pupil Aleksey Kovalev regarding the origins and migration of the Tocharians. The written texts of the Tocharians from Xinjiang northwest of China, dated to the sixth–eighth centuries C.E., suggest that they spoke an Indo-European language but—surprisingly, given their location—linguists believe that the Tocharian language was one of the first to have broken away from the Indo-European stem. Kovalev argues that the ancestors of the Tocharians are to be found in certain Neolithic settlements in present-day France and that they slowly migrated to Xinjiang via the Chemurchek culture in Mongolia (2,500–1,800 B.C.E.).
11. Klejn, Abstract to *The Varangian Controversy* (2009).

Chapter 8

1. Klejn, Abstract to *The Montelius Formula* (2010). According to Klejn, Malmer, Binford, and David Clarke are 'neorationalists' (Klejn 2010: 208).
2. Klejn, Abstract to *The Montelius Formula* (2010).
3. Ibid.; see also Malmer and Bartholin (1993).
4. Klejn, Abstract to *The Montelius Formula* (2010).
5. Ibid.
6. Ibid.
7. Klejn has recently returned to the problems of classification and typology in a recent two-volume work, *Archaeological Studies* (2012–2013).
8. Klejn, Abstract to *The Montelius Formula* (2010).
9. At about the same time as Klejn, in 2001, Bruce Trigger was found to have contracted cancer. Trigger died in 2006.
10. Klejn, Abstract to *The History of Archaeological Thought* (2012).
11. Klejn, Abstract to *A History of Anthropological Ideas and Theories*.
12. Ibid.
13. Ibid.
14. Ibid.
15. Ibid.
16. Ibid.
17. Ibid. (Klejn follows Propp in his criticism of Lévi-Strauss.)
18. In 1954 in 'Archaeological Theory and Method: Some Suggestions from the Old World', *American Anthropologist* 56(2): 155–68, Christopher Hawkes proposed that archaeologists know most about past technologies, less about past economic systems, less yet about political institutions, and least of all about past beliefs. This theory become known as 'Hawkes' ladder'.
19. Klejn, Abstract to *Soviet Archaeology*; see also Klejn (2012b): 144–49. Klejn points out that neither Marx nor Engels regarded archaeology as a political discipline (Kristiansen 1993: 192).
20. G. P. Grigoryev (1972): 'Kultura I tip v arkheologii: kategorii analiza ili realnost?' in *Tezisy dokladov na sektsiyakh . . .* (1971). Moscow: 5–9; quoted in Klejn (2012b): 95.

Chapter 9

1. *Metaarchaeology* (2001a) was published in Russia in 2004 under the title *Introduction to Theoretical Archaeology*
2. As explained in Chapter 7, Klejn believes that the idea of a common origin is the primary distinguishing characteristic of an ethnos—other attributes are discussed only in order to shed light upon this—and there is no inevitable coincidence between language and culture. Likewise, cultural genesis may to some extent reflect ethnogenesis, but it does not invariably coincide with it.
3. C. Renfrew (1969); a review of Clarke and Binford in *Antiquity* 43: 241–44.
4. This saying, often misattributed, seems to have first been coined by a late nineteenth-century archaeologist of Hadrian's Wall, Collingwood Bruce.
5. With Klejn's approval I have here corrected 'conscience' in the original text to 'consciousness', from the Russian 'soznanie'.
6. Quoted in Collingwood (1993): 269 and Collingwood (1999): 24.
7. Figure 4 from *Metaarchaeology*.
8. I trace the ancestry of the idea in 'Arkheolog i detektiv: Ot Leningrada do Sent-Mary Mid' ['The Archaeologist and the Detective: From Leningrad to St. Mary Mead'] in *Rossiyskiy Arkheologicheskiy Ezhegodnik* 1 (2011): 70–72.
9. Collingwood, like Klejn, was a keen reader of detective fiction; Collingwood favoured Agatha Christie and Dorothy L. Sayers; Klejn favours Boris Akunin (Klejn, pers. comm.). (In 1939, having read Agatha Christie's *Murder in Mesopotamia,* Collingwood remarked in a letter to his sister Barbara that he thought Agatha Christie's involvement in archaeology—she was married to the archaeologist Max Mallowan—had had the effect of improving her abilities as a writer of detective novels.)
10. In *Metaarchaeology* the editor of *Acta Archaeologica*, Klavs Randsborg, interpreted Klejn as comparing the archaeologist to the criminologist (a form of sociologist), but it became apparent in conversation with Klejn that Klejn is in fact comparing the archaeologist to a detective, and comparing archaeology to forensic science.
11. Klejn first expounded his views on the principles of archaeology at the David Clarke memorial lecture in 1993.
12. As commentators on Collingwood have many times pointed out, the posthumous *Idea of History* was published in a form unintended by Collingwood. As such it gives a misleading impression of his meaning.
13. B. Trigger, 'The Future of Archaeology Is the Past' in *Research and Theory in Current Archaeology*, C. L. Redman (Ed.) (1973): 103; quoted by Klejn in *Metaarchaeology* (2001a): 49.
14. Heider, K. 'Archaeological Assumptions and Ethnographical Facts: A Cautionary Tale from New Guinea' in *Southwestern Journal of Archaeology* 23 (1967): 52–64, 52, quoted by Klejn in *Metaarchaeology* (2001a): 53.
15. U. Fischer, 'Zur Ratio der prähistorischen Archäologie' in *Germania* 65(1) (1987): 175–95; 184, quoted by Klejn in *Metaarchaeology* (2001a): 53.
16. K. C. Chang, 'Major Aspects of the Interrelationship of Archaeology and Ethnology' in *Current Anthropology* 8(3) (1967): 227–34, 230, quoted by Klejn in *Metaarchaeology* (2001a): 53.

17. R. E. M. Wheeler, 'Archaeology and the Transmission of Ideas' in *Antiquity* 2 (104) (1952): 180–92: 180f, quoted by Klejn in *Metaarchaeology* (2001a): 54.
18. 'Hawkes was right'; Klejn in S. Leach, 'In Conversation with Leo S. Klejn' (2011).
19. Figure 9 in *Metaarchaeology*.

Chapter 10

1. C. F. C. Hawkes (1973), 'Innocence retrieval in archaeology', *Antiquity* 187: 176–78 (177), quoted by Klejn in *Metaarchaeology* 2001a: 61.
2. H. Härke, 'The Hun is a methodical chap', in P. J. Ucko (Ed.), *Theory in Archaeology: A World Perspective* 1995: 46–60 (48), quoted by Klejn in *Metaarchaeology* (2001a): 62.
3. U. Fischer, Zur Ratio der prähistorischen Archäologie', *Germania* 65(1): 175–95 (194), quoted by Klejn in *Metaarchaeology* (2001a): 64.
4. Figure 10 in *Metaarchaeology*.
5. D. L. Clarke, 'Analytical archaeology: Epilogue', *Norwegian Archaeological Review* 3: 25–34 (29), quoted by Klejn in *Metaarchaeology* (2001a): 87.

Chapter 11

1. http://www.adgarrett.com/articles/basic-principles-of-forensic-science/; accessed May 25, 2015. Barclay is here alluding to what is widely recognised as one of the most basic principles of forensic archaeology: every contact leaves a trace. This principle (also known as Locard's exchange principle or the transfer principle) was formulated in the 1920s by the famous French detective Edmond Locard. Locard also noted the similarity between forensic science and archaeology: 'the criminologist [detective] re-creates the criminal from traces the latter leaves behind, just as the archaeologist reconstructs prehistoric beings from his finds' (in E. Locard, 'The Analysis of Dust Traces. II', *American Journal of Police Science* 1930, 1[4]: 401–18, originally published in *Revue Internationale de Criminalistique* 1929 [1]: 4–5).
2. W. W. Taylor, *A Study of Archaeology* 1948: 44; 1967: 41; quoted by Klejn in *Metaarchaeology* 2001a: 41.
3. In *An Essay on Philosophical Method* (1933) when Collingwood discusses scientific systems of non-overlapping classification he would have had recent first-hand experience of this form of classification in the writing of *The Archaeology of Roman Britain* (1930).
4. Attempts to interpret Collingwood's philosophy as an illustrious forerunner of post-processual theoretical archaeology—for example, I. Hodder and S. Hutson, *Reading the Past* (3rd ed.), 2003—have tended to ignore this aspect of Collingwood's views.

References

Abstracts to all Klejn's major monographs can be found at www.archaeology.ru.

Anthony, D. W. 2007. *The Horse, the Wheel, and Language: How Bronze-Age Riders from the Eurasian Steppes Shaped the Modern World.* Princeton, NJ: Princeton University Press.

Arnold, B., and Hassmann, H. 1995. 'Archaeology in Nazi Germany: The legacy of the Faustian bargain', in *Nationalism Politics and the Practice of Archaeology*, pp. 70–81. New York: Cambridge University Press.

Barclay, D. 2013. Basic principles of forensic science, http://www.adgarrett.com/articles/basic-principles-of-forensic-science/, September 12. 2014.

Barford, P. M. 2001. *The Early Slavs.* Ithaca, NY: Cornell University Press.

Broeders, A. P. A. 2007. Principles of forensic identification science, in *Handbook of Criminal Investigation*, T. Newburn, T. Williamson, and A. Wright (Eds.), pp. 303–37. Abingdon: Routledge.

Bulkin, V. A., Klejn, L. S., and Lebedev, G. S. 1982. Attainments and problems of Soviet archaeology. *World Archaeology* 13(3): 272–95.

Burström, M. 1994. An ivory tower in archaeology? A conversation with Leo S. Klejn. *Current Swedish Archaeology* 2: 7–12.

Chernykh, E. N. 1995. Postscript: Russian archaeology after the collapse of the USSR: Infrastructural crisis and the resurgence of old and new nationalisms, in *Nationalism, Politics, and the Practice of Archaeology*, pp. 139–48. New York: Cambridge University Press.

Chrisomalis, S., and Costopoulos, A. (Eds.) 2013. *Human Expeditions: Inspired by Bruce Trigger.* Toronto: University of Toronto Press.

Clark, J. G. D. 1939. *Archaeology and Society.* London: Methuen.

Collingwood, R. G. 1930. *The Archaeology of Roman Britain.* London: Methuen.

———. 1933. *An Essay on Philosophical Method.* Oxford: Clarendon Press.

———. 1940. *An Essay on Metaphysics.* Oxford: Clarendon Press.

———. 1993. *The Idea of History* (revised ed., with an introduction by Jan van der Dussen). Oxford: Oxford University Press.

———. 1999. *The Principles of History,* W. H. Dray and Jan van der Dussen (Eds.). Oxford: Oxford University Press.

Curta, F. 2001. *The Making of the Slavs: History and archaeology of the Lower Danube Region.* New York: Cambridge University Press.

Dawkins, R. 1976. *The Selfish Gene.* Oxford: Oxford University Press.

Dolukhanov, P. M. 1993. Archaeology in the ex-USSR: Post-perestroyka problems. *Antiquity* 67(254): 150–56.
———. 2009. Introduction to *The East European Plain on the Eve of Agriculture,* P. M. Dolukhanov, G. R. Sarson, and A. M. Shukharov (Eds.). British Archaeological Reports, Series 1964.
Embree, L. 1989. The Structure of American archaeology: A preliminary report, in *Critical Traditions in Contemporary Archaeology,* V. Pinsky and A. Wylie (Eds.), pp. 28–37. New York: Cambridge University Press.
Freud, S. 2002 [1930]. *Civilization and Its Discontents.* London: Penguin.
Gazeau, V., and Musin, A. 2010. Normannism and anti-Normannism, Liberté pour l'histoire: http://www.lph-asso.fr/index.php?option=com_content&view=article&id=139%3Anormannisme-et-antinormannisme&catid=31%3Adossier-russie&Itemid=78&lang=en, March 2010.
Gray, J. 2009. *Gray's Anatomy*. London: Penguin.
Hawkes, C. 1954. Archaeological theory and method: Some suggestions from the Old World. *American Anthropologist* 56(2): 155–68.
Hodder, I., and Hutson, S. 2003. *Reading the Past* (3rd ed.). New York: Cambridge University Press.
Hrouda, B. 1978. Einleitung und Beweggrunde, in *Methoden der Archäologie.* München: Beck.
Immonen, V. 2003. The Stratigraphy of a life: An archaeological dialogue with Leo Klejn. *Archaeological Dialogues* 10(1): 57–75.
Klejn, L. S. 1971. Why not history? *Current Anthropology* 12(2): 120.
———. 1976. The behavior of peoples: A review article. *Current Anthropology* 17(1): 132–36. (A review of Thorne Deuel's *The Human Factor in the Behavior of Peoples* [1971].)
———. 1977. A panorama of theoretical archaeology. *Current Anthropology* 18(1): 1–42.
———. 1982. *Archaeological Typology.* British Archaeological Reports (BAR International Series, no. 153) (errata and corrigenda in a separate pamphlet).
———. 1992. Current political situation in Russia and the position of archaeology in the country. *Oxford Magazine* 84: 26–32.
———. 1996. History of archaeology before 1900: European archaeology, in *Oxford Companion to Archaeology,* Brian M. Fagan (Ed.), pp. 286–87. Oxford: Oxford University Pres.
———. 1998. Archaeologists and migrations: A problem of attitude? Comment on H. Härke. *Current Anthropology* 39(1): 30–31.
———. 1999. The early evolution of dice between the Danube and the Indus: Contributions to the Early History of Mathematics. *Acta Archaeologica* 70: 113–35.
———. 2001a. *Metaarchaeology* (supplementary edition of *Acta Archaeologica*). Munksgaard: Blackwell.
———. 2001b. Russia, in *Encyclopedia of Archaeology: History and Discoveries,* T. Murray (Ed.), pp. 1127–45. Santa Barbara, CA: ABC-CLIO.
———. 2006. Figures, Figurines, and Colin Renfrew. *Antiquity* 80: 980–84.
———. 2008a. Bruce Trigger in world archaeology. *Bulletin of the History of Archaeology* 18(2): 4–12.

Klejn, L. S. 2008b. Gustav Kossinna (1858–1931), in *Histories of Archaeology: A Reader in the History of Archaeology*, T. Murray and C. Evans (Eds.), pp. 233–46. Oxford: Oxford University Press; first published in *Encyclopaedia of Archaeology: The Great Archaeologists*, T. Murray (Ed.). Santa Barbara, CA: ABC-CLIO.

———. 2008c. Review of David W. Anthony, *The Horse, the Wheel, and Language* (2007). *Journal of Indo-European Studies* 36(3 & 4): 464–80.

———. 2010. *Trudno byt' Klejnom: Avtobiografiya v monologakh i dialogakh* [*It's Hard to Be Klejn: Autobiography in Monologues and Dialogues*]. St. Petersburg: Nestor-Istoriya.

———. 2012a. *Incorporeal Heroes: The Origins of Homeric Images*. Newcastle: Cambridge Scholars Publishing.

———. 2012b. *Soviet Archaeology: Trends, Schools, and History*. Oxford: Oxford University Press.

———. 2013a. Otkuda u chechentsev Pir"on—iz Irana ili Rusi? [From whence came Chechen Pir"on—from Iran or from Rus?]. *Stratum plus* 5.

———. 2013b. Figurative activity in an evolutionary perspective, in *Human Expeditions: Inspired by Bruce Trigger*, S. Chrisomalis and A. Costopoulos (Eds.). Toronto: University of Toronto Press.

———. 2014. *Vremya v arkheologii* [*Time in Archaeology*]. St. Petersburg: Evraziya.

Kristiansen, K. 1993. Exploring the limits: An interview with Leo Klejn. *Journal of European Archaeology* 1(1): 184–94.

Lajoye, P. 2012. There is no 'Perun in the Caucasus' . . . but maybe an ancient Iranian thunder demon. *Studia Mythologica Slavica* XV: 179–84.

Leach, S. 2011a. V besedakh c L. S. Klejnom [In conversation with Leo. S. Klejn]. *Aktual'nye problemy Sibiri i Dalnego Vostoka*. Ussuriysk, UGPI: 36–44; *Archaeological Dialogues* 22(2).

———. 2011b. Arkheolog i detektiv: Ot Leningrada do Sent-Mary Mid [The archaeologist and the detective: From Leningrad to St. Mary Mead]. *Rossiyskiy Arkheologicheskiy Ezhegodnik* 1. St. Petersburg, Universities' Publishing Consortium: 70–72.

———. 2013a. Mezhdunarodnaya konferentsiya 2011 g. v Birmingeme: Vklad L. S. Klejna v arkheologiyu in *Arkheologicheskie Vesti* 19: 268–69. Sankt-Petersburg, Dmitriya Bulavina [Discussion of L. S. Klejn's archaeological theories at Birmingham Conference (2011), *Arkheologicheskie Vesti*].

———. 2013b. Leo S. Klejn and the dictatorship of 'why?' over 'what?' (with Alexey Elyashevich). *Antiquity* (Project Gallery) 87(336), http://antiquity.ac.uk/projgall/elyashevich336/.

———. Forthcoming. Metodologicheskaya priroda arkheologii [The methodological nature of archaeology], in *Klejn: A Guide,* M. Kashuba (Ed.).

Leroi-Gourhan, A. 1961. In *L'histoire et ses méthodes*, C. Samaran (Ed.). Paris: Galimard.

Malmer, M. P., and Bartholin, T. 1993. On theoretical realism in archaeology. *Current Swedish Archaeology* 1: 145–48.

Mongait, A. L. 1961. *Archaeology in the USSR* (2nd ed., translated and adapted by M. W. Thompson). Harmondsworth: Pelican.

Pinker, S. 2011. *The Better Angels of Our Nature: Why Violence Has Declined,* New York: Penguin.

Renfrew, C. 1987. *Archaeology and Language: The Puzzle of Indo-European Origins*. London: Jonathan Cape.

Renfrew, C., and Bahn, P. 2000. *Archaeology: Theories, Methods, and Practice* (3rd ed.). London: Thames and Hudson.

Renfrew, C., Rowlands, M. J., and Segraves, B. A. (Eds.) 1982. *Theory and Explanation in Archaeology*. New York: Academic Press.

Rybakov, B. 1965. *Early Centuries of Russian History*. Moscow: Progress Publishers.

Shanks, M., and Tilley, C. 1987. *Reconstructing Archaeology*. New York: Cambridge University Press.

Shelov, D. B. 1975. Scythians, Sarmatians, and Greeks: Recent work, in *Recent Archaeological Excavations in Europe*, R. Bruce-Mitford (Ed.). London: Routledge & Kegan Paul.

Shnirelman, V. A. 1995. From Internationalism to Nationalism: Forgotten pages of Soviet archaeology in the 1930s and 1940s, in *Nationalism, Politics, and the Practice of Archaeology*, P. L. Kohl and C. Fawcett (Eds.), pp. 120–38. New York: Cambridge University Press.

Smolla, G. 1979/1980. Das Kossinna-Syndrome. *Fundberichte aus Hessen* 19/20: 1–9.

Sørensen, M. L. S. 2002. Mats P. Malmer: An intellectual biography. *Current Swedish Archaeology* 10:163–77.

Taylor, T. 1994. Conversations with Leo Klejn. *Current Anthropology* 34(5): 723–35.

Tikhonov, I. L. 2007. Archaeology at St. Petersburg University (from 1724 until today). *Antiquity* 81(312): 446–56.

Trigger, B. 1978. No longer from another planet. *Antiquity* 50(206): 193–98.

———. 1989. *A History of Archeological Thought*. New York: Cambridge University Press.

Van der Dussen, J. 1981. *History as a Science: The Philosophy of R. G. Collingwood*. The Hague: Martinus Nijhoff.

Vishniatsky, L. B. 2011. Antropogenez.ru/book/9.

Yoffe, M., and Krafczik, J. 2003. *Perun the God of Thunder*. New York: Peter Lang.

Index

absolute and relative dating, 49
Aesop, 45
Afanasyev, A. N., 71, 77
Akunin, B., 211n9
Amalrik, A., 93
Ani, 27
Anichov, E. V., 71, 73
Anthony, D., 88, 89, 90, 92
Aristotle, 99
Arnold, B., 84
Artamonov, M., 25–6, 28, 30, 32, 83, 88
artefactology, 104
Artsikhovsky, A. V., 31, 104, 109, 111
Astruc, J., 64
atheism, 50-1
autochthonism, 27–9
Azadovski, 37

Bacon, F., 114, 117
Baden culture, 91
Ballard, J.G., 55
Bannikov, K. L., 57, 58
Barclay, D., 136
Bergk, T., 65
Bethe, E., 65
Binford, 95, 210n1
Bochkarev, V. S., 206n22
Bohr, N., 123
Brezhnev, 36
Broeders, 136
Bryusov, A.Y., 82–83, 104
Bulkin, V. A., 42, 206n22

Catacomb-grave culture, 26, 34, 82–83, 89, 90, 136
Chekhov, 41
Cherny, S., 25
Chernyakhov culture, 31
Childe, G., 43, 47, 81, 86, 89, 95
Christie, A., 120, 211n9
Clarke, D., 95, 109, 128, 210n1
Collingwood, R. G., 108, 113, 114, 120, 121, 122, 137–42
Collingwood Bruce, 137
Compte, A., 117
Corded ware culture, 89
Cuceteni-Tripolye culture, 89
Current Anthropology, 33–4, 35
Curta, F., 27, 86

Daniel, G., 100
Darwinism, 56
Da Vinci, L., 60
Dawkins, R., 59
Death, 52
Deniken, 17
Derzhavin, N.S., 72
Dice, 87, 209n18
Dlugosch, 70
Dniestr, 76
Doctors' Plot, 31
Dolukhanov, P., 115
Don, 34, 89
Donets, 34, 89
Dostoyevsky, 41
Dunnel, R., 118
Düntzer, H., 65
Dyakanov, I. M., 63

Eggers, H.-J., 83, 115
Elyashevish, A., 48
Embree, L., 109
Endoarchaeological theory, 109–10
Ethnogenesis, 105

Faier, V. V., 68
Famintsyn, A. S., 71
Fatayano culture, 96
Feit, U., 84
Fick, A., 65
Fischer, U., 126
Freud, S., 56
Funnel Beaker culture, 89, 91

Galkovsky, N. M., 71
Gardin, J.-C., 97
Gerhardt, 130
Gibadullin-Klejn, D., 48
Gimbutas, M., 89, 90
Glinka, G., 71
Glozel fake, 121
Golding, W., 55
Gray, J., 55
Grekov, B. D., 72
Grigoryev, G. P., 106
Gumilev, N., 25

Haak, W., 89
Hachmann, 83
Hägerstrand, T., 98
Härke, H., 87, 125
Hassmann, 84
Häusler, A., 33
Hawkes, C., 123, 212n18
Hawkes' ladder, 104, 212n18
Haydn, 20
Herodotus, 27
historical materialism, 103–4
Hodder, I., 212n4
Holmes, S., 120, 137
Hutson, S., 212n4

Ilf and Petrov, 140
Isle of Man, 58
Ivanov, V., 73
Ivan the Terrible, 60

Jagić, W., 71
Jankuhn, H., 84
Japhetic theory, 27
jazz, 48
Johnson, S., 49
Journal of Theoretical Archaeology, 51

Kabo, V. R., 57, 58
Kaisarov, A. S., 71
Kakheti, 75
Katnelson, 27
Kareev, N. I., 71
Kastorsky, M., 71
Kauer, P., 65
KGB, 22, 36–37, 40, 43, 45, 48
Kiev Institute of Archaeology, 31
Kirpichnikov, A., 71
Klejn, B., 34, 47
Kolpakov, E. M., 206n22
Kon, I., 60
Kondakov, N. P., 48
Korzukhina, G. F., 206n22
Kosovo Polje, 63
Kossinna, 31, 81–87, 91, 92
Kossinna Syndrome, 83–84
Kostomarov, N., 71, 93
Kovalev, A., 210n10
Kozintsev, A. G., 41, 57–58
Krushchev, 34
Kurgan hypothesis, 89
Kupalo, 73, 78–79

Lajoyje, P., 209n25
Lazaridis, I., 89
Language, 59, 86, 87–92
Lebedev, G. S., 32, 42, 206n22
Leger, L., 71
Lenin, 23
Leningrad Tribune, 40, 49
Lermontov, 22
Leroi-Gourhan, 111
Lévi-Strauss, C., 73, 101, 210n17
Levitan, 29
Lewis-Williams, J. D., 207n18
Lincoln, A., 60
Liszt, 20
Locard, E., 212n1
Lomonsov, 92, 93
Lorenz, K., 56
Lowmiański, H., 71, 76

Lyapushkin, I. I., 26

Machál, H., 71
Mallory, J. M., 89, 90, 92
Mallowan, M., 211n9
Malmer, M. P., 96–99, 118, 210n1
Mansikka, V. J., 71
Marr, N., 27, 86, 92
Marrism, 27–28
Marx, K., 23, 33, 46–47, 56–57, 106
Marxism, 124, 125
Maslenitsa, 77–78
Mavrodin, 83
Meilakh, 37
mermaids, 77
Mervan II, 75
Meschaninov, I. I., 27
Metaarchaeological theory, 110
migration, 59
Miller, 92, 93
Mirek, 37
modesty (in academic life), 207n23
Molière, 118
Montelius, O., 86, 96–99
Morris, D., 56
Moszyński, 71
Müller, S., 97
Munchausen, 134

Nalimov, V. V., 123
Nature, 89
Neva, 40
New Archaeology, 95–96, 97, 103, 105
Niederle, L., 71, 73
Nilsson, M. P., 66
Nosov, E. N., 206n22
numismatics, 97
Nureyev, R., 60

Ores, B., 97

Page, D., 62
Paraarchaeological theory, 110
Peter the Great, 70
Petrie, F., 140
philosophy, 140
Phrygian migration, 87
Pinker, S., 55, 58
Piotrovsky, B. B., 34
Piotrovsky, Y. Y., 206n22
Pogodin, 93
Poliochi, 63
Pol Pot, 46
Popov, 28, 205n12
Post-processual archaeology, 95, 96, 103, 118
Pravda, 28–29
Procopius, 70
Prometheus, 22
Propp, V. L., 23–25, 72, 78, 210n17
Pskov, 76
Pushkin, 22, 77, 205n1
Putin, 49–50, 94

Renfrew, C., 89, 91, 92, 110
Rennaisance antiquaries, 110
Rickert, H., 116
rock, 48
Rod, 75–76
Roginski, 37
Romanov, 36
Rudenko, S. I., 205n18
Ruzhnetsky, S., 71
Rybakov, B. A., 36, 72, 73–74, 75, 76, 79, 80, 109
Ryurikovich dynasty, 32

Saitapharnes tiara, 121
Safronova, V. A., 206n22
Sakharov, A., 36
Sakharov, A. (Director of the Institute of Russian History), 94
Sayers, D. L., 211n9
Schlusselburg, 58
Schnapp, A., 100
Schuchhardt, C., 83
Shaskolsky, 93
Shchukin, M. B., 42, 206n22
Scythians, 27, 34
Shaskolsky, I. P., 32
Shatkov, G., 33–34
Shennan, S., 118

Shepping, D. O., 71
Sher, Y. A., 207n18
Shevchenko, T., 111
Shilov, V. P., 26
Simpson, G., 137
Smirnov, 104
Smirnova, 26
Smolla, G., 83, 84
Solovyev, S. M., 71
Solzhenitsyn, 41
Sovietskaya Archaeologiya, 31, 83
Srtryjkovski, 70
Stadialist theories, 86, 105
Stalin, 23, 29, 31, 34
starina, 115
Stolyar, A.D., 26
Strabo, 67
Stroev, P., 71
Strugatsky, 51
Sumtsov, N. F., 71
Svyatki, 79
Szafrański, W., 71

Taylor, W., 136
Thomsen, 130
Tikhonova, M. A., 206n22
Time, 49
Tocharians, 210n10
Tolstoy, L., 19
Tolstoy, N., 73
Toporov, V., 73
Trapeznikov, 36
Trigger, B., 35, 38, 42, 47, 99, 100–01
Troitsky Variant, 49
Tsar Saltan, 77
Tsymbursky, 66, 68
Tukhachevsky, 17
Tulchinsky, G., 140
typology, 96–99, 118, 129

Vainakh (Chechen-Ingush) folklore, 75–77
Veles, 73
Veles's Book, 74
Veselovsky, A. N., 71, 73
Vishniatsky, L. B., 101
Vladimir I, 75, 76, 80, 209n15
Vladimirov, Y. M., 43
Vlas, 73
Vlasius, 73
Volos, 73
Volos-Veles, 73
Von Ranke, 113
Voronin, 26
Voyinovich, 50
Voznesensky, A. A., 25

Wahle, 83, 84, 90
Wheeler, M., 123
Wilde, O., 37
Winckelmann, J. J., 48, 130
Windelband, W., 116
Worsaae, 130
Wolf, A. A., 62

Yamnaya (Pit-grave) culture, 82, 90, 91
Yarilo, 73
Yesenin, S., 25

Zbruch idol, 76
Zelenin, D., 73
zoomorphic sceptres, 87
Zubrow, E., 38

About the Author

Stephen Leach is Senior Research Assistant in Philosophy at Keele University. He is the author of *The Foundations of History: Collingwood's Analysis of Historical Explanation* (2009) and coauthor of (with Alan Whitworth) *Saving the Wall: The Conservation of Hadrian's Wall* (2012) and (with James Connelly and Peter Johnson) *R. G. Collingwood: A Research Companion* (2014). He is also the editor of Leo Klejn's *Incorporeal Heroes: The Origins of Homeric Images* (2012).